ORDNANCE SURVEY

STREET ATLAS
East Essex

Contents

PHILIP'S

First published 1990
Second edition published 1994 by

Ordnance Survey
Romsey Road
Maybush
Southampton SO9 4DH

and

Philip's
an imprint of Reed Consumer Books Limited
Michelin House, 81 Fulham Road, London, SW3 6RB
and Auckland, Melbourne, Singapore and Toronto

ISBN 0-540-05848-3 (Philip's, hardback)
ISBN 0-540-05866-1 (Philip's, softback)
ISBN 0-319-00400-7 (Ordnance Survey, hardback)
ISBN 0-319-00401-5 (Ordnance Survey, softback)

To the best of the Publishers' knowledge, the information in this atlas was correct at the time of going to press. No responsibility can be accepted for any errors or their consequences.

The representation in this atlas of a road, track or path is no evidence of the existence of a right of way.

Printed and bound in Great Britain by
Butler & Tanner Ltd, Frome and London

Key to map symbols

British Rail station

London transport station

Private railway station

Bus or coach station

Heliport

Police station (may not be open 24 hours)

Hospital with casualty facilities
(may not be open 24 hours)

Post office

Place of worship

Important building

Parking

120 Adjoining page indicator

Motorway or dual carriageway

A27(T) **Main or through road** (with Department of Transport number)

Gate or obstruction to traffic (restrictions may not apply at all times or to all vehicles)

Footpath

Bridleway

Path

Track

The representation in this atlas of a road, track or path is no evidence of the existence of a right of way

Amb Sta	Ambulance station	LC	Level crossing
Coll	College	Liby	Library
FB	Footbridge	Mus	Museum
F Sta	Fire station	Sch	School
Hospl	Hospital	TH	Town hall

0	¼	½	¾	1 mile
0	250m	500m	250m	1 Kilometre

The scale of the maps is 3½ inches to 1 mile (1:18103)

Key to map pages

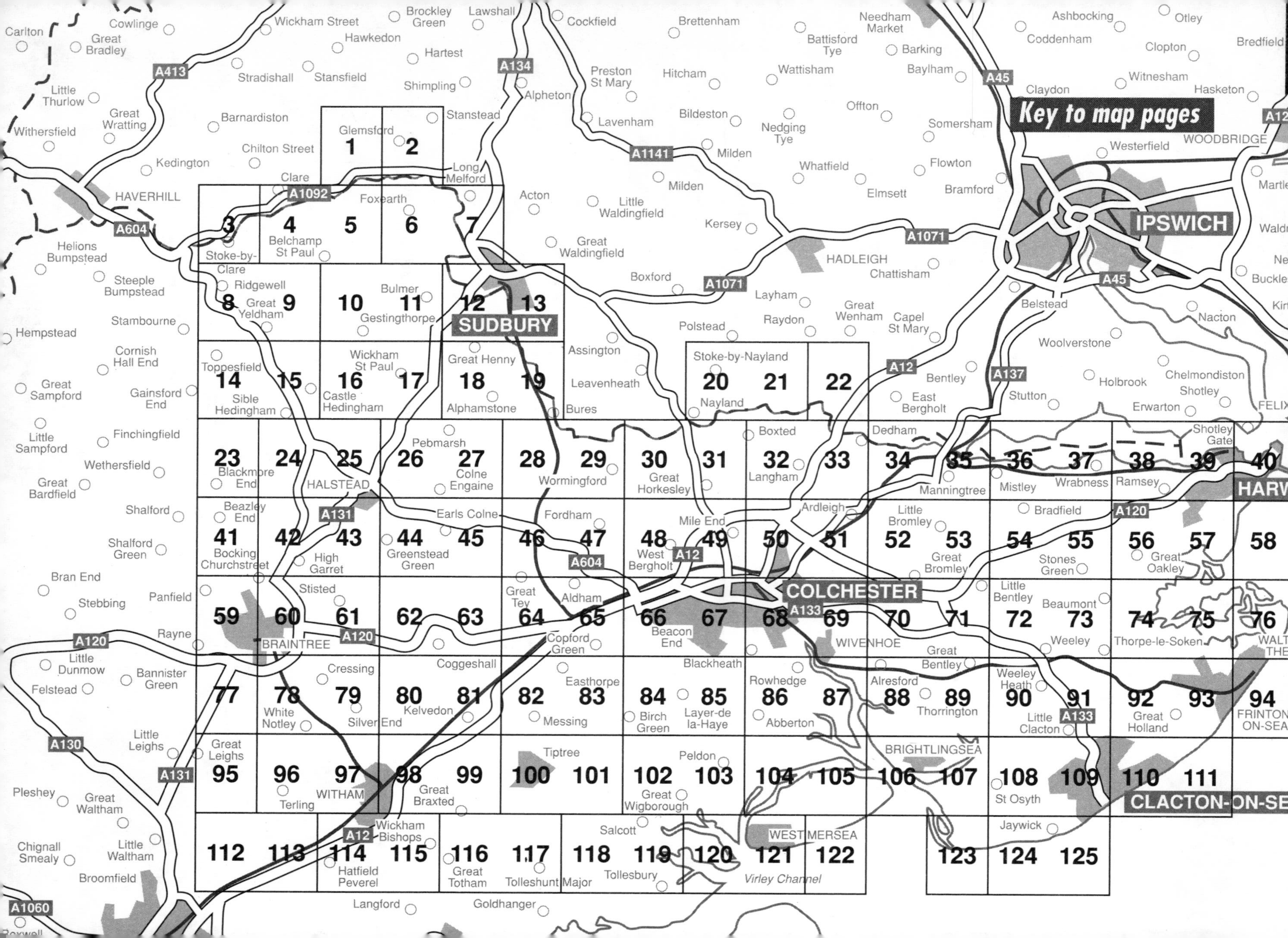
IPSWICH
COLCHESTER
SUDBURY
HARWICH
CLACTON-ON-SEA
HAVERHILL
HADLEIGH
HALSTEAD
BRAINTREE
WITHAM
WIVENHOE
BRIGHTLINGSEA
WEST MERSEA
FELIXSTOWE
WOODBRIDGE
WALTON-ON-THE-NAZE
FRINTON-ON-SEA
A12
A45
A134
A1141
A1071
A137
A120
A133
A604
A131
A1092
A413
A130
A1060
Carlton
Cowlinge
Great Bradley
Little Thurlow
Great Wratting
Withersfield
Kedington
Wickham Street
Hawkedon
Stradishall
Stansfield
Barnardiston
Chilton Street
Clare
Brockley Green
Hartest
Shimpling
Lawshall
Stanstead
Glemsford
Long Melford
Alpheton
Cockfield
Preston St Mary
Lavenham
Brettenham
Hitcham
Bildeston
Milden
Battisford Tye
Wattisham
Nedging Tye
Whatfield
Needham Market
Barking
Baylham
Offton
Somersham
Flowton
Elmsett
Bramford
Ashbocking
Coddenham
Claydon
Otley
Clopton
Witnesham
Hasketon
Bredfield
Westerfield
Martlesham
Waldringfield
Newbourne
Bucklesham
Kirton
Nacton
Belstead
Woolverstone
Holbrook
Chelmondiston
Shotley
Erwarton
Shotley Gate
Stutton
Bentley
East Bergholt
Capel St Mary
Great Wenham
Chattisham
Raydon
Layham
Kersey
Polstead
Boxford
Acton
Little Waldingfield
Great Waldingfield
Foxearth
Belchamp St Paul
Stoke-by-Clare
Ridgewell
Great Yeldham
Bulmer
Gestingthorpe
Helions Bumpstead
Steeple Bumpstead
Stambourne
Hempstead
Cornish Hall End
Great Sampford
Gainsford End
Toppesfield
Sible Hedingham
Wickham St Paul
Castle Hedingham
Great Henny
Alphamstone
Assington
Leavenheath
Bures
Stoke-by-Nayland
Nayland
Little Sampford
Finchingfield
Wethersfield
Great Bardfield
Blackmore End
Pebmarsh
Colne Engaine
Wormingford
Great Horkesley
Boxted
Langham
Dedham
Manningtree
Mistley
Wrabness
Ramsey
Shalford
Shalford Green
Beazley End
Bocking Churchstreet
High Garret
Earls Colne
Greenstead Green
Fordham
Mile End
West Bergholt
Ardleigh
Little Bromley
Great Bromley
Bradfield
Stones Green
Great Oakley
Bran End
Stebbing
Panfield
Stisted
Great Tey
Aldham
Copford Green
Beacon End
Little Bentley
Beaumont
Weeley
Thorpe-le-Soken
Rayne
Little Dunmow
Felstead
Bannister Green
Cressing
Coggeshall
Easthorpe
Blackheath
Rowhedge
Great Bentley
Alresford
Weeley Heath
White Notley
Silver End
Kelvedon
Messing
Birch Green
Layer-de la-Haye
Abberton
Thorrington
Little Clacton
Great Holland
Little Leighs
Great Leighs
Terling
Great Braxted
Tiptree
Peldon
Great Wigborough
St Osyth
Pleshey
Great Waltham
Chignall Smealy
Little Waltham
Broomfield
Wickham Bishops
Hatfield Peverel
Great Totham
Tolleshunt Major
Salcott
Tollesbury
Virley Channel
Jaywick
Langford
Goldhanger
Roxwell
1
2
3
4
5
6
7
8
9
10
11
12
13
14
15
16
17
18
19
20
21
22
23
24
25
26
27
28
29
30
31
32
33
34
35
36
37
38
39
40
41
42
43
44
45
46
47
48
49
50
51
52
53
54
55
56
57
58
59
60
61
62
63
64
65
66
67
68
69
70
71
72
73
74
75
76
77
78
79
80
81
82
83
84
85
86
87
88
89
90
91
92
93
94
95
96
97
98
99
100
101
102
103
104
105
106
107
108
109
110
111
112
113
114
115
116
117
118
119
120
121
122
123
124
125

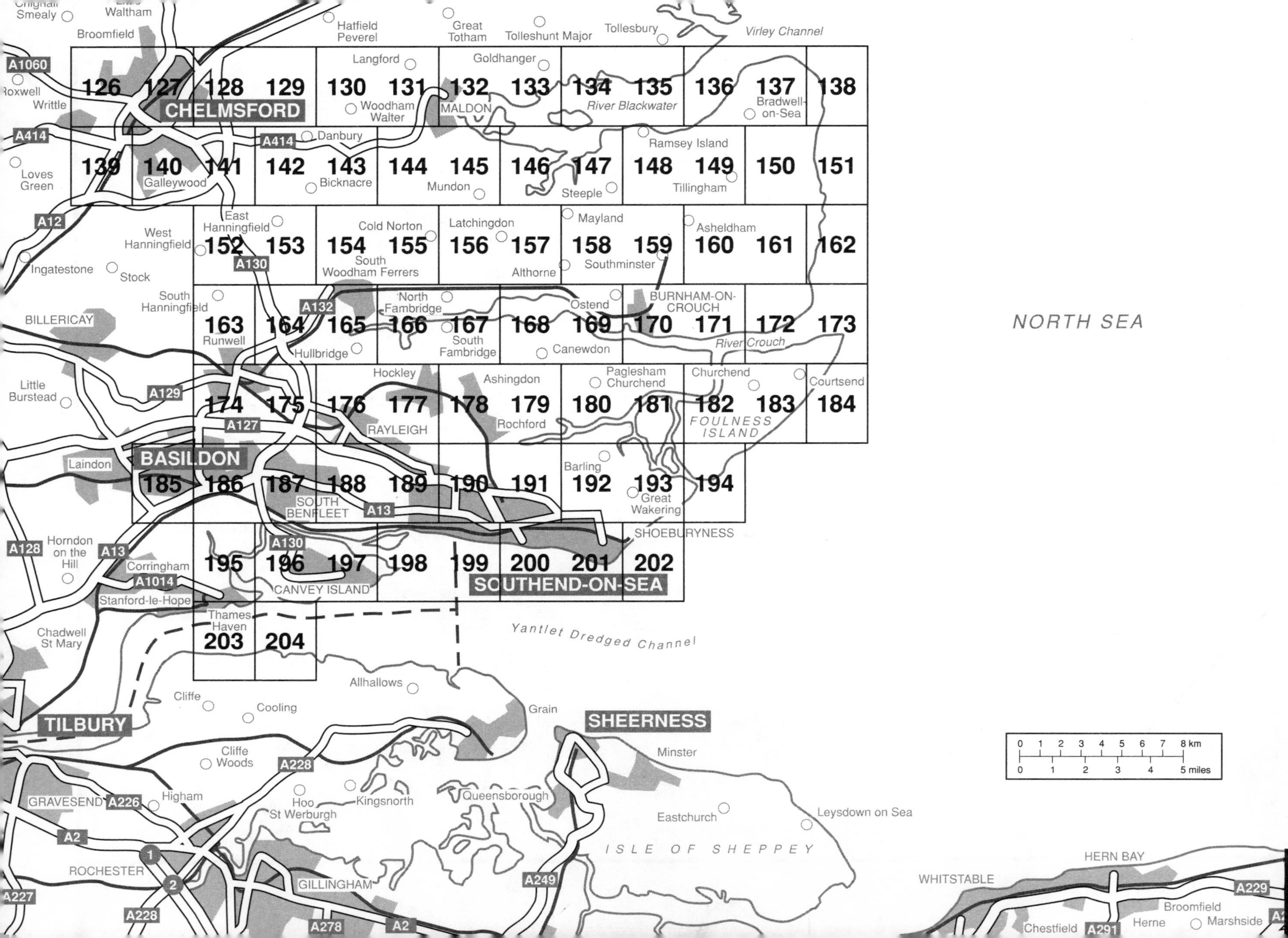

NORTH SEA
CHELMSFORD
BASILDON
SOUTHEND-ON-SEA
SHEERNESS
TILBURY
126 127 128 129 130 131 132 133 134 135 136 137 138
139 140 141 142 143 144 145 146 147 148 149 150 151
152 153 154 155 156 157 158 159 160 161 162
163 164 165 166 167 168 169 170 171 172 173
174 175 176 177 178 179 180 181 182 183 184
185 186 187 188 189 190 191 192 193 194
195 196 197 198 199 200 201 202
203 204
Smealy
Waltham
Broomfield
Hatfield Peverel
Great Totham
Tolleshunt Major
Tollesbury
Virley Channel
Langford
Goldhanger
Woodham Walter
MALDON
River Blackwater
Bradwell-on-Sea
Roxwell
Writtle
Danbury
Ramsey Island
Galleywood
Bicknacre
Mundon
Steeple
Tillingham
Loves Green
East Hanningfield
West Hanningfield
Cold Norton
Latchingdon
Mayland
Asheldham
South Woodham Ferrers
Althorne
Southminster
Ingatestone
Stock
South Hanningfield
North Fambridge
Ostend
BURNHAM-ON-CROUCH
BILLERICAY
Runwell
Hullbridge
South Fambridge
Canewdon
River Crouch
Little Burstead
Hockley
Ashingdon
Paglesham Churchend
Churchend
Courtsend
RAYLEIGH
Rochford
FOULNESS ISLAND
Laindon
Barling
SOUTH BENFLEET
Great Wakering
SHOEBURYNESS
Horndon on the Hill
Corringham
CANVEY ISLAND
Stanford-le-Hope
Thames Haven
Chadwell St Mary
Yantlet Dredged Channel
Allhallows
Cliffe
Cooling
Grain
Minster
Cliffe Woods
GRAVESEND
Higham
Hoo St Werburgh
Kingsnorth
Queensborough
Eastchurch
Leysdown on Sea
ISLE OF SHEPPEY
ROCHESTER
GILLINGHAM
WHITSTABLE
HERN BAY
Broomfield
Chestfield
Herne
Marshside
A1060
A414
A12
A130
A132
A129
A127
A13
A128
A1014
A228
A226
A2
A227
A278
A249
A229
A291
1
2
0 1 2 3 4 5 6 7 8 km
0 1 2 3 4 5 miles

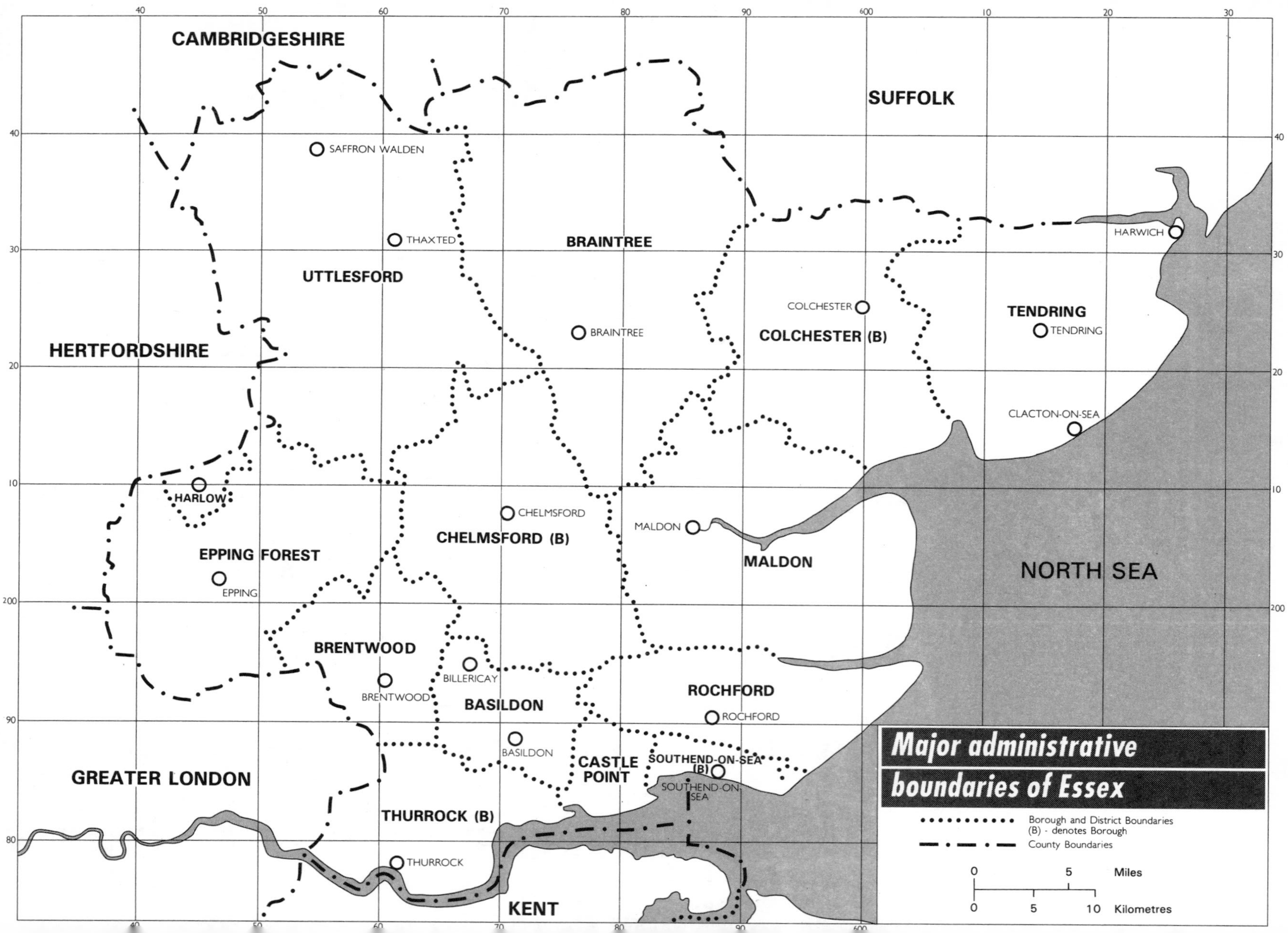
Major administrative boundaries of Essex
Borough and District Boundaries
(B) - denotes Borough
County Boundaries
Miles
Kilometres
CAMBRIDGESHIRE
SUFFOLK
HERTFORDSHIRE
GREATER LONDON
KENT
NORTH SEA
UTTLESFORD
BRAINTREE
COLCHESTER (B)
TENDRING
EPPING FOREST
CHELMSFORD (B)
MALDON
BRENTWOOD
BASILDON
ROCHFORD
CASTLE POINT
SOUTHEND-ON-SEA (B)
THURROCK (B)
SAFFRON WALDEN
THAXTED
BRAINTREE
COLCHESTER
TENDRING
HARWICH
CLACTON-ON-SEA
HARLOW
EPPING
CHELMSFORD
MALDON
BILLERICAY
BRENTWOOD
BASILDON
ROCHFORD
SOUTHEND-ON-SEA
THURROCK

not continued, see key diagram

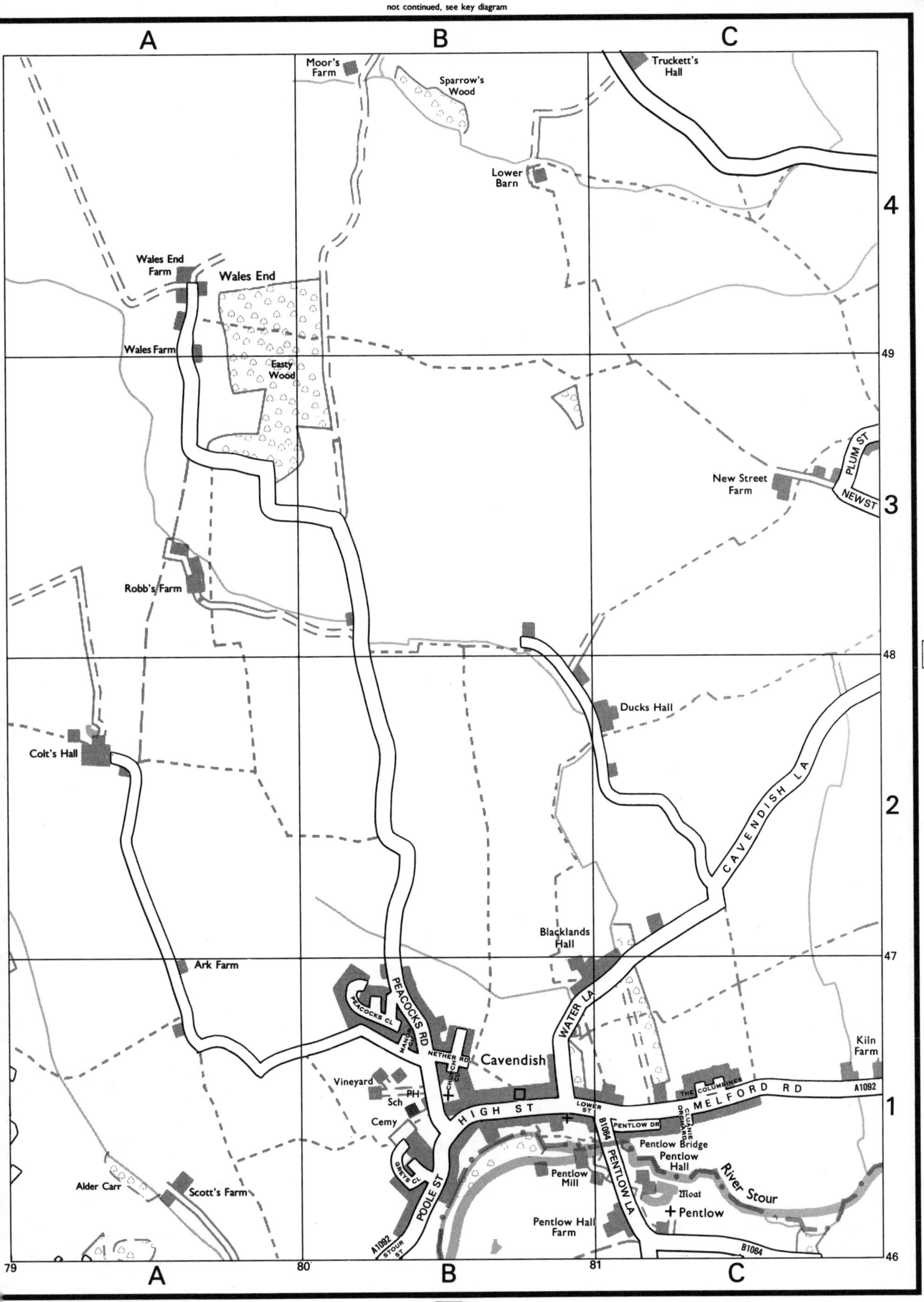
A
B
C
Moor's Farm
Sparrow's Wood
Truckett's Hall
Lower Barn
4
Wales End Farm
Wales End
Wales Farm
Easty Wood
49
New Street Farm
PLUM ST
NEW ST
3
Robb's Farm
48
2
Ducks Hall
Colt's Hall
CAVENDISH LA
2
Blacklands Hall
47
Ark Farm
PEACOCKS RD
PEACOCKS CL
MANOR
NETHER RD
CHURCH CL
Cavendish
WATER LA
Kiln Farm
Vineyard
PH
Sch
Cemy
HIGH ST
LOWER ST
B1064
PENTLOW DR
THE COLUMBINES
MELFORD RD
A1092
1
CLUANIE ORCHARD
Pentlow Bridge
Pentlow Hall
Pentlow Mill
PENTLOW LA
GREYS CL
River Stour
Moat
Pentlow
Alder Carr
Scott's Farm
POOLE ST
Pentlow Hall Farm
A1092
STOUR ST
B1064
46
79
80
81
A
B
C

5

not continued, see key diagram

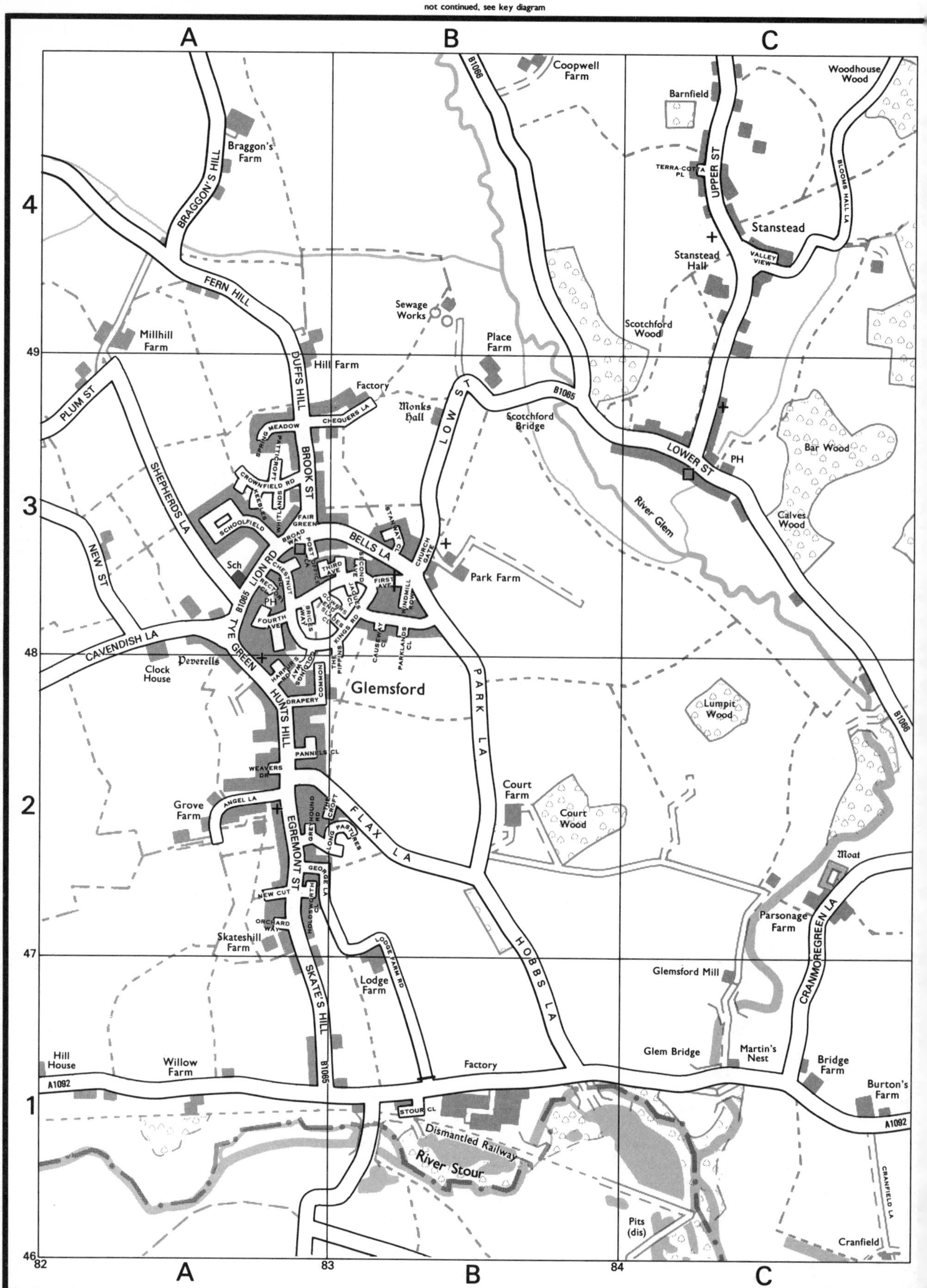
A
B
C
Coopwell Farm
Barnfield
Woodhouse Wood
Braggon's Farm
BRAGGON'S HILL
TERRA-COTTA PL
UPPER ST
BLOOMS HALL LA
Stanstead
Stanstead Hall
VALLEY VIEW
FERN HILL
Sewage Works
Scotchford Wood
Millhill Farm
Place Farm
DUFFS HILL
Hill Farm
Factory
PLUM ST
CHEQUERS LA
Monks Hall
LOW ST
B1065
Scotchford Bridge
LOWER ST
PH
Bar Wood
SPRING MEADOW
PATTICROFT
BROOK ST
CROWNFIELD RD
SHEPHERDS LA
River Glem
SCHOOLFIELD
FAIR GREEN
BROAD WAY
BELLS LA
CHURCH GATE
Calves Wood
NEW ST
Sch
LION RD
CHESTNUT
THIRD AVE
SECOND AVE
FIRST AVE
WINDMILL ROW
Park Farm
RECTORY
PH
JACQUES CL
FOURTH AVE
BRICKS WAY
KINGS RD
THE PIPPINS
CAUSEWAY CL
PARKLANDS CL
CAVENDISH LA
TYE GREEN
Clock House
Peverells
HUNTS HILL
COMMON
Glemsford
PARK LA
DRAPERY
Lumpit Wood
B1066
PANNELS CL
WEAVERS DR
Court Farm
Court Wood
Grove Farm
ANGEL LA
EGREMONT ST
GREYHOUND RD
THE CROFT
LONG PASTURES
FLAX LA
Moat
NEW CUT
GEORGE LA
Parsonage Farm
ORCHARD WAY
Skateshill Farm
LODGE FARM RD
Lodge Farm
SKATE'S HILL
HOBBS LA
Glemsford Mill
CRANMOREGREEN LA
Hill House
Willow Farm
B1065
Factory
Glem Bridge
Martin's Nest
Bridge Farm
Burton's Farm
A1092
STOUR CL
Dismantled Railway
River Stour
A1092
CRANFIELD LA
Pits (dis)
Cranfield
4
3
2
1
49
48
47
46
82
83
84

1

6

not continued, see key diagram

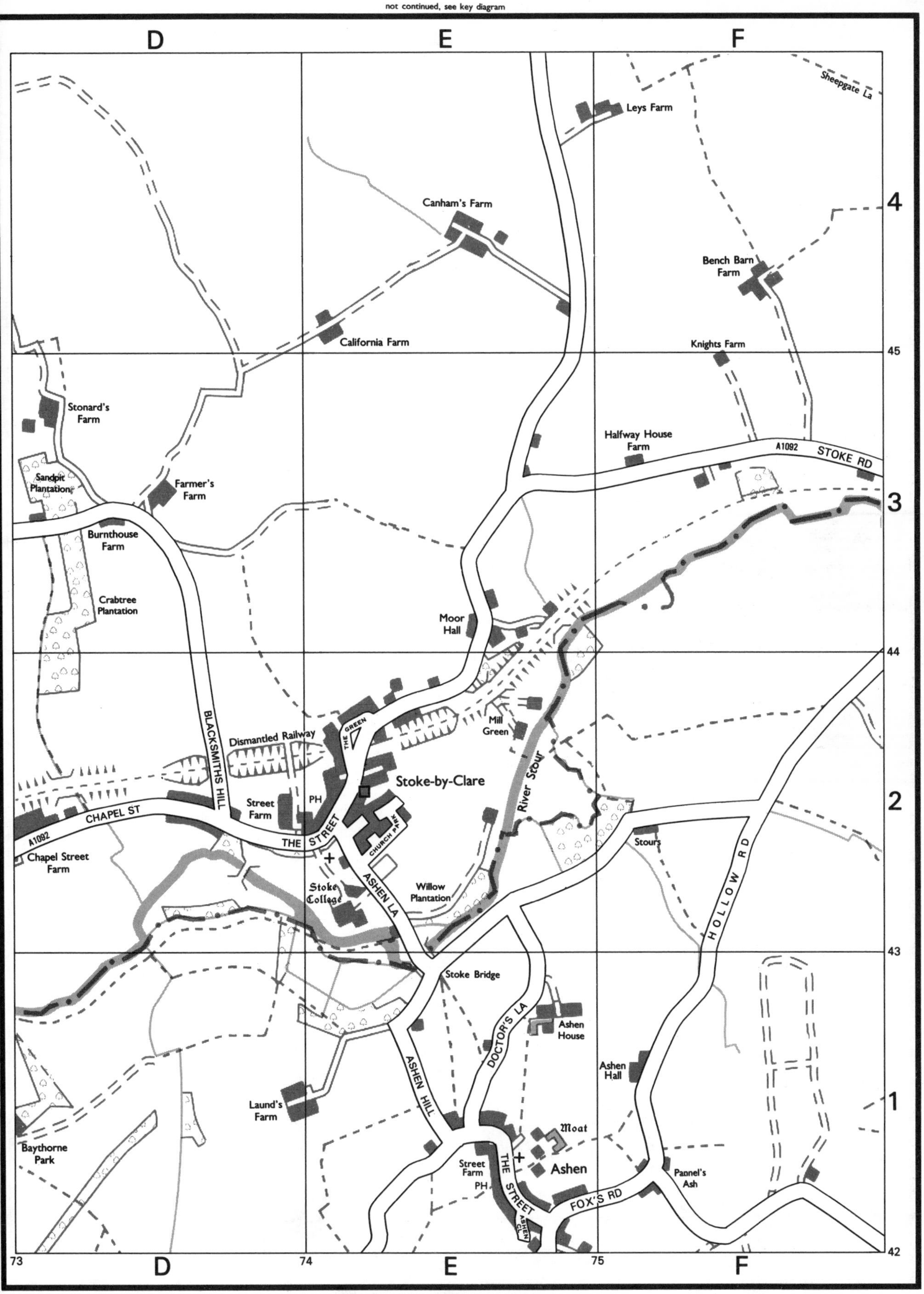
D
E
F
Sheepgate La
Leys Farm
Canham's Farm
4
Bench Barn Farm
California Farm
Knights Farm
45
Stonard's Farm
Halfway House Farm
A1092
STOKE RD
Sandpit Plantation
Farmer's Farm
3
Burnthouse Farm
Crabtree Plantation
Moor Hall
44
BLACKSMITHS HILL
THE GREEN
Mill Green
Dismantled Railway
Stoke-by-Clare
River Stour
2
Street Farm
PH
CHAPEL ST
CHURCH PK
Stours
A1092
THE STREET
Chapel Street Farm
ASHEN LA
HOLLOW RD
Stoke College
Willow Plantation
43
Stoke Bridge
DOCTOR'S LA
Ashen House
ASHEN HILL
Ashen Hall
Laund's Farm
1
Moat
Baythorne Park
Street Farm
PH
THE STREET
Ashen
Pannel's Ash
FOX'S RD
ASHEN CL
42
73
74
75
D
E
F

4

8

not continued, see key diagram

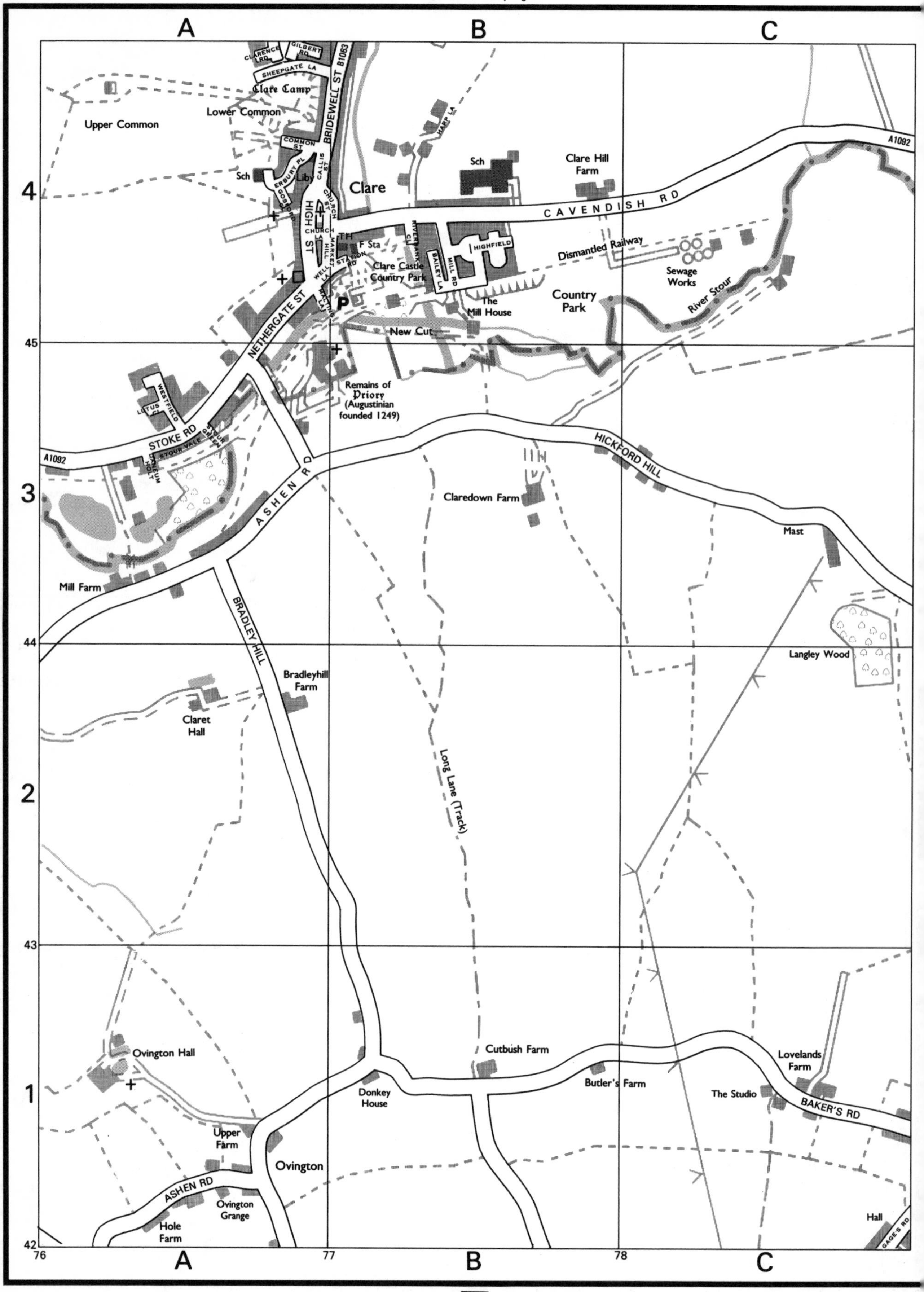

A
B
C
4
45
3
44
2
43
1
42
76
77
78
A
B
C
CLARENCE RD
GILBERT RD
SHEEPGATE LA
Clare Camp
BRIDEWELL ST B1063
Upper Common
Lower Common
HARP LA
COMMON ST
CALLIS ST
Sch
Clare Hill Farm
A1092
Sch
Liby
Clare
CHURCH ST
HIGH ST
CAVENDISH RD
CHURCH
TH
RIVERBANK CL
F Sta
HIGHFIELD
Dismantled Railway
Sewage Works
Clare Castle Country Park
BAILEY LA
MILL RD
WELL LA
STATION RD
The Mill House
Country Park
River Stour
P
NETHERGATE ST
New Cut
Remains of Priory (Augustinian founded 1249)
WESTFIELD
LOTUS CL
STOKE RD
STOUR VALE
STOUR GREEN
A1092
HICKFORD HILL
ASHEN RD
Claredown Farm
Mast
Mill Farm
BRADLEY HILL
Langley Wood
Bradleyhill Farm
Claret Hall
Long Lane (Track)
Ovington Hall
Cutbush Farm
Lovelands Farm
Butler's Farm
Donkey House
The Studio
BAKER'S RD
Upper Farm
Ovington
ASHEN RD
Ovington Grange
Hole Farm
Hall
GAGE'S RD

3

9

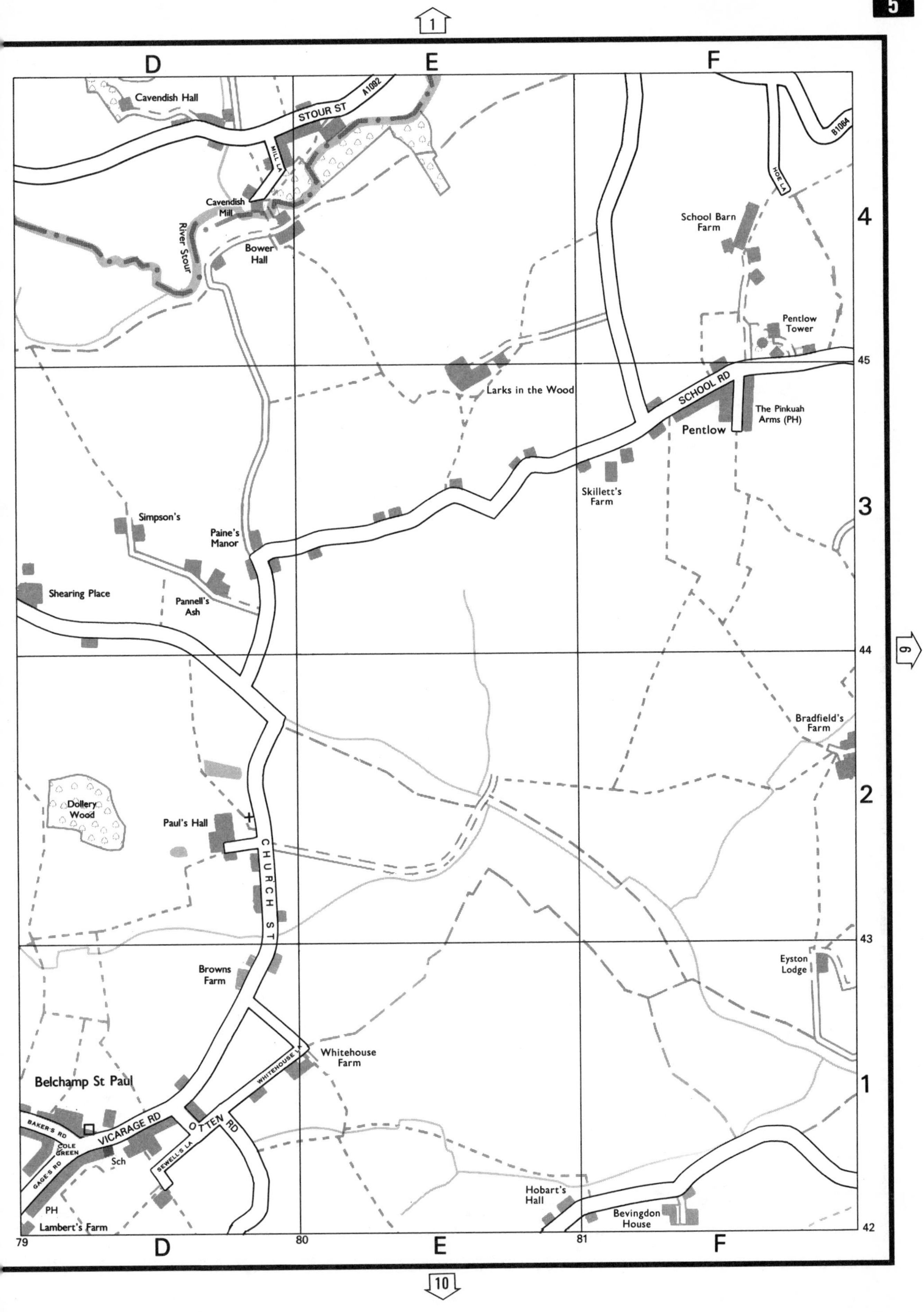

1
D
E
F
Cavendish Hall
STOUR ST
A1092
MILL LA
Cavendish Mill
River Stour
Bower Hall
B1064
HOE LA
School Barn Farm
Pentlow Tower
Larks in the Wood
SCHOOL RD
The Pinkuah Arms (PH)
Pentlow
Skillett's Farm
Simpson's
Paine's Manor
Shearing Place
Pannell's Ash
Bradfield's Farm
Dollery Wood
Paul's Hall
CHURCH ST
Eyston Lodge
Browns Farm
Whitehouse Farm
WHITEHOUSE LA
Belchamp St Paul
BAKER'S RD
VICARAGE RD
COLE GREEN
GAGE'S RD
Sch
OTTEN RD
SEWELL'S LA
PH
Lambert's Farm
Hobart's Hall
Bevingdon House
79
80
81
42
43
44
45
4
3
2
1
6
10

2

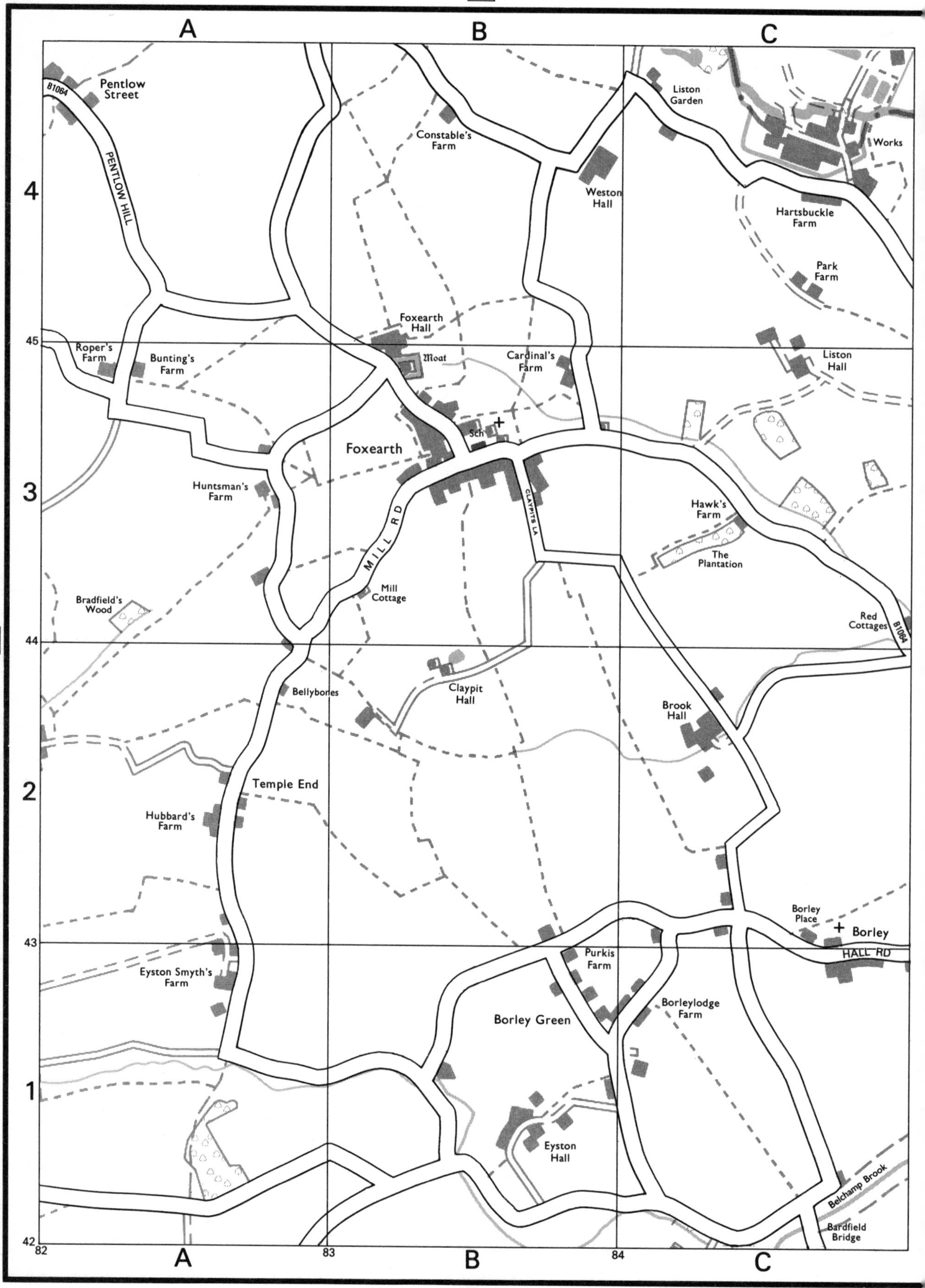

A
B
C
Pentlow Street
B1064
PENTLOW HILL
Constable's Farm
Liston Garden
Works
Weston Hall
Hartsbuckle Farm
Park Farm
Foxearth Hall
Roper's Farm
Bunting's Farm
Moat
Cardinal's Farm
Liston Hall
Sch
Foxearth
Huntsman's Farm
MILL RD
CLAYPITS LA
Hawk's Farm
The Plantation
Mill Cottage
Bradfield's Wood
Red Cottages
Bellybones
Claypit Hall
Brook Hall
Temple End
Hubbard's Farm
Borley Place
Borley
HALL RD
Purkis Farm
Eyston Smyth's Farm
Borleylodge Farm
Borley Green
Eyston Hall
Belchamp Brook
Bardfield Bridge
4
3
2
1
45
44
43
42
82
83
84

5

11

not continued, see key diagram

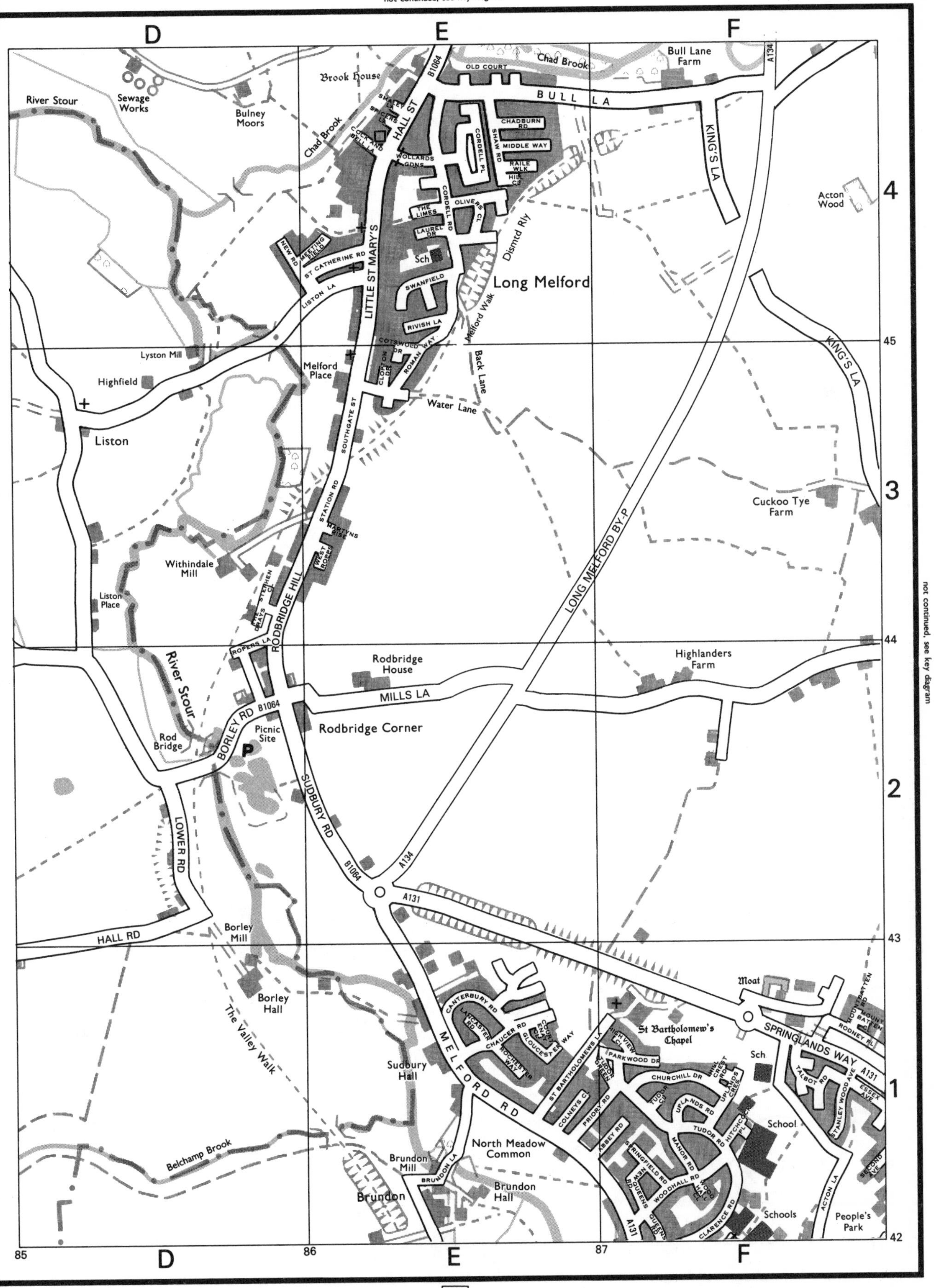

not continued, see key diagram

12

3

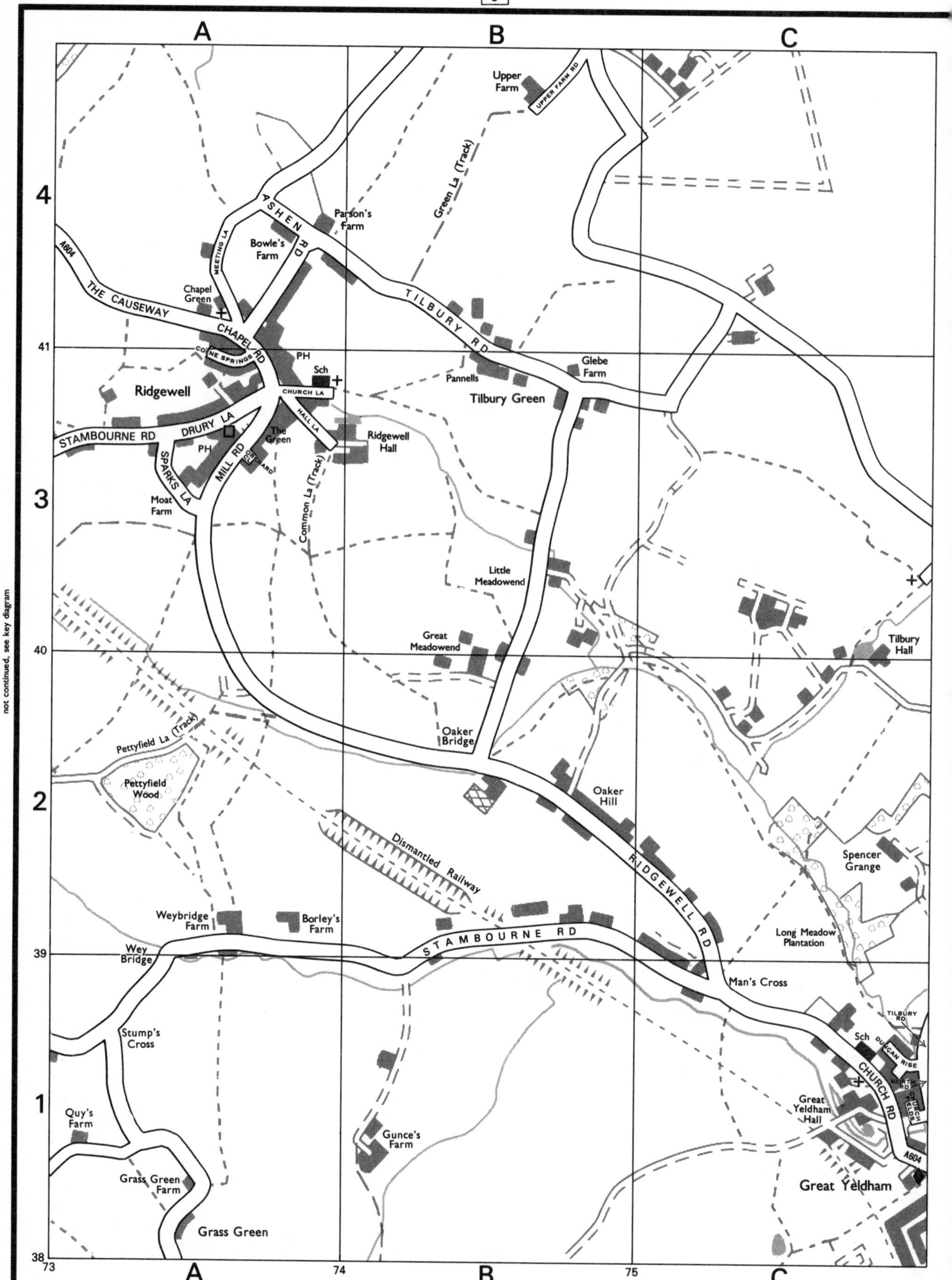
A
B
C
4
3
2
1
41
40
39
38
73
74
75
Upper Farm
UPPER FARM RD
Green La (Track)
ASHEN RD
Parson's Farm
MEETING LA
Bowle's Farm
A604
THE CAUSEWAY
Chapel Green
CHAPEL RD
COLNE SPRINGS
TILBURY RD
PH
Sch
CHURCH LA
HALL LA
Ridgewell
Pannells
Glebe Farm
Tilbury Green
STAMBOURNE RD
DRURY LA
PH
MILL RD
ORCHARD
The Green
Ridgewell Hall
SPARKS LA
Moat Farm
Common La (Track)
Little Meadowend
Tilbury Hall
Great Meadowend
Oaker Bridge
Pettyfield La (Track)
Pettyfield Wood
Oaker Hill
Dismantled Railway
RIDGEWELL RD
Spencer Grange
Weybridge Farm
Borley's Farm
Long Meadow Plantation
Wey Bridge
STAMBOURNE RD
Man's Cross
Stump's Cross
TILBURY RD
Sch
DUNCAN RISE
CHURCH RD
NORTH RD
CHURCH FIELDS
Great Yeldham Hall
Quy's Farm
Gunce's Farm
A604
Grass Green Farm
Great Yeldham
Grass Green
A
B
C

not continued, see key diagram

14

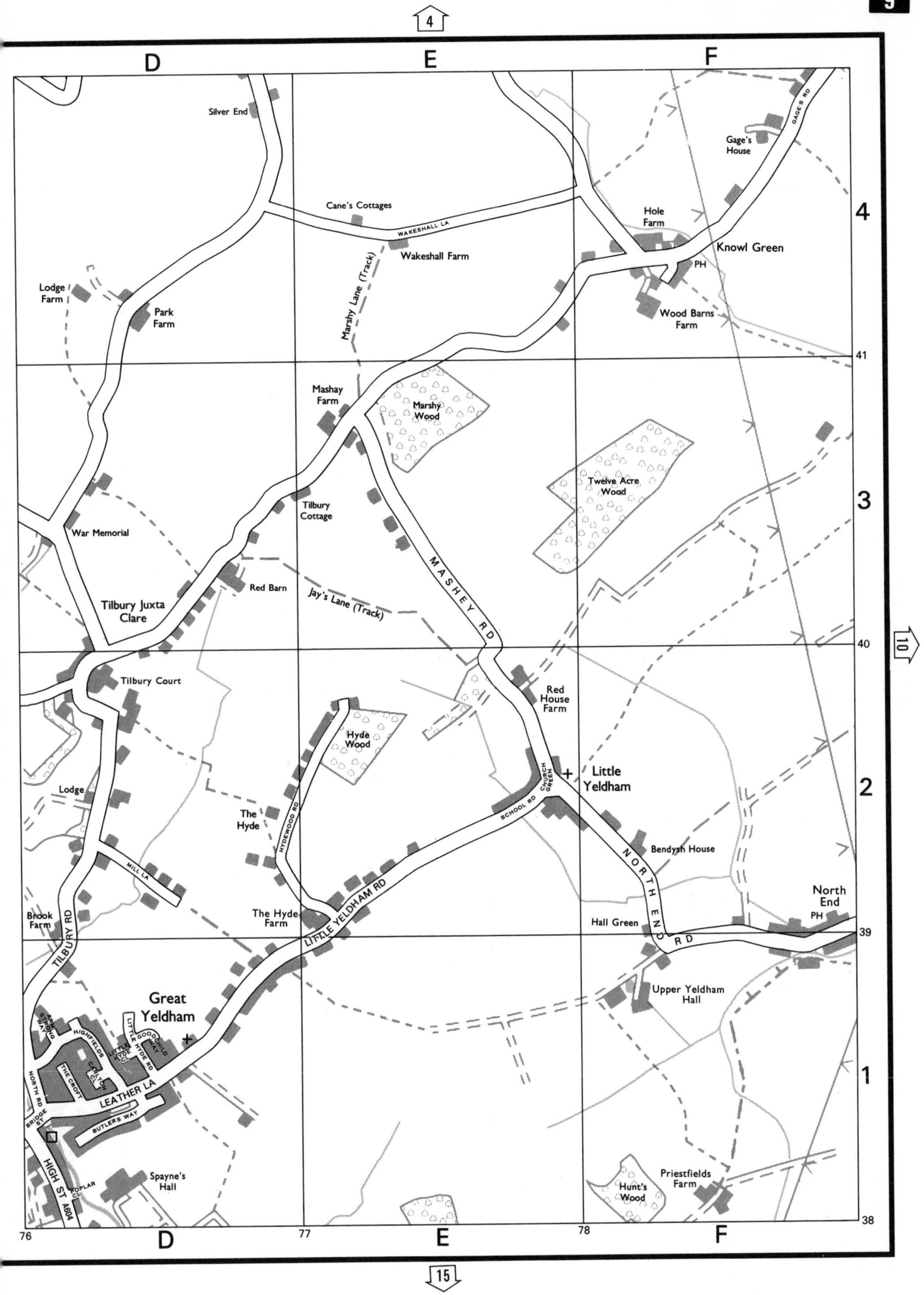
4
D
E
F
Silver End
Cane's Cottages
WAKESHALL LA
Wakeshall Farm
Marshy Lane (Track)
Gage's House
GAGES RD
Hole Farm
Knowl Green
PH
Wood Barns Farm
Lodge Farm
Park Farm
4
41
Mashay Farm
Marshy Wood
Twelve Acre Wood
Tilbury Cottage
3
War Memorial
MASHEY RD
Red Barn
Jay's Lane (Track)
Tilbury Juxta Clare
40
10
Tilbury Court
Red House Farm
Hyde Wood
CHURCH GREEN
Little Yeldham
Lodge
The Hyde
HYDEWOOD RD
SCHOOL RD
2
Bendysh House
MILL LA
NORTH END RD
North End
PH
Brook Farm
The Hyde Farm
Hall Green
LITTLE YELDHAM RD
TILBURY RD
39
Upper Yeldham Hall
Great Yeldham
ARMSTRONG WAY
HIGHFIELDS
LITTLE HYDE CL
LITTLE HYDE RD
GOODCHILD WAY
CARLTON CL
THE CROFT
NORTH RD
LEATHER LA
BUTLERS WAY
BRIDGE ST
1
HIGH ST A604
Spayne's Hall
POPLAR CL
Hunt's Wood
Priestfields Farm
38
76
77
78
D
E
F
15

5

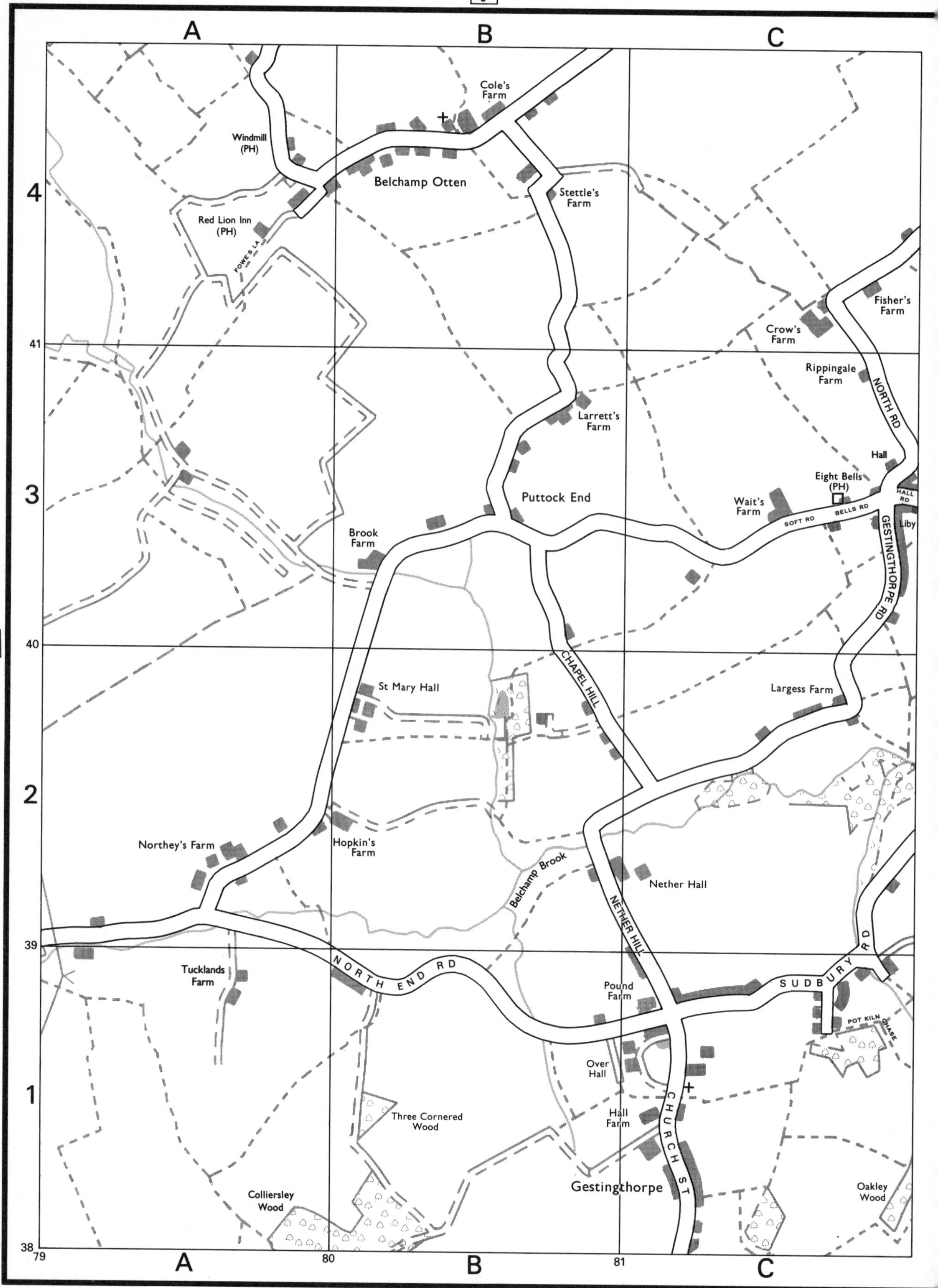
A
B
C
4
3
2
1
41
40
39
38
79
80
81
Windmill (PH)
Cole's Farm
Belchamp Otten
Stettle's Farm
Red Lion Inn (PH)
FOWE'S LA
Fisher's Farm
Crow's Farm
Rippingale Farm
NORTH RD
Larrett's Farm
Hall
Eight Bells (PH)
Puttock End
Wait's Farm
SOFT RD
BELLS RD
HALL RD
Liby
GESTINGTHORPE RD
Brook Farm
St Mary Hall
CHAPEL HILL
Largess Farm
Northey's Farm
Hopkin's Farm
Belchamp Brook
Nether Hall
NETHER HILL
Tucklands Farm
NORTH END RD
Pound Farm
SUDBURY RD
POT KILN CHASE
Over Hall
Three Cornered Wood
Hall Farm
CHURCH ST
Colliersley Wood
Gestingthorpe
Oakley Wood

9

16

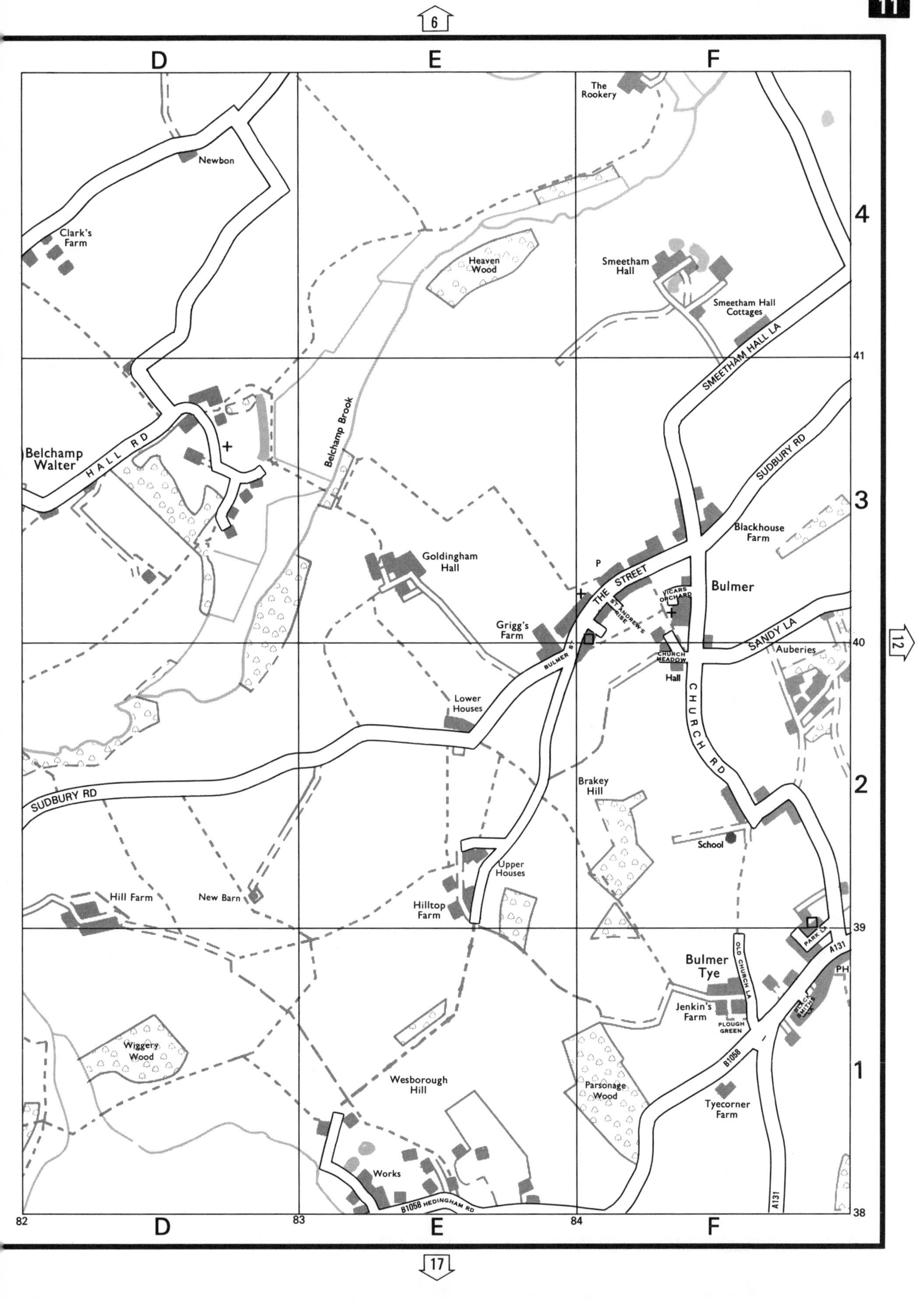
6
D
E
F
The Rookery
Newbon
Clark's Farm
Heaven Wood
Smeetham Hall
Smeetham Hall Cottages
SMEETHAM HALL LA
Belchamp Walter
HALL RD
Belchamp Brook
SUDBURY RD
Goldingham Hall
Blackhouse Farm
P
THE STREET
VICARS ORCHARD
ST ANDREW'S RISE
Bulmer
Grigg's Farm
BULMER ST
SANDY LA
Auberies
CHURCH MEADOW
Hall
CHURCH RD
Lower Houses
SUDBURY RD
Brakey Hill
School
Upper Houses
Hill Farm
New Barn
Hilltop Farm
PARK LA
A131
Bulmer Tye
OLD CHURCH LA
PH
Jenkin's Farm
PLOUGH GREEN
BLACKSMITHS LA
Wiggery Wood
B1058
Wesborough Hill
Parsonage Wood
Tyecorner Farm
Works
B1058 HEDINGHAM RD
A131
4
41
3
40
2
39
1
38
82
83
84
12
17

7

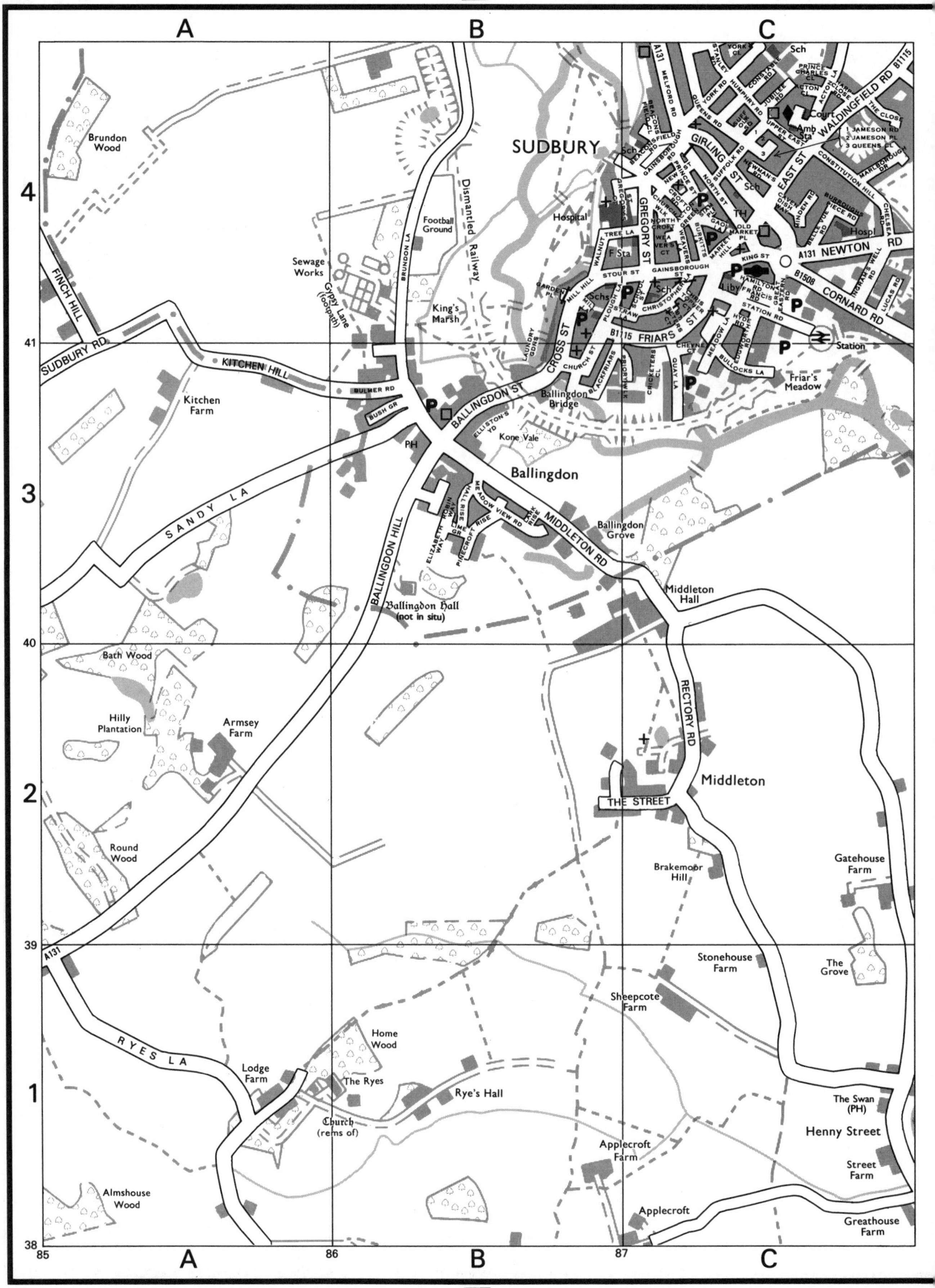
A
B
C
SUDBURY
Brundon Wood
Football Ground
Dismantled Railway
Sewage Works
Gypsy Lane (footpath)
BRUNDON LA
King's Marsh
Hospital
F Sta
Sch
Schs
TH
Court
Amb Sta
Hospl
Liby
Station
Friar's Meadow
FINCH HILL
SUDBURY RD
KITCHEN HILL
BULMER RD
BUSH GR
Kitchen Farm
PH
BALLINGDON ST
ELLISTON'S YD
Kone Vale
Ballingdon Bridge
Ballingdon
SANDY LA
BALLINGDON HILL
HALL RISE
MEADOW VIEW RD
MIDDLETON RD
PINECROFT RISE
ELIZABETH WAY
ROBIN WAY
LIME GR
Ballingdon Grove
Middleton Hall
Ballingdon Hall (not in situ)
GREGORY ST
CROSS ST
FRIARS ST
B1115
STOUR ST
GAINSBOROUGH ST
MILL HILL
WALNUT TREE LA
CHURCH ST
BLACKFRIARS
PRIORY WLK
CRICKETERS CL
QUAY LA
MEADOW LA
BULLOCKS LA
STATION RD
HAMILTON RD
FRANCIS RD
NEWTON RD
A131
CORNARD RD
B1508
EAST ST
GIRLING ST
SUFFOLK RD
NORTH ST
WALDINGFIELD RD B1115
CONSTITUTION HILL
MELFORD RD
QUEENS RD
YORK RD
STANLEY RD
HUMPHRY RD
THE CLOSE
1 JAMESON RD
2 JAMESON PL
3 QUEENS CL
INGRAM'S WELL RD
LUCAS RD
CHELSEA RD
MARLBOROUGH DR
41
40
39
38
4
3
2
1
85
86
87
Bath Wood
Hilly Plantation
Armsey Farm
Round Wood
RECTORY RD
Middleton
THE STREET
Brakemoor Hill
Gatehouse Farm
Stonehouse Farm
Sheepcote Farm
The Grove
RYES LA
Home Wood
Lodge Farm
The Ryes
Rye's Hall
Church (rems of)
Applecroft Farm
Applecroft
The Swan (PH)
Henny Street
Street Farm
Greathouse Farm
Almshouse Wood

11

18

not continued, see key diagram

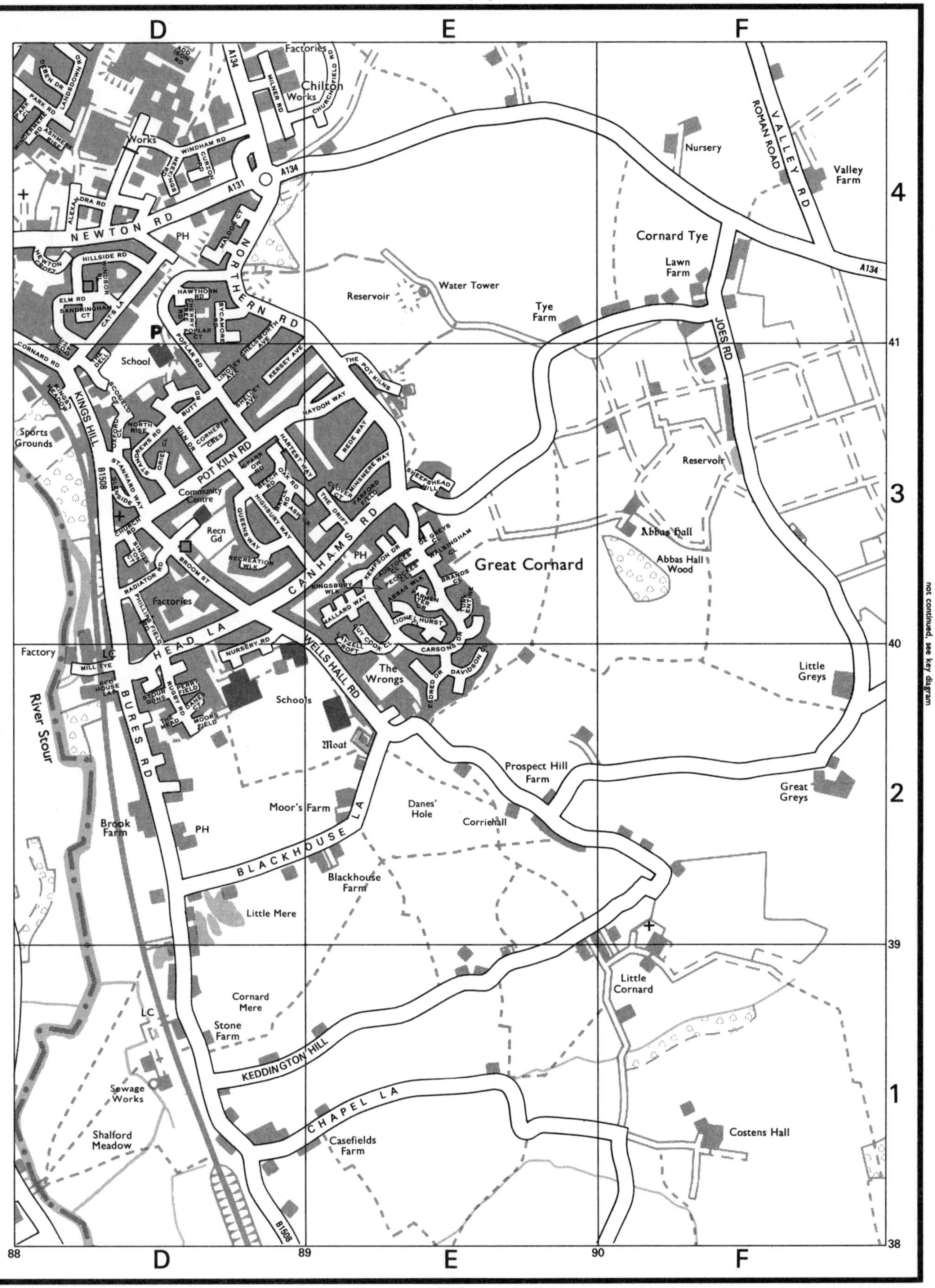

not continued, see key diagram

19

8

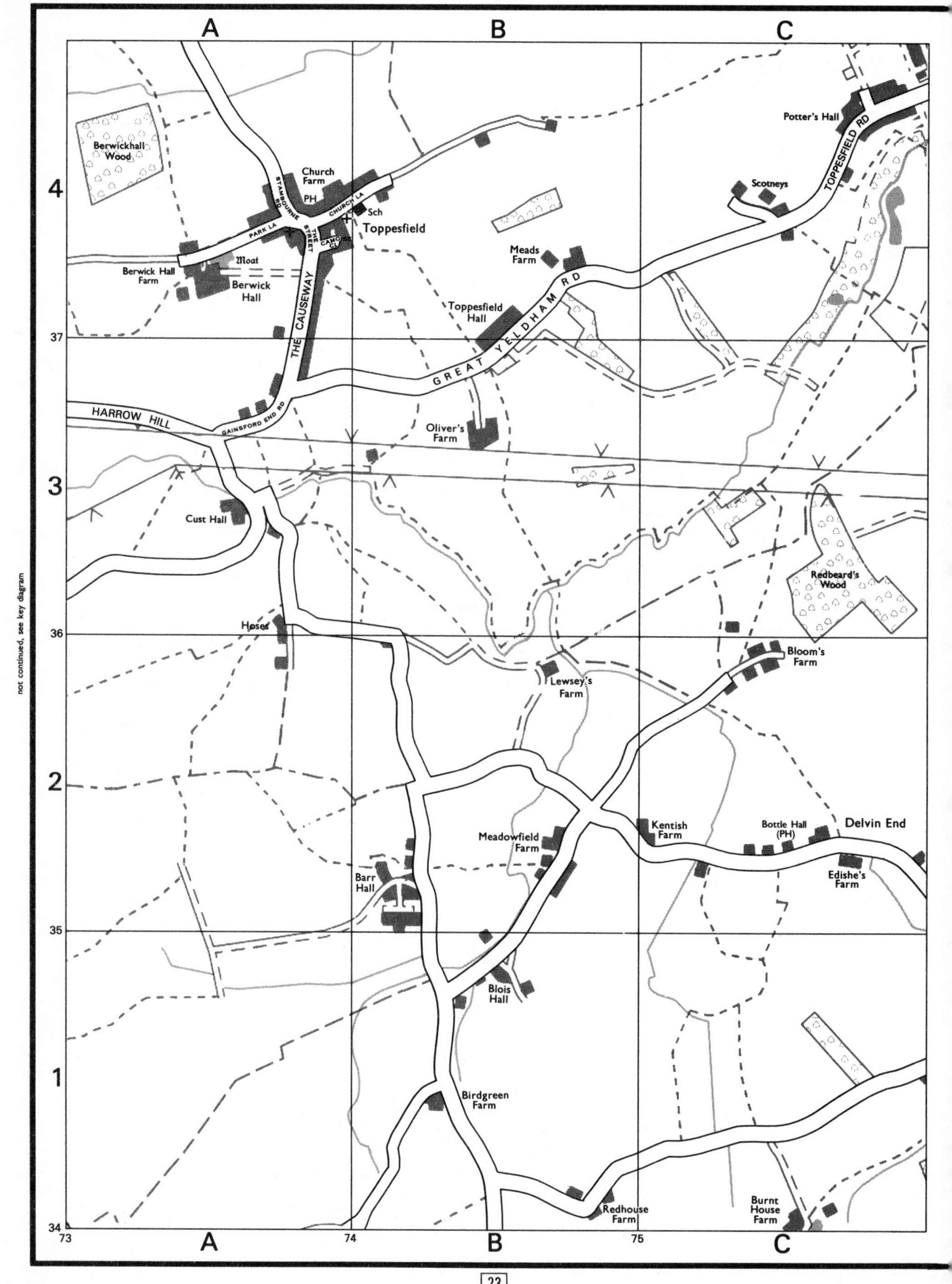
A
B
C
4
3
2
1
37
36
35
34
73
74
75
Berwickhall Wood
Church Farm
PH
Sch
Toppesfield
STAMBOURNE RD
CHURCH LA
PARK LA
THE STREET
CAMOISE CL
Moat
Berwick Hall Farm
Berwick Hall
THE CAUSEWAY
Meads Farm
Toppesfield Hall
GREAT YELDHAM RD
Potter's Hall
TOPPESFIELD RD
Scotneys
HARROW HILL
GAINSFORD END RD
Oliver's Farm
Cust Hall
Redbeard's Wood
Hoses
Bloom's Farm
Lewsey's Farm
Meadowfield Farm
Kentish Farm
Bottle Hall (PH)
Delvin End
Edishe's Farm
Barr Hall
Blois Hall
Birdgreen Farm
Redhouse Farm
Burnt House Farm
not continued, see key diagram

23

9

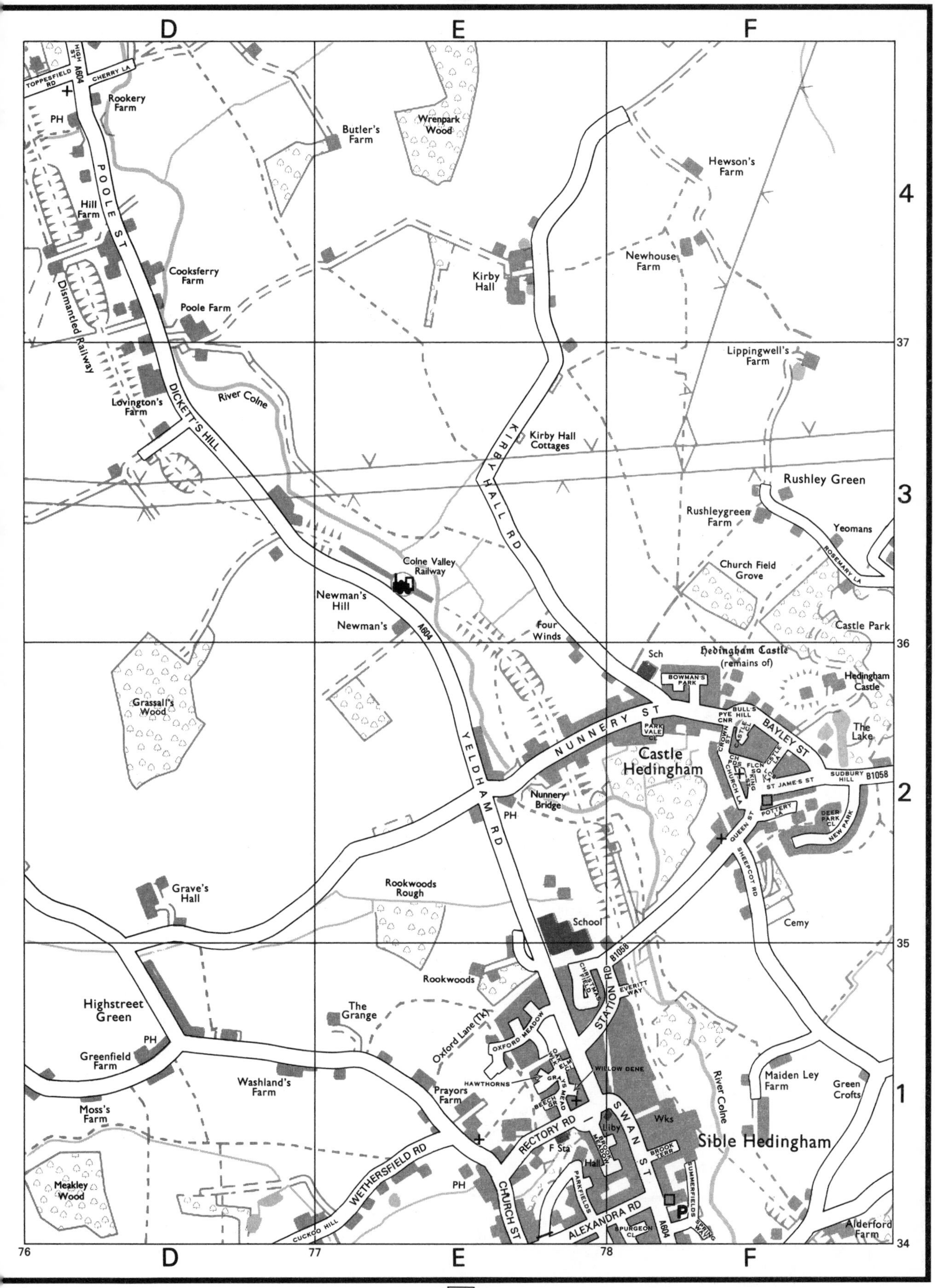

D
E
F
4
3
2
1
37
36
35
34
76
77
78
TOPPESFIELD RD
HIGH ST
A604
CHERRY LA
Rookery Farm
PH
Butler's Farm
Wrenpark Wood
Hewson's Farm
POOLE ST
Hill Farm
Cooksferry Farm
Poole Farm
Dismantled Railway
Kirby Hall
Newhouse Farm
Lippingwell's Farm
Lovington's Farm
DICKETT'S HILL
River Colne
KIRBY HALL RD
Kirby Hall Cottages
Rushley Green
Rushleygreen Farm
Yeomans
ROSEMARY LA
Church Field Grove
Colne Valley Railway
Newman's Hill
Newman's
Four Winds
Castle Park
Sch
Hedingham Castle (remains of)
Hedingham Castle
BOWMAN'S PARK
Grassall's Wood
YELDHAM RD
NUNNERY ST
PARK VALE CL
PYE CNR
BULL'S HILL
CROWN ST
CASTLE ST
BAYLEY ST
The Lake
Castle Hedingham
CH PDS
CHURCH LA
FLCN SQ
KING ST
CASTLE LA
SUDBURY HILL
B1058
ST JAMES'S ST
Nunnery Bridge
POTTERY LA
DEER PARK CL
NEW PARK
QUEEN ST
SHEEPCOT RD
Rookwoods Rough
Grave's Hall
School
Cemy
Rookwoods
CHRISTMAS FIELD
STATION RD
EVERITT WAY
Highstreet Green
The Grange
Oxford Lane (Tk)
OXFORD MEADOW
OAK WALK
ELM
WILLOW DENE
Greenfield Farm
Washland's Farm
HAWTHORNS
GR
HAYS MEAD
BEECH GR
Prayors Farm
River Colne
Maiden Ley Farm
Green Crofts
Moss's Farm
SWAN ST
Wks
RECTORY RD
Liby
BROOK MEADOW
Sible Hedingham
F Sta
Hall
BROOK TERR
WETHERSFIELD RD
PARKFIELDS
SUMMERFIELDS
Meakley Wood
PH
CHURCH ST
ALEXANDRA RD
P
CUCKOO HILL
SPURGEON CL
SPRING WAY
Alderford Farm

16

24

10

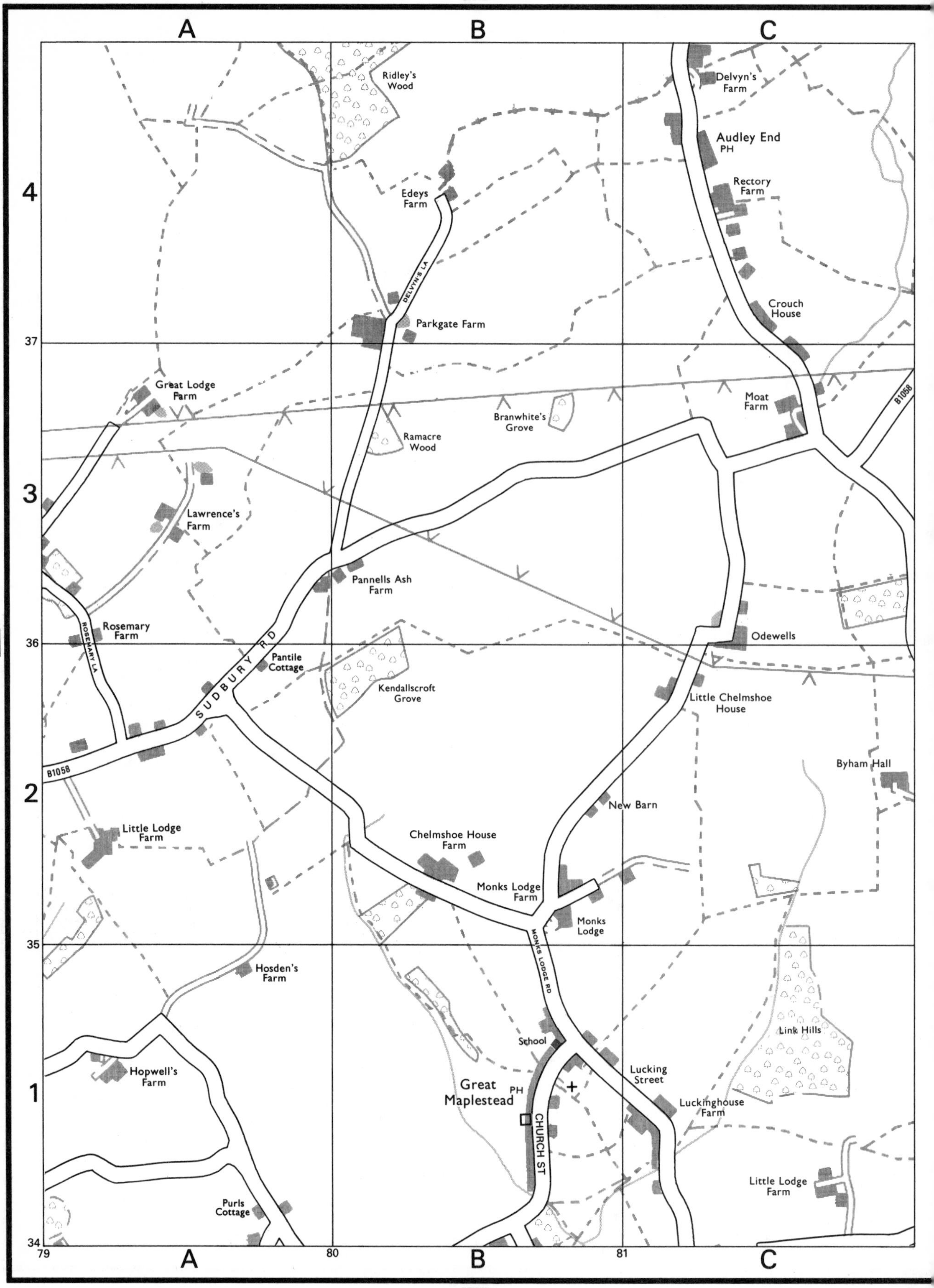
A
B
C
4
3
2
1
37
36
35
34
79
80
81
Ridley's Wood
Delvyn's Farm
Audley End
PH
Rectory Farm
Edeys Farm
DELVYN'S LA
Crouch House
Parkgate Farm
Great Lodge Farm
Moat Farm
B1058
Branwhite's Grove
Ramacre Wood
Lawrence's Farm
Pannells Ash Farm
Rosemary Farm
ROSEMARY LA
Odewells
Pantile Cottage
SUDBURY RD
Kendallscroft Grove
Little Chelmshoe House
B1058
Byham Hall
New Barn
Little Lodge Farm
Chelmshoe House Farm
Monks Lodge Farm
Monks Lodge
MONKS LODGE RD
Hosden's Farm
Link Hills
School
Lucking Street
Hopwell's Farm
Great Maplestead
PH
Luckinghouse Farm
CHURCH ST
Little Lodge Farm
Purls Cottage

15

25

11

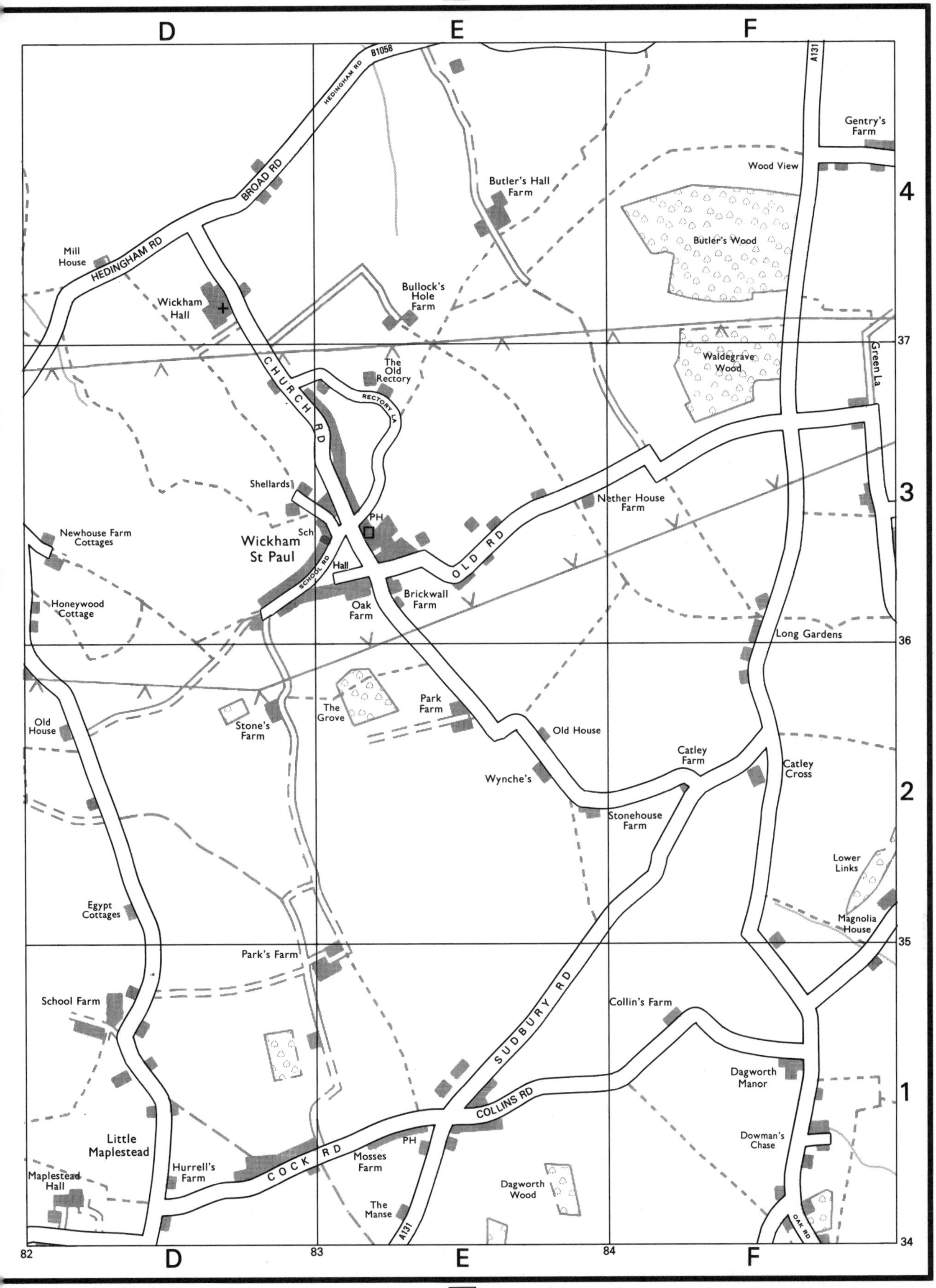
D
E
F
B1058
HEDINGHAM RD
BROAD RD
HEDINGHAM RD
Mill House
Wickham Hall
CHURCH RD
The Old Rectory
RECTORY LA
Bullock's Hole Farm
Butler's Hall Farm
A131
Gentry's Farm
Wood View
Butler's Wood
Waldegrave Wood
Green La
4
37
3
Shellards
Wickham St Paul
Sch
PH
Hall
SCHOOL RD
Newhouse Farm Cottages
Honeywood Cottage
Oak Farm
Brickwall Farm
OLD RD
Nether House Farm
Long Gardens
36
The Grove
Park Farm
Stone's Farm
Old House
Old House
Catley Farm
Catley Cross
Wynche's
Stonehouse Farm
2
Lower Links
Magnolia House
Egypt Cottages
35
Park's Farm
School Farm
SUDBURY RD
Collin's Farm
Dagworth Manor
1
COLLINS RD
Little Maplestead
Dowman's Chase
Hurrell's Farm
COCK RD
PH
Mosses Farm
Maplestead Hall
The Manse
A131
Dagworth Wood
OAK RD
34
82
83
84
D
E
F

18

26

12

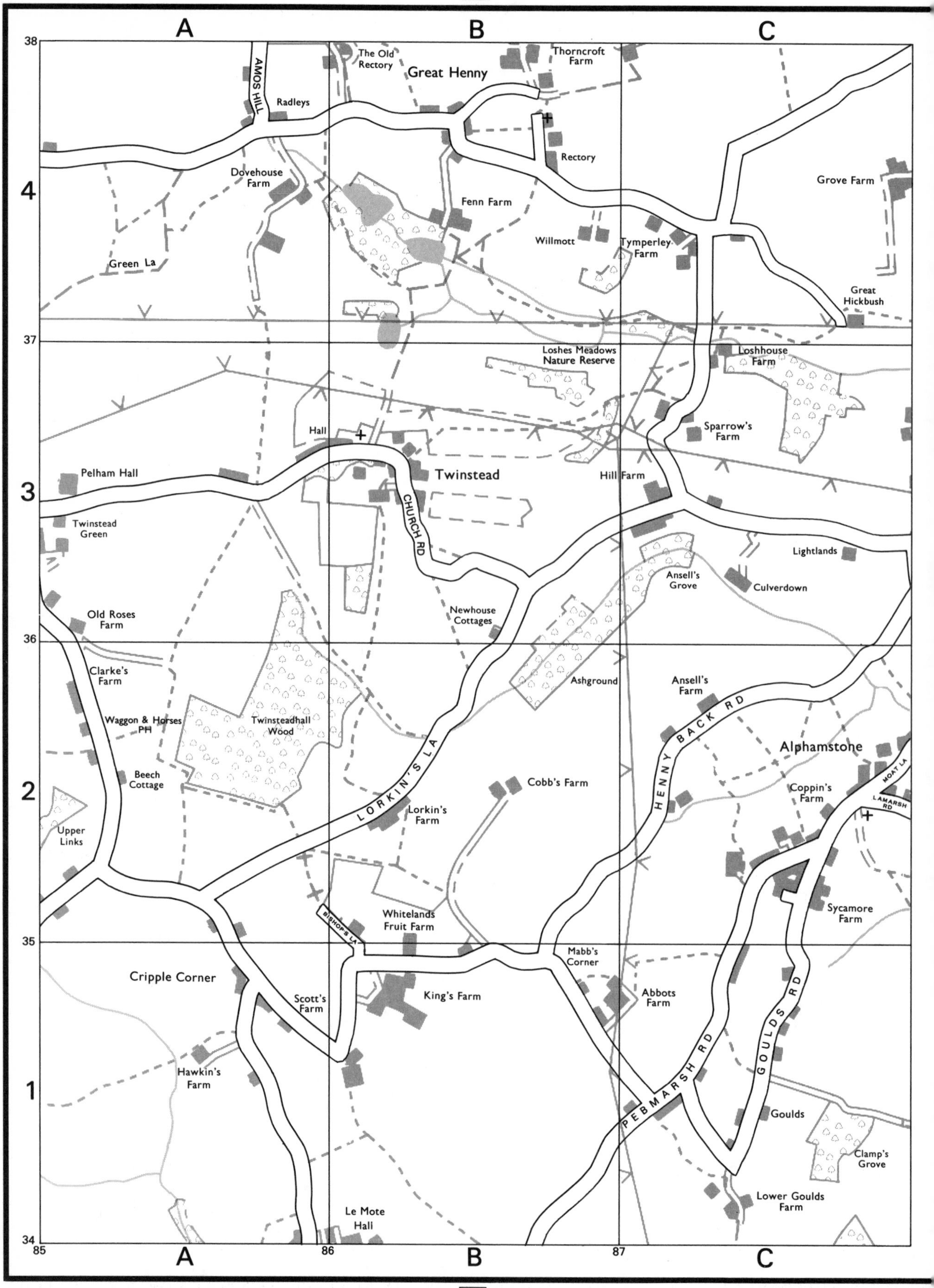

A
B
C
38
37
36
35
34
85
86
87
4
3
2
1
AMOS HILL
Radleys
The Old Rectory
Great Henny
Thorncroft Farm
Rectory
Dovehouse Farm
Fenn Farm
Grove Farm
Willmott
Tymperley Farm
Green La
Great Hickbush
Loshes Meadows Nature Reserve
Loshhouse Farm
Sparrow's Farm
Hall
Twinstead
Hill Farm
Pelham Hall
Twinstead Green
CHURCH RD
Lightlands
Ansell's Grove
Culverdown
Old Roses Farm
Newhouse Cottages
Clarke's Farm
Ashground
Ansell's Farm
Waggon & Horses PH
Twinsteadhall Wood
HENNY BACK RD
Alphamstone
Beech Cottage
Cobb's Farm
Coppin's Farm
MOAT LA
LAMARSH RD
Upper Links
LORKIN'S LA
Lorkin's Farm
Sycamore Farm
BISHOPS LA
Whitelands Fruit Farm
Mabb's Corner
Cripple Corner
King's Farm
Abbots Farm
Scott's Farm
GOULDS RD
PEBMARSH RD
Hawkin's Farm
Goulds
Clamp's Grove
Lower Goulds Farm
Le Mote Hall

17

27

13

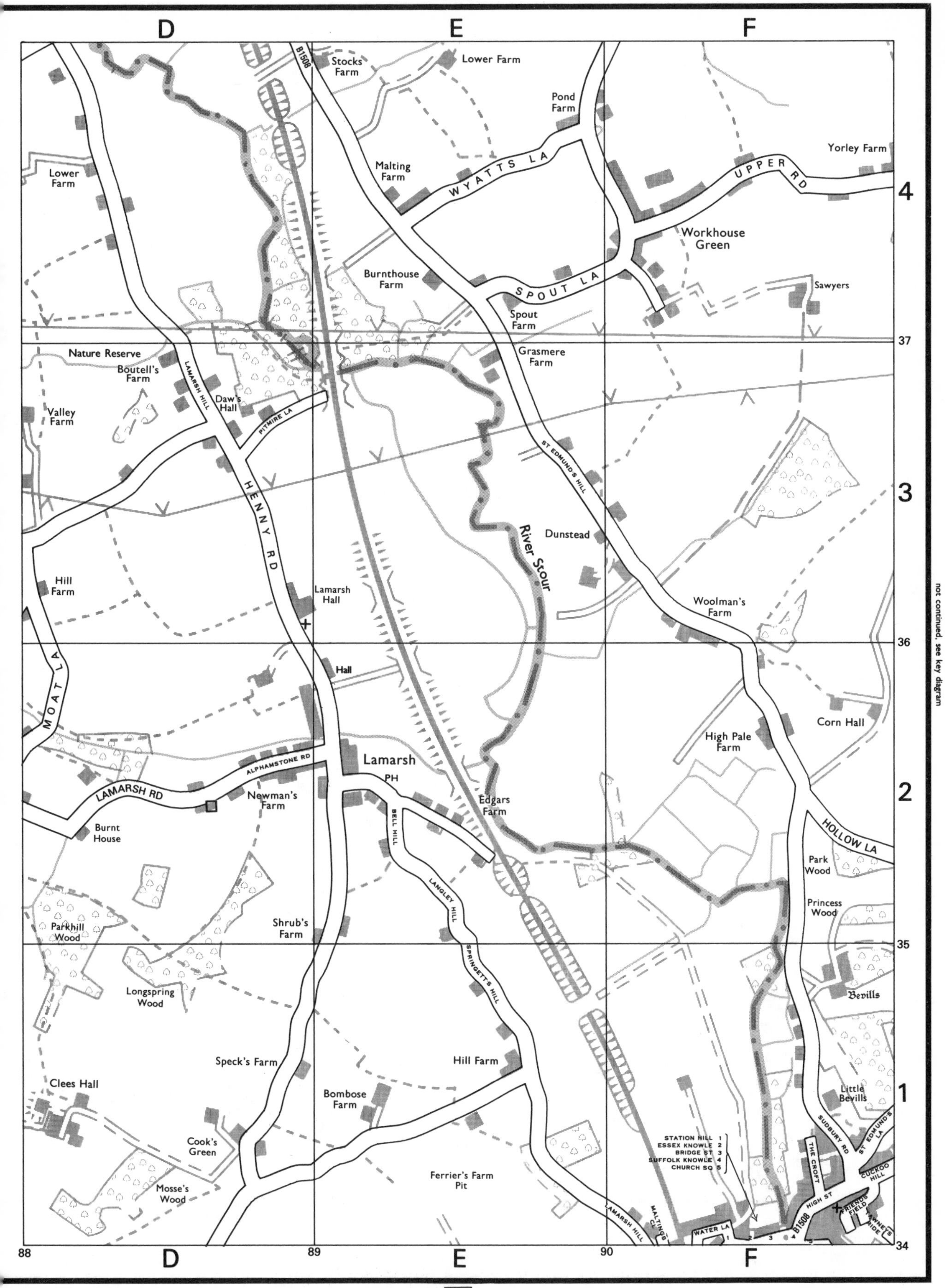
D
E
F
Stocks Farm
Lower Farm
Pond Farm
Yorley Farm
Lower Farm
Malting Farm
WYATTS LA
UPPER RD
Workhouse Green
Burnthouse Farm
SPOUT LA
Sawyers
Spout Farm
Nature Reserve
Boutell's Farm
Grasmere Farm
Valley Farm
Daw's Hall
LAMARSH HILL
PITMIRE LA
ST EDMUND'S HILL
HENNY RD
River Stour
Dunstead
Hill Farm
Lamarsh Hall
Woolman's Farm
Hall
MOAT LA
Corn Hall
High Pale Farm
Lamarsh
ALPHAMSTONE RD
LAMARSH RD
PH
Newman's Farm
Edgars Farm
BELL HILL
HOLLOW LA
Burnt House
Park Wood
LANGLEY HILL
Princess Wood
Parkhill Wood
Shrub's Farm
SPRINGETT'S HILL
Bevills
Longspring Wood
Speck's Farm
Hill Farm
Clees Hall
Bombose Farm
Little Bevills
Cook's Green
STATION HILL 1
ESSEX KNOWLE 2
BRIDGE ST 3
SUFFOLK KNOWLE 4
CHURCH SQ 5
SUDBURY RD
ST EDMUND'S LA
THE CROFT
CUCKOO HILL
Ferrier's Farm Pit
Mosse's Wood
HIGH ST
FRIENDS FIELD
FAWNES RIDE
LAMARSH HILL
MALTINGS CL
WATER LA
B1508
4
37
3
36
2
35
1
34
88
89
90
not continued, see key diagram

28

not continued, see key diagram

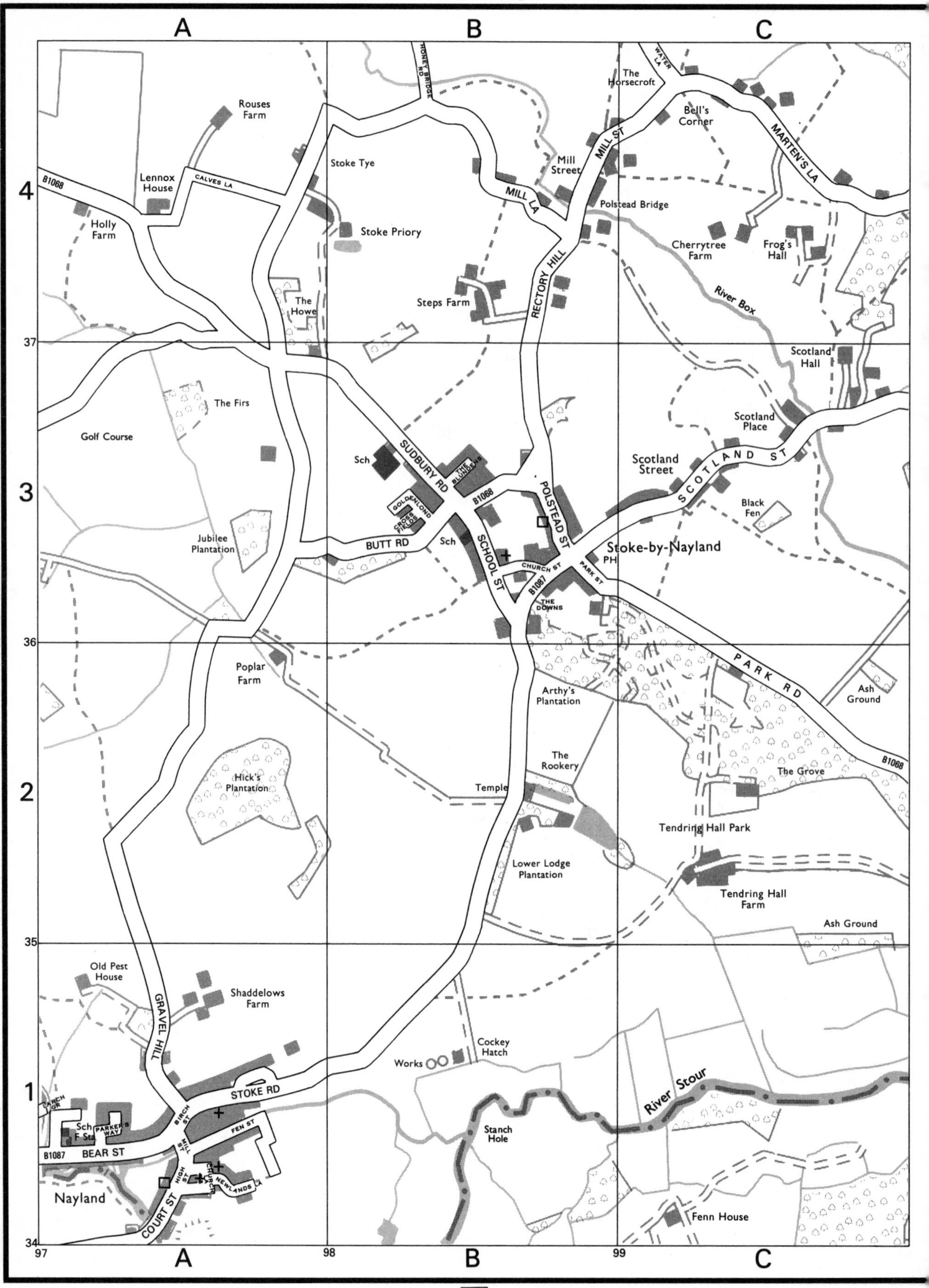

not continued, see key diagram

31

not continued, see key diagram

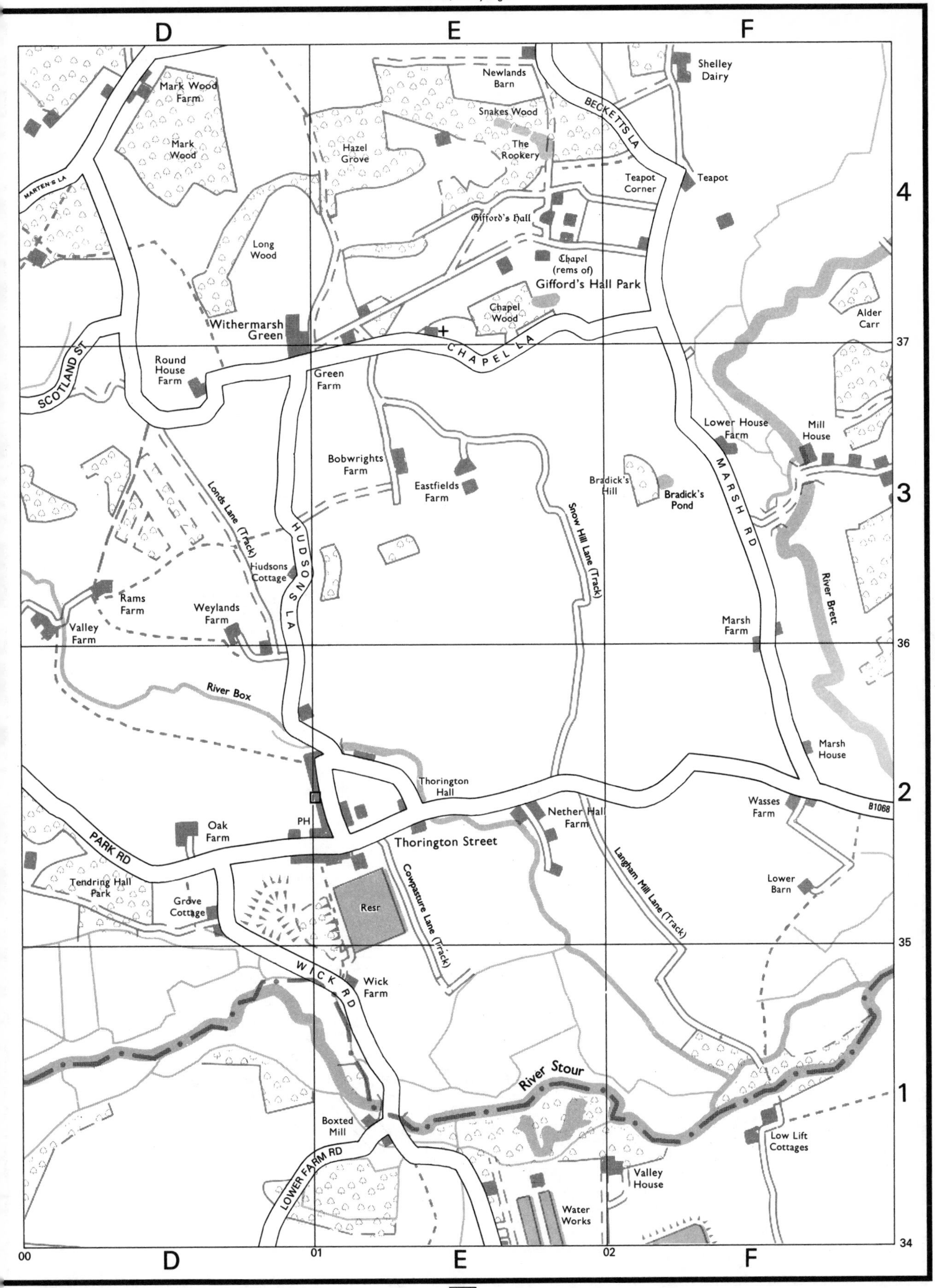

D
E
F
Shelley Dairy
Newlands Barn
Mark Wood Farm
Snakes Wood
BECKETTS LA
Mark Wood
Hazel Grove
The Rookery
Teapot Corner
Teapot
4
MARTEN'S LA
Gifford's Hall
Long Wood
Chapel (rems of)
Gifford's Hall Park
Chapel Wood
Alder Carr
Withermarsh Green
37
CHAPEL LA
Round House Farm
Green Farm
SCOTLAND ST
Lower House Farm
Mill House
Bobwrights Farm
Eastfields Farm
Bradick's Hill
Bradick's Pond
3
Londs Lane (Track)
HUDSONS LA
Snow Hill Lane (Track)
MARSH RD
River Brett
Hudsons Cottage
Rams Farm
Weylands Farm
Valley Farm
Marsh Farm
36
River Box
Marsh House
Thorington Hall
2
Wasses Farm
B1068
Nether Hall Farm
PH
Oak Farm
PARK RD
Thorington Street
Compasture Lane (Track)
Langham Mill Lane (Track)
Lower Barn
Tendring Hall Park
Grove Cottage
Resr
35
WICK RD
Wick Farm
River Stour
1
Boxted Mill
Low Lift Cottages
LOWER FARM RD
Valley House
Water Works
00
01
02
34
D
E
F

22

not continued, see key diagram

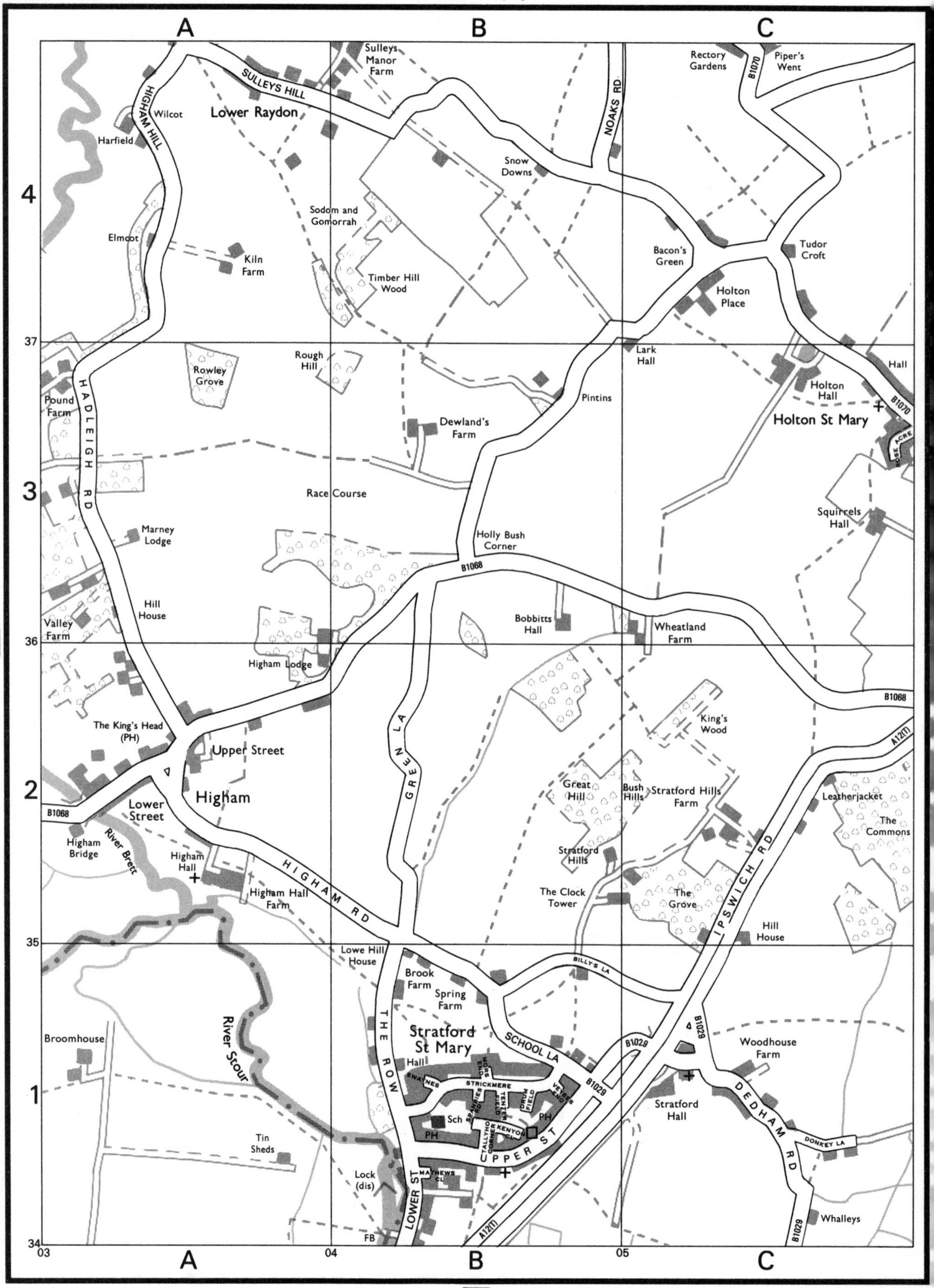

A
B
C
4
3
2
1
37
36
35
34
03
04
05
Sulleys Manor Farm
SULLEYS HILL
Lower Raydon
Wilcot
Harfield
HIGHAM HILL
NOAKS RD.
Rectory Gardens
Piper's Went
B1070
Snow Downs
Sodom and Gomorrah
Elmcot
Kiln Farm
Timber Hill Wood
Bacon's Green
Tudor Croft
Holton Place
Lark Hall
Hall
Holton Hall
Holton St Mary
ROSE ACRE
Rough Hill
Rowley Grove
Pound Farm
HADLEIGH RD
Pintins
Dewland's Farm
Race Course
Squirrels Hall
Marney Lodge
Holly Bush Corner
B1068
Hill House
Valley Farm
Bobbitts Hall
Wheatland Farm
Higham Lodge
The King's Head (PH)
Upper Street
King's Wood
A12(T)
GREEN LA
Higham
Lower Street
Great Hill
Bush Hills
Stratford Hills Farm
Leatherjacket
The Commons
Higham Bridge
River Brett
Higham Hall
Stratford Hills
IPSWICH RD
HIGHAM RD
Higham Hall Farm
The Clock Tower
The Grove
Hill House
Lowe Hill House
BILLY'S LA
Brook Farm
Spring Farm
River Stour
Broomhouse
THE ROW
Stratford St Mary
SCHOOL LA
B1029
Woodhouse Farm
Hall
SWAYNES
STRICKMERE
MORS END
TENTER FIELD
DRUM FIELD
VESEYS END
SPANBIES RD
Sch
KENYON CL
PH
TALLYHO CORNER
UPPER ST
DEDHAM RD
Stratford Hall
DONKEY LA
Tin Sheds
Lock (dis)
MATHEWS CL
LOWER ST
Whalleys
FB

21

33

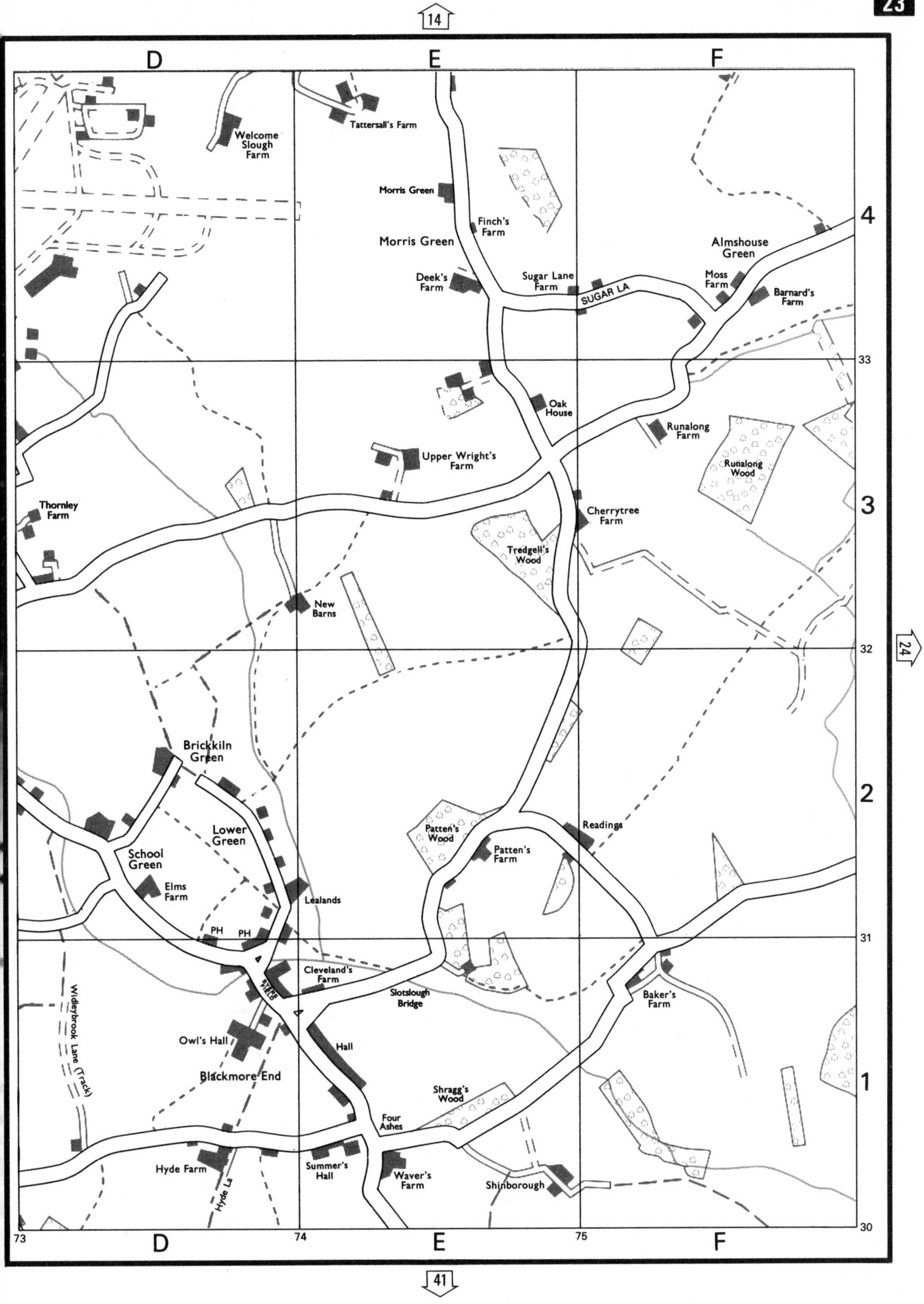
14
D
E
F
Welcome Slough Farm
Tattersall's Farm
Morris Green
Finch's Farm
Morris Green
Almshouse Green
Deek's Farm
Sugar Lane Farm
SUGAR LA
Moss Farm
Barnard's Farm
4
33
Oak House
Runalong Farm
Upper Wright's Farm
Runalong Wood
Thornley Farm
Cherrytree Farm
3
Tredgell's Wood
New Barns
32
24
Brickkiln Green
2
Lower Green
Readings
Patten's Wood
Patten's Farm
School Green
Elms Farm
Lealands
PH
PH
31
Cleveland's Farm
Baker's Farm
Slotslough Bridge
Widleybrook Lane (Track)
Owl's Hall
Hall
Blackmore End
1
Shragg's Wood
Four Ashes
Hyde Farm
Summer's Hall
Waver's Farm
Shinborough
Hyde La
30
73
74
75
41

15

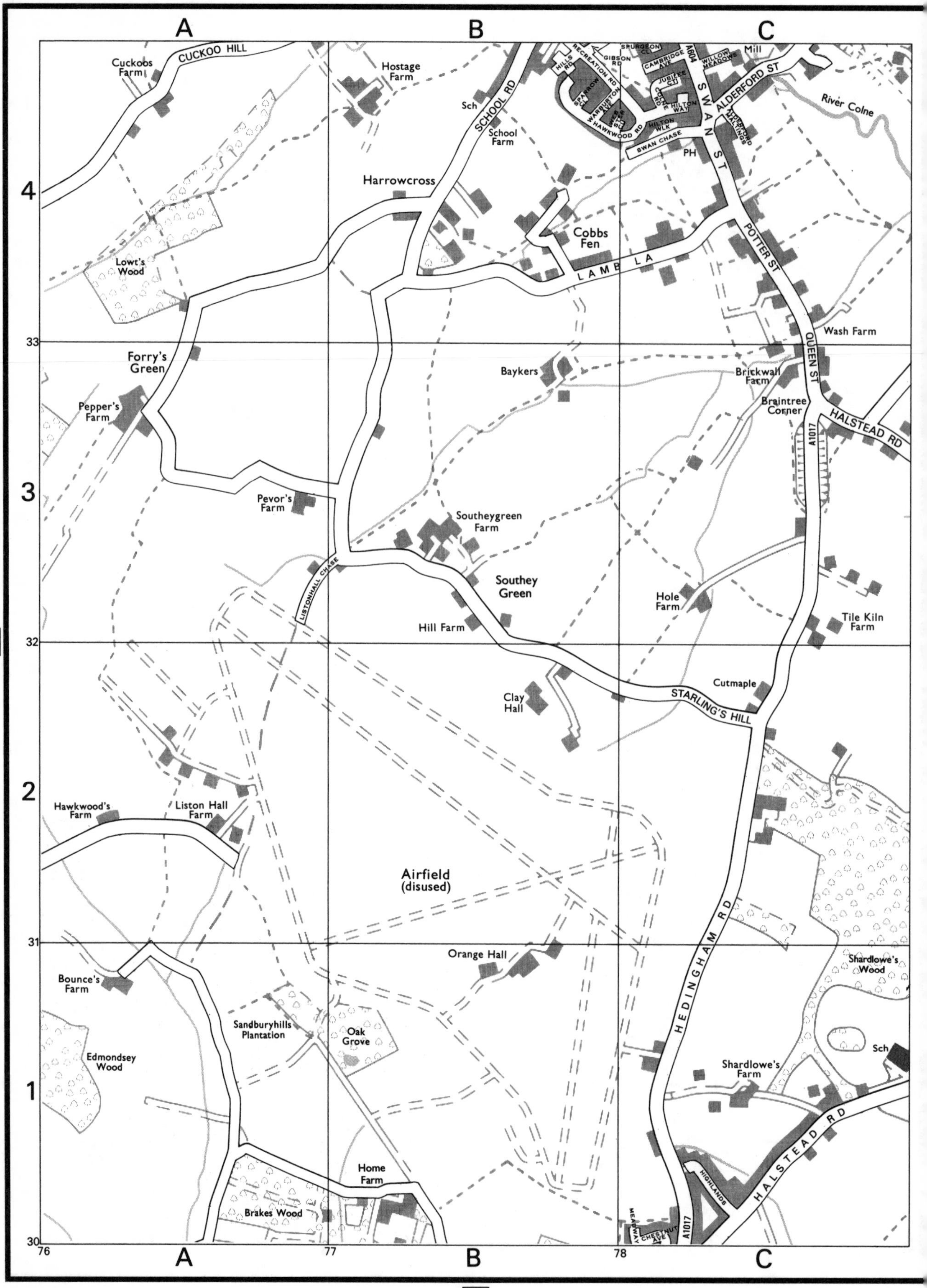

A
B
C
CUCKOO HILL
Cuckoos Farm
Hostage Farm
Sch
SCHOOL RD
School Farm
Harrowcross
RECREATION RD
GIBSON RD
SPURGEON CL
HILLS RD
CAMBRIDGE AVE
JUBILEE CT
A604
WILLOW MEADOWS
Mill
ALDERFORD ST
River Colne
SPARROW CL
WARBURTON AVE
HAWKWOOD RD
HILTON WAY
HILTON WLK
SWAN CHASE
SWAN ST
ALDERFORD MALTINGS
PH
Cobbs Fen
LAMB LA
POTTER ST
Lowt's Wood
Wash Farm
QUEEN ST
Forry's Green
Baykers
Brickwall Farm
Braintree Corner
Pepper's Farm
HALSTEAD RD
A1017
Pevor's Farm
Southeygreen Farm
LISTONHALL CHASE
Southey Green
Hole Farm
Hill Farm
Tile Kiln Farm
Cutmaple
Clay Hall
STARLING'S HILL
Hawkwood's Farm
Liston Hall Farm
Airfield (disused)
HEDINGHAM RD
Orange Hall
Shardlowe's Wood
Bounce's Farm
Sandburyhills Plantation
Oak Grove
Edmondsey Wood
Shardlowe's Farm
Sch
HALSTEAD RD
HIGHLANDS
Home Farm
Brakes Wood
MEADWAY
CHESTNUT AVE
A1017
4
33
3
32
2
31
1
30
76
77
78
23

42

16

D
E
F
Purlshill
Purlshill Plantation
Barrett's Hall
DYNE'S HALL RD
MILL LA
Mill Farm
Chestnut Grove
Mill
Wallace's Plantation
Dyne's Hall
Wallace's Farm
Bennett's Park
Bennett's Farm
A604 HALSTEAD RD
Sparrows Farm
Valley Farm
Foxborough Hill Farm
Dismantled Railway
Hepworth Hall
Fitz John's Farm
Fitz John's Grove
Doe's Corner
A604
Brook Street Farm
River Colne
HOWE CHASE
The Howe
HEDINGHAM RD
ASHLONG GR
Broak's Wood
Box Mill Plantation
Wash Farm
CHURCHILL AVE
SUDBURY RD
A131
Sloe House
BOX MILL LA
COURTAULD HOMES
Hospl
Whitehouse Farm
Whiteash Green
Sch
SLOE HILL
SLOUGH FARM RD
BELLEVUE TERR
MILL CHASE
HEAD ST
COLNE RD
BOIS FIELD TERR
CHIPPING HILL
FLEECE YD
MORLEY RD
PRETORIA RD
EAST MILL
STANLEY RD
BUTLER RD
ROSEMARY LA
CHAPEL ST
UPPER CHAPEL ST
MARKET HILL
COLCHESTER RD A604
BERIDGE RD
BROTON DR
HIGH ST
BROOM HILL
MANFIELD
HIGHBURY TERR
Little Spansey Wood
HALSTEAD RD
Sch
CHAPEL HILL
TRINITY ST A131
BRIDGE ST
Great Spansey Wood
MALLOW FIELD
HARVEY ST
MIDDLEFIELD
RUSSELL'S RD
ORCHARD AVE
DOOLEY RD
Liby
FACTORY TERR
ST ANDREWS RD
WEAVERS ROW
KINGS RD
FACTORY LA E
VICARAGE MEADOW
GARDENERS RD
NEW ST
TRINITY RD
FACTORY LA W
MARTIN'S RD
Sch
PARSONAGE ST
COURTAULD CL
WINDMILL RD
MONKLANDS CT
MOUNT HILL
GODWIN CL
WARREN
HALSTEAD
SPANSEY CT
ACORN AVE
MOUNT PLEASANT
MITCHELL AVE
F Sta
The Grange
Blamster's Farm
A131
DE VERES RD
OXFORD RD
TIDINGS HILL
ELM DR
RAVENS AVE
RIVER CL
79
80
81
33
32
31
30
4
3
2
1

26

43

17

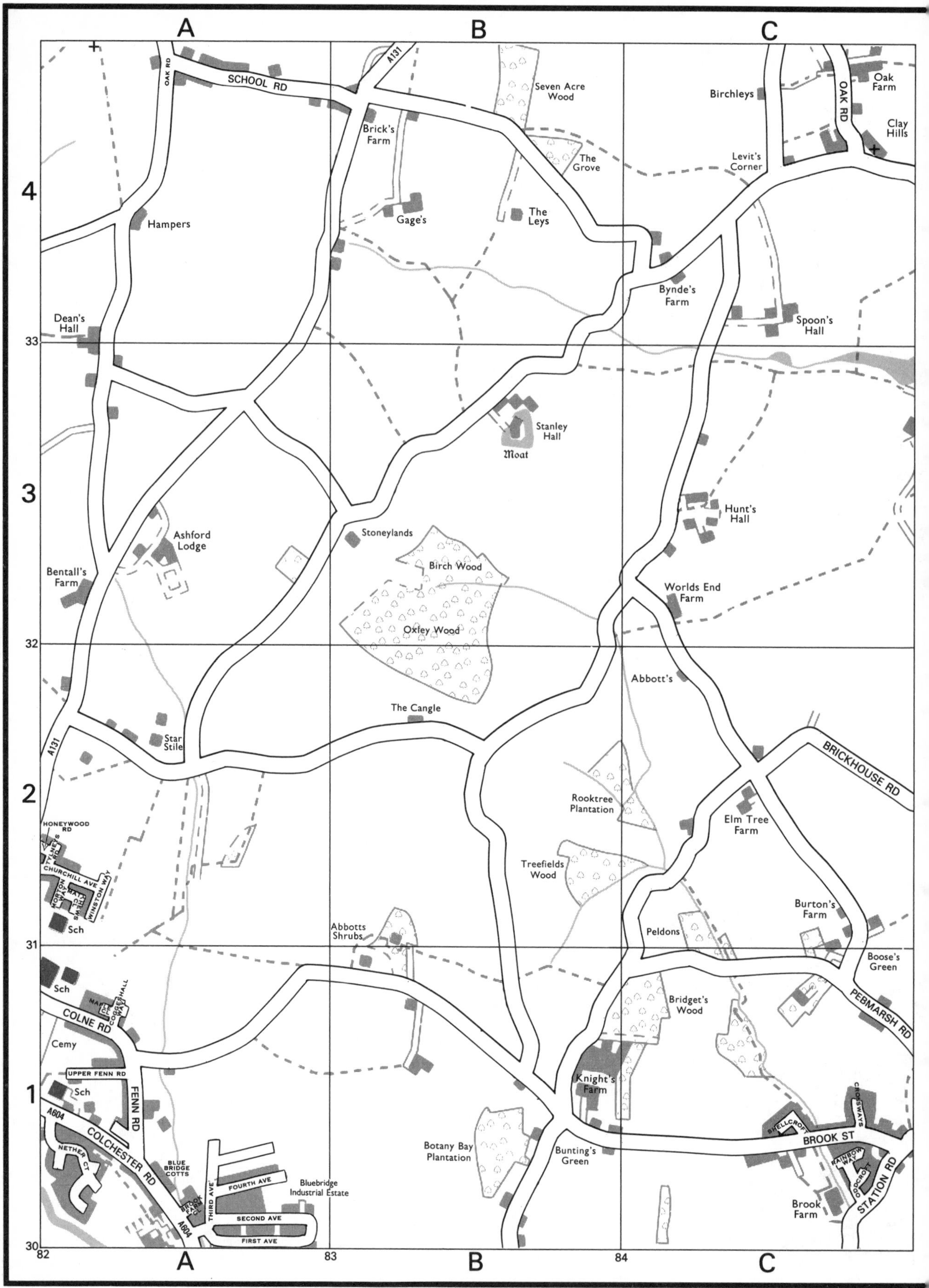
A
B
C
SCHOOL RD
OAK RD
A131
Seven Acre Wood
Birchleys
Oak Farm
Clay Hills
Brick's Farm
The Grove
Levit's Corner
4
Hampers
Gage's
The Leys
Bynde's Farm
Spoon's Hall
Dean's Hall
33
Stanley Hall
Moat
3
Hunt's Hall
Ashford Lodge
Stoneylands
Birch Wood
Bentall's Farm
Worlds End Farm
Oxley Wood
32
Abbott's
The Cangle
Star Stile
BRICKHOUSE RD
2
Rooktree Plantation
Elm Tree Farm
HONEYWOOD RD
CHURCHILL AVE
WINSTON WAY
Treefields Wood
Burton's Farm
Sch
Peldons
Abbotts Shrubs
31
Boose's Green
Sch
COGGESHALL
COLNE RD
Bridget's Wood
PEBMARSH RD
Cemy
UPPER FENN RD
Knight's Farm
1
Sch
FENN RD
A604
COLCHESTER RD
NETHER CT
CROSSWAYS
SHELLCROFT
BROOK ST
Botany Bay Plantation
Bunting's Green
RAINBOW WAY
BLUE BRIDGE COTTS
FOURTH AVE
Bluebridge Industrial Estate
THIRD AVE
STATION RD
Brook Farm
SECOND AVE
FIRST AVE
A604
30
82
83
84

25

44

18

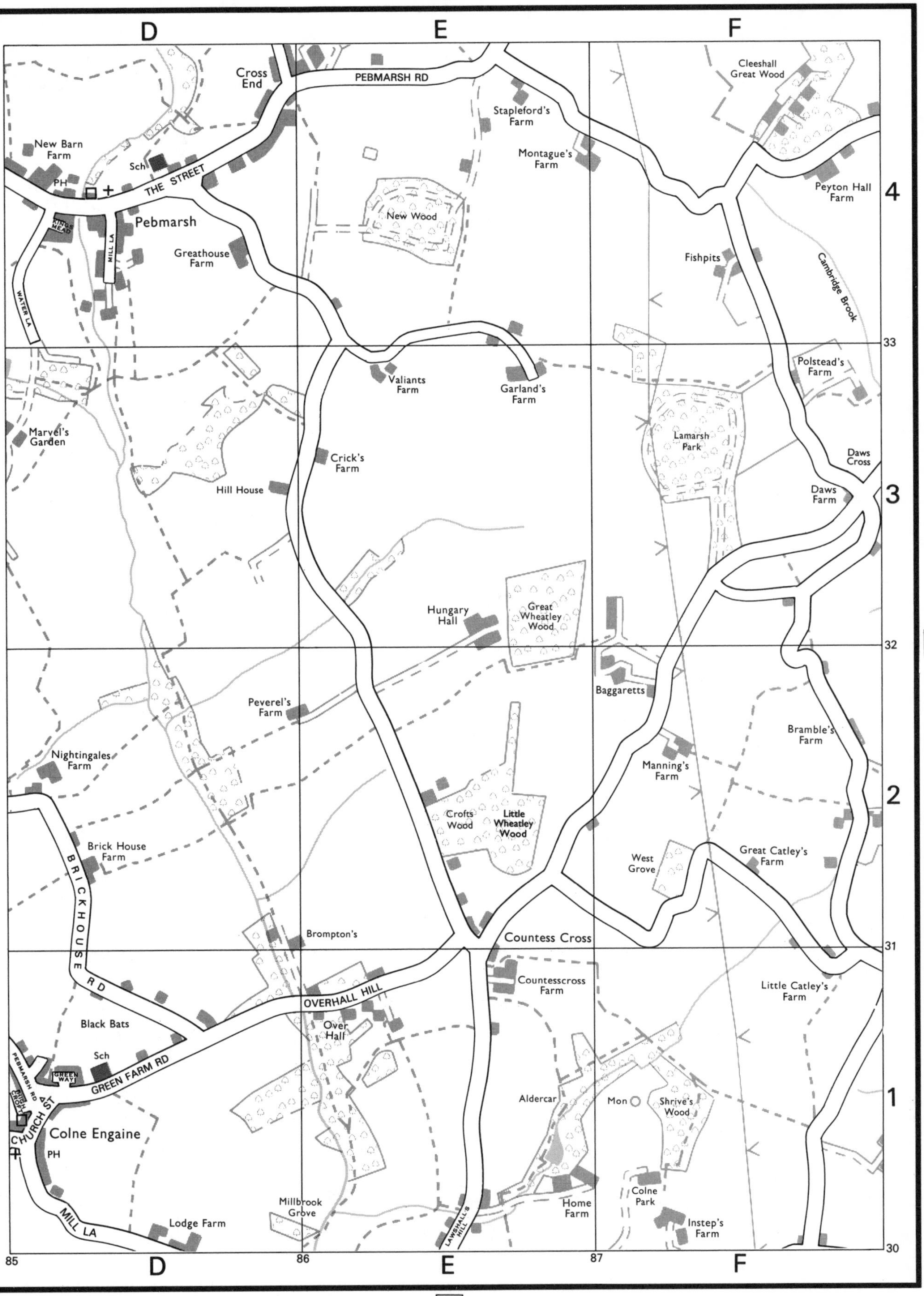

D
E
F
Cross End
PEBMARSH RD
Stapleford's Farm
Cleeshall Great Wood
New Barn Farm
Sch
PH
THE STREET
Montague's Farm
Peyton Hall Farm
4
KINGS MEAD
MILL LA
Pebmarsh
New Wood
Greathouse Farm
Fishpits
Cambridge Brook
WATER LA
33
Polstead's Farm
Valiants Farm
Garland's Farm
Marvel's Garden
Lamarsh Park
Crick's Farm
Daws Cross
Hill House
Daws Farm
3
Hungary Hall
Great Wheatley Wood
32
Baggaretts
Peverel's Farm
Bramble's Farm
Nightingales Farm
Manning's Farm
2
Crofts Wood
Little Wheatley Wood
Brick House Farm
West Grove
Great Catley's Farm
BRICKHOUSE RD
Brompton's
Countess Cross
31
Countesscross Farm
Little Catley's Farm
OVERHALL HILL
Black Bats
Over Hall
Sch
GREEN WAY
GREEN FARM RD
PEBMARSH RD
CHURCH ST
Aldercar
Mon
Shrive's Wood
1
Colne Engaine
PH
Millbrook Grove
Home Farm
Colne Park
Instep's Farm
LAWSHALL'S HILL
MILL LA
Lodge Farm
30
85
86
87
D
E
F

28

45

19

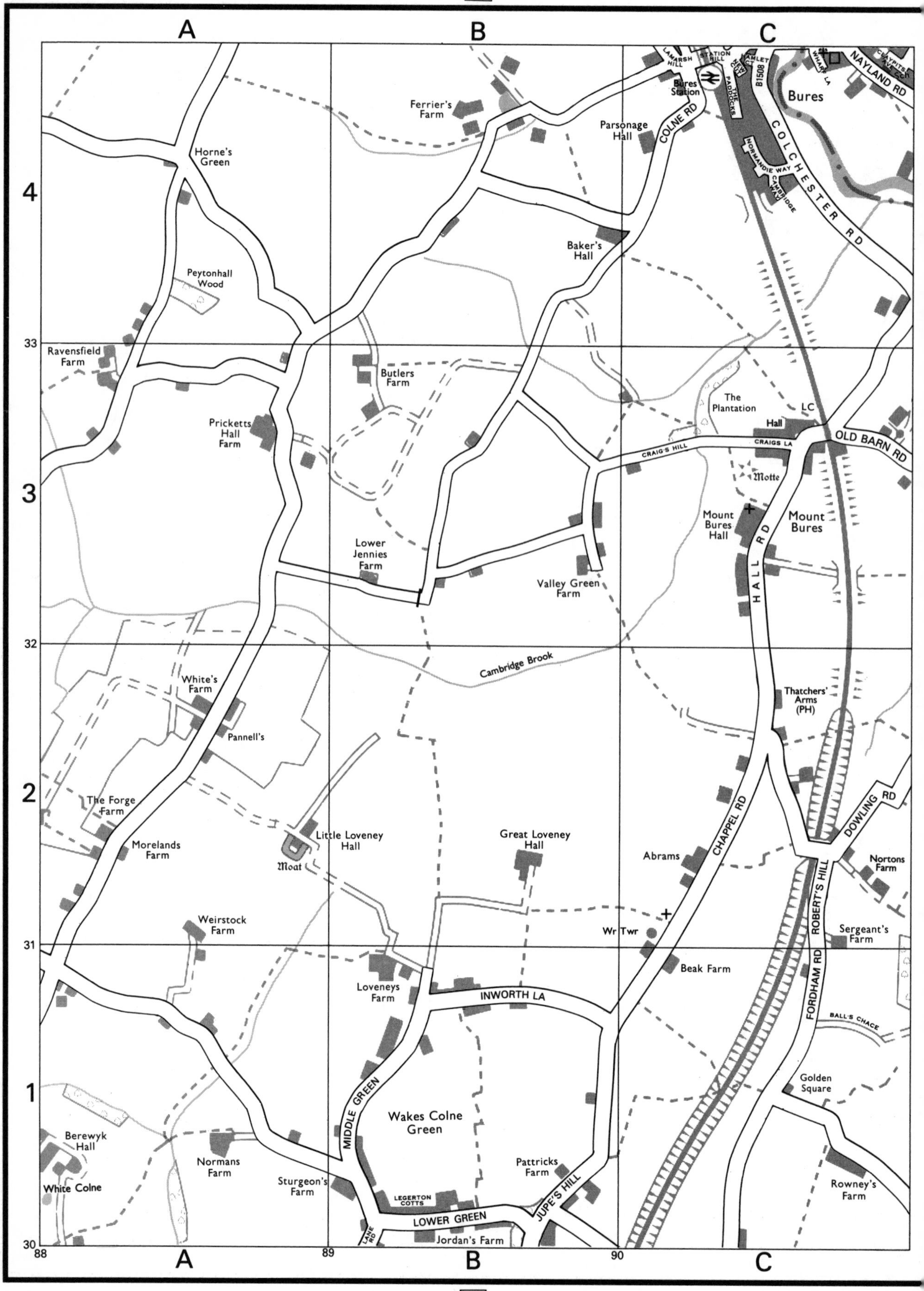
A
B
C
4
3
2
1
33
32
31
30
88
89
90
Horne's Green
Ferrier's Farm
Parsonage Hall
COLNE RD
LAMARSH HILL
STATION HILL
Bures Station
NEW CUT
HAMLET CT
THE PADDOCKS
B1508
WHARF LA
NAYLAND RD
CLAYPITS AVE
Sch
Bures
COLCHESTER RD
NORMANDIE WAY
CAMBRIDGE WAY
Baker's Hall
Peytonhall Wood
Ravensfield Farm
Butlers Farm
The Plantation
LC
Hall
OLD BARN RD
CRAIGS LA
CRAIG'S HILL
Pricketts Hall Farm
Motte
Mount Bures Hall
Mount Bures
HALL RD
Lower Jennies Farm
Valley Green Farm
Cambridge Brook
White's Farm
Pannell's
Thatchers' Arms (PH)
The Forge Farm
Morelands Farm
Little Loveney Hall
Moat
Great Loveney Hall
Abrams
CHAPPEL RD
DOWLING RD
Nortons Farm
ROBERT'S HILL
Weirstock Farm
Wr Twr
Sergeant's Farm
Beak Farm
FORDHAM RD
Loveneys Farm
INWORTH LA
BALL'S CHACE
Golden Square
MIDDLE GREEN
Wakes Colne Green
Berewyk Hall
White Colne
Normans Farm
Sturgeon's Farm
Pattricks Farm
JUPE'S HILL
Rowney's Farm
LEGERTON COTTS
LOWER GREEN
LANE RD
Jordan's Farm

27

46

not continued, see key diagram
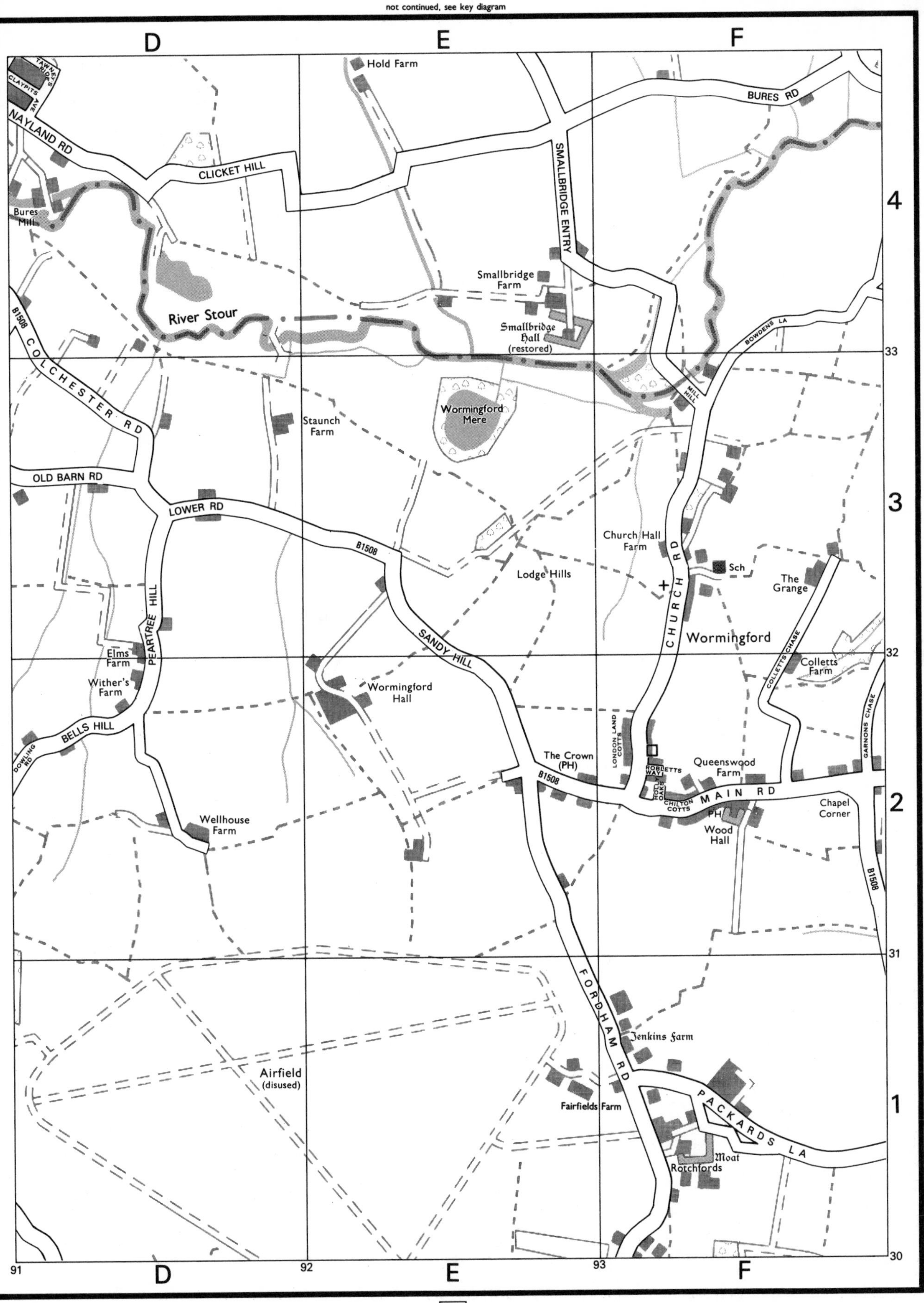
D
E
F
Hold Farm
TAWNEY RISE
CLAYPITS AVE
NAYLAND RD
BURES RD
CLICKET HILL
SMALLBRIDGE ENTRY
Bures Mill
4
Smallbridge Farm
River Stour
Smallbridge Hall (restored)
B1508
COLCHESTER RD
BOWDENS LA
33
MILL HILL
Wormingford Mere
Staunch Farm
OLD BARN RD
LOWER RD
3
Church Hall Farm
CHURCH RD
Sch
The Grange
Lodge Hills
SANDY HILL
PEARTREE HILL
Wormingford
COLLETTS CHASE
Colletts Farm
32
Elms Farm
Wither's Farm
Wormingford Hall
GARNONS CHASE
BELLS HILL
DOWLING RD
LONDON LAND COTTS
The Crown (PH)
ROBLETTS WAY
HOLLY OAKS
Queenswood Farm
CHILTON COTTS
MAIN RD
PH
Wood Hall
Chapel Corner
2
Wellhouse Farm
31
FORDHAM RD
Jenkins Farm
Airfield (disused)
PACKARDS LA
1
Fairfields Farm
Moat
Rotchfords
30
91
92
93
30
47

not continued, see key diagram

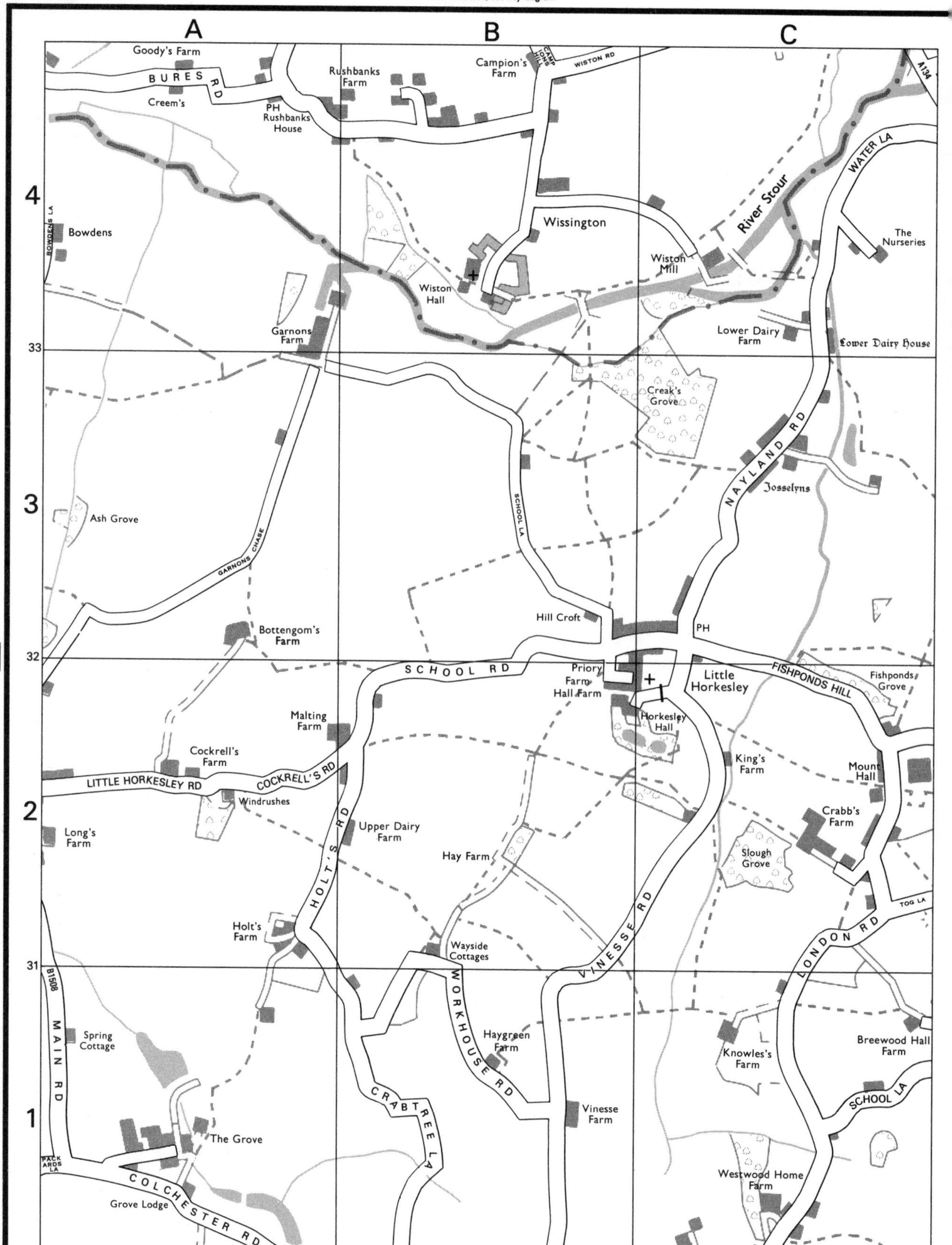
A
B
C
4
3
2
1
33
32
31
30
94
95
96
Goody's Farm
BURES RD
Creem's
PH
Rushbanks House
Rushbanks Farm
Campion's Farm
WISTON RD
A134
WATER LA
River Stour
Bowdens
BOWDENS LA
Wissington
Wiston Mill
The Nurseries
Wiston Hall
Garnons Farm
Lower Dairy Farm
Lower Dairy House
Creak's Grove
NAYLAND RD
Josselyns
SCHOOL LA
Ash Grove
GARNONS CHASE
Hill Croft
PH
Bottengom's Farm
SCHOOL RD
Priory Farm
Hall Farm
Little Horkesley
FISHPONDS HILL
Fishponds Grove
Horkesley Hall
Malting Farm
Cockrell's Farm
LITTLE HORKESLEY RD
COCKRELL'S RD
Windrushes
King's Farm
Mount Hall
Long's Farm
Upper Dairy Farm
HOLT'S RD
Hay Farm
Crabb's Farm
Slough Grove
VINESSE RD
TOG LA
LONDON RD
Holt's Farm
Wayside Cottages
B1508
MAIN RD
Spring Cottage
WORKHOUSE RD
Haygreen Farm
Knowles's Farm
Breewood Hall Farm
CRABTREE LA
Vinesse Farm
SCHOOL LA
The Grove
PACKARDS LA
COLCHESTER RD
Grove Lodge
B1508
Westwood Home Farm

29

48

20

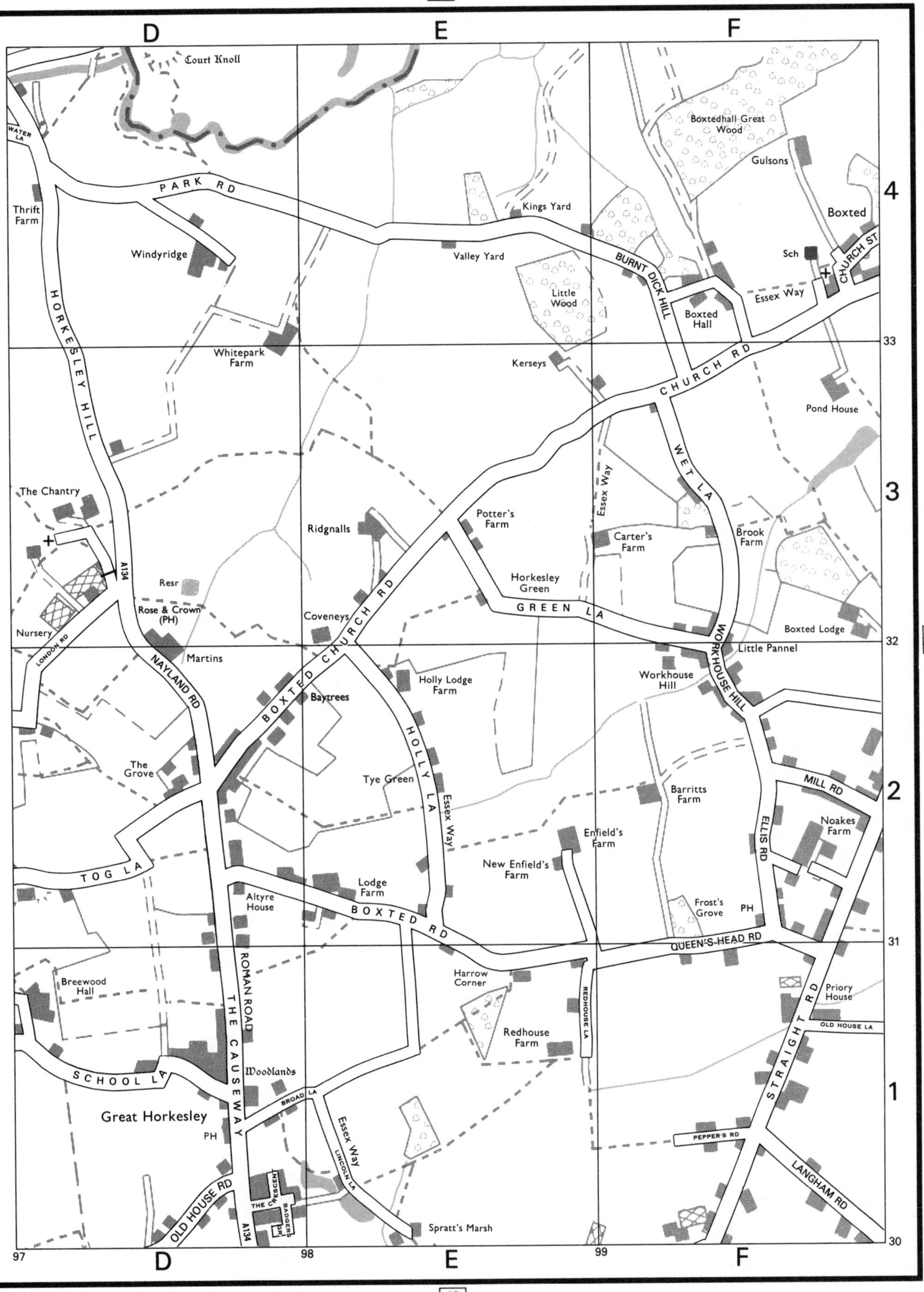
D
E
F
Court Knoll
Water La
Park Rd
Thrift Farm
Windyridge
Horkesley Hill
Kings Yard
Valley Yard
Boxtedhall Great Wood
Gulsons
Boxted
Sch
Church St
Essex Way
Burnt Dick Hill
Little Wood
Boxted Hall
4
33
Whitepark Farm
Kerseys
Church Rd
Pond House
Wet La
The Chantry
Essex Way
3
Potter's Farm
Ridgnalls
Carter's Farm
Brook Farm
A134
Resr
Horkesley Green
Green La
Rose & Crown (PH)
Coveneys
Boxted Church Rd
Nursery
London Rd
Boxted Lodge
32
Workhouse Hill
Little Pannel
Martins
Nayland Rd
Holly Lodge Farm
Workhouse Hill
Baytrees
Holly La
The Grove
Tye Green
Mill Rd
2
Barritts Farm
Essex Way
Noakes Farm
Ellis Rd
Enfield's Farm
New Enfield's Farm
Tog La
Lodge Farm
Altyre House
Boxted Rd
Frost's Grove
PH
Queen's Head Rd
31
Roman Road
Harrow Corner
Breewood Hall
Priory House
Redhouse La
Old House La
The Causeway
Redhouse Farm
Straight Rd
School La
Woodlands
1
Broad La
Great Horkesley
PH
Essex Way
Pepper's Rd
Lincoln La
Langham Rd
Old House Rd
The Crescent
Badgers Gr
A134
Spratt's Marsh
30
97
98
99
D
E
F

32

49

21

31

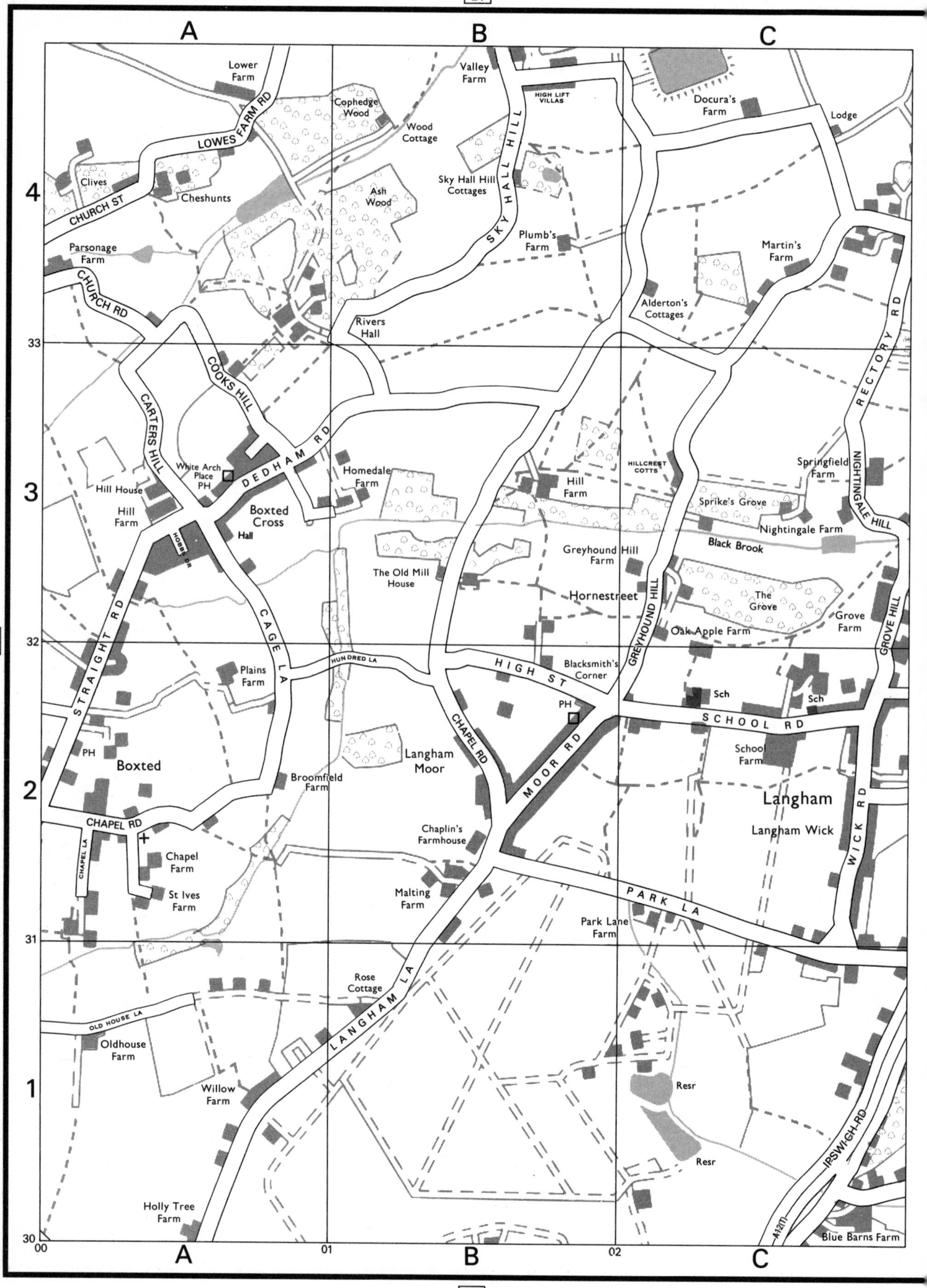
A
B
C
4
3
2
1
33
32
31
30
00
01
02
Lower Farm
Lowes Farm Rd
Church St
Clives
Cheshunts
Parsonage Farm
Church Rd
Cophedge Wood
Wood Cottage
Ash Wood
Valley Farm
High Lift Villas
Sky Hall Hill
Sky Hall Hill Cottages
Plumb's Farm
Rivers Hall
Docura's Farm
Lodge
Martin's Farm
Alderton's Cottages
Rectory Rd
Cooks Hill
Carters Hill
Dedham Rd
White Arch Place PH
Hill House
Hill Farm
Boxted Cross
Hall
Hobbs Dr
Homedale Farm
Hillcrest Cotts
Hill Farm
Springfield Farm
Nightingale Hill
Sprike's Grove
Nightingale Farm
Black Brook
Greyhound Hill Farm
Greyhound Hill
The Old Mill House
Hornestreet
The Grove
Grove Farm
Grove Hill
Oak Apple Farm
Straight Rd
Cage La
Plains Farm
Hundred La
High St
Blacksmith's Corner
Sch
Sch
PH
School Rd
School Farm
Chapel Rd
Moor Rd
Langham Moor
Broomfield Farm
PH
Boxted
Langham
Langham Wick
Wick Rd
Chapel Rd
Chapel La
Chapel Farm
St Ives Farm
Chaplin's Farmhouse
Malting Farm
Park La
Park Lane Farm
Rose Cottage
Old House La
Oldhouse Farm
Langham La
Willow Farm
Resr
Resr
Ipswich Rd
A12(T)
Holly Tree Farm
Blue Barns Farm

50

22

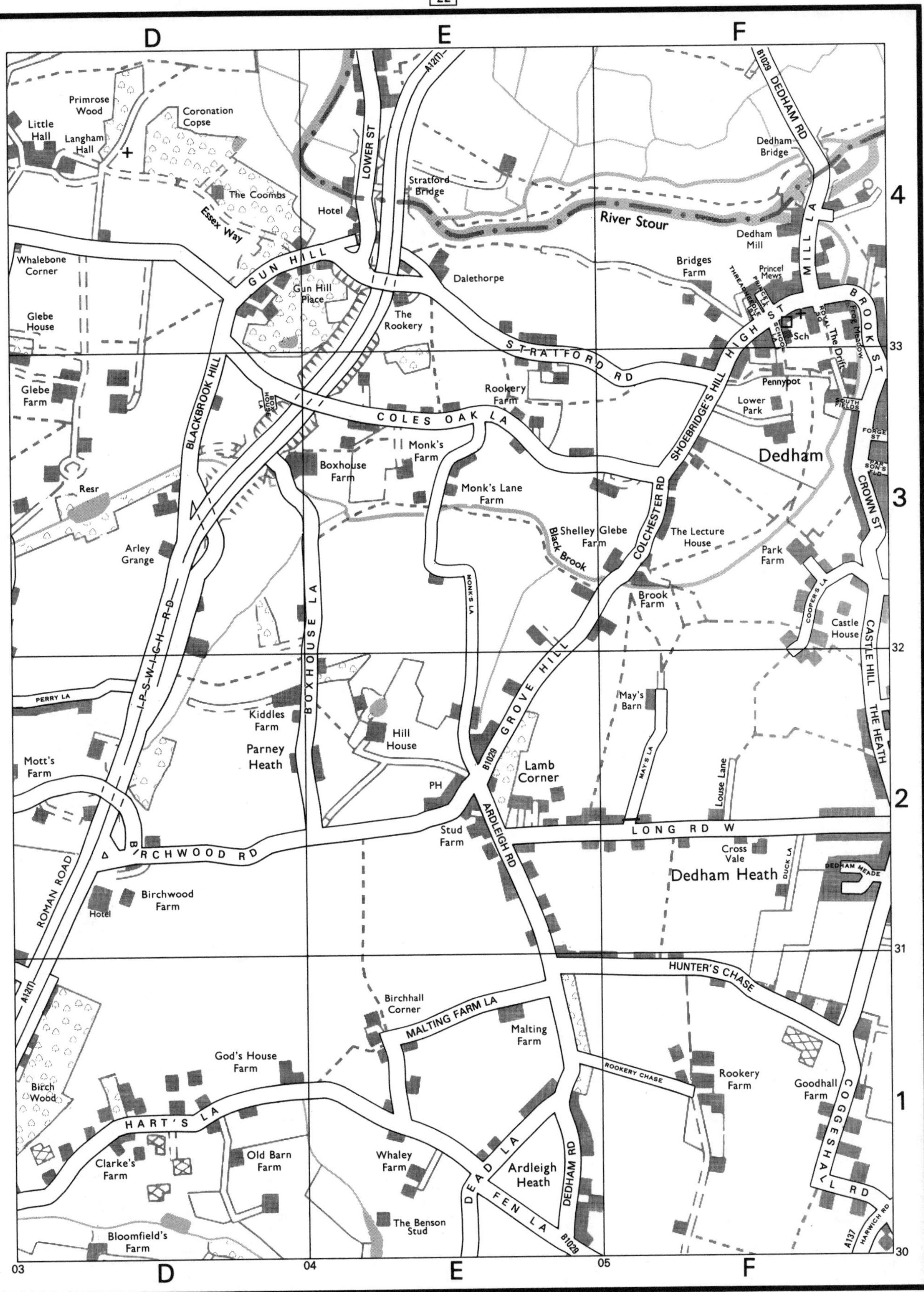
D
E
F
Primrose Wood
Coronation Copse
Little Hall
Langham Hall
The Coombs
Essex Way
Lower St
A12(T)
Stratford Bridge
Hotel
River Stour
Dedham Bridge
B1029 Dedham Rd
Dedham Mill
Mill La
Whalebone Corner
Gun Hill
Gun Hill Place
Dalethorpe
Bridges Farm
Princel Mews
Threadneedle St
Princel St
School La
Royal Sq
Brook St
Frog Meadow
The Drift
Sch
Glebe House
The Rookery
Stratford Rd
33
Glebe Farm
Blackbrook Hill
Boxhouse La
Rookery Farm
High St
Shoebridge's Hill
Pennypot
Lower Park
South Fields
Coles Oak La
Forge St
Parson's Fld
Monk's Farm
Boxhouse Farm
Dedham
Resr
Monk's Lane Farm
Colchester Rd
Crown St
3
Arley Grange
Shelley Glebe Farm
Black Brook
The Lecture House
Park Farm
Cooper's La
Ipswich Rd
Monk's La
Brook Farm
Castle House
Castle Hill
32
Perry La
Grove Hill
May's Barn
Kiddles Farm
Hill House
The Heath
Mott's Farm
Parney Heath
B1029
Lamb Corner
May's La
Louse Lane
PH
2
Ardleigh Rd
Long Rd W
Stud Farm
Cross Vale
Roman Road
Birchwood Rd
Duck La
Dedham Meade
Dedham Heath
Birchwood Farm
Hotel
31
A12(T)
Hunter's Chase
Birchhall Corner
Malting Farm La
Malting Farm
God's House Farm
Rookery Chase
Rookery Farm
Goodhall Farm
1
Birch Wood
Hart's La
Coggeshall Rd
Old Barn Farm
Clarke's Farm
Whaley Farm
Dead La
Ardleigh Heath
Dedham Rd
Fen La
The Benson Stud
Harwich Rd
A137
Bloomfield's Farm
B1029
30
03
04
05
D
E
F

34

51

not continued, see key diagram

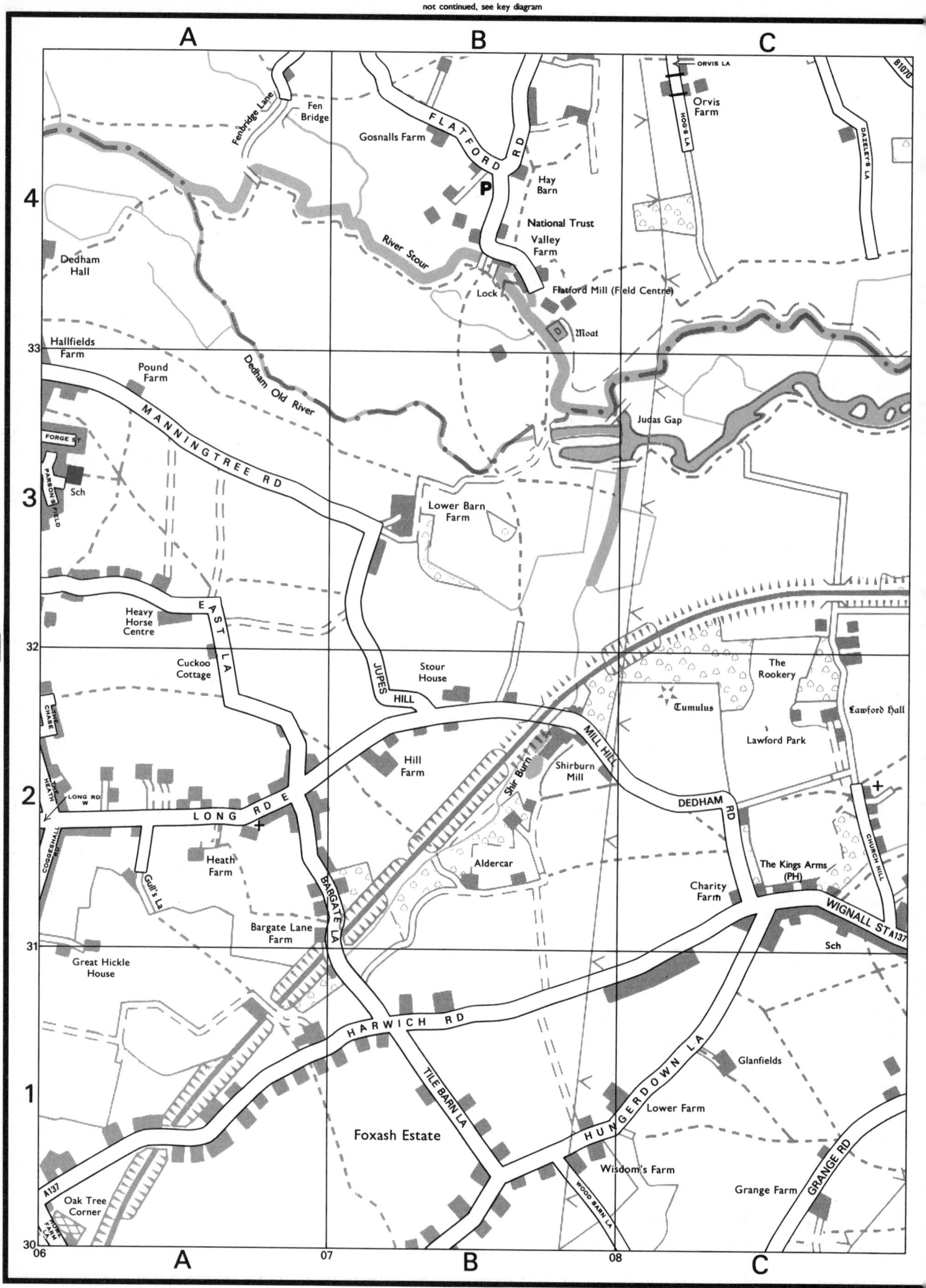
A
B
C
Fenbridge Lane
Fen Bridge
Gosnalls Farm
FLATFORD RD
Orvis Farm
ORVIS LA
HOG'S LA
DAZELEY'S LA
B1070
Hay Barn
National Trust
Valley Farm
River Stour
Dedham Hall
Lock
Flatford Mill (Field Centre)
Moat
Hallfields Farm
Pound Farm
Dedham Old River
MANNINGTREE RD
Judas Gap
FORGE ST
PARSON'S FIELD
Sch
Lower Barn Farm
Heavy Horse Centre
EAST LA
Cuckoo Cottage
JUPES HILL
Stour House
The Rookery
Tumulus
Lawford Hall
Lawford Park
THE CHASE
Hill Farm
MILL HILL
Shir Burn
Shirburn Mill
THE HEATH
LONG RD W
LONG RD E
DEDHAM RD
COGGESHALL RD
Heath Farm
Gull's La
Aldercar
BARGATE LA
Bargate Lane Farm
Charity Farm
The Kings Arms (PH)
CHURCH HILL
WIGNALL ST A137
Sch
Great Hickle House
HARWICH RD
Glanfields
HUNGERDOWN LA
TILE BARN LA
Lower Farm
Foxash Estate
Wisdom's Farm
WOOD BARN LA
GRANGE RD
Grange Farm
A137
Oak Tree Corner
HOME FARM LA
4
3
2
1
33
32
31
30
06
07
08

33

52

not continued, see key diagram

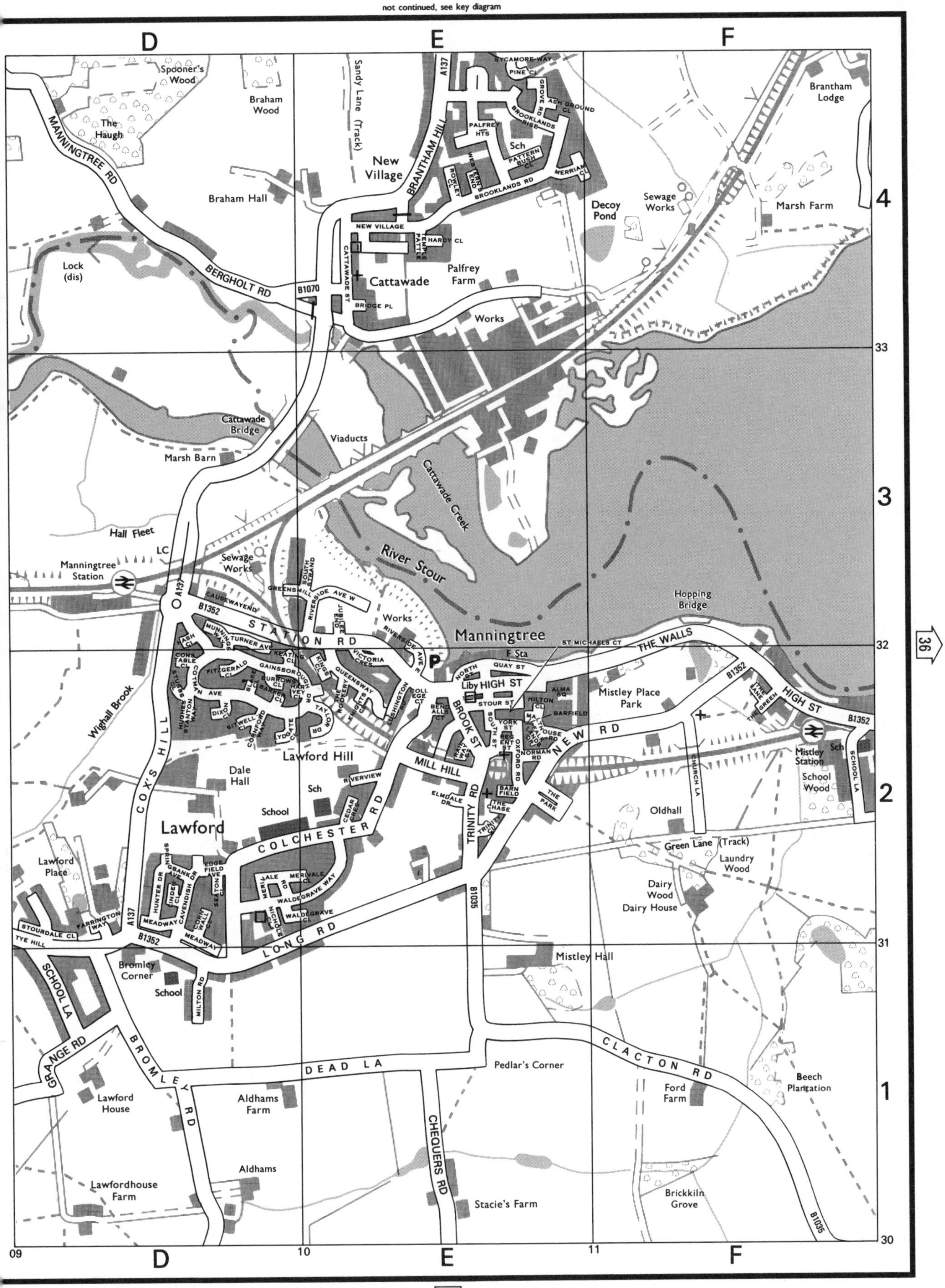

D
E
F
Spooner's Wood
Braham Wood
The Haugh
MANNINGTREE RD
Sandy Lane (Track)
A137
BRANTHAM HILL
New Village
SYCAMORE WAY
PINE CL
GROVE RD
ASH GROUND CL
BROOKLANDS RISE
PALFREY HTS
Sch
PATTERN BUSH CL
MERRIAM CL
ROWLEY
WESTERN'S END
BROOKLANDS RD
Brantham Lodge
Braham Hall
NEW VILLAGE
HARDY CL
TEMPLE PATTLE
CATTAWADE ST
Decoy Pond
Sewage Works
Marsh Farm
4
Lock (dis)
BERGHOLT RD
B1070
Cattawade
Palfrey Farm
BRIDGE PL
Works
33
Cattawade Bridge
Viaducts
Marsh Barn
Cattawade Creek
3
Hall Fleet
LC
River Stour
Manningtree Station
Sewage Works
A137
SOUTH STRAND
GREENSHILL
RIVERSIDE AVE W
CAUSEWAYEND
JUBILEE END
Works
Hopping Bridge
B1352
STATION RD
RIVERSIDE AVE E
Manningtree
ST MICHAELS CT
THE WALLS
32
36
NASH CL
MUNNINGS WAY
TURNER AVE
KEATING CL
KINGS CL
VICTORIA CRES
P
F Sta
QUAY ST
NORTH ST
CONSTABLE CL
COTMAN AVE
FITZGERALD CL
GAINSBOROUGH CL
QUEENSWAY
COLL EGE CT
Liby HIGH ST
ALMA SQ
Mistley Place Park
B1352
THE LANE
THE GREEN
HIGH ST
STUBBS CL
WARNER WAY
HUGHES STAYS
BLAKE CL
BURROWS CL
BARKER CL
HARVEY DR
TAYLOR DR
LUSHINGTON RD
BEND ALLS CT
STOUR ST
HILTON CL
BARFIELD
B1352
DIXON
SITWELL CL
CORNFORD WAY
LYDGATE CL
BROOK ST
SOUTH ST
YORK ST
REGENT ST
MALTHOUSE RD
NEW RD
Mistley Station
Sch
SCHOOL LA
Wighall Brook
Lawford Hill
MILL HILL
NORMAN RD
OXFORD RD
CHURCH LA
School Wood
COX'S HILL
Dale Hall
RIVERVIEW
Sch
ELMDALE DR
BARN FIELD
THE PARK
THE CHASE
TRINITY RD
TRINITY CL
2
School
CEDAR CRES
Oldhall
Lawford
COLCHESTER RD
Green Lane (Track)
Laundry Wood
Lawford Place
SPRING ROAD
BANK AVE
HUNTER DR
LINDEN CL
CAVENDISH DR
EDGE FIELD AVE
MERIVALE RD
MERIVALE CL
WALDEGRAVE WAY
SEXTON CL
CORN WALL CL
B1035
Dairy Wood
Dairy House
A137
STOURDALE CL
FARRINGTON WAY
MEADWAY
NICHOLS CL
WALDEGRAVE
TYE HILL
B1352
MEADWAY
LONG RD
31
SCHOOL LA
Bromley Corner
School
MILTON RD
Mistley Hall
GRANGE RD
BROMLEY RD
DEAD LA
Pedlar's Corner
CLACTON RD
Beech Plantation
1
Lawford House
Aldhams Farm
CHEQUERS RD
Ford Farm
Aldhams
Lawfordhouse Farm
Stacie's Farm
Brickkiln Grove
B1035
30
09
10
11

53

not continued, see key diagram

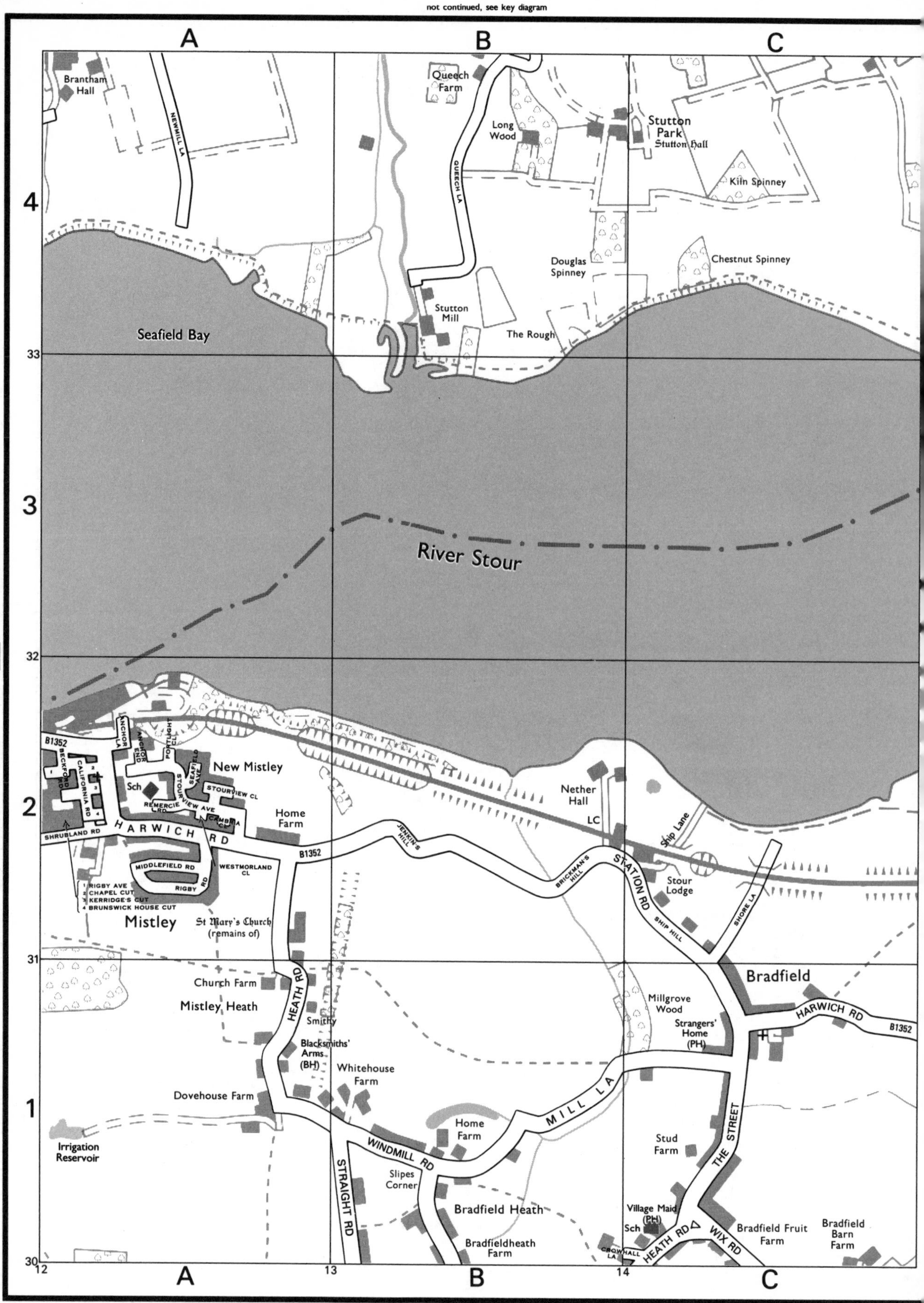

A
B
C
4
3
2
1
33
32
31
30
12
13
14
Brantham Hall
Queech Farm
Long Wood
Stutton Park
Stutton Hall
Kiln Spinney
NEWMILL LA
QUEECH LA
Douglas Spinney
Chestnut Spinney
Stutton Mill
The Rough
Seafield Bay
River Stour
B1352
ANCHOR LA
ANCHOR END
PORTLIGHT CL
SEAFIELD AVE
BECKFORD RD
CALIFORNIA RD
New Mistley
Sch
STOURVIEW CL
STOURVIEW AVE
REMERCIE RD
CAMBRIA CL
HARWICH RD
SHRUBLAND RD
Home Farm
JENKIN'S HILL
Nether Hall
LC
Ship Lane
BRICKMAN'S HILL
STATION RD
Stour Lodge
SHIP HILL
SHORE LA
MIDDLEFIELD RD
WESTMORLAND CL
RIGBY RD
1 RIGBY AVE
2 CHAPEL CUT
3 KERRIDGE'S CUT
4 BRUNSWICK HOUSE CUT
Mistley
St Mary's Church (remains of)
Bradfield
HARWICH RD
B1352
Church Farm
Mistley Heath
HEATH RD
Smithy
Millgrove Wood
Strangers' Home (PH)
Blacksmiths' Arms (BH)
Whitehouse Farm
MILL LA
Dovehouse Farm
Home Farm
THE STREET
Stud Farm
Irrigation Reservoir
WINDMILL RD
STRAIGHT RD
Slipes Corner
Bradfield Heath
Village Maid (PH)
Sch
HEATH RD
WIX RD
CROWHALL LA
Bradfield Fruit Farm
Bradfield Barn Farm
Bradfieldheath Farm

35

54

not continued, see key diagram

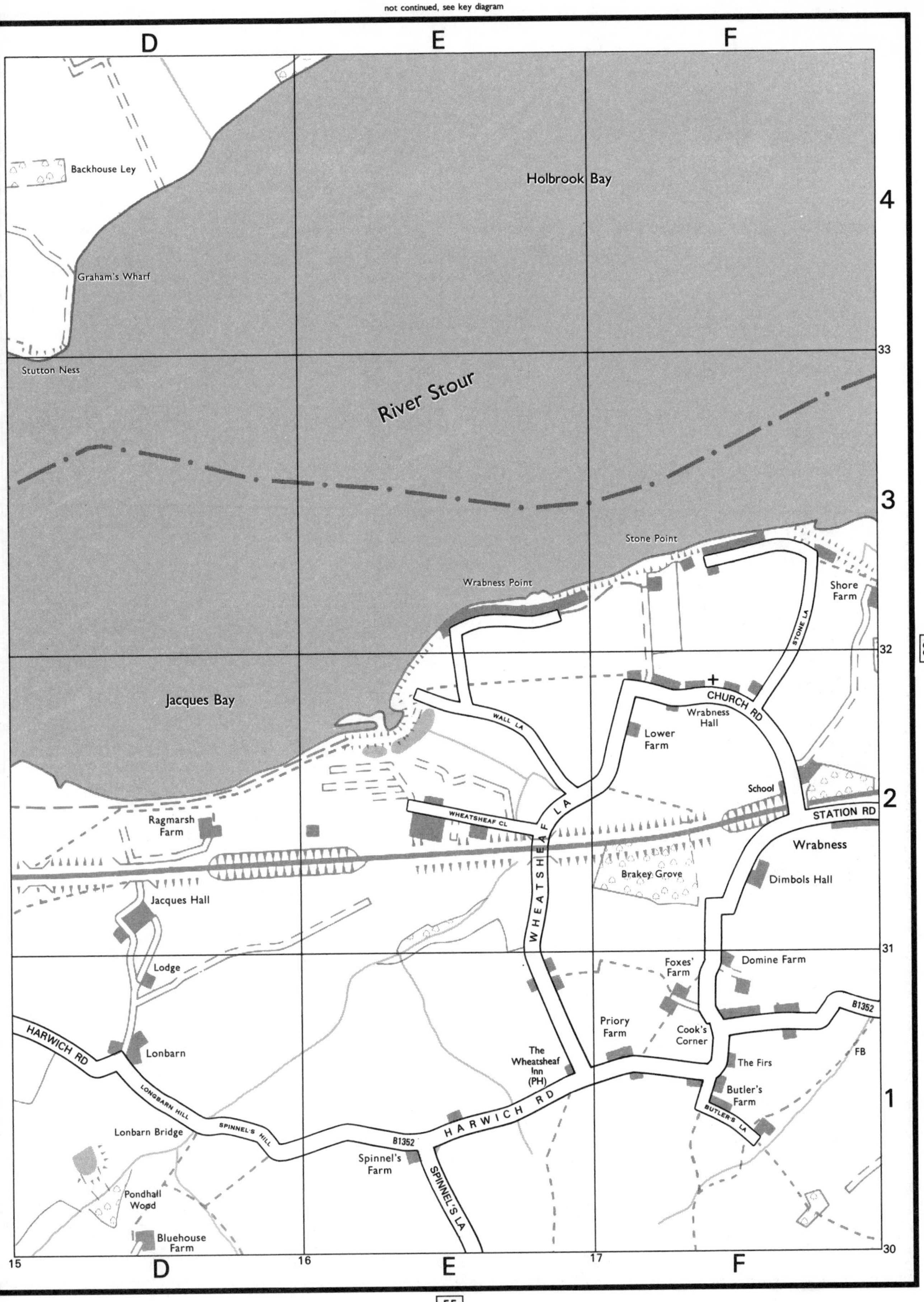
D
E
F
Backhouse Ley
Holbrook Bay
4
Graham's Wharf
33
Stutton Ness
River Stour
3
Stone Point
Wrabness Point
Shore Farm
STONE LA
32
Jacques Bay
CHURCH RD
Wrabness Hall
WALL LA
Lower Farm
School
2
STATION RD
Ragmarsh Farm
WHEATSHEAF CL
WHEATSHEAF LA
Wrabness
Brakey Grove
Dimbols Hall
Jacques Hall
31
Domine Farm
Lodge
Foxes' Farm
B1352
Priory Farm
Cook's Corner
HARWICH RD
Lonbarn
The Wheatsheaf Inn (PH)
FB
The Firs
1
Butler's Farm
LONGBARN HILL
BUTLER'S LA
SPINNEL'S HILL
HARWICH RD
Lonbarn Bridge
B1352
Spinnel's Farm
SPINNEL'S LA
Pondhall Wood
Bluehouse Farm
30
15
D
16
E
17
F

38

55

not continued, see key diagram

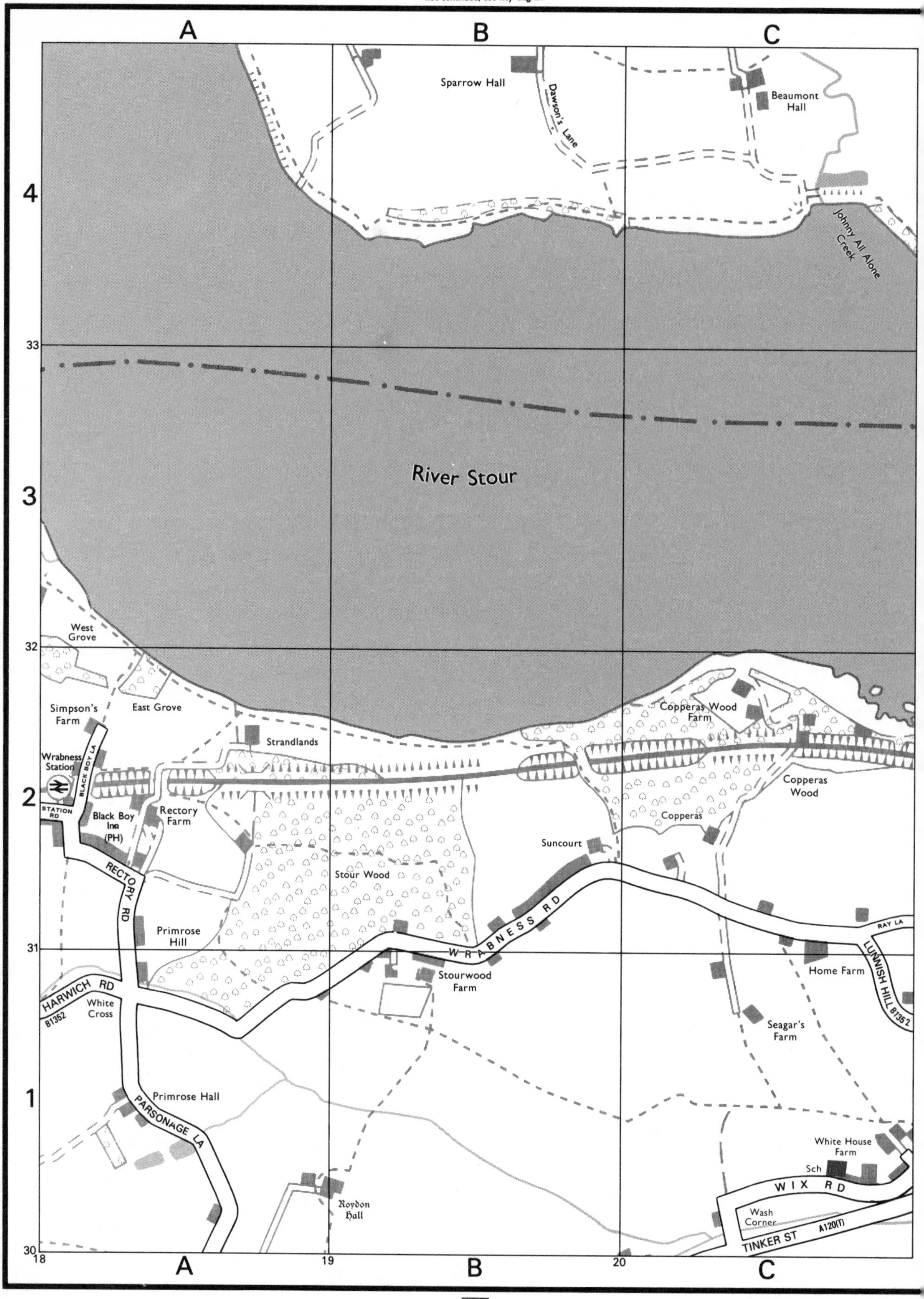
A
B
C
4
3
2
1
33
32
31
30
18
19
20
Sparrow Hall
Dawson's Lane
Beaumont Hall
Johnny All Alone Creek
River Stour
West Grove
East Grove
Simpson's Farm
Copperas Wood Farm
Strandlands
Wrabness Station
BLACK BOY LA
STATION RD
Black Boy Inn (PH)
Rectory Farm
Copperas Wood
Copperas
Suncourt
RECTORY RD
Stour Wood
Primrose Hill
WRABNESS RD
RAY LA
LUNNISH HILL B1352
Home Farm
Stourwood Farm
HARWICH RD
B1352
White Cross
Seagar's Farm
Primrose Hall
PARSONAGE LA
White House Farm
Sch
WIX RD
Roydon Hall
Wash Corner
A120(T)
TINKER ST

37

56

not continued, see key diagram

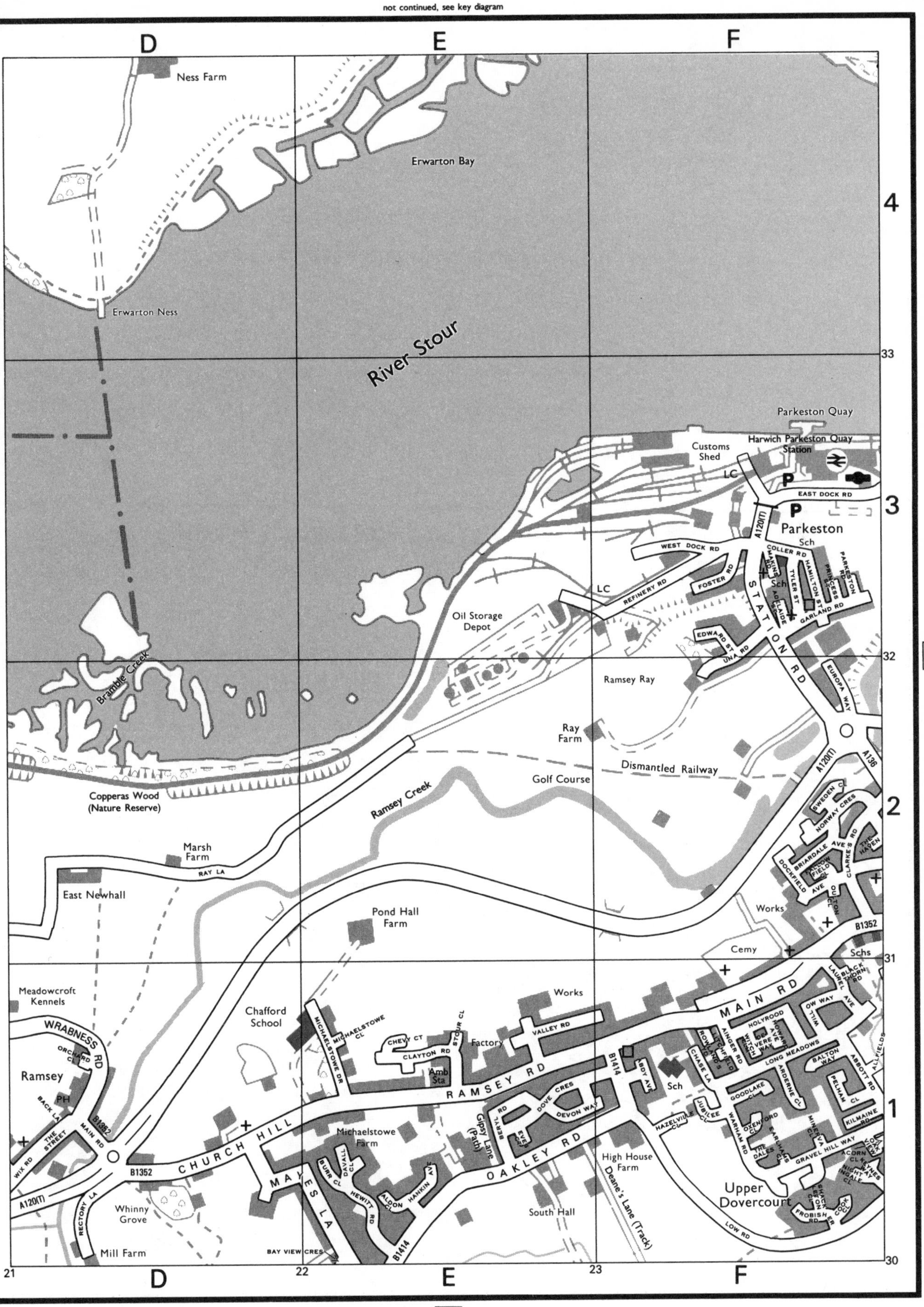

D
E
F
Ness Farm
Erwarton Bay
Erwarton Ness
River Stour
Parkeston Quay
Customs Shed
Harwich Parkeston Quay Station
EAST DOCK RD
Parkeston
WEST DOCK RD
REFINERY RD
FOSTER RD
STATION RD
GARLAND RD
Oil Storage Depot
Ramsey Ray
Ray Farm
Dismantled Railway
Golf Course
Ramsey Creek
Bramble Creek
Copperas Wood (Nature Reserve)
Marsh Farm
RAY LA
East Newhall
Pond Hall Farm
Works
Cemy
Schs
Meadowcroft Kennels
Chafford School
WRABNESS RD
Ramsey
MAIN RD
RAMSEY RD
CHURCH HILL
OAKLEY RD
Michaelstowe Farm
Gipsy Lane (Path)
High House Farm
Deane's Lane (Track)
South Hall
Whinny Grove
Mill Farm
Upper Dovercourt
LOW RD
MAYES LA
B1352
B1414
A120(T)
A136
4
3
2
1
33
32
31
30
21
22
23
40

not continued, see key diagram

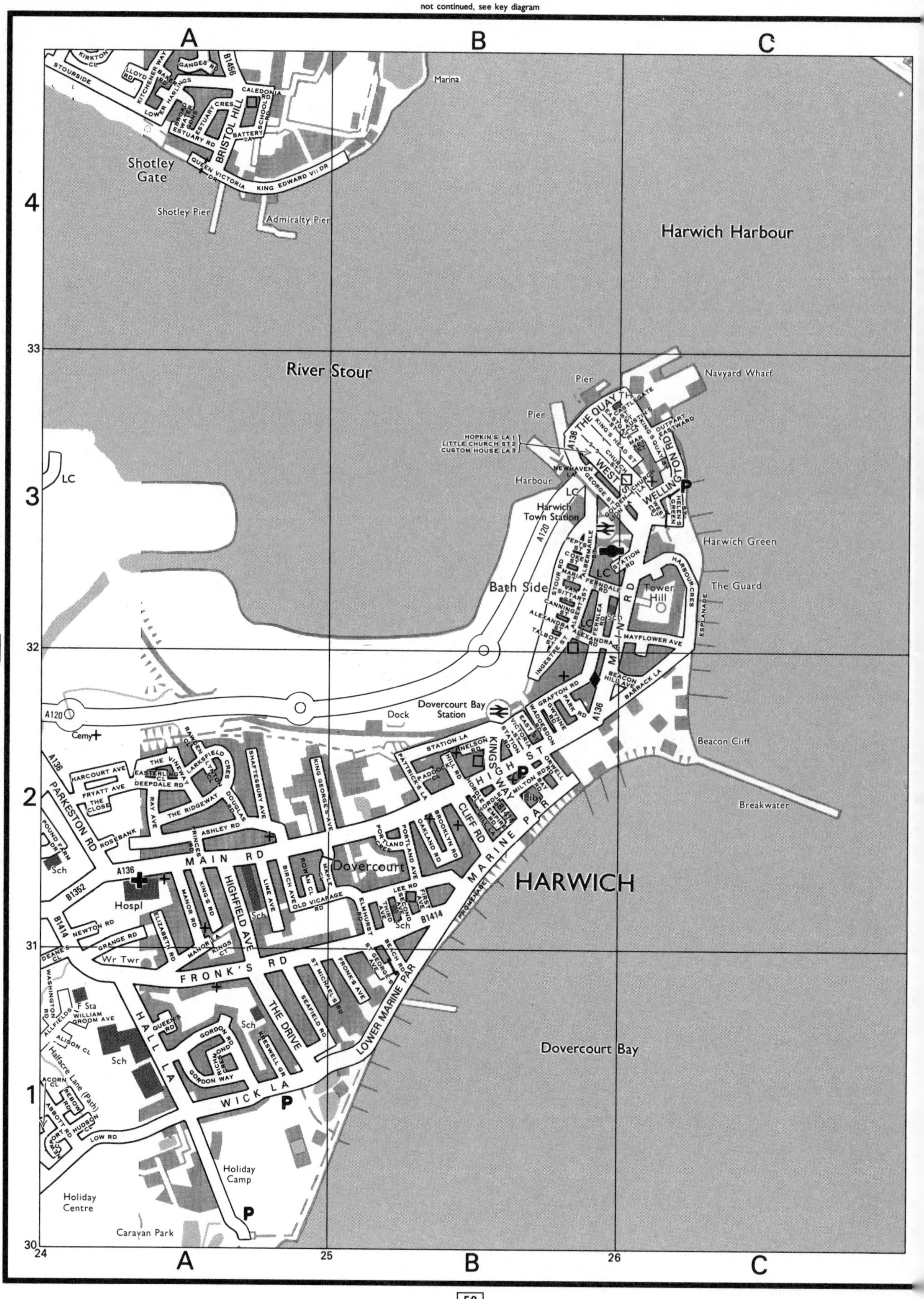
A
B
C
4
3
2
1
33
32
31
30
24
25
26
Marina
Shotley Gate
Shotley Pier
Admiralty Pier
BRISTOL HILL
KING EDWARD VII DR
QUEEN VICTORIA DR
STOURSIDE
KITCHENER WAY
GANGES RD
CALEDONIA RD
SCHOOL CRES
BATTERY LA
ESTUARY RD
ESTUARY CRES
LOWER HARLINGS
B1456
Harwich Harbour
River Stour
Navyard Wharf
Pier
Pier
HOPKIN'S LA 1
LITTLE CHURCH ST 2
CUSTOM HOUSE LA 3
THE QUAY
A136
CASTLEGATE
KING'S HEAD ST
CHURCH ST
WEST ST
WELLINGTON RD
OUTPART EASTWARD
NEWHAVEN LA
GEORGE ST
Harbour
LC
Harwich Town Station
Harwich Green
The Guard
Bath Side
Tower Hill
HARBOUR CRES
ESPLANADE
MAYFLOWER AVE
STATION RD
MAIN RD
FERNDALE RD
FERNLEA RD
ALEXANDRA RD
STOUR RD
CANNING ST
ALBERT ST
SITTART ST
INGESTRE ST
TALBOT ST
A120
LC
Sch
BEACON HILL AVE
BARRACK LA
Beacon Cliff
Breakwater
GRAFTON RD
PARK RD
Dovercourt Bay Station
Dock
A120
Cemy
STATION LA
NELSON RD
KINGSWAY
HIGH ST
ORWELL
MILTON RD
Lib
MARINE PAR
CLIFF RD
PATTRICK'S LA
PADDOCK CL
HILL RD
HARWICH
PROMENADE
A136
HARCOURT AVE
FRYATT AVE
DEEPDALE RD
EASTERLING CL
THE VINEYARD
LARKSFIELD CRES
THE RIDGEWAY
DOUGLAS RD
RAY AVE
THE CLOSE
PARKESTON RD
ROSEBANK
POUND FARM DR
Sch
ASHLEY RD
PRINCES RD
SHAFTESBURY AVE
KING GEORGE'S AVE
PORTLAND AVE
PORTLAND CRES
OAKLAND RD
BROOKLYN RD
MAIN RD
A136
B1352
Hospl
Dovercourt
MANOR RD
KING'S RD
HIGHFIELD AVE
LIME AVE
BIRCH AVE
ROWAN CL
MAPLE CL
OLD VICARAGE RD
ELMHURST RD
LEE RD
SECOND AVE
THIRD AVE
FIRST AVE
B1414
Sch
Sch
B1414
NEWTON RD
GRANGE RD
ELIZABETH RD
MANOR LA
KINGS CT
DEANE'S CL
Wr Twr
FRONK'S RD
ST MICHAEL'S RD
FRONKS AVE
ST GEORGE'S AVE
BEACH RD
LOWER MARINE PAR
WASHINGTON RD
F Sta
WILLIAM GROOM AVE
ALLFIELDS
ALISON CL
Halfacre Lane (Path)
Sch
HALL LA
QUEEN'S RD
GORDON RD
RICHMOND RD
GORDON WAY
Sch
KESWELL GR
THE DRIVE
SEAFIELD RD
WICK LA
Dovercourt Bay
ACORN CL
REBOW RD
ABBOTT RD
HUDSON CL
NEWPORT RD
LOW RD
Holiday Camp
Holiday Centre
Caravan Park
P

39

23

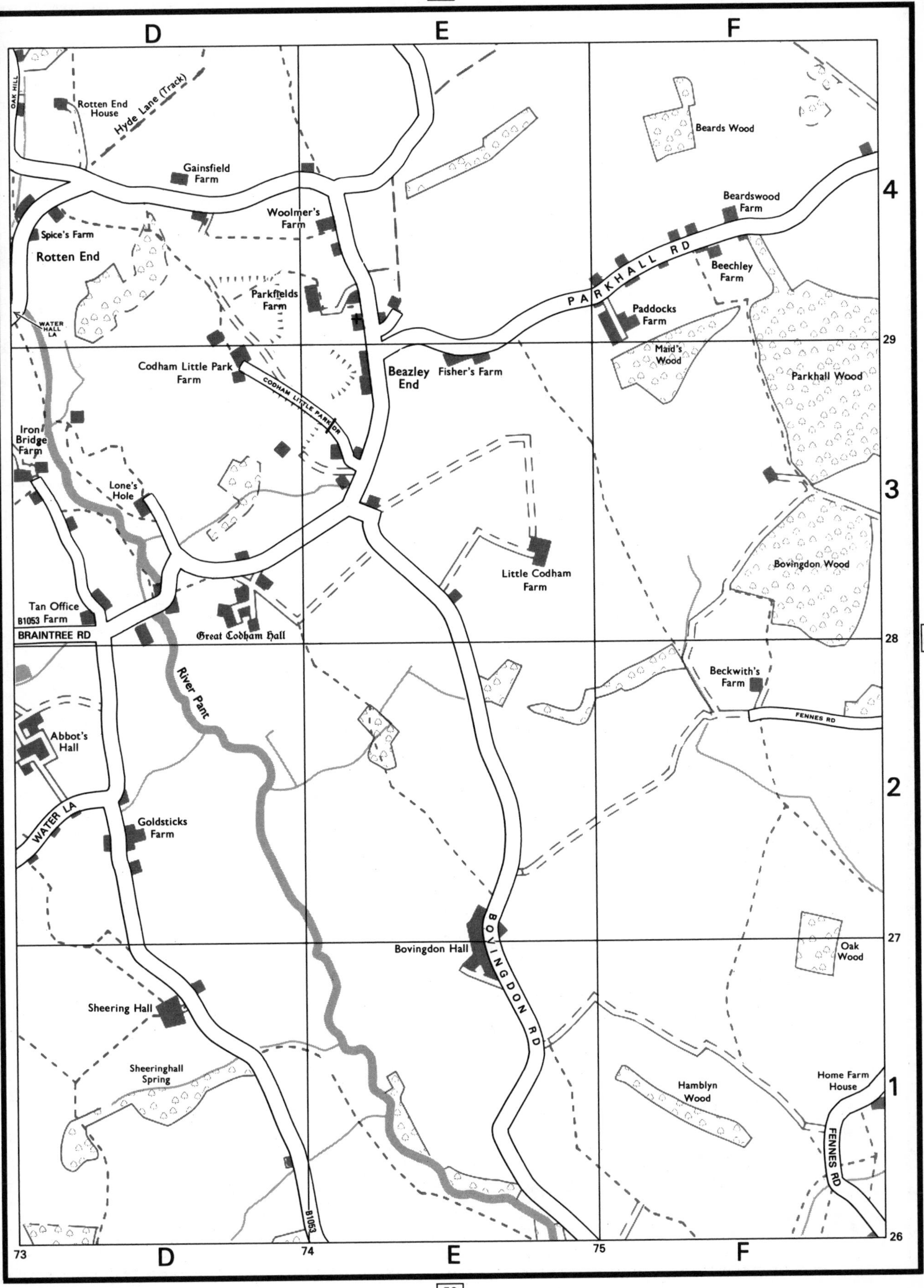

D
E
F
Rotten End House
Hyde Lane (Track)
OAK HILL
Gainsfield Farm
Beards Wood
Woolmer's Farm
Spice's Farm
Rotten End
Beardswood Farm
PARKHALL RD
Beechley Farm
Parkfields Farm
Paddocks Farm
WATER HALL LA
Maid's Wood
Codham Little Park Farm
CODHAM LITTLE PARK DR
Beazley End
Fisher's Farm
Parkhall Wood
Iron Bridge Farm
Lone's Hole
Little Codham Farm
Bovingdon Wood
Tan Office Farm
B1053
BRAINTREE RD
Great Codham Hall
River Pant
Beckwith's Farm
FENNES RD
Abbot's Hall
WATER LA
Goldsticks Farm
BOVINGDON RD
Bovingdon Hall
Oak Wood
Sheering Hall
Sheeringhall Spring
Hamblyn Wood
Home Farm House
FENNES RD
B1053
4
3
2
1
29
28
27
26
73
74
75

42

59

24

41

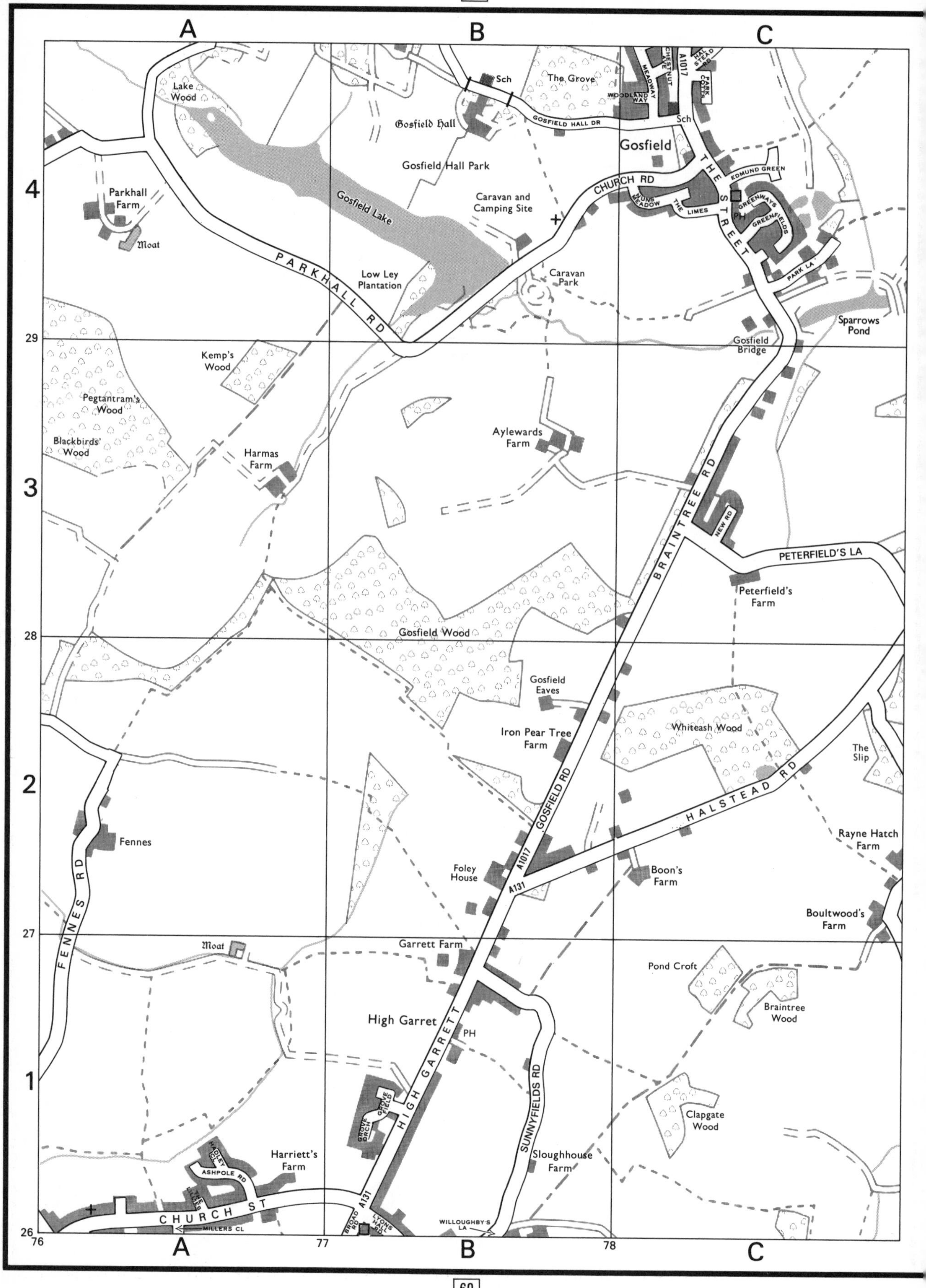
A
B
C
4
3
2
1
29
28
27
26
76
77
78
Lake Wood
Sch
The Grove
Gosfield Hall
GOSFIELD HALL DR
MEADWAY
CHESTNUT AVE
A1017
HALSTEAD RD
PARK CORNER
WOODLAND WAY
Gosfield
Gosfield Hall Park
Gosfield Lake
Parkhall Farm
Moat
PARKHALL RD
Caravan and Camping Site
CHURCH RD
NUNS MEADOW
THE LIMES
THE STREET
EDMUND GREEN
GREENWAYS
GREENFIELDS
PH
PARK LA
Low Ley Plantation
Caravan Park
Sparrows Pond
Gosfield Bridge
Kemp's Wood
Pegtantram's Wood
Blackbirds' Wood
Harmas Farm
Aylewards Farm
BRAINTREE RD
NEW RD
PETERFIELD'S LA
Peterfield's Farm
Gosfield Wood
Gosfield Eaves
Iron Pear Tree Farm
Whiteash Wood
The Slip
HALSTEAD RD
GOSFIELD RD
Fennes
FENNES RD
Rayne Hatch Farm
Foley House
A1017
A131
Boon's Farm
Boultwood's Farm
Moat
Garrett Farm
Pond Croft
Braintree Wood
High Garret
PH
HIGH GARRETT
SUNNYFIELDS RD
GROVE ORCH
GROVE FIELD
Clapgate Wood
Harriett's Farm
HADLEY CL
ASHPOLE RD
THE LIMES
Sloughhouse Farm
CHURCH ST
MILLERS CL
BROAD RD
LYONS HALL RD
WILLOUGHBY'S LA

60

25

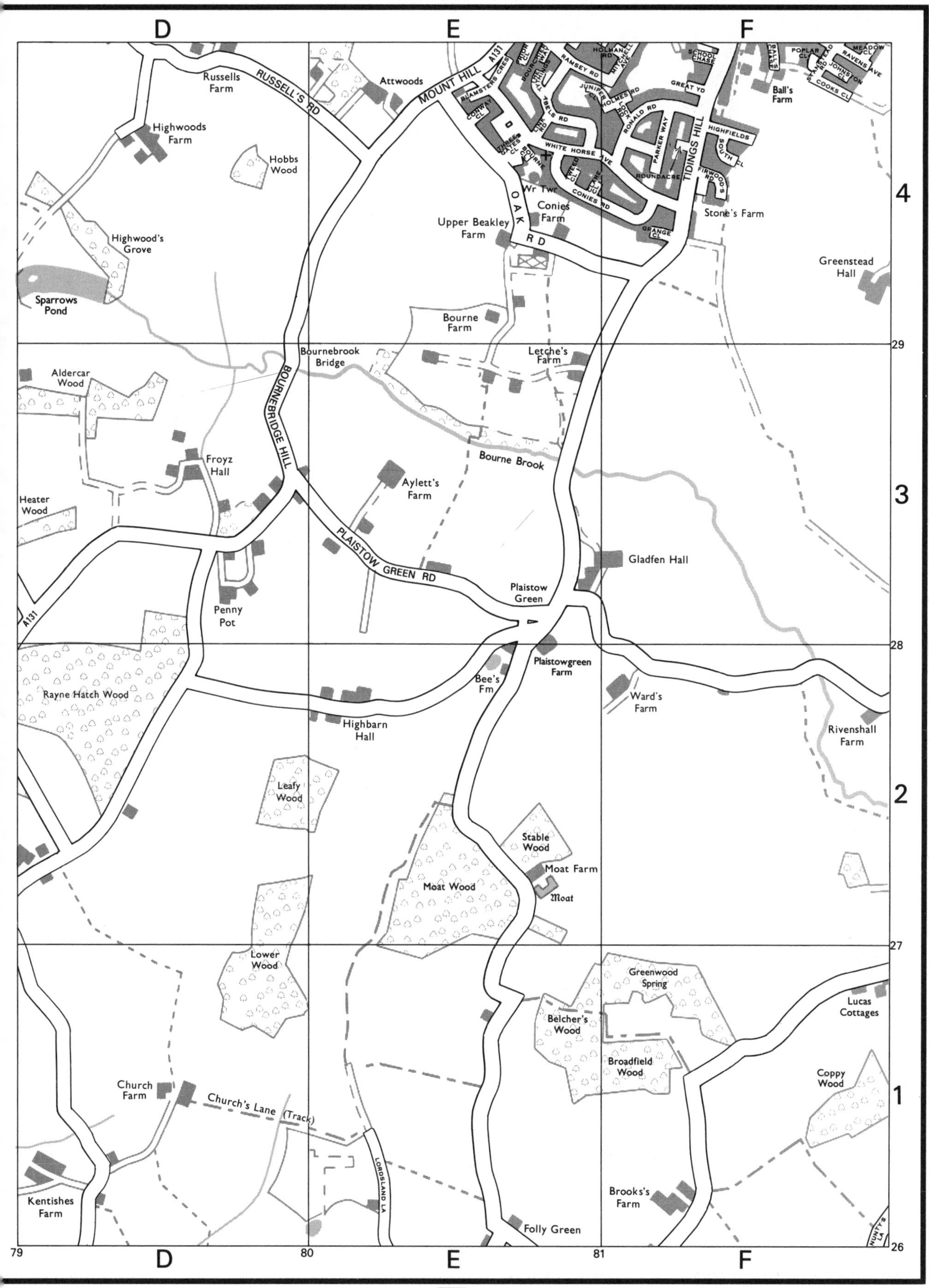
D
E
F
Russells Farm
RUSSELL'S RD
Attwoods
MOUNT HILL
A131
Highwoods Farm
Hobbs Wood
Highwood's Grove
Sparrows Pond
BLAMSTERS CRES
CONWAY CL
PRIOR CL
BOURCHIER WAY
THE TYTHINGS
RAMSEY RD
HOLMAN RD
MITCHELL AVE
SCHOOL CHASE
GREAT YD
JUNIPER CL
HOLMES RD
LOCK RD
BELS RD
LINK RD
THREE GATES CL
BOURNE CL
WHITE HORSE AVE
RONALD RD
PARKER WAY
TIDINGS HILL
HIGHFIELDS
SOUTH CL
TWEED CL
CLARE CL
ROUNDACRE
FIRWOODS RD
CONIES RD
GRANGE CL
BALL'S CHASE
POPLAR CL
STANSTEAD RD
MEADOW CL
RAVENS AVE
JOHNSTON CL
COOKS CL
Ball's Farm
Wr Twr
OAK RD
Conies Farm
Upper Beakley Farm
Stone's Farm
Greenstead Hall
4
Bourne Farm
Bournebrook Bridge
Letche's Farm
29
Aldercar Wood
BOURNEBRIDGE HILL
Bourne Brook
Froyz Hall
Aylett's Farm
Heater Wood
3
PLAISTOW GREEN RD
Gladfen Hall
Plaistow Green
Penny Pot
A131
28
Plaistowgreen Farm
Bee's Fm
Ward's Farm
Rayne Hatch Wood
Highbarn Hall
Rivenshall Farm
Leafy Wood
2
Stable Wood
Moat Farm
Moat
Moat Wood
27
Lower Wood
Greenwood Spring
Belcher's Wood
Lucas Cottages
Broadfield Wood
Church Farm
Coppy Wood
1
Church's Lane (Track)
LORDSLAND LA
Brooks's Farm
Kentishes Farm
Folly Green
NUNTY'S LA
79
80
81
26
D
E
F

44

61

26

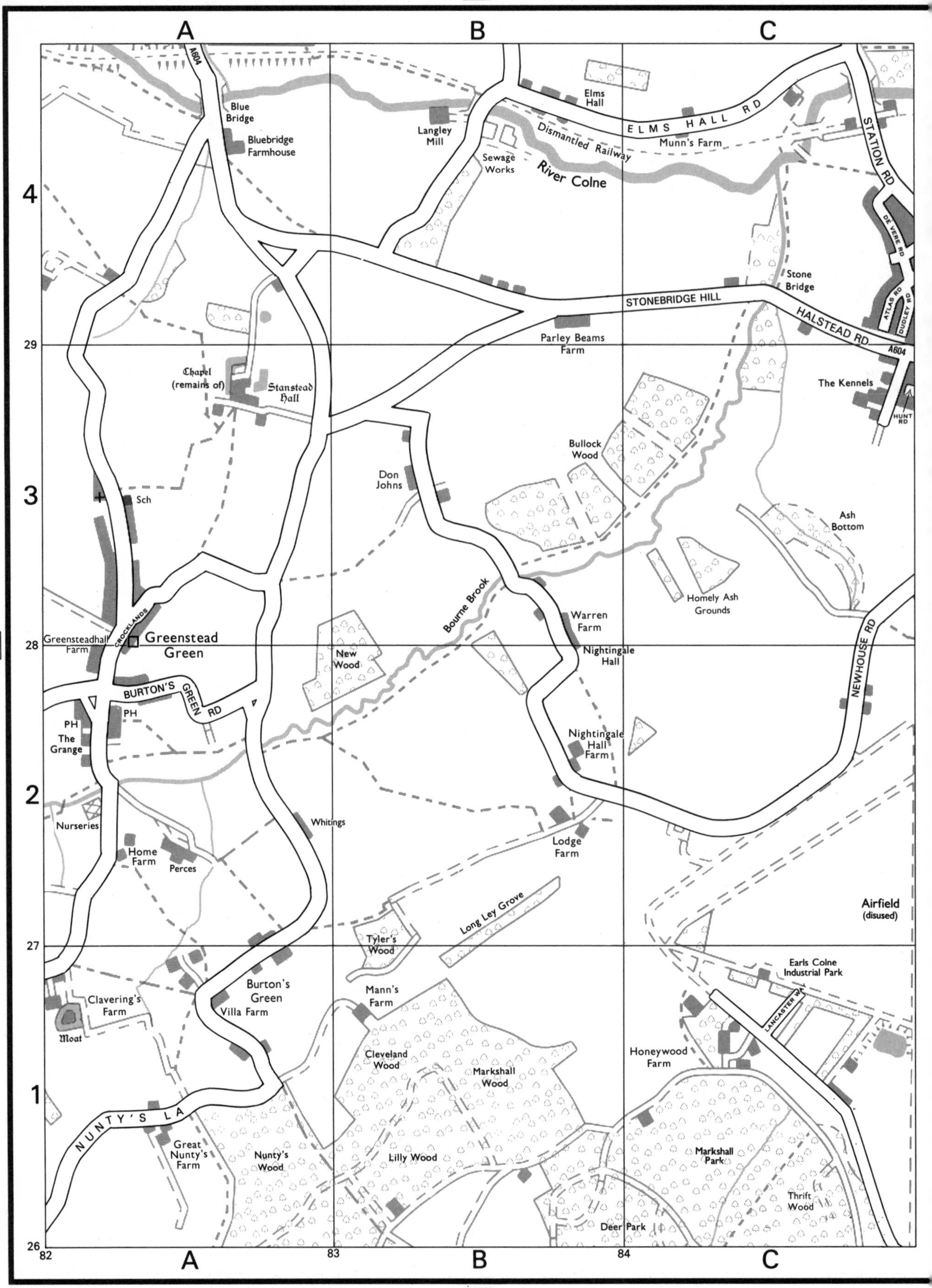
A
B
C
4
3
2
1
29
28
27
26
82
83
84
A604
Blue Bridge
Bluebridge Farmhouse
Langley Mill
Elms Hall
ELMS HALL RD
Dismantled Railway
Munn's Farm
Sewage Works
River Colne
STATION RD
DE VERE RD
Stone Bridge
STONEBRIDGE HILL
HALSTEAD RD
ATLAS RD
DUDLEY RD
Parley Beams Farm
The Kennels
HUNT RD
Chapel (remains of)
Stanstead Hall
Bullock Wood
Don Johns
Sch
Ash Bottom
Homely Ash Grounds
Bourne Brook
Warren Farm
CROCKLANDS
Greenstead Green
Greensteadhall Farm
Nightingale Hall
New Wood
NEWHOUSE RD
BURTON'S GREEN RD
PH
The Grange
Nightingale Hall Farm
Nurseries
Whitings
Home Farm
Perces
Lodge Farm
Airfield (disused)
Long Ley Grove
Tyler's Wood
Earls Colne Industrial Park
LANCASTER WAY
Clavering's Farm
Moat
Burton's Green
Villa Farm
Mann's Farm
Honeywood Farm
Cleveland Wood
Markshall Wood
NUNTY'S LA
Great Nunty's Farm
Nunty's Wood
Lilly Wood
Markshall Park
Thrift Wood
Deer Park

43

62

27

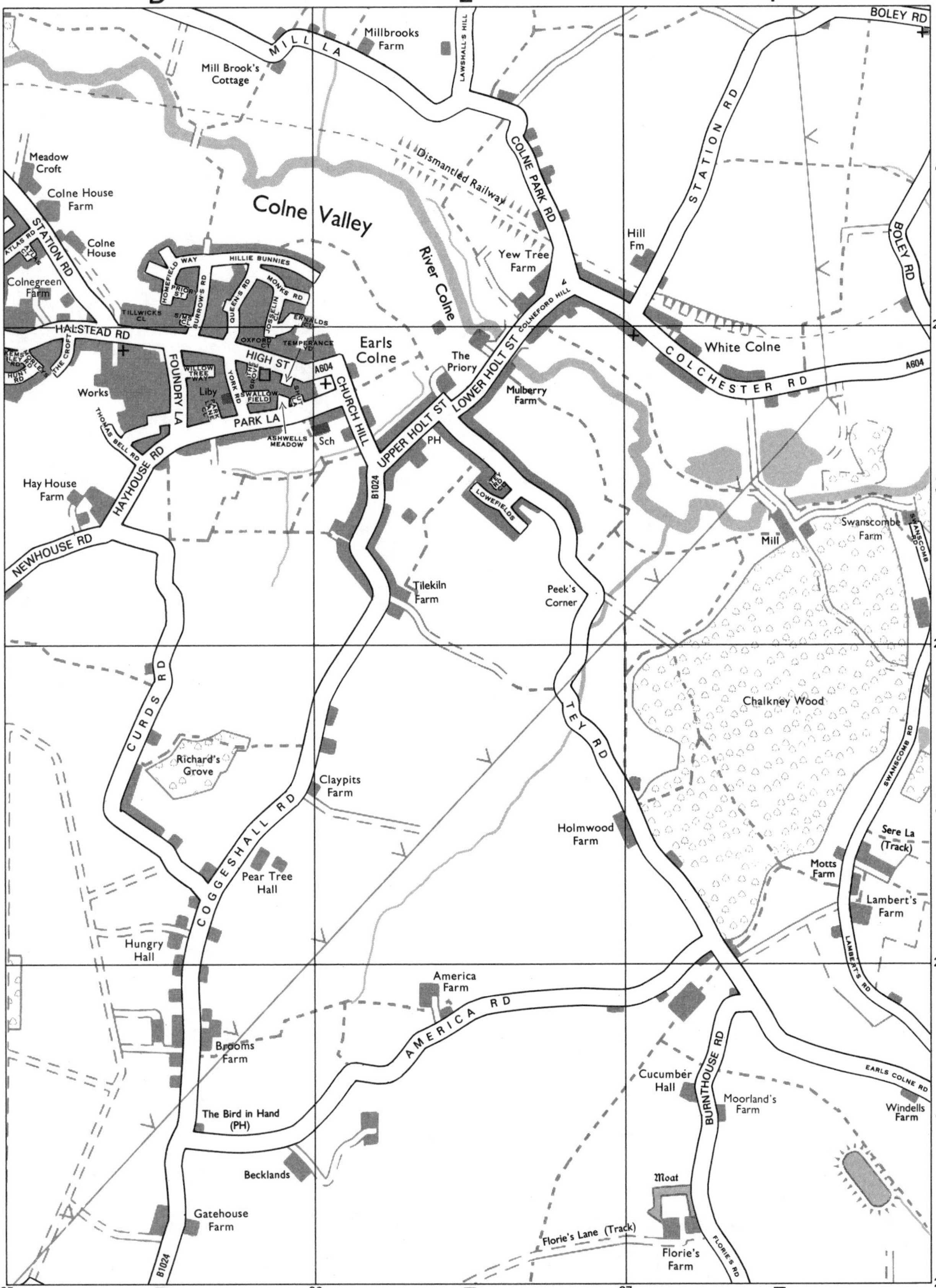

D
E
F
BOLEY RD
Millbrooks Farm
MILL LA
LAWSHALL'S HILL
Mill Brook's Cottage
STATION RD
Meadow Croft
Colne House Farm
Dismantled Railway
COLNE PARK RD
Colne Valley
Colne House
Colnegreen Farm
River Colne
Yew Tree Farm
Hill Fm
BOLEY RD
HOMEFIELD WAY
HILLIE BUNNIES
PRIORY ST
QUEEN'S RD
MONKS RD
JOSSELIN CT
ERNALDS
TILLWICKS CL
BURROW'S RD
HALSTEAD RD
OXFORD CT
TEMPERANCE YD
Earls Colne
The Priory
COLNEFORD HILL
LOWER HOLT ST
White Colne
COLCHESTER RD
A604
HIGH ST
THE CROFT
WILLOW TREE WAY
THE GROVE
YORK RD
A604
CHURCH HILL
Works
FOUNDRY LA
Liby
SWALLOW FIELD
PARK LA
ASHWELLS MEADOW
Sch
UPPER HOLT ST
PH
Mulberry Farm
THOMAS BELL RD
HAYHOUSE RD
Hay House Farm
B1024
LOWEFIELDS
Mill
Swanscombe Farm
SWANSCOMB RD
NEWHOUSE RD
Tilekiln Farm
Peek's Corner
CURDS RD
TEY RD
Chalkney Wood
Richard's Grove
Claypits Farm
SWANSCOMB RD
COGGESHALL RD
Holmwood Farm
Sere La (Track)
Pear Tree Hall
Motts Farm
Lambert's Farm
Hungry Hall
LAMBERT'S RD
America Farm
AMERICA RD
Brooms Farm
BURNTHOUSE RD
EARLS COLNE RD
Cucumber Hall
Moorland's Farm
Windells Farm
The Bird in Hand (PH)
Becklands
Moat
Gatehouse Farm
Florie's Lane (Track)
Florie's Farm
FLORIES RD
B1024
4
3
2
1
29
28
27
26
85
86
87

46

63

28

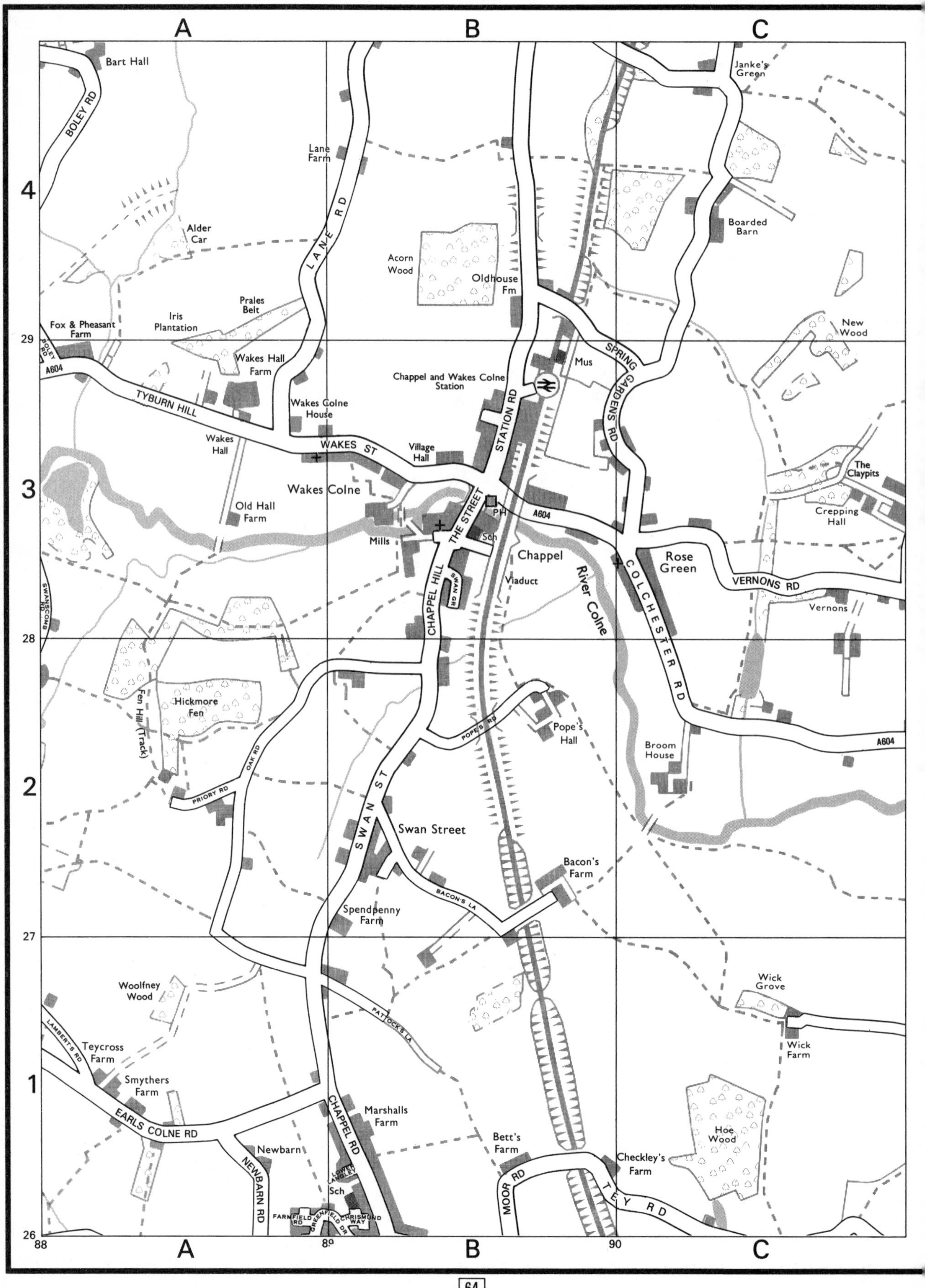
A
B
C
4
3
2
1
29
28
27
26
88
89
90
Bart Hall
BOLEY RD
Lane Farm
LANE RD
Janke's Green
Boarded Barn
Alder Car
Acorn Wood
Oldhouse Fm
Prales Belt
Iris Plantation
Fox & Pheasant Farm
BOLEY RD
New Wood
Wakes Hall Farm
Mus
SPRING GARDENS RD
Chappel and Wakes Colne Station
A604
TYBURN HILL
Wakes Colne House
STATION RD
Wakes Hall
WAKES ST
Village Hall
The Claypits
Wakes Colne
Old Hall Farm
THE STREET
PH
A604
Crepping Hall
Mills
Sch
Chappel
Rose Green
COLCHESTER RD
VERNONS RD
SWANSCOMB RD
CHAPPEL HILL
SWAN GR
Viaduct
River Colne
Vernons
Hickmore Fen
Fen Hill (Track)
POPE'S RD
Pope's Hall
OAK RD
Broom House
A604
PRIORY RD
SWAN ST
Swan Street
Bacon's Farm
BACON'S LA
Spendpenny Farm
Wick Grove
Woolfney Wood
PATTOCK'S LA
LAMBERT'S RD
Teycross Farm
Wick Farm
Smythers Farm
EARLS COLNE RD
Marshalls Farm
CHAPPEL RD
Bett's Farm
Hoe Wood
Newbarn
NEWBARN RD
MOOR RD
Checkley's Farm
TEY RD
LOWER LANGLEY
Sch
FARMFIELD RD
GREENFIELD DR
CHRISMUND WAY

45

64

29

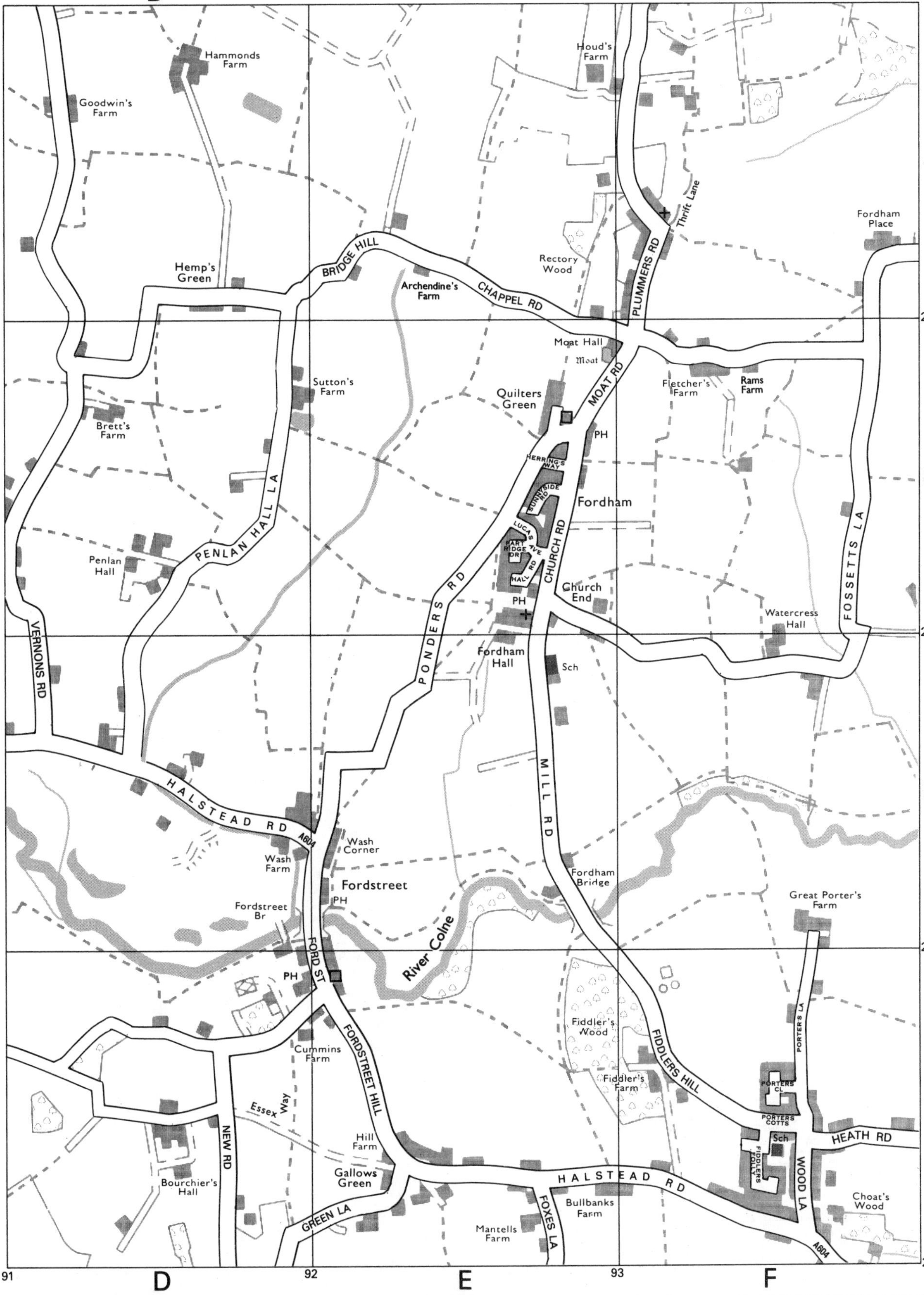
D
E
F
Hammonds Farm
Goodwin's Farm
Houd's Farm
Thrift Lane
Fordham Place
Hemp's Green
BRIDGE HILL
Archendine's Farm
CHAPPEL RD
Rectory Wood
PLUMMERS RD
Moat Hall
Moat
MOAT RD
Sutton's Farm
Quilters Green
Fletcher's Farm
Rams Farm
Brett's Farm
PH
HERRING'S WAY
SUNNYSIDE RD
Fordham
LUCAS AVE
PART RIDGE DR
HALL RD
CHURCH RD
PENLAN HALL LA
Penlan Hall
PONDERS RD
Church End
Watercress Hall
FOSSETTS LA
VERNONS RD
Fordham Hall
Sch
MILL RD
HALSTEAD RD
A604
Wash Corner
Wash Farm
Fordstreet
Fordham Bridge
Great Porter's Farm
Fordstreet Br
FORD ST
River Colne
Fiddler's Wood
PORTER'S LA
Cummins Farm
FORDSTREET HILL
Fiddler's Farm
FIDDLERS HILL
PORTERS CL
PORTERS COTTS
Essex Way
NEW RD
Hill Farm
FIDDLERS FOLLY
HEATH RD
WOOD LA
Gallows Green
HALSTEAD RD
Bourchier's Hall
Bullbanks Farm
Choat's Wood
FOXES LA
GREEN LA
Mantells Farm
1
2
3
4
26
27
28
29
91
92
93

48

65

30

47

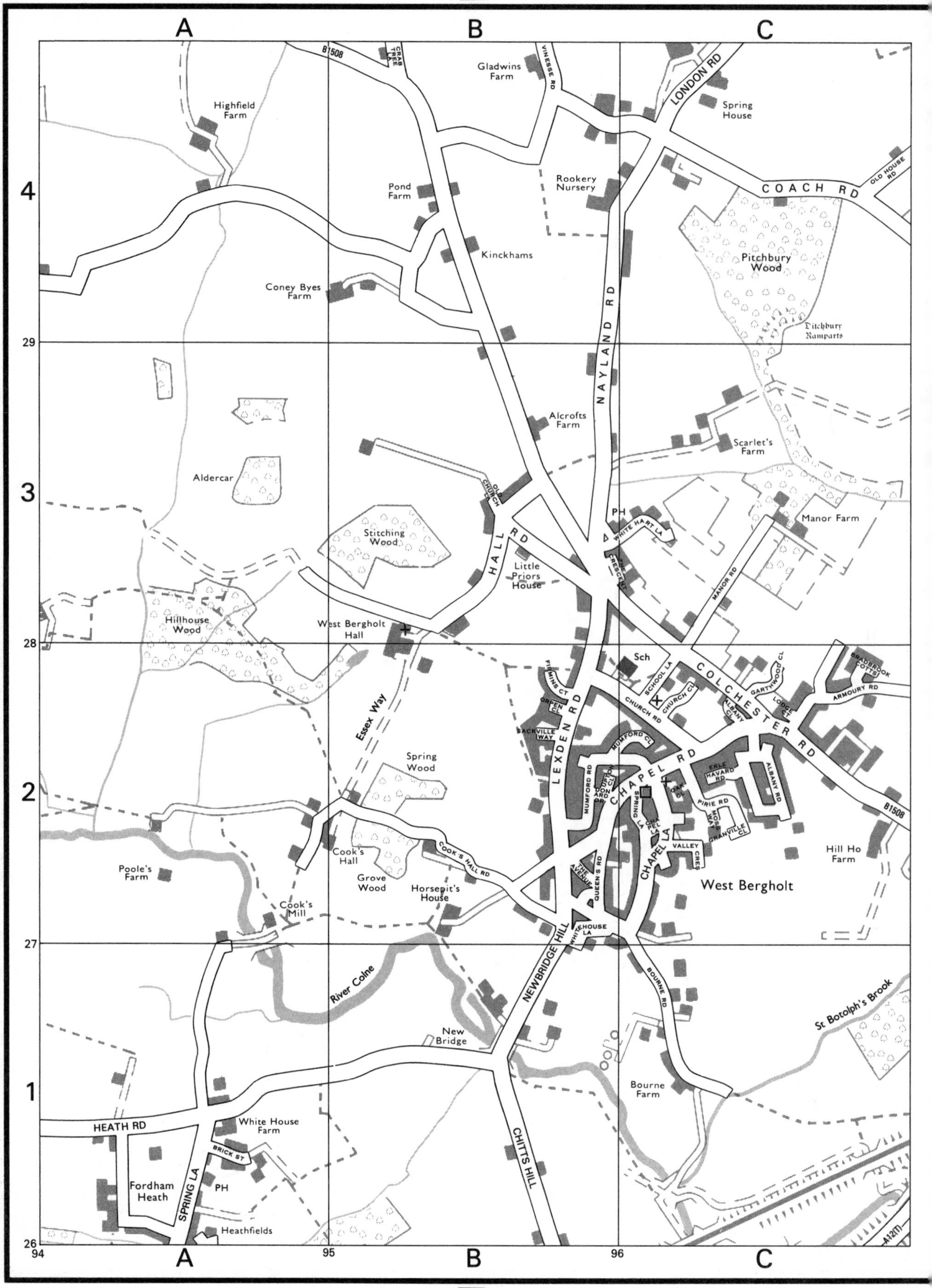
A
B
C
4
3
2
1
29
28
27
26
94
95
96
B1508
CRAB TREE LA
Gladwins Farm
VINESSE RD
LONDON RD
Spring House
Highfield Farm
Rookery Nursery
Pond Farm
COACH RD
OLD HOUSE RD
Kinckhams
Pitchbury Wood
Coney Byes Farm
Ditchbury Ramparts
NAYLAND RD
Alcrofts Farm
Scarlet's Farm
Aldercar
OLD CHURCH
PH
WHITE HART LA
Manor Farm
Stitching Wood
HALL RD
Little Priors House
THE CRESCENT
MANOR RD
Hillhouse Wood
West Bergholt Hall
Sch
FIRMINS CT
SCHOOL LA
COLCHESTER RD
BRADBROOK COTTS
ARMOURY RD
GARTHWOOD CL
GREEN CL
CHURCH CL
CHURCH RD
ALBANY CL
LODGE CT
Essex Way
SACKVILLE WAY
LEXDEN RD
MUMFORD CL
Spring Wood
MUMFORD RD
CHAPEL RD
ERLE HAVARD RD
ALBANY RD
OAK CL
PIRIE RD
MOSS WAY
GRANVILLE CL
B1508
SPRING LA
CHAPEL LA
VALLEY CRES
Hill Ho Farm
Poole's Farm
Cook's Hall
COOK'S HALL RD
Grove Wood
Horsepit's House
THE AVENUE
QUEEN'S RD
West Bergholt
Cook's Mill
NEWBRIDGE HILL
WHITEHOUSE LA
BOURNE RD
River Colne
St Botolph's Brook
New Bridge
Bourne Farm
HEATH RD
White House Farm
BRICK ST
CHITTS HILL
Fordham Heath
SPRING LA
PH
Heathfields
A12(T)

66

31

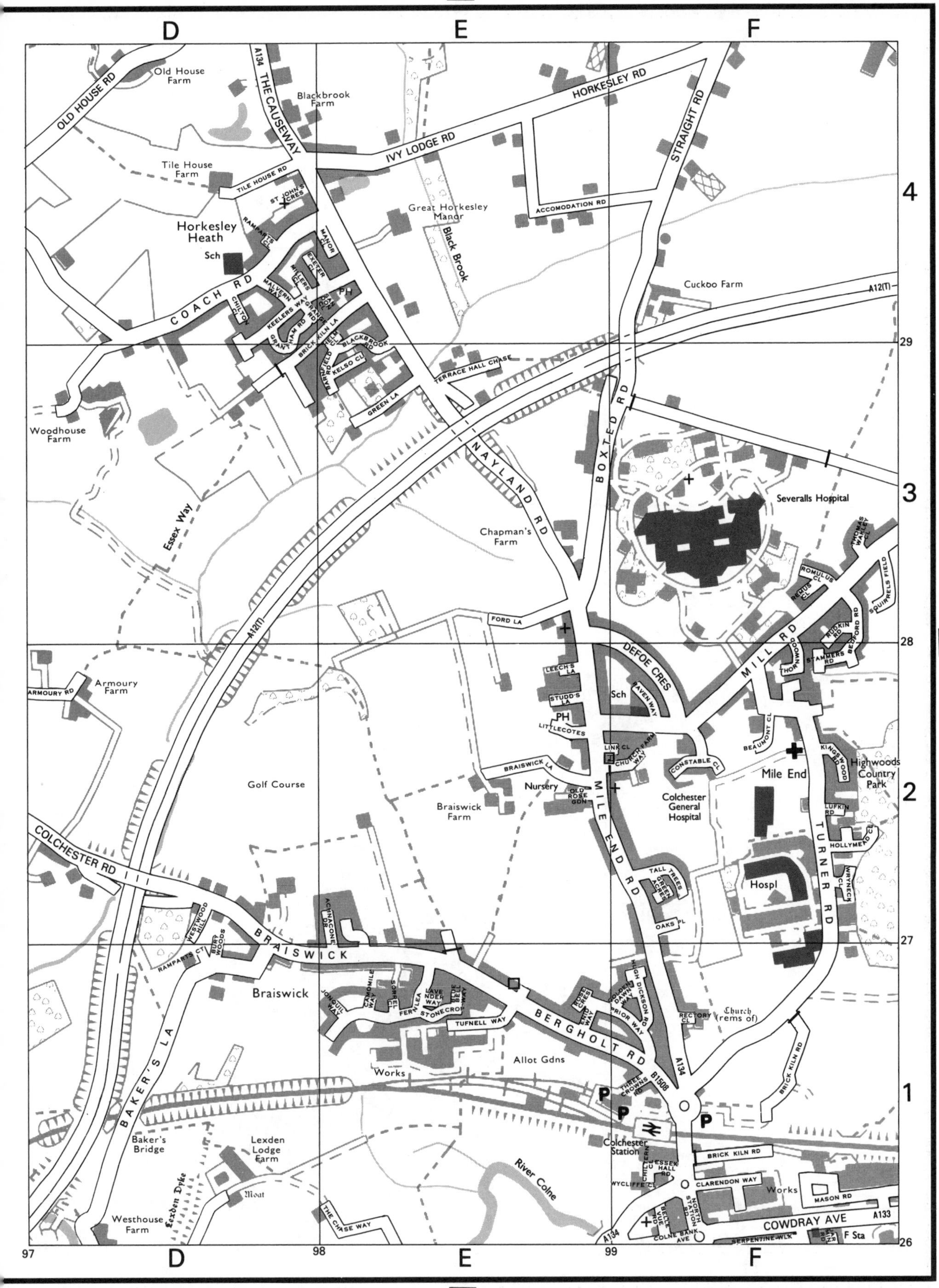
D
E
F
Old House Farm
OLD HOUSE RD
A134 THE CAUSEWAY
Blackbrook Farm
HORKESLEY RD
STRAIGHT RD
IVY LODGE RD
Tile House Farm
TILE HOUSE RD
ST JOHN'S CRES
Great Horkesley Manor
ACCOMODATION RD
4
Horkesley Heath
Sch
RAMPARTS CL
MANOR CL
EXETER CL
MILLERS CL
MALVERN WAY
PH
Black Brook
Cuckoo Farm
A12(T)
COACH RD
CHILTON CL
KEELERS WAY
GRANTHAM RD
BRICK KILN LA
HELM CL
BLACKBROOK RD
BARNFIELD RD
KELSO CL
TERRACE HALL CHASE
GREEN LA
29
Woodhouse Farm
BOXTED RD
NAYLAND RD
Severalls Hospital
3
Essex Way
Chapman's Farm
THOMAS WAKLEY CL
ROMULUS CL
REMUS CL
SQUIRRELS FIELD
FORD LA
A12(T)
MILL RD
HORNWOOD
RUCKIN RD
BEDFORD RD
STAMMERS RD
28
DEFOE CRES
Armoury Farm
ARMOURY RD
LEECH'S LA
STUDD'S LA
Sch
RAVEN WAY
PH
LITTLECOTES
BEAUMONT CL
LINK CL
CHURCH FARM WAY
CONSTABLE CL
KINGSWOOD
Highwoods Country Park
Mile End
BRAISWICK LA
Golf Course
Nursery
OLD ROSE GDN
MILE END RD
Colchester General Hospital
2
Braiswick Farm
LUFKIN RD
HOLLYMEAD CL
COLCHESTER RD
TALL TREES
GREEN ACRES
Hospl
TURNER RD
WRYNECK CL
WESTWOOD HILL
BURY WOODS
ACHNACONE DR
OAKS PL
RAMPARTS CT
BRAISWICK
27
Braiswick
JONQUIL WAY
CAMOMILE WAY
SORREL CL
FERNLEA
LAVENDER WAY
STONECROP
TUFNELL WAY
ROSE CRES
EMLY WAY
GOLDEN DAWN WAY
HIGH DICKSON RD
PRIOR WAY
RECTORY CL
Church (rems of)
BERGHOLT RD
BAKER'S LA
Allot Gdns
Works
B1508
A134
THREE CROWNS RD
BRICK KILN RD
1
P
P
P
Baker's Bridge
Lexden Lodge Farm
River Colne
Colchester Station
BRICK KILN RD
ESSEX HALL RD
CHILTERN CL
WYCLIFFE CL
CLARENDON WAY
Works
Lexden Dyke
Moat
NORTH STATION RD
BELLE VUE RD
MASON RD
Westhouse Farm
THE CHASE WAY
A134
COLNE BANK AVE
COWDRAY AVE
A133
SERPENTINE WLK
F Sta
26
97
98
99
D
E
F

50
67

32

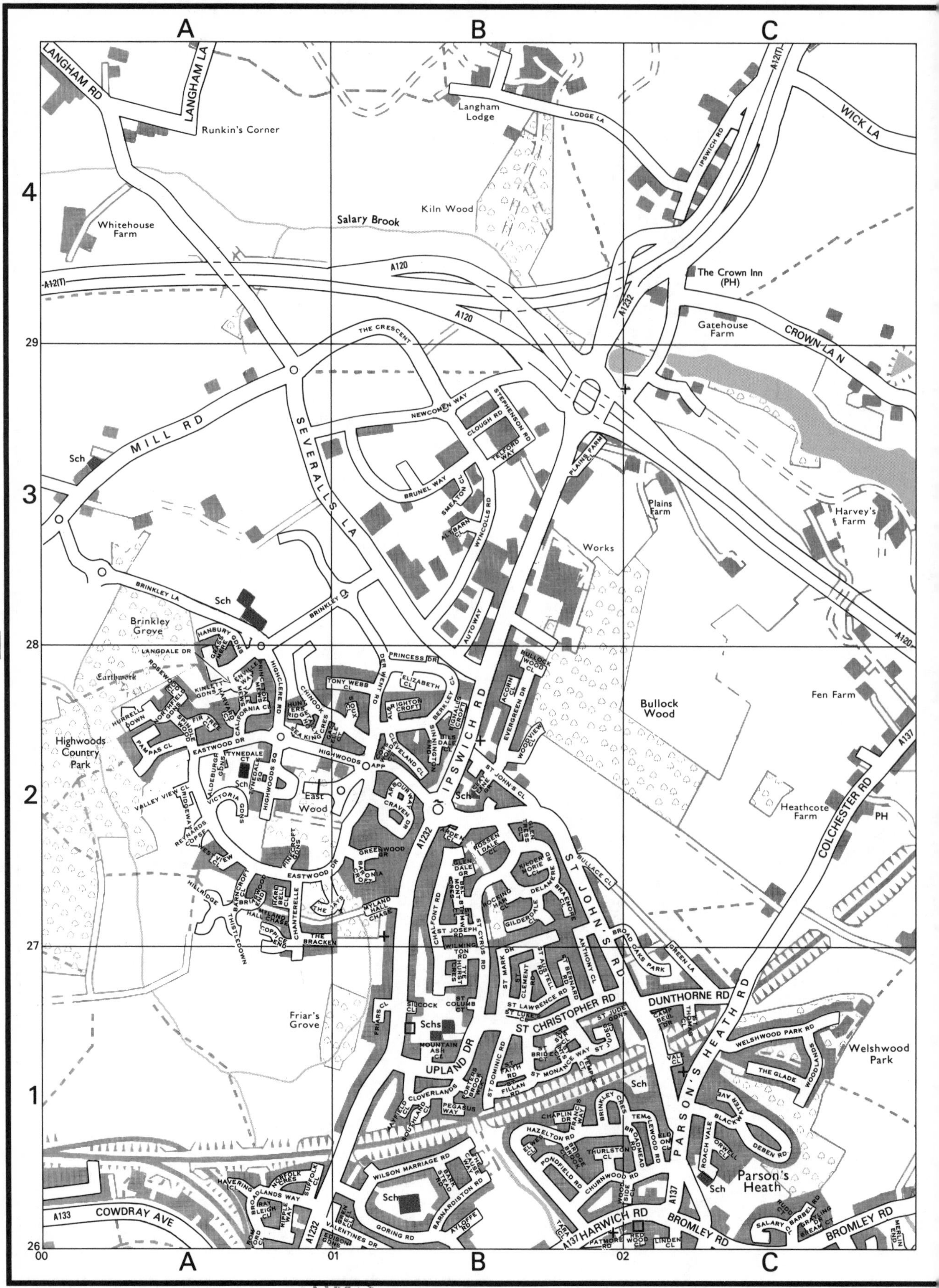
A
B
C
4
3
2
1
29
28
27
26
00
01
02
LANGHAM RD
LANGHAM LA
Runkin's Corner
Langham Lodge
LODGE LA
WICK LA
A12(T)
IPSWICH RD
Whitehouse Farm
Salary Brook
Kiln Wood
A120
A12(T)
The Crown Inn (PH)
A1232
Gatehouse Farm
CROWN LA N
THE CRESCENT
NEWCOMEN WAY
STEPHENSON RD
CLOUGH RD
TELFORD WAY
MILL RD
SEVERALLS LA
Sch
BRUNEL WAY
SMEATON CL
ALTBARN CL
WYNCOLLS RD
PLAINS FARM CL
Plains Farm
Harvey's Farm
Works
BRINKLEY LA
Sch
BRINKLEY CRES
AUTOWAY
Brinkley Grove
A120
HANBURY GDNS
LANGDALE DR
PRINCESS DR
DERWENT RD
BULLOCK WOOD CL
Earthwork
TONY WEBB CL
ELIZABETH WAY
BERKLEY CL
Bullock Wood
Fen Farm
ACORN CL
EVERGREEN DR
HIGHCLERE RD
CHINOOK
IPSWICH RD
HURRELL DOWN
PAMPAS CL
EASTWOOD DR
TYNEDALE CT
HIGHWOODS SQ
HIGHWOODS APP
CLEVELAND CL
WOODVIEW CL
ST JOHN'S CL
Highwoods Country Park
Sch
East Wood
CRAVEN DR
Sch
A137
COLCHESTER RD
VALLEY VIEW CL
VICTORIA GDNS
REYNARDS COPSE
WEST VIEW
HILLRIDGE
Heathcote Farm
PH
A1232
ARDEN CL
ROSSENDALE CL
GLENDALE GR
GREENWOOD GR
EASTWOOD DR
FINECROFT GDNS
ST JOHN'S RD
BULLACE CL
KINDERMORIE CL
DELAMERE RD
BRAEMORE CL
GILDERDALE CL
ST JOSEPH RD
ST CYRUS RD
WILMINGTON RD
CHALFONT RD
THE BRACKEN
THISTLEDOWN
COPPICE END
CHANTERELLE
MYLAND HALL CHASE
BROAD OAKS PARK
GREEN LA
ST MARK DR
ST AUSTELL RD
ST BERNARD RD
ANTHONY CL
ST CLEMENT RD
ST LAWRENCE RD
ST LUKE'S CL
ST CHRISTOPHER RD
DUNTHORNE RD
ST JUDE GDNS
CAMP BEUL DR
Friar's Grove
FRIARS CL
SILCOCK CL
ST COLUMB CT
Schs
MOUNTAIN ASH CL
UPLAND DR
ST DOMINIC RD
ST FAITH RD
ST FILLAN RD
BRIDE CT
ST MONANCE WAY
ST JUDE CL
PARSON'S HEATH
WELSHWOOD PARK RD
THE GLADE
WOODLANDS
Welshwood Park
Sch
CLOVERLANDS
PEGASUS WAY
SOUTHLAND CL
BRINKLEY CRES
CHAPLIN DR
HAZELTON RD
THURLSTON CL
BROOKMEAD
DEBEN RD
BLACKWATER AVE
ORWELL CL
ROACH VALE
WILSON MARRIAGE RD
PONDFIELD RD
CHURNWOOD RD
Parson's Heath
Sch
NORFOLK CRES
SUFFOLK CL
HAVERING CL
BROADLANDS WAY
RIPPLE WAY
Sch
BARNARDISTON RD
A133
COWDRAY AVE
A1232
GORING RD
AYLOFFE RD
HARWICH RD
A137
BROMLEY RD
SALARY CL
BROMLEY RD
VALENTINES DR
EDISON GDNS
PATMORE RD
REDWOOD CL
LINDEN CL
MERLIN END

49

68

33

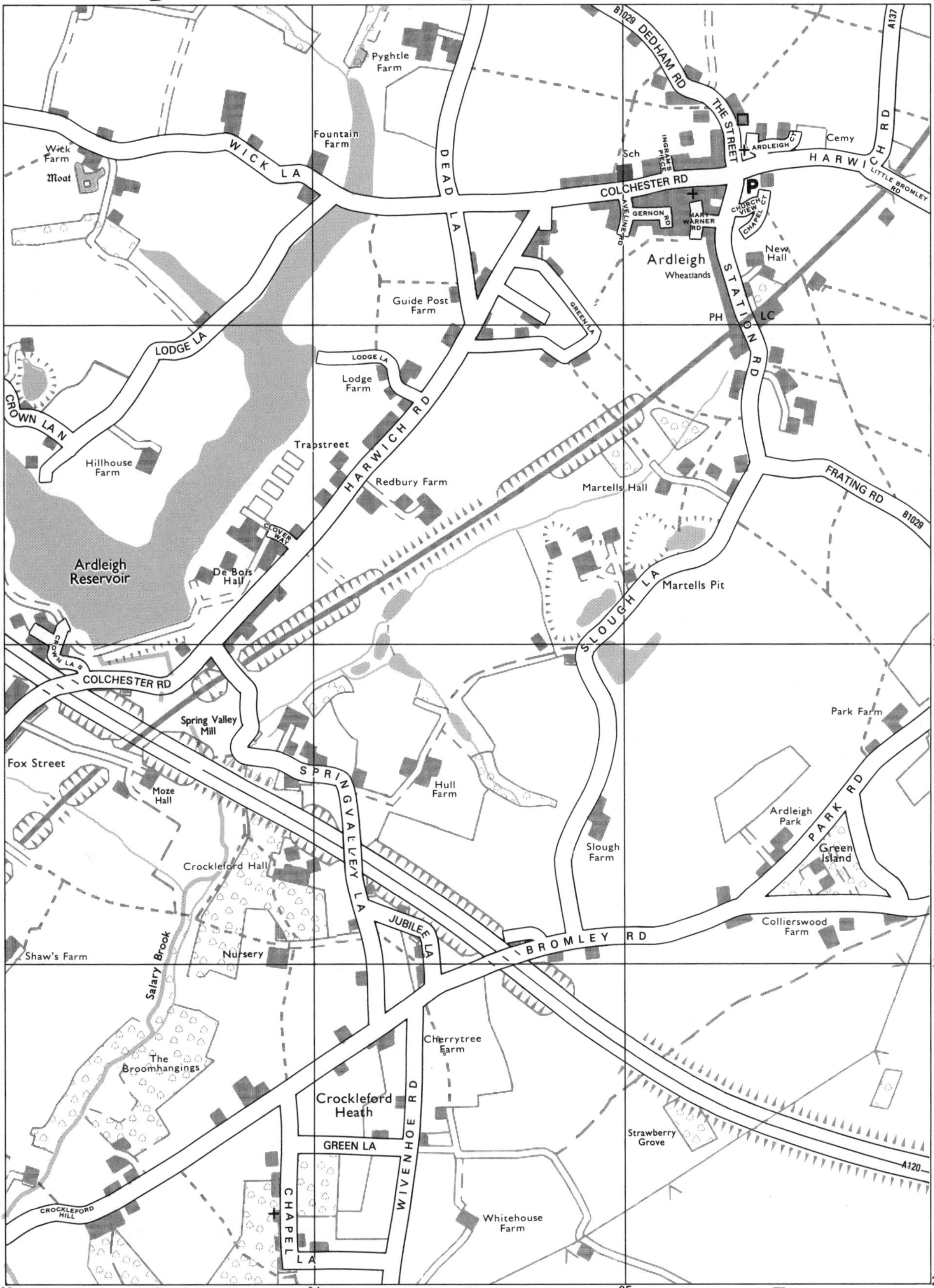
D
E
F
Pyghtle Farm
Fountain Farm
Wick Farm
Moat
WICK LA
DEAD LA
B1029 DEDHAM RD
THE STREET
INGRAMS PIECE
Sch
COLCHESTER RD
ARDLEIGH CT
Cemy
HARWICH RD
LITTLE BROMLEY RD
A137
CHURCH VIEW
CHAPEL CT
GERNON RD
MARY WARNER RD
AVELINE RD
Ardleigh
Wheatlands
New Hall
STATION RD
Guide Post Farm
GREEN LA
PH
LC
LODGE LA
Lodge Farm
CROWN LA N
Hillhouse Farm
Trapstreet
HARWICH RD
Redbury Farm
Martells Hall
FRATING RD
B1029
CLOVER WAY
Ardleigh Reservoir
De Bois Hall
SLOUGH LA
Martells Pit
CROWN LA S
COLCHESTER RD
Spring Valley Mill
Fox Street
Moze Hall
SPRING VALLEY LA
Hull Farm
Park Farm
PARK RD
Ardleigh Park
Green Island
Slough Farm
Crockleford Hall
JUBILEE LA
BROMLEY RD
Collierswood Farm
Shaw's Farm
Nursery
Salary Brook
The Broomhangings
Cherrytree Farm
Crockleford Heath
WIVENHOE RD
GREEN LA
Strawberry Grove
A120
CROCKLEFORD HILL
CHAPEL LA
Whitehouse Farm
4
3
2
1
29
28
27
26
03
04
05
D
E
F

52

34

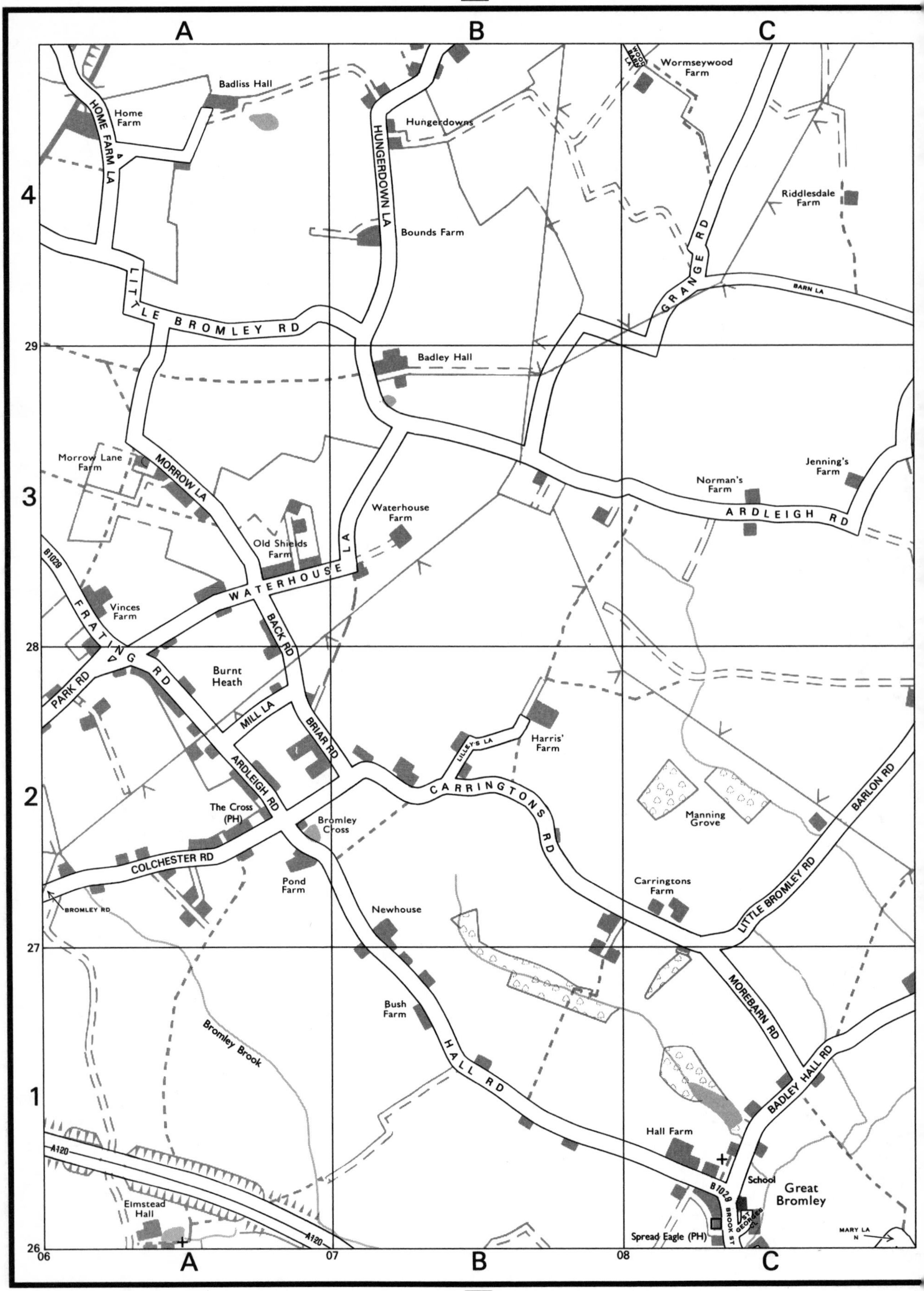
A
B
C
A
B
C
4
3
2
1
29
28
27
26
06
07
08
Badliss Hall
Home Farm
HOME FARM LA
LITTLE BROMLEY RD
HUNGERDOWN LA
Hungerdowns
Bounds Farm
Wormseywood Farm
Riddlesdale Farm
GRANGE RD
BARN LA
Badley Hall
Morrow Lane Farm
MORROW LA
Old Shields Farm
Waterhouse Farm
WATERHOUSE LA
Norman's Farm
Jenning's Farm
ARDLEIGH RD
B1029
FRATING RD
Vinces Farm
BACK RD
PARK RD
Burnt Heath
MILL LA
BRIAR RD
ARDLEIGH RD
LILLEY'S LA
Harris' Farm
CARRINGTONS RD
Manning Grove
BARLON RD
The Cross (PH)
Bromley Cross
COLCHESTER RD
BROMLEY RD
Pond Farm
Newhouse
Carringtons Farm
LITTLE BROMLEY RD
MOREBARN RD
Bush Farm
Bromley Brook
HALL RD
BADLEY HALL RD
A120
Hall Farm
School
Great Bromley
B1029
BROOK ST
ST GEORGES CL
Elmstead Hall
Spread Eagle (PH)
MARY LA N

51

70

35

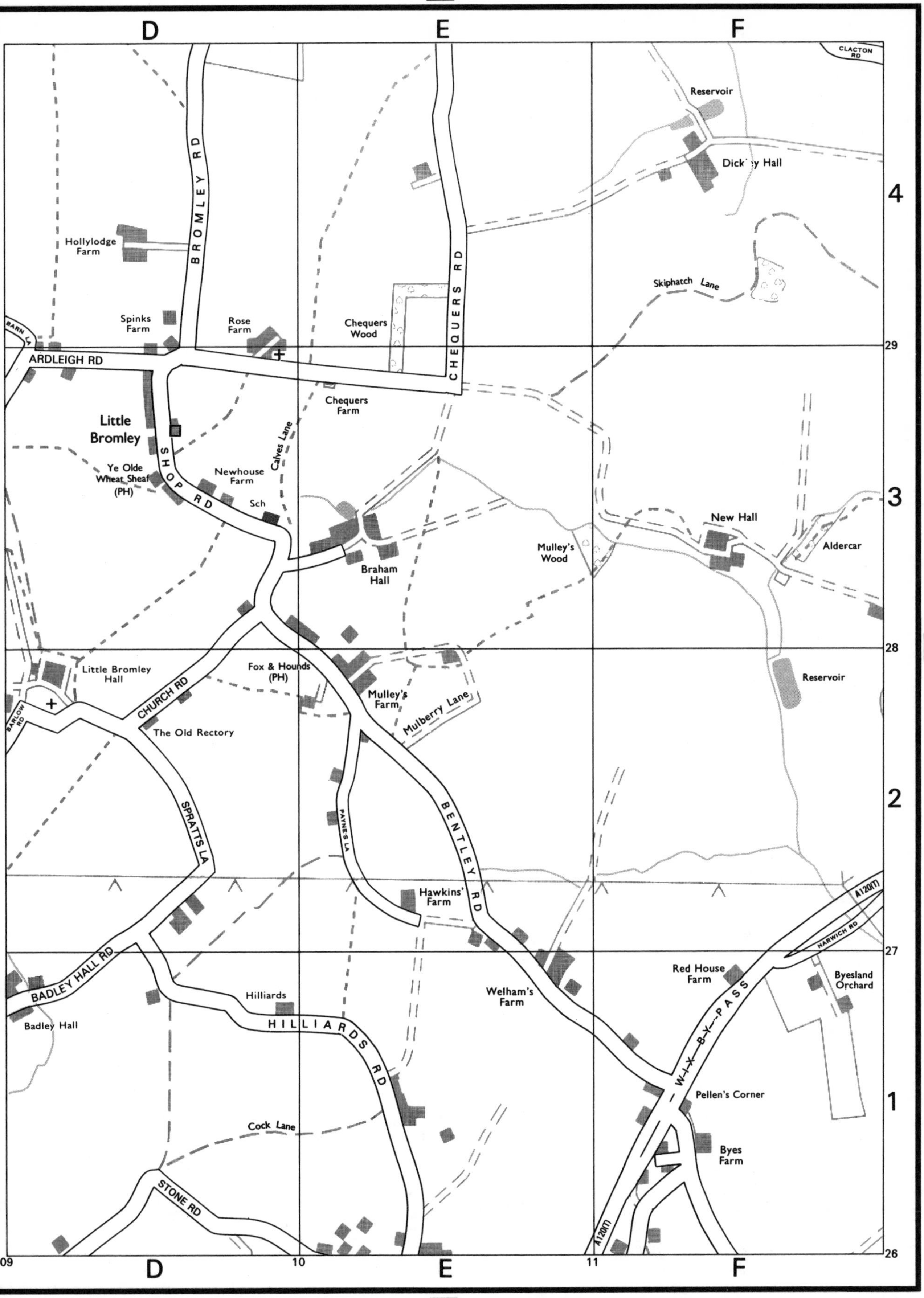
D
E
F
CLACTON RD
Reservoir
Dick'ey Hall
4
BROMLEY RD
Hollylodge Farm
CHEQUERS RD
Skiphatch Lane
Spinks Farm
Rose Farm
Chequers Wood
BARN LA
29
ARDLEIGH RD
Chequers Farm
Little Bromley
SHOP RD
Calves Lane
Ye Olde Wheat Sheaf (PH)
Newhouse Farm
Sch
3
New Hall
Aldercar
Mulley's Wood
Braham Hall
28
Little Bromley Hall
Fox & Hounds (PH)
Reservoir
CHURCH RD
Mulley's Farm
Mulberry Lane
BARLOW RD
The Old Rectory
SPRATTS LA
PAYNE'S LA
BENTLEY RD
2
A120(T)
Hawkins' Farm
HARWICH RD
BADLEY HALL RD
27
Red House Farm
Byesland Orchard
Welham's Farm
Hilliards
Badley Hall
HILLIARDS RD
WIX BY-PASS
Pellen's Corner
1
Cock Lane
Byes Farm
STONE RD
A120(T)
09
10
11
26
D
E
F

54

71

36

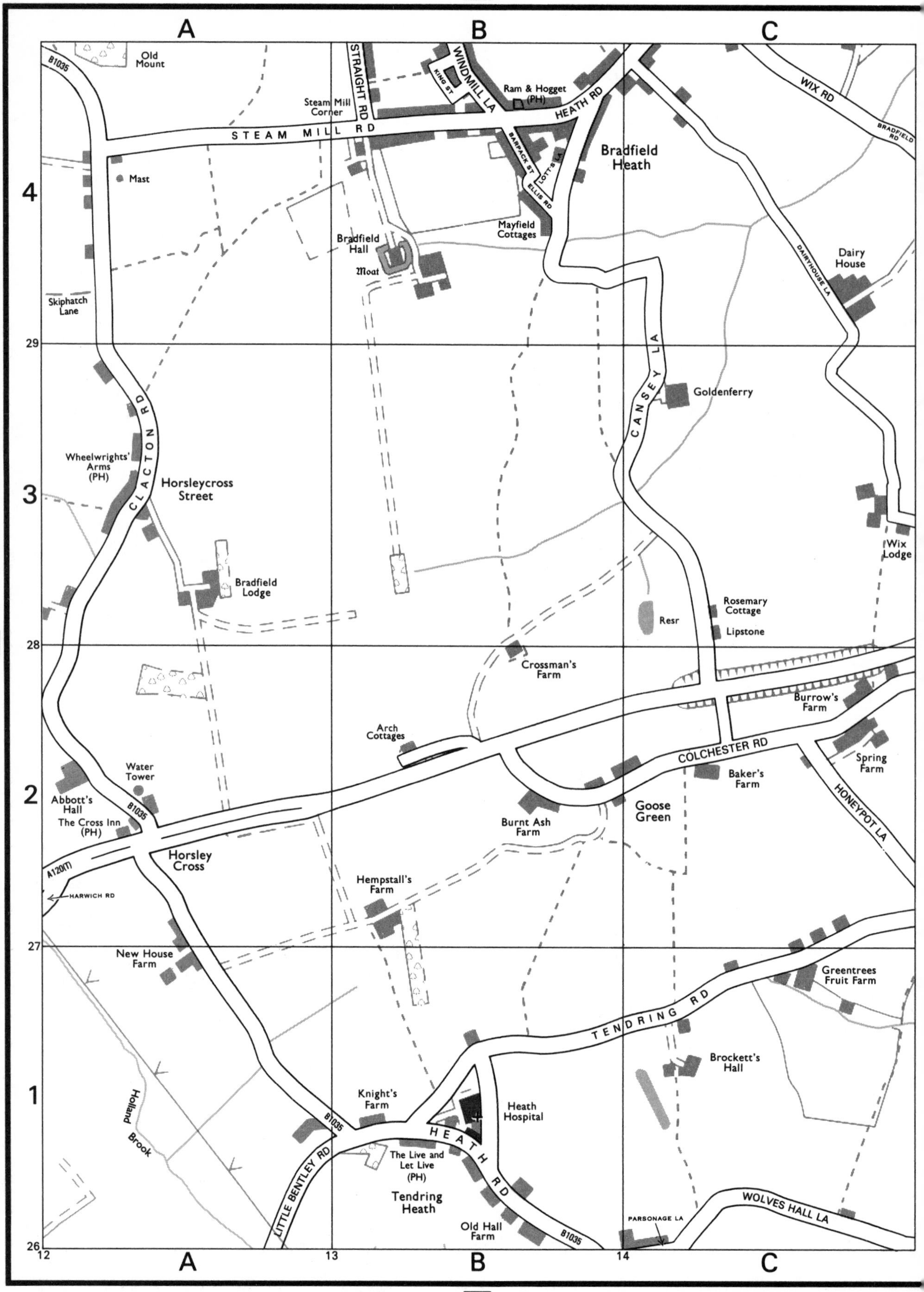

A
B
C
Old Mount
B1035
Steam Mill Corner
STRAIGHT RD
KING ST
WINDMILL LA
Ram & Hogget (PH)
HEATH RD
WIX RD
BRADFIELD RD
STEAM MILL RD
BARPACK ST
LOTT'S LA
ELLIS RD
Bradfield Heath
Mast
4
Mayfield Cottages
Bradfield Hall
Moat
Dairy House
DAIRYHOUSE LA
Skiphatch Lane
29
CANSEY LA
Goldenferry
CLACTON RD
Wheelwrights' Arms (PH)
Horsleycross Street
3
Wix Lodge
Bradfield Lodge
Rosemary Cottage
Resr
Lipstone
28
Crossman's Farm
Burrow's Farm
Arch Cottages
COLCHESTER RD
Spring Farm
Water Tower
Baker's Farm
2
Abbott's Hall
B1035
Goose Green
HONEYPOT LA
The Cross Inn (PH)
Burnt Ash Farm
Horsley Cross
A120(T)
HARWICH RD
Hempstall's Farm
27
New House Farm
Greentrees Fruit Farm
TENDRING RD
Brockett's Hall
1
Holland Brook
Knight's Farm
Heath Hospital
B1035
HEATH RD
LITTLE BENTLEY RD
The Live and Let Live (PH)
Tendring Heath
Old Hall Farm
B1035
PARSONAGE LA
WOLVES HALL LA
26
12
13
14
A
B
C

53

72

37

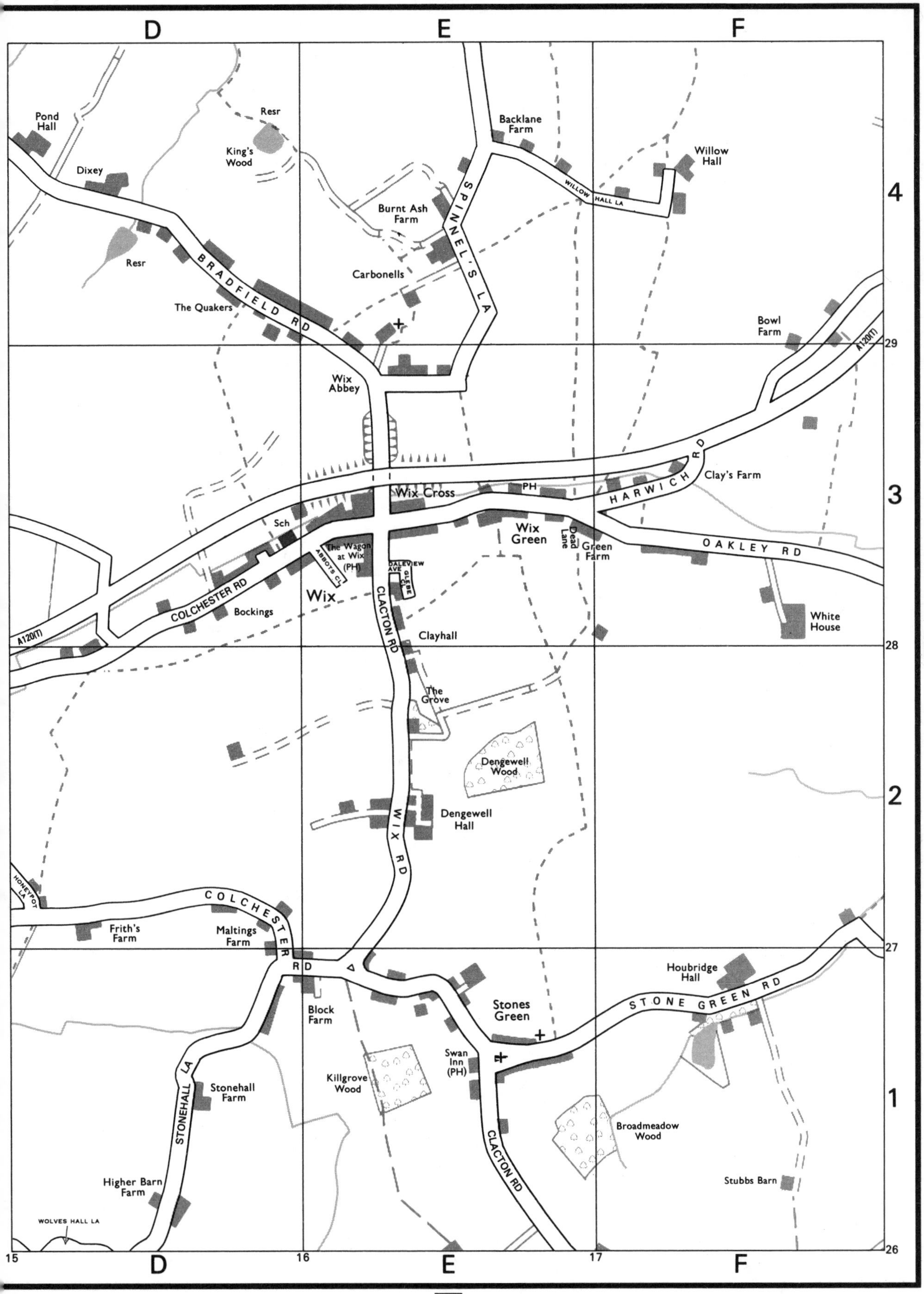
D
E
F
Pond Hall
Resr
King's Wood
Dixey
Backlane Farm
Willow Hall
WILLOW HALL LA
Burnt Ash Farm
SPINNEL'S LA
Resr
BRADFIELD RD
Carbonells
The Quakers
Bowl Farm
A120(T)
Wix Abbey
Wix Cross
PH
HARWICH RD
Clay's Farm
Sch
Wix Green
Dead Lane
Green Farm
OAKLEY RD
The Wagon at Wix (PH)
ABBOTS CL
DALEVIEW AVE
GLEBE CL
COLCHESTER RD
Bockings
Wix
CLACTON RD
White House
A120(T)
Clayhall
The Grove
Dengewell Wood
Dengewell Hall
WIX RD
HONEYPOT LA
COLCHESTER RD
Frith's Farm
Maltings Farm
Houbridge Hall
Block Farm
Stones Green
STONE GREEN RD
Swan Inn (PH)
Killgrove Wood
Stonehall Farm
STONEHALL LA
Broadmeadow Wood
CLACTON RD
Higher Barn Farm
Stubbs Barn
WOLVES HALL LA
15
16
17
29
28
27
26
4
3
2
1

56

73

38

55

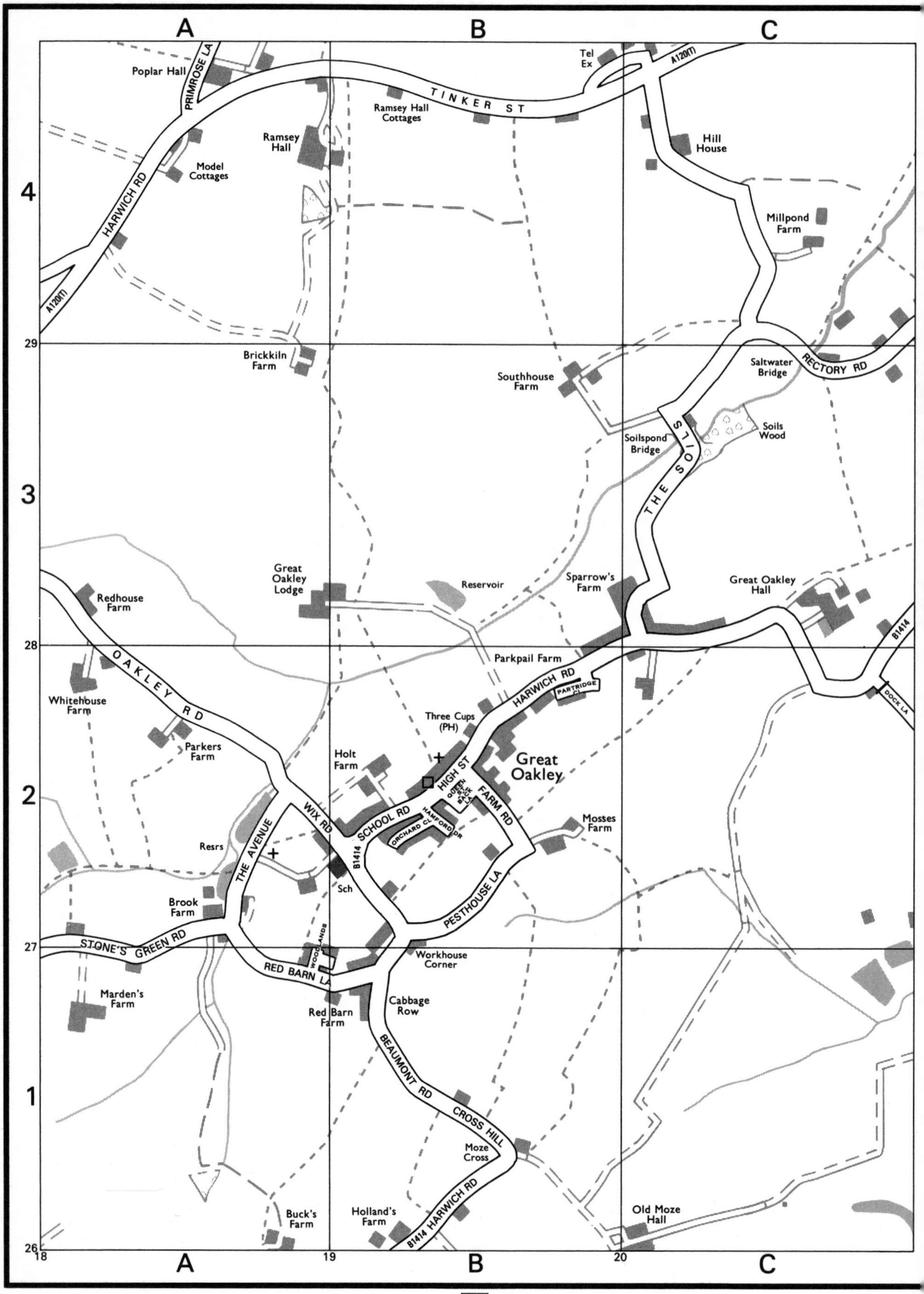

A
B
C
4
3
2
1
29
28
27
26
18
19
20
Poplar Hall
PRIMROSE LA
TINKER ST
Tel Ex
A120(T)
Ramsey Hall Cottages
Ramsey Hall
Model Cottages
HARWICH RD
Hill House
Millpond Farm
Brickkiln Farm
Southhouse Farm
Saltwater Bridge
RECTORY RD
Soilspond Bridge
THE SOILS
Soils Wood
Great Oakley Lodge
Reservoir
Sparrow's Farm
Great Oakley Hall
Redhouse Farm
B1414
Parkpail Farm
PARTRIDGE CL
DOCK LA
OAKLEY RD
Whitehouse Farm
Three Cups (PH)
Parkers Farm
Holt Farm
Great Oakley
HIGH ST
FARM RD
WIX RD
SCHOOL RD
ORCHARD CL
HAMFORD DR
Mosses Farm
Resrs
THE AVENUE
Sch
PESTHOUSE LA
Brook Farm
STONE'S GREEN RD
WOODLANDS
Workhouse Corner
RED BARN LA
Marden's Farm
Cabbage Row
Red Barn Farm
BEAUMONT RD
CROSS HILL
Moze Cross
Buck's Farm
Holland's Farm
B1414 HARWICH RD
Old Moze Hall

74

39

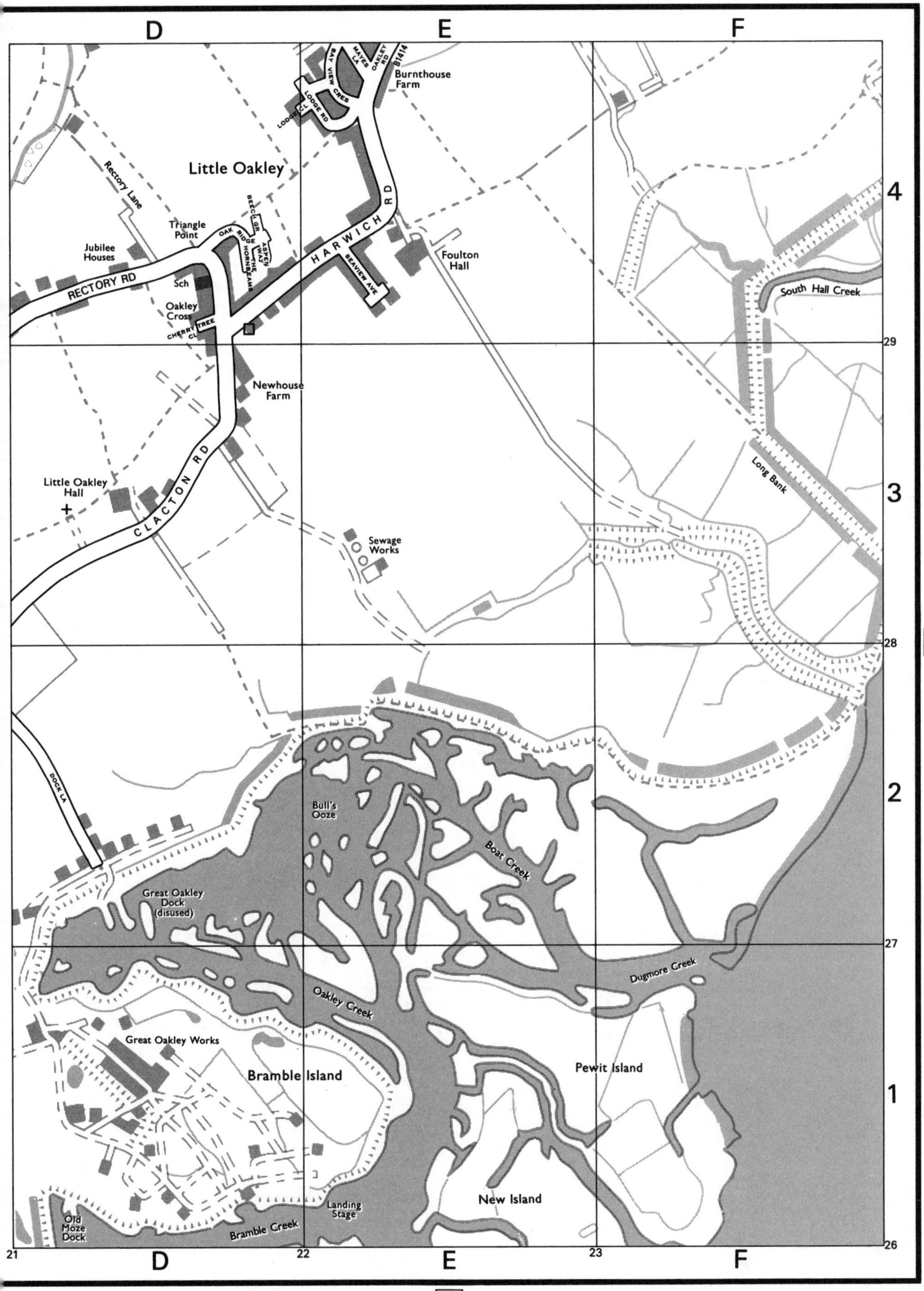
D
E
F
Burnthouse Farm
B1414
Little Oakley
Rectory Lane
Triangle Point
Jubilee Houses
RECTORY RD
Sch
Oakley Cross
HARWICH RD
Foulton Hall
South Hall Creek
Newhouse Farm
Little Oakley Hall
CLACTON RD
Sewage Works
Long Bank
DOCK LA
Bull's Ooze
Boat Creek
Great Oakley Dock (disused)
Dugmore Creek
Oakley Creek
Great Oakley Works
Bramble Island
Pewit Island
New Island
Landing Stage
Old Moze Dock
Bramble Creek
4
3
2
1
29
28
27
26
21
22
23

58

75

40

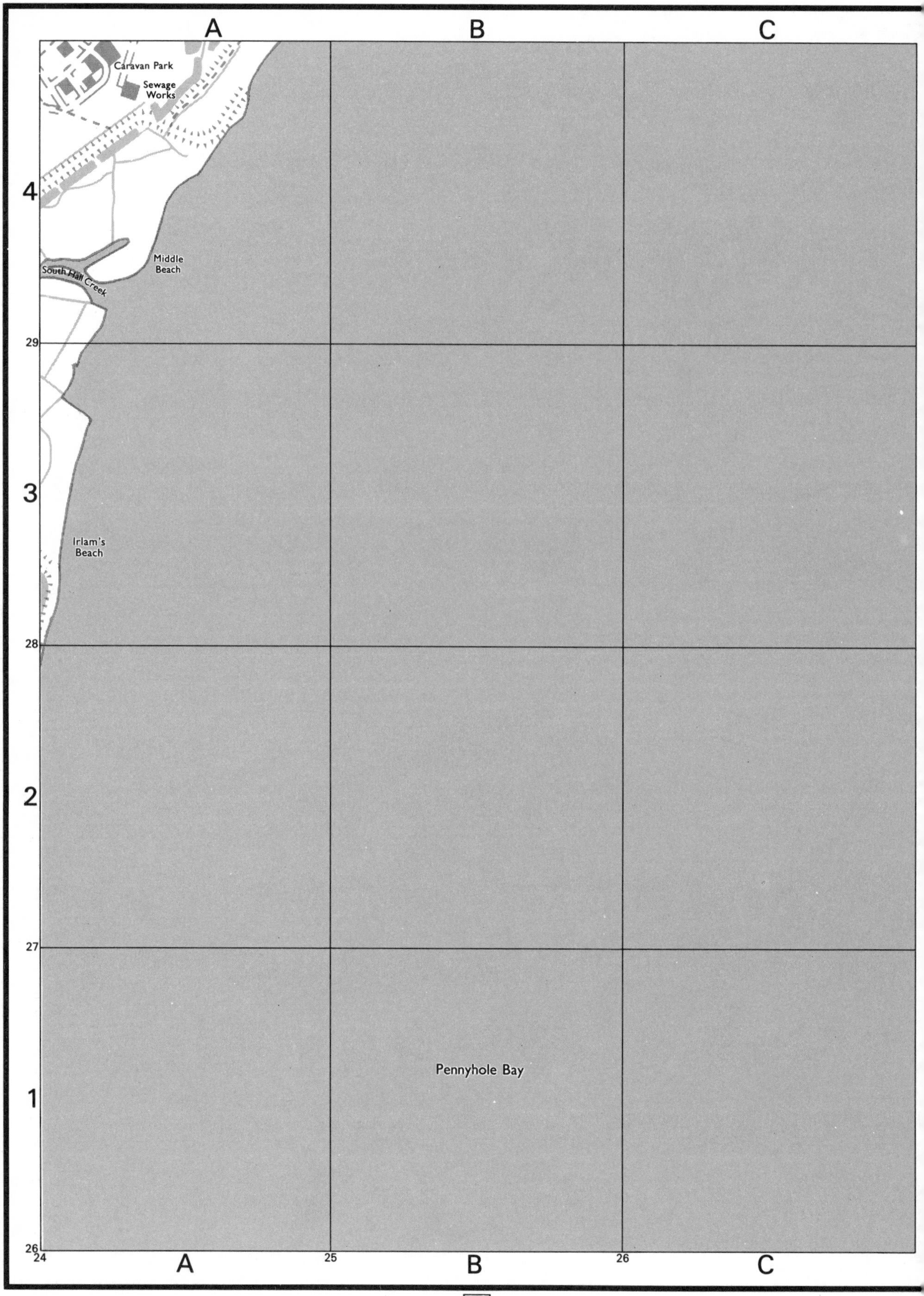
A
B
C
Caravan Park
Sewage Works
4
Middle Beach
South Hall Creek
29
3
Irlam's Beach
28
2
27
Pennyhole Bay
1
26
24
25
26

57

76

41

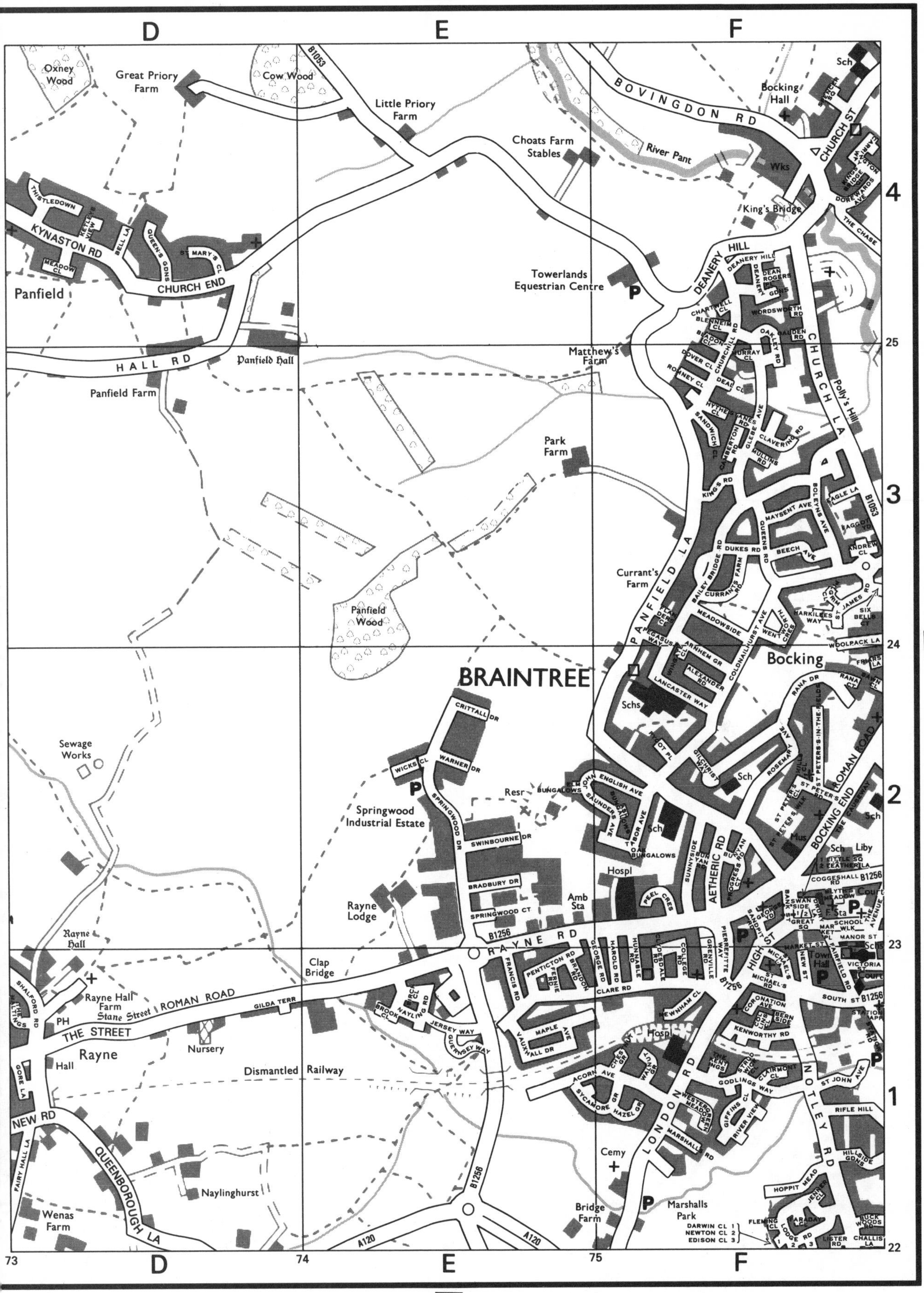

D
E
F
Oxney Wood
Great Priory Farm
Cow Wood
B1053
Little Priory Farm
Choats Farm Stables
BOVINGDON RD
River Pant
Sch
Bocking Hall
Wks
CHURCH ST
King's Bridge
4
THISTLEDOWN
KYNASTON RD
BELL LA
QUEEN'S GDNS
ST MARY'S CL
MEADOW CL
Panfield
CHURCH END
Towerlands Equestrian Centre
P
DEANERY HILL
DEAN ROGERS
WORDSWORTH RD
CHARTWELL CL
BLENHEIM CL
CHURCHILL RD
OAKLEY RD
CHURCH LA
Polly's Hill
25
HALL RD
Panfield Hall
Matthew's Farm
Panfield Farm
DOVER CL
ROMNEY CL
DEAL CL
HYTHE CL
SANDWICH CL
GLEBE AVE
CLAVERING RD
MULLINS RD
Park Farm
KING'S RD
BOLEYNS AVE
EAGLE LA
B1053
3
MAYSENT AVE
QUEENS RD
DUKES RD
BEECH AVE
BAILEY BRIDGE RD
CURRANTS FARM
Currant's Farm
PANFIELD LA
MEADOWSIDE
COLDNAILHURST AVE
HARKILEES WAY
SIX BELLS CT
Panfield Wood
PEGASUS WAY
ARNHEM GR
ALEXANDER RD
WOOLPACK LA
24
Bocking
BRAINTREE
LANCASTER WAY
RANA DR
Schs
CRITTALL DR
Sewage Works
WICKS CL
WARNER DR
P
Sch
ROSEMARY AVE
ST PETER'S-IN-THE-FIELDS
ROMAN ROAD
Resr
BUNGALOWS
JOHN ENGLISH AVE
2
Springwood Industrial Estate
SPRINGWOOD DR
SAUNDERS AVE
ARBOR AVE
Sch
BOCKING END
THE CAUSEWAY
Sch
Mus
Sch
Liby
SWINBOURNE DR
SUNNYSIDE
AETHERIC RD
OAK BUNGALOWS
LITTLE SQ
LEATHER LA
COGGESHALL RD
B1256
Court
Hospl
BRADBURY DR
PEEL CRES
PROGRESS CT
Amb Sta
Rayne Lodge
SPRINGWOOD CT
GREAT SQ
SCHOOL WLK
MANOR ST
THE AVENUE
B1256
RAYNE RD
HIGH ST
P
Rayne Hall
23
Schs
Clap Bridge
FRANCIS RD
PENTICTON RD
BRANDON RD
GEORGE RD
HAROLD RD
HUNNABLE RD
CLYDESDALE RD
COLLEGE
GRENVILLE RD
PIERREFITTE WAY
ST MICHAEL'S RD
MARKET ST
NEW ST
Town Hall
FAIRFIELD RD
VICTORIA ST
Court
B1256
CLARE RD
NEWNHAM CL
SOUTH ST
Rayne Hall Farm
Stane Street
ROMAN ROAD
GILDA TERR
BROOK CL
NAYLING RD
JERSEY WAY
GUERNSEY WAY
SHALFORD RD
PH
THE STREET
MAPLE AVE
VAUXHALL DR
CORONATION AVE
BERNSIDE
KENWORTHY RD
Rayne
Nursery
Hall
Hospl
GORE LA
Dismantled Railway
ACORN AVE
SYCAMORE GR
HAZEL GR
CLAIRMONT CL
GODLINGS WAY
ST JOHN AVE
P
1
NOTLEY RD
LONDON RD
WESTERGREEN MEADOW
GIFFINS CL
RIVER VIEW
RIFLE HILL
NEW RD
QUEENBOROUGH LA
FAIRY HALL LA
B1256
Cemy
MARSHALLS RD
HILLSIDE GDNS
Naylinghurst
HOPPIT MEAD
JENNER CL
Wenas Farm
Bridge Farm
P
Marshalls Park
DARWIN CL 1
NEWTON CL 2
EDISON CL 3
FLEMING CL
FARADAY CL
LODGE RD
LISTER RD
CHALLIS LA
BUCK WOODS RD
A120
A120
73
D
74
E
75
F
22

60

77

42

59

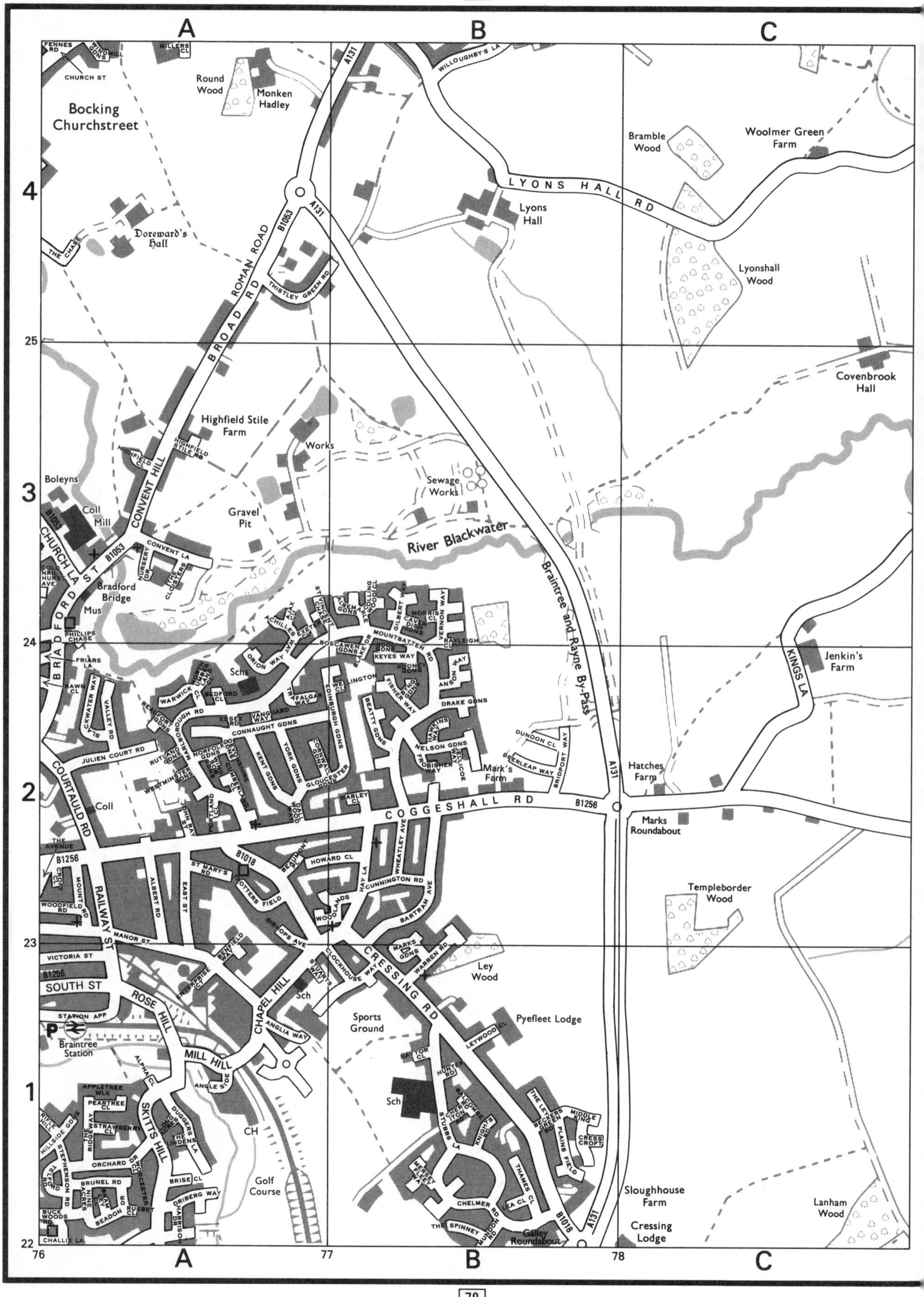
A
B
C
4
3
2
1
25
24
23
22
76
77
78
Bocking Churchstreet
Round Wood
Monken Hadley
Doreward's Hall
Bramble Wood
Woolmer Green Farm
LYONS HALL RD
Lyons Hall
Lyonshall Wood
Covenbrook Hall
Highfield Stile Farm
Works
Sewage Works
Gravel Pit
Boleyns
Coll Mill
River Blackwater
Bradford Bridge
Mus
Braintree and Rayne By-Pass
Jenkin's Farm
KINGS LA
Schs
Mark's Farm
Hatches Farm
Marks Roundabout
COGGESHALL RD
Coll
Templeborder Wood
Ley Wood
Pyefleet Lodge
Sports Ground
Sch
Braintree Station
CH
Golf Course
Sloughhouse Farm
Cressing Lodge
Lanham Wood
Galley Roundabout
BROAD RD
ROMAN ROAD
CONVENT HILL
CHURCH LA
BRADFORD ST
COURTAULD RD
RAILWAY ST
SOUTH ST
ROSE HILL
MILL HILL
CHAPEL HILL
SKITTS HILL
CRESSING RD
A131
B1053
B1256
B1018
WILLOUGHBY'S LA
THISTLEY GREEN RD
THE CHASE
CHURCH ST
CONVENT LA
JULIEN COURT RD
CONNAUGHT GDNS
EDINBURGH GDNS
MOUNTBATTEN RD
DRAKE GDNS
DUNOON CL
BEERLEAP WAY
BRIDPORT WAY
HOWARD CL
CUNNINGTON RD
BARTRAM AVE
WHEATLEY AVE
MANOR ST
VICTORIA ST
STATION APP
ALBERT RD
EAST ST
MOUNT RD
BISHOPS AVE
CLOCKHOUSE WAY
ANGLIA WAY
WARREN RD
LEYWOOD CL
HUNTER RD
STUBBS LA
CHELMER RD
THE SPINNEY
THAMES CL
PLAINS FIELD
CRESS CROFT
ORCHARD DR
BRUNEL RD
HILLSIDE GDNS
STEPHENSON RD
APPLETREE WLK
PEARTREE CL
STRAWBERRY CL
DRIBERG WAY
BRISE CL
CHALLIS LA
ANGLE SIDE

78

43

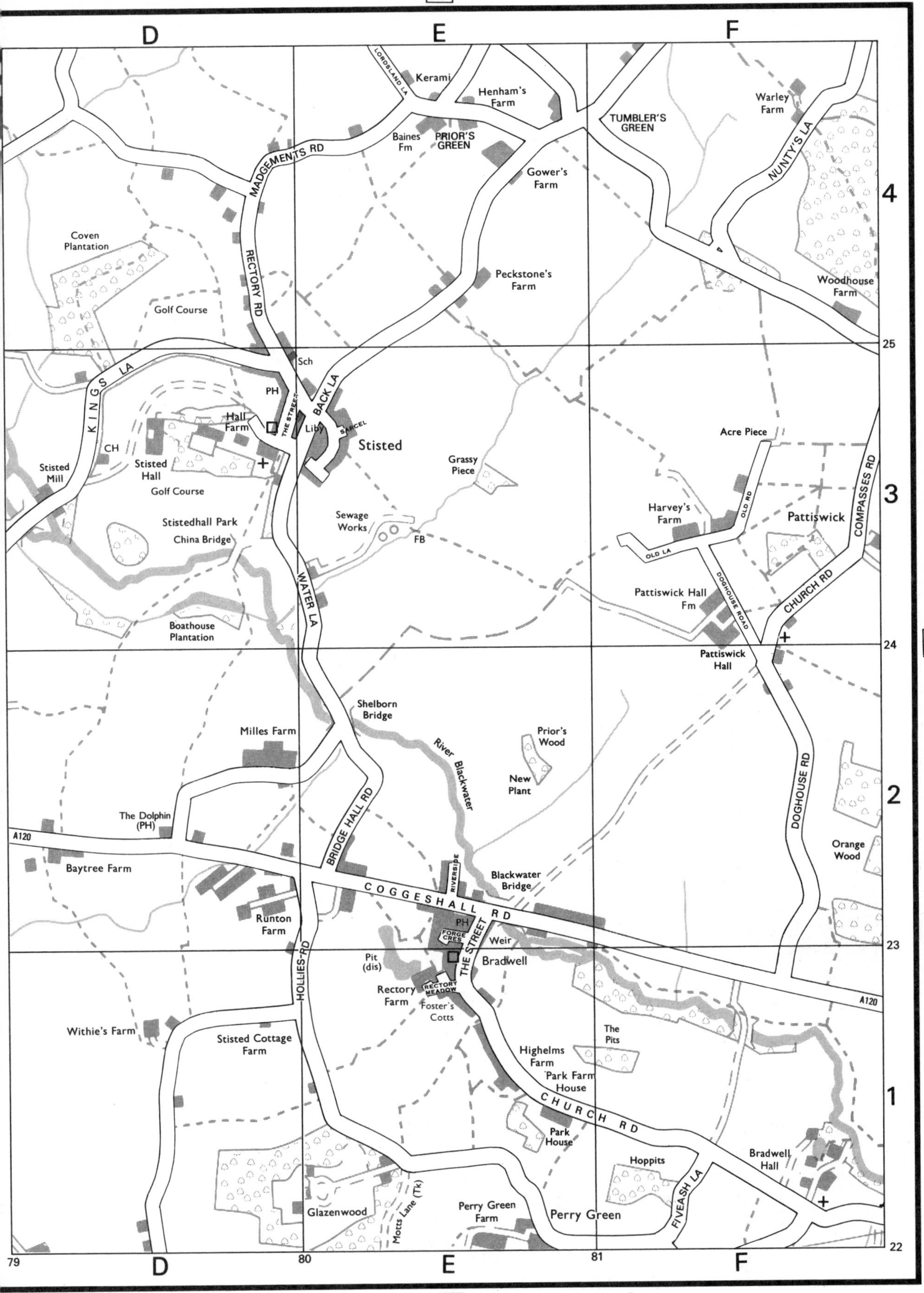
D
E
F
LORDSLAND LA
Kerami
Henham's Farm
Warley Farm
TUMBLER'S GREEN
MADGEMENTS RD
Baines Fm
PRIOR'S GREEN
NUNTY'S LA
Gower's Farm
4
Coven Plantation
RECTORY RD
Peckstone's Farm
Woodhouse Farm
Golf Course
25
Sch
KINGS LA
PH
BACK LA
Hall Farm
THE STREET
Liby
SARCEL
Stisted
Acre Piece
CH
Stisted Mill
Stisted Hall
Golf Course
Grassy Piece
COMPASSES RD
3
Harvey's Farm
OLD RD
Stistedhall Park
Sewage Works
Pattiswick
China Bridge
FB
OLD LA
WATER LA
DOGHOUSE ROAD
CHURCH RD
Pattiswick Hall Fm
Boathouse Plantation
24
Pattiswick Hall
Shelborn Bridge
Prior's Wood
Milles Farm
River Blackwater
New Plant
DOGHOUSE RD
2
BRIDGE HALL RD
The Dolphin (PH)
A120
Orange Wood
Baytree Farm
RIVERSIDE
Blackwater Bridge
COGGESHALL RD
Runton Farm
PH
FORGE CRES
Weir
23
THE STREET
Pit (dis)
Bradwell
HOLLIES RD
Rectory Farm
RECTORY MEADOW
Foster's Cotts
A120
Withie's Farm
Stisted Cottage Farm
The Pits
Highelms Farm
Park Farm House
1
CHURCH RD
Park House
Hoppits
Bradwell Hall
FIVEASH LA
Glazenwood
Motts Lane (Tk)
Perry Green Farm
Perry Green
22
79
80
81
62

79

44

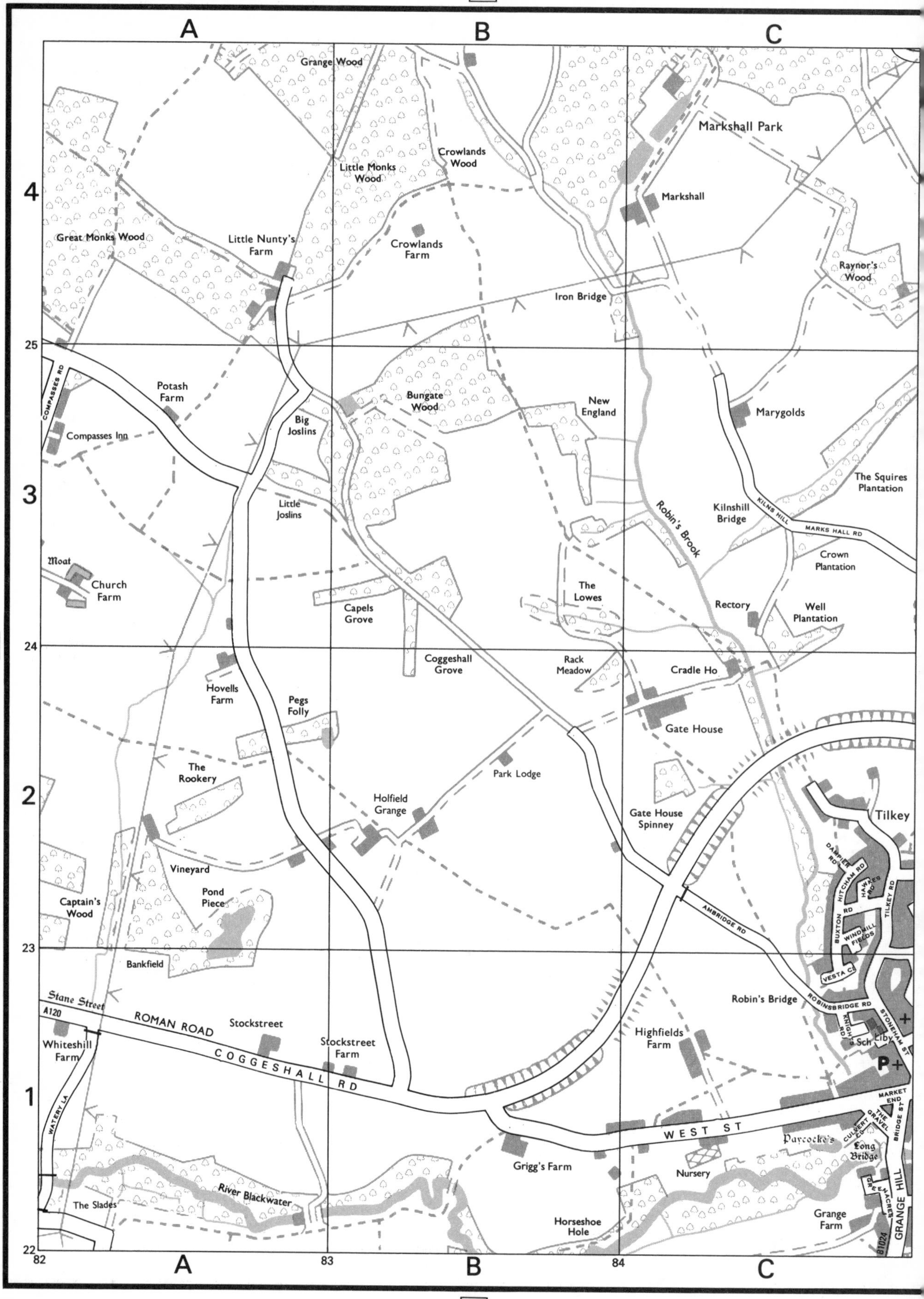
A
B
C
Grange Wood
Crowlands Wood
Little Monks Wood
Markshall Park
Markshall
Great Monks Wood
Little Nunty's Farm
Crowlands Farm
Raynor's Wood
Iron Bridge
Potash Farm
Bungate Wood
New England
Marygolds
Compasses Inn
COMPASSES RD
Big Joslins
Little Joslins
The Squires Plantation
Robin's Brook
Kilnshill Bridge
KILNS HILL
MARKS HALL RD
Crown Plantation
Moat
Church Farm
Capels Grove
The Lowes
Rectory
Well Plantation
Coggeshall Grove
Rack Meadow
Cradle Ho
Hovells Farm
Pegs Folly
Gate House
The Rookery
Park Lodge
Holfield Grange
Gate House Spinney
Tilkey
DAMPIER RD
HITCHAM RD
HAWKES RD
TILKEY RD
BUXTON RD
WINDMILL FIELDS
VESTA CL
Vineyard
Pond Piece
Captain's Wood
AMBRIDGE RD
Bankfield
Robin's Bridge
ROBINSBRIDGE RD
Stane Street
A120
ROMAN ROAD
Stockstreet
Stockstreet Farm
COGGESHALL RD
Highfields Farm
KNIGHTS RD
STONEHAM ST
Sch
Liby
Whiteshill Farm
WATERY LA
MARKET END
THE GRAVEL
BRIDGE ST
WEST ST
Paycocke's
CULVERT CT
Long Bridge
Grigg's Farm
Nursery
River Blackwater
The Slades
Horseshoe Hole
GREENACRES
Grange Farm
GRANGE HILL
B1024
4
3
2
1
25
24
23
22
82
83
84
A
B
C

61

80

45

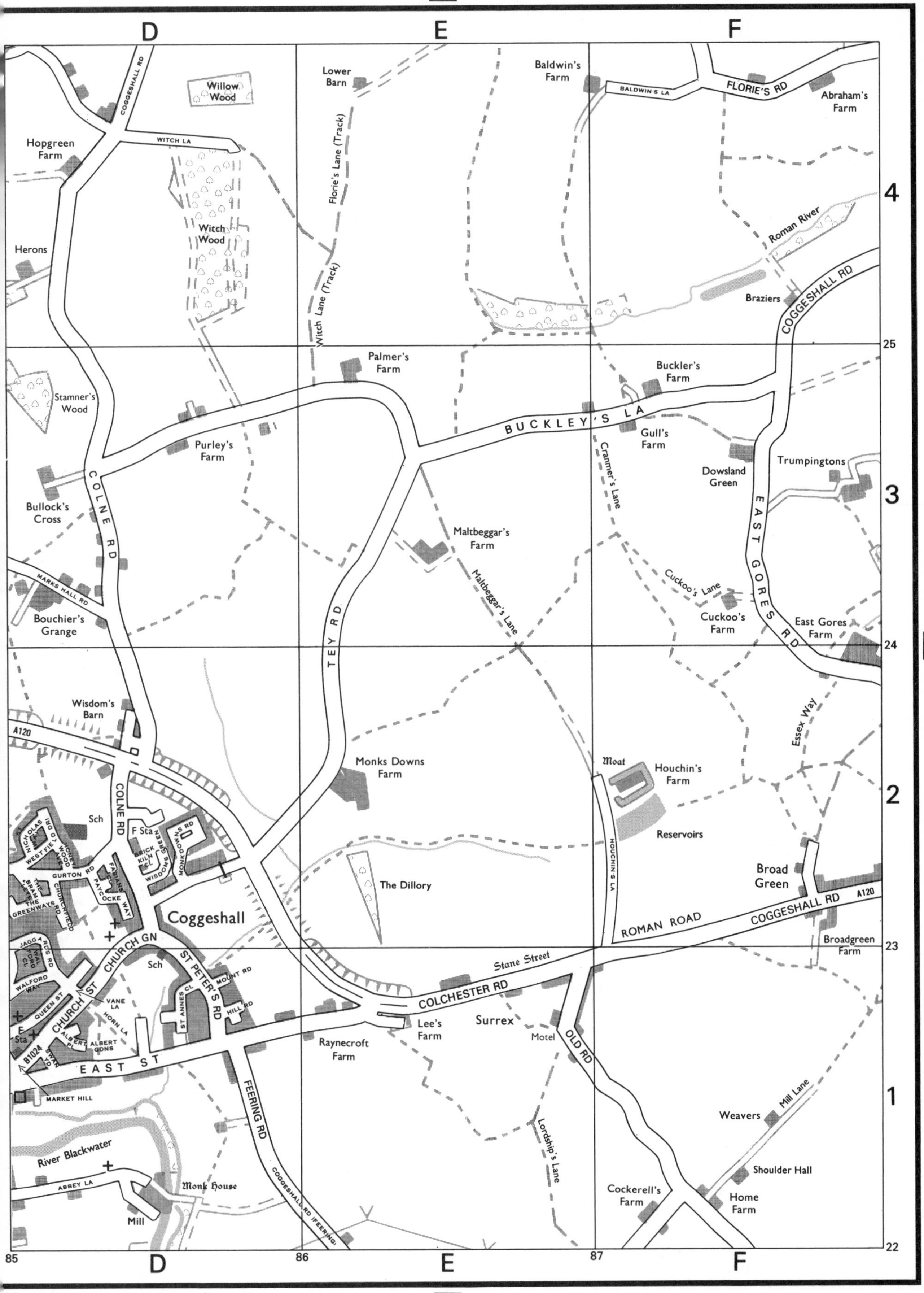

D
E
F
Willow Wood
Lower Barn
Baldwin's Farm
BALDWIN'S LA
FLORIE'S RD
Abraham's Farm
COGGESHALL RD
WITCH LA
Hopgreen Farm
Florie's Lane (Track)
Witch Wood
Herons
Witch Lane (Track)
Roman River
Braziers
COGGESHALL RD
4
25
Palmer's Farm
Buckler's Farm
Stamner's Wood
BUCKLEY'S LA
Purley's Farm
Gull's Farm
Cranmer's Lane
Dowsland Green
Trumpingtons
COLNE RD
Bullock's Cross
3
Maltbeggar's Farm
EAST GORES RD
MARKS HALL RD
Cuckoo's Lane
Cuckoo's Farm
Bouchier's Grange
TEY RD
Maltbeggar's Lane
East Gores Farm
24
Wisdom's Barn
Essex Way
A120
Moat
Houchin's Farm
Monks Downs Farm
2
COLNE RD
Sch
F Sta
Reservoirs
HOUCHIN'S LA
NICHOLAS
WESTFIELD
HONEYWOOD AVE
GURTON RD
BRICK KILN CL
WISDOMS GREEN
MONKDOWNS RD
FABIANS CL
PAYCOCKE WAY
CHURCHFIELD
THE BRAMBLES
THE GREENWAYS
Broad Green
The Dillory
A120
COGGESHALL RD
ROMAN ROAD
Coggeshall
Broadgreen Farm
23
CHURCH GN
JAGGARDS RD
WALFORD CL
WALFORD WAY
QUEEN ST
CHURCH ST
Sch
ST PETER'S RD
ST ANNES CL
MOUNT RD
HILL RD
VANE LA
HORN LA
ALBERT PL
ALBERT GDNS
Stane Street
COLCHESTER RD
Lee's Farm
Surrex
Motel
OLD RD
Raynecroft Farm
B1024
Sta
SWAN YD
EAST ST
MARKET HILL
FEERING RD
1
Mill Lane
Weavers
River Blackwater
ABBEY LA
Monk House
COGGESHALL RD (FEERING)
Lordship's Lane
Shoulder Hall
Cockerell's Farm
Home Farm
Mill
22
85
86
87
D
E
F

64

81

46

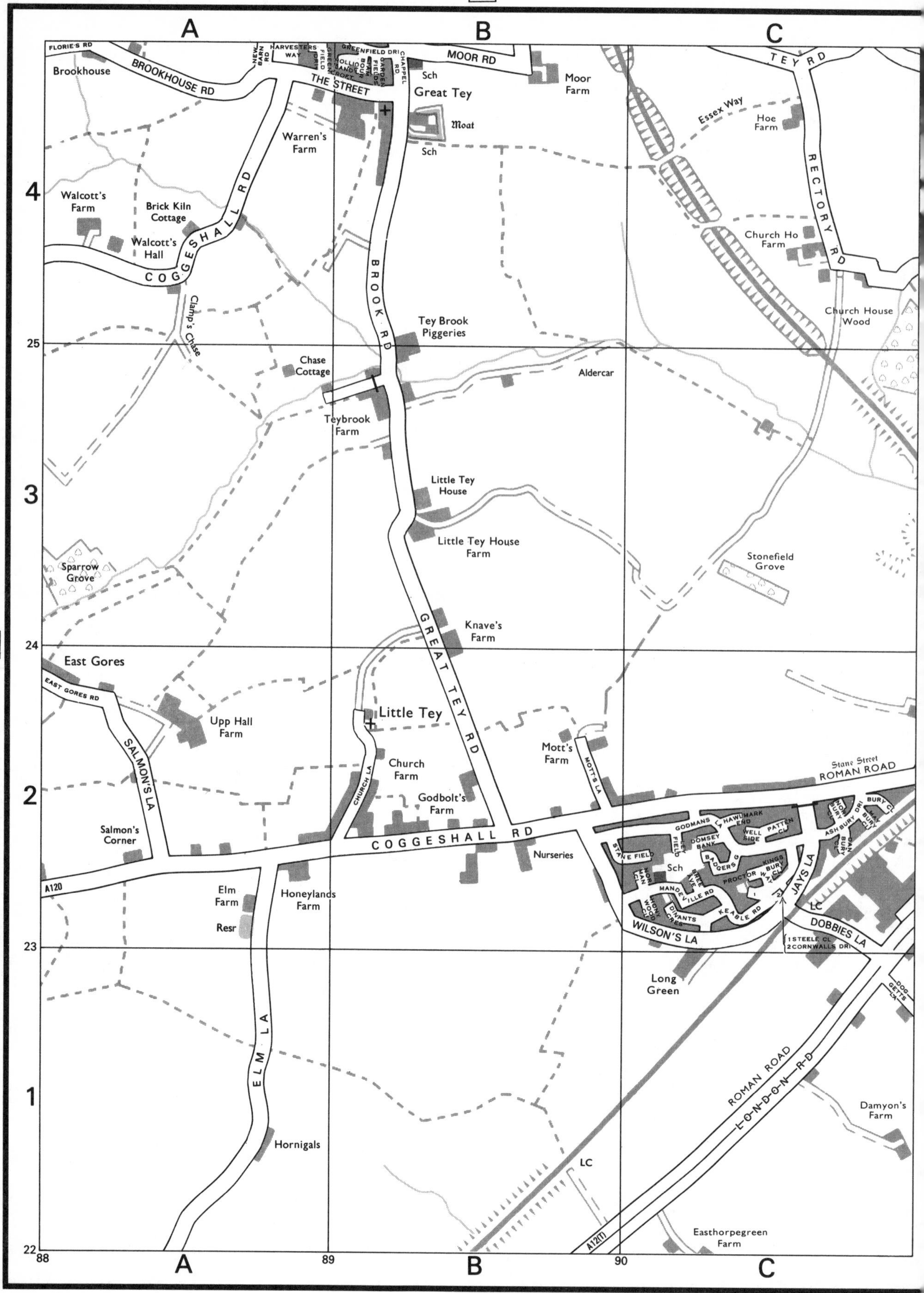
A
B
C
FLORIE'S RD
Brookhouse
BROOKHOUSE RD
HARVESTERS WAY
GREENFIELD DRI
CHAPPEL RD
MOOR RD
THE STREET
Sch
Great Tey
Moor Farm
Moat
Sch
Warren's Farm
TEY RD
Essex Way
Hoe Farm
RECTORY RD
4
Walcott's Farm
Brick Kiln Cottage
Walcott's Hall
COGGESHALL RD
Church Ho Farm
BROOK RD
Clamp's Chase
Tey Brook Piggeries
Church House Wood
25
Chase Cottage
Aldercar
Teybrook Farm
3
Little Tey House
Little Tey House Farm
Sparrow Grove
Stonefield Grove
GREAT TEY RD
Knave's Farm
24
East Gores
EAST GORES RD
Little Tey
Upp Hall Farm
SALMON'S LA
Mott's Farm
MOTT'S LA
Church Farm
CHURCH LA
Stane Street
ROMAN ROAD
2
Godbolt's Farm
Salmon's Corner
COGGESHALL RD
Nurseries
GODMANS LA
HAWKMARK END
PATTEN CL
WELL SIDE
DOMSEY BANK
BADGERS G
KINGS BURY CL
PROCTOR WAY
Sch
MANDEVILLE RD
DINANTS CRES
KEABLE RD
JAYS LA
ASH BURY DRI
BURY CL
LC
DOBBIES LA
WILSON'S LA
A120
Elm Farm
Resr
Honeylands Farm
1 STEELE CL
2 CORNWALLS DRI
23
Long Green
ELM LA
ROMAN ROAD
LONDON RD
1
Damyon's Farm
Hornigals
LC
A12(T)
Easthorpegreen Farm
22
88
89
90
A
B
C

63

82

47

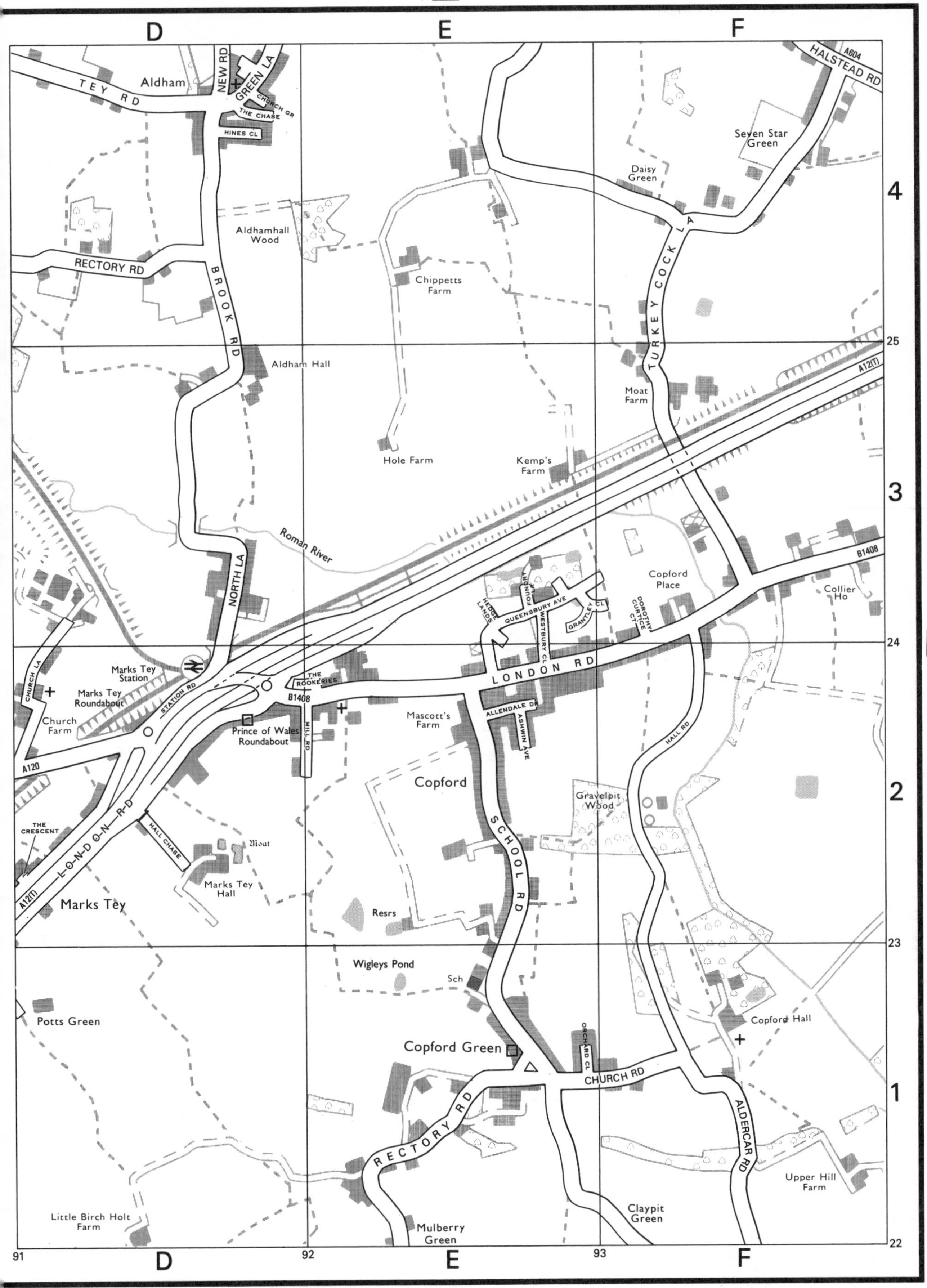
D
E
F
Aldham
TEY RD
NEW RD
GREEN LA
CHURCH GR
THE CHASE
HINES CL
HALSTEAD RD
A604
Seven Star Green
Daisy Green
Aldhamhall Wood
RECTORY RD
BROOK RD
Chippetts Farm
TURKEY COCK LA
Aldham Hall
A12(T)
Moat Farm
Hole Farm
Kemp's Farm
Roman River
NORTH LA
HEDGE LANDS
FOUNDRY LA
QUEENSBURY AVE
WESTBURY CL
GRANTLEY CL
DOROTHY CURTICE CT
Copford Place
B1408
Collier Ho
Marks Tey Station
Marks Tey Roundabout
CHURCH LA
STATION RD
THE ROOKERIES
LONDON RD
Church Farm
Prince of Wales Roundabout
MILL RD
Mascott's Farm
ALLENDALE DR
ASHWIN AVE
HALL RD
A120
Copford
Gravelpit Wood
THE CRESCENT
LONDON RD
HALL CHASE
Moat
Marks Tey Hall
SCHOOL RD
Marks Tey
Resrs
Wigleys Pond
Sch
Potts Green
Copford Hall
Copford Green
ORCHARD CL
CHURCH RD
RECTORY RD
ALDERCAR RD
Upper Hill Farm
Claypit Green
Little Birch Holt Farm
Mulberry Green
4
25
3
24
2
23
1
22
91
92
93

66

83

48

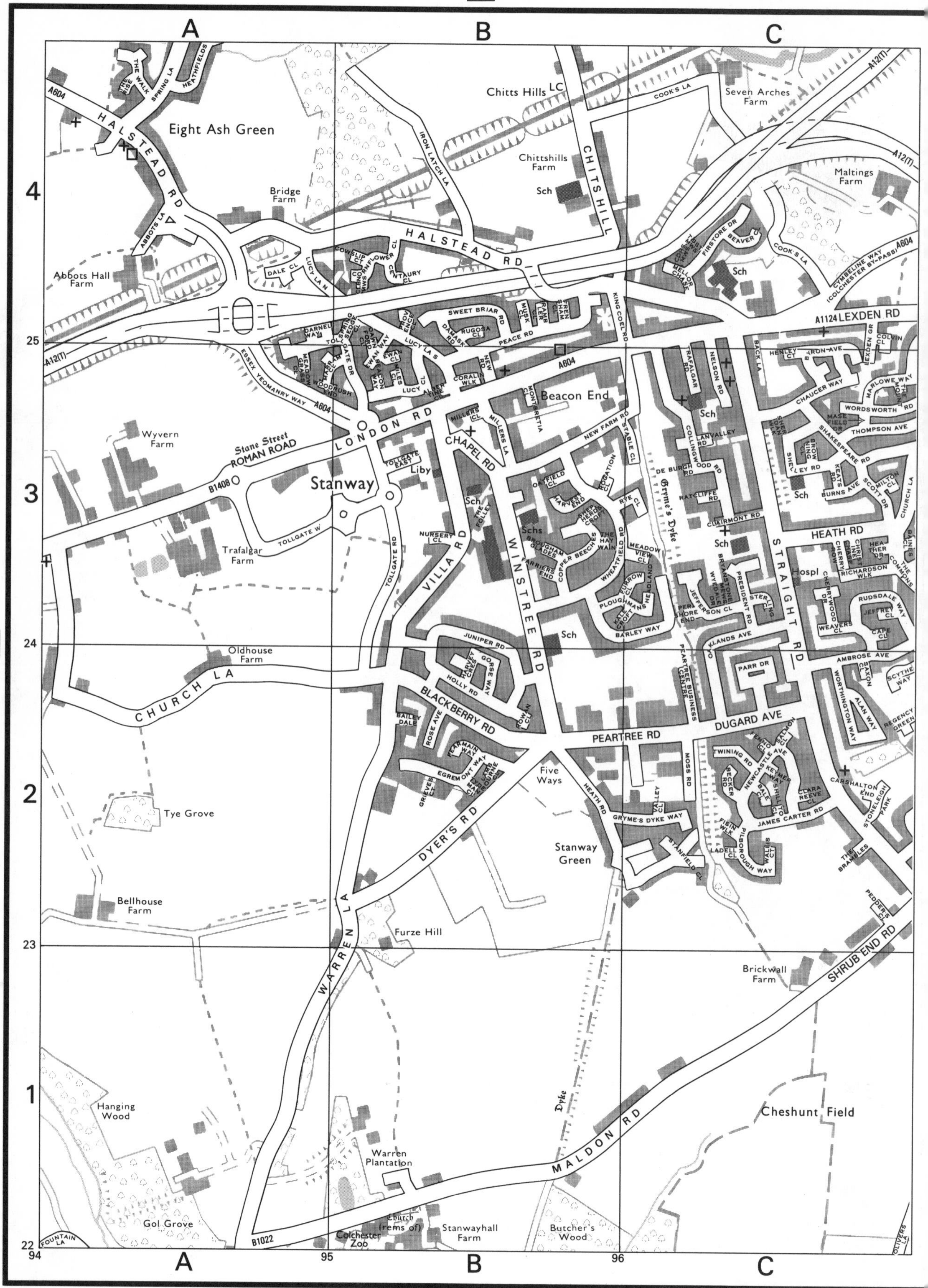
A
B
C
4
3
2
1
25
24
23
22
94
95
96
Eight Ash Green
HALSTEAD RD
SPRING LA
HEATHFIELDS
THE WALK
THE RISE
ABBOTS LA
A604
Chitts Hills
LC
Chittshills Farm
CHITTS HILL
Sch
IRON LATCH LA
COOK'S LA
Seven Arches Farm
A12(T)
Maltings Farm
Bridge Farm
Abbots Hall Farm
DALE CL
LUCY LA N
COWSLIP CL
CENTAURY CL
SWEET BRIAR RD
RUGOSA CL
DAMASK RD
PEACE RD
KING COEL RD
FIRSTORE DR
BEAVER CL
COOK'S LA
CYMBELINE WAY (COLCHESTER BY-PASS)
A1124 LEXDEN RD
ESSEX YEOMANRY WAY
DARNEL WAY
LUCY LA S
CORALIN WLK
NEW RD
Beacon End
MONTBRETIA CL
MILLERS CL
MILLERS LA
LONDON RD
CHAPEL RD
Wyvern Farm
Stane Street ROMAN ROAD
B1408
Stanway
TOLLGATE EAST
Liby
TOLLGATE W
TOLLGATE RD
Trafalgar Farm
NURSERY CL
VILLA RD
THE FOLLEY
Schs
WINSTREE RD
OATFIELD CL
HARVEST END
ROTATION CL
NEW FARM RD
STABLE CL
RYE CL
BROUGHAM GLADES
COPPER BEECHES
FARRIERS END
WHEATFIELD RD
THE HAY WAIN
MEADOW VIEW CL
BURROW CL
HEADLAND
PLOUGHMANS
BARLEY WAY
Gryme's Dyke
TRAFALGAR RD
NELSON RD
COLLINGWOOD RD
DE BURGH RD
LANVALLEY RD
RATCLIFFE RD
CLAIRMONT RD
BRYANSTONE MEWS
WYEDALE DR
PRESIDENT RD
JEFFERSON CL
OAKLANDS AVE
PEARTREE BUSINESS CENTRE
PARR DR
STRAIGHT RD
BACK LA
HENLEY CT
IRON AVE
LEXDEN GR
COLVIN CL
CHAUCER WAY
MARLOWE WAY
THE MOUNT RD
WORDSWORTH RD
MASEFIELD DR
THOMPSON AVE
SHAKESPEARE RD
SHELLEY RD
KEATS RD
BURNS AVE
SCOTT DR
MILTON CL
CHURCH LA
HEATH RD
CHERRY CHASE
CHRISTINE CHASE
HEATHER DR
Hospl
RICHARDSON WLK
RUDSDALE WAY
JEFFREY CL
WEAVERS CL
CAPE CL
AMBROSE AVE
WORTHINGTON WAY
ALAN WAY
SCYTHE WAY
REGENCY GREEN
Oldhouse Farm
CHURCH LA
JUNIPER RD
GORSE WAY
HOLLY RD
BLACKBERRY RD
ROWAN CL
BAILEY DALE
ROSE AVE
EGREMONT WAY
GRIEVES CT
PEARTREE RD
DUGARD AVE
MOSS RD
Five Ways
HEATH RD
VALLEY CL
GRYME'S DYKE WAY
STANFIELD CL
TWINING RD
BECKER RD
NEWCASTLE AVE
CLARA REEVE CL
JAMES CARTER RD
PILBOROUGH WAY
LADELL CL
CARSHALTON END
STONELEIGH PARK
THE BRAMBLES
PEDDERS CL
SHRUB END RD
Tye Grove
DYER'S RD
Stanway Green
Bellhouse Farm
Furze Hill
WARREN LA
Brickwall Farm
Dyke
Hanging Wood
MALDON RD
Cheshunt Field
Warren Plantation
Gol Grove
FOUNTAIN LA
B1022
Colchester Zoo
Church (rems of)
Stanwayhall Farm
Butcher's Wood
OLIVERS LA

65

84

49

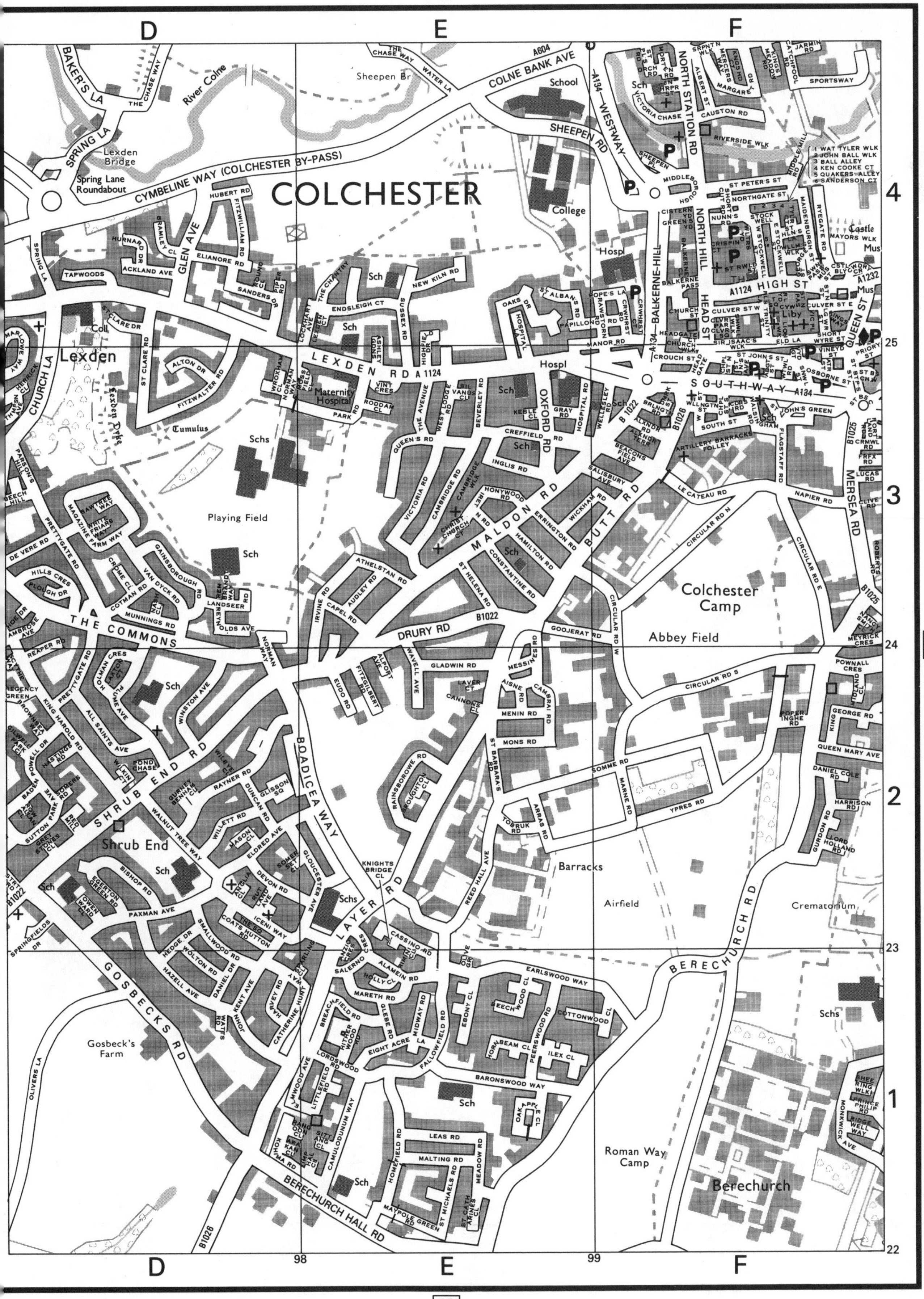
D
E
F
COLCHESTER
Lexden
Lexden Bridge
Spring Lane Roundabout
River Colne
Sheepen Br
School
College
Hospl
Castle
Mus
Lexden Dyke
Tumulus
Maternity Hospital
Playing Field
Colchester Camp
Abbey Field
Barracks
Airfield
Crematorium
Shrub End
Gosbeck's Farm
Roman Way Camp
Berechurch
CYMBELINE WAY (COLCHESTER BY-PASS)
COLNE BANK AVE
SHEEPEN RD
WESTWAY
NORTH STATION RD
NORTH HILL
HEAD ST
BALKERNE HILL
HIGH ST
LEXDEN RD
SOUTHWAY
MALDON RD
OXFORD RD
BUTT RD
DRURY RD
MERSEA RD
CIRCULAR RD E
CIRCULAR RD N
CIRCULAR RD S
CIRCULAR RD W
BOADICEA WAY
LAYER RD
SHRUB END RD
THE COMMONS
GOSBECKS RD
BERECHURCH RD
BERECHURCH HALL RD
CHURCH LA
SPRING LA
BAKER'S LA
GLEN AVE
QUEEN ST
1 WAT TYLER WLK
2 JOHN BALL WLK
3 BALL ALLEY
4 KEN COOKE CT
5 QUAKERS ALLEY
6 SANDERSON CT
4
3
2
1
25
24
23
22
98
99
B1022
B1026
B1025
A1124
A134
A604
A1232

68

85

50

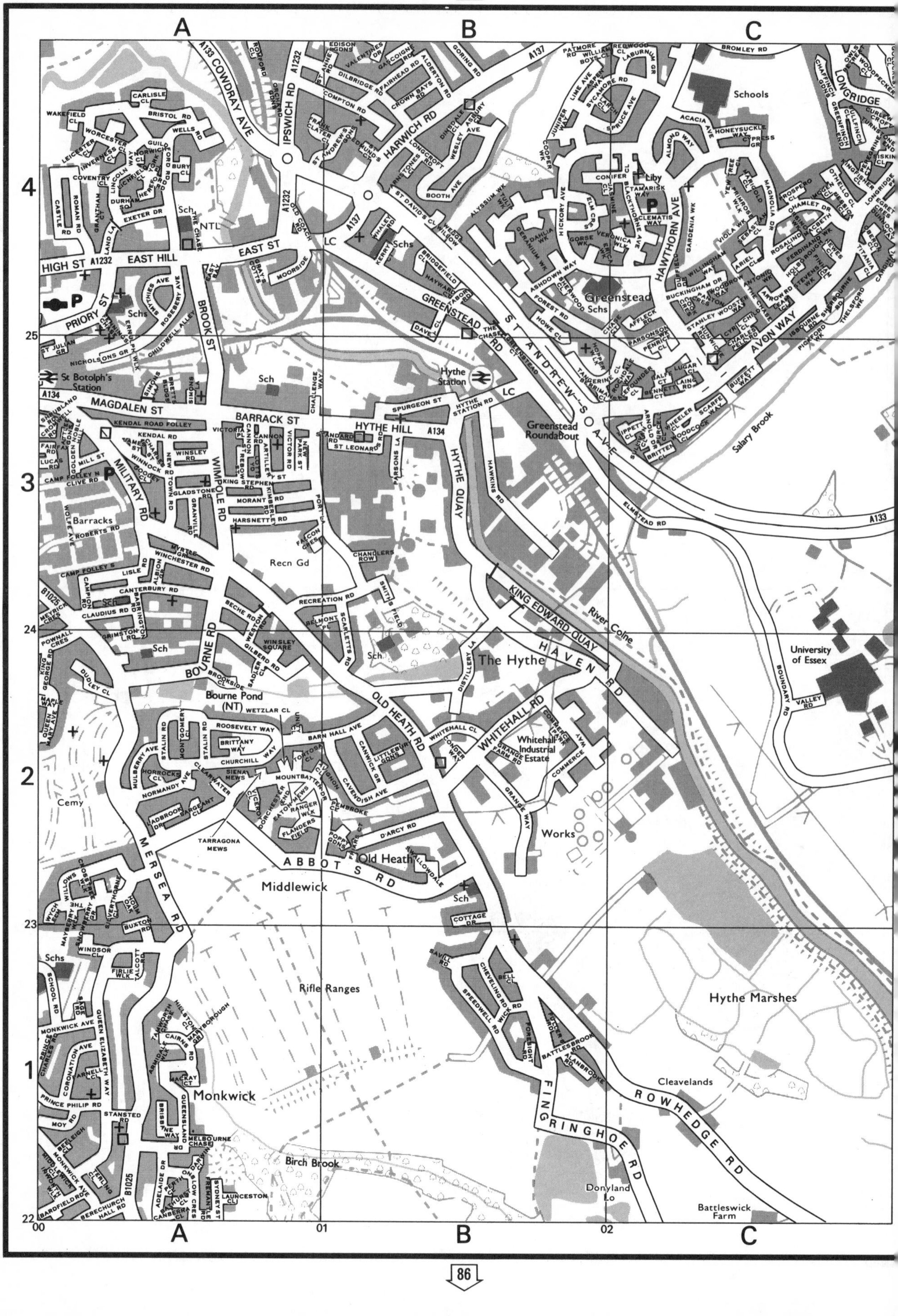

A
B
C
4
3
2
1
25
24
23
22
00
01
02
A133 COWDRAY AVE
IPSWICH RD
A1232
HARWICH RD
A137
Schools
LONGRIDGE
HAWTHORN AVE
Greenstead
Schs
ST ANDREW'S AVE
AVON WAY
Salary Brook
HIGH ST
EAST HILL
EAST ST
PRIORY ST
BROOK ST
St Botolph's Station
A134
MAGDALEN ST
BARRACK ST
HYTHE HILL
Hythe Station
GREENSTEAD RD
Greenstead Roundabout
HYTHE QUAY
ELMSTEAD RD
A133
Barracks
MILITARY RD
WIMPOLE RD
Recn Gd
KING EDWARD QUAY
River Colne
University of Essex
BOUNDARY RD
The Hythe
HAVEN RD
BOURNE RD
Bourne Pond (NT)
OLD HEATH RD
WHITEHALL RD
Whitehall Industrial Estate
Works
Cemy
MERSEA RD
ABBOTS RD
Old Heath
Middlewick
Rifle Ranges
Hythe Marshes
Monkwick
QUEEN ELIZABETH WAY
FINGRINGHOE RD
ROWHEDGE RD
Cleavelands
Birch Brook
Donyland Lo
Battleswick Farm
B1025
Sch
NTL
LC
Liby

67

86

51

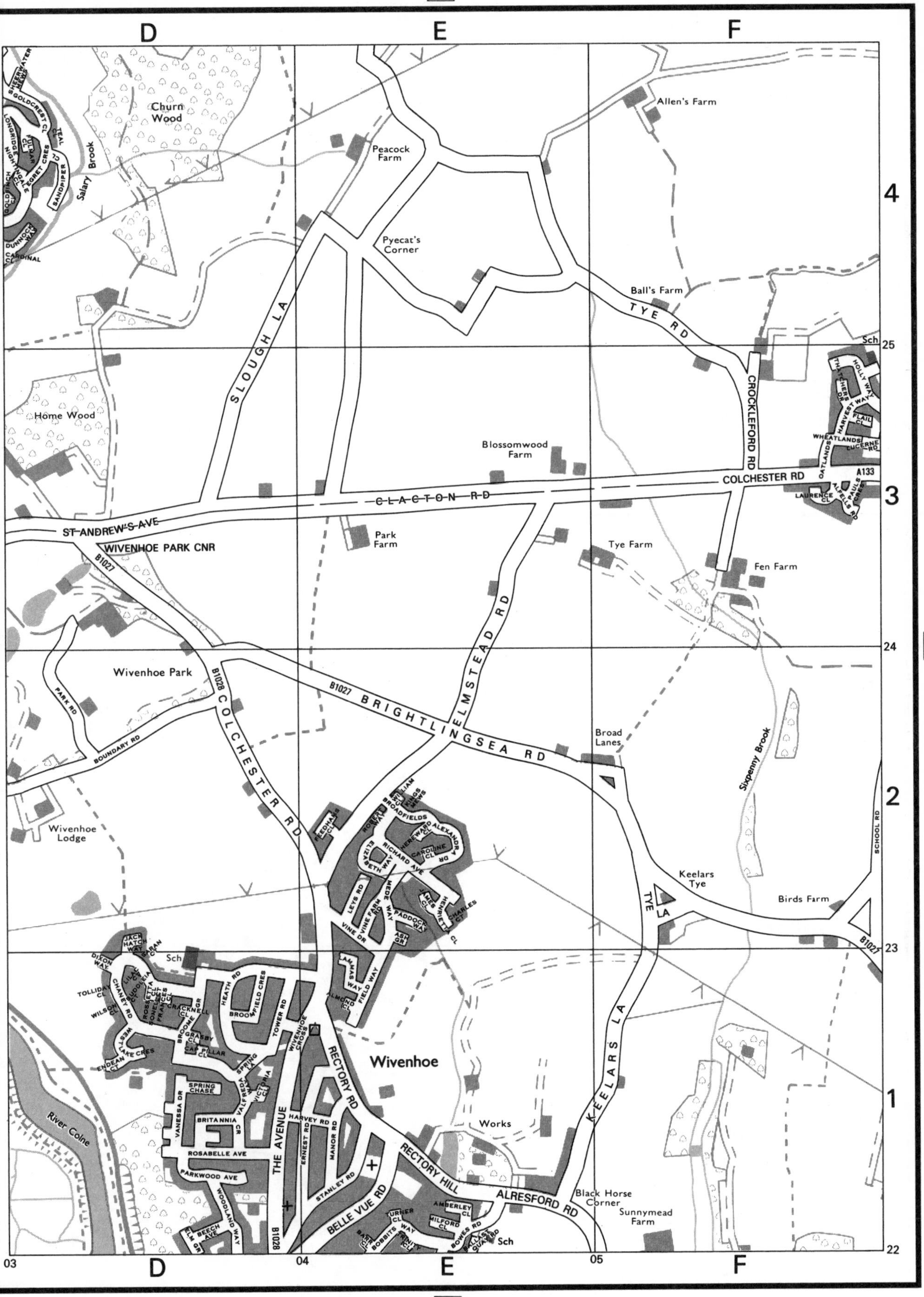

D
E
F
4
3
2
1
25
24
23
22
03
04
05
Churn Wood
Salary Brook
Home Wood
Peacock Farm
Pyecat's Corner
Allen's Farm
Ball's Farm
TYE RD
CROCKLEFORD RD
Sch
Blossomwood Farm
COLCHESTER RD
A133
CLACTON RD
ST ANDREW'S AVE
WIVENHOE PARK CNR
B1027
SLOUGH LA
Park Farm
Tye Farm
Fen Farm
ELMSTEAD RD
Wivenhoe Park
PARK RD
BOUNDARY RD
B1028
COLCHESTER RD
B1027 BRIGHTLINGSEA RD
Broad Lanes
Sixpenny Brook
SCHOOL RD
Wivenhoe Lodge
Keelars Tye
TYE LA
Birds Farm
B1027
KEELARS LA
Wivenhoe
RECTORY RD
RECTORY HILL
ALRESFORD RD
Works
Black Horse Corner
Sunnymead Farm
River Colne
THE AVENUE
B1028
BELLE VUE RD
Sch
HOLLY WAY
HARVEST WAY
FLAIL CL
WHEATLANDS
LUCERNE RD
OATLANDS
LAURENCE CL
ALFELLS RD
PAULS CRES
THATCHERS DR
GOLDCREST CL
TEAL CL
LONGRIDGE
NIGHTINGALE CL
EGRET CRES
SANDPIPER CL
GOLDFINCH CL
DUNNOCK WAY
CARDINAL CL
FEEDHAMS CL
BROADFIELDS
ROBERTS WAY
ALEXANDRA DR
HEREWARD CL
CAROLINE CL
RICHARD AVE
ELIZABETH WAY
LEYS RD
MEDE WAY
VINE FARM RD
JAMES CL
HENRIETTA CL
CHARLES CT
PADDOCK WAY
VINE DR
ASH GR
LAMMAS WAY
FIELD WAY
ALMOND CL
JACK HATCH WAY
DIXON WAY
TOLLIDAY CL
WILSON CL
CHANEY RD
ROSSETTA CL
LILAC CL
BUDDLEIA CL
FRANCES CL
CRACKNELL
BROOME GR
GRASBY CL
CAP PILLAR CL
WEST LAKE CRES
ENDEAN CT
HEATH RD
BROOMFIELD CRES
TOWER RD
WIVENHOE CROSS
SPRING LA
SPRING CHASE
VALFREDA WAY
VICTORIA CL
VANESSA DR
BRITANNIA CR
ROSABELLE AVE
PARKWOOD AVE
WOODLAND WAY
BEECH AVE
ELM GR
HARVEY RD
ERNEST RD
MANOR RD
STANLEY RD
AMBERLEY CL
MILFORD CL
TURNER CL
BOBBITS WAY
TRINITY CL
BOWES RD
BALLAST QUAY RD

70

52

69

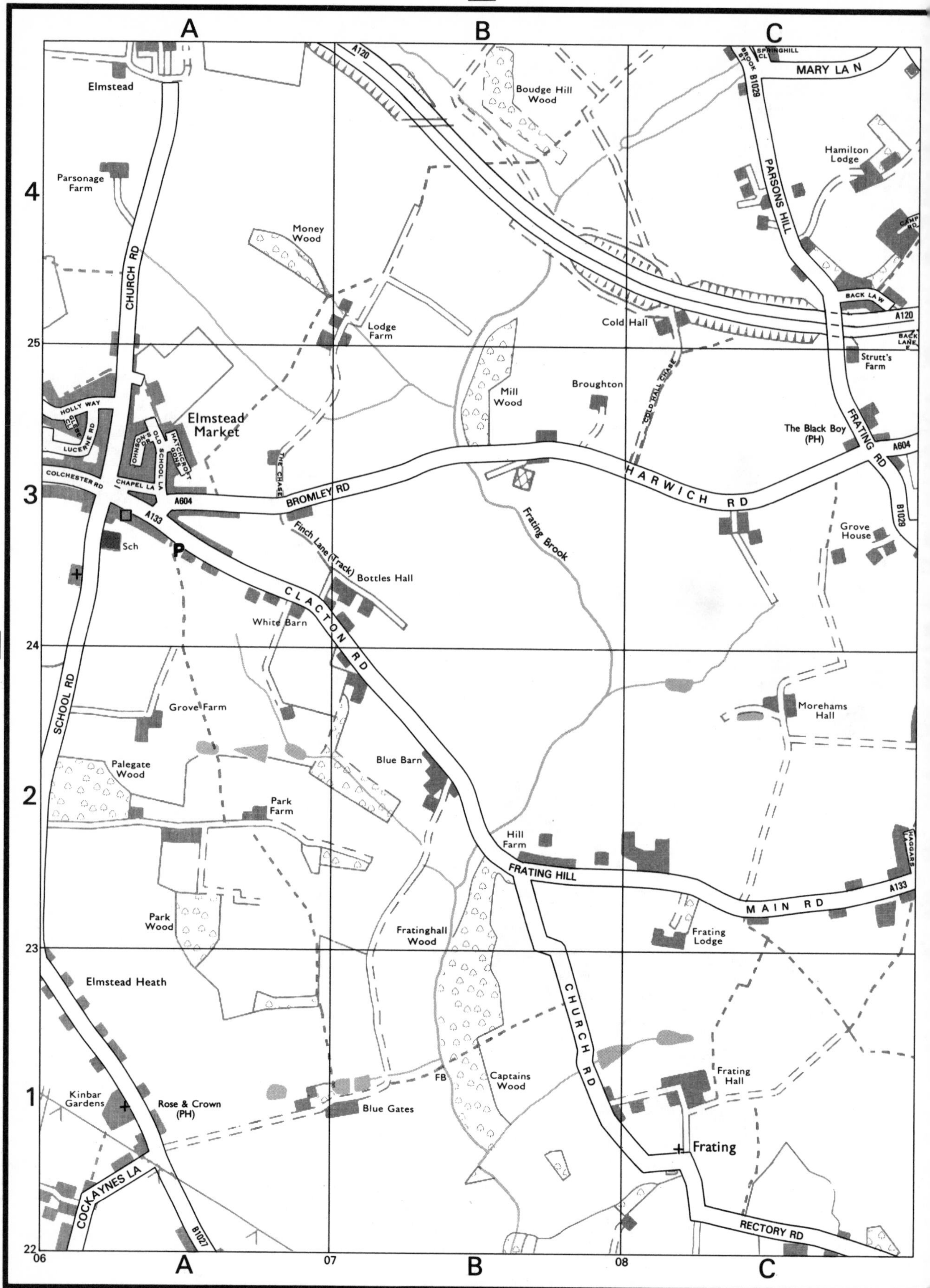
A
B
C
4
3
2
1
25
24
23
22
06
07
08
Elmstead
Parsonage Farm
CHURCH RD
A120
Boudge Hill Wood
Money Wood
Lodge Farm
Cold Hall
SPRINGHILL CL
BROOK ST B1029
MARY LA N
Hamilton Lodge
PARSONS HILL
BACK LA W
BACK LANE E
Strutt's Farm
Mill Wood
Broughton
COLD HALL CHASE
HOLLY WAY
GLEBE CL
LUCERNE RD
Elmstead Market
OLD SCHOOL LA
HATCHCROFT GDNS
COLCHESTER RD
CHAPEL LA
A604
A133
THE CHASE
BROMLEY RD
HARWICH RD
The Black Boy (PH)
FRATING RD
B1029
Grove House
Sch
P
Finch Lane (Track)
Bottles Hall
Frating Brook
CLACTON RD
White Barn
SCHOOL RD
Grove Farm
Morehams Hall
Palegate Wood
Blue Barn
Park Farm
Hill Farm
FRATING HILL
MAIN RD
HAGGARS LA
Park Wood
Fratinghall Wood
Frating Lodge
Elmstead Heath
CHURCH RD
FB
Captains Wood
Frating Hall
Kinbar Gardens
Rose & Crown (PH)
Blue Gates
Frating
COCKAYNES LA
B1027
RECTORY RD

88

53

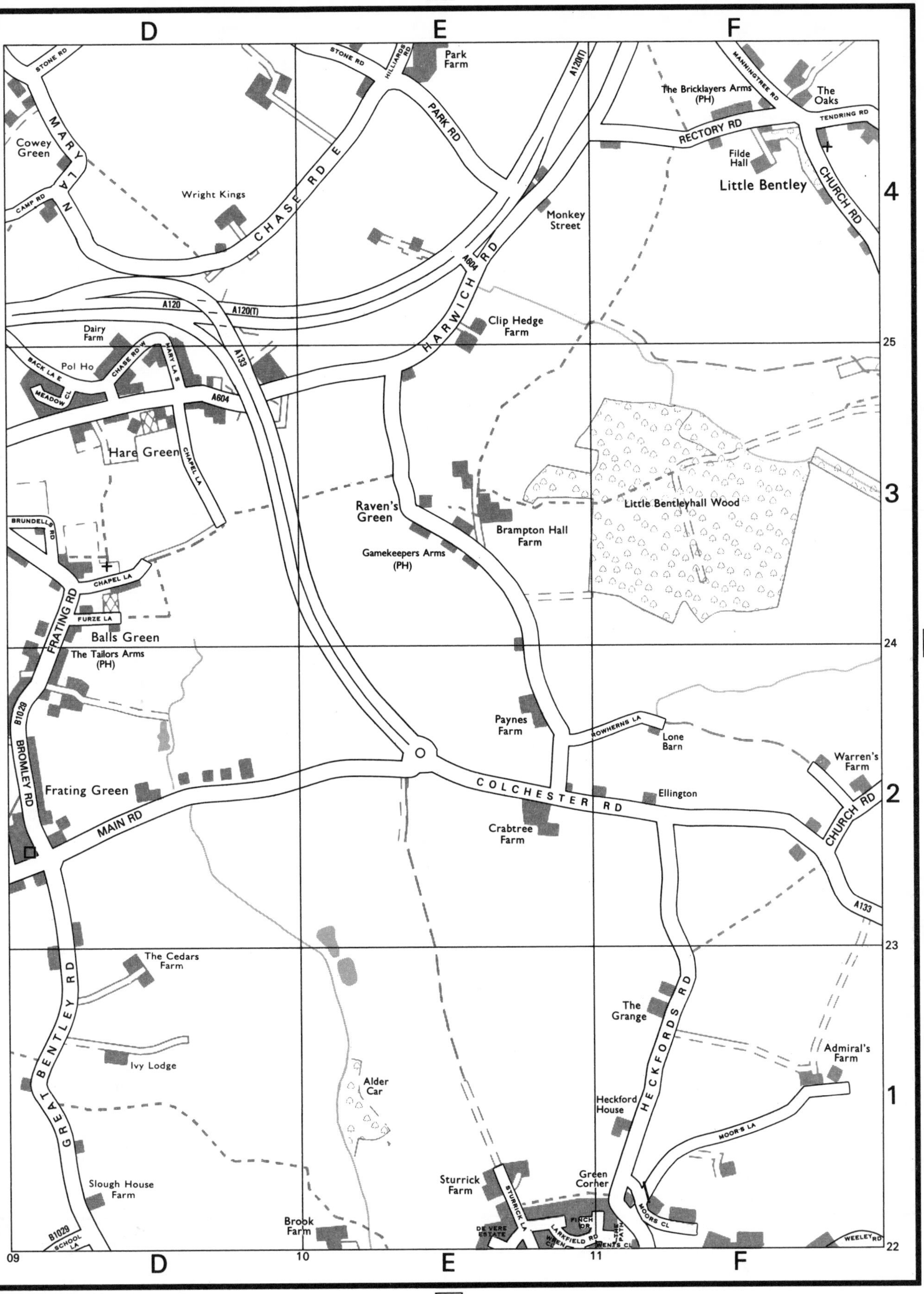
D
E
F
Park Farm
STONE RD
HILLIARDS RD
A120(T)
MANNINGTREE RD
The Bricklayers Arms (PH)
The Oaks
TENDRING RD
RECTORY RD
Filde Hall
Little Bentley
CHURCH RD
Cowey Green
MARY LAN
CAMP RD
Wright Kings
CHASE RD E
PARK RD
Monkey Street
A604
HARWICH RD
A120
Clip Hedge Farm
Dairy Farm
Pol Ho
BACK LA E
MEADOW CL
CHASE RD W
MARY LA S
A133
Hare Green
CHAPEL LA
Raven's Green
Brampton Hall Farm
Little Bentleyhall Wood
Gamekeepers Arms (PH)
BRUNDELLS RD
FRATING RD
FURZE LA
Balls Green
The Tailors Arms (PH)
B1029
BROMLEY RD
Paynes Farm
ROWHERNS LA
Lone Barn
Warren's Farm
Frating Green
COLCHESTER RD
Ellington
MAIN RD
Crabtree Farm
A133
The Cedars Farm
GREAT BENTLEY RD
The Grange
HECKFORDS RD
Admiral's Farm
Ivy Lodge
Alder Car
Heckford House
MOOR'S LA
Slough House Farm
Sturrick Farm
STURRICK LA
Green Corner
MOORS CL
Brook Farm
DE VERE ESTATE
FINCH DR
LARKFIELD RD
WREN CL
WENTS CL
WEELEY RD
B1029
SCHOOL LA
25
24
23
22
4
3
2
1
09
10
11

72

89

54

71

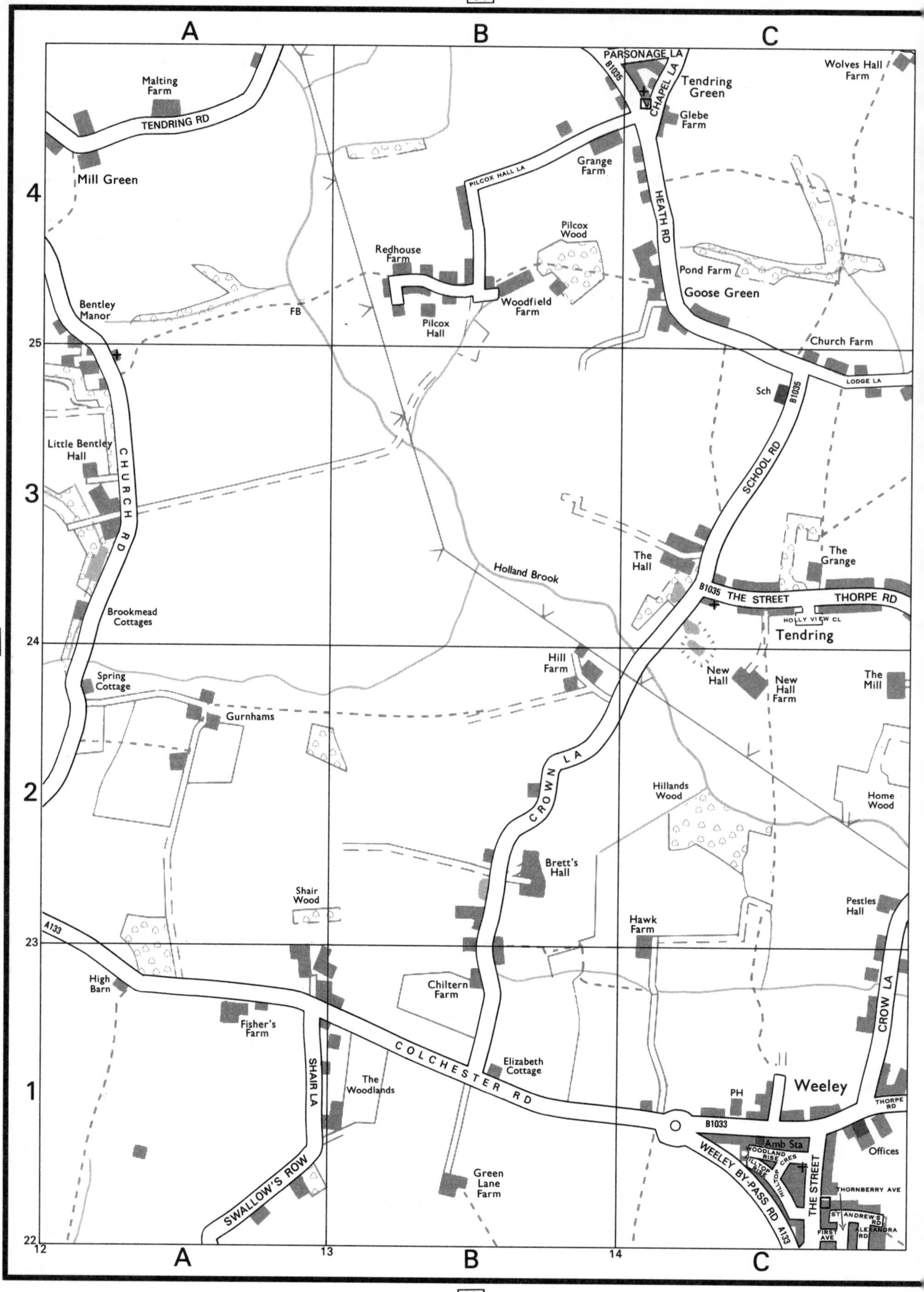
A
B
C
4
3
2
1
25
24
23
22
12
13
14
Malting Farm
TENDRING RD
Mill Green
PARSONAGE LA
B1035
CHAPEL LA
Tendring Green
Glebe Farm
Wolves Hall Farm
Grange Farm
PILCOX HALL LA
HEATH RD
Pilcox Wood
Redhouse Farm
Pond Farm
Goose Green
Bentley Manor
FB
Pilcox Hall
Woodfield Farm
Church Farm
LODGE LA
Sch
SCHOOL RD
Little Bentley Hall
CHURCH RD
The Hall
The Grange
Holland Brook
THE STREET
THORPE RD
HOLLY VIEW CL
Tendring
Brookmead Cottages
Hill Farm
New Hall
New Hall Farm
The Mill
Spring Cottage
Gurnhams
CROWN LA
Hillands Wood
Home Wood
Brett's Hall
Shair Wood
Pestles Hall
A133
Hawk Farm
High Barn
Chiltern Farm
CROW LA
Fisher's Farm
SHAIR LA
COLCHESTER RD
Elizabeth Cottage
The Woodlands
PH
Weeley
THORPE RD
B1033
Amb Sta
WOODLAND RISE
CRES
HILLTOP RISE
HILLTOP
WEELEY BY-PASS RD
THE STREET
Offices
THORNBERRY AVE
ST ANDREW'S RD
ALEXANDRA RD
FIRST AVE
Green Lane Farm
SWALLOW'S ROW

90

55

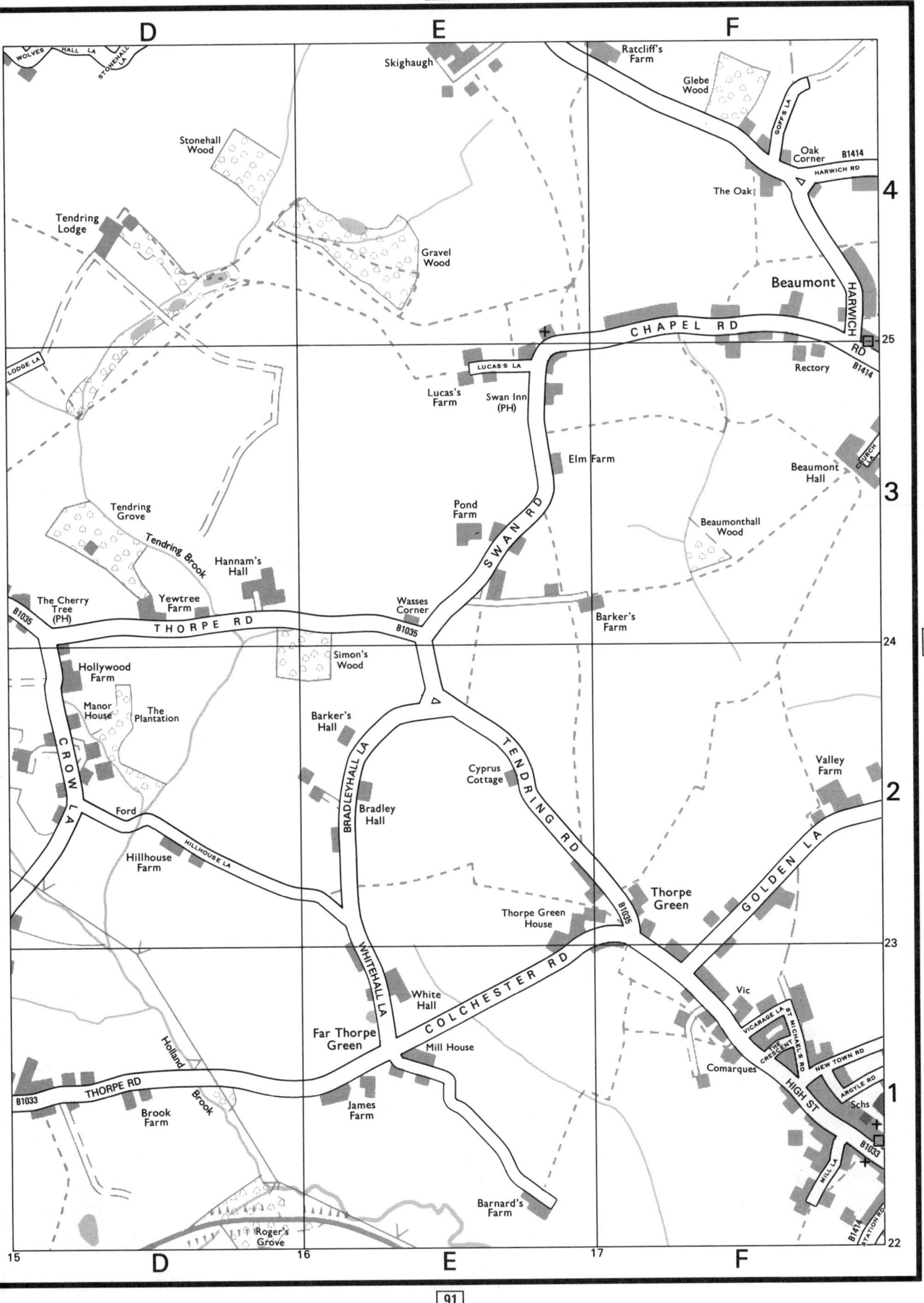
D
E
F
WOLVES HALL LA
STONEHALL LA
Skighaugh
Ratcliff's Farm
Glebe Wood
GOFF'S LA
Oak Corner
B1414
HARWICH RD
The Oak
4
Stonehall Wood
Tendring Lodge
Gravel Wood
Beaumont
HARWICH RD
CHAPEL RD
25
B1414
Rectory
LODGE LA
LUCAS'S LA
Lucas's Farm
Swan Inn (PH)
Elm Farm
CHURCH LA
Beaumont Hall
3
Pond Farm
Tendring Grove
Tendring Brook
SWAN RD
Beaumonthall Wood
Hannam's Hall
The Cherry Tree (PH)
Yewtree Farm
Wasses Corner
B1035
THORPE RD
B1035
Barker's Farm
24
Hollywood Farm
Simon's Wood
Manor House
The Plantation
Barker's Hall
CROW LA
BRADLEYHALL LA
TENDRING RD
Cyprus Cottage
Valley Farm
2
Bradley Hall
Ford
HILLHOUSE LA
Hillhouse Farm
GOLDEN LA
Thorpe Green
B1035
Thorpe Green House
23
WHITEHALL LA
COLCHESTER RD
White Hall
Vic
VICARAGE LA
THE CRESCENT
ST MICHAEL'S RD
Far Thorpe Green
Mill House
NEW TOWN RD
ARGYLE RD
Comarques
HIGH ST
1
Holland Brook
THORPE RD
B1033
Schs
B1033
Brook Farm
James Farm
MILL LA
Barnard's Farm
STATION RD
B1414
Roger's Grove
22
15
16
17
D
E
F

74

91

56

73

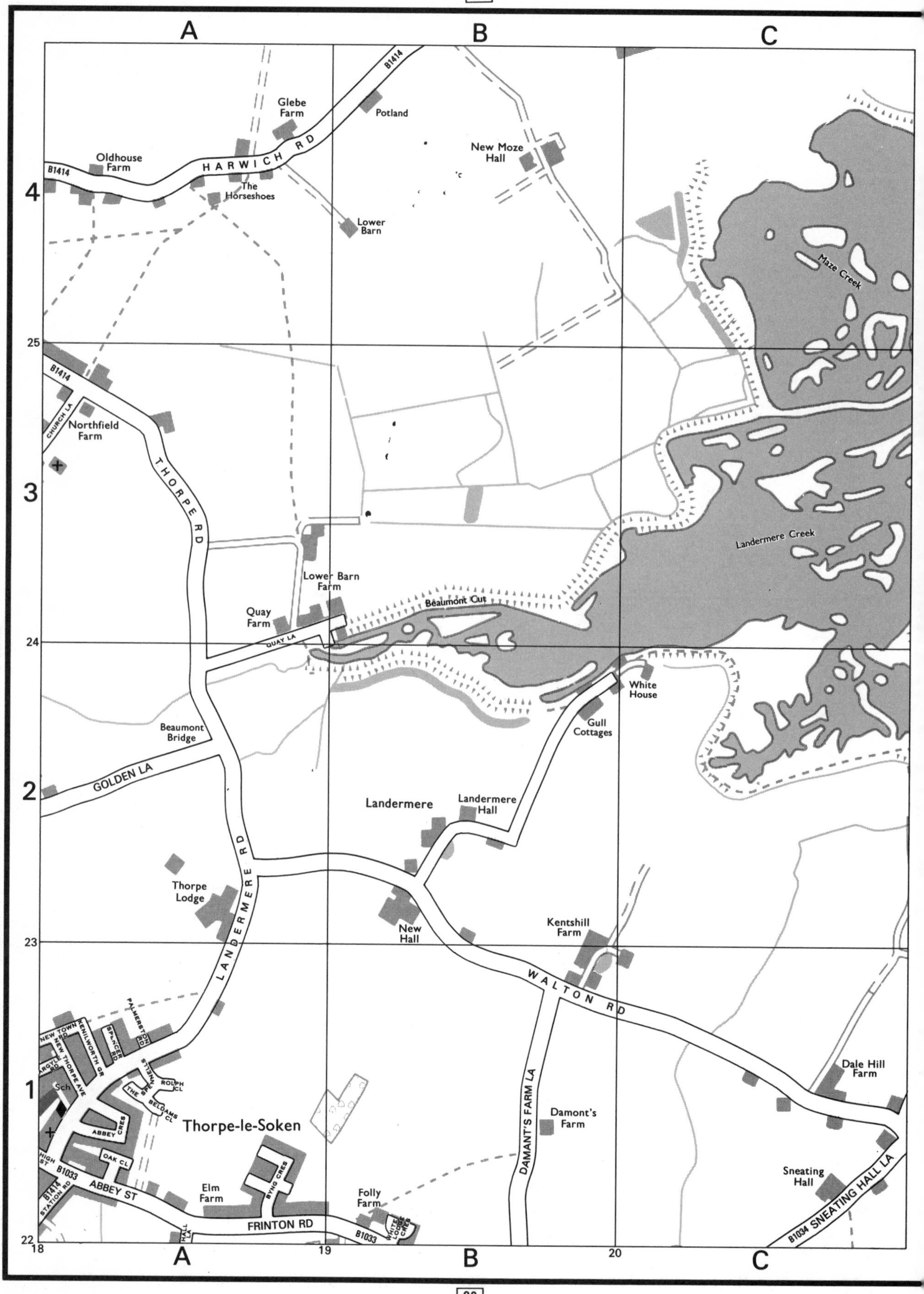
A
B
C
4
3
2
1
25
24
23
22
18
19
20
B1414
HARWICH RD
Glebe Farm
Potland
New Moze Hall
Oldhouse Farm
The Horseshoes
Lower Barn
Maze Creek
Northfield Farm
CHURCH LA
THORPE RD
Landermere Creek
Lower Barn Farm
Quay Farm
QUAY LA
Beaumont Cut
White House
Gull Cottages
Beaumont Bridge
GOLDEN LA
Landermere
Landermere Hall
LANDERMERE RD
Thorpe Lodge
New Hall
Kentshill Farm
WALTON RD
PALMERSTON RD
NEW TOWN RD
KENILWORTH GR
SPENCER RD
NEW THORPE AVE
ARGYLE RD
THE SPENNELLS
ROLPH CL
THE BELDAMS CL
Sch
ABBEY CRES
OAK CL
HIGH ST
B1033
ABBEY ST
B1414 STATION RD
Thorpe-le-Soken
Elm Farm
BYNG CRES
Folly Farm
HALL LA
FRINTON RD
WHITE LODGE CRES
DAMANT'S FARM LA
Damont's Farm
Dale Hill Farm
Sneating Hall
B1034 SNEATING HALL LA

92

57

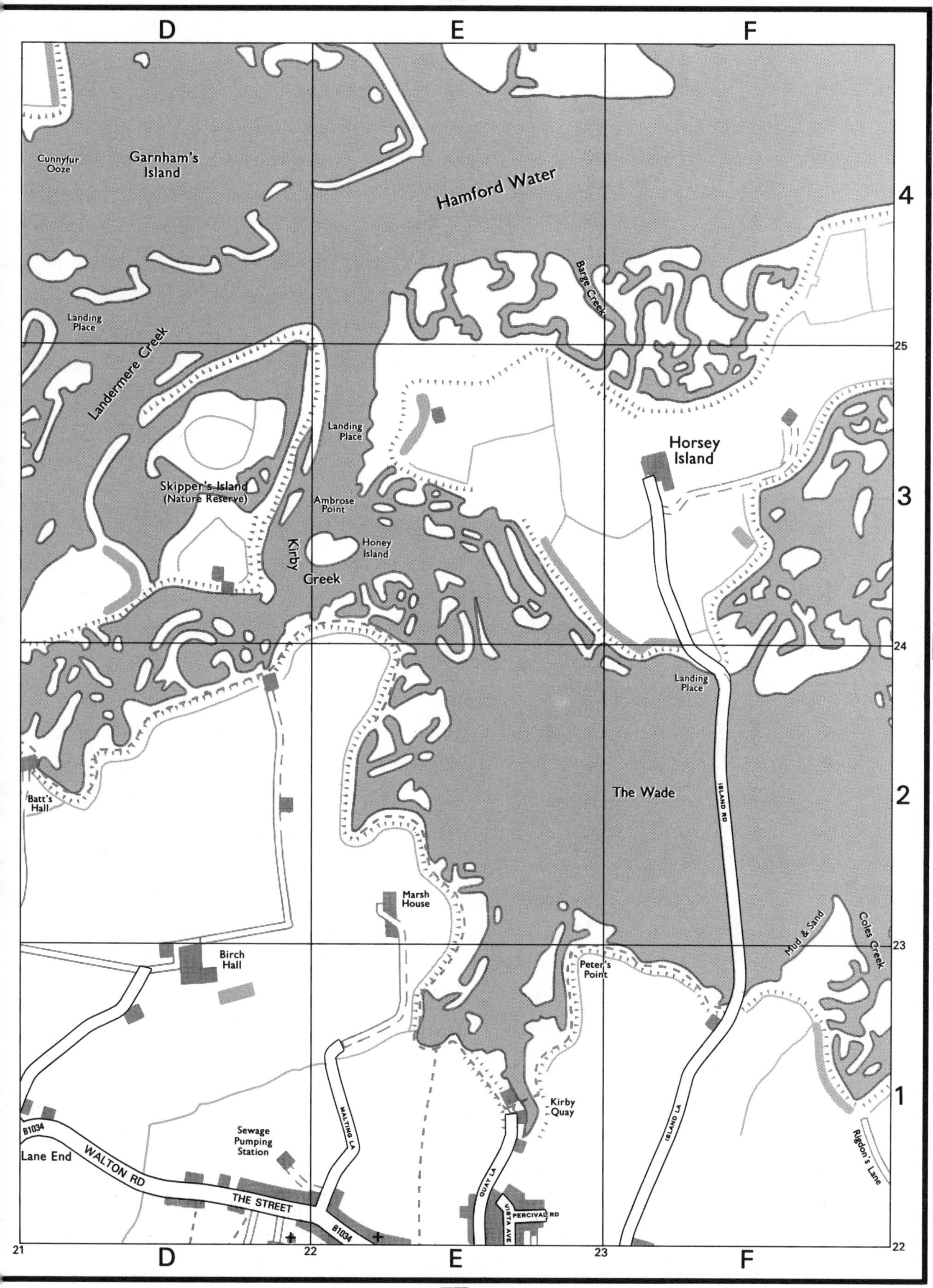
D
E
F
Cunnyfur Ooze
Garnham's Island
Hamford Water
4
Landing Place
Landermere Creek
Barge Creek
25
Landing Place
Horsey Island
Skipper's Island (Nature Reserve)
Ambrose Point
3
Kirby Creek
Honey Island
24
Landing Place
The Wade
ISLAND RD
2
Batt's Hall
Marsh House
Mud & Sand
Coles Creek
23
Birch Hall
Peter's Point
Kirby Quay
1
ISLAND LA
Rigdon's Lane
MALTING LA
Sewage Pumping Station
B1034
Lane End
WALTON RD
THE STREET
B1034
QUAY LA
VISTA AVE
PERCIVAL RD
21
22
23
22
D
E
F

76

93

58

75

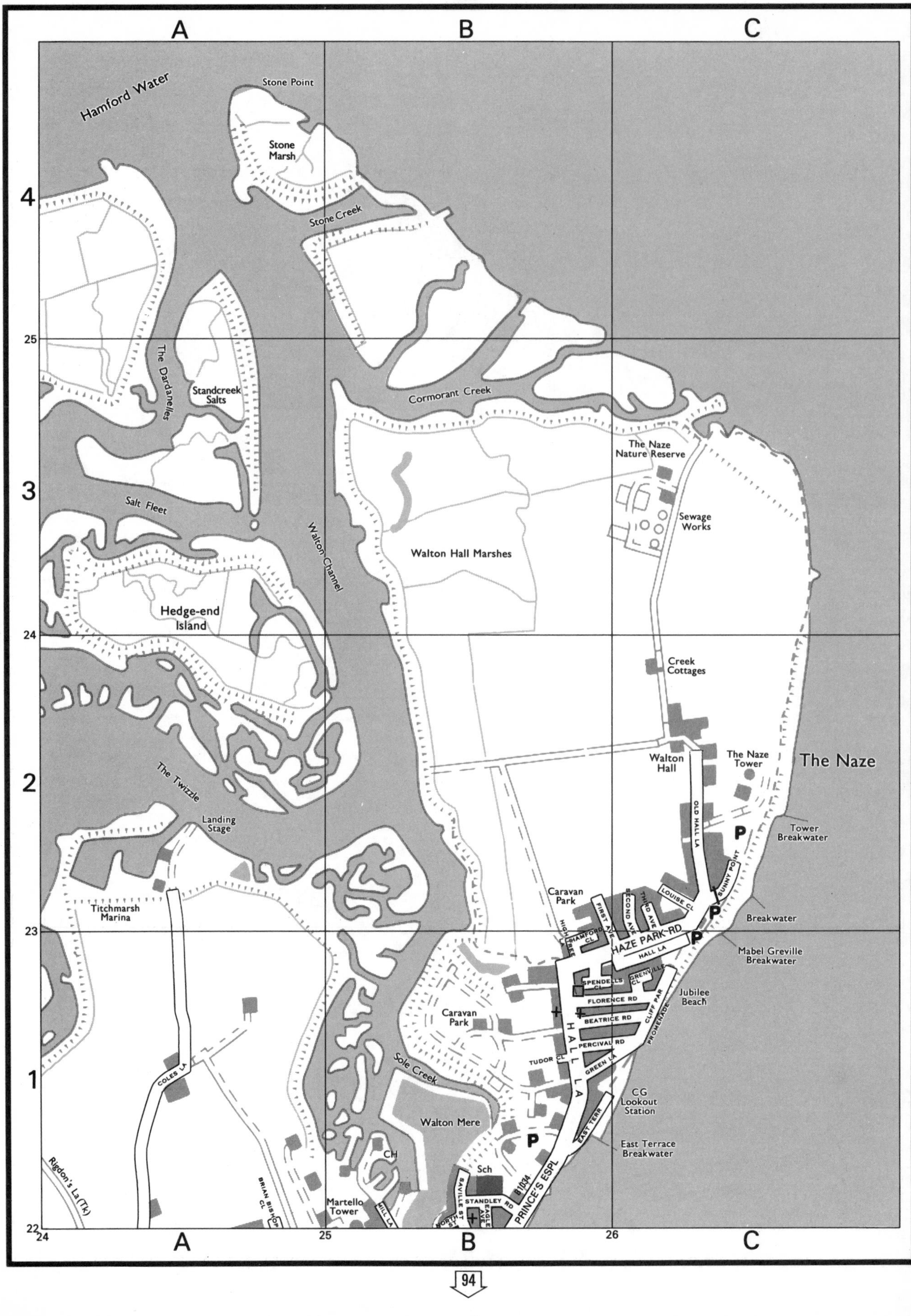

A
B
C
4
3
2
1
25
24
23
22
24
25
26
Hamford Water
Stone Point
Stone Marsh
Stone Creek
The Dardanelles
Standcreek Salts
Cormorant Creek
Salt Fleet
Walton Channel
Walton Hall Marshes
The Naze Nature Reserve
Sewage Works
Hedge-end Island
Creek Cottages
The Twizzle
Walton Hall
The Naze Tower
The Naze
Landing Stage
OLD HALL LA
Tower Breakwater
P
Titchmarsh Marina
Caravan Park
SECOND AVE
THIRD AVE
LOUISE CL
SUNNY POINT
FIRST AVE
HAMFORD CL
HIGH TREES
HAZE PARK RD
HALL LA
Breakwater
Mabel Greville Breakwater
SPENDELLS CL
GRENVILLE CL
Jubilee Beach
FLORENCE RD
BEATRICE RD
CLIFF PAR
PROMENADE
Caravan Park
PERCIVAL RD
TUDOR CL
GREEN LA
HALL LA
COLES LA
Sole Creek
CG Lookout Station
Walton Mere
EAST TERR
East Terrace Breakwater
CH
Sch
Rigdon's La (Tk)
BRIAN BISHOP CL
Martello Tower
MILL LA
SAVILLE ST
NORTH ST
STANDLEY RD
EAGLE AVE
B1034
PRINCE'S ESPL

94

59

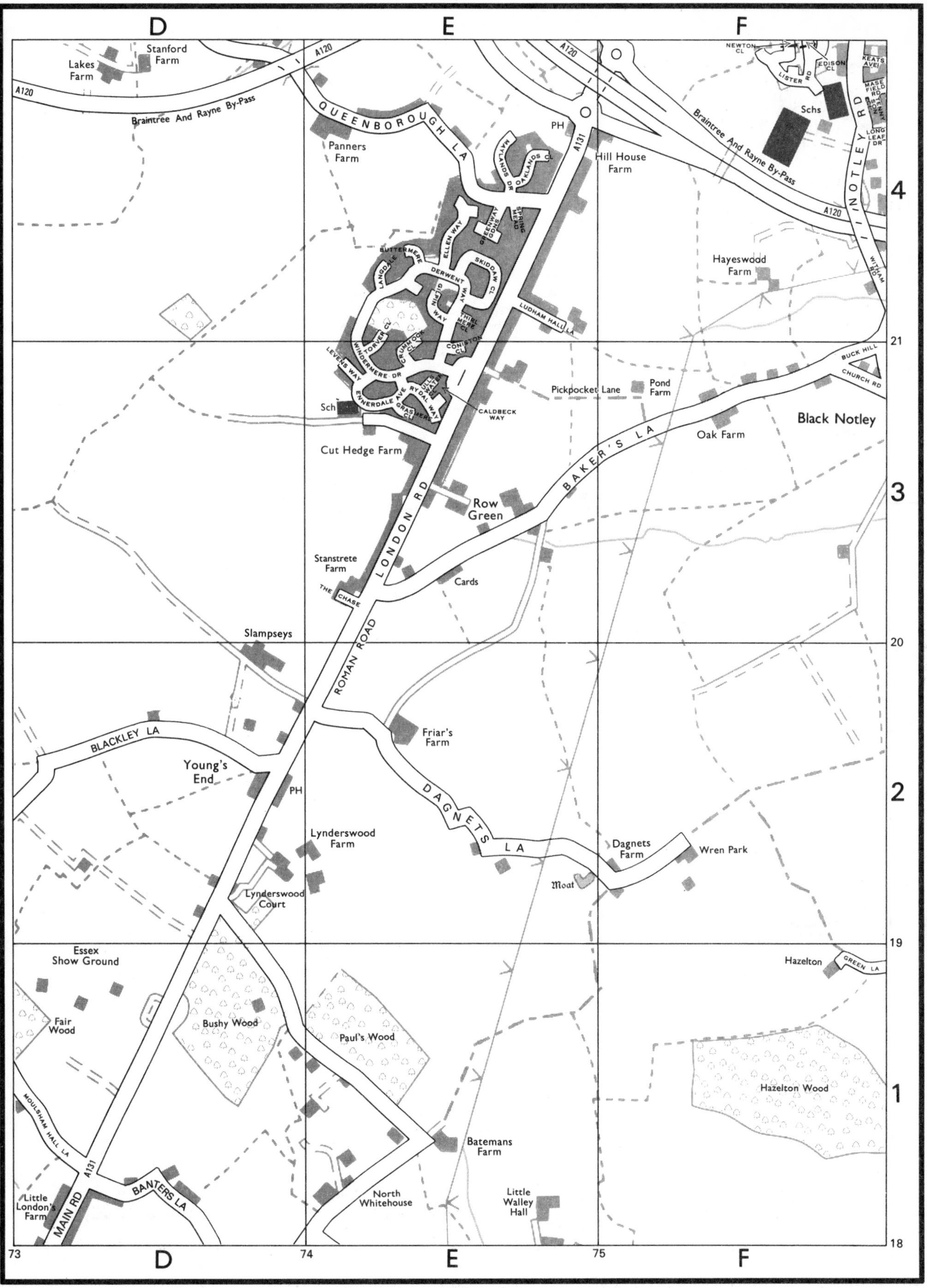
D
E
F
Stanford Farm
Lakes Farm
A120
Braintree And Rayne By-Pass
QUEENBOROUGH LA
Panners Farm
PH
A131
Hill House Farm
NEWTON CL
EDISON CL
LISTER RD
KEATS AVE
Schs
MASEFIELD RD
LONG LEAF DR
NOTLEY RD
MAYLANDS DR
OAKLANDS CL
SPRING MEAD
GREENWAY GDNS
ELLEN WAY
BUTTERMERE
LANGDALE
DERWENT WAY
SKIDDAW CL
GILPIN WAY
THIRLMERE CL
LUDHAM HALL LA
Hayeswood Farm
WITHAM RD
CONISTON CL
CRUMMOCK CL
TORVER CL
WINDERMERE DR
LEVENS WAY
ENNERDALE AVE
RYDAL WAY
GRASMERE CL
CALDBECK WAY
Sch
Pickpocket Lane
Pond Farm
BUCK HILL
CHURCH RD
Black Notley
Oak Farm
BAKER'S LA
Cut Hedge Farm
LONDON RD
Row Green
Stanstrete Farm
THE CHASE
Cards
ROMAN ROAD
Slampseys
Friar's Farm
BLACKLEY LA
Young's End
PH
DAGNETS LA
Lynderswood Farm
Dagnets Farm
Wren Park
Moat
Lynderswood Court
Essex Show Ground
Hazelton
GREEN LA
Fair Wood
Bushy Wood
Paul's Wood
Hazelton Wood
MOULSHAM HALL LA
Batemans Farm
A131
BANTERS LA
North Whitehouse
Little Walley Hall
Little London's Farm
MAIN RD
4
3
2
1
21
20
19
18
73
74
75
D
E
F

78

95

60

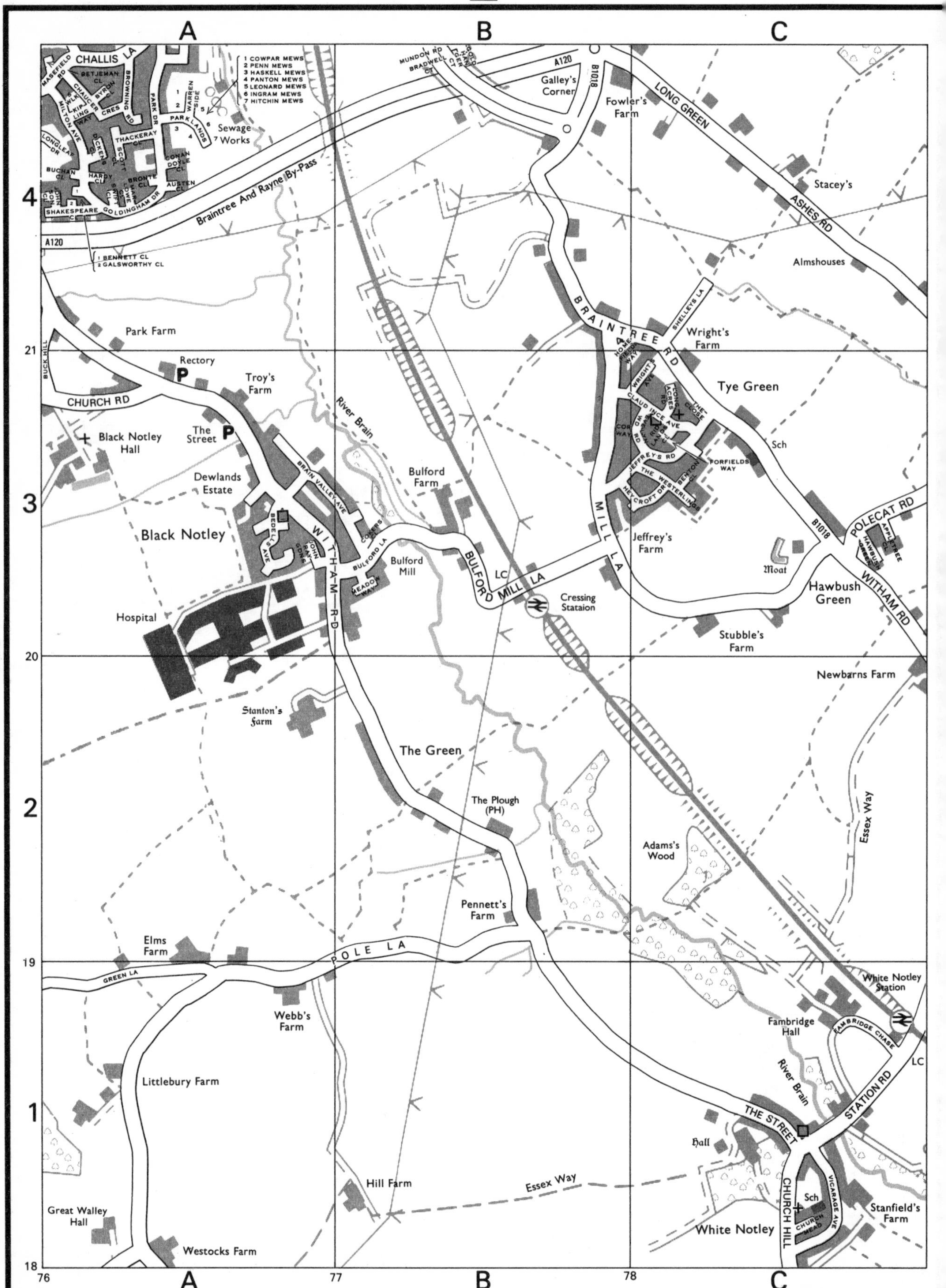

A
B
C
4
3
2
1
21
20
19
18
76
77
78
CHALLIS LA
MASEFIELD RD
BETJEMAN CL
CHAUCER
BYRON
BROWNING RD
PARK DR
WARREN SIDE
1 COWPAR MEWS
2 PENN MEWS
3 HASKELL MEWS
4 PANTON MEWS
5 LEONARD MEWS
6 INGRAM MEWS
7 HITCHIN MEWS
PARKLANDS
Sewage Works
MILTON AVE
KIPLING WAY
CRES
THACKERAY CL
LONGLEAT DR
DICKENS
SCOTT
CONAN DOYLE CL
BUCHAN CL
HARDY CL
BRONTE CL
AUSTEN CL
SHAKESPEARE
GOLDINGHAM DR
Braintree And Rayne By-Pass
A120
1 BENNETT CL
2 GALSWORTHY CL
MUNDON RD
BRADWELL CT
A120
Galley's Corner
B1018
Fowler's Farm
LONG GREEN
Stacey's
ASHES RD
Almshouses
BRAINTREE RD
SHELLEYS LA
Wright's Farm
Tye Green
Sch
CLAUD INCE AVE
JEFFREY'S RD
THE WESTERLINGS
HEYCROFT DR
FORFIELDS WAY
THE CLOSE
MILL LA
Jeffrey's Farm
Moat
B1018
POLECAT RD
WITHAM RD
Hawbush Green
Stubble's Farm
Newbarns Farm
Park Farm
BUCK HILL
Rectory
CHURCH RD
Troy's Farm
Black Notley Hall
The Street
River Brain
Dewlands Estate
BRAIN VALLEY AVE
Bulford Farm
Black Notley
BEDELLS AVE
WITHAM RD
BULFORD LA
Bulford Mill
BULFORD MILL LA
LC
Cressing Stataion
Hospital
Stanton's Farm
The Green
The Plough (PH)
Adams's Wood
Essex Way
Pennett's Farm
Elms Farm
POLE LA
GREEN LA
Webb's Farm
White Notley Station
Fambridge Hall
FAMBRIDGE CHASE
LC
River Brain
Littlebury Farm
THE STREET
STATION RD
Hall
CHURCH HILL
Sch
CHURCH MEAD
VICARAGE AVE
Stanfield's Farm
Hill Farm
Essex Way
Great Walley Hall
White Notley
Westocks Farm

77

96

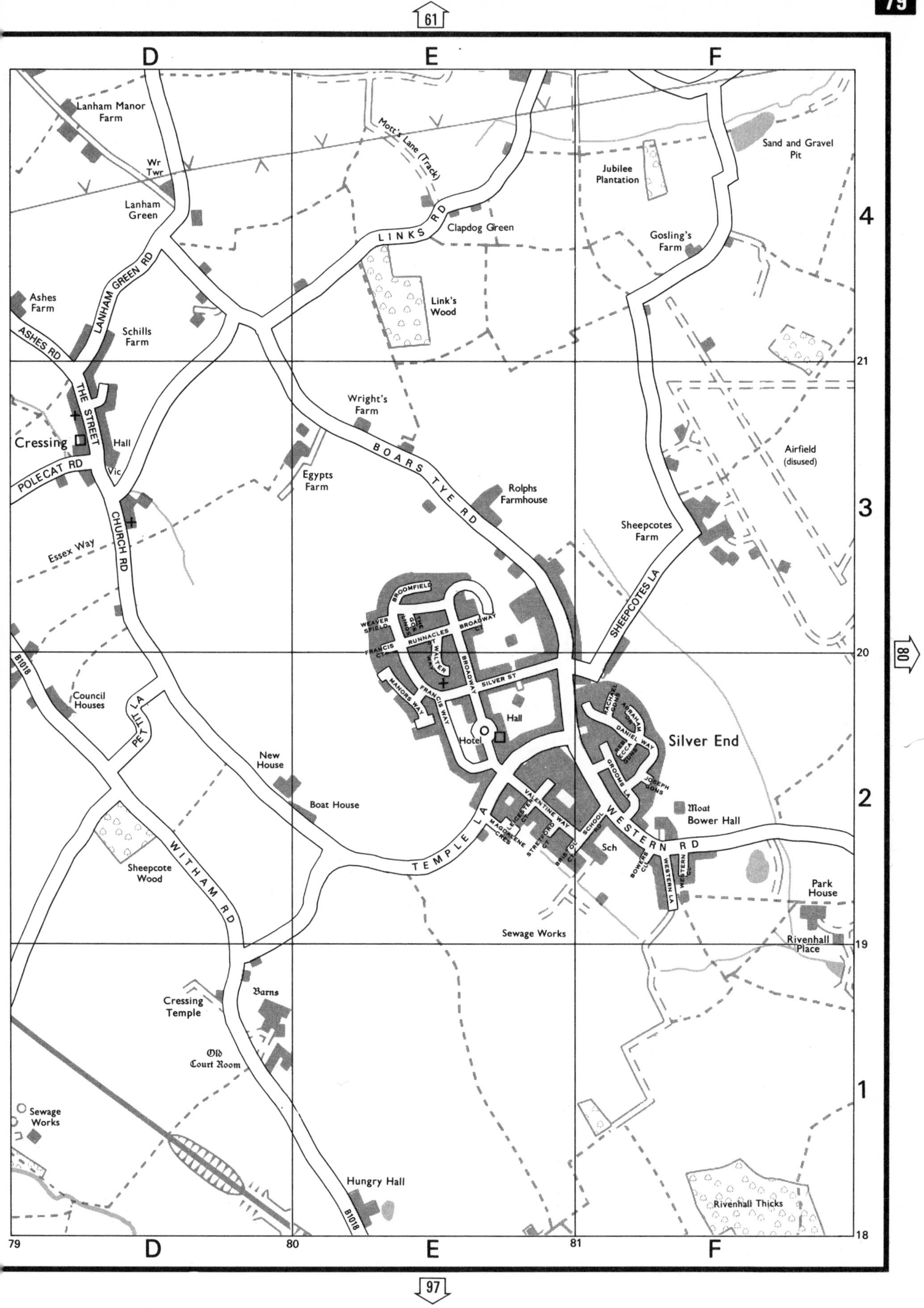
61
D
E
F
Lanham Manor Farm
Wr Twr
Lanham Green
Mott's Lane (Track)
LINKS RD
Clapdog Green
Jubilee Plantation
Sand and Gravel Pit
Gosling's Farm
LANHAM GREEN RD
Ashes Farm
Schills Farm
Link's Wood
ASHES RD
THE STREET
Cressing
Hall
Vic
POLECAT RD
Wright's Farm
BOARS TYE RD
Egypts Farm
Rolphs Farmhouse
Airfield (disused)
Sheepcotes Farm
CHURCH RD
Essex Way
SHEEPCOTES LA
BROOMFIELD
WEAVER SFIELD
THE GOSLINGS
RUNNACLES
BROADWAY CT
FRANCIS CT
ST WALTER WAY
BROADWAY
SILVER ST
MANORS WAY
FRANCIS WAY
Hall
Hotel
B1018
Council Houses
PETTIT LA
RACHAEL GDNS
ABRAHAM DR
DANIEL WAY
Silver End
REBECCA GDNS
GROOMS LA
JOSEPH GDNS
New House
Boat House
VALENTINE WAY
LEICESTER CT
Moat
Bower Hall
MAGDALENE CRES
STRETFORD CT
SCHOOL RD
WESTERN RD
TEMPLE LA
BRISTOL CT
Sch
BOWERS CL
WESTERN LA
WESTERN CL
Park House
Sheepcote Wood
WITHAM RD
Sewage Works
Rivenhall Place
Barns
Cressing Temple
Old Court Room
Sewage Works
Hungry Hall
B1018
Rivenhall Thicks
4
3
2
1
21
20
19
18
79
80
81
80
97

62

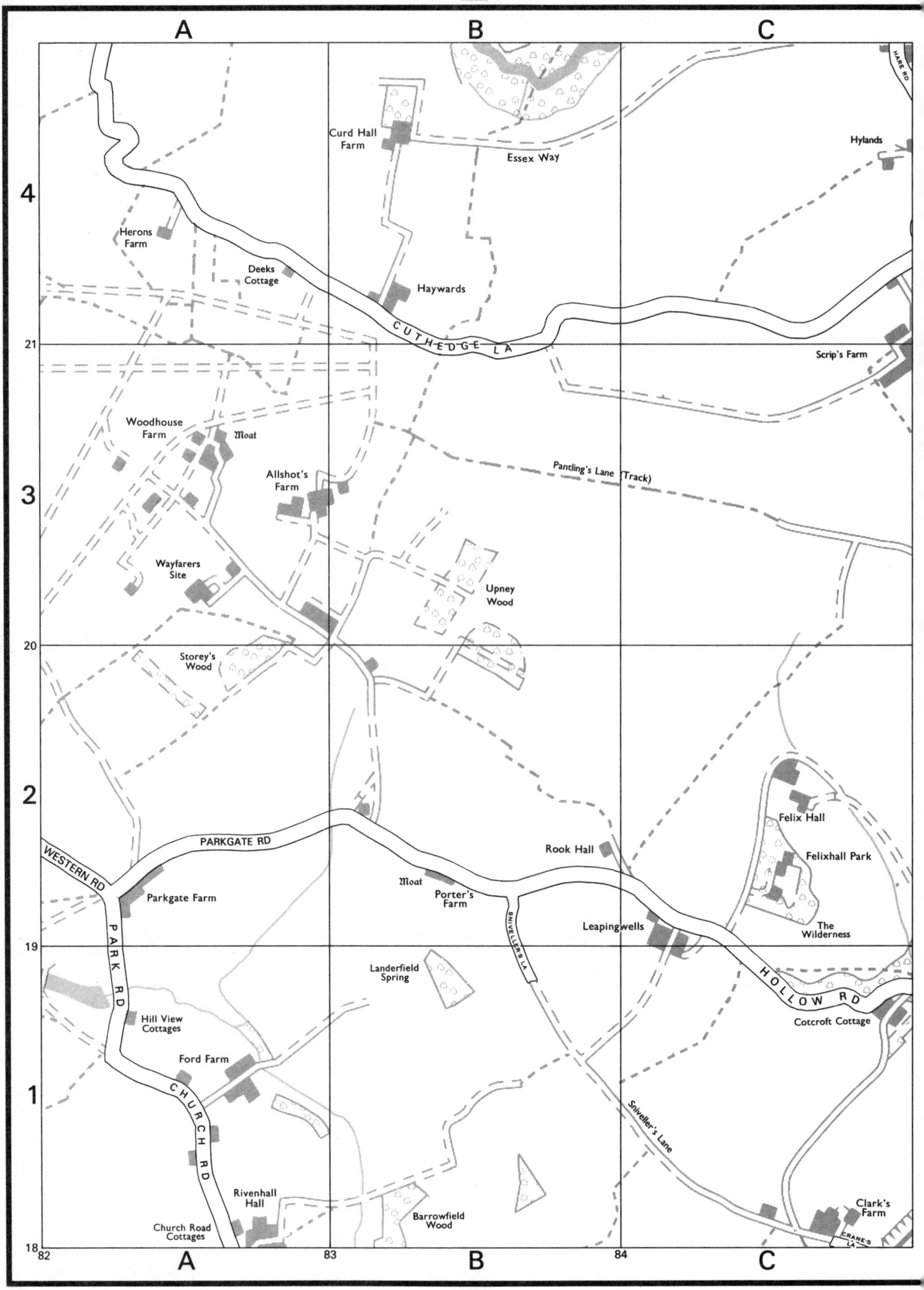
A
B
C
4
3
2
1
21
20
19
18
82
83
84
HARE RD
Curd Hall Farm
Essex Way
Hylands
Herons Farm
Deeks Cottage
Haywards
CUTHEDGE LA
Scrip's Farm
Woodhouse Farm
Moat
Allshot's Farm
Pantling's Lane (Track)
Wayfarers Site
Upney Wood
Storey's Wood
Felix Hall
Felixhall Park
Rook Hall
PARKGATE RD
WESTERN RD
Parkgate Farm
Moat
Porter's Farm
SNIVELLERS LA
Leapingwells
The Wilderness
PARK RD
Landerfield Spring
HOLLOW RD
Cotcroft Cottage
Hill View Cottages
Ford Farm
CHURCH RD
Sniveller's Lane
Rivenhall Hall
Barrowfield Wood
Church Road Cottages
Clark's Farm
CRANE'S LA

79

98

63

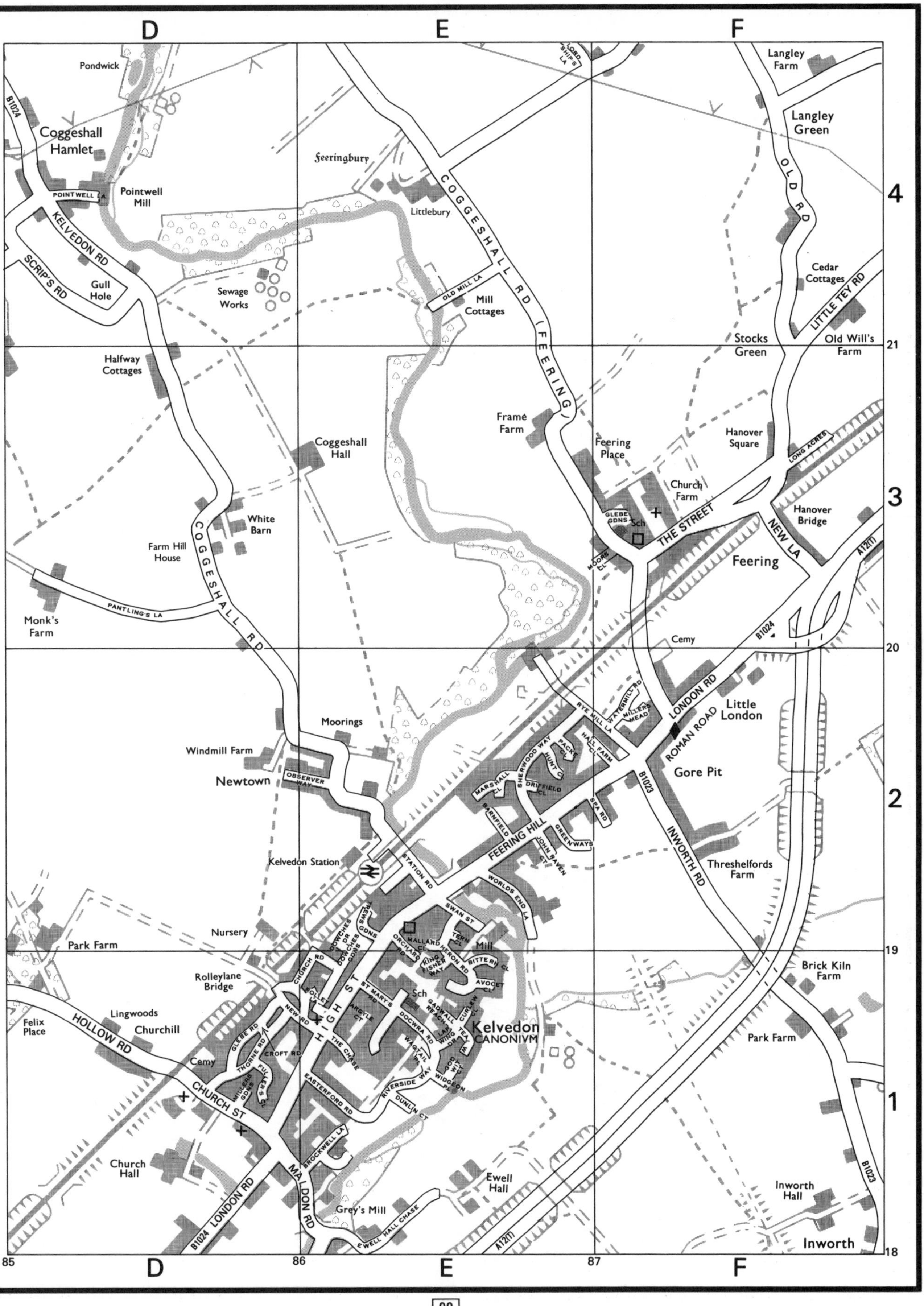
D
E
F
Pondwick
B1024
Coggeshall
Hamlet
POINTWELL LA
Pointwell
Mill
KELVEDON RD
SCRIP'S RD
Gull
Hole
Feeringbury
Littlebury
LORDSHIP'S LA
COGGESHALL RD (FEERING)
OLD MILL LA
Mill
Cottages
Sewage
Works
Langley
Farm
Langley
Green
OLD RD
Cedar
Cottages
LITTLE TEY RD
Stocks
Green
Old Will's
Farm
4
21
Halfway
Cottages
Frame
Farm
Feering
Place
Hanover
Square
LONG ACRES
Coggeshall
Hall
Church
Farm
Hanover
Bridge
3
White
Barn
Farm Hill
House
COGGESHALL RD
GLEBE GDNS
Sch
THE STREET
NEW LA
Feering
A12(T)
MOORS CL
Monk's
Farm
PANTLING'S LA
Cemy
B1024
20
RYE MILL LA
WATERMILL RD
MILLERS MEAD
LONDON RD
Little
London
ROMAN ROAD
Gore Pit
Moorings
Windmill Farm
Newtown
OBSERVER WAY
HALL FARM CL
PACKE CL
HUNT CL
SHERWOOD WAY
MARSHALL CL
DRIFFIELD CL
SPA RD
B1023
BARNFIELD
FEERING HILL
GREEN WAYS
2
INWORTH RD
Kelvedon Station
STATION RD
JOHN RAVEN CT
WORLDS END LA
Threshelfords
Farm
SWAN ST
TREWS GDNS
DOUCHES DR
DOUCHES GDNS
Nursery
Park Farm
ORCHARD RD
MALLARD CL
TERN CL
Mill
HERON RD
KINGFISHER WAY
BITTERN CL
AVOCET CL
19
Brick Kiln
Farm
Rolleylane
Bridge
CHURCH RD
HIGH ST
ST MARY'S RD
Sch
GADWALL REACH
CURLEW CL
Felix
Place
Lingwoods
Churchill
HOLLOW RD
GLEBE RD
THORNE RD
CROFT RD
NEW RD
ARGYLE CT
DOCWRA RD
LAPWING WAY
TEAL WAY
Kelvedon
CANONIVM
Park Farm
Cemy
MILLERS GDNS
FULLERS CL
THE CHASE
WAGTAIL WAY
RIVERSIDE WAY
WIDGEON PL
1
CHURCH ST
EASTERFORD RD
DUNLIN CT
BROCKWELL LA
Church
Hall
MALDON RD
Ewell
Hall
B1023
Inworth
Hall
B1024 LONDON RD
Grey's Mill
EWELL HALL CHASE
A12(T)
Inworth
18
85
86
87
D
E
F

82

99

64

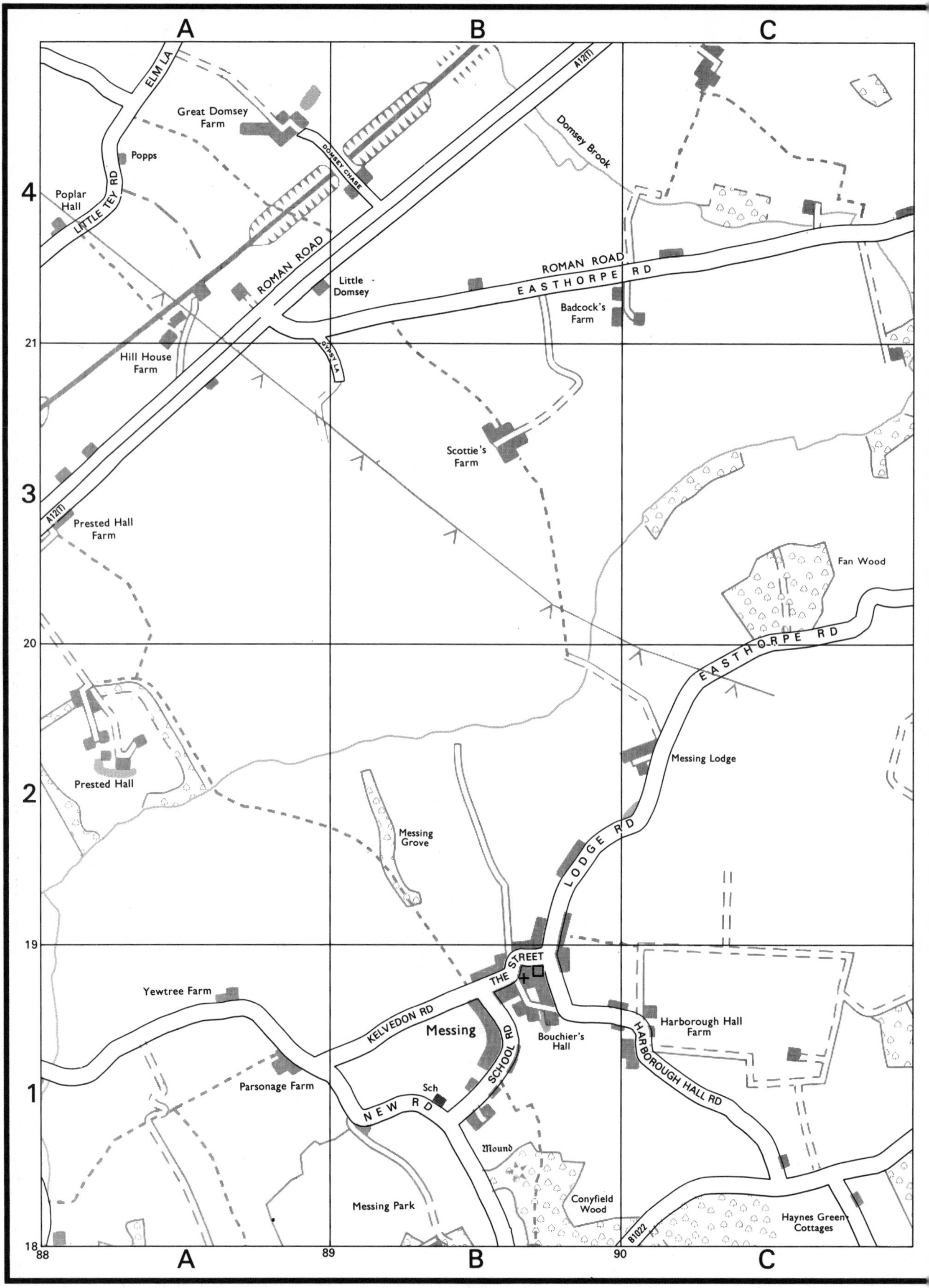
A
B
C
4
3
2
1
21
20
19
18
88
89
90
ELM LA
Great Domsey Farm
Popps
Poplar Hall
LITTLE TEY RD
DOMSEY CHASE
A12(T)
Domsey Brook
ROMAN ROAD
Little Domsey
ROMAN ROAD
EASTHORPE RD
Badcock's Farm
GYPSY LA
Hill House Farm
Scottie's Farm
Prested Hall Farm
Fan Wood
EASTHORPE RD
Messing Lodge
Prested Hall
Messing Grove
LODGE RD
THE STREET
Yewtree Farm
KELVEDON RD
Messing
SCHOOL RD
Bouchier's Hall
Harborough Hall Farm
HARBOROUGH HALL RD
Parsonage Farm
Sch
NEW RD
Mound
Conyfield Wood
Messing Park
B1022
Haynes Green Cottages

81

100

65

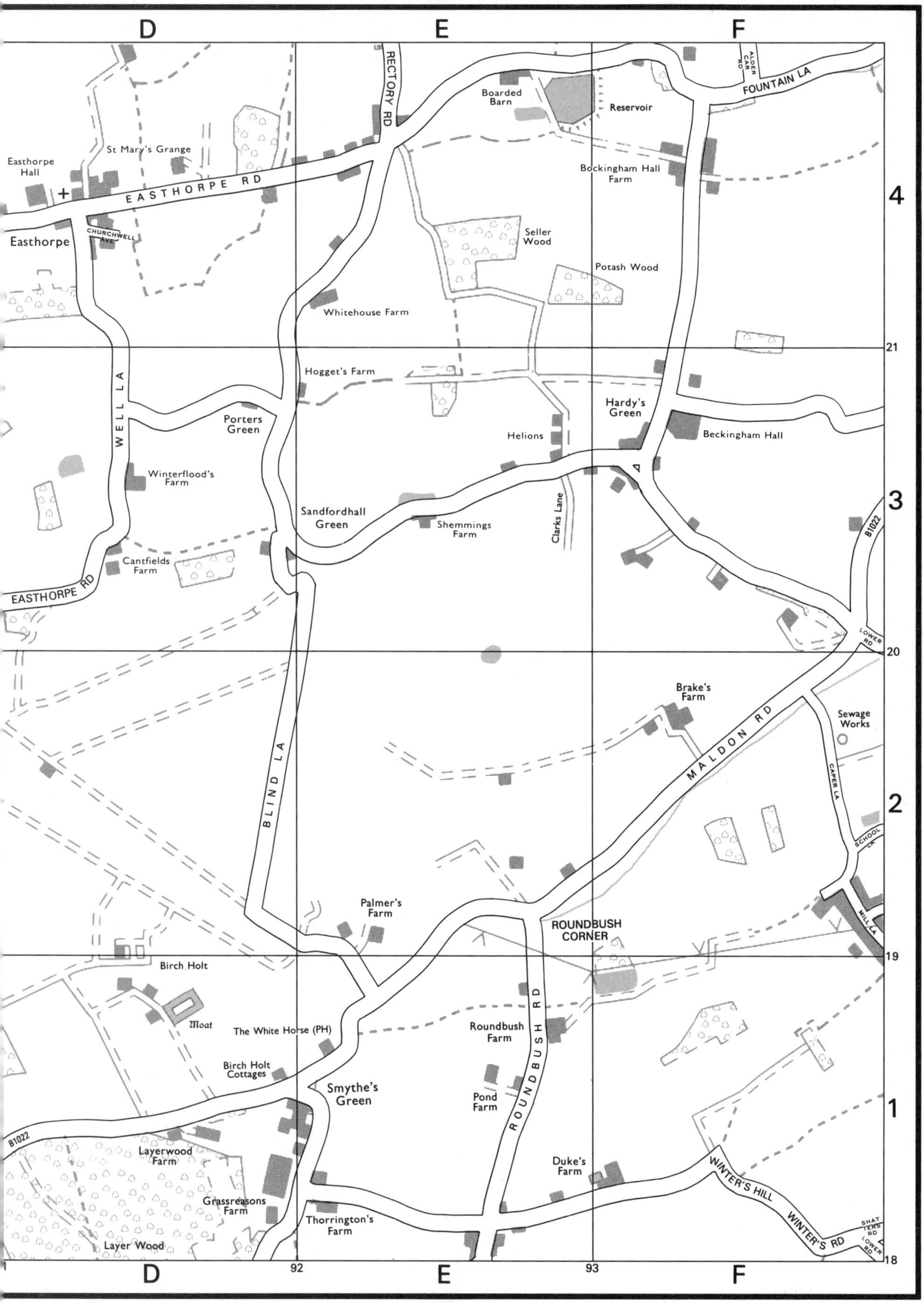
D
E
F
RECTORY RD
ALDER CAR RD
FOUNTAIN LA
Boarded Barn
Reservoir
St Mary's Grange
Easthorpe Hall
EASTHORPE RD
Bockingham Hall Farm
4
Easthorpe
CHURCHWELL AVE
Seller Wood
Potash Wood
Whitehouse Farm
21
Hogget's Farm
WELL LA
Porters Green
Hardy's Green
Helions
Beckingham Hall
Winterflood's Farm
Sandfordhall Green
Shemmings Farm
Clarks Lane
3
B1022
Cantfields Farm
EASTHORPE RD
LOWER RD
20
Brake's Farm
MALDON RD
Sewage Works
CAPER LA
BLIND LA
2
SCHOOL LA
Palmer's Farm
MILL LA
ROUNDBUSH CORNER
19
Birch Holt
Moat
The White Horse (PH)
Roundbush Farm
ROUNDBUSH RD
Birch Holt Cottages
Smythe's Green
Pond Farm
1
B1022
Layerwood Farm
Duke's Farm
WINTER'S HILL
Grassreasons Farm
Thorrington's Farm
WINTER'S RD
SHATTERS RD
LOWER RD
Layer Wood
18
92
93
D
E
F

84

101

66

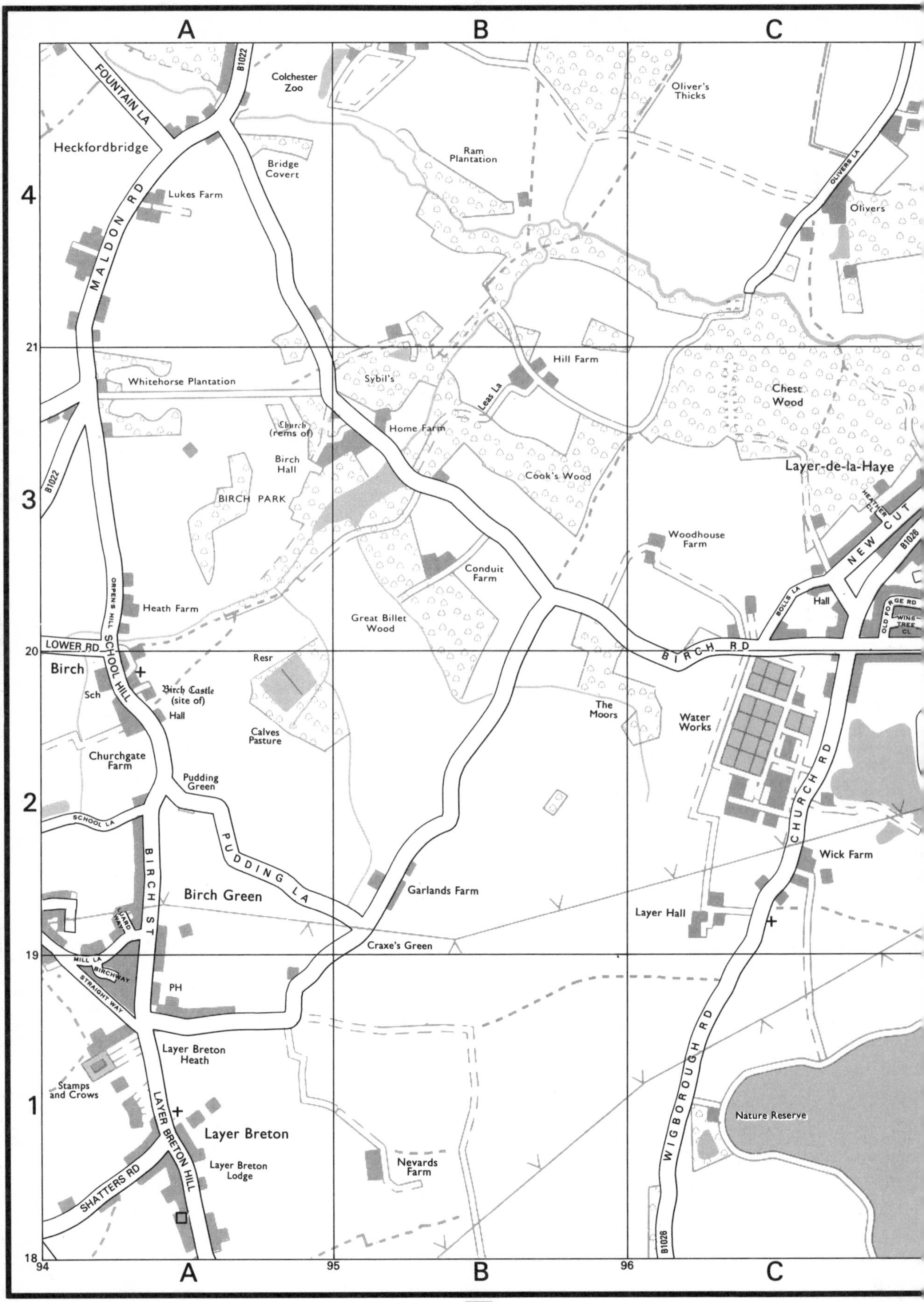
A
B
C
FOUNTAIN LA
B1022
Colchester Zoo
Oliver's Thicks
Heckfordbridge
Ram Plantation
Bridge Covert
OLIVERS LA
4
Lukes Farm
Olivers
MALDON RD
21
Hill Farm
Whitehorse Plantation
Sybil's
Leas La
Chest Wood
Church (rems of)
Home Farm
Birch Hall
Layer-de-la-Haye
B1022
3
BIRCH PARK
Cook's Wood
HEATHER CL
Woodhouse Farm
NEW CUT
B1026
Conduit Farm
ORPEN'S HILL
BOLLS LA
Hall
OLD FORGE RD
WINS-TREE CL
Heath Farm
Great Billet Wood
LOWER RD
SCHOOL HILL
BIRCH RD
20
Birch
Resr
Sch
Birch Castle (site of)
Hall
The Moors
Water Works
Churchgate Farm
Calves Pasture
CHURCH RD
Pudding Green
2
SCHOOL LA
BIRCH ST
PUDDING LA
Wick Farm
Garlands Farm
Birch Green
Layer Hall
LUARD WAY
Craxe's Green
19
MILL LA
BIRCHWAY
STRAIGHT WAY
PH
Layer Breton Heath
WIGBOROUGH RD
Stamps and Crows
1
LAYER BRETON HILL
Layer Breton
Nature Reserve
Layer Breton Lodge
Nevards Farm
SHATTERS RD
B1026
18
94
95
96

83

102

67

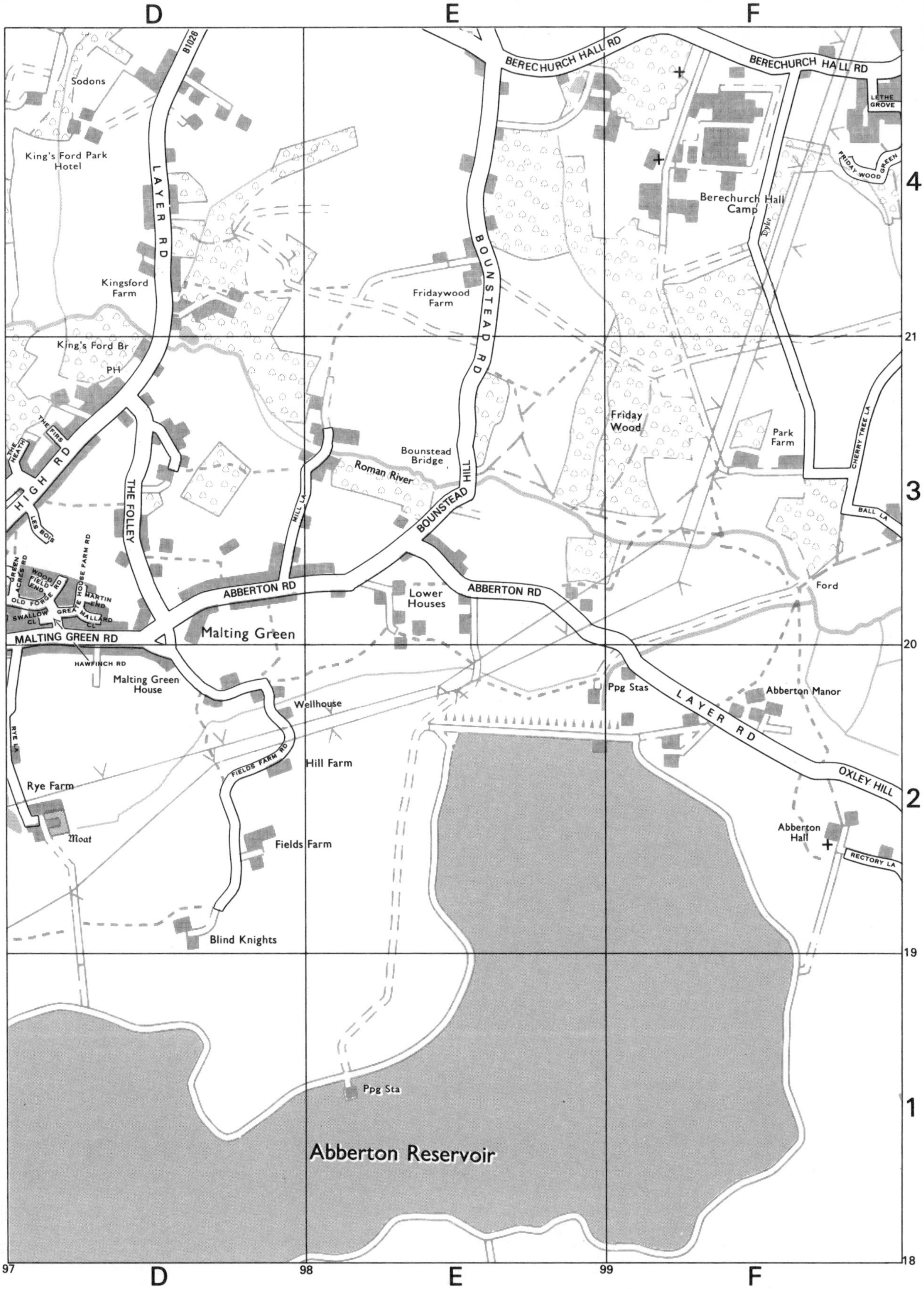
D
E
F
B1026
Sodons
King's Ford Park Hotel
LAYER RD
Kingsford Farm
King's Ford Br
PH
THE FIRS
THE HEATH
HIGH RD
LES BOIS
THE FOLLEY
GREEN ACRES RD
WOOD FIELD END
OLD FORGE RD
WHITE HOUSE FARM RD
MARTIN END
SWALLOW CL
MALLARD CL
MALTING GREEN RD
HAWFINCH RD
Malting Green
Malting Green House
ABBERTON RD
MILL LA
Roman River
Bounstead Bridge
BOUNSTEAD HILL
BOUNSTEAD RD
Fridaywood Farm
BERECHURCH HALL RD
LETHE GROVE
FRIDAY WOOD GREEN
Berechurch Hall Camp
Dyke
Friday Wood
Park Farm
CHERRY TREE LA
BALL LA
Ford
Lower Houses
Wellhouse
Ppg Stas
LAYER RD
Abberton Manor
OXLEY HILL
Abberton Hall
RECTORY LA
Hill Farm
FIELDS FARM RD
Rye Farm
RYE LA
Moat
Fields Farm
Blind Knights
Ppg Sta
Abberton Reservoir
4
3
2
1
21
20
19
18
97
98
99

99

103

68

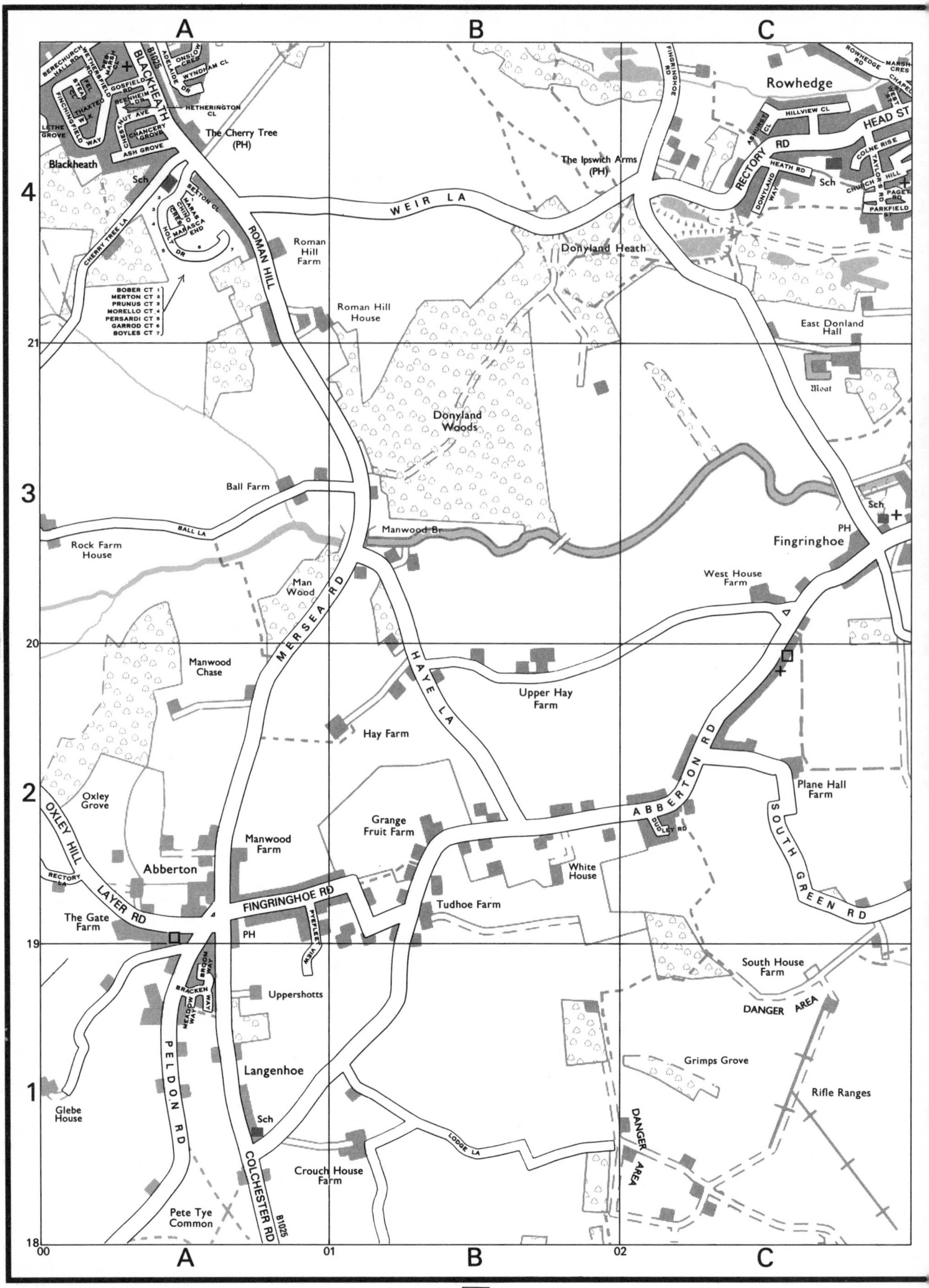
A
B
C
4
3
2
1
21
20
19
18
00
01
02
Blackheath
BLACKHEATH
B1025
The Cherry Tree (PH)
HETHERINGTON CL
WYNDHAM CL
ONSLOW CRES
ADELAIDE DR
GOSFIELD RD
CHESTNUT AVE
CHANCERY GROVE
ASH GROVE
FINCHINGFIELD WAY
LETHE GROVE
BERECHURCH HALL RD
Sch
CHERRY TREE LA
SEXTON CL
HOLT DR
BOBER CT 1
MERTON CT 2
PRUNUS CT 3
MORELLO CT 4
PERSARDI CT 5
GARROD CT 6
BOYLES CT 7
ROMAN HILL
Roman Hill Farm
Roman Hill House
WEIR LA
The Ipswich Arms (PH)
Donyland Heath
FINGRINGHOE RD
Rowhedge
ROWHEDGE RD
MARSH CRES
HILLVIEW CL
HEAD ST
RECTORY RD
ASHURST CL
HEATH RD
DONYLAND WAY
COLNE RISE
TAYLORS RD
CHURCH HILL
PAGET RD
PARKFIELD
CHAPEL ST
Sch
East Donland Hall
Moat
Donyland Woods
Ball Farm
BALL LA
Rock Farm House
Manwood Br
Man Wood
MERSEA RD
HAYE LA
Sch
PH
Fingringhoe
West House Farm
Manwood Chase
Upper Hay Farm
Hay Farm
ABBERTON RD
DUDLEY RD
Plane Hall Farm
SOUTH GREEN RD
Oxley Grove
OXLEY HILL
Grange Fruit Farm
Manwood Farm
Abberton
RECTORY LA
LAYER RD
FINGRINGHOE RD
White House
Tudhoe Farm
The Gate Farm
PH
PYEFLEET VIEW
BROOM WAY
BRACKEN WAY
MEADOW WAY
Uppershotts
South House Farm
DANGER AREA
Grimps Grove
Rifle Ranges
Langenhoe
PELDON RD
Glebe House
Sch
COLCHESTER RD
B1025
LODGE LA
DANGER AREA
Crouch House Farm
Pete Tye Common

85

104

69

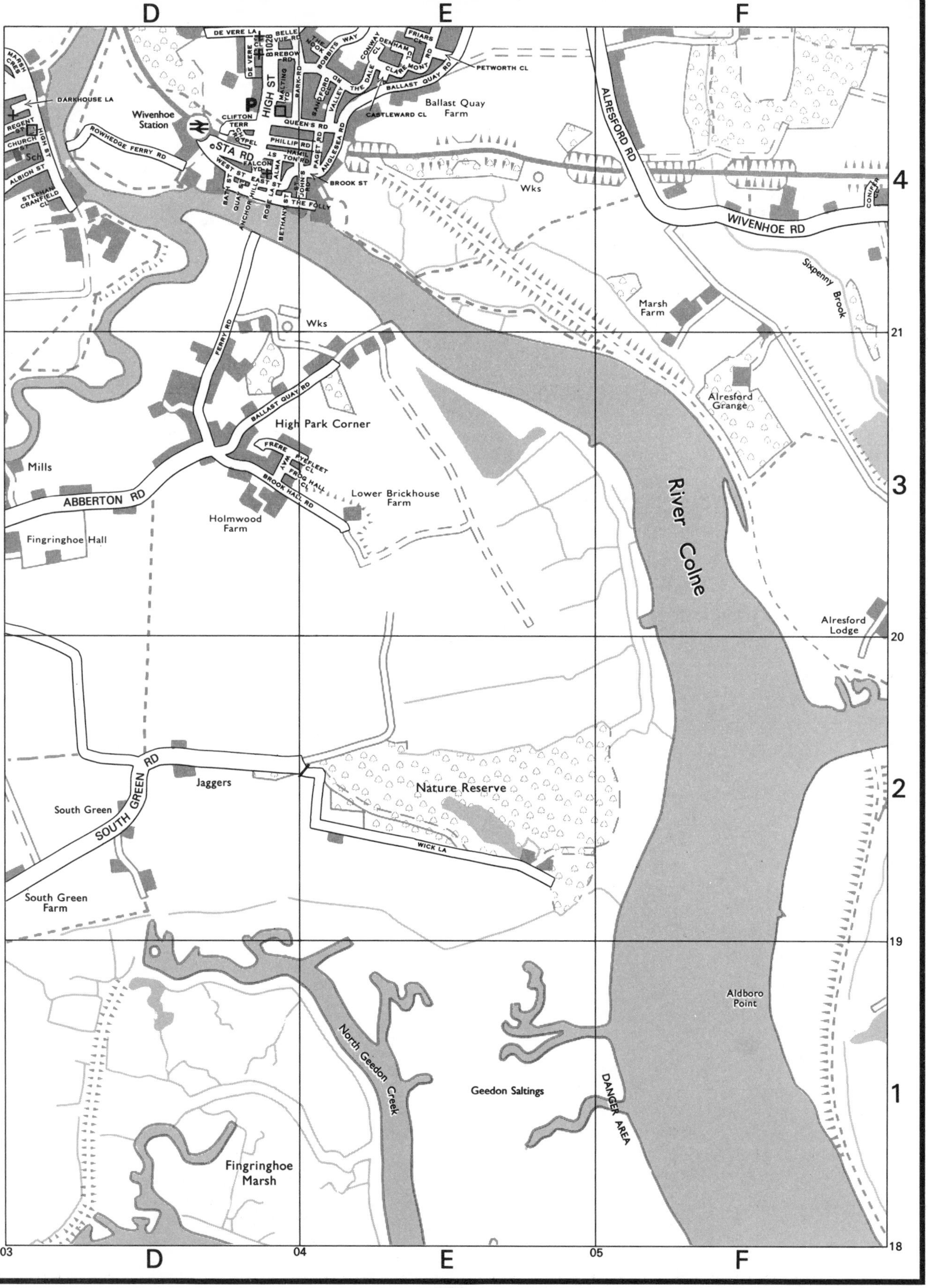
D
E
F
DE VERE LA
BELLE VUE RD
REBOW RD
HIGH ST
B1028
MALTING YD
PARK RD
SANDFORD CL
VALLEY RD
THE DALE
CLARE MONT
CONWAY CL
DENHAM CL
FRIARS CL
BOBBITS WAY
THE NOOK
PETWORTH CL
BALLAST QUAY RD
CASTLEWARD CL
Ballast Quay Farm
DARKHOUSE LA
Wivenhoe Station
CLIFTON TERR
QUEEN'S RD
STA RD
PHILLIP RD
HAMILTON RD
ANGLESEA RD
PAGET RD
ROWHEDGE FERRY RD
REGENT ST
CHURCH ST
HIGH ST
Sch
ALBION ST
STEPHAN CRANFIELD CL
WEST ST
FALCON YD
ALMA ST
EAST ST
BATH ST
QUAY ST
ANCHOR HILL
ROSE LA
BETHANY ST
ST JOHN'S RD
BROOK ST
THE FOLLY
Wks
ALRESFORD RD
WIVENHOE RD
CONIFER CL
4
Sixpenny Brook
Marsh Farm
Wks
FERRY RD
21
BALLAST QUAY RD
High Park Corner
Alresford Grange
Mills
FRERE WAY
PYEFLEET CL
FROG HALL CL
BROOK HALL RD
ABBERTON RD
Lower Brickhouse Farm
Holmwood Farm
3
Fingringhoe Hall
River Colne
Alresford Lodge
20
RD
SOUTH GREEN
Jaggers
Nature Reserve
South Green
2
WICK LA
South Green Farm
19
Aldboro Point
North Geedon Creek
Geedon Saltings
DANGER AREA
1
Fingringhoe Marsh
03
04
05
18
D
E
F

88

105

70

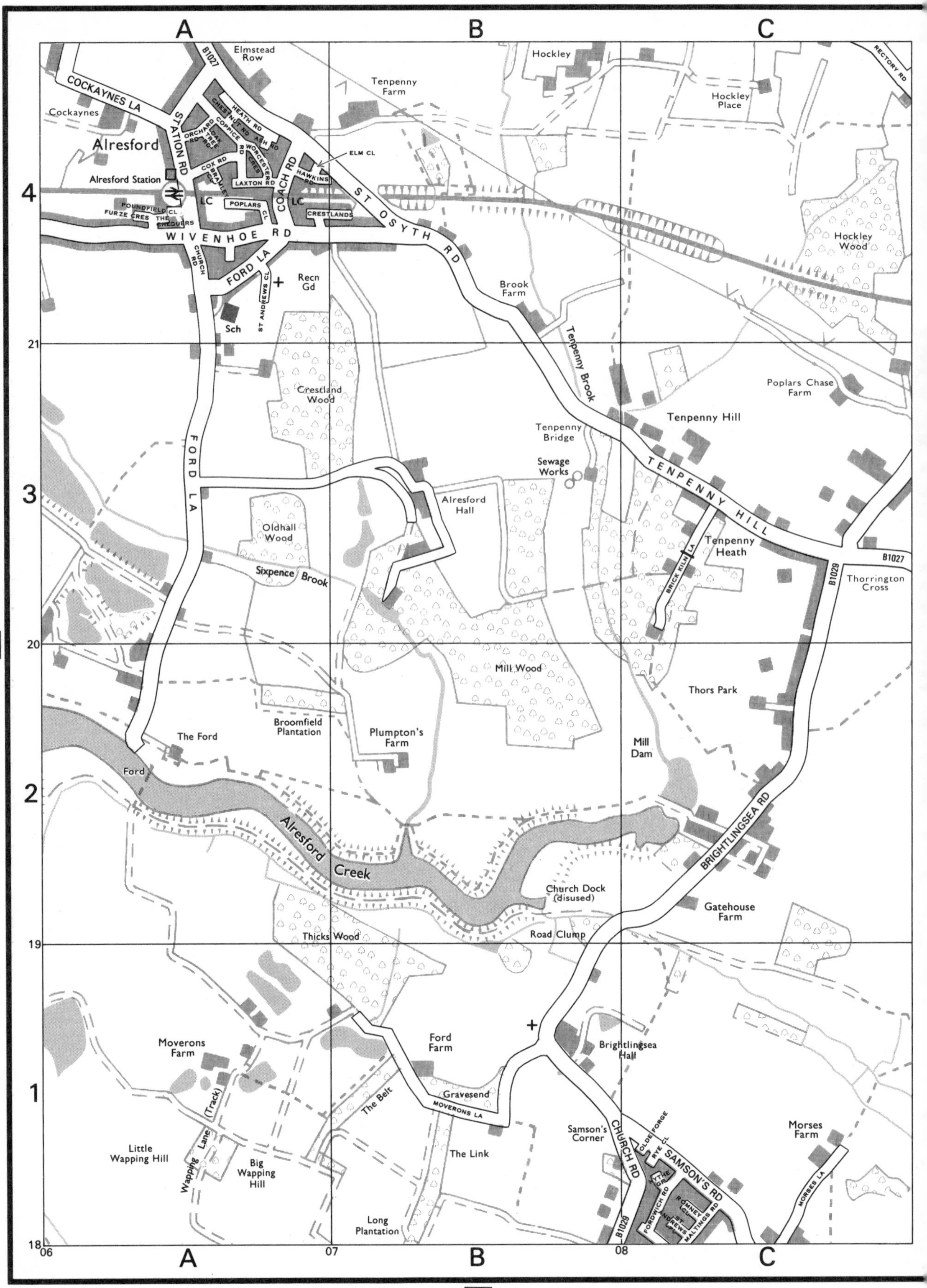
A
B
C
Elmstead Row
Hockley
Tenpenny Farm
Hockley Place
RECTORY RD
B1027
COCKAYNES LA
Cockaynes
Alresford
STATION RD
HEATH RD
CHESTNUT RD
ASH RD
ORCHARD RD
COPPICE RD
OAK TREE RD
WORCESTER CRES
ELM CL
HAWKINS
COACH RD
COX RD
BRAMLEY CL
LAXTON RD
Alresford Station
LC
POPLARS
CL
CRESTLANDS
ST OSYTH RD
POUNDFIELD CL
FURZE CRES
THE CHEQUERS
WIVENHOE RD
CHURCH RD
FORD LA
ST ANDREWS CL
Recn Gd
Sch
Hockley Wood
Brook Farm
Tenpenny Brook
Poplars Chase Farm
Crestland Wood
Tenpenny Hill
Tenpenny Bridge
Sewage Works
TENPENNY HILL
Alresford Hall
Oldhall Wood
Tenpenny Heath
BRICK KILN LA
B1027
B1029
Thorrington Cross
Sixpence Brook
Mill Wood
Thors Park
Broomfield Plantation
Plumpton's Farm
The Ford
Mill Dam
Ford
BRIGHTLINGSEA RD
Alresford Creek
Church Dock (disused)
Gatehouse Farm
Thicks Wood
Road Clump
Ford Farm
Moverons Farm
Brightlingsea Hall
(Track)
The Belt
Gravesend
MOVERONS LA
Samson's Corner
CHURCH RD
OLDE FORGE
RYE CL
SAMSON'S RD
Morses Farm
Little Wapping Hill
Wapping Lane
Big Wapping Hill
The Link
MORSES LA
FORDWICH RD
ROMNEY CL
ST ANDREWS CL
MALTINGS RD
Long Plantation
B1029
4
3
2
1
21
20
19
18
06
07
08

87

106

71

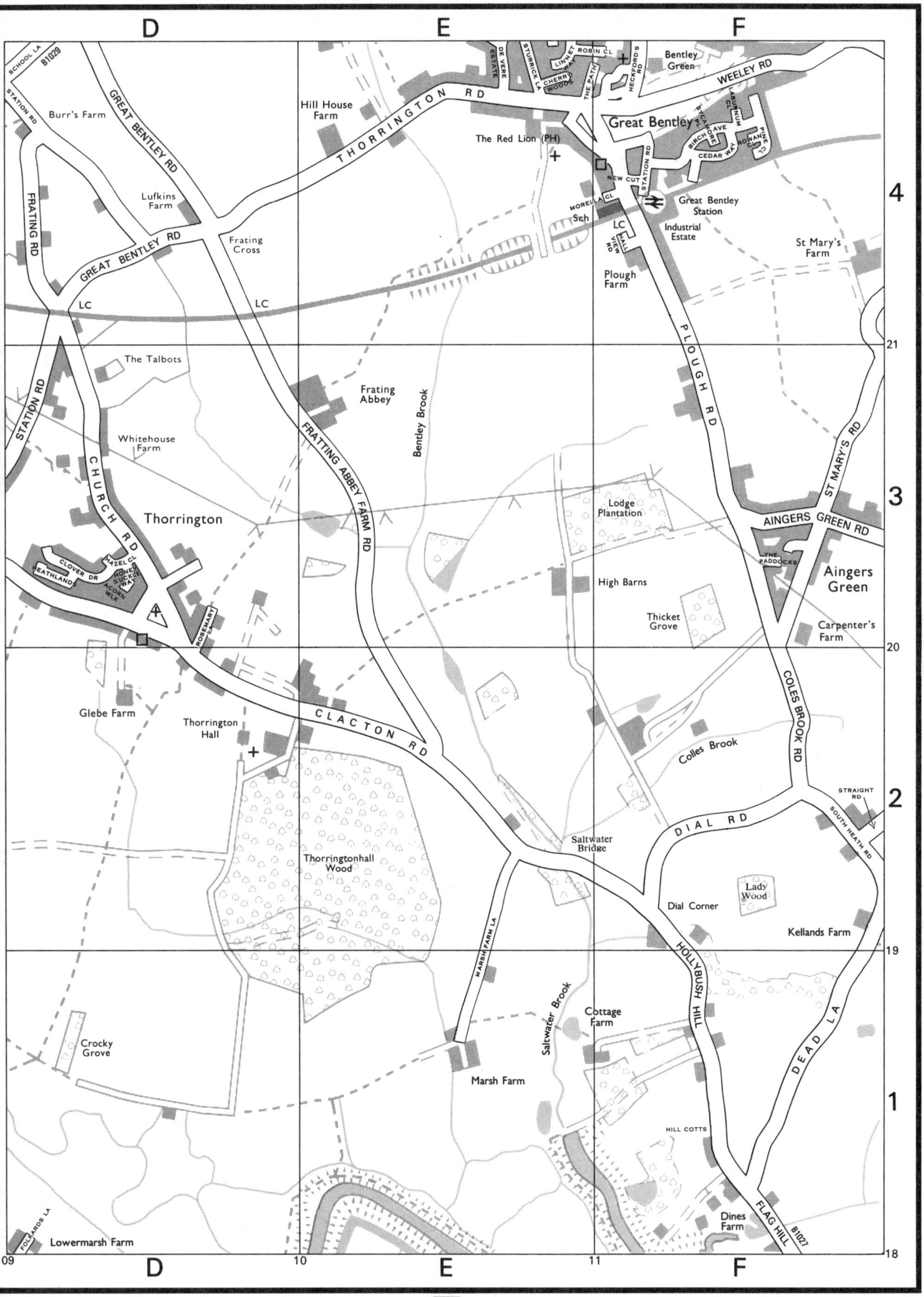
D
E
F
4
3
2
1
21
20
19
18
09
10
11
SCHOOL LA
B1029
STATION RD
Burr's Farm
GREAT BENTLEY RD
FRATING RD
Lufkins Farm
GREAT BENTLEY RD
Frating Cross
LC
LC
Hill House Farm
THORRINGTON RD
DE VERE ESTATE
STURRICK LA
LINNET WAY
ROBIN CL
CHERRY WOODS
THE PATH
HECKFORD'S RD
Bentley Green
WEELEY RD
Great Bentley
SYCAMORE PL
LABURNUM CL
BIRCH AVE
CEDAR WAY
ROWAN CL
PINE CL
The Red Lion (PH)
NEW CUT
STATION RD
MORELLA CL
Sch
LC
HALL VIEW RD
Great Bentley Station
Industrial Estate
St Mary's Farm
Plough Farm
PLOUGH RD
The Talbots
STATION RD
Frating Abbey
Bentley Brook
Whitehouse Farm
CHURCH RD
FRATTING ABBEY FARM RD
ST MARY'S RD
Thorrington
Lodge Plantation
AINGERS GREEN RD
CLOVER DR
HAZEL CL
HONEYSUCKLE WAY
HEATHLANDS
ACORN WLK
THE PADDOCKS
Aingers Green
High Barns
ROSEMARY LA
Thicket Grove
Carpenter's Farm
Glebe Farm
Thorrington Hall
CLACTON RD
COLES BROOK RD
Colles Brook
STRAIGHT RD
SOUTH HEATH RD
DIAL RD
Saltwater Bridge
Thorringtonhall Wood
Lady Wood
Dial Corner
Kellands Farm
MARSH FARM LA
HOLLYBUSH HILL
Saltwater Brook
Cottage Farm
DEAD LA
Crocky Grove
Marsh Farm
HILL COTTS
FOLKARDS LA
Lowermarsh Farm
Dines Farm
FLAG HILL
B1027

90

107

72

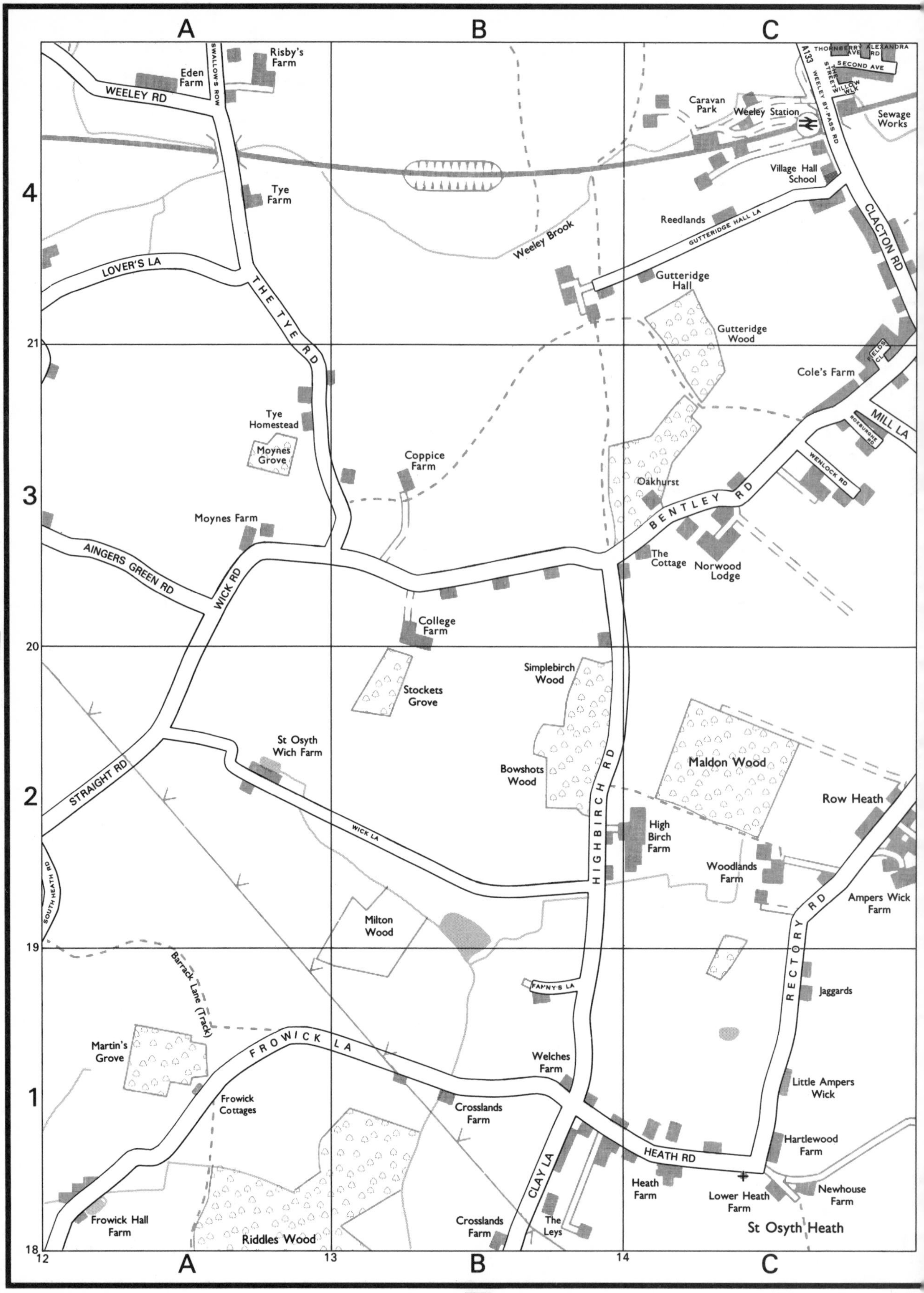
A
B
C
4
3
2
1
21
20
19
18
12
13
14
Eden Farm
Risby's Farm
SWALLOW'S ROW
WEELEY RD
Tye Farm
LOVER'S LA
THE TYE RD
Tye Homestead
Moynes Grove
Moynes Farm
AINGERS GREEN RD
WICK RD
STRAIGHT RD
SOUTH HEATH RD
St Osyth Wich Farm
WICK LA
Coppice Farm
College Farm
Stockets Grove
Milton Wood
Barrack Lane (Track)
Martin's Grove
FROWICK LA
Frowick Cottages
Frowick Hall Farm
Riddles Wood
Crosslands Farm
Crosslands Farm
CLAY LA
The Leys
Welches Farm
FANNY'S LA
HIGHBIRCH RD
Simplebirch Wood
Bowshots Wood
Weeley Brook
Caravan Park
Weeley Station
A133
WEELEY BY-PASS RD
THE STREET
WILLOW WLK
THORNBERRY AVE
ALEXANDRA RD
SECOND AVE
Sewage Works
Village Hall
School
Reedlands
GUTTERIDGE HALL LA
Gutteridge Hall
Gutteridge Wood
CLACTON RD
FIELDS CL
Cole's Farm
MILL LA
ROXBURGHE RD
WENLOCK RD
Oakhurst
BENTLEY RD
The Cottage
Norwood Lodge
Maldon Wood
Row Heath
High Birch Farm
Woodlands Farm
Ampers Wick Farm
RECTORY RD
Jaggards
Little Ampers Wick
Hartlewood Farm
HEATH RD
Heath Farm
Lower Heath Farm
Newhouse Farm
St Osyth Heath

89

108

73

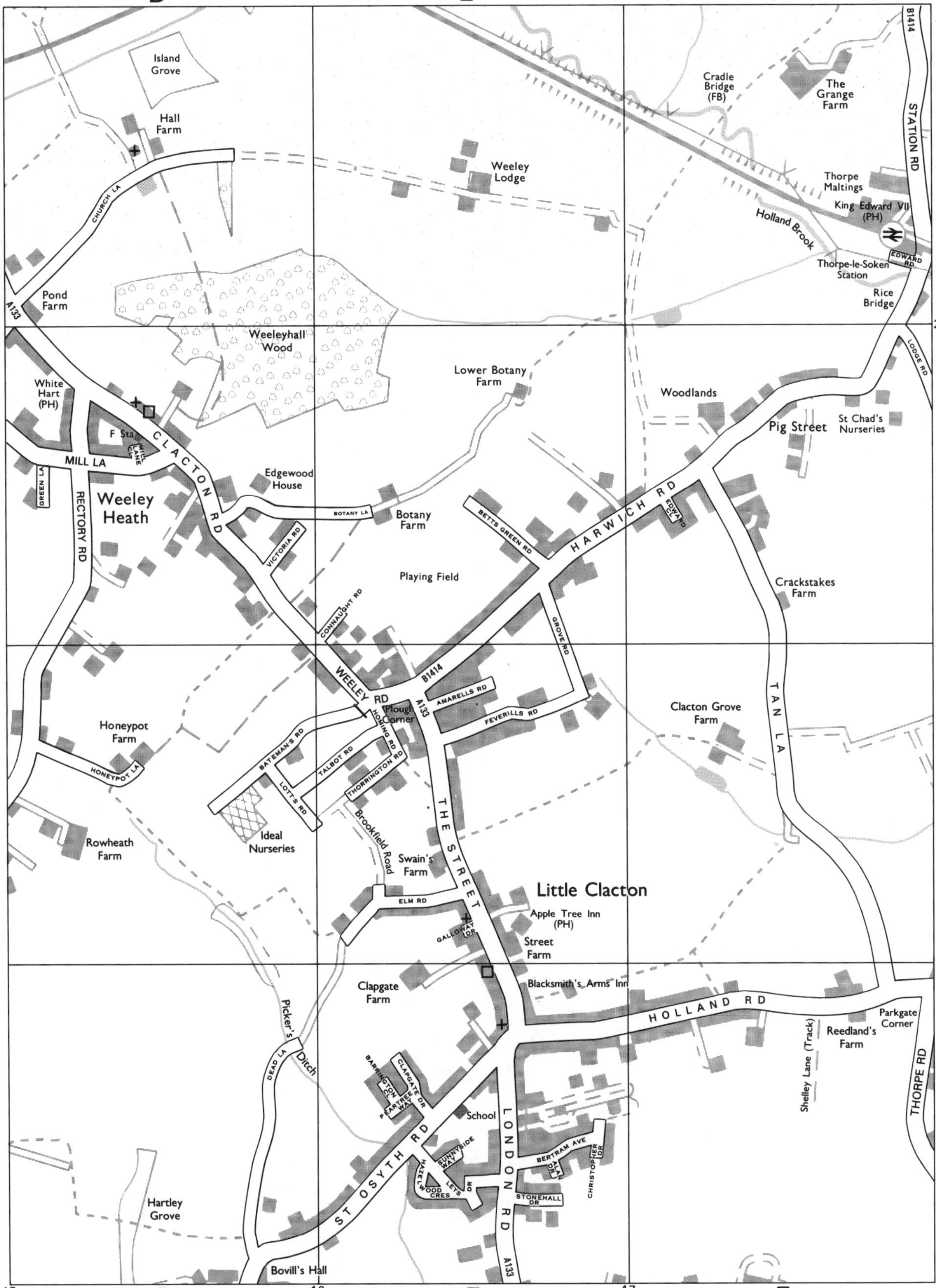
D
E
F
Island Grove
Hall Farm
Church La
Pond Farm
A133
Weeleyhall Wood
Weeley Lodge
Cradle Bridge (FB)
The Grange Farm
Station Rd
B1414
Thorpe Maltings
King Edward VII (PH)
Holland Brook
Thorpe-le-Soken Station
Edward Rd
Rice Bridge
Lodge Rd
Lower Botany Farm
Woodlands
White Hart (PH)
F Sta
Mill Lane
Clacton Rd
Pig Street
St Chad's Nurseries
Mill La
Green La
Edgewood House
Weeley Heath
Rectory Rd
Botany La
Botany Farm
Victoria Rd
Betts Green Rd
Harwich Rd
Edward Cl
Playing Field
Crackstakes Farm
Connaught Rd
Grove Rd
Weeley Rd
B1414
Amarells Rd
Plough Corner
Feverills Rd
Honeypot Farm
Honeypot La
Bateman's Rd
Talbot Rd
Thorrington Rd
Lott's Rd
Clacton Grove Farm
Tan La
Ideal Nurseries
Brookfield Road
The Street
Rowheath Farm
Swain's Farm
Little Clacton
Elm Rd
Apple Tree Inn (PH)
Galloway Dr
Street Farm
Clapgate Farm
Blacksmith's Arms Inn
Holland Rd
Parkgate Corner
Reedland's Farm
Picker's Ditch
Dead La
Barrington Cl
Clapgate Dr
Peartree Way
School
Shelley Lane (Track)
Thorpe Rd
St Osyth Rd
Sunnyside Way
Bertram Ave
Alan Dr
Christopher Dr
Hazelwood Cres
Leys Dr
London Rd
Stonehall Dr
Hartley Grove
Bovill's Hall
A133
4
3
2
1
21
20
19
18
15
16
17
D
E
F

92

109

74

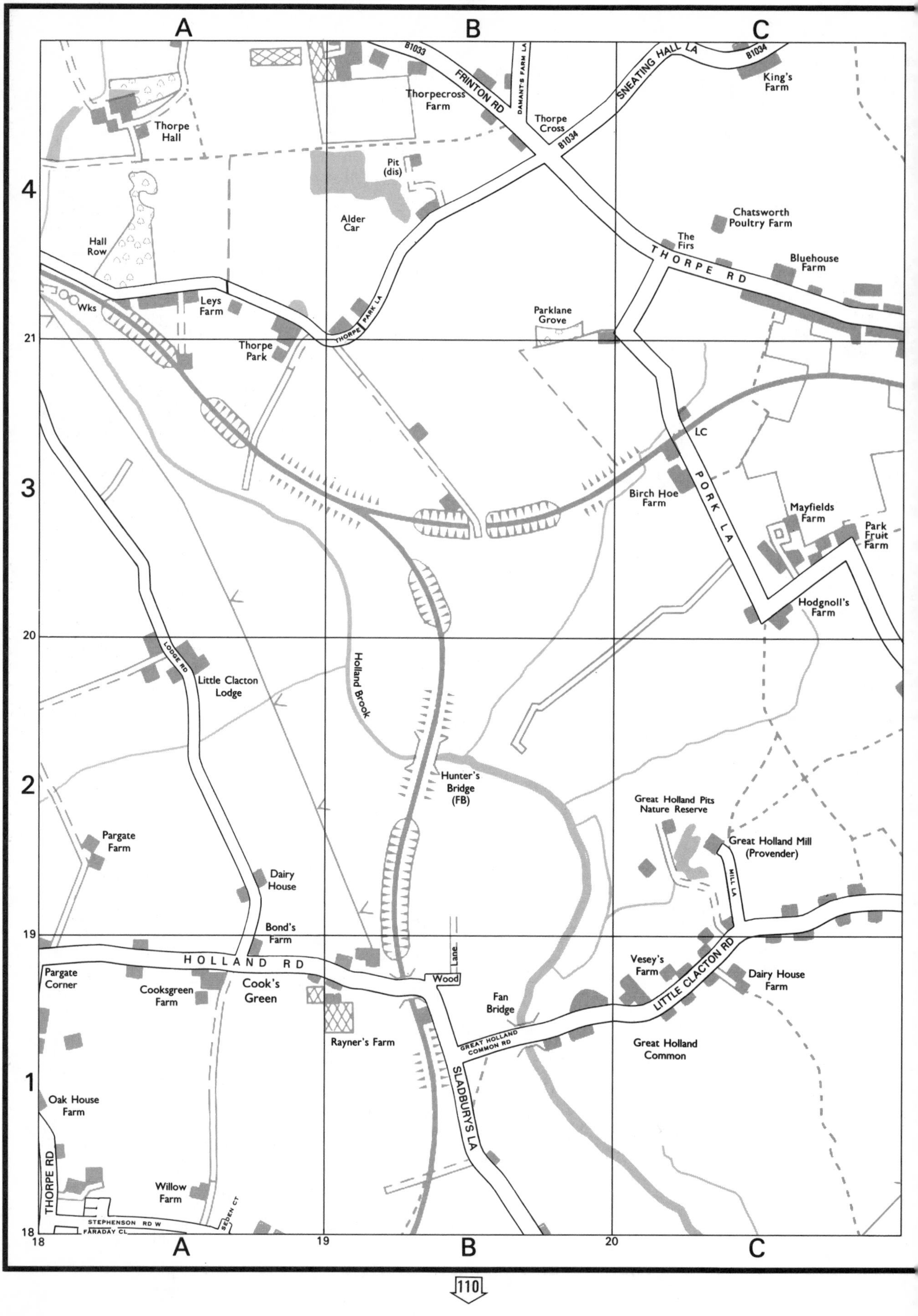
A
B
C
4
3
2
1
21
20
19
18
Thorpe Hall
Hall Row
Wks
Leys Farm
Thorpe Park
Thorpecross Farm
FRINTON RD
B1033
DAMANT'S FARM LA
Thorpe Cross
B1034
SNEATING HALL LA
King's Farm
Pit (dis)
Alder Car
THORPE PARK LA
Chatsworth Poultry Farm
The Firs
THORPE RD
Bluehouse Farm
Parklane Grove
LC
Birch Hoe Farm
PORK LA
Mayfields Farm
Park Fruit Farm
Hodgnoll's Farm
LODGE RD
Little Clacton Lodge
Holland Brook
Hunter's Bridge (FB)
Great Holland Pits Nature Reserve
Great Holland Mill (Provender)
MILL LA
Pargate Farm
Dairy House
Bond's Farm
HOLLAND RD
Lane
Wood
Pargate Corner
Cooksgreen Farm
Cook's Green
Rayner's Farm
Fan Bridge
GREAT HOLLAND COMMON RD
Vesey's Farm
LITTLE CLACTON RD
Dairy House Farm
Great Holland Common
SLADBURYS LA
Oak House Farm
THORPE RD
Willow Farm
SEDEN CT
STEPHENSON RD W
FARADAY CL

91

110

75

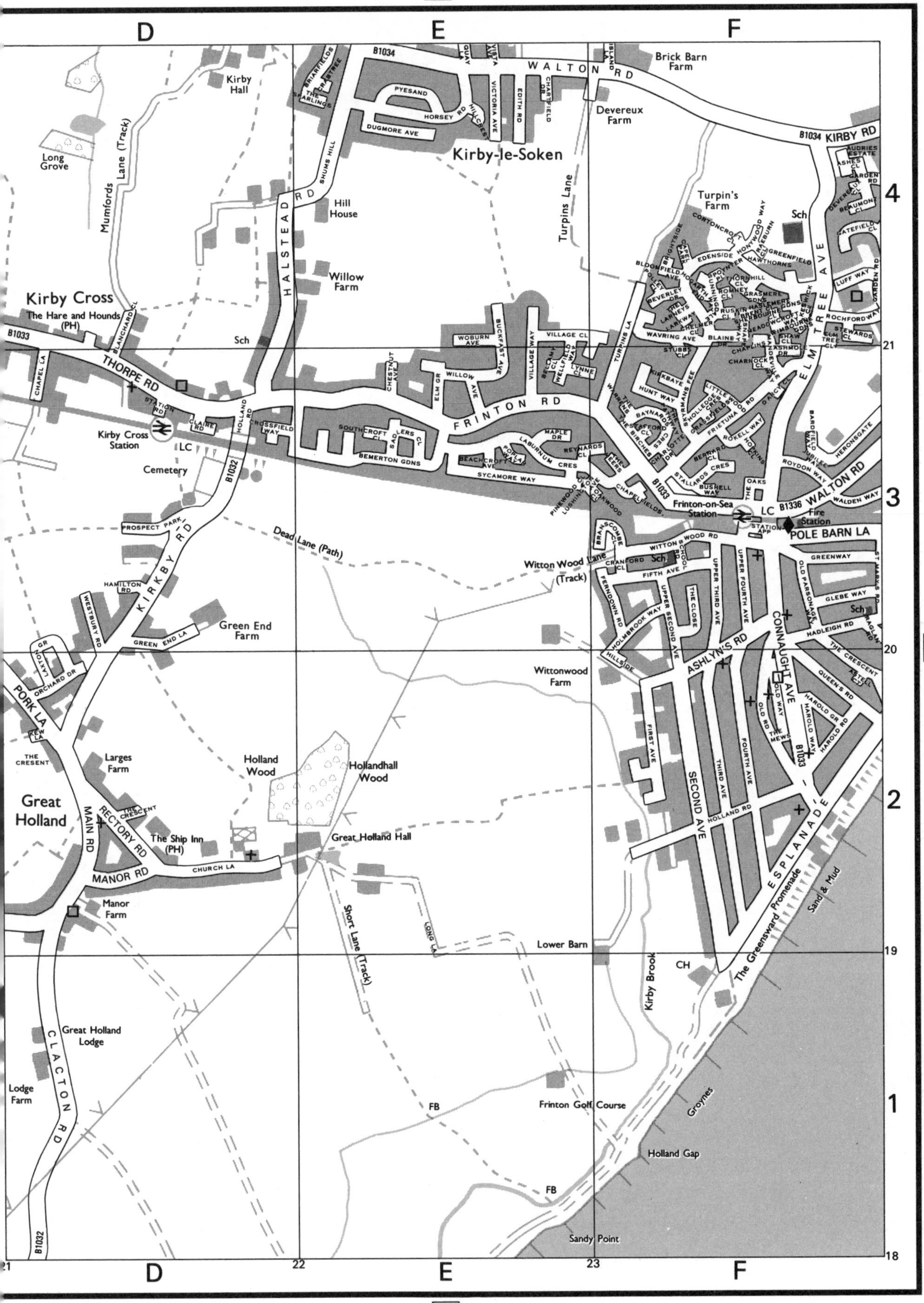
D
E
F
Kirby-le-Soken
Kirby Cross
Great Holland
Brick Barn Farm
Devereux Farm
Kirby Hall
Long Grove
Mumfords Lane (Track)
Hill House
Willow Farm
Turpins Lane
Turpin's Farm
The Hare and Hounds (PH)
Kirby Cross Station
Cemetery
Frinton-on-Sea Station
Fire Station
Dead Lane (Path)
Witton Wood Lane (Track)
Green End Farm
Wittonwood Farm
Larges Farm
Holland Wood
Hollandhall Wood
Great Holland Hall
The Ship Inn (PH)
Manor Farm
Short Lane (Track)
Lower Barn
Kirby Brook
Great Holland Lodge
Lodge Farm
Frinton Golf Course
Holland Gap
Sandy Point
Groynes
Sand & Mud
The Greensward Promenade
WALTON RD
KIRBY RD
THORPE RD
HALSTEAD RD
FRINTON RD
KIRBY RD
POLE BARN LA
WALTON RD
ELM TREE AVE
CONNAUGHT AVE
ASHLYN'S RD
SECOND AVE
ESPLANADE
MAIN RD
CLACTON RD
MANOR RD
RECTORY RD
CHURCH LA
PORK LA
B1032
B1033
B1034
B1336
4
3
2
1
21
20
19
18
22
23

94

111

76

93

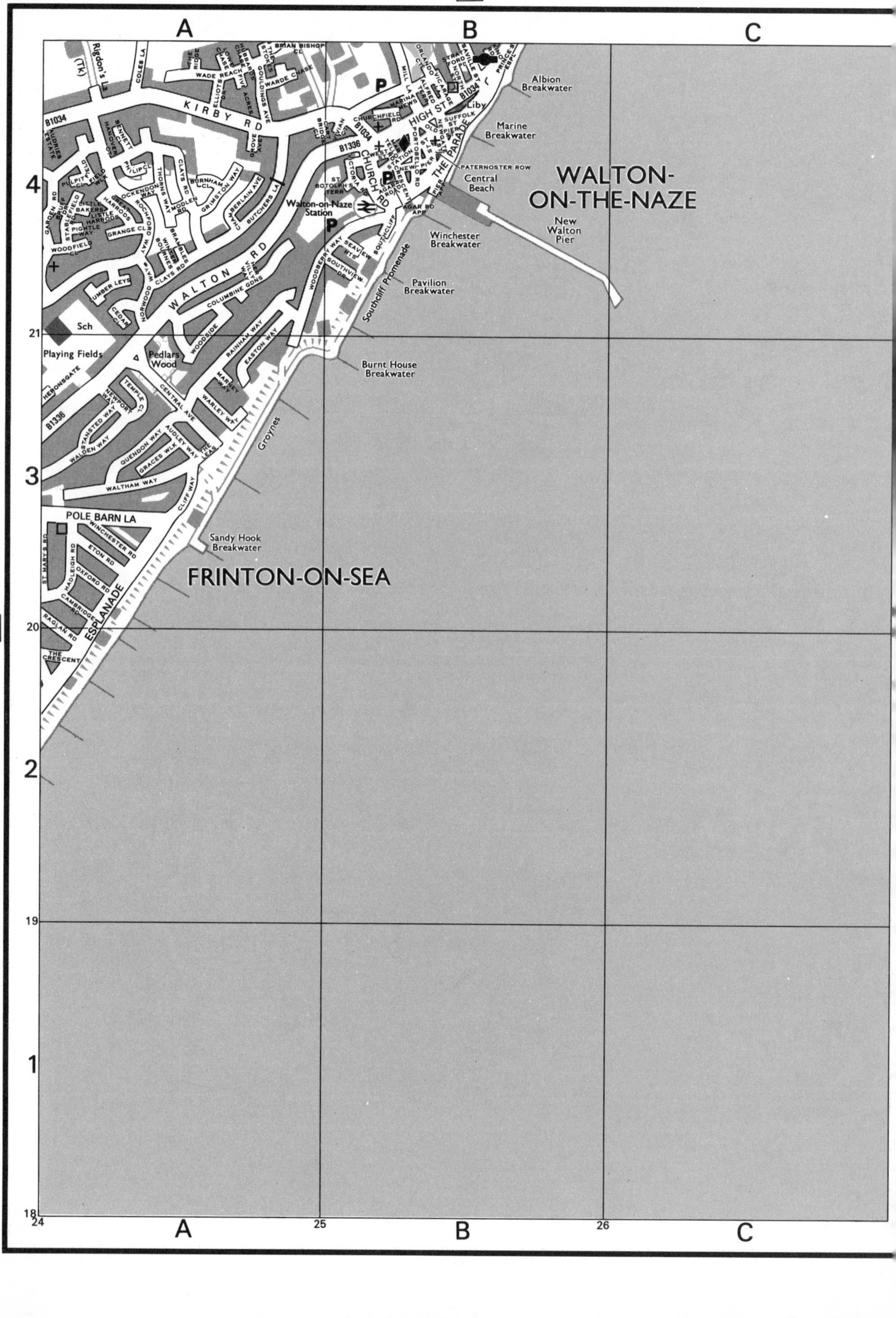

A
B
C
4
3
2
1
21
20
19
18
24
25
26
WALTON-ON-THE-NAZE
FRINTON-ON-SEA
KIRBY RD
WALTON RD
HIGH ST
THE PARADE
CHURCH RD
B1034
B1336
Walton-on-Naze Station
Albion Breakwater
Marine Breakwater
PATERNOSTER ROW
Central Beach
New Walton Pier
Winchester Breakwater
Pavilion Breakwater
Southcliff Promenade
Burnt House Breakwater
Groynes
Sandy Hook Breakwater
Liby
Sch
Playing Fields
Pedlars Wood
POLE BARN LA
ESPLANADE
CENTRAL AVE
WALTHAM WAY
CLIFF WAY
RAINHAM WAY
EASTON WAY
WOODSIDE
COLUMBINE GDNS
HERONSGATE
WALDEN WAY
QUENDON WAY
GRACES WLK
AUDLEY WAY
WARLEY WAY
WINCHESTER RD
ETON RD
OXFORD RD
HADLEIGH RD
CAMBRIDGE RD
RAGLAN RD
ST MARY'S RD
THE CRESCENT
Rigdon's La
COLES LA
WADE REACH
WARDE CHASE
BRIAN BISHOP CL
GOULDINGS AVE
CLAYS RD
BURNHAM CL
GRIMSTON WAY
CHAMBERLAIN AVE
BUTCHERS LA
ROCKFORD WAY
GRANGE CL
WOODFIELD CL
NORWOOD WAY
CEDAR CL
LUMBER LEYS
SOUTHCLIFF
SEAVIEW HTS
SOUTHVIEW DR
WOODBERRY WAY
AGAR RD
MILL LA
CHURCHFIELD RD

77

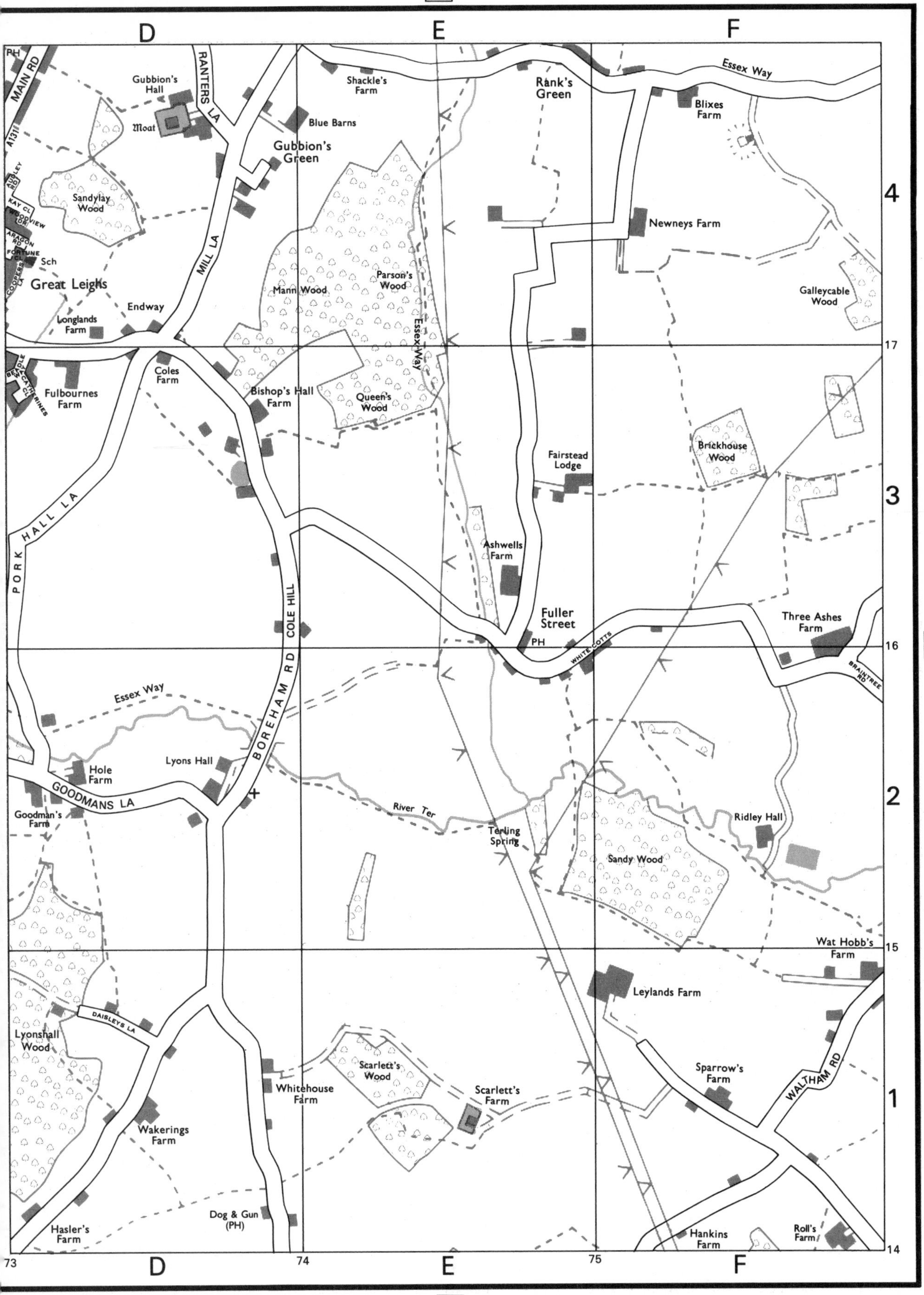

D
E
F
PH
MAIN RD
A131
RANTERS LA
Gubbion's Hall
Moat
Sandylay Wood
Great Leighs
Sch
KAY CL
WOODVIEW
ARAGON RD
FORTUNE CL
Endway
Longlands Farm
MILL LA
Gubbion's Green
Shackle's Farm
Blue Barns
Mann Wood
Parson's Wood
Essex Way
Queen's Wood
Bishop's Hall Farm
Coles Farm
Fulbournes Farm
Rank's Green
Essex Way
Blixes Farm
Newneys Farm
Galleycable Wood
Fairstead Lodge
Brickhouse Wood
Ashwells Farm
Fuller Street
PH
WHITE COTTS
Three Ashes Farm
BRAINTREE RD
PORK HALL LA
COLE HILL
BOREHAM RD
Essex Way
Lyons Hall
Hole Farm
GOODMANS LA
Goodman's Farm
River Ter
Terling Spring
Sandy Wood
Ridley Hall
Wat Hobb's Farm
Leylands Farm
Sparrow's Farm
WALTHAM RD
DAISLEYS LA
Lyonshall Wood
Wakerings Farm
Whitehouse Farm
Scarlett's Wood
Scarlett's Farm
Dog & Gun (PH)
Hasler's Farm
Hankins Farm
Roll's Farm
4
3
2
1
17
16
15
14
73
74
75

96

112

78

95

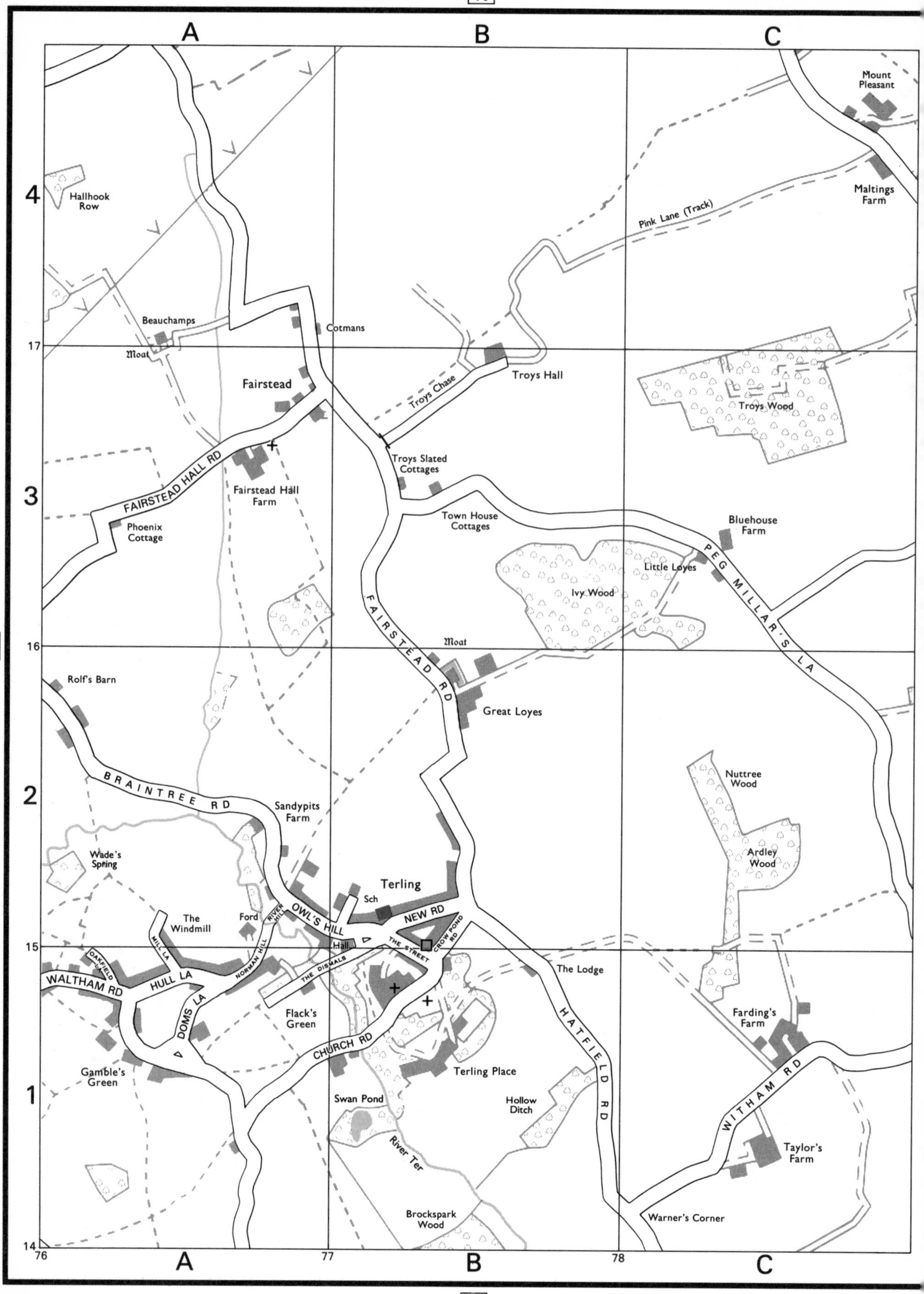
A
B
C
4
3
2
1
17
16
15
14
76
77
78
Mount Pleasant
Maltings Farm
Hallhook Row
Pink Lane (Track)
Beauchamps
Cotmans
Moat
Fairstead
Troys Chase
Troys Hall
Troys Wood
Troys Slated Cottages
FAIRSTEAD HALL RD
Fairstead Hall Farm
Phoenix Cottage
Town House Cottages
Bluehouse Farm
Little Loyes
Ivy Wood
PEG MILLAR'S LA
FAIRSTEAD RD
Moat
Rolf's Barn
Great Loyes
BRAINTREE RD
Sandypits Farm
Nuttree Wood
Ardley Wood
Wade's Spring
Terling
Sch
NEW RD
OWL'S HILL
RIVER HILL
Ford
The Windmill
MILL LA
Hall
THE STREET
CROW POND RD
THE DISMALS
NORMAN HILL
OAKFIELD
WALTHAM RD
HULL LA
DOMS LA
Flack's Green
The Lodge
CHURCH RD
Terling Place
HATFIELD RD
Farding's Farm
WITHAM RD
Gamble's Green
Swan Pond
Hollow Ditch
River Ter
Taylor's Farm
Brockspark Wood
Warner's Corner

113

79

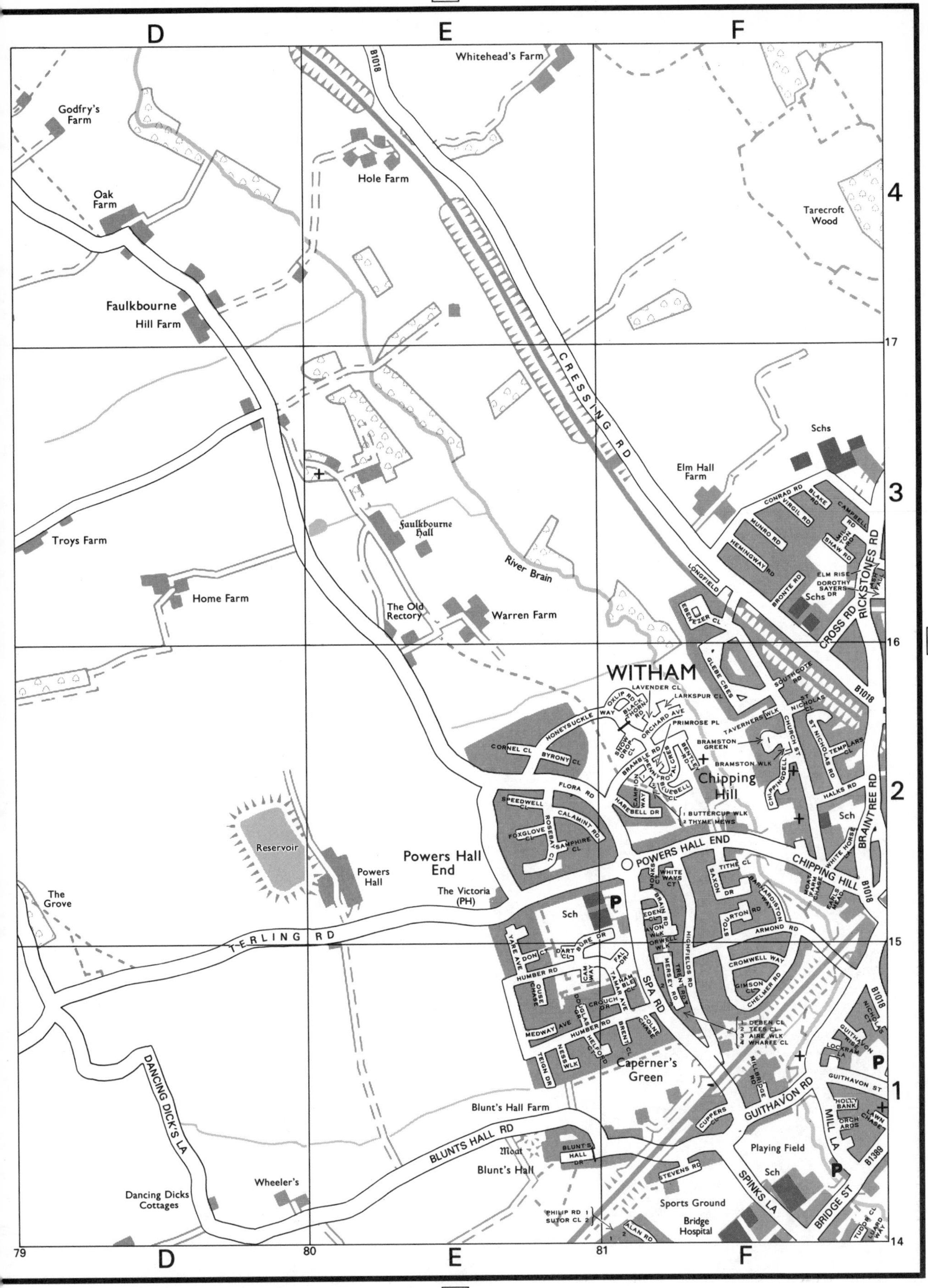

D
E
F
Whitehead's Farm
B1018
Godfry's Farm
Hole Farm
Oak Farm
4
Tarecroft Wood
Faulkbourne
Hill Farm
17
CRESSING RD
Schs
Elm Hall Farm
3
CONRAD RD
VIRGIL RD
BLAKE RD
CAMPBELL
MUNRO RD
SHAW RD
HEMINGWAY RD
RICKSTONES RD
LONGFIELD
ELM RISE
DOROTHY SAYERS DR
Schs
BRONTE RD
CROSS RD
Troys Farm
Faulkbourne Hall
River Brain
Home Farm
The Old Rectory
Warren Farm
EBENEZER CL
16
SOUTHCOTE RD
B1018
WITHAM
LAVENDER CL
LARKSPUR CL
GLEBE CRES
OXLIP RD
HONEYSUCKLE WAY
ORCHARD AVE
PRIMROSE PL
TAVERNERS WLK
ST NICHOLAS CL
CORNEL CL
BYRONY CL
SNOWDROP CL
BRAMBLE RD
BENTLEY RD
BRAMSTON GREEN
BRAMSTON WLK
ST NICHOLAS RD
TEMPLARS CL
CHURCH ST
Chipping Hill
CHIPPINGDELL
BRAINTREE RD
2
FLORA RD
SPEEDWELL CL
CALAMINT RD
HAREBELL DR
1 BUTTERCUP WLK
2 THYME MEWS
HALKS RD
Sch
FOXGLOVE CL
ROSEBAY CL
SAMPHIRE CL
Reservoir
Powers Hall End
POWERS HALL END
WHITE WAYS CT
TITHE CL
SAXON DR
WHITE HORSE LA
CHIPPING HILL
B1018
Powers Hall
The Victoria (PH)
The Grove
Sch
P
BRAIN RD
EDEN CL
AVON WLK
ORWELL WLK
HIGHFIELDS RD
STOURTON RD
ARMOND RD
BARNARDISTON WAY
MOAT FARM CHASE
TERLING RD
15
YARE AVE
DON CT
DART CL
BURE DR
HUMBER RD
TAMAR AVE
SPA RD
MERSEY RD
TRENT RD
CROMWELL WAY
GIMSON CL
CHELMER RD
OUSE CHASE
CROUCH DR
DOUGLAS DR
B1018
NICHOLAS CT
MEDWAY AVE
HUMBER RD
BRENT CL
COLNE CHASE
1 DEBEN CL
2 TEES CL
3 AIRE WLK
4 WHARFE CL
GUITHAVON RISE
LOCKRAM LA
P
DANCING DICK'S LA
TEIGN DR
NESS WLK
HELFORD CT
Caperner's Green
MILLBRIDGE RD
GUITHAVON ST
1
HOLLY BANK
ORCHARDS
LAWN CHASE
Blunt's Hall Farm
CUPPERS CL
GUITHAVON RD
MILL LA
BLUNTS HALL RD
Moat
BLUNT'S HALL DR
Playing Field
B1389
Blunt's Hall
STEVENS RD
SPINKS LA
Sch
P
Wheeler's
Sports Ground
BRIDGE ST
Dancing Dicks Cottages
PHILIP RD 1
SUTOR CL 2
ALAN RD
Bridge Hospital
TUDOR CL
LUARD WAY
14
79
D
80
E
81
F

98

114

80

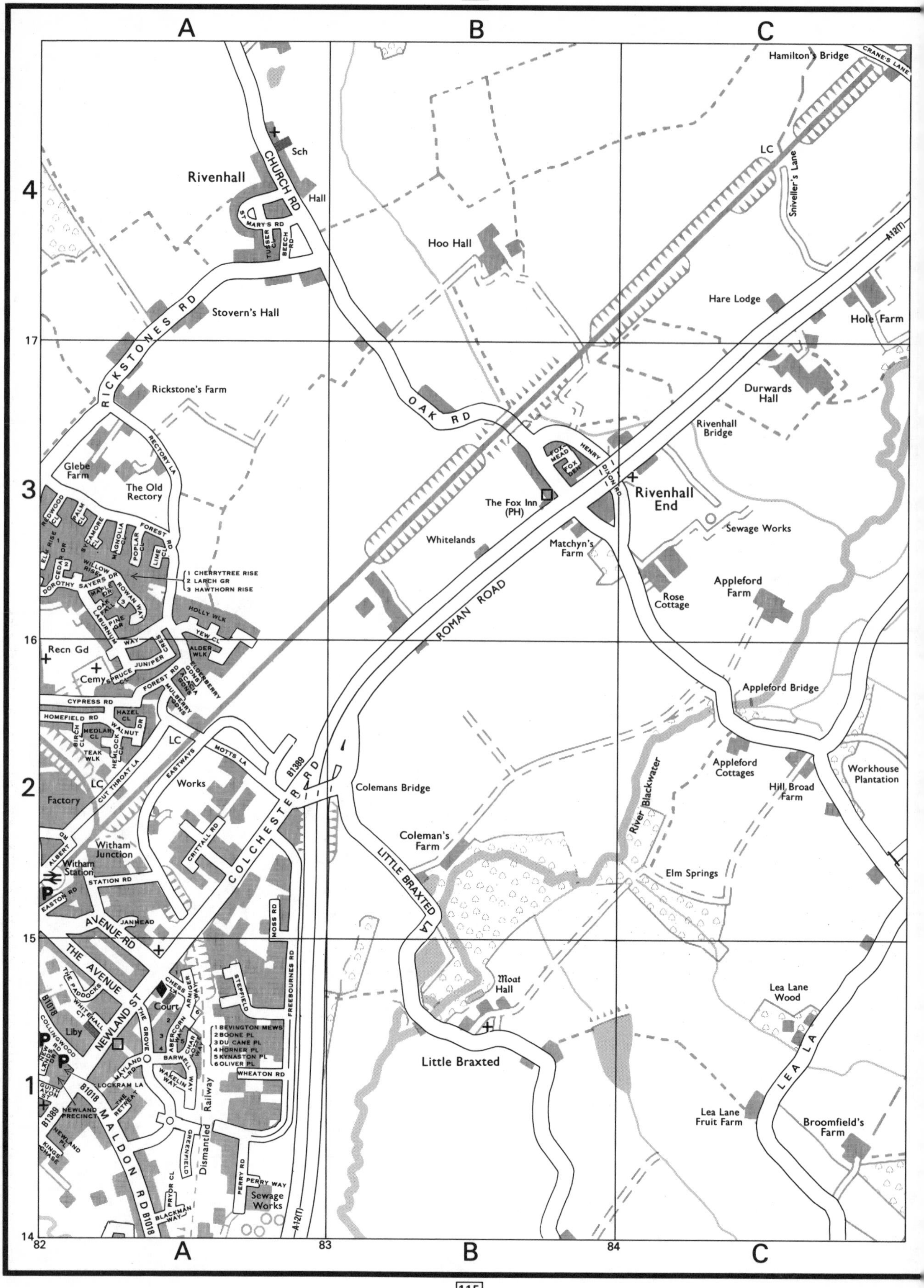
A
B
C
4
3
2
1
17
16
15
14
82
83
84
Hamilton's Bridge
CRANE'S LANE
Sch
CHURCH RD
Rivenhall
Hall
ST MARY'S RD
TUSSER CL
BEECH RD
LC
Sniveller's Lane
Hoo Hall
A12(T)
Hare Lodge
Hole Farm
Stovern's Hall
RICKSTONES RD
Rickstone's Farm
Durwards Hall
OAK RD
Rivenhall Bridge
RECTORY LA
Glebe Farm
The Old Rectory
FOX MEAD
FOX DEN
HENRY DIXON RD
Rivenhall End
The Fox Inn (PH)
Whitelands
Matchyn's Farm
Sewage Works
REDWOOD CL
ELM RISE
PALM CL
SYCAMORE CL
MAGNOLIA CL
POPLAR CL
LIME CL
FOREST RD
CEDAR DR
WILLOW RISE
DOROTHY SAYERS DR
ROWAN WAY
MAPLE DR
OAK CL
PINE DR
LABURNUM WAY
1 CHERRYTREE RISE
2 LARCH GR
3 HAWTHORN RISE
HOLLY WLK
YEW CL
ALDER WLK
JUNIPER
Rose Cottage
Appleford Farm
ROMAN ROAD
Recn Gd
Cemy
SPRUCE CL
ELDERBERRY GDNS
ACACIA GDNS
MULBERRY GDNS
CYPRESS RD
HOMEFIELD RD
HAZEL CL
MEDLAR CL
WALNUT DR
BIRCH CL
HEMLOCK CL
TEAK WLK
LC
CUT THROAT LA
Appleford Bridge
MOTTS LA
EASTWAYS
B1389
Works
Colemans Bridge
Appleford Cottages
Workhouse Plantation
Hill Broad Farm
River Blackwater
Factory
ALBERT RD
Witham Junction
CRITTALL RD
COLCHESTER RD
Coleman's Farm
Witham Station
STATION RD
EASTON RD
LITTLE BRAXTED LA
Elm Springs
JANMEAD
AVENUE RD
MOSS RD
THE AVENUE
FREEBOURNES RD
THE PADDOCKS
WHITEHALL CT
B1018
COLLINGWOOD RD
NEWLAND ST
CHESS LA
Court
ARMIGER WAY
STEPFIELD
THE GROVE
ABERCORN WAY
CHAR WAY
1 BEVINGTON MEWS
2 BOONE PL
3 DU CANE PL
4 HORNER PL
5 KYNASTON PL
6 OLIVER PL
Moat Hall
Lea Lane Wood
Liby
BARWELL WAY
WHEATON RD
Little Braxted
WAYLAND RD
WAKELIN WAY
LOCKRAM LA
THE RETREAT
Railway
Dismantled
MALDON RD
NEWLAND PRECINCT
NEWLAND PL
KINGS CHASE
GREENFIELD
LEA LA
Lea Lane Fruit Farm
Broomfield's Farm
PRYOR CL
PERRY RD
PERRY WAY
Sewage Works
BLACKMAN WAY
A12(T)

97

115

81

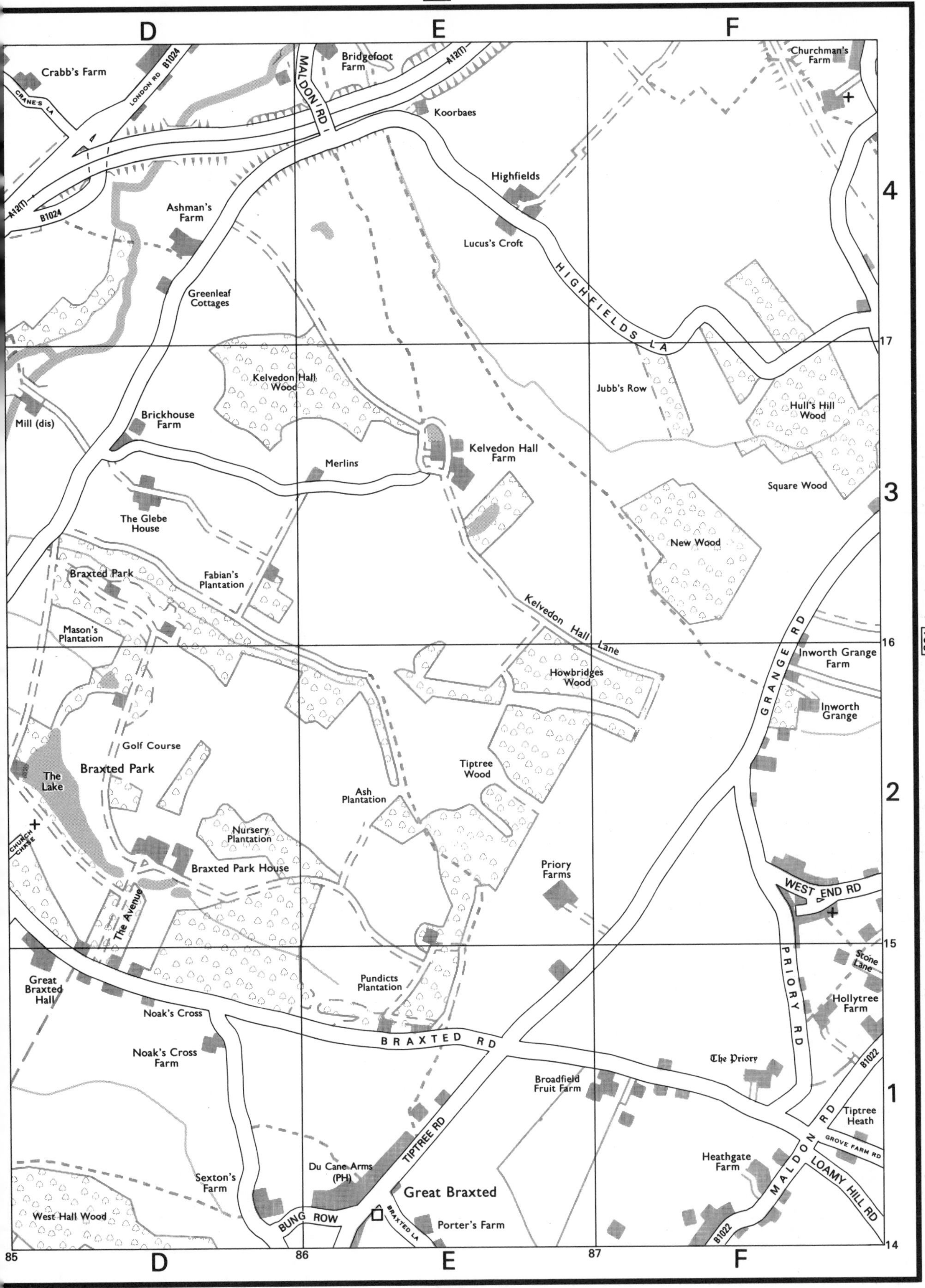
D
E
F
Crabb's Farm
CRANE'S LA
LONDON RD B1024
A12(T)
B1024
MALDON RD
Bridgefoot Farm
Koorbaes
Churchman's Farm
Ashman's Farm
Highfields
Lucus's Croft
HIGHFIELDS LA
Greenleaf Cottages
Kelvedon Hall Wood
Jubb's Row
Hull's Hill Wood
Mill (dis)
Brickhouse Farm
Merlins
Kelvedon Hall Farm
Square Wood
The Glebe House
New Wood
Braxted Park
Fabian's Plantation
Kelvedon Hall Lane
Mason's Plantation
Howbridges Wood
GRANGE RD
Inworth Grange Farm
Inworth Grange
Golf Course
Braxted Park
The Lake
Tiptree Wood
Ash Plantation
CHURCH CHASE
Nursery Plantation
Braxted Park House
Priory Farms
WEST END RD
The Avenue
PRIORY RD
Stone Lane
Great Braxted Hall
Pundicts Plantation
Hollytree Farm
Noak's Cross
BRAXTED RD
Noak's Cross Farm
The Priory
B1022
Broadfield Fruit Farm
Tiptree Heath
GROVE FARM RD
Heathgate Farm
MALDON RD
LOAMY HILL RD
Sexton's Farm
Du Cane Arms (PH)
TIPTREE RD
Great Braxted
West Hall Wood
BUNG ROW
BRAXTED LA
Porter's Farm
B1022
4
3
2
1
17
16
15
14
85
86
87
D
E
F

100

116

82

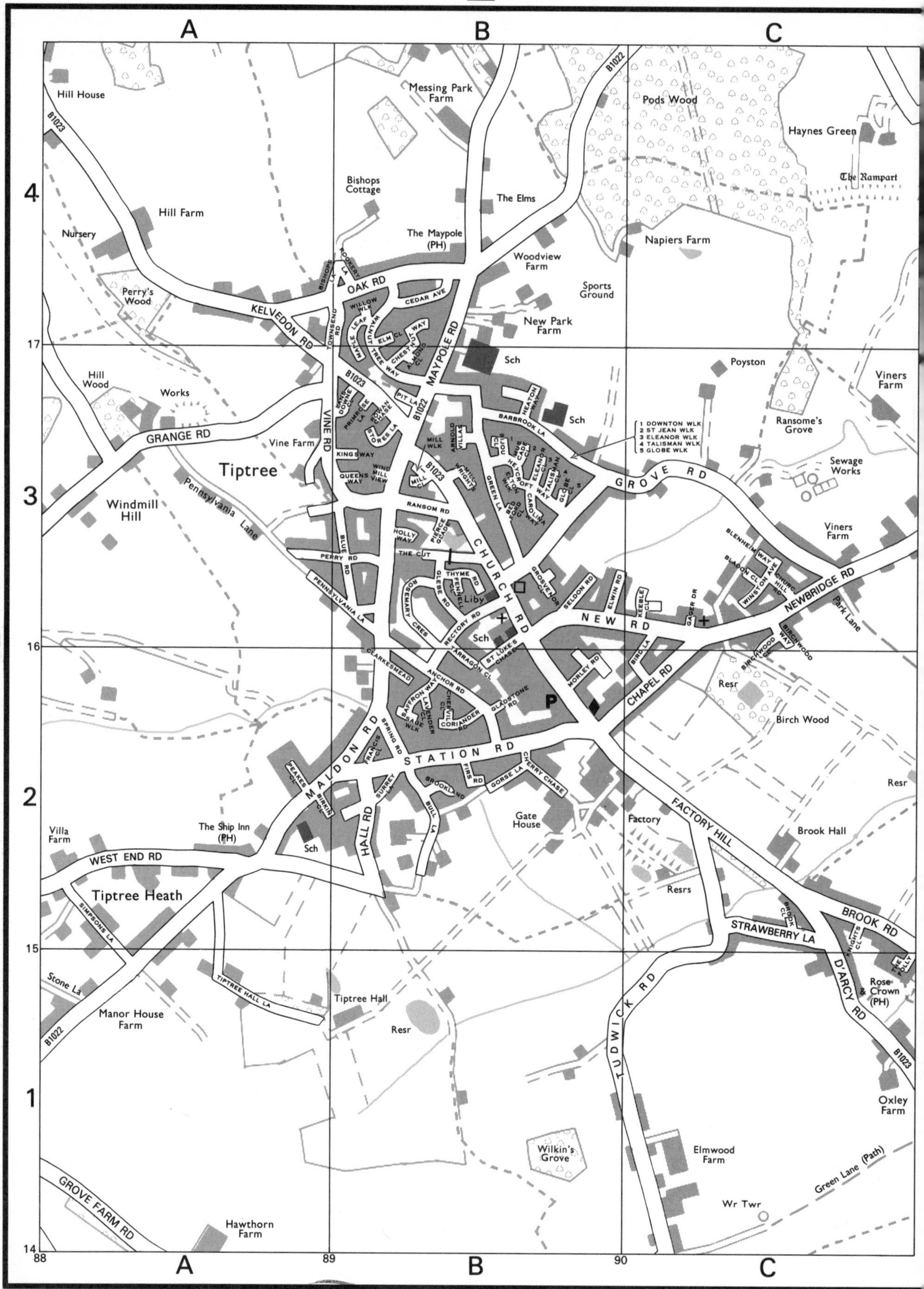
A
B
C
4
3
2
1
17
16
15
14
88
89
90
Hill House
B1023
Messing Park Farm
B1022
Pods Wood
Haynes Green
The Rampart
Bishops Cottage
Hill Farm
The Elms
Nursery
The Maypole (PH)
Napiers Farm
Woodview Farm
Sports Ground
Perry's Wood
OAK RD
CEDAR AVE
KELVEDON RD
New Park Farm
Sch
Poyston
Viners Farm
Hill Wood
Works
MAYPOLE RD
B1023
VINE RD
GRANGE RD
Vine Farm
Tiptree
Windmill Hill
Pennsylvania Lane
HEATON WAY
BARBROOK LA
1 DOWNTON WLK
2 ST JEAN WLK
3 ELEANOR WLK
4 TALISMAN WLK
5 GLOBE WLK
Ransome's Grove
Sewage Works
GROVE RD
KINGSWAY
QUEENS WAY
RANSOM RD
HOLLY WAY
THE CUT
PERRY RD
BLUE RD
CHURCH RD
GREEN LA
Viners Farm
BLENHEIM WAY
WINSTON AVE
NEWBRIDGE RD
Park Lane
PENNSYLVANIA LA
GROSVENOR
SELDON RD
ELWIN RD
KEEBLE CL
GAGER DR
NEW RD
Liby
RECTORY RD
ROSEMARY CRES
Sch
ST LUKE'S CHASE
TARRAGON CL
CLARKESMEAD
ANCHOR RD
MORLEY RD
BIRD LA
CHAPEL RD
BIRCHWOOD RD
Resr
Birch Wood
GLADSTONE RD
P
CORIANDER RD
MALDON RD
SPRING RD
FRANCIS CL
STATION RD
FIRS RD
GORSE LA
CHERRY CHASE
BROOKLAND
PEAKES CL
BIRKIN CL
HALL RD
SURREY LA
BULL LA
Gate House
Factory
FACTORY HILL
Resr
Brook Hall
Villa Farm
The Ship Inn (PH)
Sch
WEST END RD
Tiptree Heath
Resrs
SIMPSONS LA
STRAWBERRY LA
BROOK RD
KNIGHTS CL
D'ARCY RD
Stone La
TIPTREE HALL LA
Tiptree Hall
TUDWICK RD
Rose & Crown (PH)
Manor House Farm
Resr
B1022
B1023
Oxley Farm
Wilkin's Grove
Elmwood Farm
Green Lane (Path)
GROVE FARM RD
Wr Twr
Hawthorn Farm

99

117

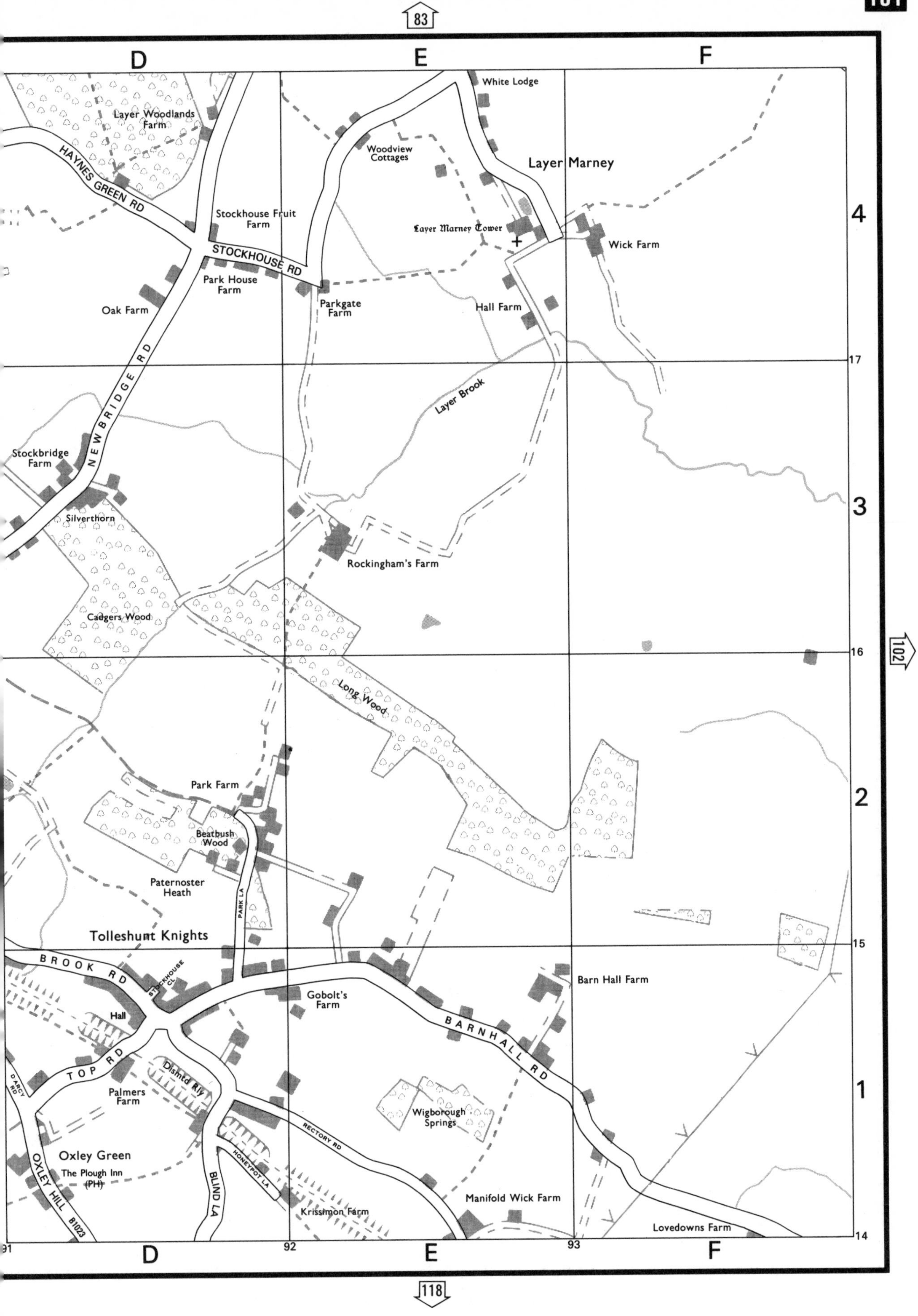
83
D
E
F
White Lodge
Layer Woodlands Farm
HAYNES GREEN RD
Woodview Cottages
Layer Marney
Stockhouse Fruit Farm
Layer Marney Tower
Wick Farm
STOCKHOUSE RD
Park House Farm
Oak Farm
Parkgate Farm
Hall Farm
NEWBRIDGE RD
Layer Brook
Stockbridge Farm
Silverthorn
Rockingham's Farm
Cadgers Wood
Long Wood
Park Farm
Beatbush Wood
Paternoster Heath
PARK LA
Tolleshunt Knights
BROOK RD
STOCKHOUSE CL
Hall
Gobolt's Farm
Barn Hall Farm
BARNHALL RD
TOP RD
Dismtd Rly
Palmers Farm
DARCY RD
Wigborough Springs
RECTORY RD
Oxley Green
The Plough Inn (PH)
OXLEY HILL
B1023
BLIND LA
HONEYPOT LA
Krissimon Farm
Manifold Wick Farm
Lovedowns Farm
4
3
2
1
17
16
15
14
102
91
92
93
118

84

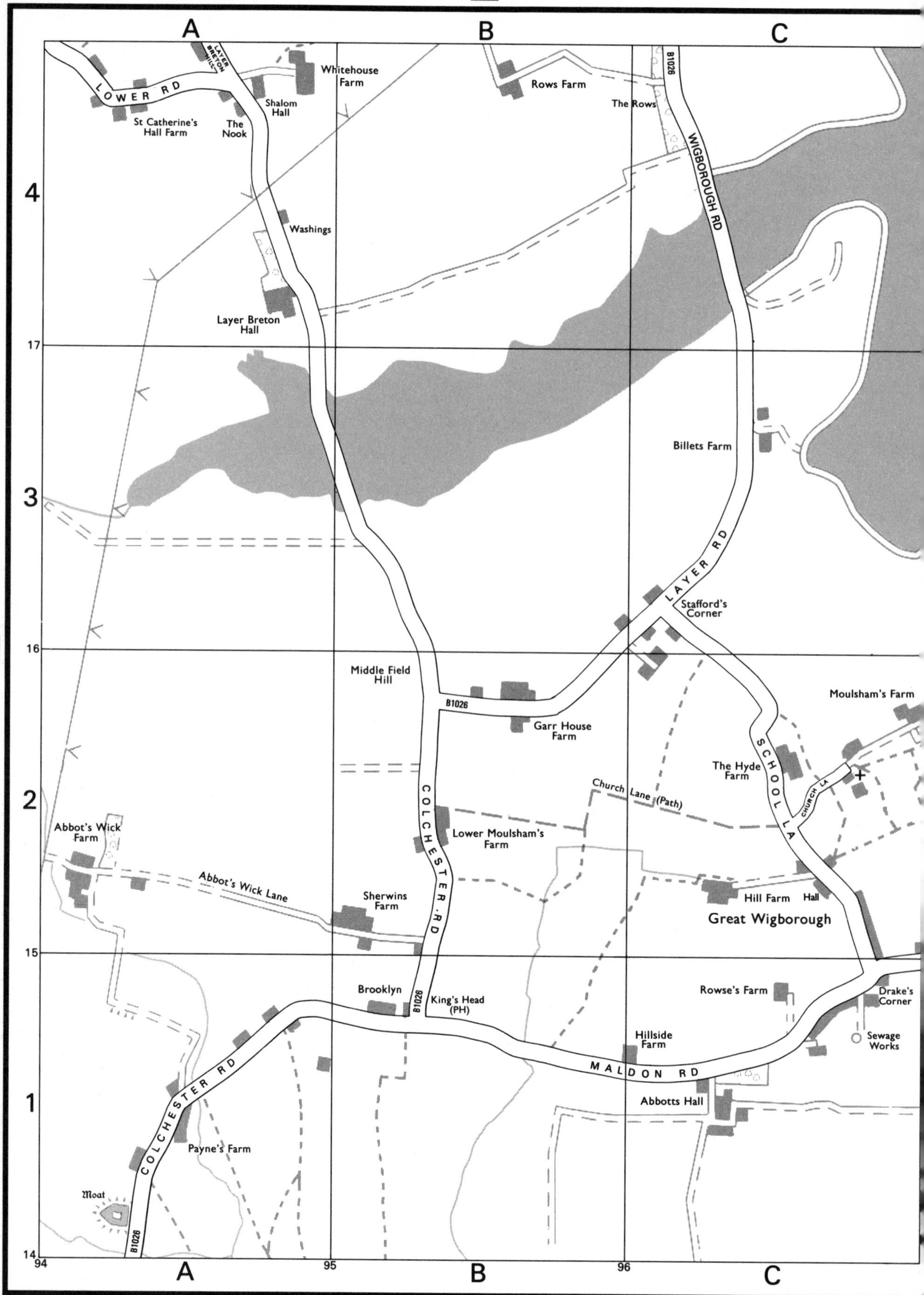
A
B
C
LOWER RD
LAYER BRETON HILL
Whitehouse Farm
Rows Farm
B1026
Shalom Hall
St Catherine's Hall Farm
The Nook
The Rows
WIGBOROUGH RD
4
Washings
Layer Breton Hall
17
Billets Farm
3
LAYER RD
Stafford's Corner
16
Middle Field Hill
B1026
Garr House Farm
Moulsham's Farm
SCHOOL LA
The Hyde Farm
CHURCH LA
Church Lane (Path)
COLCHESTER RD
2
Abbot's Wick Farm
Lower Moulsham's Farm
Abbot's Wick Lane
Sherwins Farm
Hill Farm
Hall
Great Wigborough
15
Brooklyn
B1026
King's Head (PH)
Rowse's Farm
Drake's Corner
Sewage Works
Hillside Farm
MALDON RD
COLCHESTER RD
1
Abbotts Hall
Payne's Farm
Moat
B1026
14
94
95
96
A
B
C

101

119

85

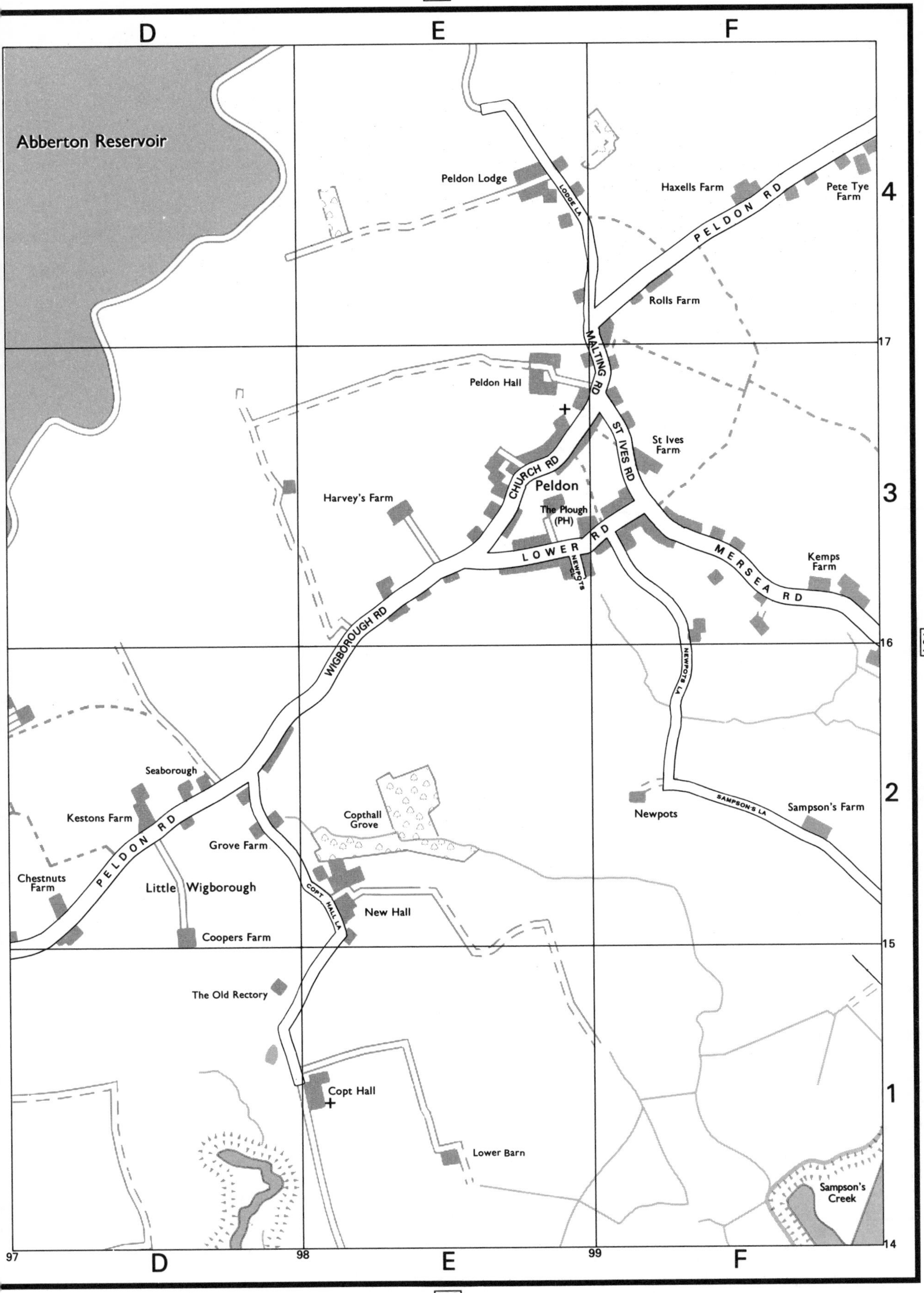
D
E
F
Abberton Reservoir
Peldon Lodge
LODGE LA
Haxells Farm
PELDON RD
Pete Tye Farm
4
Rolls Farm
17
MALTING RD
Peldon Hall
ST IVES RD
St Ives Farm
CHURCH RD
Peldon
3
Harvey's Farm
The Plough (PH)
LOWER RD
NEWPOTS CL
MERSEA RD
Kemps Farm
WIGBOROUGH RD
16
NEWPOTS LA
Seaborough
Copthall Grove
2
Kestons Farm
PELDON RD
Grove Farm
Newpots
SAMPSON'S LA
Sampson's Farm
Chestnuts Farm
Little Wigborough
COPT HALL LA
New Hall
Coopers Farm
15
The Old Rectory
Copt Hall
1
Lower Barn
Sampson's Creek
14
97
98
99
D
E
F

104

120

86

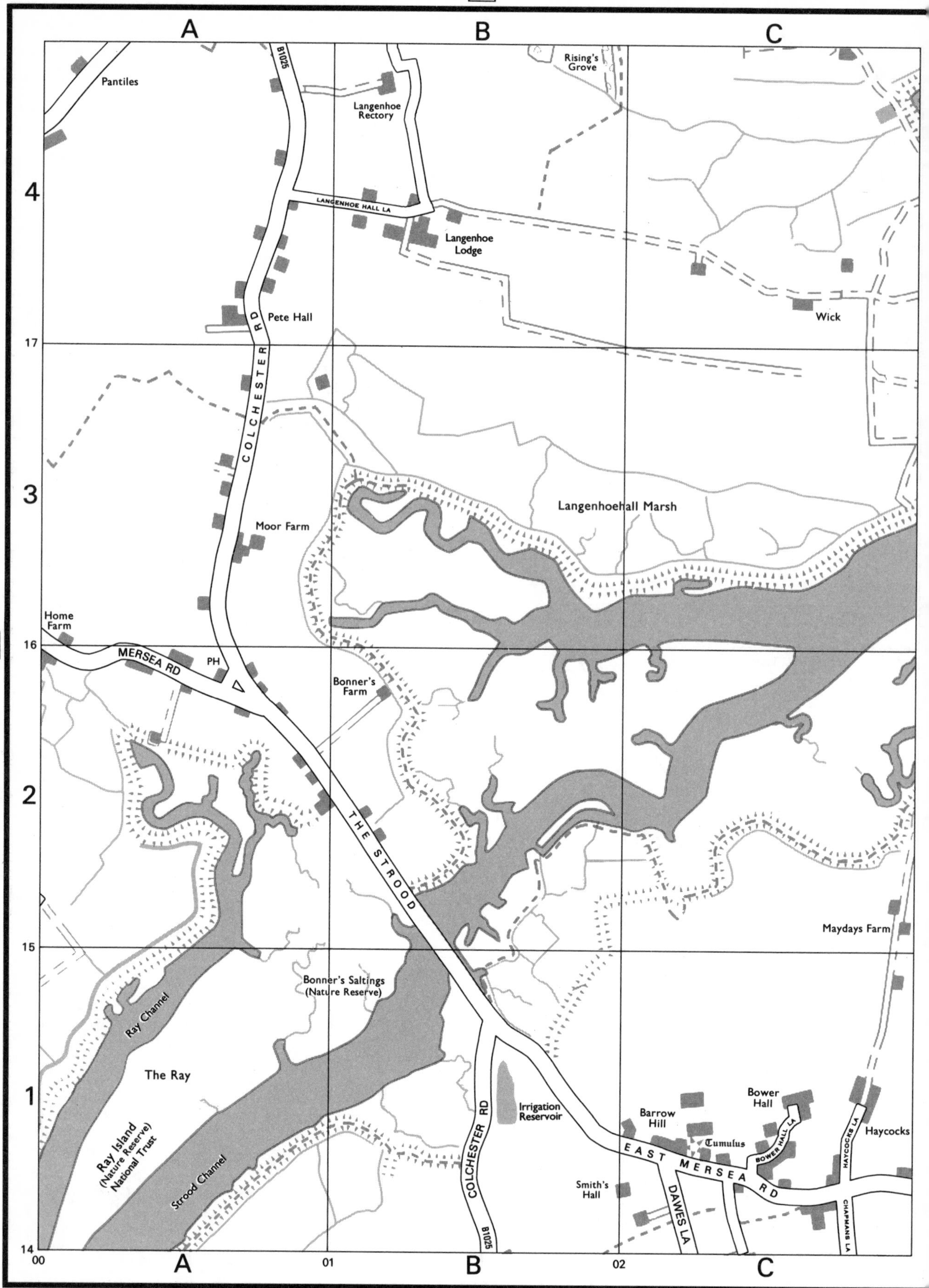
A
B
C
Pantiles
B1025
Langenhoe Rectory
Rising's Grove
LANGENHOE HALL LA
Langenhoe Lodge
Pete Hall
Wick
COLCHESTER RD
Langenhoehall Marsh
Moor Farm
Home Farm
MERSEA RD
PH
Bonner's Farm
THE STROOD
Maydays Farm
Bonner's Saltings (Nature Reserve)
Ray Channel
The Ray
Irrigation Reservoir
Ray Island (Nature Reserve) National Trust
Strood Channel
COLCHESTER RD
B1025
Barrow Hill
Bower Hall
Cumulus
BOWER HALL LA
HAYCOCKS LA
Haycocks
EAST MERSEA RD
Smith's Hall
DAWES LA
CHAPMANS LA
4
17
3
16
2
15
1
14
00
01
02

103

121

87

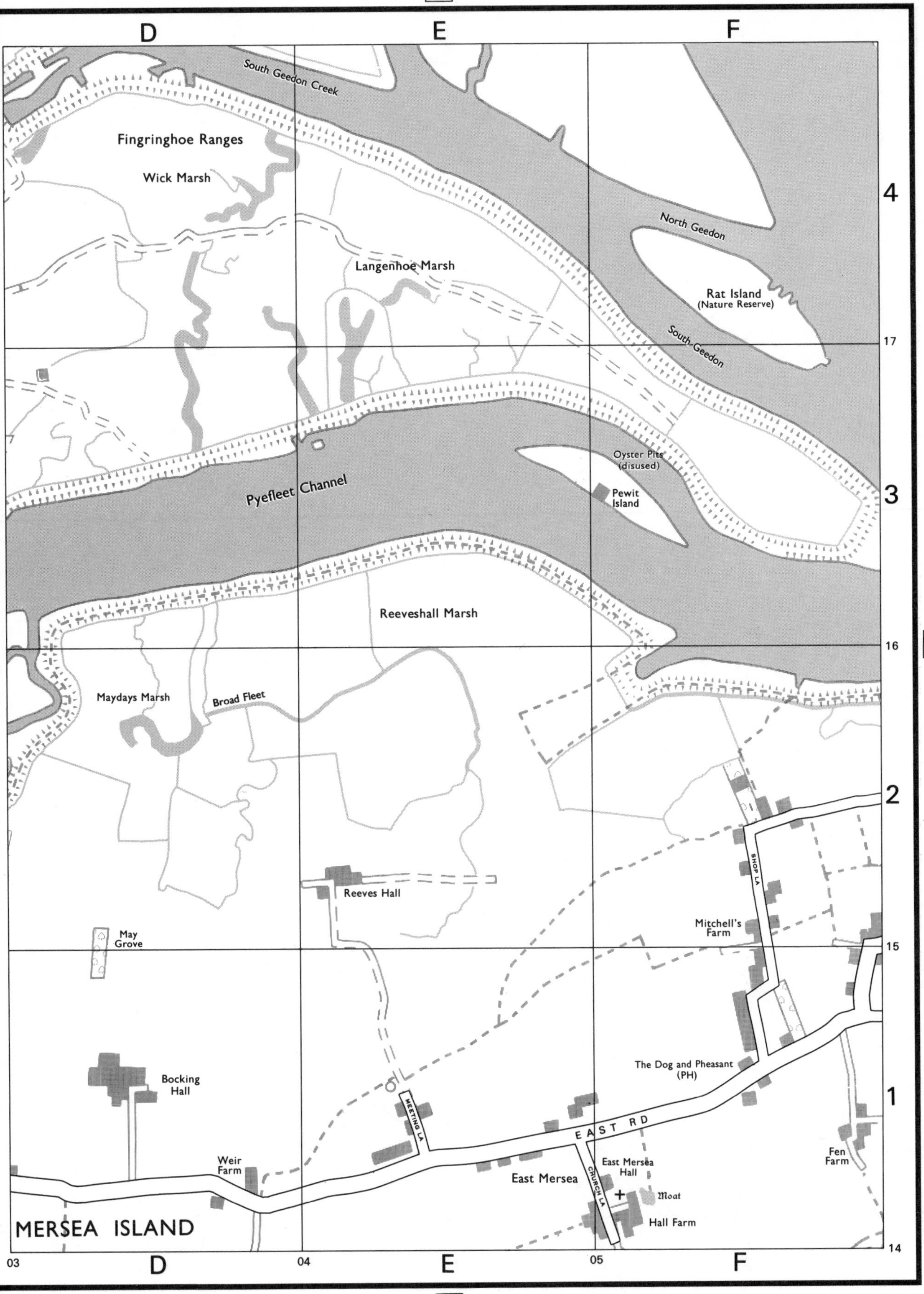
D
E
F
South Geedon Creek
Fingringhoe Ranges
Wick Marsh
4
North Geedon
Langenhoe Marsh
Rat Island
(Nature Reserve)
South Geedon
17
Oyster Pits
(disused)
Pyefleet Channel
Pewit
Island
3
Reeveshall Marsh
16
Maydays Marsh
Broad Fleet
2
SHOP LA
Reeves Hall
Mitchell's
Farm
May
Grove
15
The Dog and Pheasant
(PH)
Bocking
Hall
MEETING LA
1
EAST RD
Fen
Farm
Weir
Farm
East Mersea
East Mersea
Hall
CHURCH LA
Moat
Hall Farm
MERSEA ISLAND
14
03
D
04
E
05
F

106

122

88

105

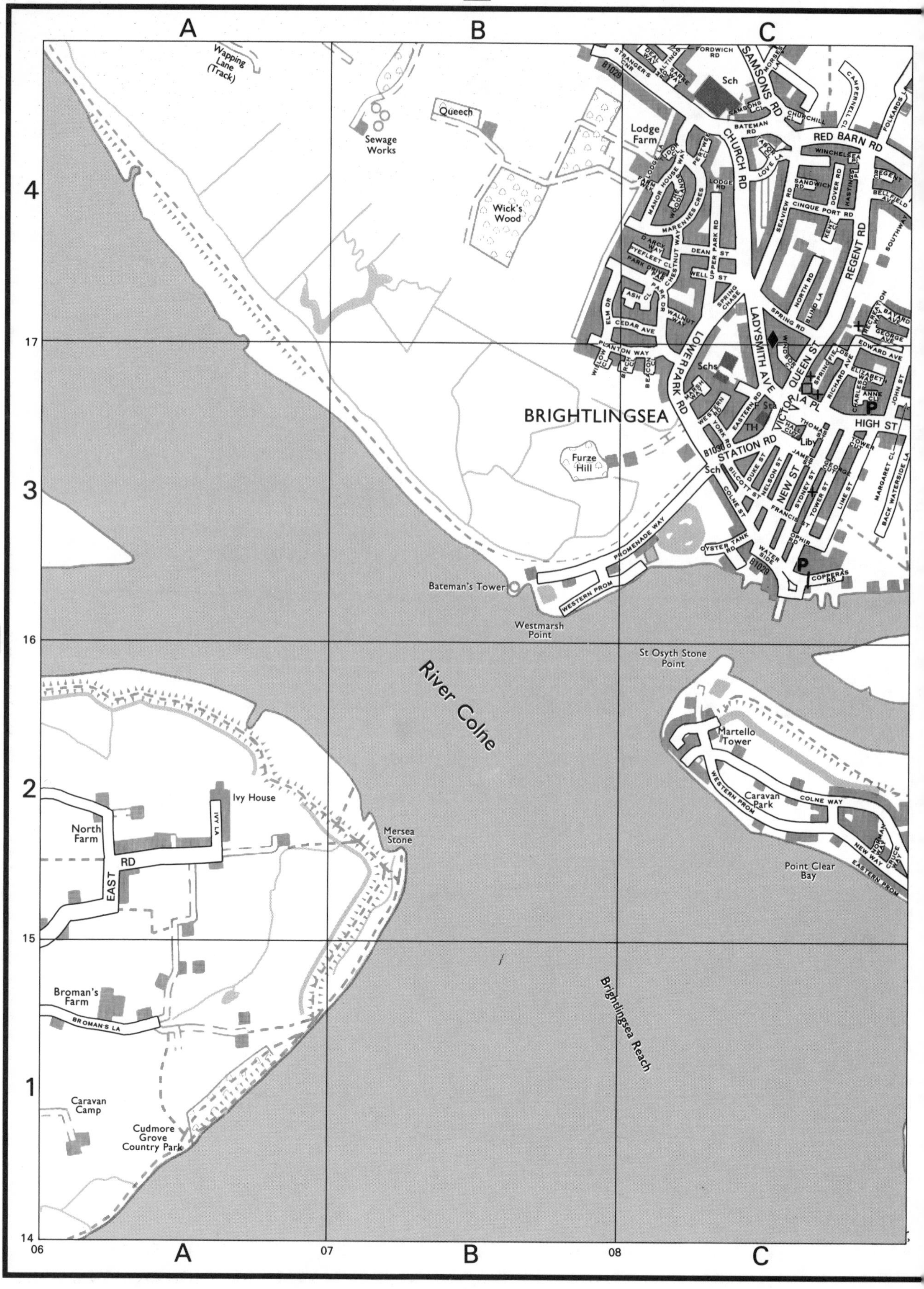

A
B
C
4
3
2
1
17
16
15
14
06
07
08
Wapping Lane (Track)
Sewage Works
Queech
Wick's Wood
Lodge Farm
Sch
Schs
BRIGHTLINGSEA
Furze Hill
Bateman's Tower
Westmarsh Point
PROMENADE WAY
WESTERN PROM
River Colne
St Osyth Stone Point
Martello Tower
Caravan Park
WESTERN PROM
COLNE WAY
NEW WAY
EASTERN PROM
Point Clear Bay
Ivy House
IVY LA
North Farm
EAST RD
Mersea Stone
Broman's Farm
BROMAN'S LA
Caravan Camp
Cudmore Grove Country Park
Brightlingsea Reach
B1029
B1030
FORDWICH RD
SAMSONS RD
CHURCHILL
CAMPERNELL CL
FOLKARDS LA
RED BARN RD
CHURCH RD
BATEMAN RD
LOVE LA
WINCHELSEA
SANDWICH RD
DOVER RD
HASTINGS PL
REGENT RD
BELLFIELD AVE
SOUTHWAY
CINQUE PORT RD
SEAVIEW RD
KENT
NORTH RD
BLIND LA
LODGE RD
MANOR HOUSE WAY
MARENNES CRES
DEAN ST
UPPER PARK RD
WELL ST
SPRING CHASE
SPRING RD
LADYSMITH AVE
LOWER PARK RD
QUEEN ST
VICTORIA PL
ASH CL
ELM DR
CEDAR AVE
WALNUT WAY
PARK DR
PLANTON WAY
BEACON
RECREATION WAY
BAYARD AVE
GEORGE AVE
EDWARD AVE
RICHARD AVE
ELIZABETH WAY
ANNE CL
JOHN ST
P
HIGH ST
Sta
TH
Liby
STATION RD
WESTERN RD
YORK RD
EASTERN RD
DUKE ST
NELSON ST
NEW ST
SYDNEY ST
TOWER ST
LIME ST
SILCOTT ST
FRANCIS ST
COLNE ST
OYSTER TANK RD
WATER SIDE
OPHIR RD
COPPERAS RD
MARGARET CL
BACK WATERSIDE LA
TOWER CUT

89

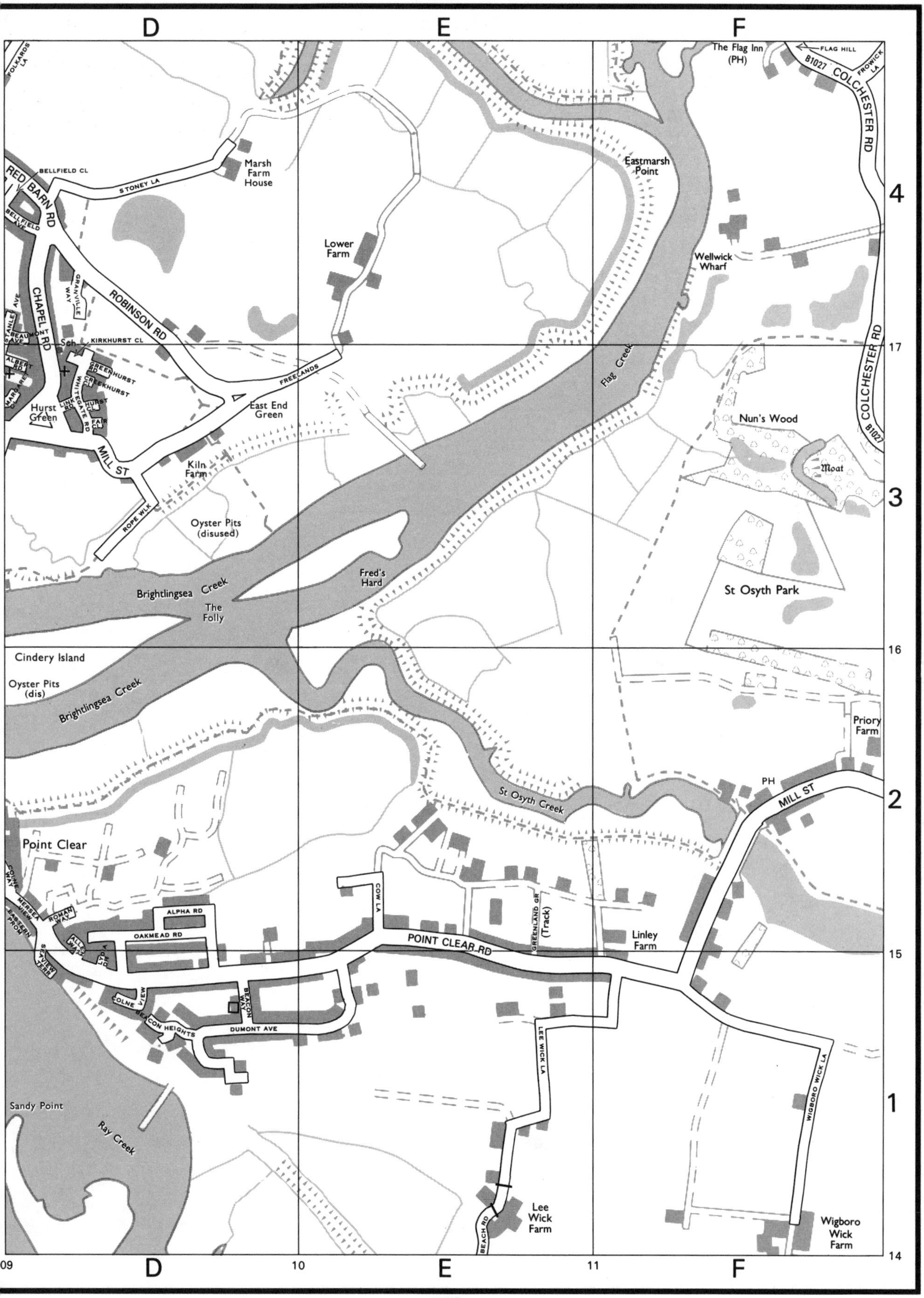
D
E
F
4
3
2
1
17
16
15
14
09
10
11
The Flag Inn (PH)
FLAG HILL
B1027
COLCHESTER RD
FROWICK LA
FOLKARDS LA
Marsh Farm House
BELLFIELD CL
STONEY LA
RED BARN RD
BELLFIELD AVE
Eastmarsh Point
Lower Farm
Wellwick Wharf
GRANVILLE WAY
ROBINSON RD
CHAPEL RD
STANLEY AVE
BEAUMONT AVE
ALBERT RD
Sch
KIRKHURST CL
GREENHURST RD
CREEKHURST
FREELANDS
Flag Creek
East End Green
Hurst Green
WHITEGATE RD
Nun's Wood
Moat
MILL ST
Kiln Farm
ROPE WLK
Oyster Pits (disused)
Brightlingsea Creek
Fred's Hard
The Folly
St Osyth Park
Cindery Island
Oyster Pits (dis)
Brightlingsea Creek
Priory Farm
PH
MILL ST
St Osyth Creek
Point Clear
COLNE WAY
MERSEA VIEW
EASTERN PROM
ROMAN WAY
ALPHA RD
OAKMEAD RD
COW LA
GREENLAND GR
(Track)
Linley Farm
POINT CLEAR RD
SEAVIEW TERR
LYDIA DR
COLNE VIEW
BEACON WAY
BEACON HEIGHTS
DUMONT AVE
LEE WICK LA
WIGBORO WICK LA
Sandy Point
Ray Creek
Lee Wick Farm
BEACH RD
Wigboro Wick Farm

108
123

90

107

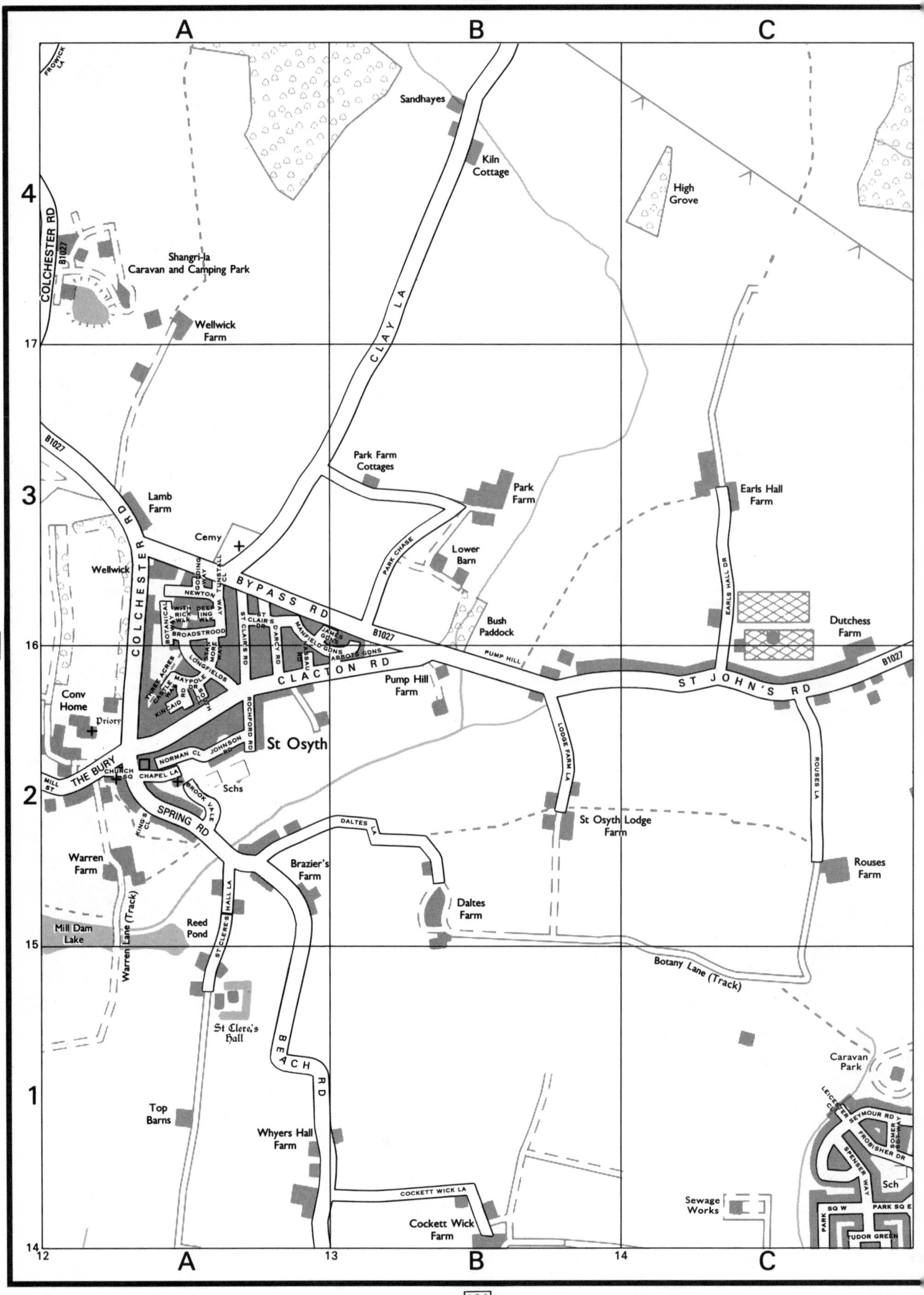
A
B
C
4
3
2
1
17
16
15
14
12
13
14
FROWICK LA
Sandhayes
Kiln Cottage
High Grove
COLCHESTER RD
B1027
Shangri-la Caravan and Camping Park
Wellwick Farm
CLAY LA
Park Farm Cottages
Park Farm
Earls Hall Farm
Lamb Farm
Cemy
Lower Barn
PARK CHASE
Wellwick
BYPASS RD
TUNSTALL CL
NEWTON WAY
BROADSTROOD
LONGFIELDS
ST CLAIR'S RD
D'ARCY RD
MANFIELD GDNS
JAMES GDNS
ABBOTS GDNS
Bush Paddock
PUMP HILL
EARLS HALL DR
Dutchess Farm
CLACTON RD
Pump Hill Farm
ST JOHN'S RD
Conv Home
Priory
St Osyth
ROCHFORD RD
JOHNSON RD
NORMAN CL
CHAPEL LA
CHURCH SQ
THE BURY
MILL ST
Schs
BROOK VALE
SPRING RD
KING'S CL
LODGE FARM LA
St Osyth Lodge Farm
ROUSES LA
DALTES LA
Brazier's Farm
Rouses Farm
Warren Farm
Daltes Farm
Mill Dam Lake
Warren Lane (Track)
Reed Pond
ST CLERE'S HALL LA
Botany Lane (Track)
St Clere's Hall
BEACH RD
Caravan Park
Top Barns
Whyers Hall Farm
LEICESTER CL
SEYMOUR RD
FROBISHER DR
SPENSER WAY
Sch
Sewage Works
COCKETT WICK LA
Cockett Wick Farm
PARK SQ W
PARK SQ E
TUDOR GREEN

124

91

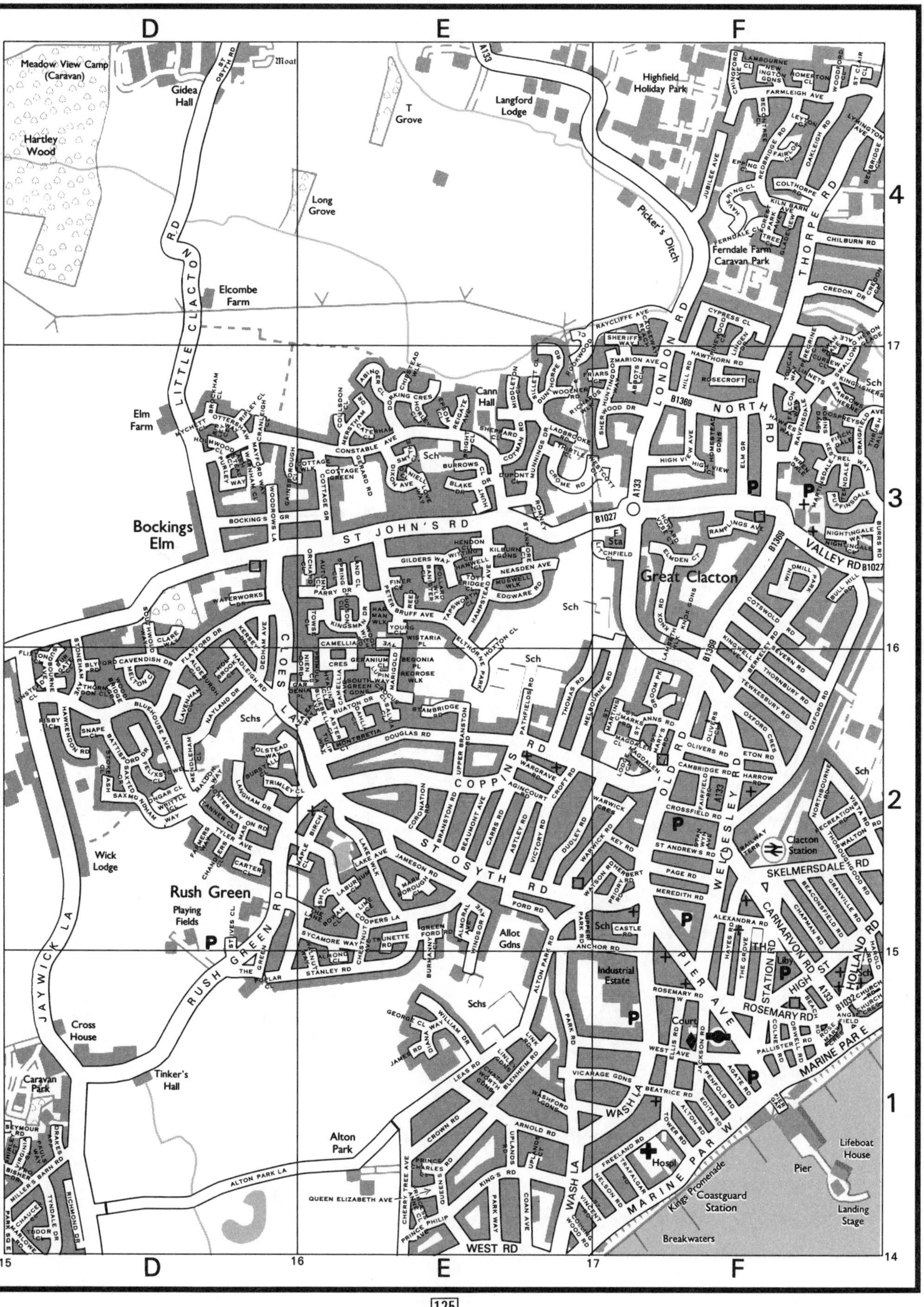
D
E
F
Meadow View Camp (Caravan)
Gidea Hall
Moat
Hartley Wood
T Grove
Langford Lodge
Highfield Holiday Park
Long Grove
Picker's Ditch
Ferndale Farm Caravan Park
Elcombe Farm
LITTLE CLACTON RD
ST OSYTH RD
A133
LONDON RD
THORPE RD
NORTH RD
B1369
B1027
Elm Farm
Cann Hall
Sch
Bockings Elm
ST JOHN'S RD
Great Clacton
VALLEY RD
Sta
Schs
CLOES LA
COPPINS RD
ST OSYTH RD
OLD RD
WELLESLEY RD
Clacton Station
SKELMERSDALE RD
Wick Lodge
Rush Green
Playing Fields
RUSH GREEN RD
JAYWICK LA
Allot Gdns
Industrial Estate
PIER AVE
CARNARVON RD
HIGH ST
HOLLAND RD
STATION RD
ROSEMARY RD
Court
Liby
Cross House
Schs
MARINE PARADE E
Caravan Park
Tinker's Hall
WASH LA
Alton Park
ALTON PARK LA
Hospl
MARINE PAR W
Kings Promenade
Coastguard Station
Lifeboat House
Pier
Landing Stage
Breakwaters
QUEEN ELIZABETH AVE
WEST RD
15
16
17
14
1
2
3
4

110

125

92

109

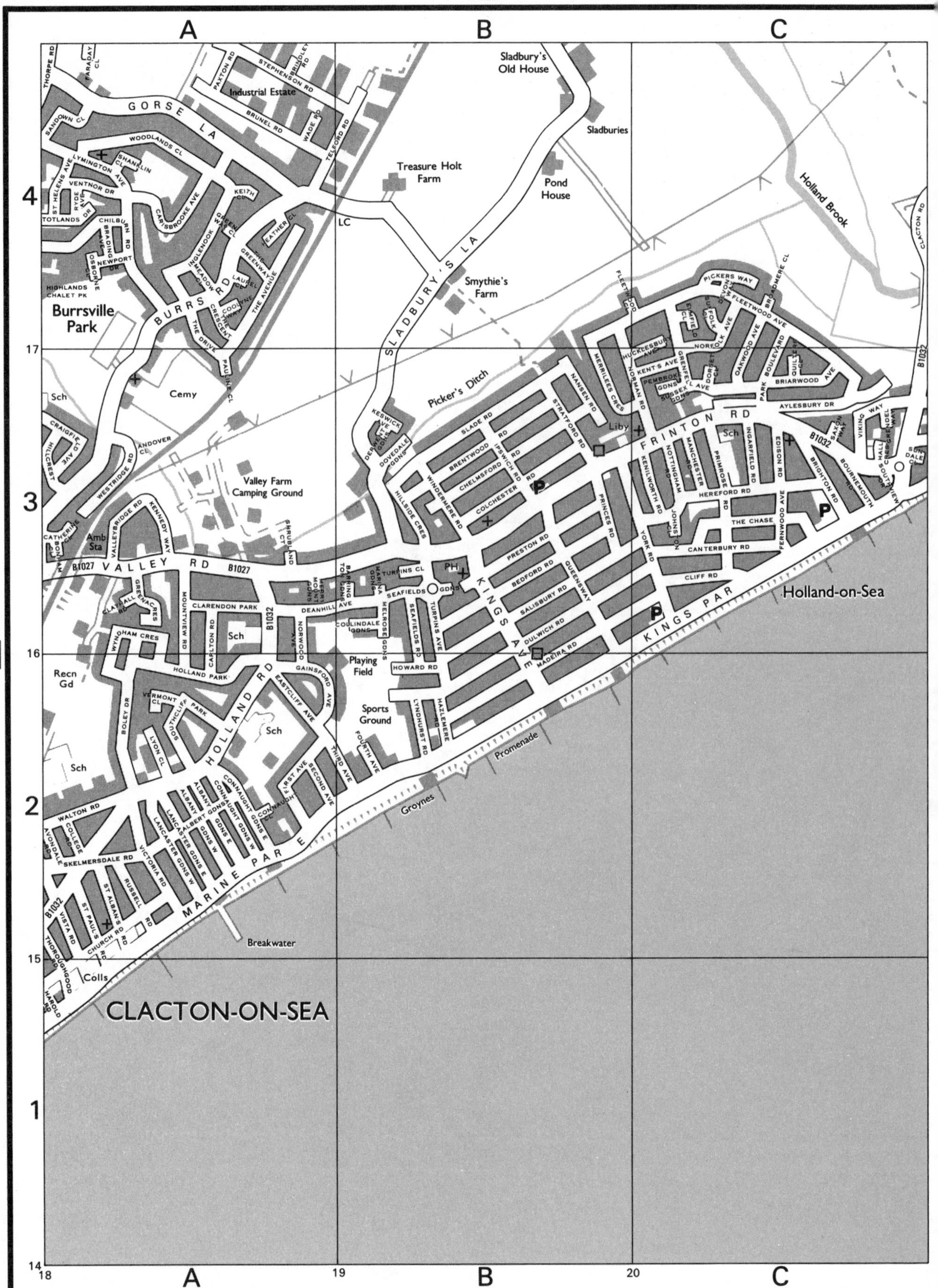
A
B
C
4
3
2
1
17
16
15
14
18
19
20
CLACTON-ON-SEA
Holland-on-Sea
Burrsville Park
Industrial Estate
Sladbury's Old House
Sladburies
Treasure Holt Farm
Pond House
Holland Brook
Smythie's Farm
Picker's Ditch
Valley Farm Camping Ground
Cemy
Sch
Recn Gd
Amb Sta
Playing Field
Sports Ground
Promenade
Groynes
Breakwater
Colls
Liby
PH
LC
HIGHLANDS CHALET PK
GORSE LA
BURRS RD
SLADBURY'S LA
VALLEY RD
B1027
B1032
HOLLAND RD
KINGS AVE
KINGS PAR
MARINE PARADE
FRINTON RD
CLACTON RD
WOODLANDS CL
LYMINGTON AVE
SHANKLIN CL
CARISBROOKE AVE
ST HELENS AVE
VENTNOR DR
TOTLANDS
CHILBURN RD
BRADING AVE
NEWPORT DR
OSBORNE CL
SANDOWN CL
THORPE RD
FARADAY CL
PAXTON RD
STEPHENSON RD
BRINDLEY RD
BRUNEL RD
WADE RD
TELFORD RD
KEITH CL
GREENWAY CL
INGLENOOK
MEADOW CL
HEATHER CL
THE GREENWAY
THE AVENUE
LAUREL CL
COOLYNE WAY
CRESCENT
THE DRIVE
PAULINE CL
ANDOVER CL
WESTRIDGE RD
CRAIGFIELD AVE
HILLCREST
CATHERINE
VALLEYBRIDGE RD
KENNEDY WAY
SHRUBLAND CT
BARRINGTON GDNS
MERRYMOUNT GDNS
MARINA GDNS
TURPINS CL
SEAFIELDS GDNS
DEANHILL AVE
COULINDALE GDNS
MELROSE GDNS
SEAFIELDS RD
TURPINS AVE
NORWOOD AVE
GAINSFORD AVE
EASTCLIFF AVE
HOWARD RD
LYNDHURST RD
HAZLEMERE RD
FOURTH AVE
THIRD AVE
SECOND AVE
FIRST AVE
CONNAUGHT GDNS E
CONNAUGHT GDNS W
CONNAUGHT AVE
ALBANY GDNS E
ALBANY GDNS W
ALBERT GDNS
LANCASTER GDNS E
LANCASTER GDNS W
CLARENDON PARK
MOUNTVIEW RD
CARLTON RD
HOLLAND PARK
WYNDHAM CRES
CLAYHALL RD
GREENACRES
VERMONT CL
SOUTHCLIFF PARK
BOLEY DR
LYON CL
WALTON RD
COLLEGE RD
AVONDALE RD
SKELMERSDALE RD
VICTORIA RD
RUSSELL RD
ST ALBANS RD
ST PAULS RD
CHURCH RD
VISTA RD
THOROUGHGOOD RD
HAROLD RD
KESWICK AVE
DERWENT GDNS
DOVEDALE GDNS
HILLSIDE CRES
WINDERMERE RD
BRENTWOOD RD
CHELMSFORD RD
IPSWICH RD
COLCHESTER RD
SLADE RD
STRATFORD RD
NANSEN RD
MERRILEES CRES
PRINCES RD
PRESTON RD
BEDFORD RD
SALISBURY RD
DULWICH RD
MADEIRA RD
QUEENSWAY
YORK RD
KENILWORTH RD
NOTTINGHAM RD
MANCHESTER RD
JOHNSTON CL
PRIMROSE RD
INGARFIELD RD
HEREFORD RD
THE CHASE
CANTERBURY RD
CLIFF RD
FERNWOOD AVE
EDISON RD
BRIGHTON RD
BOURNEMOUTH RD
SAXON WAY
VIKING WAY
AYLESBURY DR
BRIARWOOD AVE
QUILTERS CL
PARK BOULEVARD
OAKWOOD AVE
NORFOLK AVE
SUFFOLK AVE
SUSSEX GDNS
PEMBROKE GDNS
GRENFELL AVE
DORSET CL
KENT'S AVE
HUCKLESBURY AVE
NORMAN RD
FLEETWOOD CL
FLEETWOOD AVE
PICKERS WAY
DEVON WAY
BROADMERE CL
ENFIELD CL
SOUTHVIEW DR
HALL CRES
GRENDEL WAY
SUNDALE CL

93

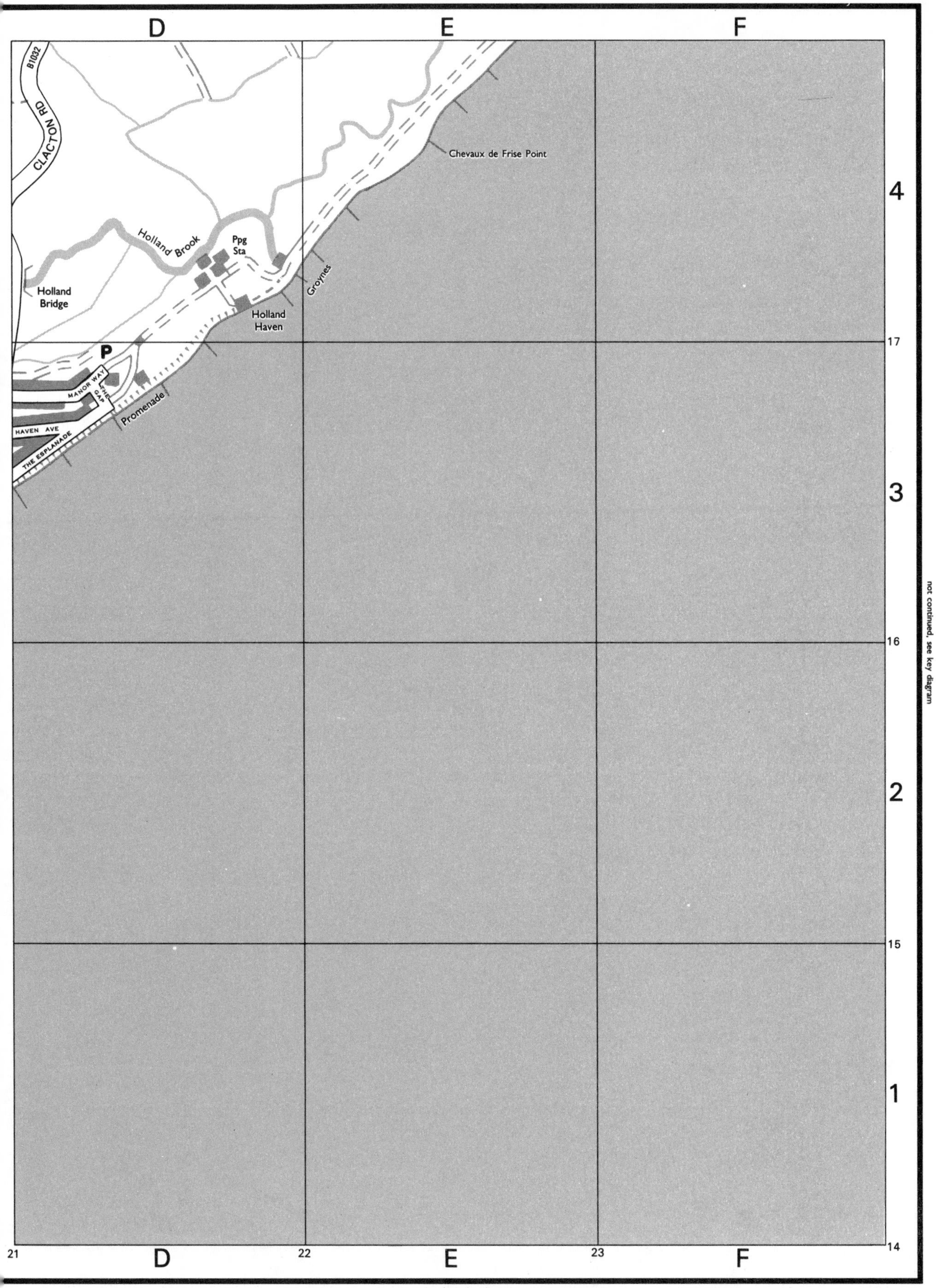

not continued, see key diagram

not continued, see key diagram

95

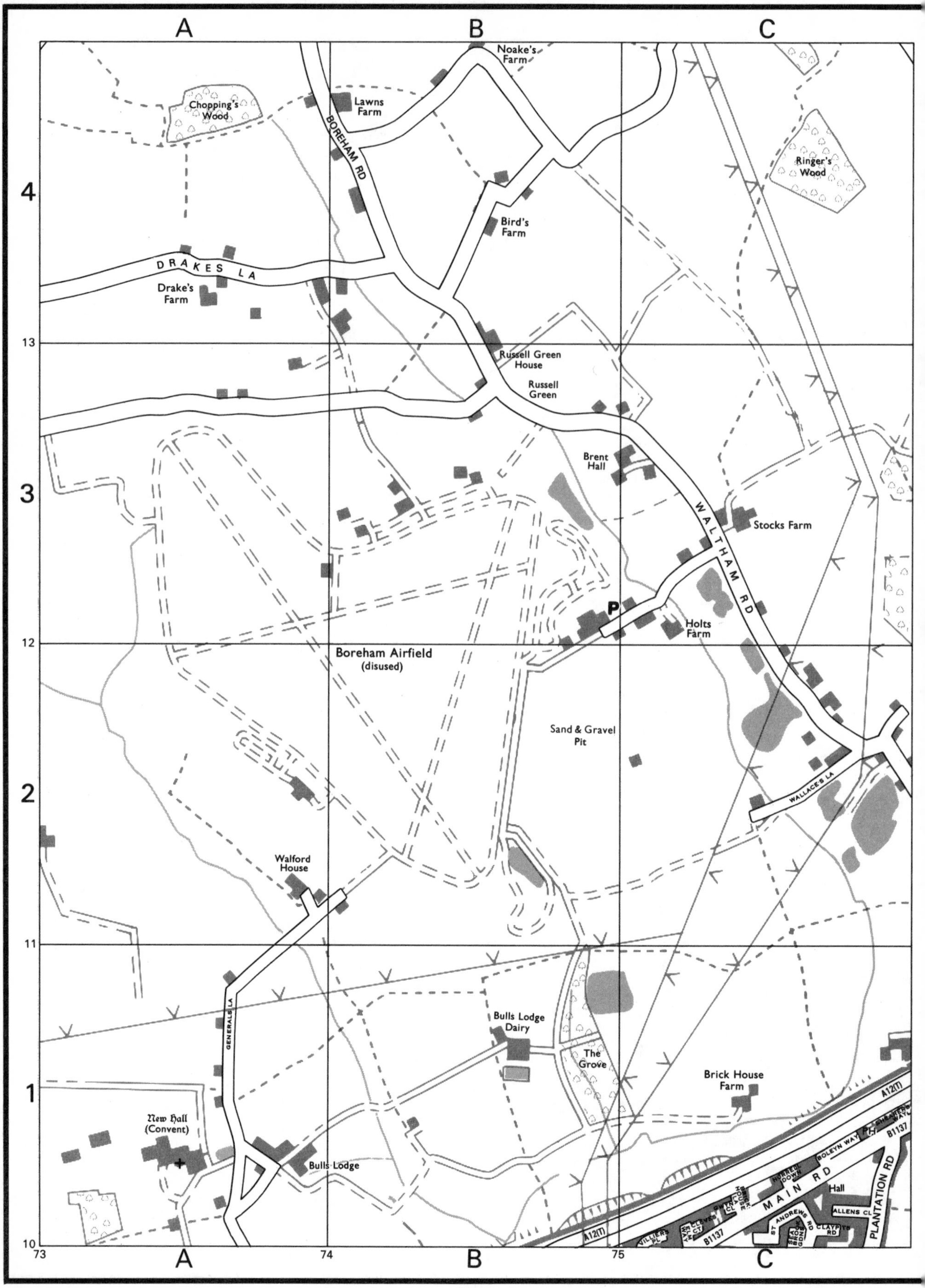
A
B
C
4
3
2
1
13
12
11
10
73
74
75
Noake's Farm
Chopping's Wood
Lawns Farm
BOREHAM RD
Ringer's Wood
Bird's Farm
DRAKES LA
Drake's Farm
Russell Green House
Russell Green
Brent Hall
WALTHAM RD
Stocks Farm
P
Holts Farm
Boreham Airfield
(disused)
Sand & Gravel Pit
WALLACE'S LA
Walford House
GENERALS LA
Bulls Lodge Dairy
The Grove
Brick House Farm
New Hall
(Convent)
Bulls Lodge
A12(T)
B1137
BOLEYN WAY
MAIN RD
Hall
ALLENS CL
PLANTATION RD
ST ANDREWS RD
CLAYPITS RD
VILLIERS PL

not continued, see key diagram

128

96

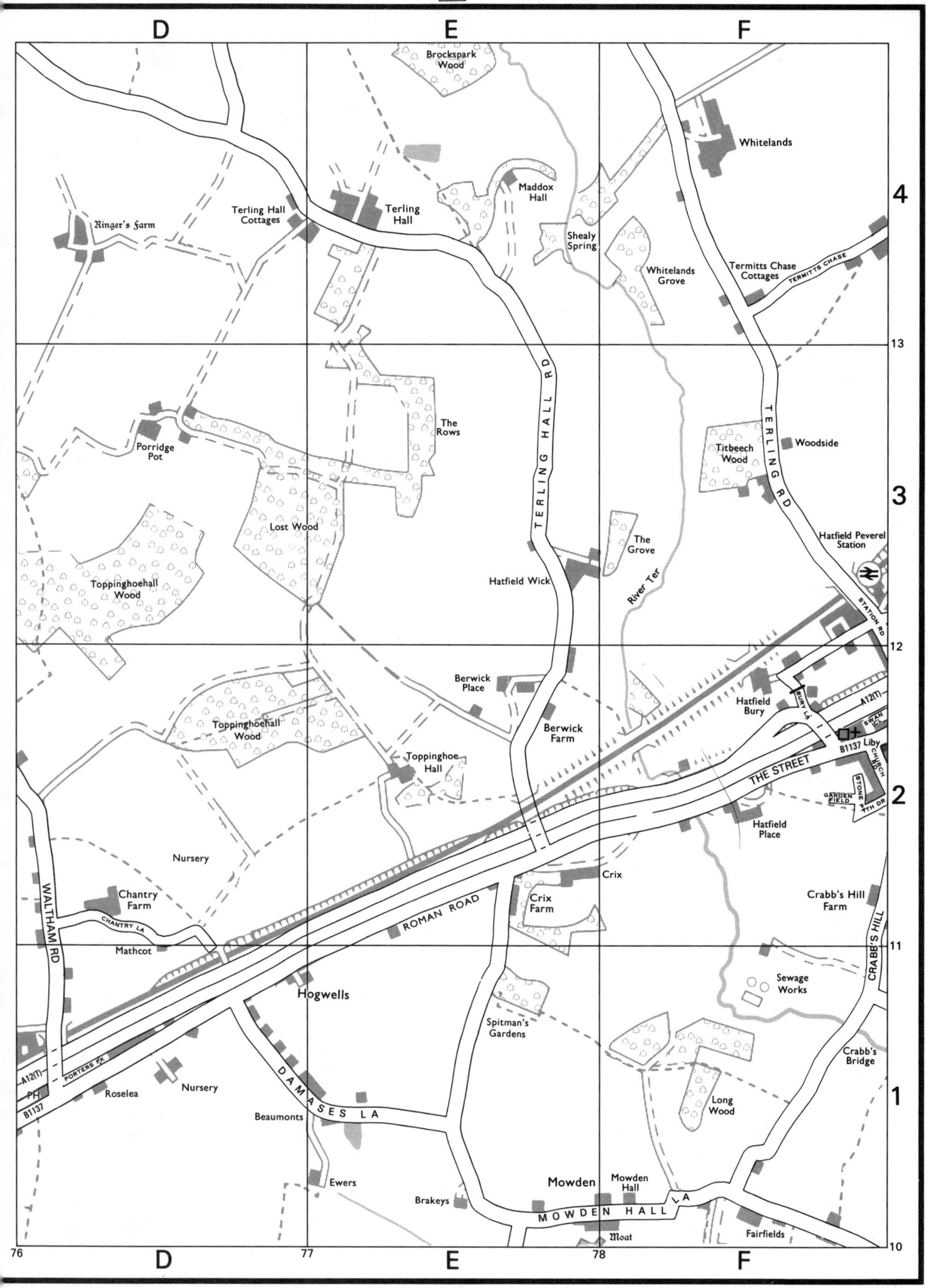
D
E
F
Brockspark Wood
Whitelands
Maddox Hall
Terling Hall Cottages
Terling Hall
Ringer's Farm
Shealy Spring
Whitelands Grove
Termitts Chase Cottages
TERMITTS CHASE
4
13
TERLING HALL RD
The Rows
Porridge Pot
TERLING RD
Woodside
Titbeech Wood
3
Lost Wood
The Grove
Hatfield Peverel Station
Toppinghoehall Wood
Hatfield Wick
River Ter
STATION RD
12
Berwick Place
Hatfield Bury
BURY LA
A12(T)
SWAN CL
Berwick Farm
Toppinghoehall Wood
Toppinghoe Hall
B1137
Liby
CHURCH RD
THE STREET
GARDEN FIELD
STONE PATH DR
2
Hatfield Place
Nursery
Crix
WALTHAM RD
Chantry Farm
CHANTRY LA
Crix Farm
Crabb's Hill Farm
ROMAN ROAD
Mathcot
11
CRABB'S HILL
Sewage Works
Hogwells
Spitman's Gardens
Crabb's Bridge
A12(T)
PORTERS PK
PH
B1137
Roselea
Nursery
DAMASES LA
Long Wood
1
Beaumonts
Ewers
Brakeys
Mowden
Mowden Hall
MOWDEN HALL LA
Fairfields
Moat
76
77
78
10
D
E
F

114

129

97

113

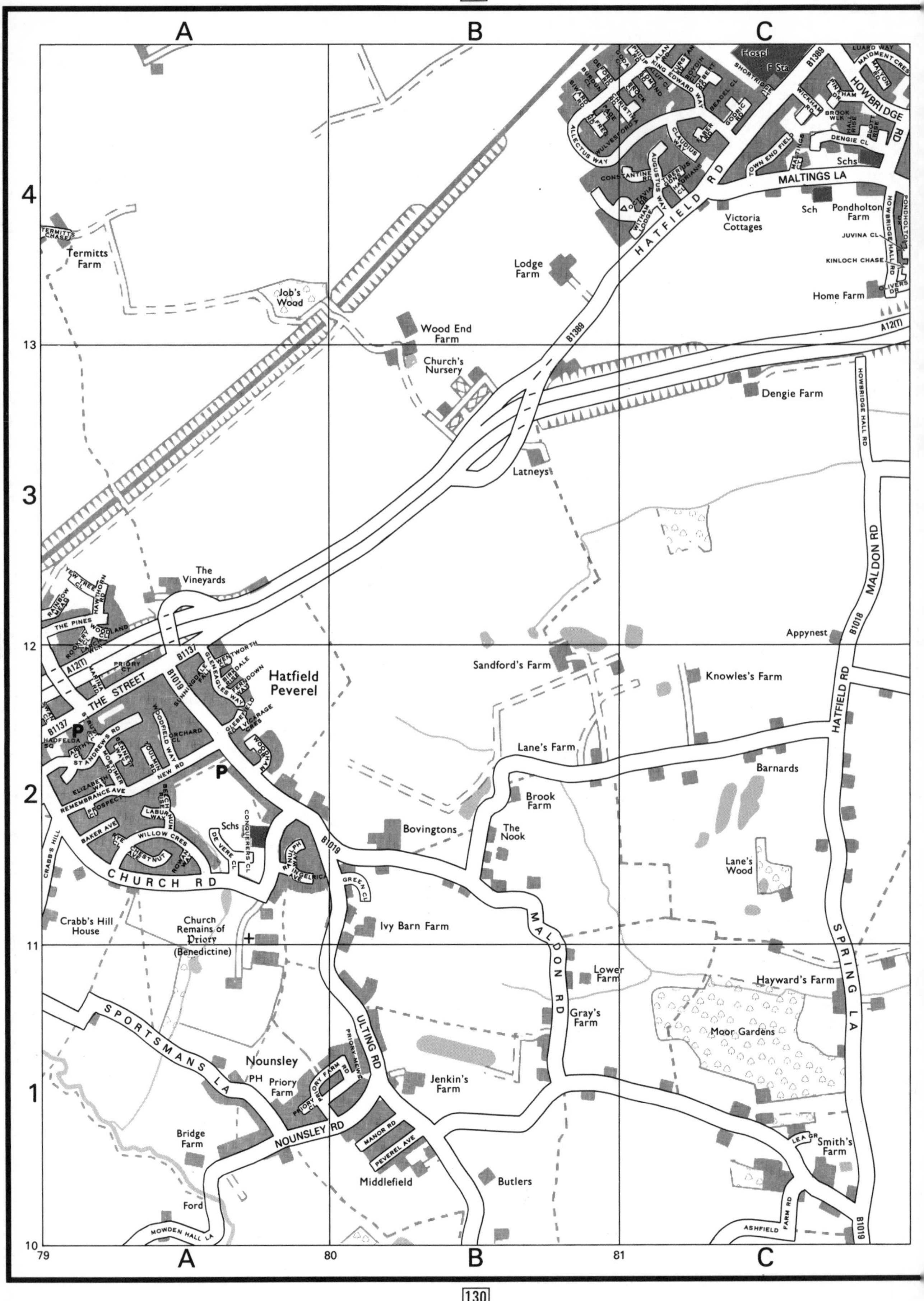
A
B
C
4
3
2
1
13
12
11
10
79
80
81
Hospl
F Sta
B1389
LUARD WAY
HOWBRIDGE RD
MALTINGS LA
Schs
Sch
Pondholton Farm
Victoria Cottages
HATFIELD RD
JUVINA CL
KINLOCH CHASE
Home Farm
A12(T)
Lodge Farm
Termitts Farm
TERMITTS CHASE
Job's Wood
Wood End Farm
Church's Nursery
Dengie Farm
HOWBRIDGE HALL RD
Latneys
The Vineyards
MALDON RD
B1018
Appynest
Sandford's Farm
Knowles's Farm
Hatfield Peverel
THE STREET
B1137
B1019
P
Lane's Farm
Barnards
Brook Farm
The Nook
Bovingtons
Schs
CHURCH RD
Lane's Wood
Crabb's Hill House
Church
Remains of Priory (Benedictine)
Ivy Barn Farm
Lower Farm
Hayward's Farm
Gray's Farm
Moor Gardens
SPRING LA
ULTING RD
SPORTSMANS LA
Nounsley
PH
Priory Farm
Jenkin's Farm
Bridge Farm
NOUNSLEY RD
Smith's Farm
Middlefield
Butlers
Ford
MOWDEN HALL LA
ASHFIELD
FARM RD

130

98

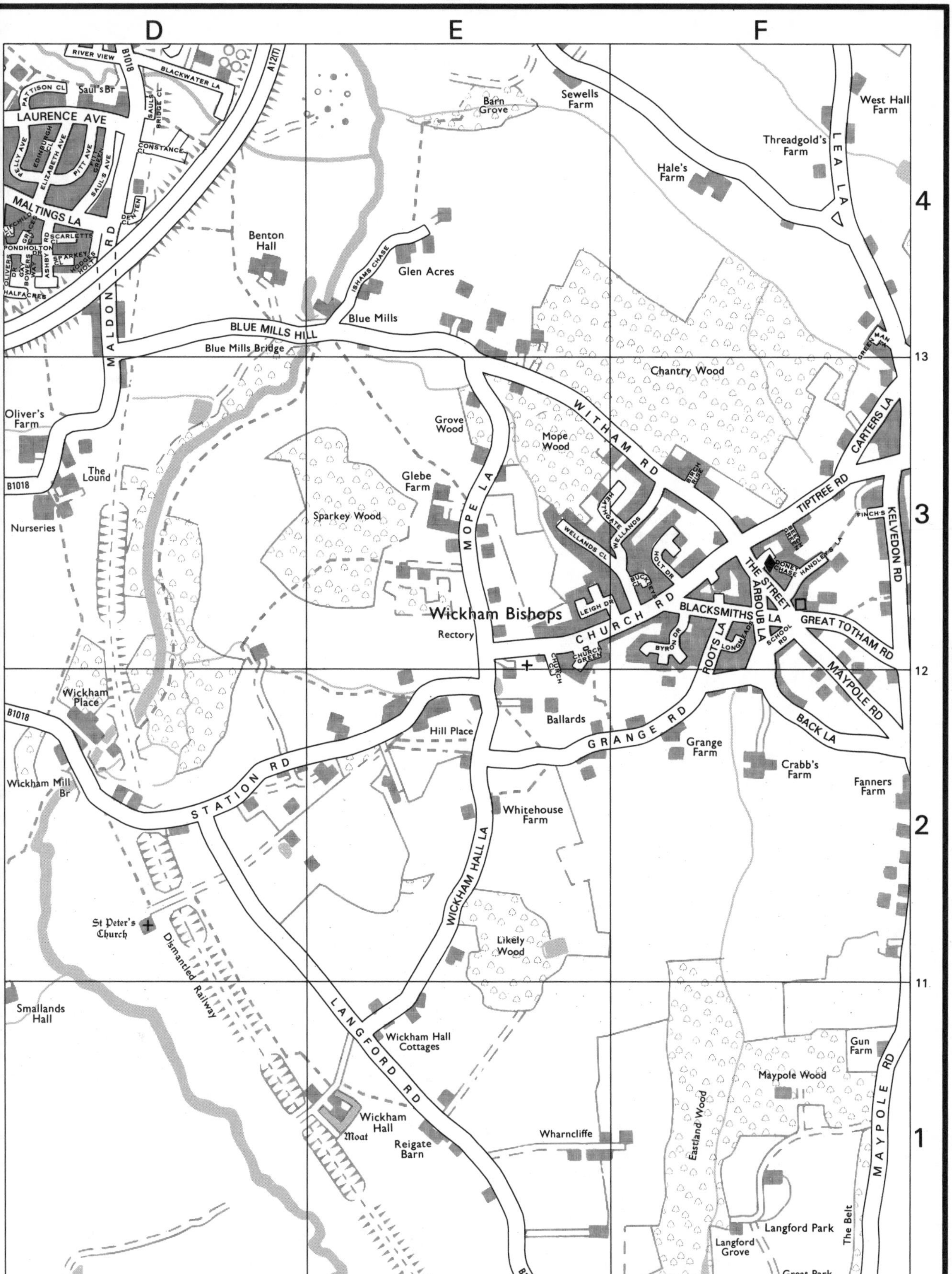
D
E
F
RIVER VIEW
B1018
BLACKWATER LA
A12(T)
PATTISON CL
Saul's Br
LAURENCE AVE
SAUL'S BRIDGE CL
CONSTANCE CL
MALTINGS LA
SCARLETTS
ASHBY RD
HALFACRES
MALDON RD
Benton Hall
Barn Grove
Sewells Farm
West Hall Farm
Threadgold's Farm
LEA LA
Hale's Farm
4
Glen Acres
ISHAMS CHASE
Blue Mills
BLUE MILLS HILL
Blue Mills Bridge
GREEN MAN LA
13
Chantry Wood
Oliver's Farm
Grove Wood
Mope Wood
WITHAM RD
CARTERS LA
B1018
The Lound
Glebe Farm
BIRCH RISE
TIPTREE RD
Nurseries
Sparkey Wood
MOPE LA
HEATHGATE
WELLANDS
WELLANDS CL
HOLT DR
BUCKLEYS CL
FINCH'S
KELVEDON RD
3
THE STREET
HANDLEY'S LA
DONEY CHASE
LEIGH DR
CHURCH RD
BLACKSMITHS LA
THE ARBOUR LA
Wickham Bishops
Rectory
GREAT TOTHAM RD
BYRON DR
ROOTS LA
LONGMEADS
SCHOOL RD
CHURCH GREEN
12
MAYPOLE RD
Wickham Place
B1018
Ballards
Hill Place
GRANGE RD
BACK LA
Grange Farm
Crabb's Farm
STATION RD
Wickham Mill Br
Fanners Farm
Whitehouse Farm
2
WICKHAM HALL LA
St Peter's Church
Dismantled Railway
Likely Wood
11
Smallands Hall
LANGFORD RD
Wickham Hall Cottages
Gun Farm
Maypole Wood
MAYPOLE RD
Eastland Wood
Wickham Hall
Moat
Reigate Barn
Wharncliffe
1
Langford Park
The Belt
Langford Grove
Great Park
B1018
10
82
83
84

116

131

99

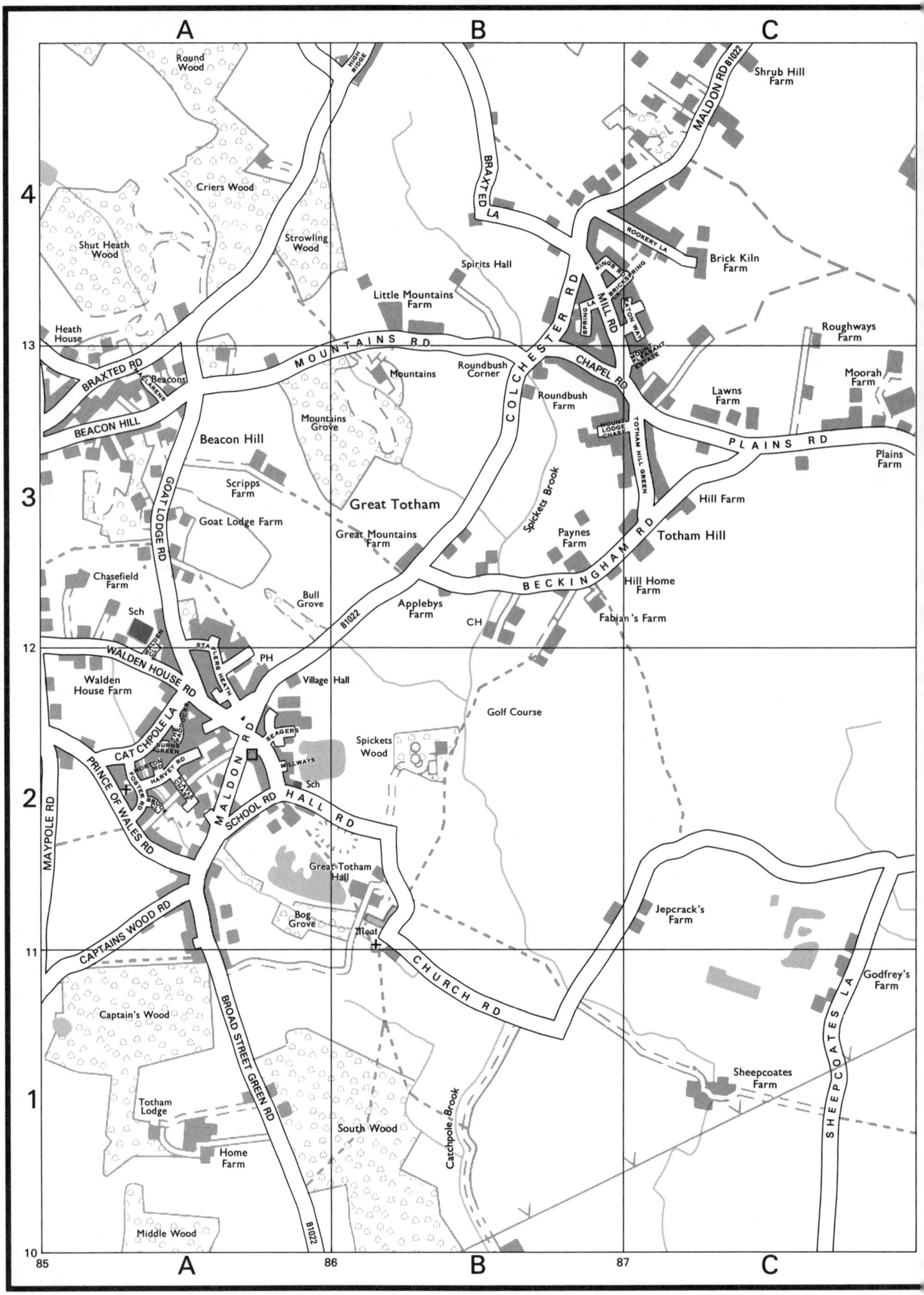

A
B
C
4
3
2
1
13
12
11
10
85
86
87
Round Wood
Criers Wood
Shut Heath Wood
Strowling Wood
HIGH RIDGE
BRAXTED LA
MALDON RD B1022
Shrub Hill Farm
ROOKERY LA
Brick Kiln Farm
Spirits Hall
Little Mountains Farm
KINGS RD
BRICKSPRING LA
SPRING LA
MILL RD
EATON WAY
MOUNT PLEASANT ESTATE
COLCHESTER RD
CHAPEL RD
Roughways Farm
Moorah Farm
Lawns Farm
Heath House
BRAXTED RD
MACLARENS
Beacons
MOUNTAINS RD
Mountains
Roundbush Corner
Roundbush Farm
MOUNT LODGE CHASE
TOTHAM HILL GREEN
PLAINS RD
Plains Farm
BEACON HILL
Beacon Hill
Mountains Grove
Scripps Farm
GOAT LODGE RD
Goat Lodge Farm
Great Totham
Spickets Brook
Paynes Farm
Hill Farm
Totham Hill
Great Mountains Farm
BECKINGHAM RD
Hill Home Farm
Chasefield Farm
Sch
Bull Grove
B1022
Applebys Farm
CH
Fabian's Farm
WALDEN CL
STAPLERS HEATH
PH
WALDEN HOUSE RD
Walden House Farm
Village Hall
Golf Course
CATCHPOLE LA
THE PADDOCKS
BURNS GREEN
SEAGERS
Spickets Wood
MORTON RD
HARVEY RD
FOSTER RD
PLAYLE CHASE
BROOK CL
MALDON RD
MILLWAYS
Sch
PRINCE OF WALES RD
MAYPOLE RD
SCHOOL RD
HALL RD
Great Totham Hall
Bog Grove
Moat
CAPTAINS WOOD RD
Jepcrack's Farm
CHURCH RD
Godfrey's Farm
Captain's Wood
BROAD STREET GREEN RD
SHEEPCOATES LA
Sheepcoates Farm
Totham Lodge
Home Farm
South Wood
Catchpole Brook
Middle Wood
B1022

115

132

100

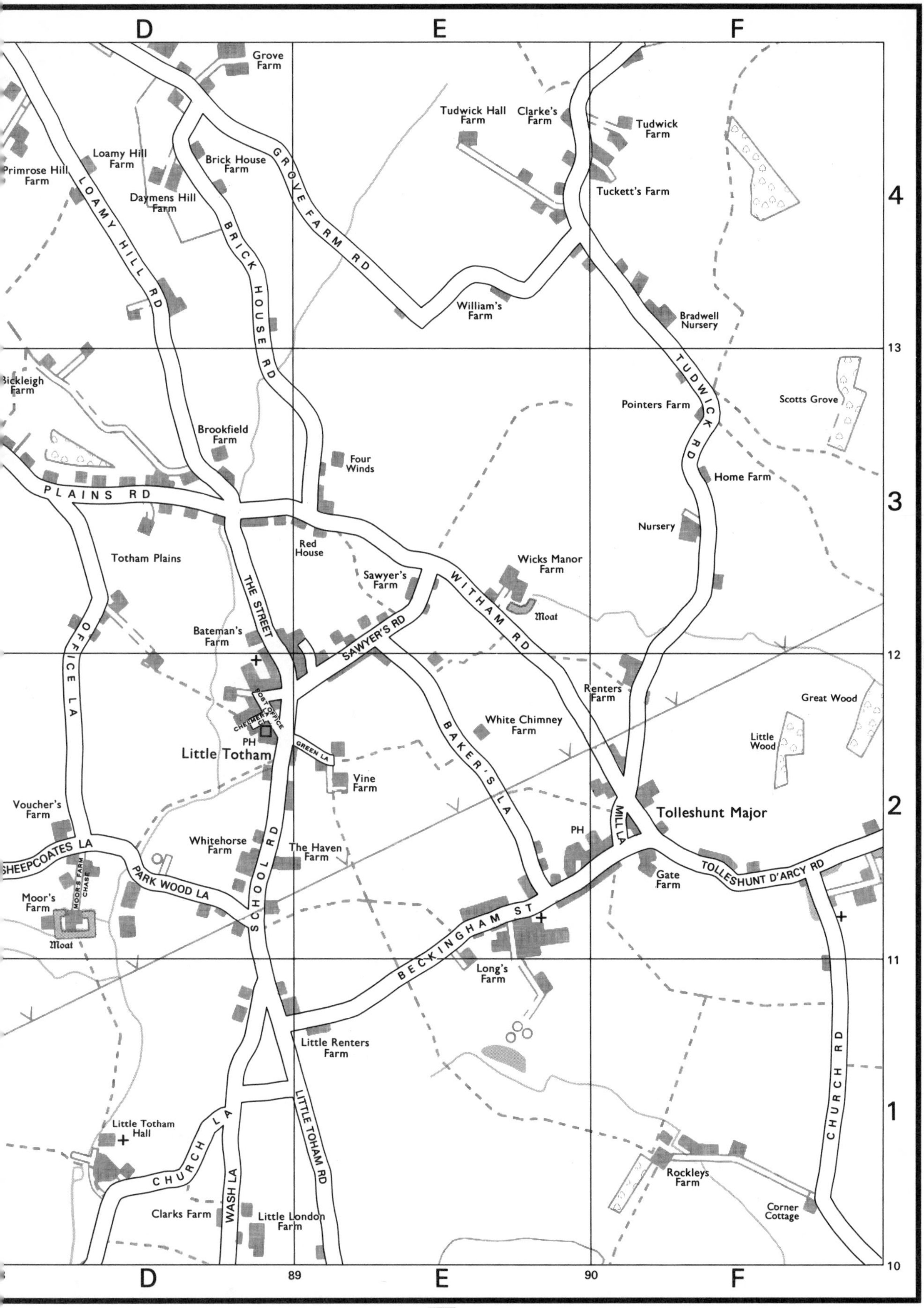
D
E
F
Grove Farm
Tudwick Hall Farm
Clarke's Farm
Tudwick Farm
Loamy Hill Farm
Primrose Hill Farm
Brick House Farm
Daymens Hill Farm
LOAMY HILL RD
GROVE FARM RD
BRICK HOUSE RD
Tuckett's Farm
William's Farm
Bradwell Nursery
Bickleigh Farm
TUDWICK RD
Pointers Farm
Scotts Grove
Brookfield Farm
Four Winds
Home Farm
PLAINS RD
Nursery
Red House
Totham Plains
Sawyer's Farm
Wicks Manor Farm
THE STREET
WITHAM RD
Moat
OFFICE LA
Bateman's Farm
SAWYER'S RD
Renters Farm
Great Wood
POST OFFICE
CHELMER
PH
White Chimney Farm
BAKER'S LA
Little Wood
Little Totham
GREEN LA
Vine Farm
Voucher's Farm
MILL LA
Tolleshunt Major
PH
Whitehorse Farm
SHEEPCOATES LA
The Haven Farm
SCHOOL RD
PARK WOOD LA
Gate Farm
TOLLESHUNT D'ARCY RD
MOOR'S FARM CHASE
Moor's Farm
Moat
BECKINGHAM ST
Long's Farm
Little Renters Farm
CHURCH RD
Little Totham Hall
CHURCH LA
LITTLE TOTHAM RD
WASH LA
Rockleys Farm
Clarks Farm
Little London Farm
Corner Cottage
4
13
3
12
2
11
1
10
89
90
D
E
F
118

133

101
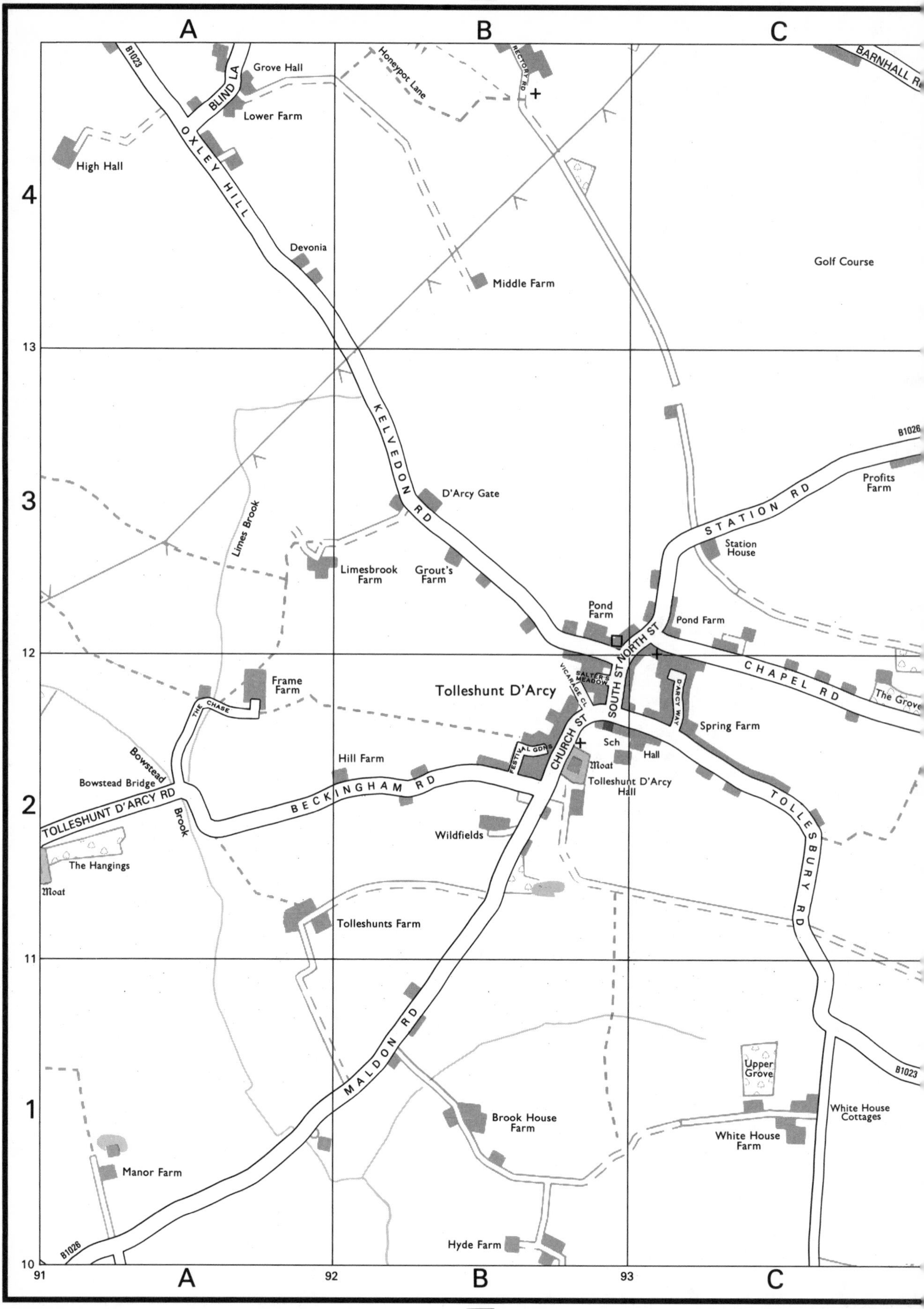
A
B
C
4
3
2
1
13
12
11
10
91
92
93
B1023
BLIND LA
Grove Hall
Lower Farm
High Hall
OXLEY HILL
Honeypot Lane
RECTORY RD
BARNHALL RD
Devonia
Middle Farm
Golf Course
KELVEDON RD
B1026
Profits Farm
D'Arcy Gate
STATION RD
Station House
Limes Brook
Limesbrook Farm
Grout's Farm
Pond Farm
Pond Farm
NORTH ST
CHAPEL RD
The Grove
Frame Farm
THE CHASE
Tolleshunt D'Arcy
SALTERS MEADOW
VICARAGE CL
SOUTH ST
D'ARCY WAY
Spring Farm
CHURCH ST
Sch
Hall
Hill Farm
FESTIVAL GDNS
Moat
Bowstead Brook
Bowstead Bridge
TOLLESHUNT D'ARCY RD
BECKINGHAM RD
Tolleshunt D'Arcy Hall
TOLLESBURY RD
Wildfields
The Hangings
Moat
Tolleshunts Farm
MALDON RD
Upper Grove
B1023
White House Cottages
White House Farm
Brook House Farm
Manor Farm
Hyde Farm
B1026
117
134

102

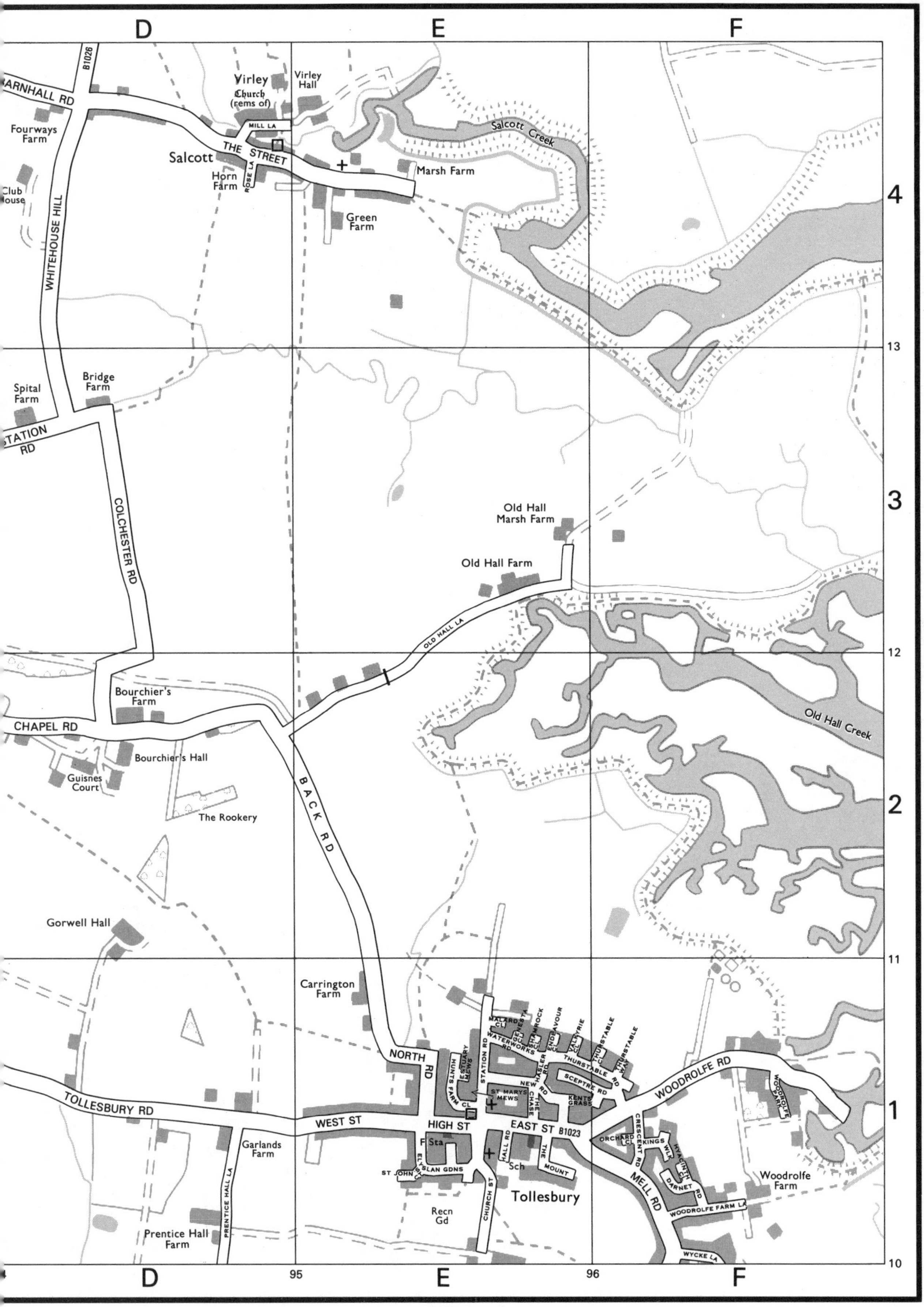

D
E
F
4
3
2
1
13
12
11
10
95
96
B1026
BARNHALL RD
Fourways Farm
Club House
WHITEHOUSE HILL
Virley
Church (rems of)
Virley Hall
MILL LA
THE STREET
Salcott
Horn Farm
ROSE LA
Marsh Farm
Salcott Creek
Green Farm
Spital Farm
Bridge Farm
STATION RD
COLCHESTER RD
Old Hall Marsh Farm
Old Hall Farm
OLD HALL LA
Old Hall Creek
Bourchier's Farm
CHAPEL RD
Bourchier's Hall
Guisnes Court
The Rookery
BACK RD
Gorwell Hall
Carrington Farm
NORTH RD
TOLLESBURY RD
WEST ST
HIGH ST
EAST ST
B1023
Garlands Farm
PRENTICE HALL LA
Prentice Hall Farm
ESTUARY MEWS
HUNTS FARM CL
STATION RD
MALARD CL
WATERWORKS RD
GENESTA CL
SHAMROCK
HASLER RD
ENDEAVOUR
CALLYRIE CL
THURSTABLE CL
THURSTABLE RD
THURSTABLE WAY
SCEPTRE RD
KENTS GRASS
NEW RD
THE CHASE
ST MARYS MEWS
F Sta
ST JOHNS
ELYSLAN GDNS
HALL RD
Sch
THE MOUNT
CHURCH ST
Recn Gd
Tollesbury
WOODROLFE RD
WOODROLFE PARK
ORCHARD CL
CRESCENT RD
KINGS WLK
HYACINTH CL
DARNET RD
MELL RD
WOODROLFE FARM LA
Woodrolfe Farm
WYCKE LA

120

135

103

119

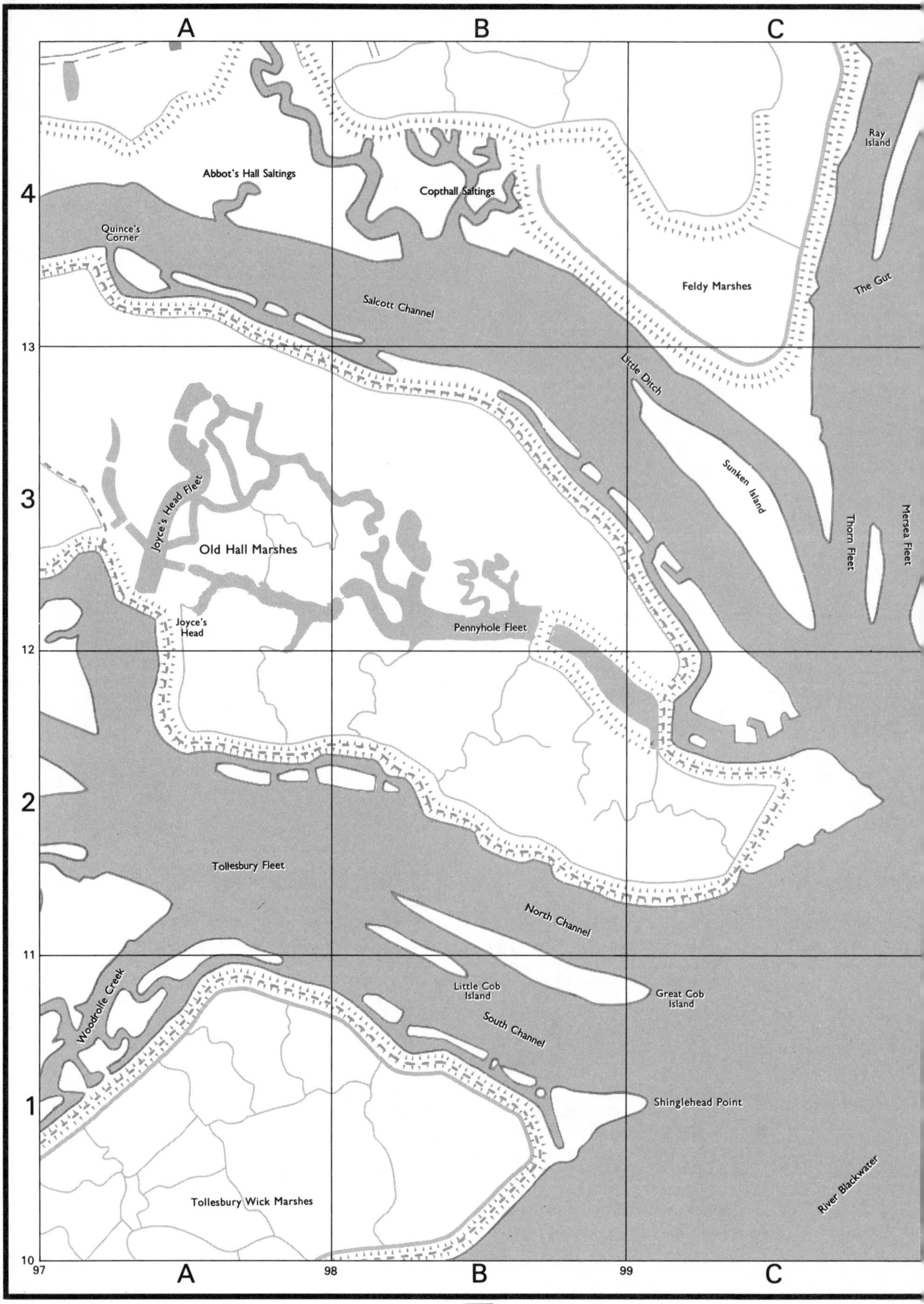
A
B
C
4
3
2
1
13
12
11
10
97
98
99
Abbot's Hall Saltings
Copthall Saltings
Quince's Corner
Salcott Channel
Feldy Marshes
Ray Island
The Gut
Little Ditch
Sunken Island
Thorn Fleet
Mersea Fleet
Joyce's Head Fleet
Old Hall Marshes
Joyce's Head
Pennyhole Fleet
Tollesbury Fleet
North Channel
Woodrolfe Creek
Little Cob Island
Great Cob Island
South Channel
Shinglehead Point
Tollesbury Wick Marshes
River Blackwater

136

104

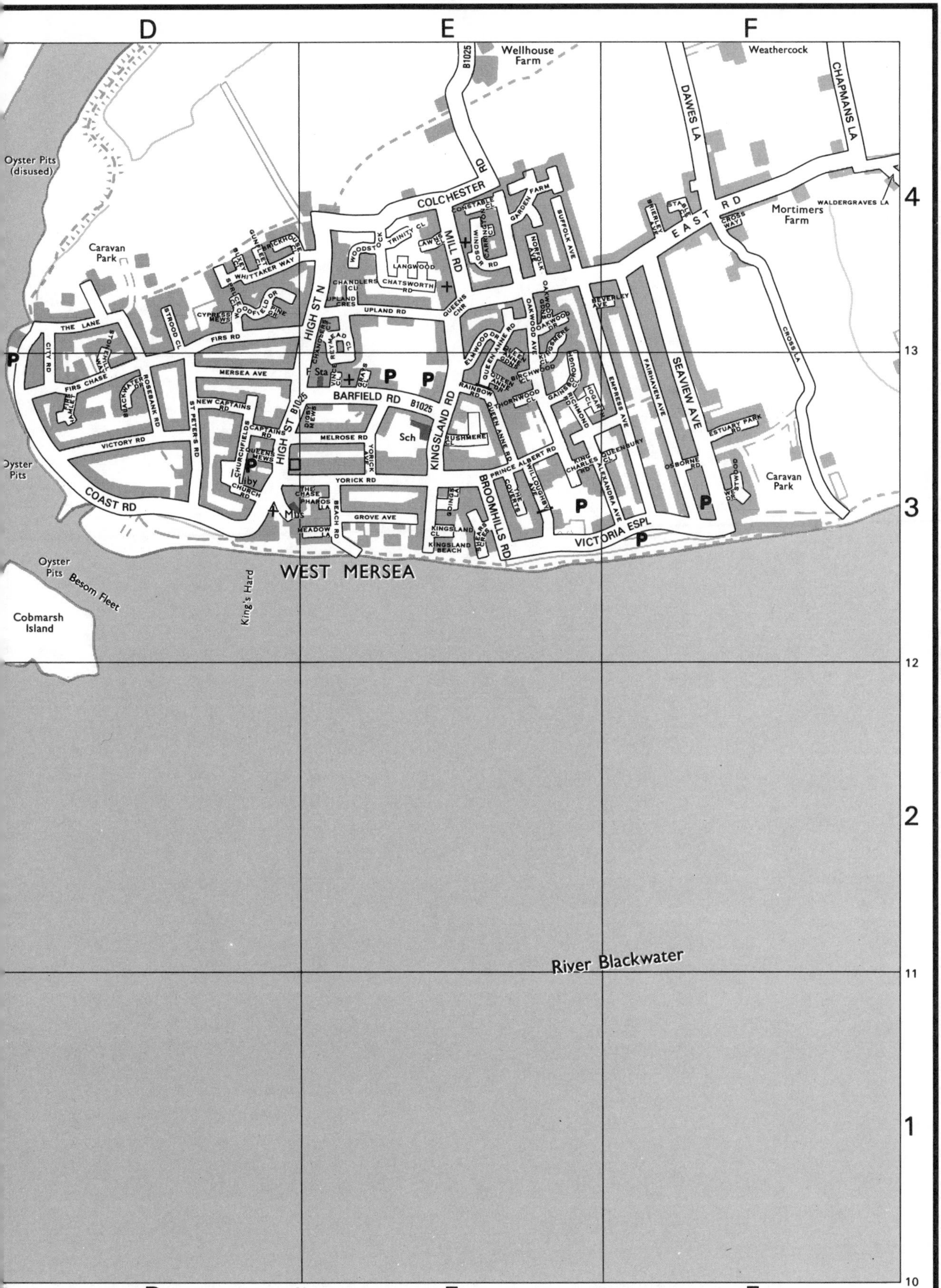
D
E
F
Wellhouse Farm
Weathercock
B1025
DAWES LA
CHAPMANS LA
Oyster Pits (disused)
Caravan Park
COLCHESTER RD
CONSTABLE CL
GARDEN FARM
EAST RD
Mortimers Farm
WALDERGRAVES LA
CROSS WAY
STABLE CL
BRIERLEY AVE
SUFFOLK AVE
NORFOLK AVE
CARRINGTON CL
ROBSON RD
MILL RD
TRINITY CL
LANGWOOD
WOODSTOCK
CHATSWORTH RD
CHANDLERS CL
UPLAND CRES
UPLAND RD
QUEENS CNR
BRICKHOUSE CL
WHITTAKER WAY
WOODFIELD DR
PINE CL
CYPRESS MEWS
STROOD CL
THE LANE
FIRS RD
CITY RD
FIRS CHASE
MERSEA AVE
HIGH ST N
BEVERLEY AVE
OAKWOOD AVE
OAKWOOD DR
ELMWOOD DR
QUEEN ANNE RD
KINGSMERE
BIRCHWOOD
GAINSBOROUGH
HOGARTH CL
EMPRESS AVE
FAIRHAVEN AVE
SEAVIEW AVE
CROSS LA
Sta
BARFIELD RD
B1025
RAINBOW RD
THORNWOOD CL
RICHMOND
BLACKWATER DR
ROSEBANK RD
NEW CAPTAINS RD
ST PETER'S RD
VICTORY RD
CAPTAINS RD
CHURCHFIELDS
QUEENS MEWS
HIGH ST B1025
DIGBY MEWS
MELROSE RD
Sch
KINGSLAND RD
RUSHMERE CL
YORICK AVE
YORICK RD
PRINCE ALBERT RD
KING CHARLES RD
QUEENBURY CL
ALEXANDRA AVE
OSBORNE RD
ESTUARY PARK RD
Caravan Park
Oyster Pits
COAST RD
Liby
CHURCH RD
Mus
THE CHASE
PHAROS LA
BEACH RD
GROVE AVE
MEADOW LA
KINGSLAND CL
KINGSLAND BEACH
BROOMHILLS RD
COVERTS
WILLOUGHBY AVE
VICTORIA ESPL
P
WEST MERSEA
Oyster Pits
Besom Fleet
King's Hard
Cobmarsh Island
River Blackwater
4
13
3
12
2
11
1
10
01
02

122

137

105

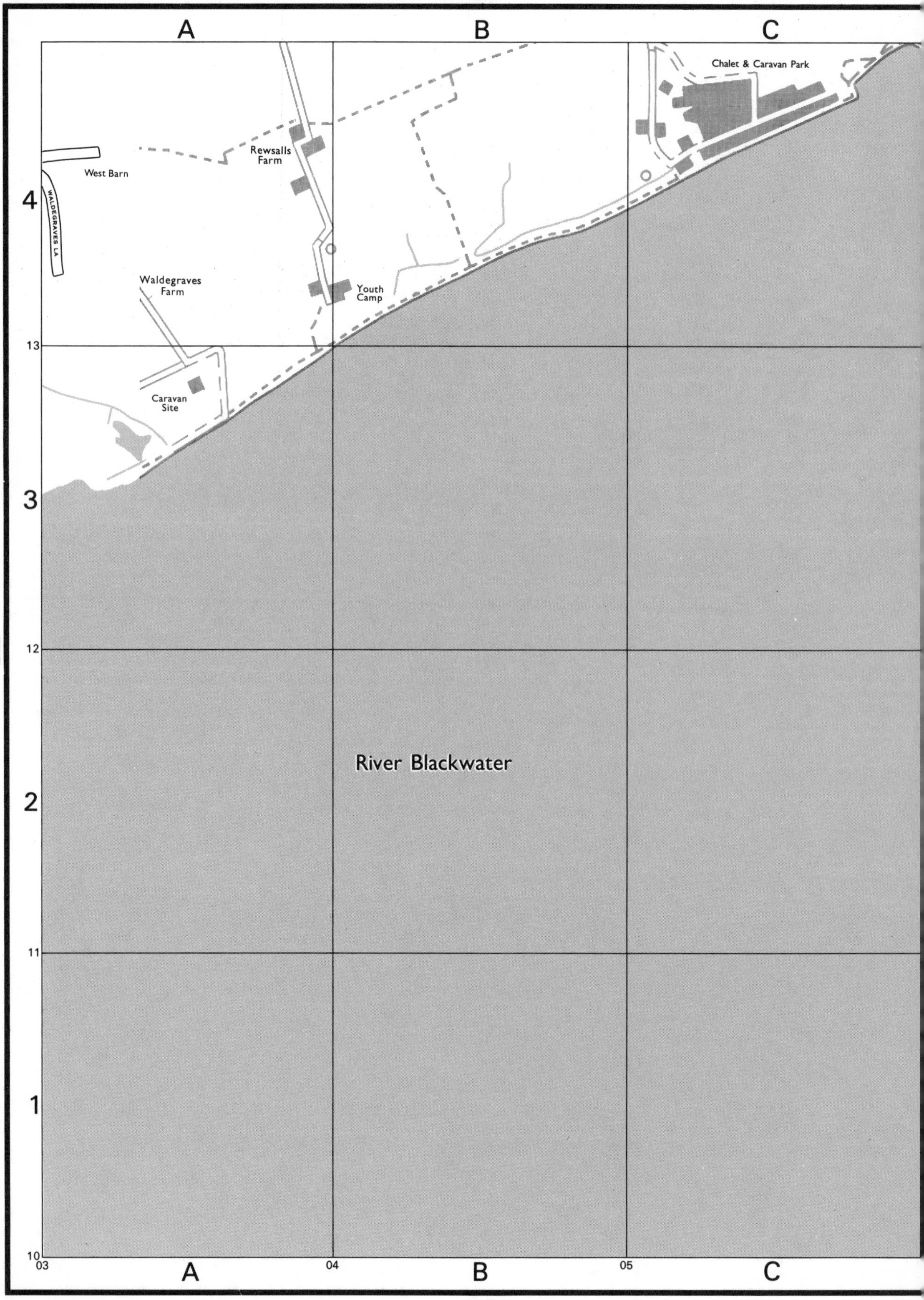
A
B
C
Chalet & Caravan Park
Rewsalls Farm
West Barn
WALDEGRAVES LA
4
Waldegraves Farm
Youth Camp
13
Caravan Site
3
12
River Blackwater
2
11
1
10
03
04
05
A
B
C

121

138

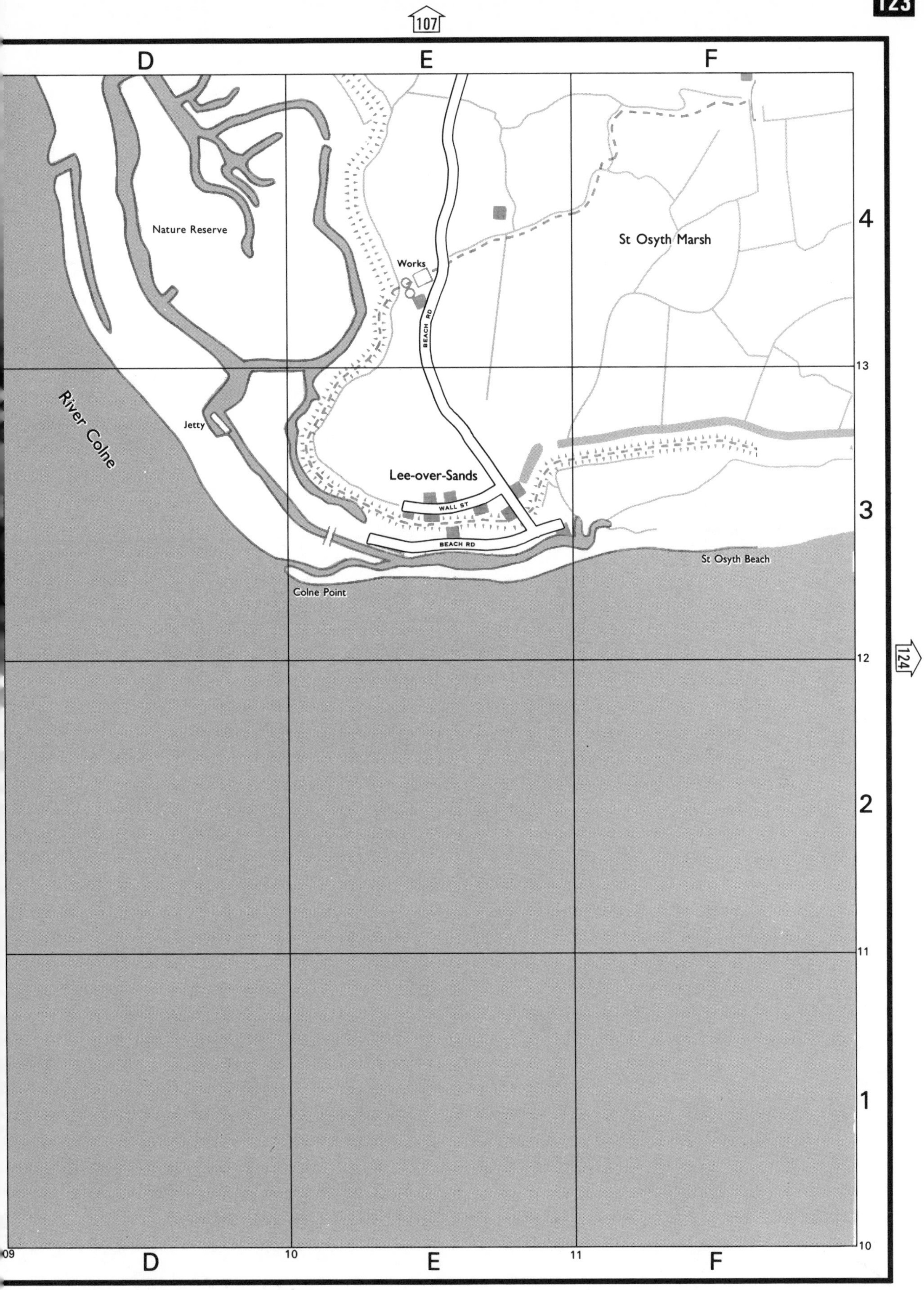
107
D
E
F
Nature Reserve
Works
BEACH RD
St Osyth Marsh
River Colne
Jetty
Lee-over-Sands
WALL ST
BEACH RD
St Osyth Beach
Colne Point
4
13
3
12
124
2
11
1
10
09
10
11
D
E
F

108

123

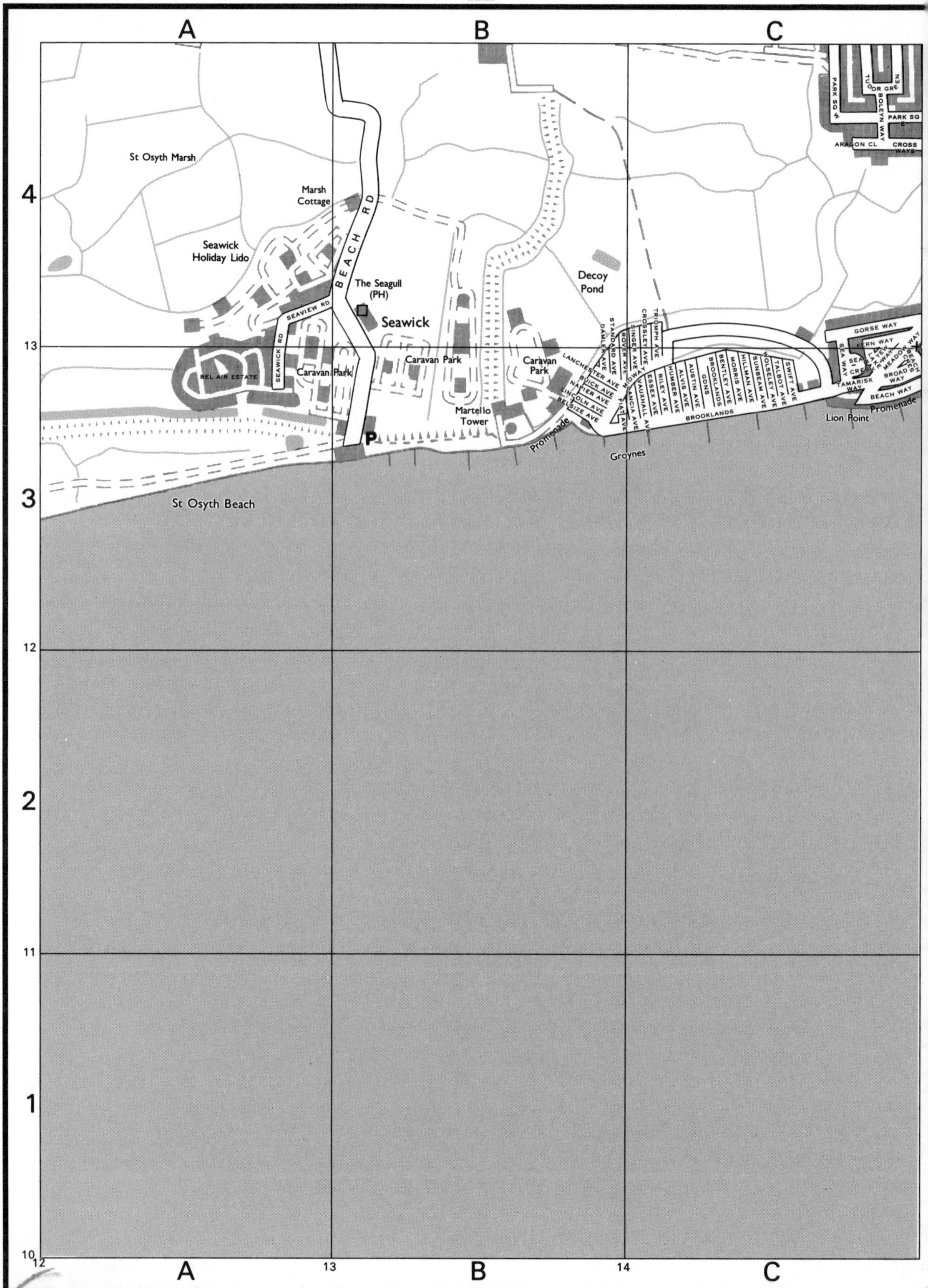
A
B
C
4
3
2
1
13
12
11
10
12
13
14
St Osyth Marsh
Marsh Cottage
Seawick Holiday Lido
BEACH RD
The Seagull (PH)
Seawick
SEAVIEW RD
SEAWICK RD
BEL AIR ESTATE
Caravan Park
Caravan Park
Caravan Park
Martello Tower
Decoy Pond
P
St Osyth Beach
Promenade
Groynes
LANCHESTER AVE
BUICK AVE
NAPIER AVE
LINCOLN AVE
BELSIZE AVE
DAIMLER AVE
STANDARD AVE
ROVER AVE
SINGER AVE
CROSSLEY AVE
TRIUMPH AVE
MIDWAY
FIAT AVE
LANCIA AVE
VAUXHALL AVE
ESSEX AVE
RILEY AVE
HUMBER AVE
ALVIS AVE
AUSTIN AVE
GDNS
BROOKLANDS
BENTLEY AVE
MORRIS AVE
HILLMAN AVE
SUNBEAM AVE
WOLSELEY AVE
TALBOT AVE
SWIFT AVE
BROOKLANDS
PARK SQ W
TUDOR GREEN
BOLEYN WAY
PARK SQ E
ARAGON CL
CROSS WAYS
GORSE WAY
FERN WAY
SEA WAY
TAMARISK WAY
BROAD WAY
BEACH WAY
MEADOW WAY
Lion Point
Promenade

not continued, see key diagram

109

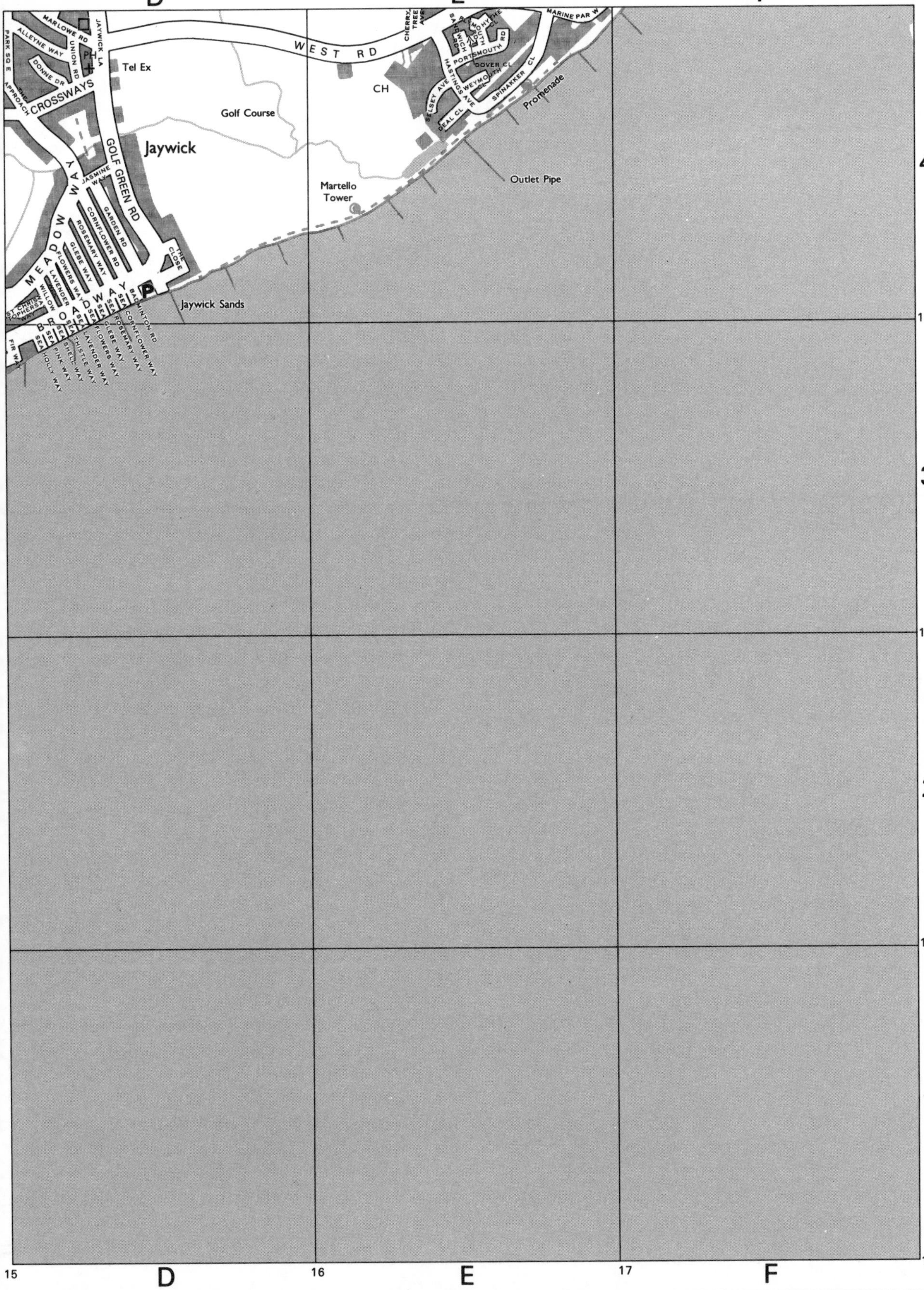

not continued, see key diagram

not continued, see key diagram

not continued, see key diagram

A
B
C
4
3
2
1
09
08
07
06
67
68
69
not continued, see key diagram
Clatterfoot
PH
Brittons Hall Farm
Beaumont Otes
Chobbing's Farm
Broom Wood
HOLLOW LA
Priors
Scot's Green
SCHOOL LA
PATCHING HALL LA
MICAWBER WAY
STEERFORTH CL
COPPERFIELD RD
TROTWOOD CL
CHUZZLEWIT DR
WELLER GR
LITTLE NELL
LITTLE DORRIT
BARNABY RUDGE
SOWERBERRY CL
QUILP DR
DOMBEY CL
LONGLEAT CL
OLIVER WAY
DROOD CL
TAPLEY RD
TRADDLES CL
Sch
Brickbarns Farm
PICKWICK AVE
BARKIS CL
DICKENS PL
WICKFIELD ASH
NICKLEBY RD
DARNAY RISE
MADELINE PL
BELLAWNEY
LINTWICH MANOR
BOUNDERBY GR
PEGGOTTY CL
TUGBY PL
PIPCHIN RD
Athletic Stadium
PARTRIDGE AVE
MENDIP RD
MALVERN CL
GRAMPIAN GR
CHEVIOT DR
COTSWOLD CRES
NICHOLAS CT
College Wood
P
CHIGNALL RD
WICKLOW AVE
PENNINE RD
SALERNO WAY
CASSINO RD
ST NAZAIRE RD
Schs
ARNHEM RD
MERSEY WAY
KENNET WAY
WELLAND AVE
1 SCOTTS WLK
2 PAN WLK
3 BEAUMONT WLK
MELBOURNE AVE
SPALDING AVE
TAYLOR AVE
ANDERSON AVE
WEST AVE
OCKELFORD AVE
TENNYSON RD
ARTHUR CT
EASTERN CRES
NORTH AVE
EDEN WAY
CHERWELL DR
TRENT RD
QUEENSLAND CRES
CANBERRA CL
TASMAN CT
HOBART CL
HUTCHISON
LANGTON AVE
PINES RD
SQUIRRELLS CT
Schs
AVON RD
TYNE WAY
DERWENT WAY
THAMES AVE
CLYDE CRES
FOX CRES
THE GREEN
KINGS RD
DIXON AVE
SWISS AVE
New Barns
River Can
Sch
HIGHFIELD RD
SUNNINGDALE RD
ST JAMES PARK
MEDWAY CL
SKREENS CT
ST FABIAN'S DR
LICHFIELD CL
CANTERBURY WAY
ACRES END
WARWICK SQ
TOWER AVE
PARK AVE
Offices
Thieves' Corner
A1060
ROXWELL
RD
ROXWELL RD
A1060
Manor House
PH
Warren Farm
WARREN LA
ROXWELL AVE
BEACH'S DR
CLIVEDEN CL
SACKVILLE CL
FITZWALTER PL
BUNDICK'S HILL
RAINSFORD RD
Admiral's Park
ADMIRALS WLK
RAINSFORD AVE
PRIMROSE HILL
Warren Bridge
COW WATERING LA
River Can
West Park
Lawford Lane (Path)
College
LORDSHIP RD
FOX BURROWS LA
BEECHES RD
HAWKHURST CL
BENEDICT DR
NABBOTT RD
RAVENSBOURNE DR
BEECHES CL
Schs
Offices
RAINSFORD LA
A1016
F Sta
Moat
Lordship Farm
ABBESS CL
ST PETER'S
ST CATHERINE'S RD
ASHFORD RD
PRIORY CL
DANE RD
CANUDEN RD
P
River Wid
MAYFIELD RD
ORCHARD
BRUCE RD
WEKHAM
LAWFORD LA
MELBA CT
Daws Farm
BLACKTHORN CL
BACK RD
ST JOHN'S RD
ONGAR RD
Liby
CHANCERY PL
THE GREEN
Writtle Bridge
HATFIELD GR
DEAN WAY
FOREST DR
WINDSOR WAY
WATERHOUSE LA
Sch
EXMOOR CL
ROTHBURY RD
HARewood RD
HAINAULT GR
SHERWOOD DR
STANSTED CL
EPPING CL
CHARNWOOD AVE
BILTON RD
LONG MEADS CL
PURCELL CL
LITTLE MEADOW
P
BRIDGE ST
Skeggs Farm
Wks
MILLFIELDS
LODGE RD
ROMANS PL
CHELMSFORD RD
SAVERNAKE RD
DELAMERE RD
A1016
WATERHOUSE ST
CROMPTON ST
HOME MEAD
SAWNEY BROOK
LAURENCE CROFT
ROMANS WAY
Writtle
LONG BRANDOCKS
THE COVERT
THE PRIORY
LONGACRE
WRITTLE RD
ROSSENDALE

not continued, see key diagram

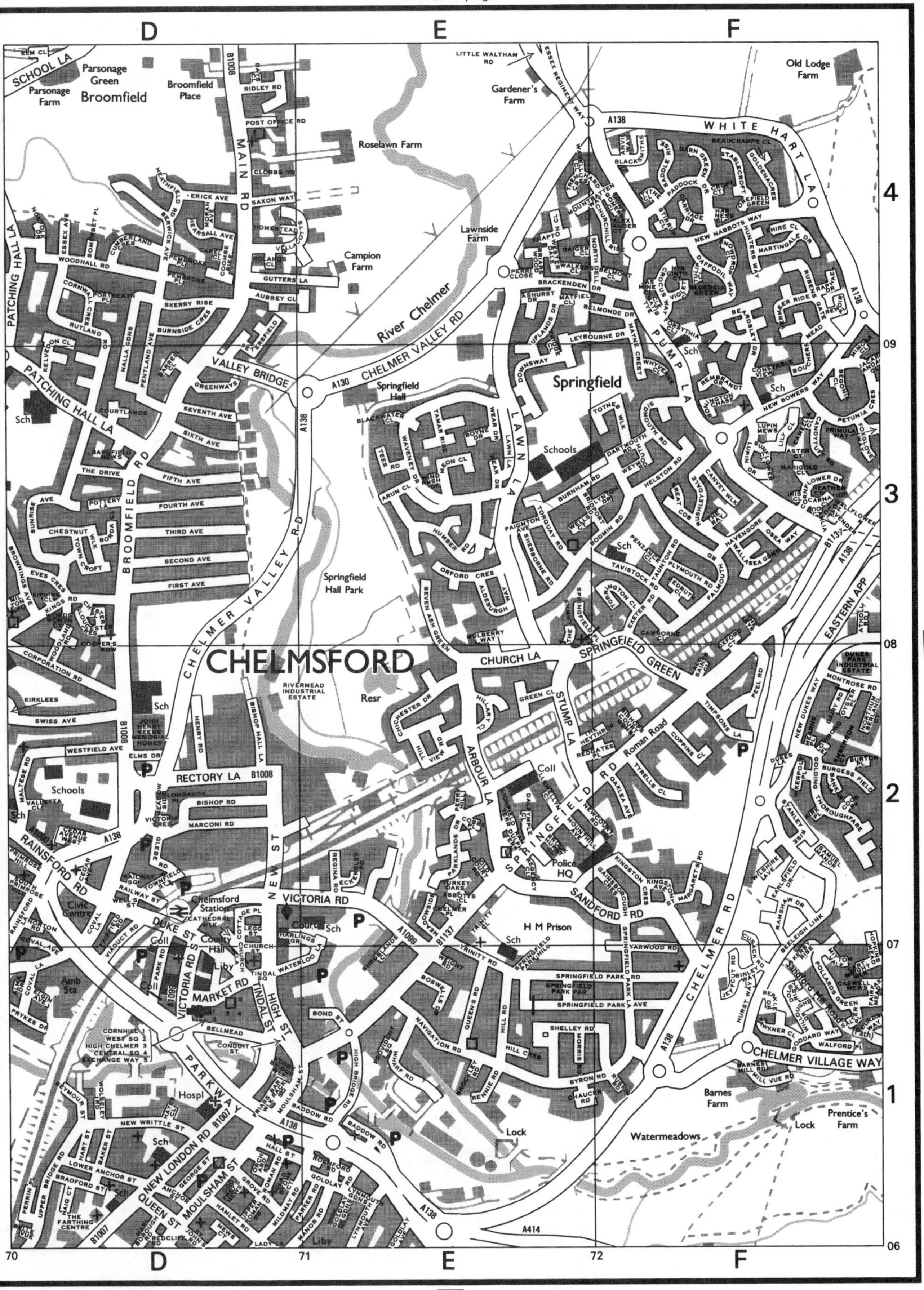
D
E
F
4
3
2
1
09
08
07
06
70
71
72
Parsonage Green
Parsonage Farm
Broomfield
Broomfield Place
SCHOOL LA
MAIN RD
RIDLEY RD
POST OFFICE RD
Roselawn Farm
LITTLE WALTHAM RD
ESSEX REGIMENT WAY
Gardener's Farm
Old Lodge Farm
WHITE HART LA
A138
ERICK AVE
SAXON WAY
Lawnside Farm
Campion Farm
WOODHALL RD
CUMBERLAND CRES
GUTTERS LA
AUBREY CL
SKERRY RISE
RUTLAND RD
PATCHING HALL LA
River Chelmer
CHELMER VALLEY RD
VALLEY BRIDGE
A130
Springfield Hall
BRACKENDEN DR
BELMONDE DR
LEYBOURNE DR
PUMP LA
Springfield
NEW NABBOTS WAY
MARTINGALE DR
NEW BOWERS WAY
SEVENTH AVE
SIXTH AVE
FIFTH AVE
FOURTH AVE
THIRD AVE
SECOND AVE
FIRST AVE
COURTLANDS
THE DRIVE
BROOMFIELD RD
Sch
Schools
TAMAR RISE
LAWN LA
DARTMOUTH RD
HELSTON RD
CANVEY WLK
HUMBER RD
ORFORD CRES
SEVEN ASH GREEN
Springfield Hall Park
TAVISTOCK RD
TAUNTON RD
PLYMOUTH RD
FALMOUTH RD
EASTERN APP
B1137
CHELMSFORD
CHURCH LA
SPRINGFIELD GREEN
RIVERMEAD INDUSTRIAL ESTATE
Resr
STUMP LA
ARBOUR LA
Roman Road
TIMPSONS LA
DUKES PARK INDUSTRIAL ESTATE
MONTROSE RD
CORPORATION RD
KIRKLEES
SWISS AVE
WESTFIELD AVE
B1008
JOHN HENRY KEENE MEMORIAL HOMES
RECTORY LA
BISHOP RD
MARCONI RD
Coll
SPRINGFIELD RD
Police HQ
SANDFORD RD
KINGSTON CRES
H M Prison
CHELMER RD
RAINSFORD RD
A1060
Civic Centre
Chelmsford Station
DUKE ST
VICTORIA RD
NEW ST
County Hall
Court
Liby
Amb Sta
MARKET RD
TINDAL ST
HIGH ST
A1099
A1137
SPRINGFIELD PARK RD
SPRINGFIELD PARK AVE
SHELLEY RD
MORRIS RD
BYRON RD
CHAUCER RD
NAVIGATION RD
QUEEN'S RD
HILL RD
WHARF RD
BOND ST
CORNHILL 1
WEST SQ 2
HIGH CHELMER 3
CENTRAL SQ 4
EXCHANGE WAY 5
BELLMEAD
CONDUIT ST
PARKWAY
Hospl
NEW WRITTLE ST
NEW LONDON RD
B1007
MOULSHAM ST
QUEEN ST
BADDOW RD
HIGH BRIDGE RD
Lock
Barnes Farm
Watermeadows
Prentice's Farm
CHELMER VILLAGE WAY
BARNES MILL RD
SANDFORD MILL ROAD
WALFORD PL
GODDARD WAY
BEELEIGH LINK
A414
LOWER ANCHOR ST
BRADFORD ST
THE FARMING CENTRE
ROCHFORD RD
GOLDLAY RD
LADY LA

128

112

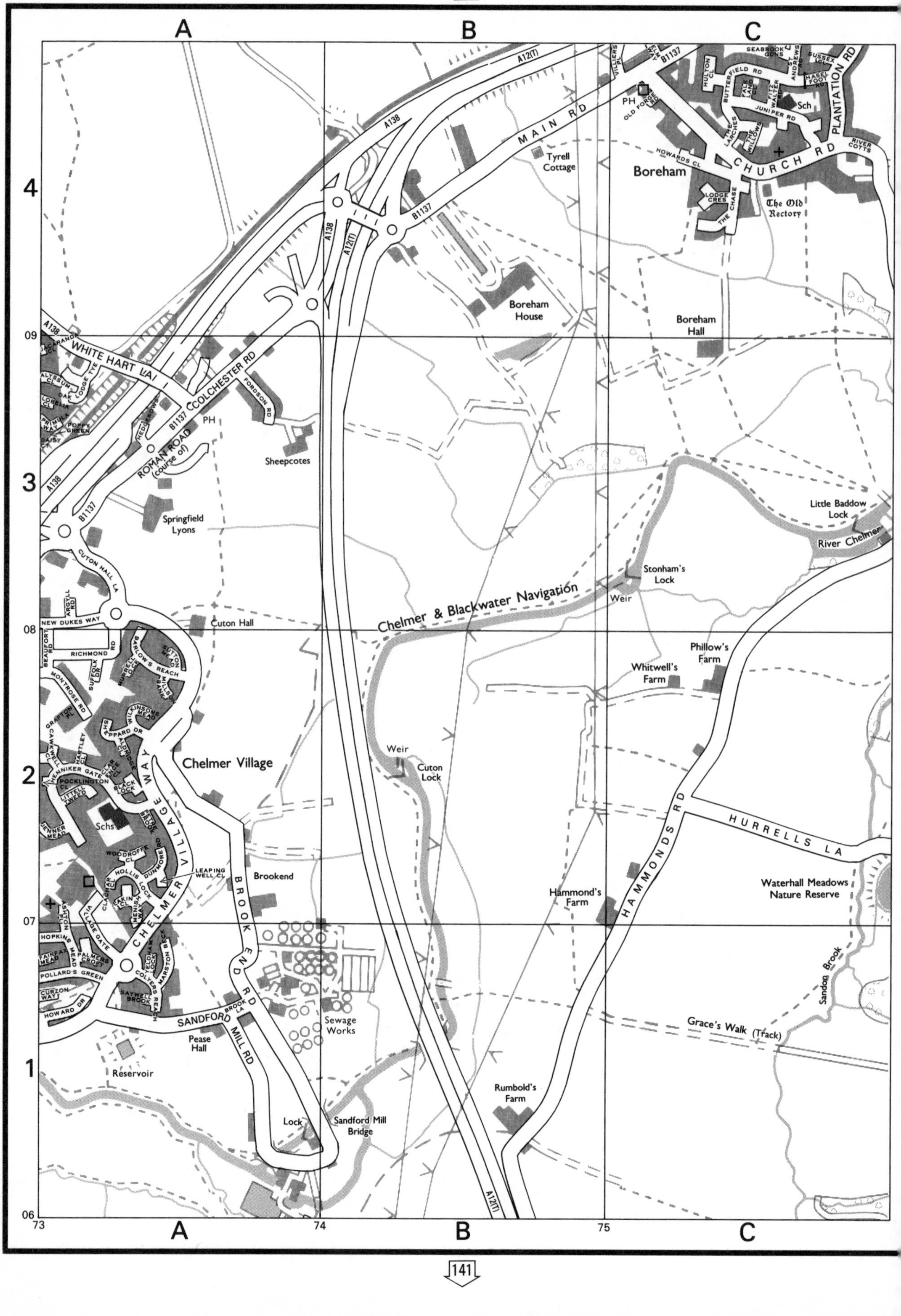
A
B
C
4
3
2
1
09
08
07
06
73
74
75
A12(T)
A138
B1137
MAIN RD
Tyrell Cottage
Boreham
CHURCH RD
PLANTATION RD
RIVER COTTS
The Old Rectory
SEABROOK GDNS
SUSSEX CL
HULTON CL
BUTTERFIELD RD
JUNIPER RD
HOWARDS CL
LODGE CRES
THE CHASE
OLD FORGE RD
PH
Sch
Boreham House
Boreham Hall
WHITE HART LA
COLCHESTER RD
FORDSON RD
ROMAN ROAD (course of)
Sheepcotes
Springfield Lyons
CUTON HALL LA
NEW DUKES WAY
Cuton Hall
RICHMOND
MONTROSE RD
Chelmer Village
CHELMER VILLAGE WAY
Schs
LEAPING WELL CL
Brookend
BROOK END RD
Chelmer & Blackwater Navigation
Little Baddow Lock
River Chelmer
Stonham's Lock
Weir
Whitwell's Farm
Phillow's Farm
Cuton Lock
HURRELLS LA
HAMMONDS RD
Hammond's Farm
Waterhall Meadows Nature Reserve
Sandon Brook
Grace's Walk (Track)
SANDFORD MILL RD
BROOK LA
Pease Hall
Reservoir
Sewage Works
Lock
Sandford Mill Bridge
Rumbold's Farm
HOWARD DR
POLLARD'S GREEN
CURZON WAY

127

141

113

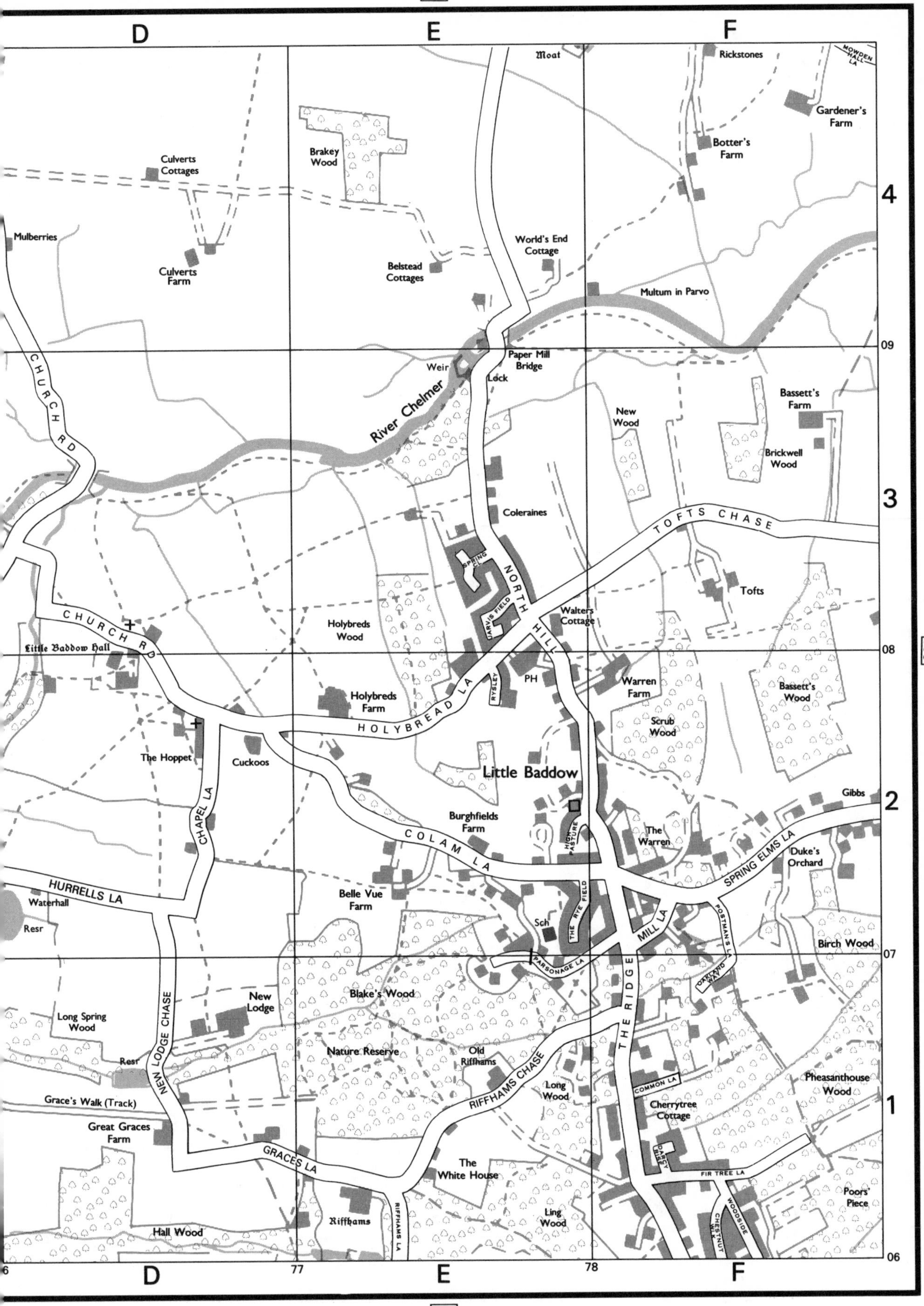
D
E
F
Moat
Rickstones
MOWDEN HALL LA
Gardener's Farm
Botter's Farm
Culverts Cottages
Brakey Wood
4
Mulberries
World's End Cottage
Belstead Cottages
Culverts Farm
Multum in Parvo
09
Paper Mill Bridge
Weir
Lock
CHURCH RD
River Chelmer
New Wood
Bassett's Farm
Brickwell Wood
3
Coleraines
TOFTS CHASE
SPRING CL
NORTH HILL
Tofts
JARVIS FIELD
Walters Cottage
CHURCH RD
Holybreds Wood
Little Baddow Hall
08
RYSLEY
PH
Warren Farm
Bassett's Wood
Holybreds Farm
Scrub Wood
HOLYBREAD LA
The Hoppet
Cuckoos
Little Baddow
Gibbs
2
CHAPEL LA
Burghfields Farm
HIGH PASTURE
The Warren
COLAM LA
Duke's Orchard
SPRING ELMS LA
HURRELLS LA
Belle Vue Farm
Waterhall
THE RYE FIELD
Sch
MILL LA
POSTMAN'S LA
Resr
Birch Wood
07
PARSONAGE LA
OAKLANDS WAY
New Lodge
Blake's Wood
THE RIDGE
Long Spring Wood
NEW LODGE CHASE
Nature Reserve
Old Riffhams
Resr
RIFFHAMS CHASE
Long Wood
Pheasanthouse Wood
Grace's Walk (Track)
COMMON LA
Cherrytree Cottage
1
Great Graces Farm
GRACES LA
The White House
DARCY RISE
FIR TREE LA
Poors' Piece
Riffhams
Ling Wood
WOODSIDE
CHESTNUT WLK
RIFFHAMS LA
Hall Wood
06
76
77
78
D
E
F

130

142

114

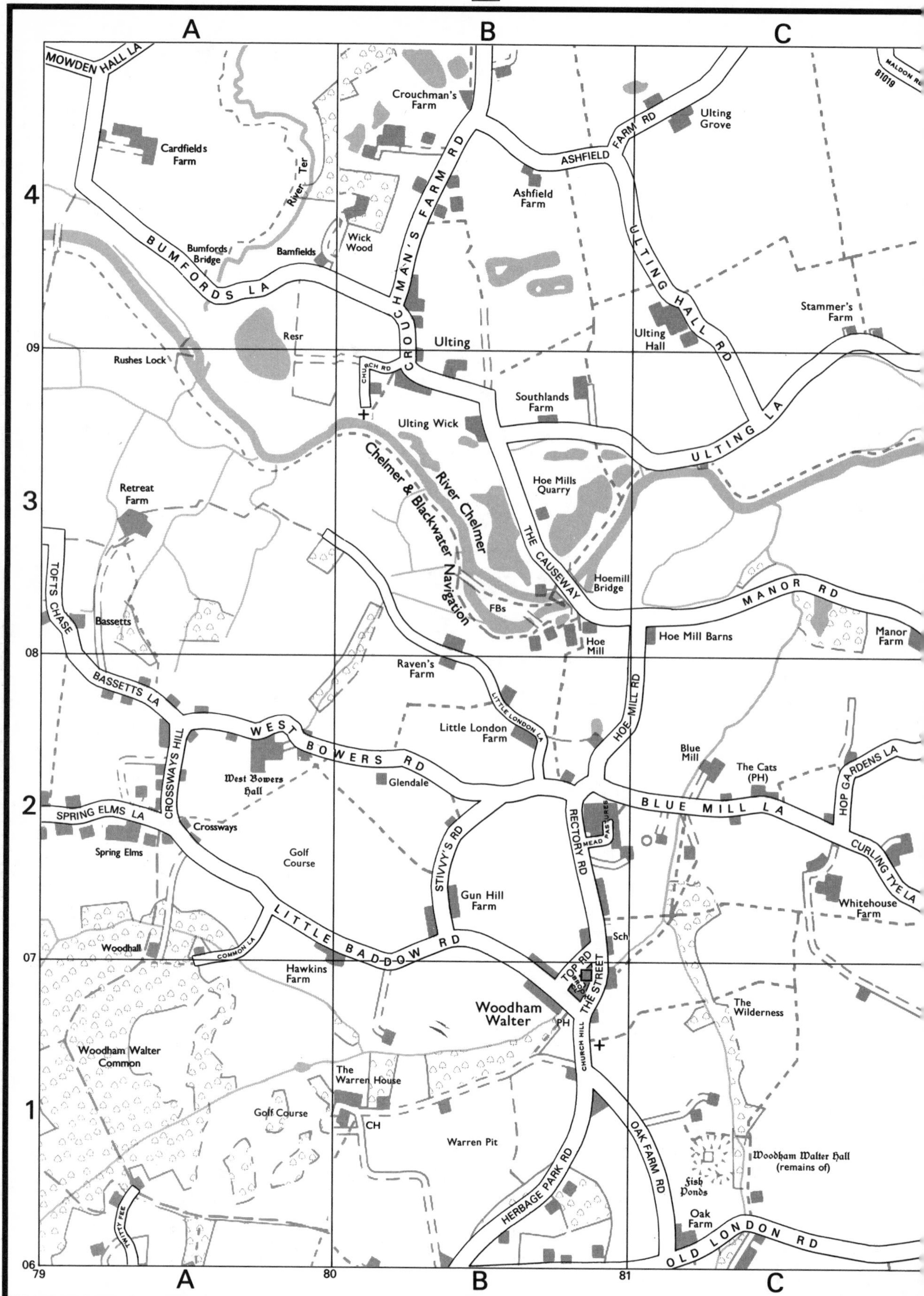
A
B
C
4
3
2
1
09
08
07
06
79
80
81
MOWDEN HALL LA
Cardfields Farm
River Ter
Crouchman's Farm
CROUCHMAN'S FARM RD
ASHFIELD FARM RD
Ulting Grove
MALDON RD
B1019
Ashfield Farm
Wick Wood
Bamfields
Bumfords Bridge
BUMFORDS LA
ULTING HALL RD
Stammer's Farm
Resr
Ulting
Ulting Hall
Rushes Lock
CHURCH RD
Southlands Farm
Ulting Wick
ULTING LA
Chelmer & Blackwater Navigation
River Chelmer
Hoe Mills Quarry
Retreat Farm
THE CAUSEWAY
Hoemill Bridge
MANOR RD
TOFTS CHASE
Bassetts
FBs
Hoe Mill
Hoe Mill Barns
Manor Farm
Raven's Farm
BASSETTS LA
LITTLE LONDON LA
HOE MILL RD
Little London Farm
WEST BOWERS RD
CROSSWAYS HILL
West Bowers Hall
Glendale
Blue Mill
The Cats (PH)
HOP GARDENS LA
SPRING ELMS LA
Crossways
STIVVY'S RD
RECTORY RD
MEAD PASTURES
BLUE MILL LA
CURLING TYE LA
Spring Elms
Golf Course
Gun Hill Farm
Whitehouse Farm
LITTLE BADDOW RD
Woodhall
COMMON LA
Sch
TOP RD
THE STREET
Hawkins Farm
The Wilderness
Woodham Walter
PH
CHURCH HILL
Woodham Walter Common
The Warren House
Golf Course
CH
Warren Pit
OAK FARM RD
HERBAGE PARK RD
Woodham Walter Hall (remains of)
Fish Ponds
Oak Farm
TWITTY FEE
OLD LONDON RD

129

143

115

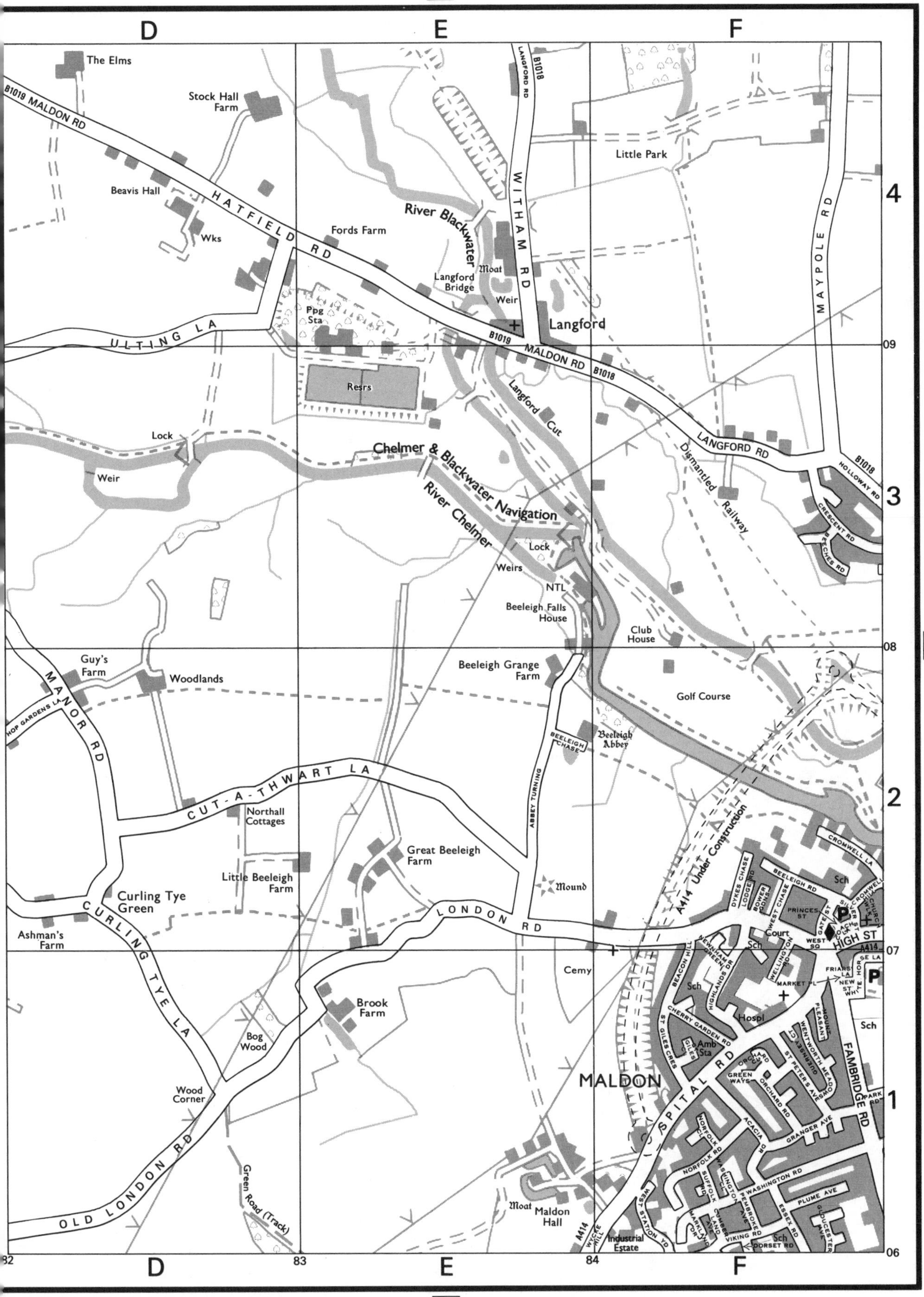
D
E
F
The Elms
B1019 MALDON RD
Stock Hall Farm
Beavis Hall
Wks
HATFIELD RD
Fords Farm
River Blackwater
Moat
Langford Bridge
Weir
LANGFORD RD
B1018
WITHAM RD
Little Park
Langford
MAYPOLE RD
Ppg Sta
ULTING LA
B1019
MALDON RD
B1018
Resrs
Langford Cut
Lock
Weir
Chelmer & Blackwater Navigation
River Chelmer
LANGFORD RD
Dismantled Railway
B1018
HOLLOWAY RD
CRESCENT RD
BEECHES RD
Lock
Weirs
NTL
Beeleigh Falls House
Club House
Guy's Farm
Woodlands
MANOR RD
HOP GARDENS LA
Beeleigh Grange Farm
Golf Course
BEELEIGH CHASE
Beeleigh Abbey
CUT-A-THWART LA
Northall Cottages
ABBEY TURNING
A414 Under Construction
CROMWELL LA
Great Beeleigh Farm
Little Beeleigh Farm
Mound
Curling Tye Green
Ashman's Farm
CURLING TYE LA
LONDON RD
DYKES CHASE
LODGE RD
BOWER GDNS
BEELEIGH RD
WEST CHASE
PRINCES ST
Sch
Court
WEST SQ
HIGH ST
A414
Cemy
BEACON HILL
NEWNHAM GREEN
HIGHLANDS DR
WELLINGTON RD
MARKET PL
NEW ST
WHITE HORSE LA
Sch
Brook Farm
Bog Wood
CHERRY GARDEN RD
Hospl
ST GILES CRES
Amb Sta
SPITAL RD
FAMBRIDGE RD
MALDON
Wood Corner
OLD LONDON RD
Green Road (Track)
NORFOLK RD
ACACIA DR
GRANGER AVE
WASHINGTON RD
PLUME AVE
GLOUCESTER AVE
ESSEX RD
Moat
Maldon Hall
A414
WEST STATION YD
Industrial Estate
VIKING RD
DORSET RD
Sch
4
3
2
1
09
08
07
06
82
83
84

132

144

116

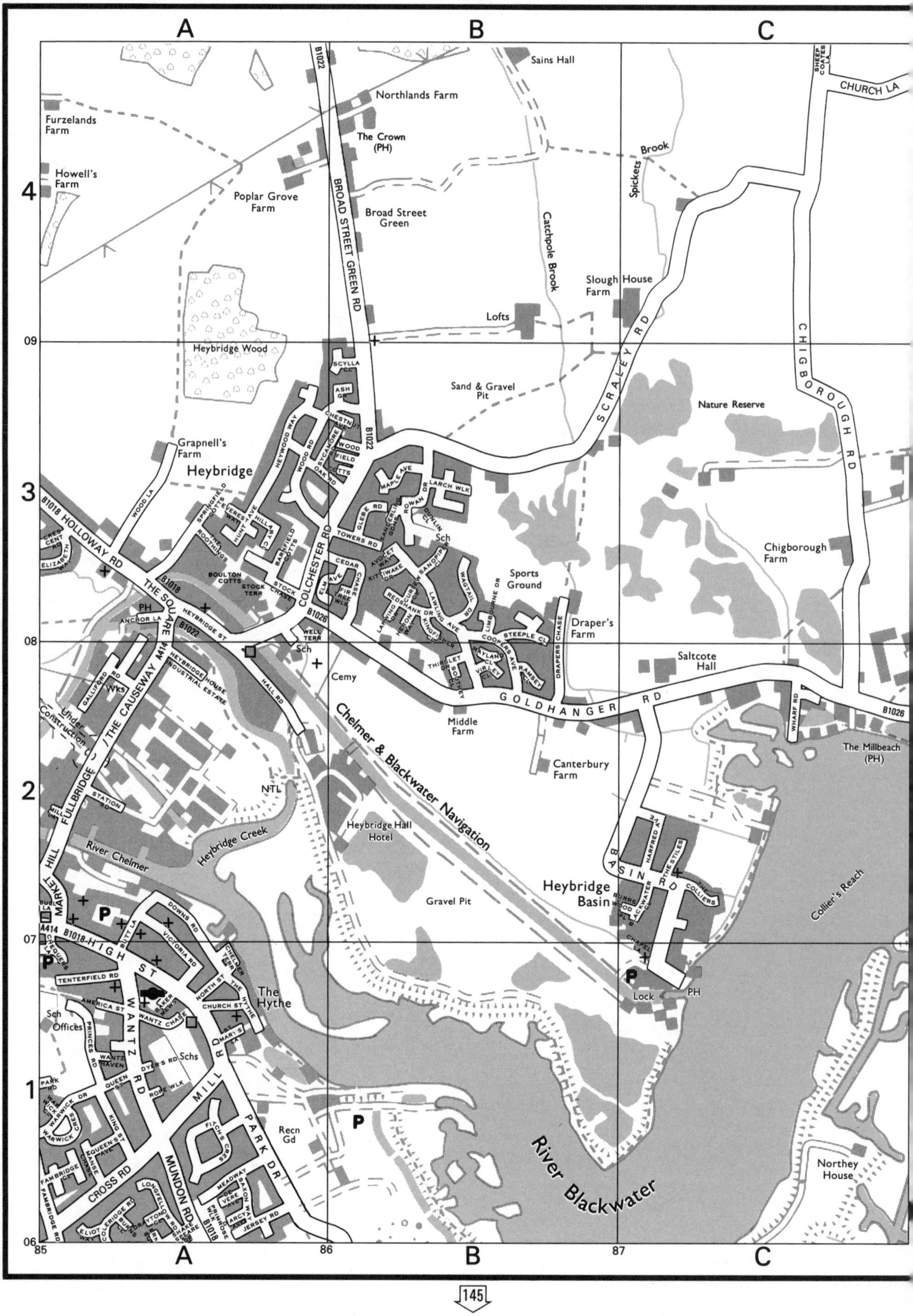
A
B
C
4
3
2
1
09
08
07
06
85
86
87
Sains Hall
Northlands Farm
Furzelands Farm
The Crown (PH)
Howell's Farm
Poplar Grove Farm
Broad Street Green
BROAD STREET GREEN RD
B1022
Catchpole Brook
Spickets Brook
CHURCH LA
SHEEP COATES LA
Slough House Farm
Lofts
Heybridge Wood
SCRALEY RD
CHIGBOROUGH RD
Sand & Gravel Pit
Nature Reserve
Grapnell's Farm
Heybridge
WOOD LA
HOLLOWAY RD
B1018
Chigborough Farm
Sports Ground
Sch
COLCHESTER RD
TOWERS RD
GLEBE RD
MAPLE AVE
LARCH WLK
THE SQUARE
PH
ANCHOR LA
HEYBRIDGE ST
B1026
Draper's Farm
DRAPERS CHASE
COOPERS AVE
STEEPLE CL
Saltcote Hall
GOLDHANGER RD
Cemy
HALL RD
HEYBRIDGE HOUSE INDUSTRIAL ESTATE
THE CAUSEWAY
A414
GALLIFORD RD
Wks
Under Construction
Middle Farm
WHARF RD
The Millbeach (PH)
Canterbury Farm
Chelmer & Blackwater Navigation
NTL
STATION RD
FULLBRIDGE
MARKET HILL
Heybridge Hall Hotel
Heybridge Creek
River Chelmer
BASIN RD
Heybridge Basin
Gravel Pit
Collier's Reach
HIGH ST
P
TENTERFIELD RD
DOWNS RD
VICTORIA RD
NORTH ST
THE HYTHE
CHURCH ST
The Hythe
Lock
PH
AMERICA ST
WANTZ CHASE
WANTZ RD
Sch
Offices
PRINCES RD
Schs
DYER'S RD
ROPE WLK
MILL RD
PARK DR
QUEEN ST
WARWICK DR
KING ST
Recn Gd
River Blackwater
CROSS RD
MUNDON RD
FAMBRIDGE RD
Northey House

131

145

117

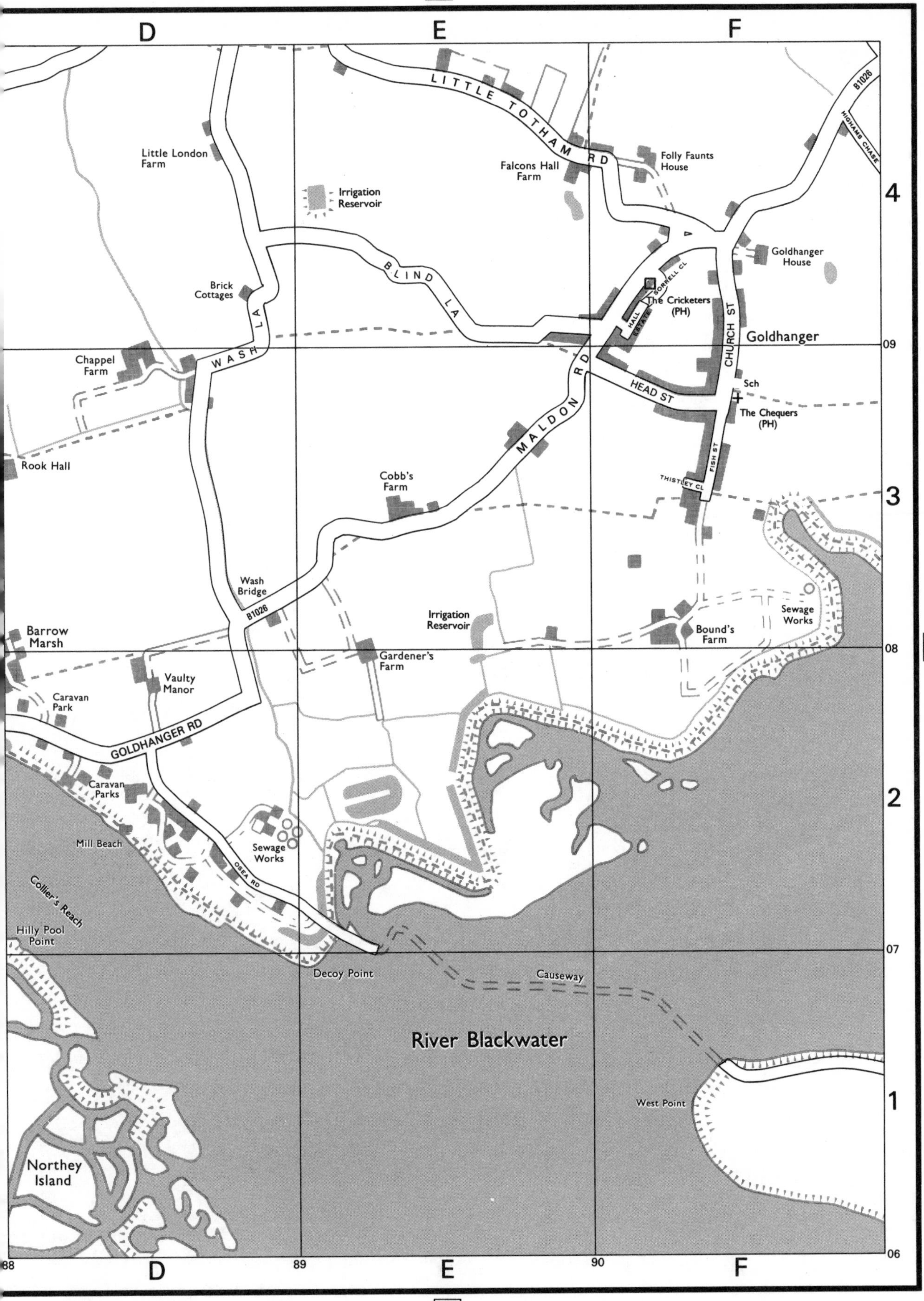
D
E
F
LITTLE TOTHAM RD
B1026
HIGHAMS CHASE
Little London Farm
Irrigation Reservoir
Falcons Hall Farm
Folly Faunts House
4
BLIND LA
Goldhanger House
Brick Cottages
SORRELL CL
The Cricketers (PH)
HALL ESTATE
CHURCH ST
WASH LA
Goldhanger
09
Chappel Farm
MALDON RD
HEAD ST
Sch
The Chequers (PH)
Rook Hall
FISH ST
Cobb's Farm
THISTLEY CL
3
Wash Bridge
Irrigation Reservoir
Sewage Works
Bound's Farm
Barrow Marsh
Gardener's Farm
08
Vaulty Manor
Caravan Park
GOLDHANGER RD
Caravan Parks
2
Mill Beach
Sewage Works
OSEA RD
Collier's Reach
Hilly Pool Point
07
Decoy Point
Causeway
River Blackwater
West Point
1
Northey Island
88
89
90
06
D
E
F

134

146

118

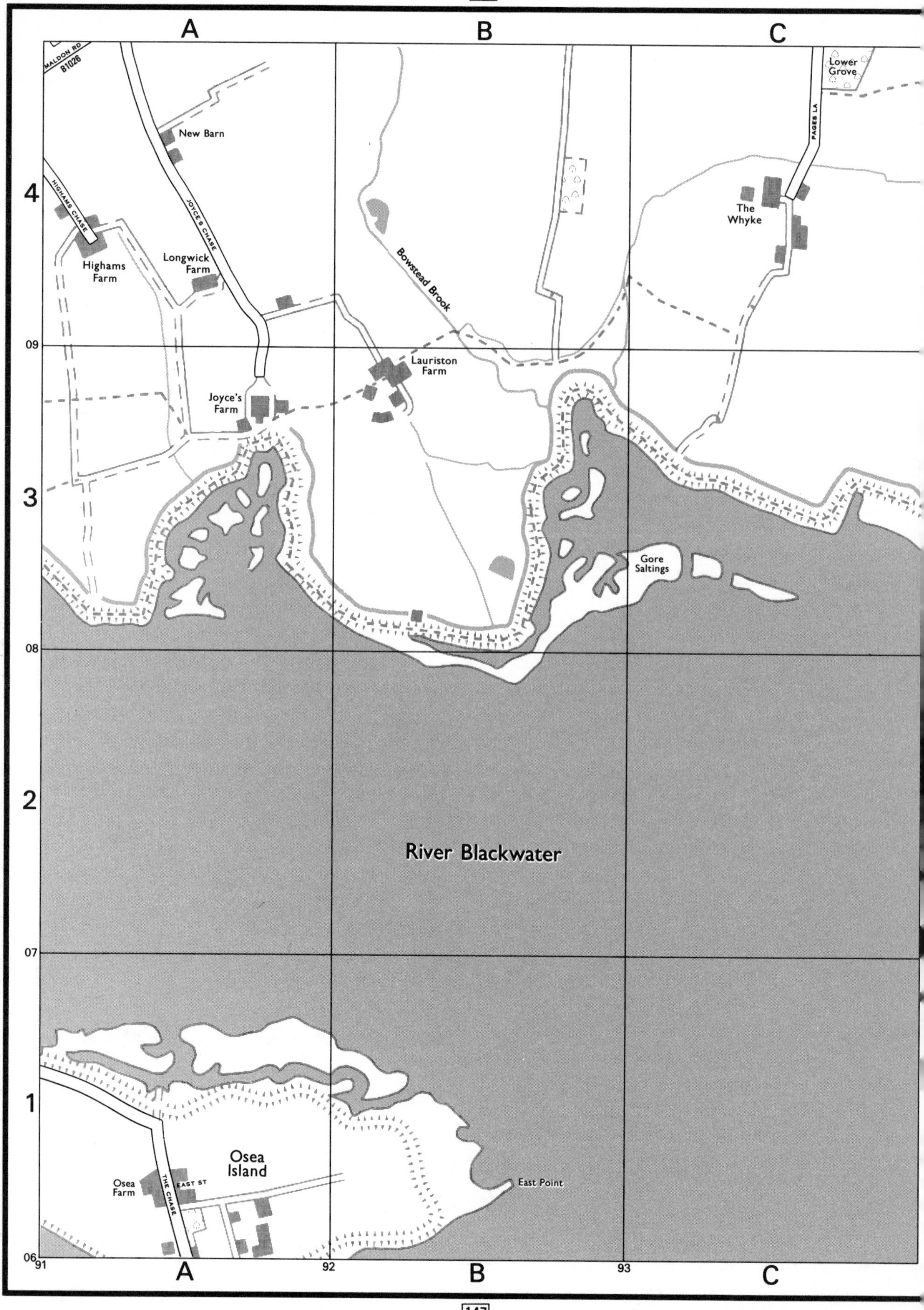
A
B
C
4
3
2
1
09
08
07
06
91
92
93
MALDON RD B1026
HIGHAMS CHASE
JOYCES CHASE
PAGES LA
New Barn
Highams Farm
Longwick Farm
Joyce's Farm
Lauriston Farm
Bowstead Brook
Lower Grove
The Whyke
Gore Saltings
River Blackwater
Osea Island
Osea Farm
THE CHASE
EAST ST
East Point

133

147

119

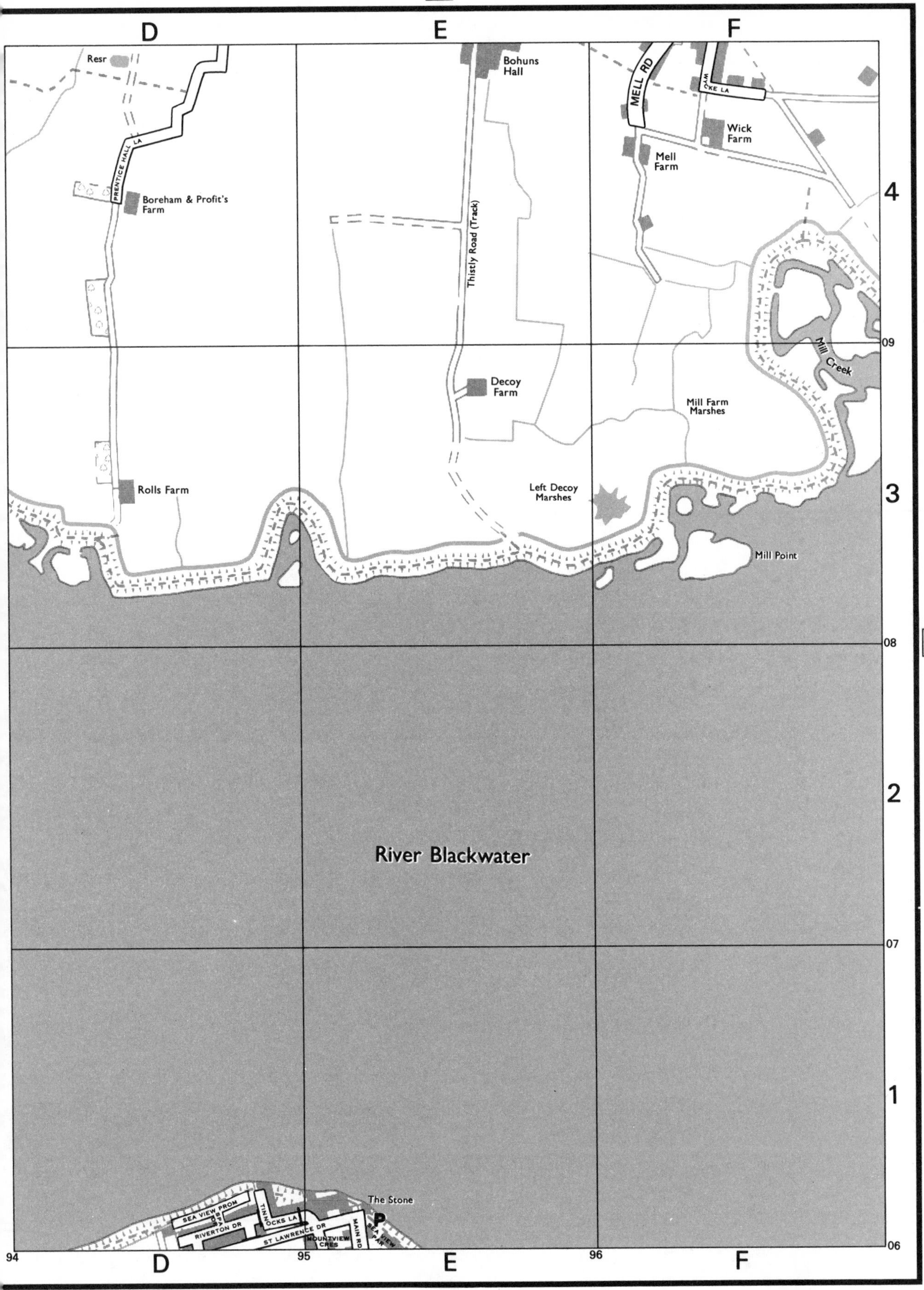
D
E
F
Resr
PRENTICE HALL LA
Boreham & Profit's Farm
Bohuns Hall
Thistly Road (Track)
MELL RD
CKE LA
Wick Farm
Mell Farm
4
09
Mill Creek
Decoy Farm
Mill Farm Marshes
Rolls Farm
Left Decoy Marshes
3
Mill Point
08
2
River Blackwater
07
1
The Stone
SEA VIEW PROM
SPA DR
TINNOCKS LA
RIVERTON DR
ST LAWRENCE DR
MOUNTVIEW CRES
MAIN RD
SEA VIEW PAR
P
06
94
95
96
D
E
F

136

148

120

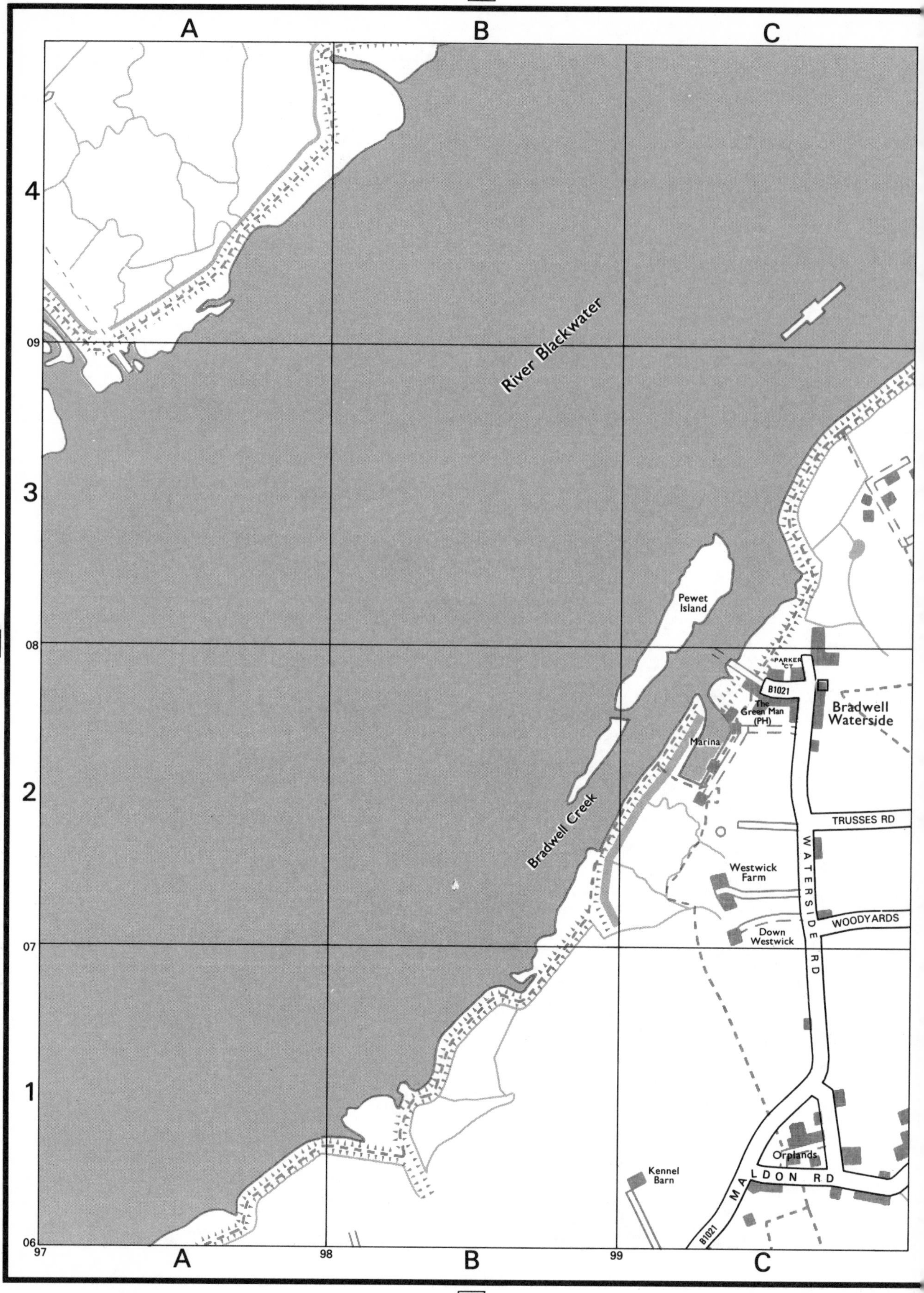
A
B
C
4
3
2
1
09
08
07
06
97
98
99
River Blackwater
Pewet Island
Bradwell Creek
PARKER CT
B1021
The Green Man (PH)
Marina
Bradwell Waterside
TRUSSES RD
WATERSIDE RD
Westwick Farm
WOODYARDS
Down Westwick
Orplands
MALDON RD
Kennel Barn
B1021

135

149

121

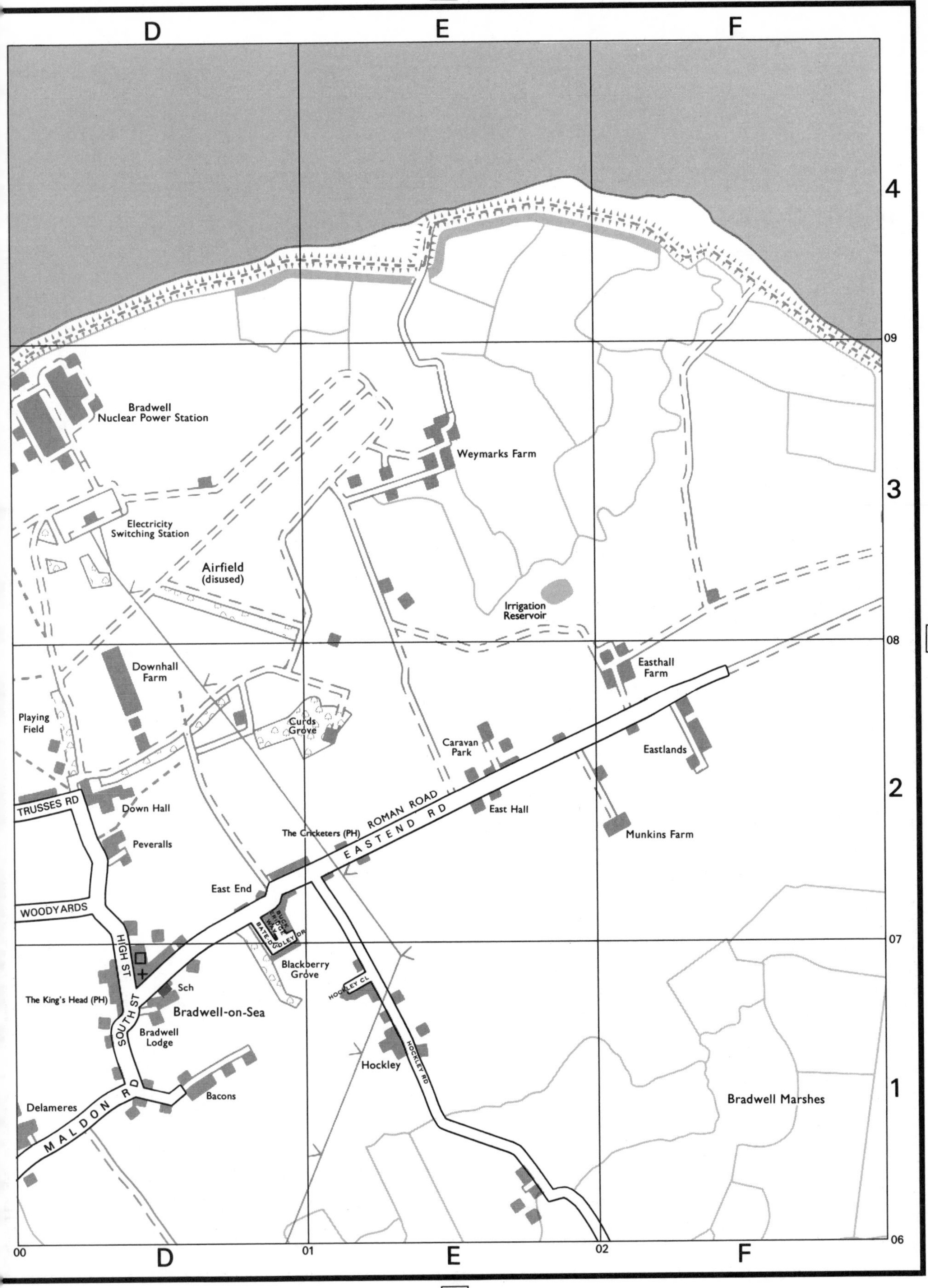
D
E
F
4
09
Bradwell
Nuclear Power Station
Weymarks Farm
3
Electricity
Switching Station
Airfield
(disused)
Irrigation
Reservoir
08
Downhall
Farm
Easthall
Farm
Playing
Field
Curds
Grove
Caravan
Park
Eastlands
TRUSSES RD
Down Hall
ROMAN ROAD
East Hall
2
Peveralls
The Cricketers (PH)
EASTEND RD
Munkins Farm
East End
WOODYARDS
HIGH ST
07
Blackberry
Grove
HOCKLEY CL
Sch
The King's Head (PH)
Bradwell-on-Sea
SOUTH ST
Bradwell
Lodge
HOCKLEY RD
Hockley
1
Delameres
MALDON RD
Bacons
Bradwell Marshes
00
D
01
E
02
F
06

138

150

122

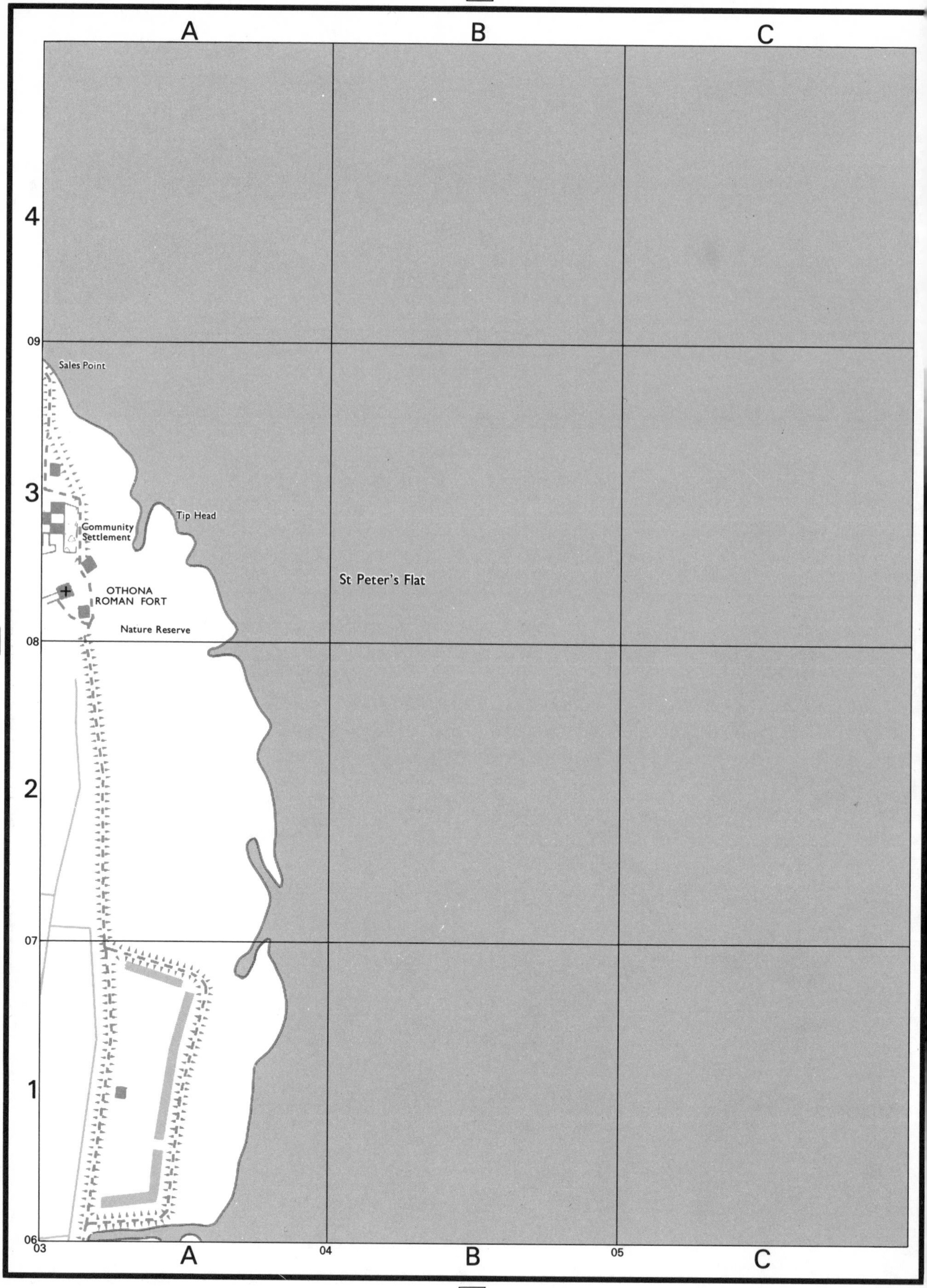
A
B
C
4
09
Sales Point
3
Tip Head
Community Settlement
OTHONA ROMAN FORT
St Peter's Flat
Nature Reserve
08
2
07
1
06
03
04
05
A
B
C

137

151

126

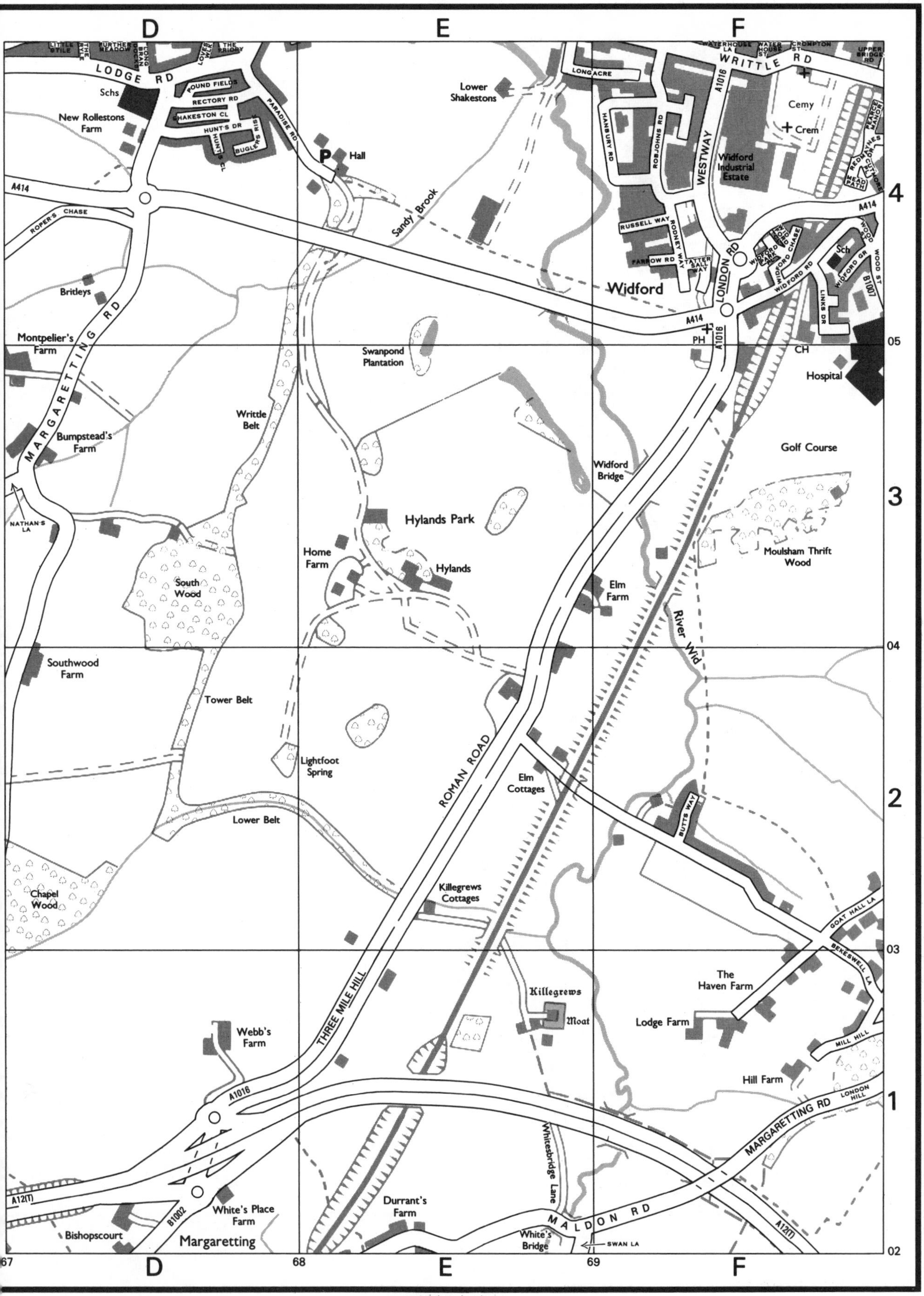
D
E
F
LODGE RD
Schs
New Rollestons Farm
ROUND FIELDS
RECTORY RD
SHAKESTON CL
HUNT'S DR
HUNT'S CL
BUGLERS RISE
PARADISE RD
P
Hall
Lower Shakestons
LONG ACRE
WRITTLE RD
A1016
HANBURY RD
ROBJOHNS RD
WESTWAY
Widford Industrial Estate
Cemy
Crem
A414
ROPER'S CHASE
Sandy Brook
RUSSELL WAY
RODNEY WAY
FARROW RD
TATTERSALL WAY
LONDON RD
WIDFORD CHASE
WIDFORD RD
Sch
LINKS DR
B1007
Britleys
Widford
Montpelier's Farm
PH
CH
Hospital
Swanpond Plantation
MARGARETTING RD
Writtle Belt
Bumpstead's Farm
Golf Course
Widford Bridge
NATHAN'S LA
Hylands Park
Moulsham Thrift Wood
Home Farm
Hylands
South Wood
Elm Farm
River Wid
Southwood Farm
Tower Belt
ROMAN ROAD
Lightfoot Spring
Elm Cottages
BUTTS WAY
Lower Belt
Chapel Wood
Killegrews Cottages
GOAT HALL LA
BEKESWELL LA
The Haven Farm
THREE MILE HILL
Killegrews
Moat
Lodge Farm
MILL HILL
Webb's Farm
Hill Farm
A1016
MARGARETTING RD
LONDON HILL
Whitesbridge Lane
A12(T)
B1002
White's Place Farm
Durrant's Farm
MALDON RD
Bishopscourt
Margaretting
White's Bridge
SWAN LA
4
05
3
04
2
03
1
02
67
68
69

140

not continued, see key diagram

127
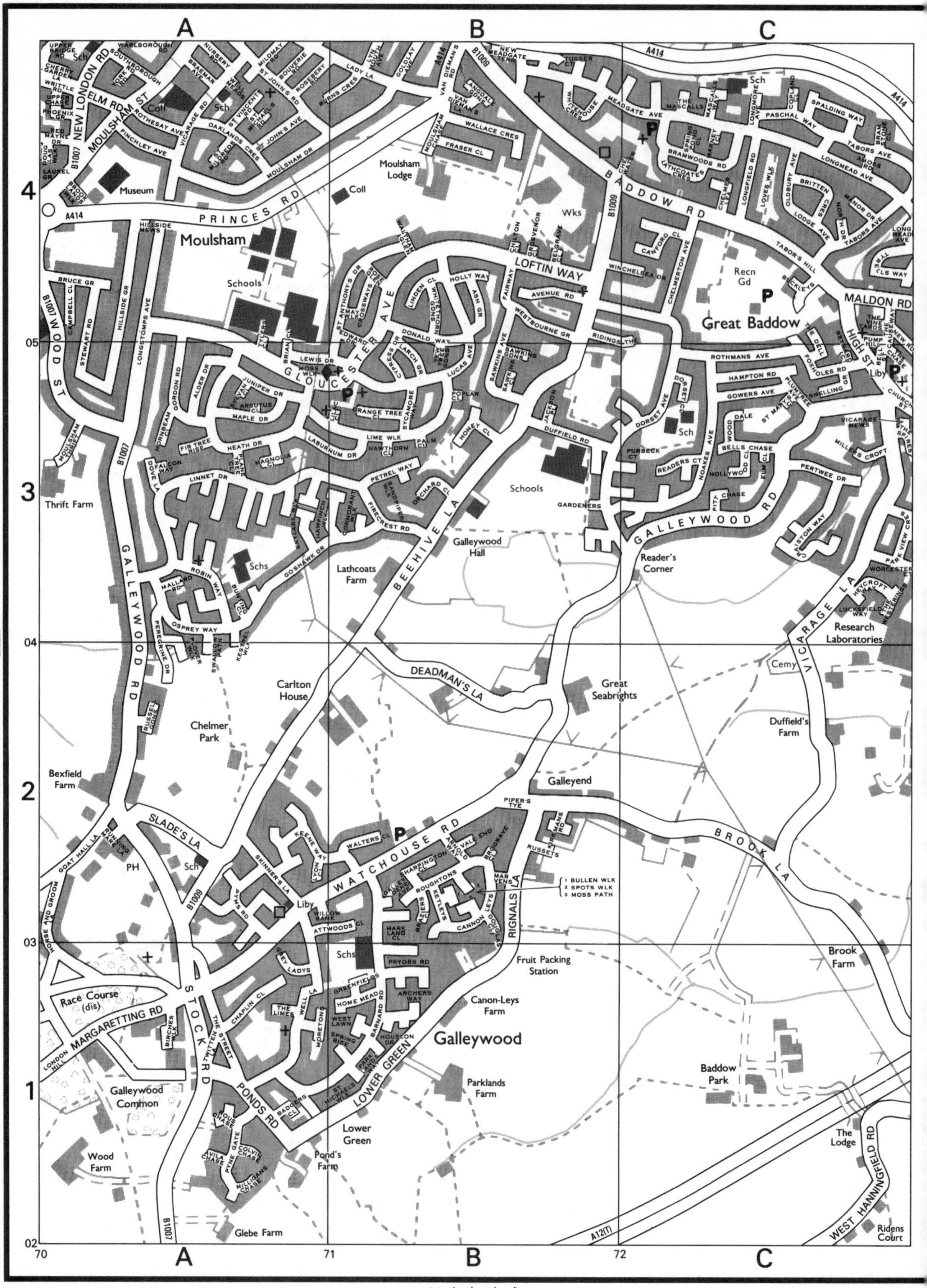
A
B
C
4
3
2
1
05
04
03
02
70
71
72
Moulsham
Schools
Museum
Moulsham Lodge
Coll
Wks
Great Baddow
Recn Gd
Schools
Galleywood Hall
Lathcoats Farm
Reader's Corner
Thrift Farm
Carlton House
Chelmer Park
Great Seabrights
Duffield's Farm
Research Laboratories
Cemy
Bexfield Farm
Galleyend
Fruit Packing Station
Canon-Leys Farm
Galleywood
Parklands Farm
Lower Green
Pond's Farm
Brook Farm
Baddow Park
The Lodge
Ridens Court
Race Course (dis)
Galleywood Common
Wood Farm
Glebe Farm
PRINCES RD
BADDOW RD
MALDON RD
LOFTIN WAY
GLOUCESTER AVE
BEEHIVE LA
GALLEYWOOD RD
DEADMAN'S LA
BROOK LA
VICARAGE LA
WATCHOUSE RD
SLADE'S LA
STOCK RD
MARGARETTING RD
PONDS RD
LOWER GREEN
RIGNALS LA
WEST HANNINGFIELD RD
WOOD ST
MOULSHAM ST
NEW LONDON RD
HIGH ST
A414
A12(T)
B1007
B1009
1 BULLEN WLK
2 SPOTS WLK
3 MOSS PATH
139
not continued, see key diagram

128

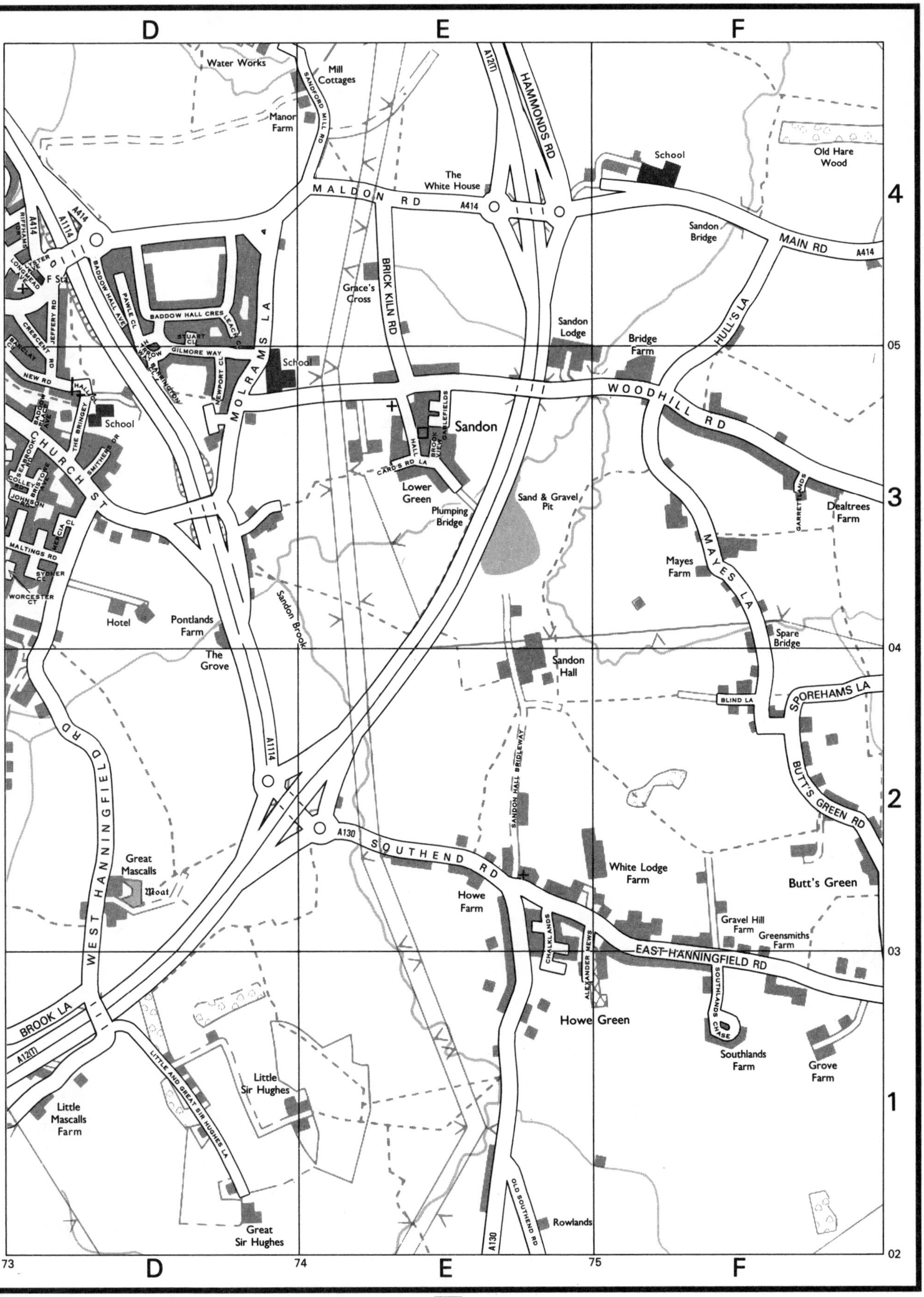
D
E
F
Water Works
Mill Cottages
SANDFORD MILL RD
Manor Farm
HAMMONDS RD
A12(T)
School
Old Hare Wood
The White House
MALDON RD
A414
4
Sandon Bridge
MAIN RD
A414
A1114
BADDOW HALL AVE
PAWLE CL
BADDOW HALL CRES
LEACH CL
STUART CL
GILMORE WAY
NEWPORT CL
BARRINGTON
MOLRAMS LA
School
Grace's Cross
BRICK KILN RD
Sandon Lodge
Bridge Farm
HULL'S LA
05
RIFFHAMS
LYSTER AVE
LONGMEAD AVE
F Sta
JEFFERY RD
CRESCENT RD
BARCLAY CL
NEW RD
HALL
BADDOW PLACE AVE
THE BRINGEY
School
SMITHERS DR
SEABROOK RD
BRISTOWE AVE
COLLEY RD
JOHNSON CL
CHURCH ST
MERCIA CL
MALTINGS RD
SYDNER CL
WORCESTER CT
WOODHILL RD
Sandon
GABLEFIELDS
BROOK VIEW
HALL LA
CARD'S RD
Lower Green
Plumping Bridge
Sand & Gravel Pit
GARRETTLANDS
Dealtrees Farm
3
Mayes Farm
MAYES LA
Sandon Brook
Hotel
Pontlands Farm
The Grove
Spare Bridge
04
Sandon Hall
BLIND LA
SPOREHAMS LA
A1114
SANDON HALL BRIDLEWAY
BUTT'S GREEN RD
2
WEST HANNINGFIELD RD
A130
SOUTHEND RD
Great Mascalls
Moat
White Lodge Farm
Howe Farm
Butt's Green
Gravel Hill Farm
Greensmiths Farm
CHALKLANDS
ALEXANDER MEWS
EAST HANNINGFIELD RD
SOUTHLANDS CHASE
03
BROOK LA
A12(T)
Howe Green
Southlands Farm
Grove Farm
LITTLE AND GREAT SIR HUGHES LA
Little Sir Hughes
1
Little Mascalls Farm
OLD SOUTHEND RD
A130
Rowlands
Great Sir Hughes
02
73
74
75
D
E
F

142

152

129

141

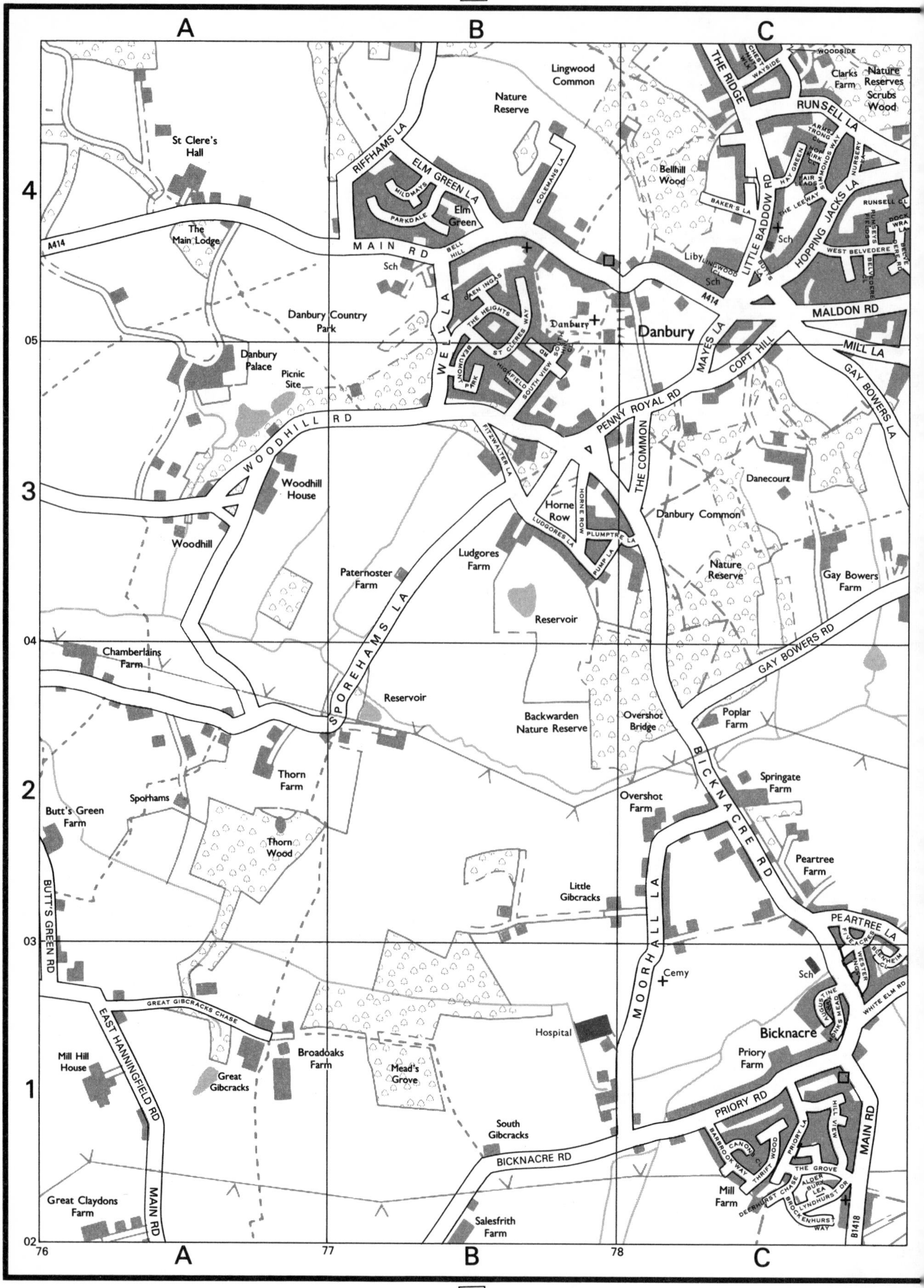
A
B
C
4
3
2
1
05
04
03
02
76
77
78
St Clere's Hall
The Main Lodge
A414
RIFFHAMS LA
ELM GREEN LA
MILDMAYS
PARKDALE
Elm Green
BELL HILL
MAIN RD
Sch
Lingwood Common
Nature Reserve
COLEMANS LA
Bellhill Wood
THE RIDGE
WAYSIDE
WOODSIDE
Clarks Farm
Nature Reserves Scrubs Wood
RUNSELL LA
HAY GREEN
THE LEEWAY
HOPPING JACKS LA
RUNSELL CL
WEST BELVEDERE
BAKER'S LA
LITTLE BADDOW RD
Liby
Danbury Country Park
THE HEIGHTS
ST CLERES WAY
Danbury
MAYES LA
MALDON RD
MILL LA
COPT HILL
Danbury Palace
Picnic Site
WELLA
BEAUMONT PARK
HIGHFIELD
SOUTH VIEW RD
GAY BOWERS LA
WOODHILL RD
PENNY ROYAL RD
FITZWALTER LA
THE COMMON
Woodhill House
Danecourt
Horne Row
HORNE ROW
LUDGORES LA
PLUMPTRE LA
PUMP LA
Danbury Common
Woodhill
Ludgores Farm
Nature Reserve
Gay Bowers Farm
Paternoster Farm
SPOREHAMS LA
Reservoir
GAY BOWERS RD
Chamberlains Farm
Reservoir
Backwarden Nature Reserve
Overshot Bridge
Poplar Farm
Thorn Farm
Springate Farm
Sporhams
Butt's Green Farm
Overshot Farm
BICKNACRE RD
Thorn Wood
Peartree Farm
BUTT'S GREEN RD
Little Gibcracks
PEARTREE LA
MOORHALL LA
Cemy
Sch
WHITE ELM RD
GREAT GIBCRACKS CHASE
EAST HANNINGFIELD RD
Hospital
Bicknacre
Mill Hill House
Broadoaks Farm
Priory Farm
Great Gibcracks
Mead's Grove
PRIORY RD
HILL VIEW
MAIN RD
South Gibcracks
BARBROOK WAY
THRIFT WOOD
PRIORY LA
BICKNACRE RD
THE GROVE
Great Claydons Farm
Mill Farm
LYNDHURST DR
MAIN RD
Salesfrith Farm
B1418

153

130
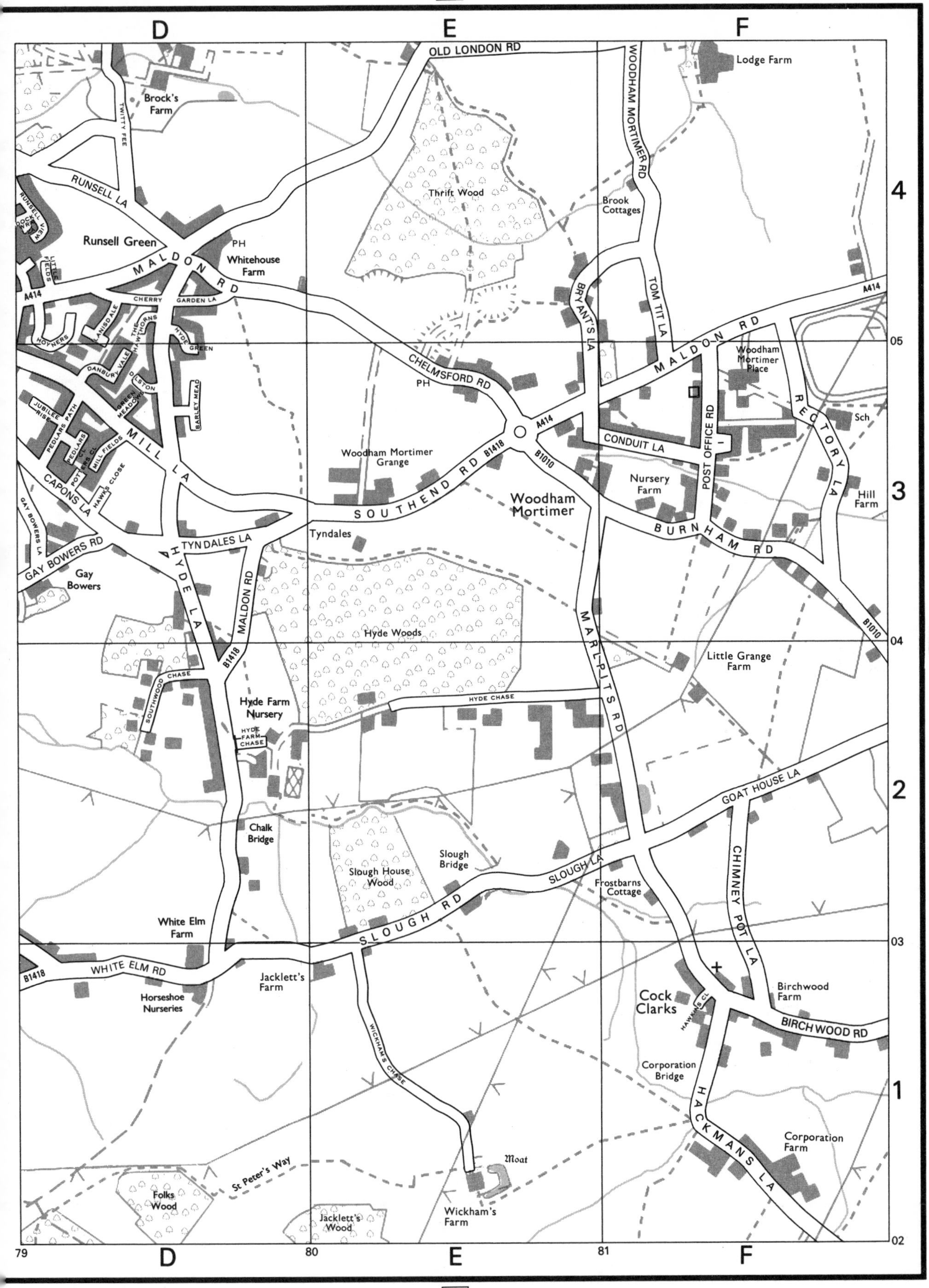
D
E
F
OLD LONDON RD
Lodge Farm
Brock's Farm
TWITTY FEE
WOODHAM MORTIMER RD
Thrift Wood
RUNSELL LA
Brook Cottages
4
Runsell Green
PH
Whitehouse Farm
MALDON RD
LITTLE FIELDS
A414
CHERRY GARDEN LA
BRYANT'S LA
TOM TIT LA
MALDON RD
A414
HOYNERS
DANBURY VALE
THE HAWTHORNS
HYDE GREEN
05
Woodham Mortimer Place
CHELMSFORD RD
PH
RECTORY LA
Sch
JUBILEE RISE
PEDLARS PATH
BARLEY MEAD
GREEN MEADOWS
A414
CONDUIT LA
POST OFFICE RD
MILL LA
MILL FIELDS
POTTERS CL
PEDLARS
Woodham Mortimer Grange
B1418
B1010
Nursery Farm
CAPONS LA
HAWKS CLOSE
SOUTHEND RD
Woodham Mortimer
Hill Farm
3
GAY BOWERS LA
TYNDALES LA
Tyndales
BURNHAM RD
GAY BOWERS RD
Gay Bowers
HYDE LA
MALDON RD
MARLPITS RD
Hyde Woods
B1010
04
Little Grange Farm
B1418
SOUTHWOOD CHASE
Hyde Farm Nursery
HYDE CHASE
HYDE FARM CHASE
GOAT HOUSE LA
2
Chalk Bridge
CHIMNEY POT LA
Slough Bridge
Slough House Wood
SLOUGH LA
Frostbarns Cottage
White Elm Farm
SLOUGH RD
03
B1418
WHITE ELM RD
Jacklett's Farm
Horseshoe Nurseries
Cock Clarks
HAWKINS CL
Birchwood Farm
BIRCHWOOD RD
WICKHAM'S CHASE
Corporation Bridge
1
HACKMANS LA
Corporation Farm
Moat
St Peter's Way
Folks Wood
Wickham's Farm
Jacklett's Wood
02
79
80
81
144
154

131

143

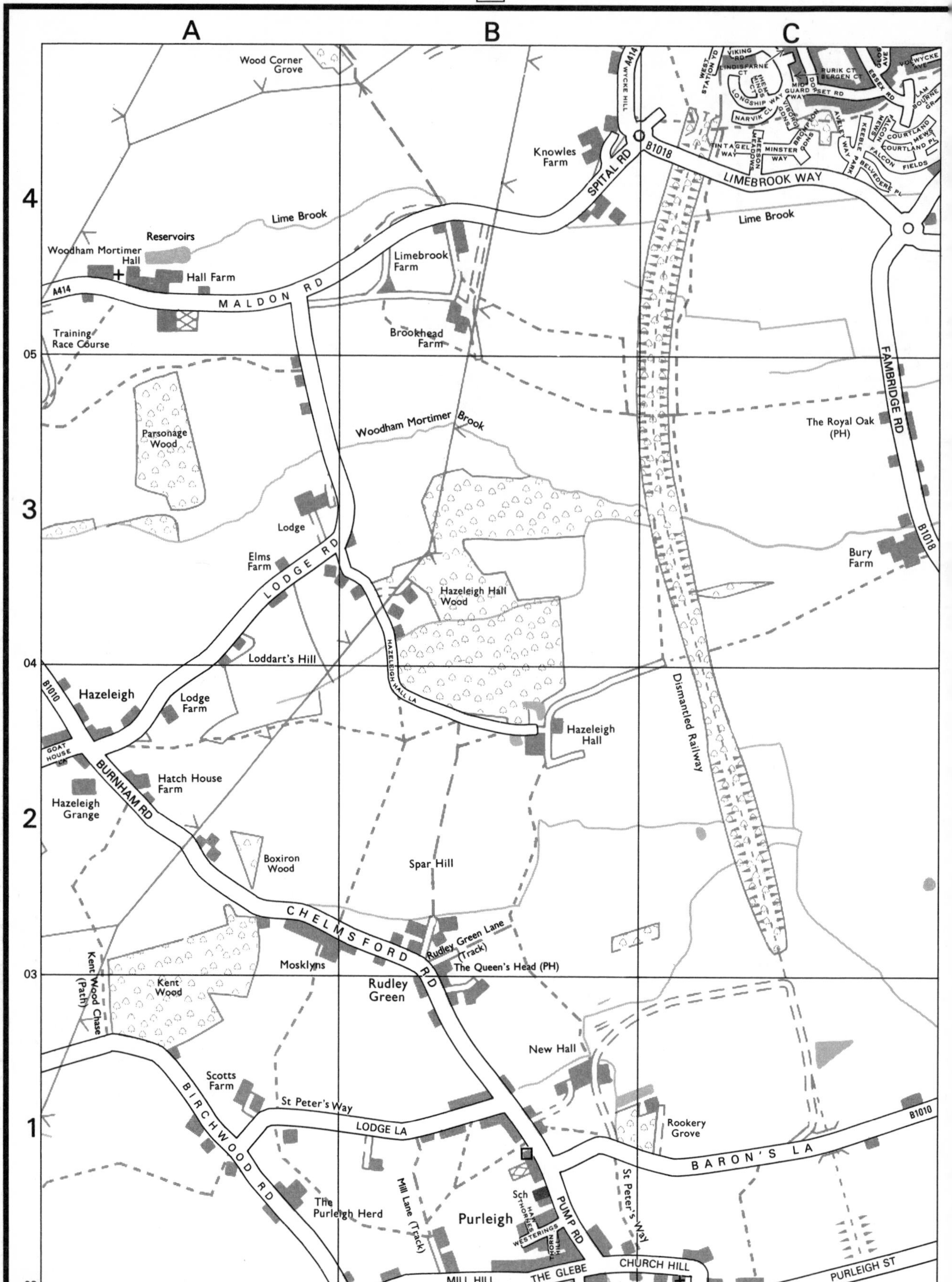
A
B
C
4
3
2
1
05
04
03
02
82
83
84
Wood Corner Grove
Knowles Farm
SPITAL RD
A414
WYCKE HILL
B1018
LIMEBROOK WAY
VIKING RD
LINDISFARNE CT
WEST STATION YD
LONGSHIP WAY
MID GUARD WAY
DORSET RD
NARVIK CL
TINTAGEL WAY
MINSTER WAY
BROMPTON GDNS
AVELEY WAY
KEEBLE PARK
COURTLAND MEWS
COURTLAND PL
FALCON FIELDS
BELVEDERE PL
ESSEX RD
Lime Brook
Reservoirs
Woodham Mortimer Hall
Hall Farm
Limebrook Farm
MALDON RD
Training Race Course
Brookhead Farm
FAMBRIDGE RD
The Royal Oak (PH)
Parsonage Wood
Woodham Mortimer Brook
Lodge
Elms Farm
LODGE RD
Hazeleigh Hall Wood
Bury Farm
Loddart's Hill
HAZELEIGH HALL LA
Hazeleigh
B1010
Lodge Farm
Hazeleigh Hall
Dismantled Railway
GOAT HOUSE LA
BURNHAM RD
Hatch House Farm
Hazeleigh Grange
Boxiron Wood
Spar Hill
CHELMSFORD RD
Rudley Green Lane (Track)
The Queen's Head (PH)
Mosklyns
Rudley Green
Kent Wood Chase (Path)
Kent Wood
New Hall
Scotts Farm
St Peter's Way
LODGE LA
BIRCHWOOD RD
Rookery Grove
BARON'S LA
B1010
The Purleigh Herd
Mill Lane (Track)
Sch
HAWTHORNES
Purleigh
WESTERINGS
PUMP RD
St Peter's Way
THE GLEBE
CHURCH HILL
MILL HILL
PURLEIGH ST

155

132

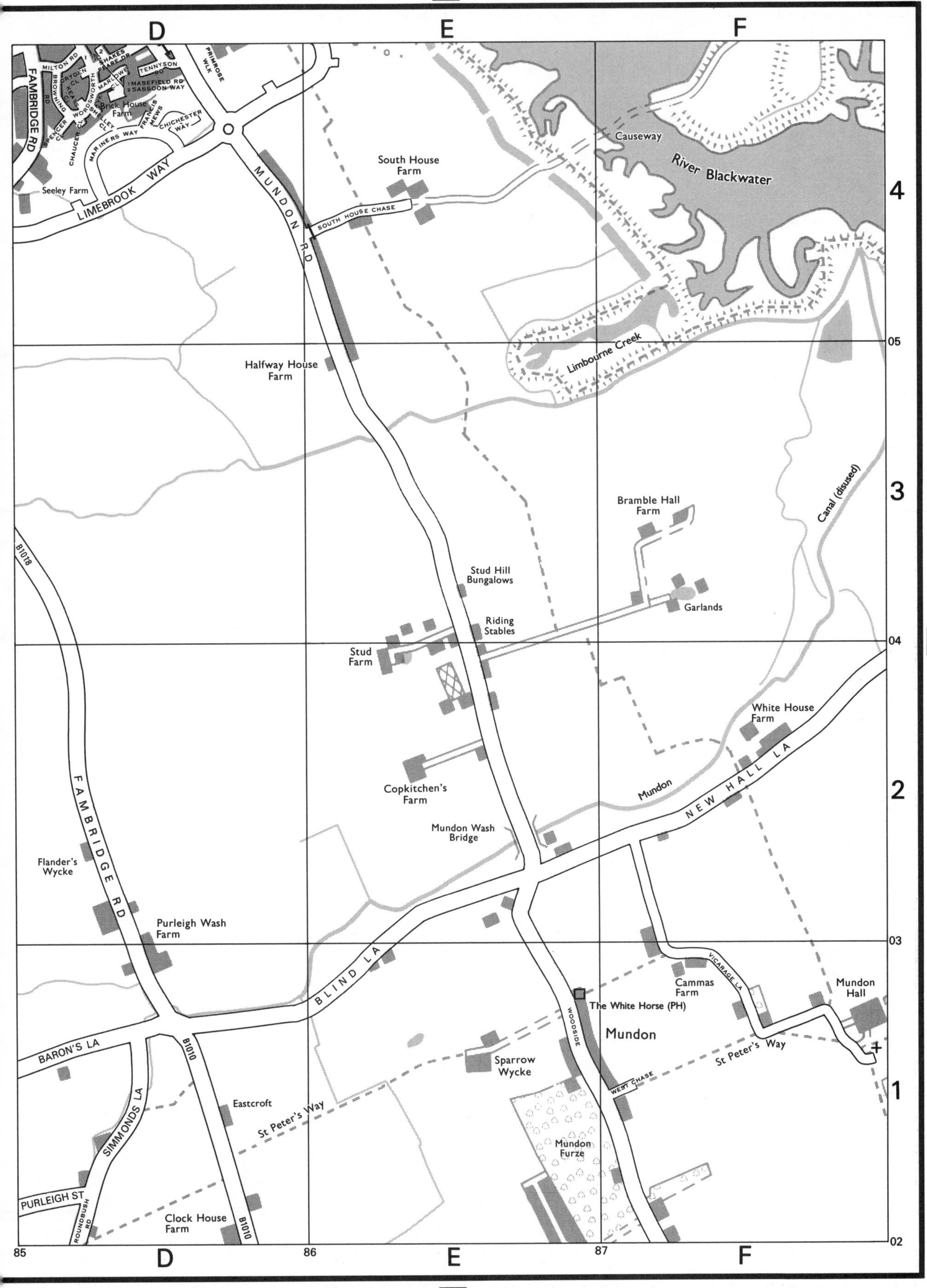

D
E
F
FAMBRIDGE RD
MILTON RD
BROWNING
DRYDEN CL
KEATS CL
SHAKESPEARE DR
MARLOWE CL
TENNYSON RD
MASEFIELD RD
SASSOON WAY
PRIMROSE WLK
Brick House Farm
SPENCER
WORDSWORTH
CHAUCER
MARINERS WAY
FRANCIS MEWS
CHICHESTER WAY
Seeley Farm
LIMEBROOK WAY
MUNDON RD
SOUTH HOUSE CHASE
South House Farm
Causeway
River Blackwater
Limbourne Creek
Halfway House Farm
Bramble Hall Farm
Canal (disused)
Stud Hill Bungalows
Garlands
Riding Stables
Stud Farm
White House Farm
Copkitchen's Farm
Mundon
NEW HALL LA
Mundon Wash Bridge
B1018
FAMBRIDGE RD
Flander's Wycke
Purleigh Wash Farm
BLIND LA
VICARAGE LA
Cammas Farm
Mundon Hall
The White Horse (PH)
WOODSIDE
Mundon
BARON'S LA
B1010
Sparrow Wycke
St Peter's Way
WEST CHASE
SIMMONDS LA
Eastcroft
St Peter's Way
Mundon Furze
PURLEIGH ST
ROUNDBUSH RD
Clock House Farm
B1010
4
05
3
04
2
03
1
02
85
86
87
D
E
F

146

156

133

145

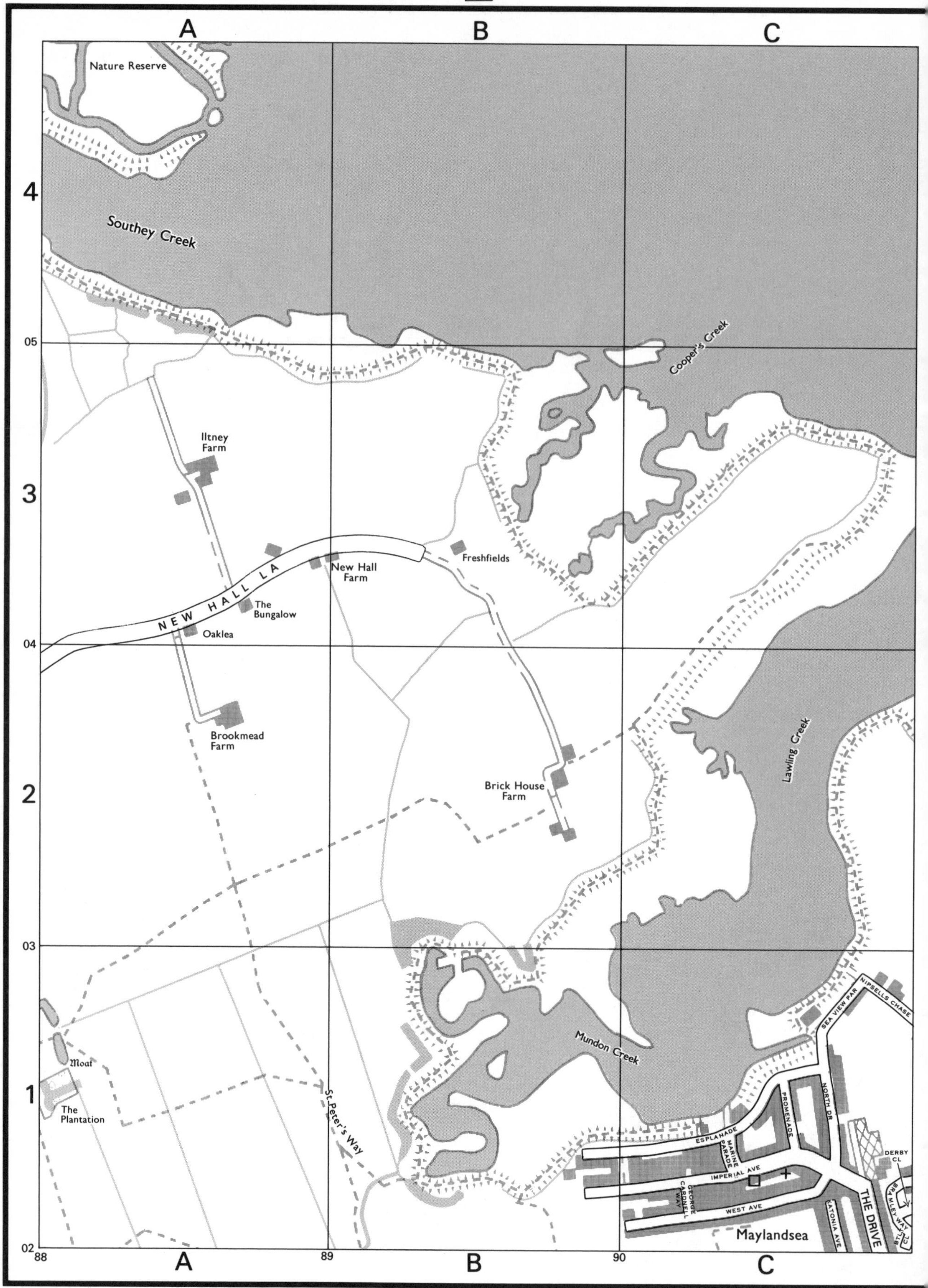
A
B
C
4
3
2
1
05
04
03
02
88
89
90
Nature Reserve
Southey Creek
Cooper's Creek
Iltney Farm
NEW HALL LA
New Hall Farm
Freshfields
The Bungalow
Oaklea
Brookmead Farm
Brick House Farm
Lawling Creek
Mundon Creek
Moat
The Plantation
St Peter's Way
SEA VIEW PAR
NIPSELLS CHASE
NORTH DR
PROMENADE
ESPLANADE
MARINE PARADE
IMPERIAL AVE
GEORGE CARDNELL WAY
WEST AVE
KATONIA AVE
THE DRIVE
DERBY CL
BRAMLEY WAY
BTL CL
Maylandsea

157

134

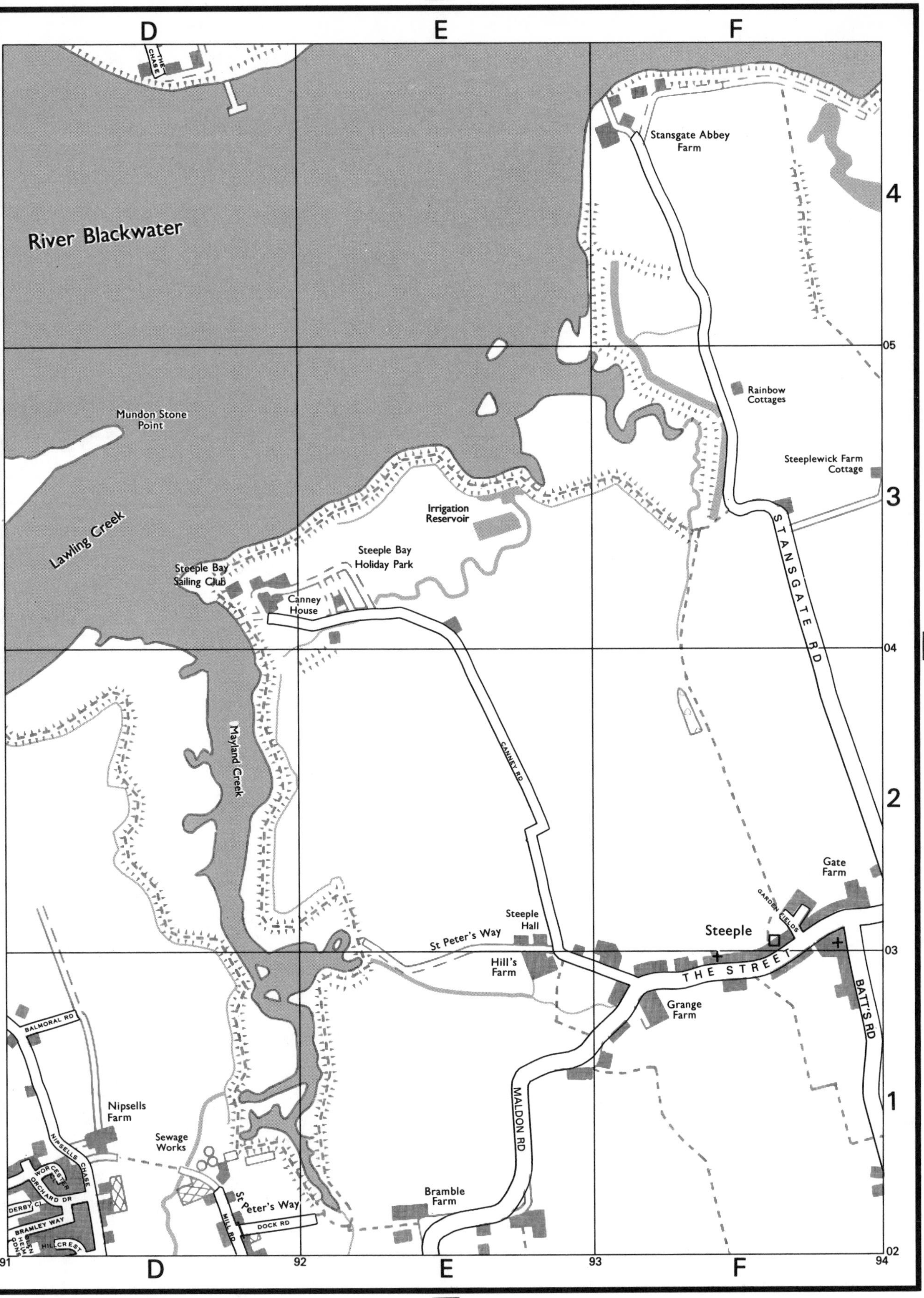
D
E
F
River Blackwater
THE CHASE
Stansgate Abbey Farm
4
05
Mundon Stone Point
Rainbow Cottages
Steeplewick Farm Cottage
Lawling Creek
3
Irrigation Reservoir
STANSGATE RD
Steeple Bay Holiday Park
Steeple Bay Sailing Club
Canney House
04
Mayland Creek
CANNEY RD
2
Gate Farm
GARDEN FIELDS
Steeple Hall
Steeple
St Peter's Way
Hill's Farm
03
THE STREET
BATT'S RD
Grange Farm
BALMORAL RD
MALDON RD
1
Nipsells Farm
Sewage Works
NIPSELLS CHASE
WORCESTER
ORCHARD DR
Bramble Farm
DERBY CL
St Peter's Way
BRAMLEY WAY
DOCK RD
MILL RD
HILLCREST
91
92
93
94
02
D
E
F

148

158

135

147

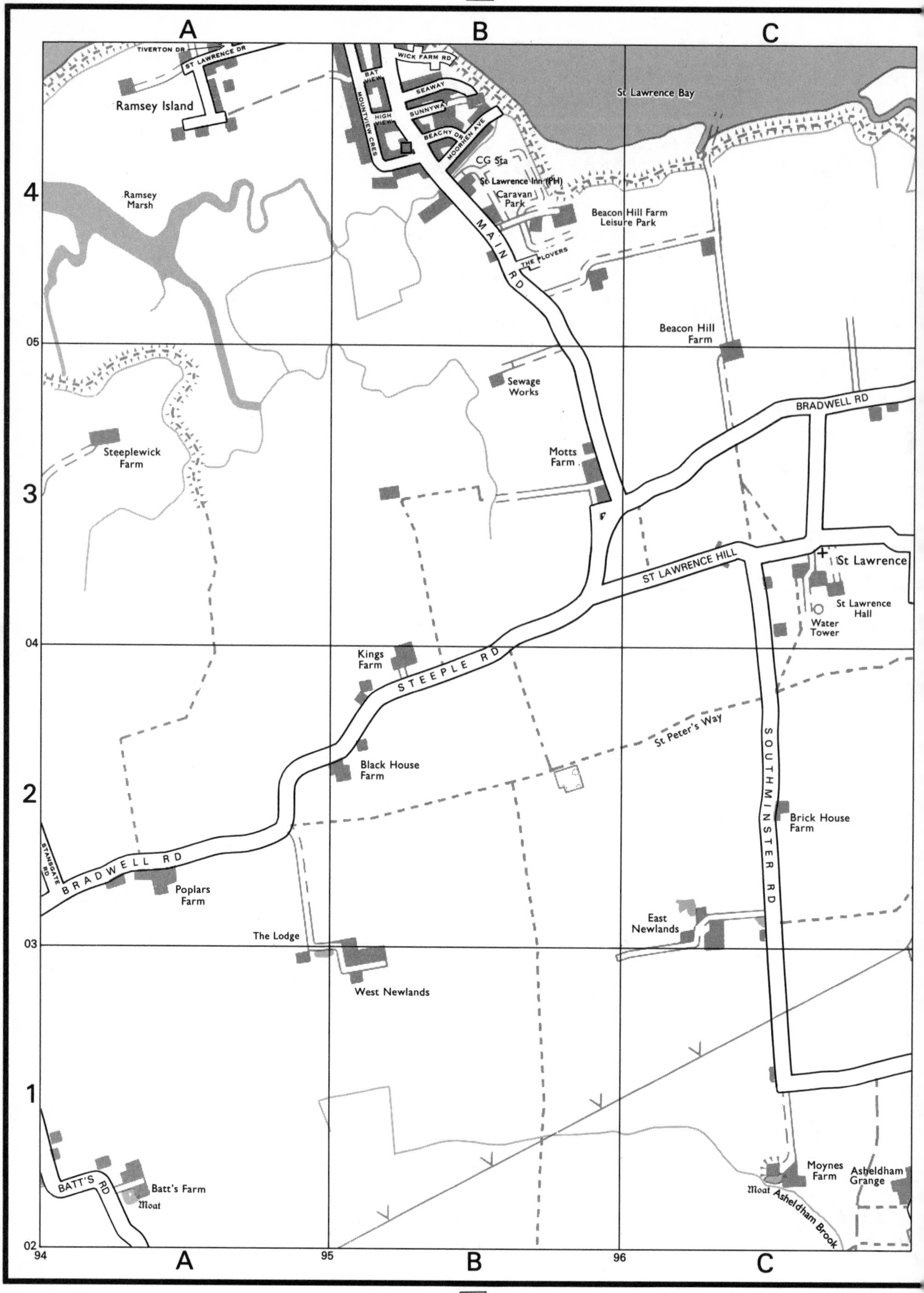
A
B
C
A
B
C
4
3
2
1
05
04
03
02
94
95
96
TIVERTON DR
ST LAWRENCE DR
Ramsey Island
WICK FARM RD
BAT VIEW
SEAWAY
SUNNYWAY
HIGH VIEW
MOUNTVIEW CRES
BEACHY DR
MOORHEN AVE
St Lawrence Bay
CG Sta
St Lawrence Inn (PH)
Caravan Park
Ramsey Marsh
Beacon Hill Farm Leisure Park
MAIN RD
THE PLOVERS
Beacon Hill Farm
Sewage Works
BRADWELL RD
Steeplewick Farm
Motts Farm
ST LAWRENCE HILL
St Lawrence
St Lawrence Hall
Water Tower
Kings Farm
STEEPLE RD
St Peter's Way
SOUTHMINSTER RD
Black House Farm
Brick House Farm
STANSGATE RD
BRADWELL RD
Poplars Farm
East Newlands
The Lodge
West Newlands
BATT'S RD
Batt's Farm
Moat
Moynes Farm
Asheldham Grange
Moat
Asheldham Brook

159

136

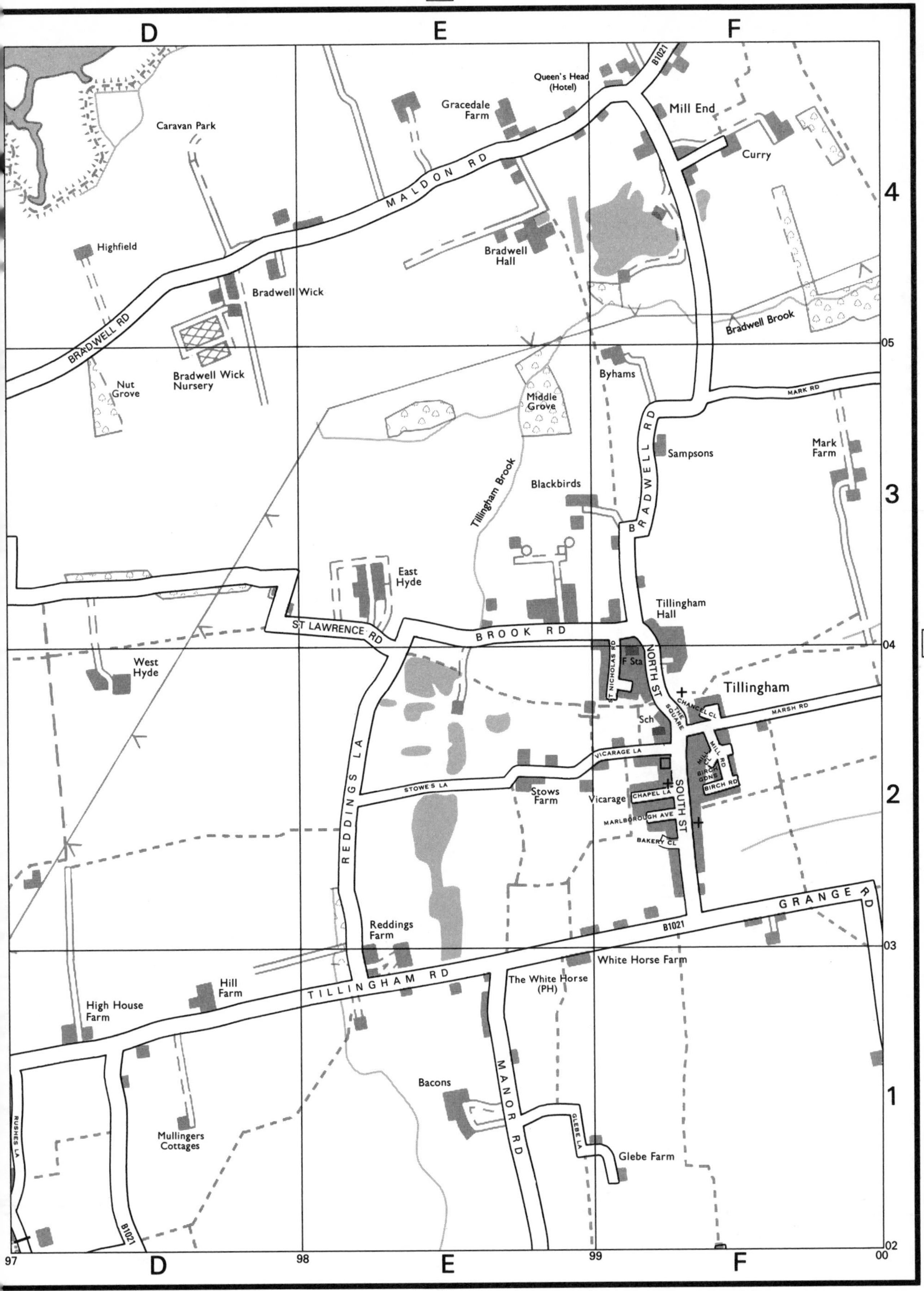
D
E
F
Caravan Park
Queen's Head (Hotel)
Gracedale Farm
Mill End
Curry
MALDON RD
B1021
Highfield
Bradwell Hall
Bradwell Wick
BRADWELL RD
Bradwell Brook
Bradwell Wick Nursery
Nut Grove
Middle Grove
Byhams
MARK RD
Sampsons
Mark Farm
Tillingham Brook
Blackbirds
BRADWELL RD
East Hyde
Tillingham Hall
ST LAWRENCE RD
BROOK RD
West Hyde
ST NICHOLAS RD
F Sta
NORTH ST
Tillingham
THE SQUARE
CHANCEL CL
MARSH RD
Sch
VICARAGE LA
MILL RD
MILL CL
BIRCH GDNS
BIRCH RD
REDDINGS LA
STOWES LA
Stows Farm
Vicarage
CHAPEL LA
SOUTH ST
MARLBOROUGH AVE
BAKERY CL
GRANGE RD
B1021
Reddings Farm
White Horse Farm
The White Horse (PH)
Hill Farm
TILLINGHAM RD
High House Farm
Bacons
MANOR RD
GLEBE LA
Glebe Farm
Mullingers Cottages
RUSHES LA
B1021
4
3
2
1
05
04
03
02
97
98
99
00

150

160

137

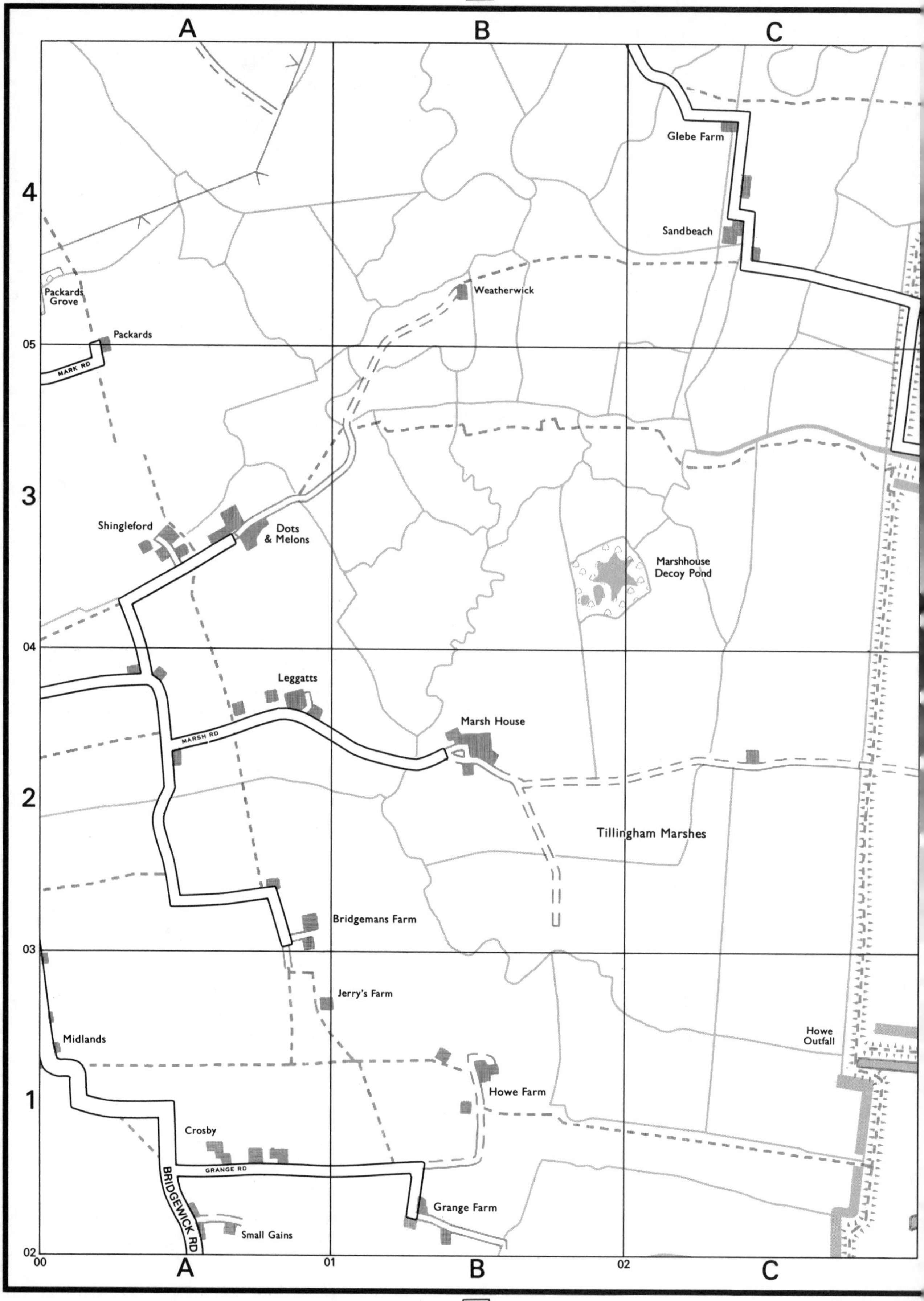
A
B
C
4
3
2
1
05
04
03
02
00
01
02
Glebe Farm
Sandbeach
Weatherwick
Packards Grove
Packards
MARK RD
Shingleford
Dots & Melons
Marshhouse Decoy Pond
Leggatts
Marsh House
MARSH RD
Tillingham Marshes
Bridgemans Farm
Jerry's Farm
Midlands
Howe Outfall
Howe Farm
Crosby
GRANGE RD
BRIDGEWICK RD
Grange Farm
Small Gains

149

161

138

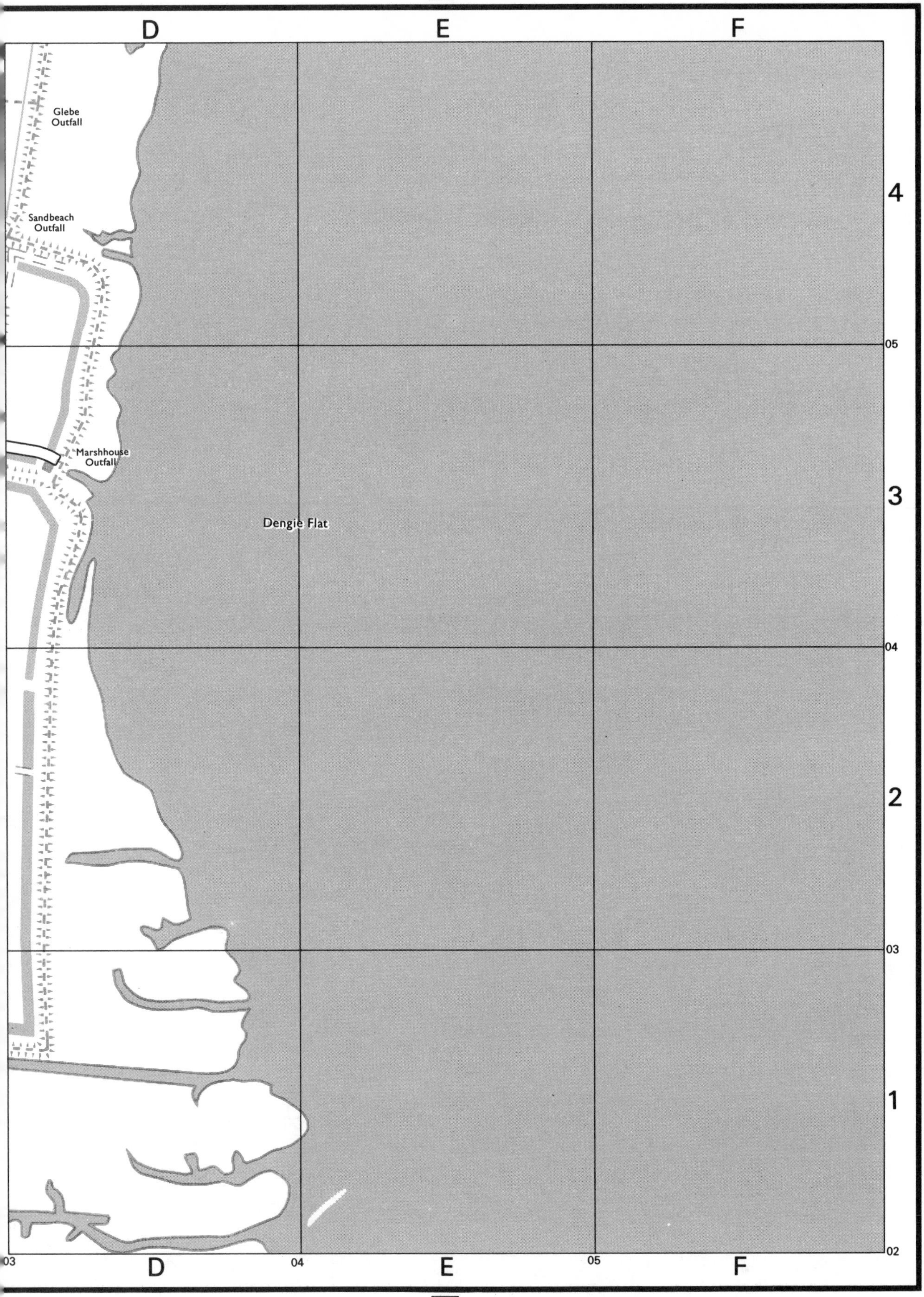
D
E
F
Glebe Outfall
Sandbeach Outfall
Marshhouse Outfall
Dengie Flat
4
05
3
04
2
03
1
02
03
D
04
E
05
F

162

141

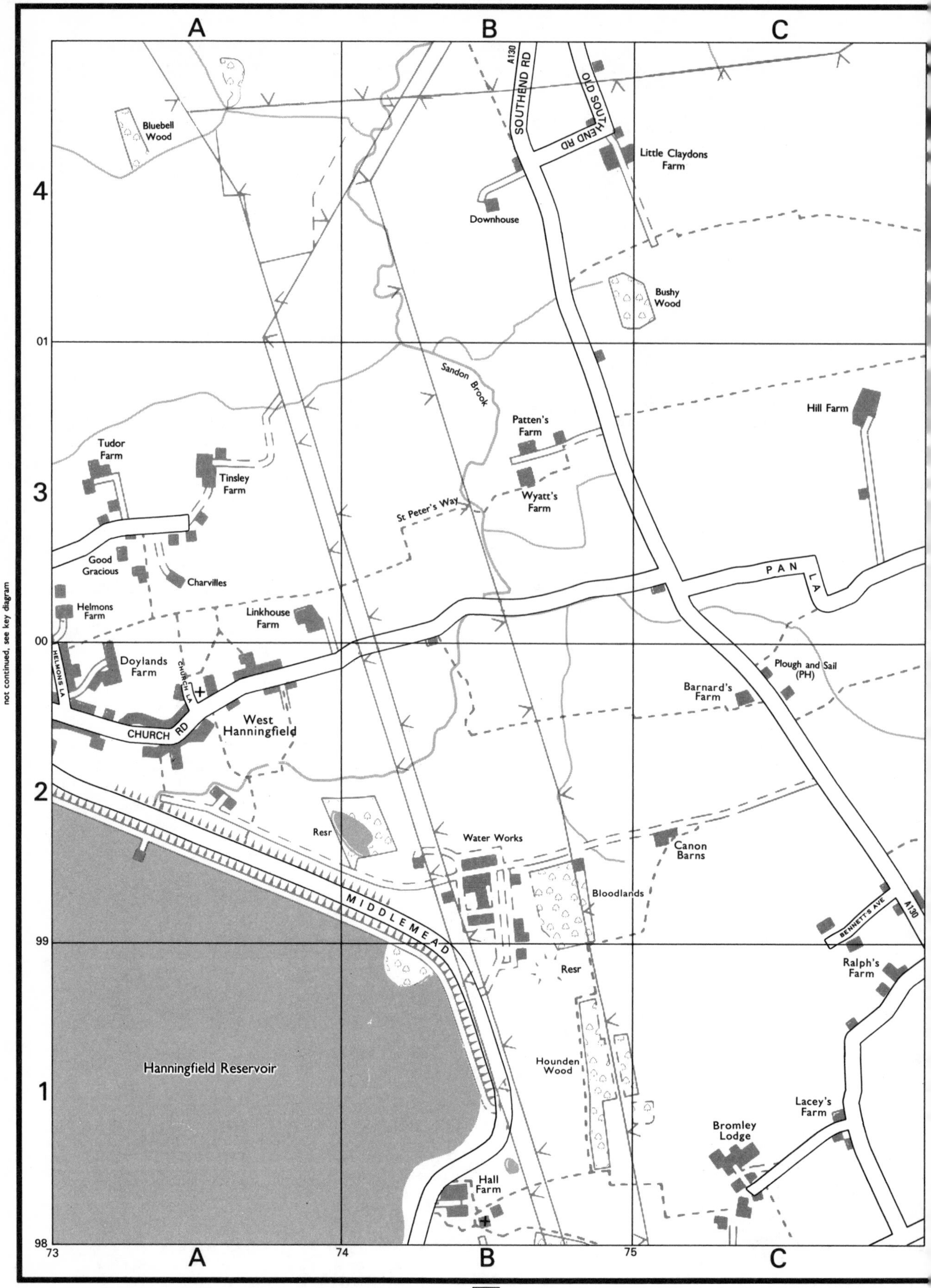
A
B
C
4
3
2
1
01
00
99
98
73
74
75
Bluebell Wood
SOUTHEND RD
A130
OLD SOUTHEND RD
Little Claydons Farm
Downhouse
Bushy Wood
Sandon Brook
Patten's Farm
Hill Farm
Tudor Farm
Tinsley Farm
Wyatt's Farm
St Peter's Way
Good Gracious
Charvilles
PAN LA
Helmons Farm
Linkhouse Farm
Doylands Farm
HELMONS LA
CHURCH LA
CHURCH RD
West Hanningfield
Plough and Sail (PH)
Barnard's Farm
Resr
Water Works
Canon Barns
Bloodlands
MIDDLEMEAD
BENNETT'S AVE
Ralph's Farm
Hanningfield Reservoir
Hounden Wood
Lacey's Farm
Bromley Lodge
Hall Farm
not continued, see key diagram

163

142

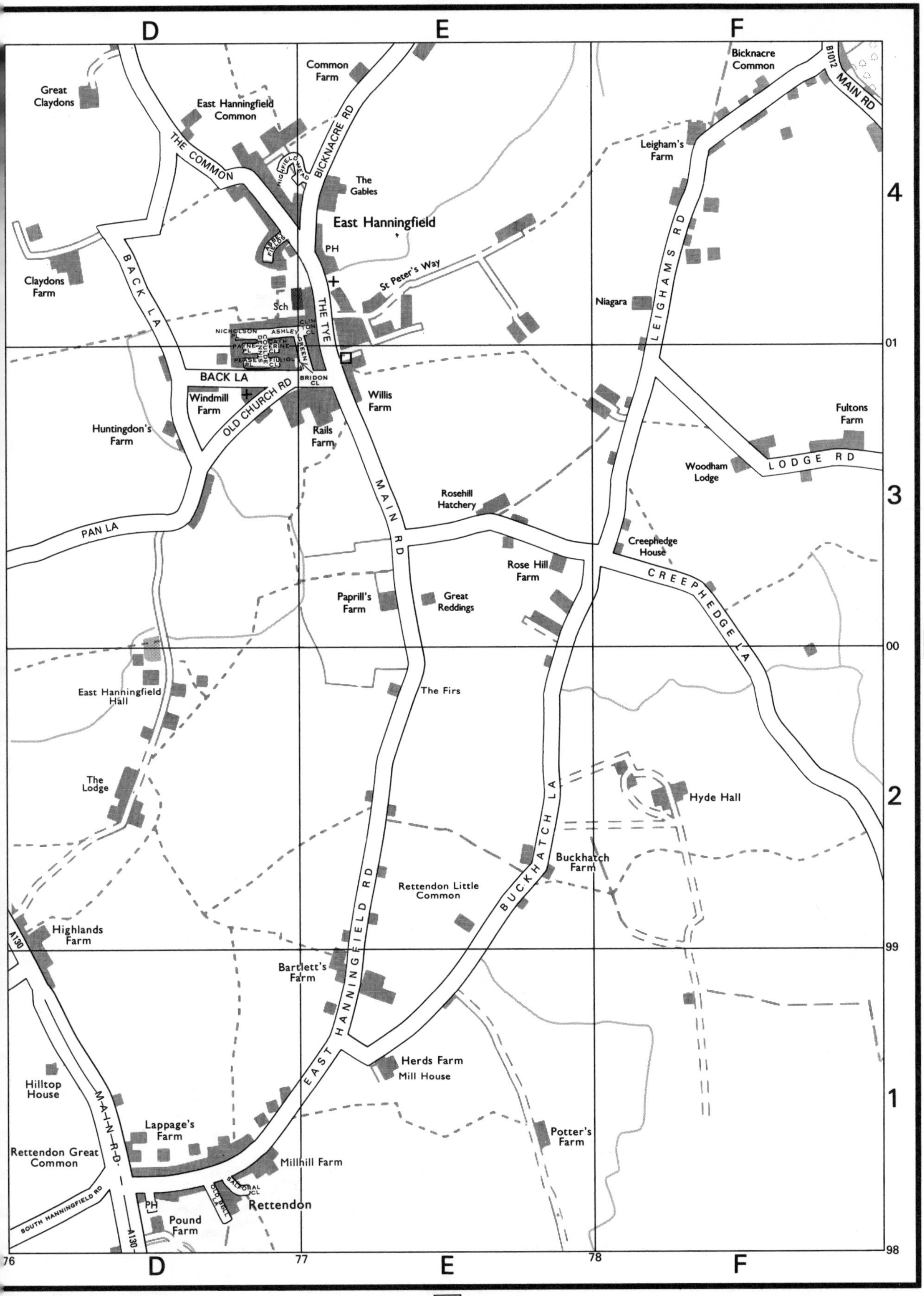
D
E
F
Great Claydons
East Hanningfield Common
Common Farm
Bicknacre Common
B1012
MAIN RD
THE COMMON
BICKNACRE RD
The Gables
Leigham's Farm
4
East Hanningfield
PH
Claydons Farm
BACK LA
St Peter's Way
LEIGHAMS RD
Sch
THE TYE
Niagara
01
BACK LA
Windmill Farm
OLD CHURCH RD
BRIDON CL
Willis Farm
Huntingdon's Farm
Rails Farm
Fultons Farm
LODGE RD
Woodham Lodge
3
Rosehill Hatchery
MAIN RD
PAN LA
Creephedge House
Rose Hill Farm
CREEPHEDGE LA
Paprill's Farm
Great Reddings
00
East Hanningfield Hall
The Firs
The Lodge
Hyde Hall
2
BUCKHATCH LA
Buckhatch Farm
Rettendon Little Common
EAST HANNINGFIELD RD
Highlands Farm
A130
99
Bartlett's Farm
Herds Farm
Mill House
Hilltop House
1
MAIN RD
Lappage's Farm
Potter's Farm
Rettendon Great Common
Millhill Farm
SOUTH HANNINGFIELD RD
PH
SALFORAL CL
Rettendon
Pound Farm
A130
98
76
D
77
E
78
F

154

164

143

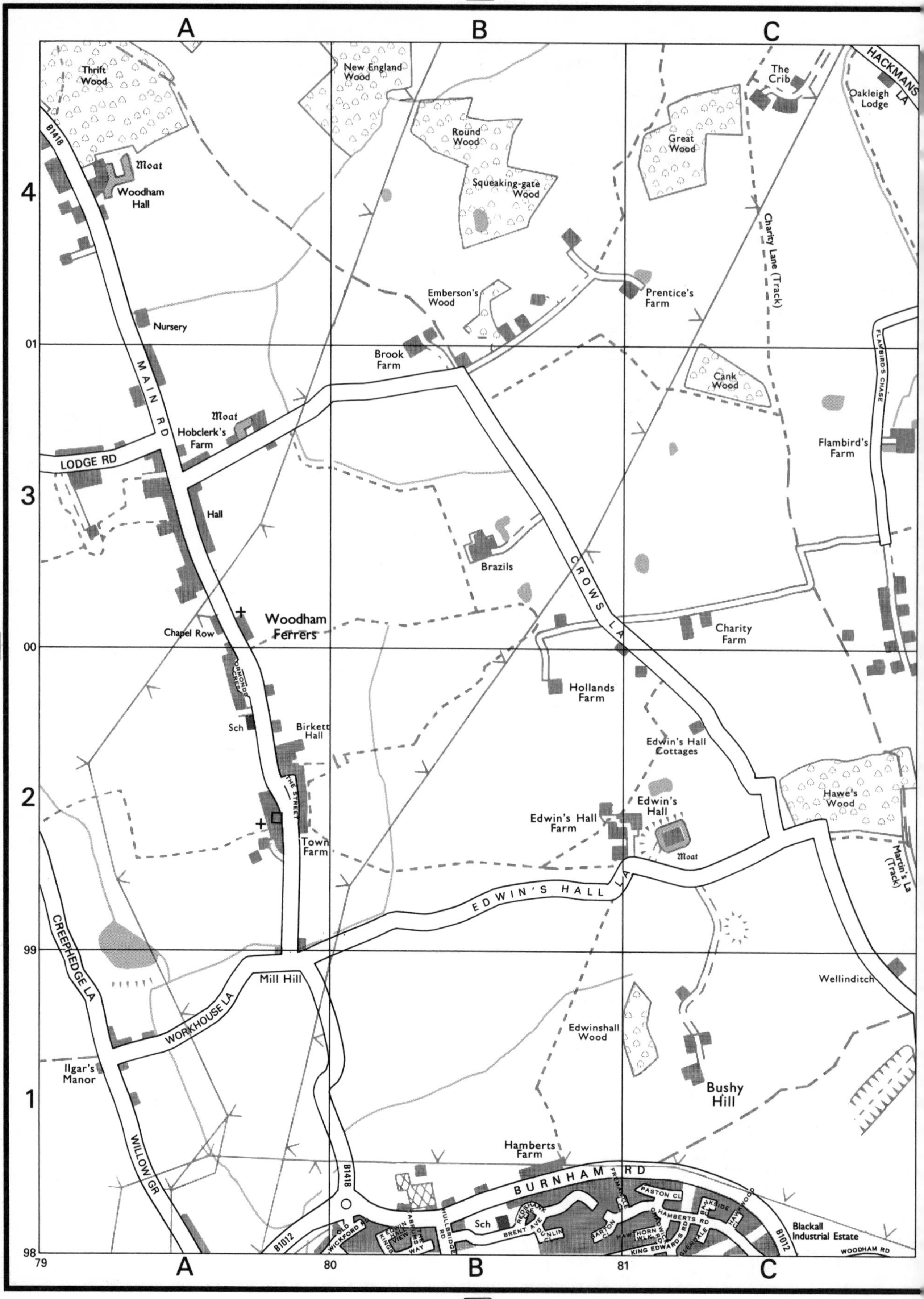
A
B
C
Thrift Wood
New England Wood
Round Wood
Squeaking-gate Wood
Great Wood
The Crib
Oakleigh Lodge
HACKMANS LA
B1418
Moat
Woodham Hall
4
Emberson's Wood
Prentice's Farm
Charity Lane (Track)
Nursery
01
Brook Farm
Cank Wood
FLAMBIRD'S CHASE
MAIN RD
Moat
Hobclerk's Farm
Flambird's Farm
LODGE RD
3
Hall
Brazils
CROWS LA
Woodham Ferrers
Chapel Row
Charity Farm
00
ORMONDS CRES
Hollands Farm
Sch
Birkett Hall
Edwin's Hall Cottages
THE STREET
2
Hawe's Wood
Edwin's Hall
Edwin's Hall Farm
Town Farm
Moat
Martin's La (Track)
EDWIN'S HALL LA
CREPHEDGE LA
99
Mill Hill
Wellinditch
WORKHOUSE LA
Edwinshall Wood
Ilgar's Manor
1
Bushy Hill
WILLOW GR
Hamberts Farm
B1418
BURNHAM RD
FREMANTLE CL
PASTON CL
BANKSIDE
HAWKWOOD CL
HAMBERTS RD
B1012
OLD WICKFORD RD
EDWIN HALL VIEW
KINGS
ABRUMS
THE WAY
HULLBRIDGE RD
Sch
REDSHANK CRES
BRENT AVE
DUNLIN CL
BARTON CL
HAWTHORN WLK
CHADWICK RD
KING EDWARD'S RD
GLENDALE
B1012
Blackall Industrial Estate
WOODHAM RD
98
79
80
81

153

165

144

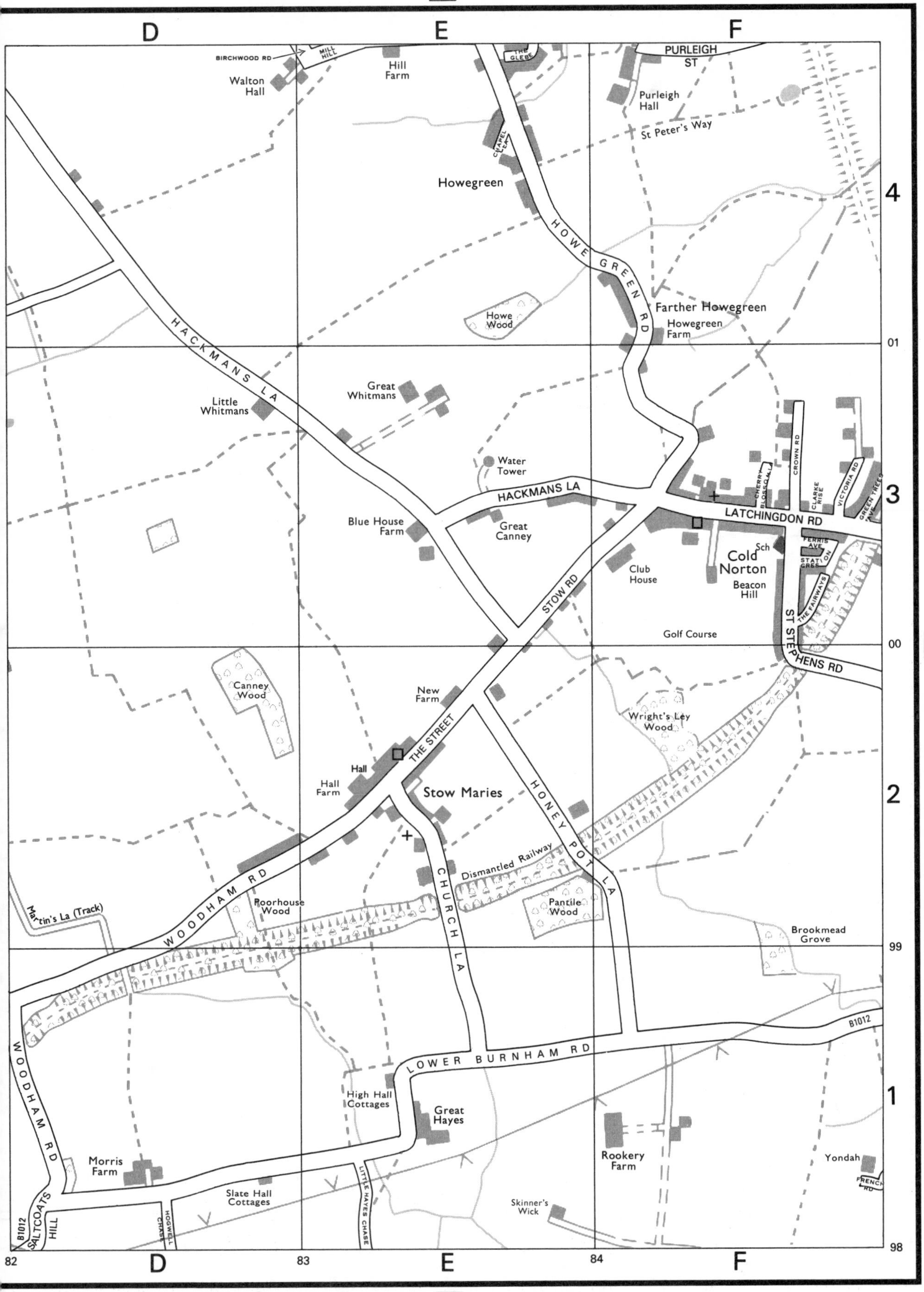
D
E
F
4
3
2
1
01
00
99
98
82
83
84
BIRCHWOOD RD
MILL HILL
THE GLEBE
PURLEIGH ST
Walton Hall
Hill Farm
Purleigh Hall
St Peter's Way
CHAPEL LA
Howegreen
HOWE GREEN RD
Farther Howegreen
Howegreen Farm
Howe Wood
HACKMANS LA
Little Whitmans
Great Whitmans
Water Tower
HACKMANS LA
Great Canney
Blue House Farm
LATCHINGDON RD
CHERRY BLOSSOM LA
CROWN RD
CLARKE RISE
VICTORIA RD
GREEN TREES AVE
FERRIS AVE
STATION CRES
THE FAIRWAYS
Sch
Cold Norton
Beacon Hill
Club House
STOW RD
Golf Course
ST STEPHENS RD
Canney Wood
New Farm
Wright's Ley Wood
THE STREET
Hall
Hall Farm
Stow Maries
HONEY POT LA
Dismantled Railway
CHURCH LA
WOODHAM RD
Poorhouse Wood
Pantile Wood
Martin's La (Track)
Brookmead Grove
B1012
LOWER BURNHAM RD
High Hall Cottages
Great Hayes
WOODHAM RD
Rookery Farm
Yondah
FRENCH RD
Morris Farm
Slate Hall Cottages
Skinner's Wick
SALTCOATS HILL
HOGWELL CHASE
LITTLE HAYES CHASE

156

166

145

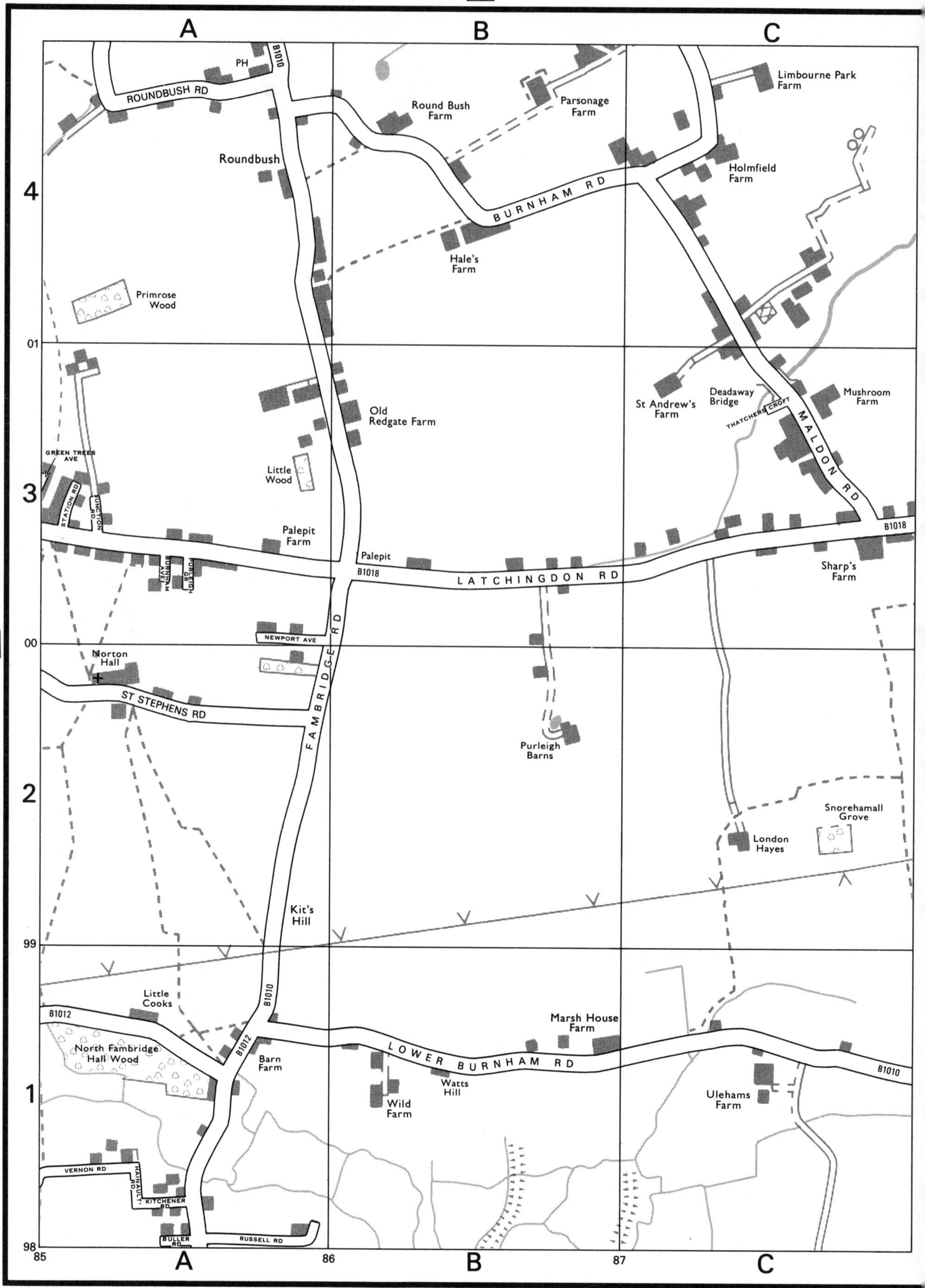
A
B
C
4
3
2
1
01
00
99
98
85
86
87
PH
B1010
ROUNDBUSH RD
Roundbush
Round Bush Farm
Parsonage Farm
Limbourne Park Farm
Holmfield Farm
BURNHAM RD
Hale's Farm
Primrose Wood
Old Redgate Farm
St Andrew's Farm
Deadaway Bridge
THATCHERS CROFT
Mushroom Farm
MALDON RD
GREEN TREES AVE
STATION RD
JUNCTION RD
Little Wood
Palepit Farm
Palepit
B1018
BURNHAM AVE
FURLEIGH GR
LATCHINGDON RD
Sharp's Farm
NEWPORT AVE
Norton Hall
ST STEPHENS RD
FAMBRIDGE RD
Purleigh Barns
Snorehamall Grove
London Hayes
Kit's Hill
Little Cooks
B1012
North Fambridge Hall Wood
Barn Farm
LOWER BURNHAM RD
Marsh House Farm
Watts Hill
Wild Farm
Ulehams Farm
VERNON RD
HAINAULT RD
KITCHENER RD
BULLER RD
RUSSELL RD

155

167

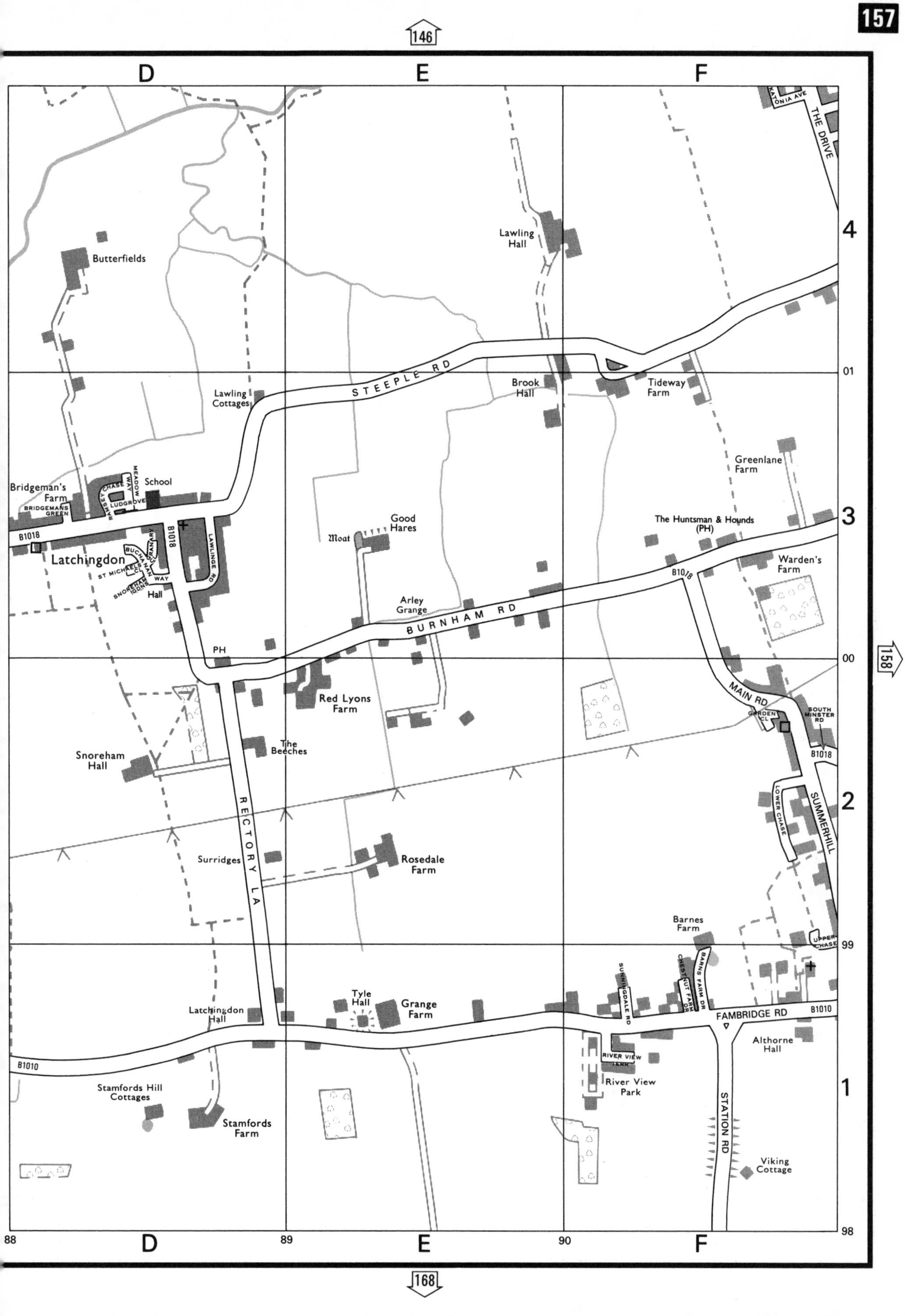
146
D
E
F
KATONIA AVE
THE DRIVE
4
Lawling Hall
Butterfields
STEEPLE RD
01
Lawling Cottages
Brook Hall
Tideway Farm
Greenlane Farm
Bridgeman's Farm
BRIDGEMANS GREEN
RAMSEY CHASE
MEADOW WAY
LUDGROVE
School
B1018
Latchingdon
BUCHANAN WAY
GRANARY
ST MICHAELS CL
SNOREHAM GDNS
Hall
LAWLINGE RD
Moat
Good Hares
The Huntsman & Hounds (PH)
3
Warden's Farm
B1018
Arley Grange
BURNHAM RD
PH
00
158
Red Lyons Farm
MAIN RD
GARDEN CL
SOUTH MINSTER RD
B1018
Snoreham Hall
The Beeches
RECTORY LA
LOWER CHASE
SUMMERHILL
2
Surridges
Rosedale Farm
Barnes Farm
UPPER CHASE
99
SUNNINGDALE RD
CHESTNUT FARM DR
BARNS FARM DR
Tyle Hall
Grange Farm
Latchingdon Hall
FAMBRIDGE RD
B1010
Althorne Hall
B1010
RIVER VIEW TERR
River View Park
STATION RD
1
Stamfords Hill Cottages
Stamfords Farm
Viking Cottage
98
88
D
89
E
90
F
168

147

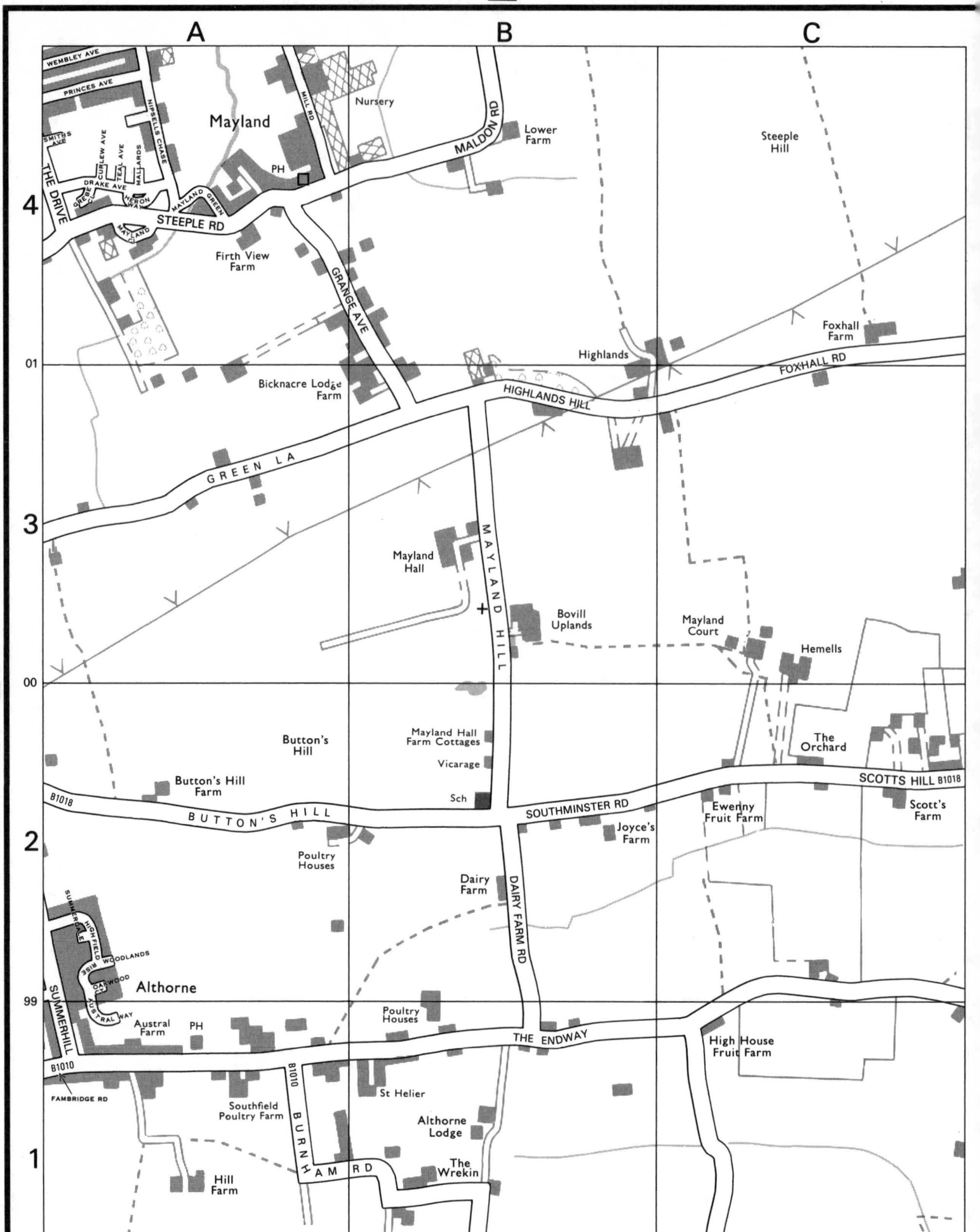
A
B
C
4
3
2
1
01
00
99
98
91
92
93
WEMBLEY AVE
PRINCES AVE
Mayland
SMITHS AVE
CURLEW AVE
TEAL AVE
NIPSELLS CHASE
MALLARDS
DRAKE AVE
GREBE CL
HERON WAY
MAYLAND GREEN
MAYLAND CL
THE DRIVE
STEEPLE RD
PH
MILL RD
Nursery
MALDON RD
Lower Farm
Steeple Hill
Firth View Farm
GRANGE AVE
Highlands
Foxhall Farm
FOXHALL RD
Bicknacre Lodge Farm
HIGHLANDS HILL
GREEN LA
Mayland Hall
MAYLAND HILL
Bovill Uplands
Mayland Court
Hemells
Button's Hill
Mayland Hall Farm Cottages
Vicarage
Sch
The Orchard
Button's Hill Farm
B1018
BUTTON'S HILL
SOUTHMINSTER RD
SCOTTS HILL B1018
Ewenny Fruit Farm
Scott's Farm
Joyce's Farm
Poultry Houses
Dairy Farm
DAIRY FARM RD
SUMMERDALE
HIGHFIELD RISE
WOODLANDS
OAKWOOD CT
AUSTRAL WAY
Althorne
SUMMERHILL
Austral Farm
PH
Poultry Houses
THE ENDWAY
High House Fruit Farm
B1010
FAMBRIDGE RD
B1010
St Helier
Southfield Poultry Farm
BURNHAM RD
Althorne Lodge
The Wrekin
Hill Farm
MALDON RD
B1010
Andrews Farm

157

148

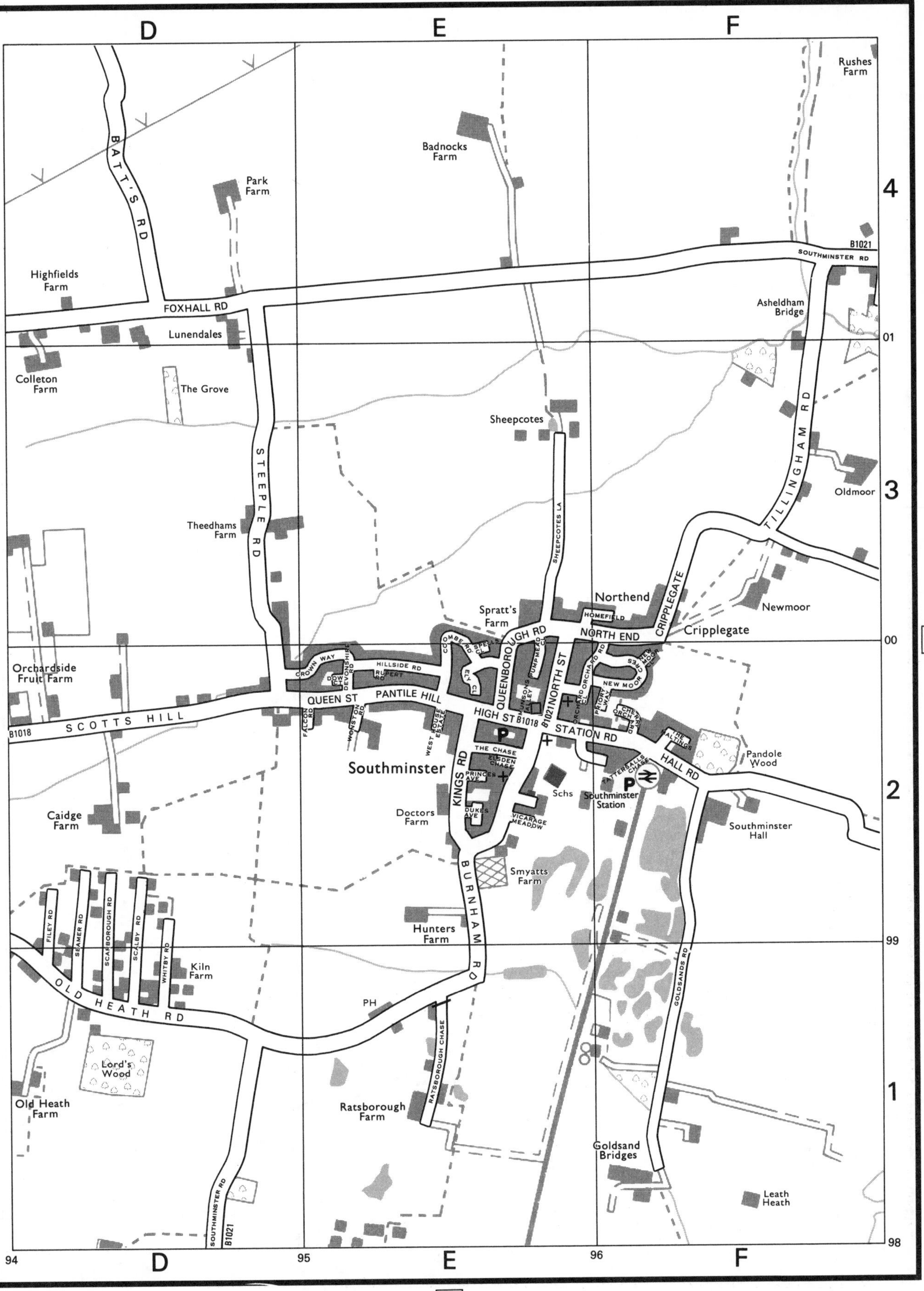
D
E
F
Rushes Farm
Badnocks Farm
Park Farm
BATT'S RD
4
B1021
SOUTHMINSTER RD
Highfields Farm
FOXHALL RD
Asheldham Bridge
Lunendales
01
Colleton Farm
The Grove
Sheepcotes
TILLINGHAM RD
STEEPLE RD
Oldmoor
3
Theedhams Farm
SHEEPCOTES LA
Northend
CRIPPLEGATE
Newmoor
Spratt's Farm
HOMEFIELD
NORTH END
Cripplegate
00
QUEENBOROUGH RD
Orchardside Fruit Farm
CROWN WAY
HILLSIDE RD
RUPERT RD
NEW MOOR
QUEEN ST
PANTILE HILL
HIGH ST B1018
NORTH ST B1021
B1018
SCOTTS HILL
STATION RD
THE CHASE
ELSDEN CHASE
HALL RD
Pandole Wood
Southminster
KINGS RD
Schs
Southminster Station
2
Caidge Farm
Doctors Farm
Southminster Hall
BURNHAM RD
Smyatts Farm
Hunters Farm
99
FILEY RD
SEAMER RD
SCARBOROUGH RD
SCALBY RD
WHITBY RD
Kiln Farm
OLD HEATH RD
PH
GOLDSANDS RD
RATSBOROUGH CHASE
Lord's Wood
1
Old Heath Farm
Ratsborough Farm
Goldsand Bridges
SOUTHMINSTER RD
B1021
Leath Heath
98
94
D
95
E
96
F

160

170

149

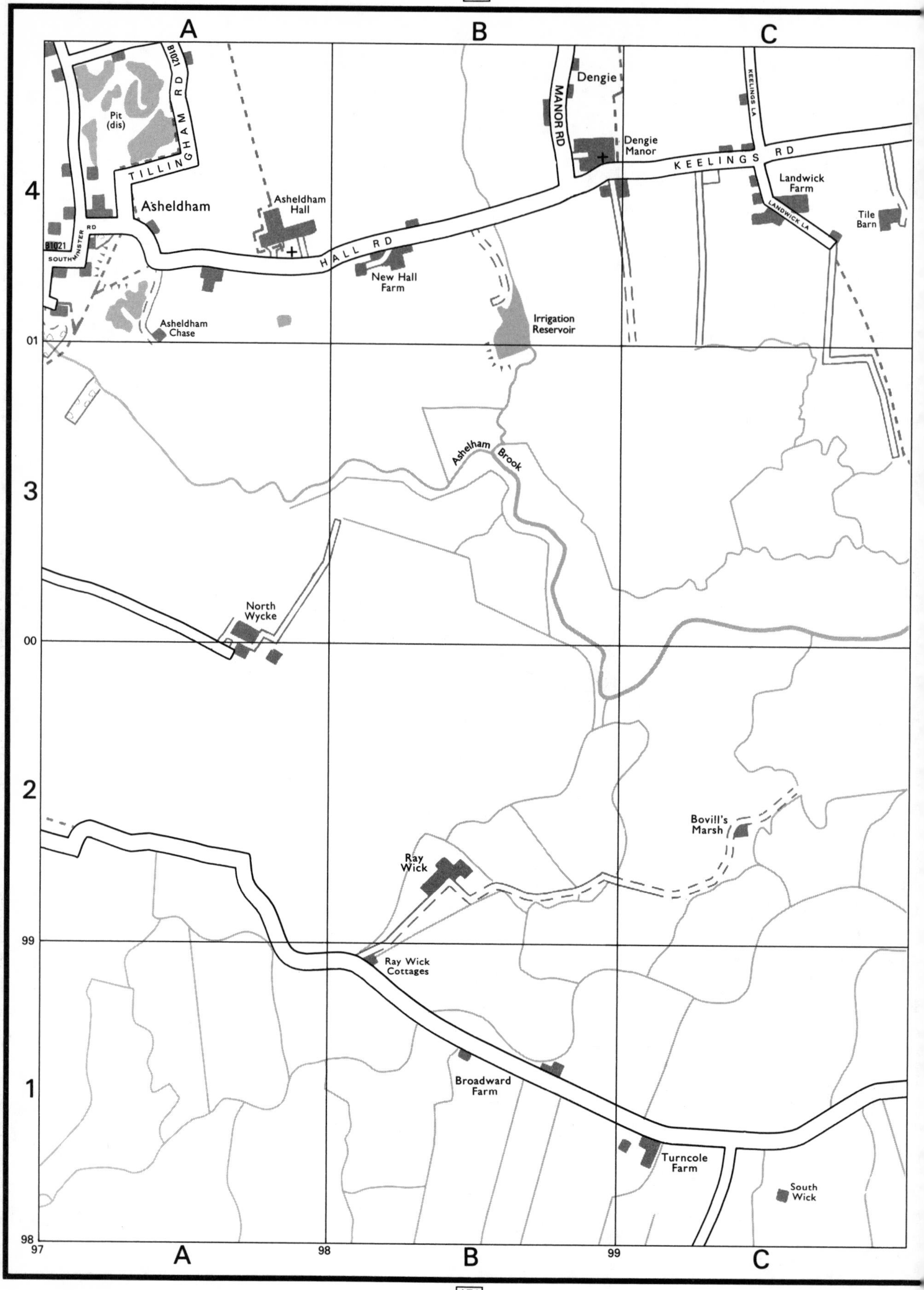
A
B
C
Dengie
MANOR RD
KEELINGS LA
Pit (dis)
TILLINGHAM RD
B1018
Dengie Manor
KEELINGS RD
4
Asheldham
Asheldham Hall
Landwick Farm
LANDWICK LA
Tile Barn
SOUTHMINSTER RD
B1021
HALL RD
New Hall Farm
Irrigation Reservoir
Asheldham Chase
01
Asheldham Brook
3
North Wycke
00
2
Bovill's Marsh
Ray Wick
99
Ray Wick Cottages
1
Broadward Farm
Turncole Farm
South Wick
98
97
98
99
A
B
C

159

171

150

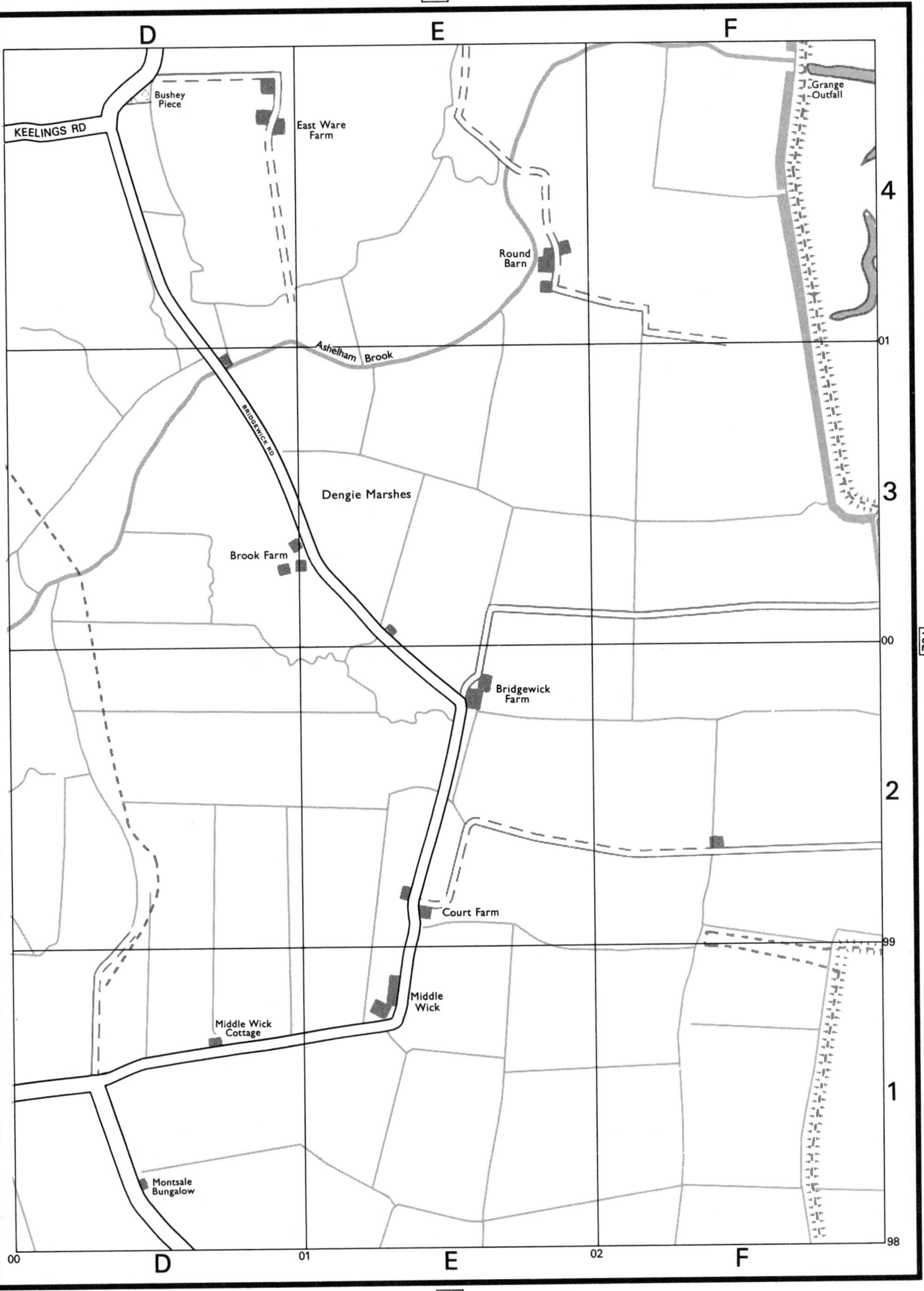
D
E
F
Bushey
Piece
KEELINGS RD
East Ware
Farm
Grange
Outfall
4
Round
Barn
01
Ashelham Brook
BRIDGEWICK RD
Dengie Marshes
3
Brook Farm
00
Bridgewick
Farm
2
Court Farm
99
Middle
Wick
Middle Wick
Cottage
1
Montsale
Bungalow
98
00
01
02
D
E
F

162

172

151

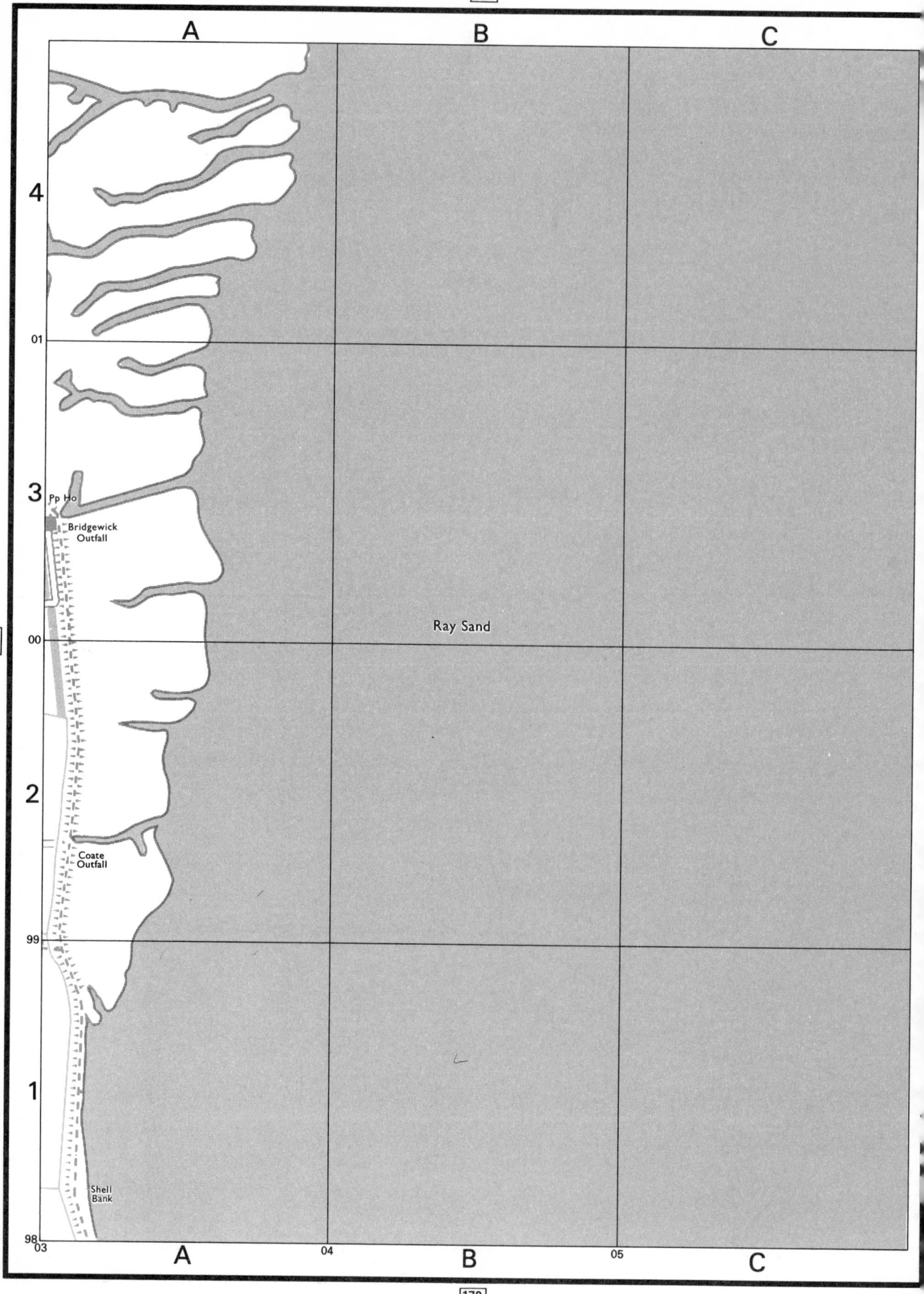
A
B
C
4
3
2
1
01
00
99
98
03
04
05
Pp Ho
Bridgewick Outfall
Ray Sand
Coate Outfall
Shell Bank

161

173

152

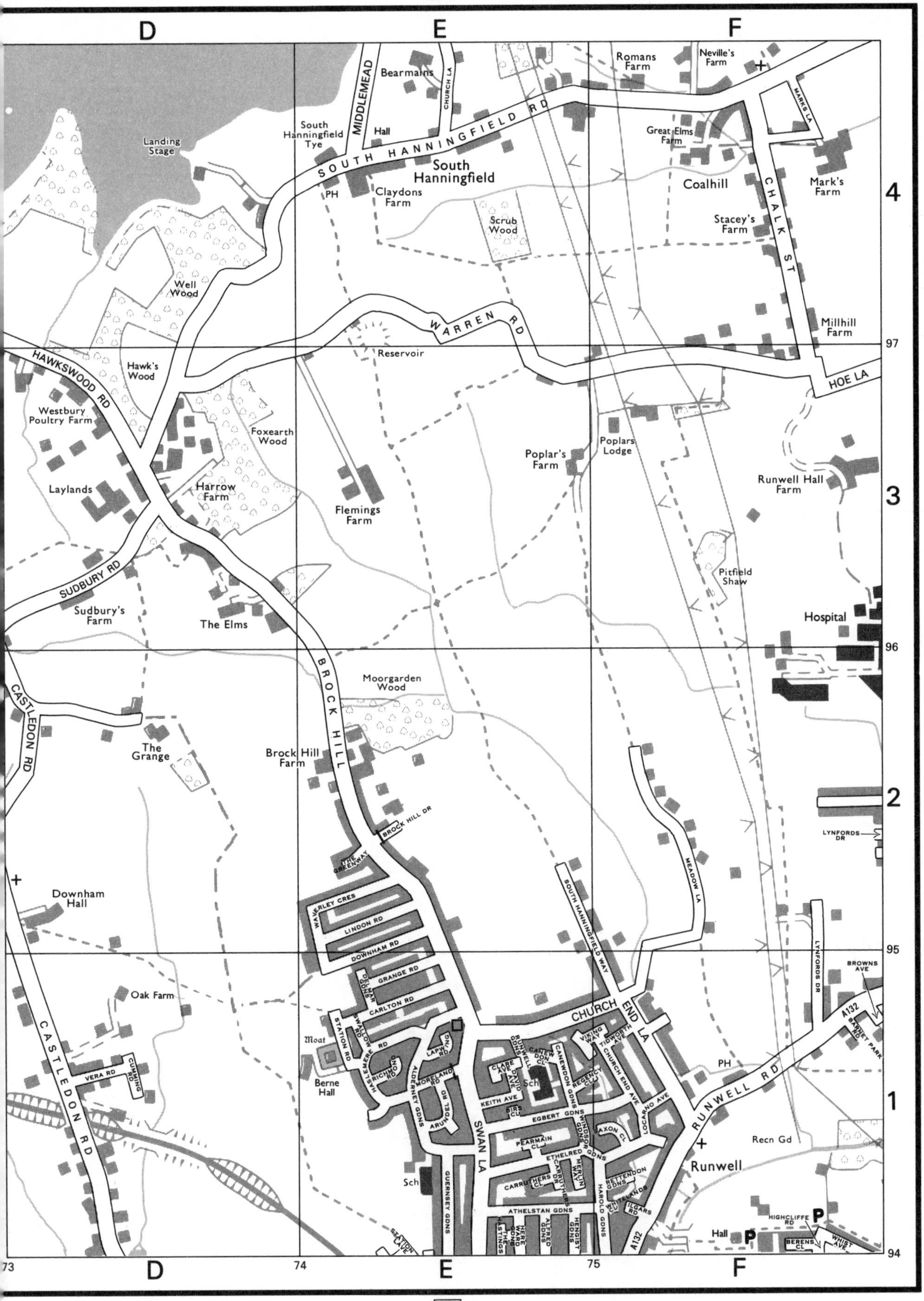
D
E
F
Landing Stage
Bearmains
MIDDLEMEAD
CHURCH LA
Hall
South Hanningfield Tye
SOUTH HANNINGFIELD RD
South Hanningfield
PH
Claydons Farm
Romans Farm
Neville's Farm
MARKS LA
Great Elms Farm
Coalhill
CHALK ST
Mark's Farm
Stacey's Farm
Scrub Wood
Well Wood
WARREN RD
Millhill Farm
Reservoir
HOE LA
HAWKSWOOD RD
Hawk's Wood
Westbury Poultry Farm
Foxearth Wood
Poplar's Farm
Poplars Lodge
Laylands
Harrow Farm
Flemings Farm
Runwell Hall Farm
SUDBURY RD
Sudbury's Farm
The Elms
Pitfield Shaw
Hospital
BROCK HILL
Moorgarden Wood
CASTLEDON RD
The Grange
Brock Hill Farm
BROCK HILL DR
LYNFORDS DR
THE GREENWAY
SOUTH HANNINGFIELD WAY
MEADOW LA
Downham Hall
WAVERLEY CRES
LINDON RD
DOWNHAM RD
GRANGE RD
DELMAR GDNS
CARLTON RD
LYNFORDS DR
BROWNS AVE
Oak Farm
CHURCH END LA
A132
BARNET PARK RD
STATION RD
SWALLOW RD
Moat
HASLEMERE RD
RICHMOND RD
LAPWING RD
CLARE AVE
RUNWELL GDNS
CANTERBURY CL
CANEWDON GDNS
VIKING WAY
TIDWORTH AVE
CHURCH END AVE
REGENCY CL
LOCARNO AVE
PH
RUNWELL RD
VERA RD
CUMMING RD
Berne Hall
ALDERNEY GDNS
MORELAND RD
ARUNDEL RD
KEITH AVE
DAVID AVE
Sch
BIRS CL
EGBERT GDNS
WINDSOR GDNS
SAXON CL
SWAN LA
PEARMAIN CL
ETHELRED GDNS
CARRUTHERS DR
MERLIN WAY
RETTENDON GDNS
WHITELANDS CL
Recn Gd
Runwell
Sch
GUERNSEY GDNS
CARRUTHERS CL
HAROLD GDNS
ILGARS RD
ATHELSTAN GDNS
HASTINGS
HEREWARD GDNS
ALFRED GDNS
HENGIST GDNS
A132
HIGHCLIFFE RD
Hall
P
P
BERENS CL
WHIST AVE
STATION AVE
4
3
2
1
97
96
95
94
73
74
75
D
E
F

164

174

153

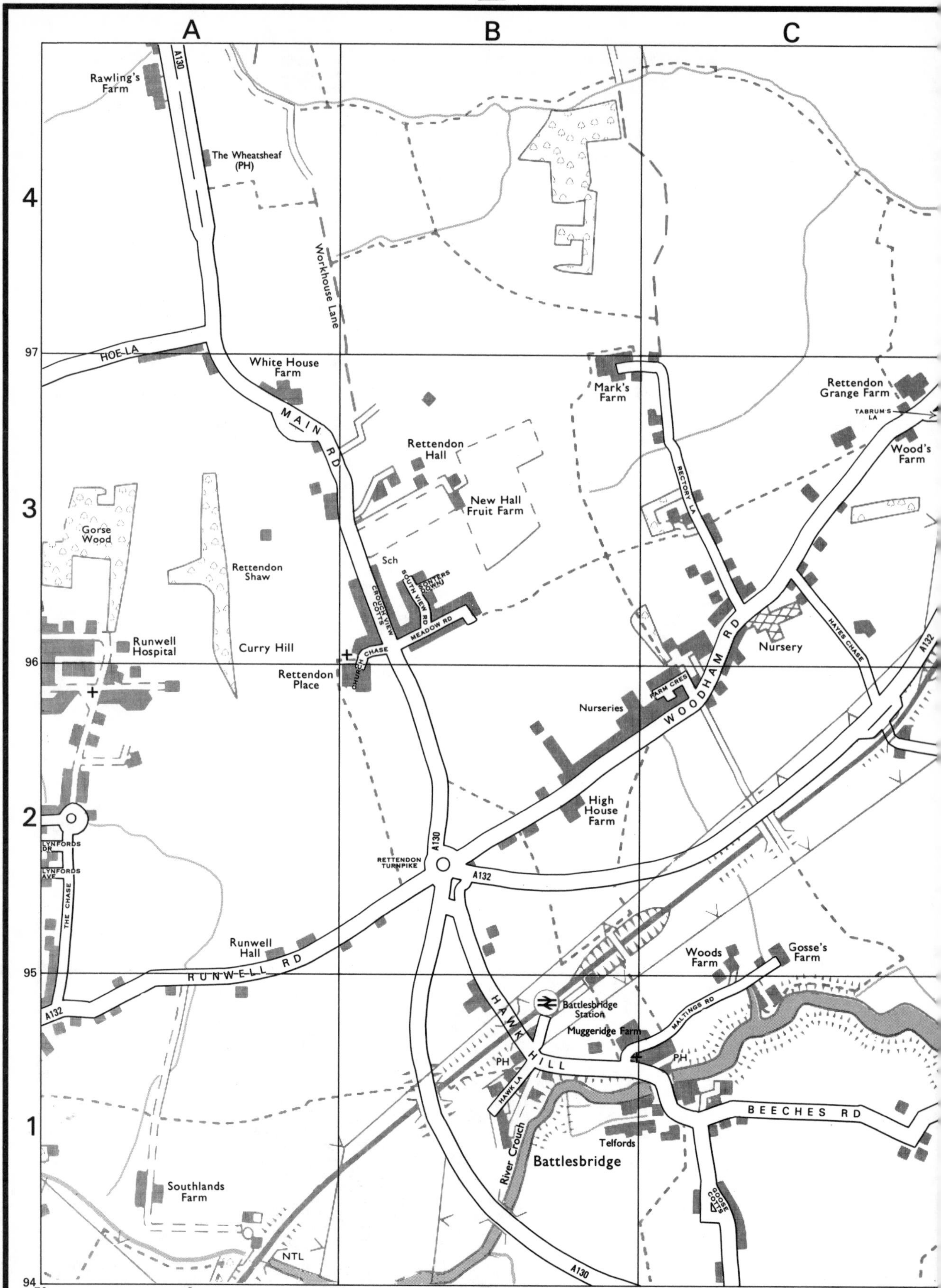
A
B
C
4
3
2
1
97
96
95
94
76
77
78
A130
Rawling's Farm
The Wheatsheaf (PH)
Workhouse Lane
HOE LA
White House Farm
MAIN RD
Rettendon Hall
New Hall Fruit Farm
Mark's Farm
Rettendon Grange Farm
TABRUM'S LA
Wood's Farm
RECTORY LA
Gorse Wood
Rettendon Shaw
Sch
CROUCH VIEW COTTS
SOUTH VIEW RD
MEADOW RD
CHASE
Runwell Hospital
Curry Hill
Rettendon Place
Nursery
HAYES CHASE
WOODHAM RD
FARM CRES
Nurseries
High House Farm
A132
LYNFORDS DR
LYNFORDS AVE
THE CHASE
RETTENDON TURNPIKE
Runwell Hall
RUNWELL RD
Woods Farm
Gosse's Farm
HAWK HILL
Battlesbridge Station
Muggeridge Farm
MALTINGS RD
PH
HAWK LA
BEECHES RD
River Crouch
Telfords
Battlesbridge
GOOSE COTTS
Southlands Farm
NTL

163

175

154

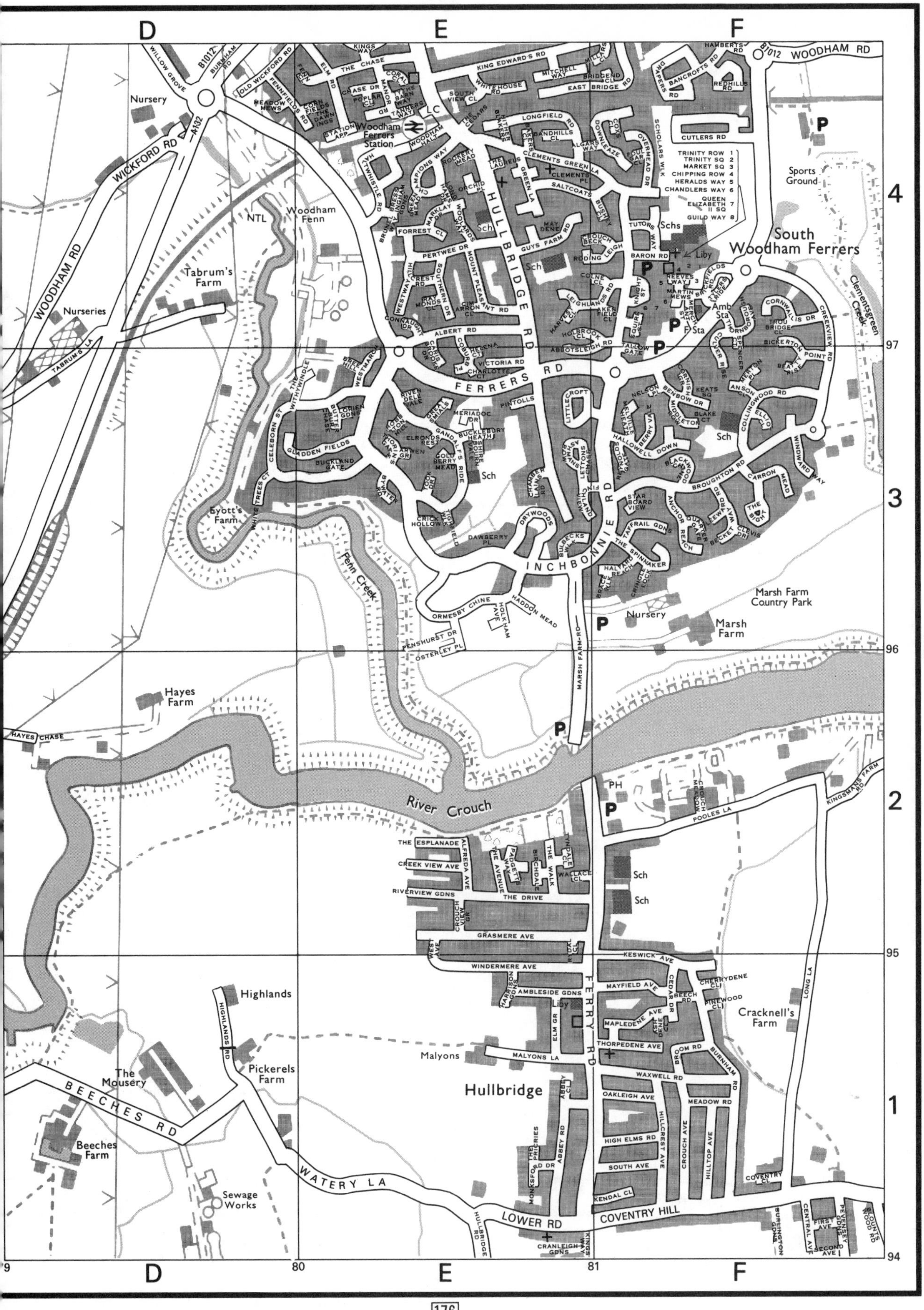

D
E
F
4
3
2
1
97
96
95
94
80
81
Woodham Ferrers Station
South Woodham Ferrers
Woodham Fenn
Tabrum's Farm
Nursery
Nurseries
Eyott's Farm
Sports Ground
Clementsgreen Creek
Marsh Farm Country Park
Marsh Farm
Hayes Farm
Fenn Creek
River Crouch
Highlands
Pickerels Farm
The Mousery
Beeches Farm
Sewage Works
Malyons
Hullbridge
Cracknell's Farm
WICKFORD RD
WOODHAM RD
HULLBRIDGE RD
FERRERS RD
INCHBONNIE RD
MARSH FARM RD
FERRY RD
POOLES LA
LONG LA
BEECHES RD
WATERY LA
LOWER RD
COVENTRY HILL
HAYES CHASE
HIGHLANDS RD
TRINITY ROW 1
TRINITY SQ 2
MARKET SQ 3
CHIPPING ROW 4
HERALDS WAY 5
CHANDLERS WAY 6
QUEEN ELIZABETH II SQ 7
GUILD WAY 8

166

176

155

165

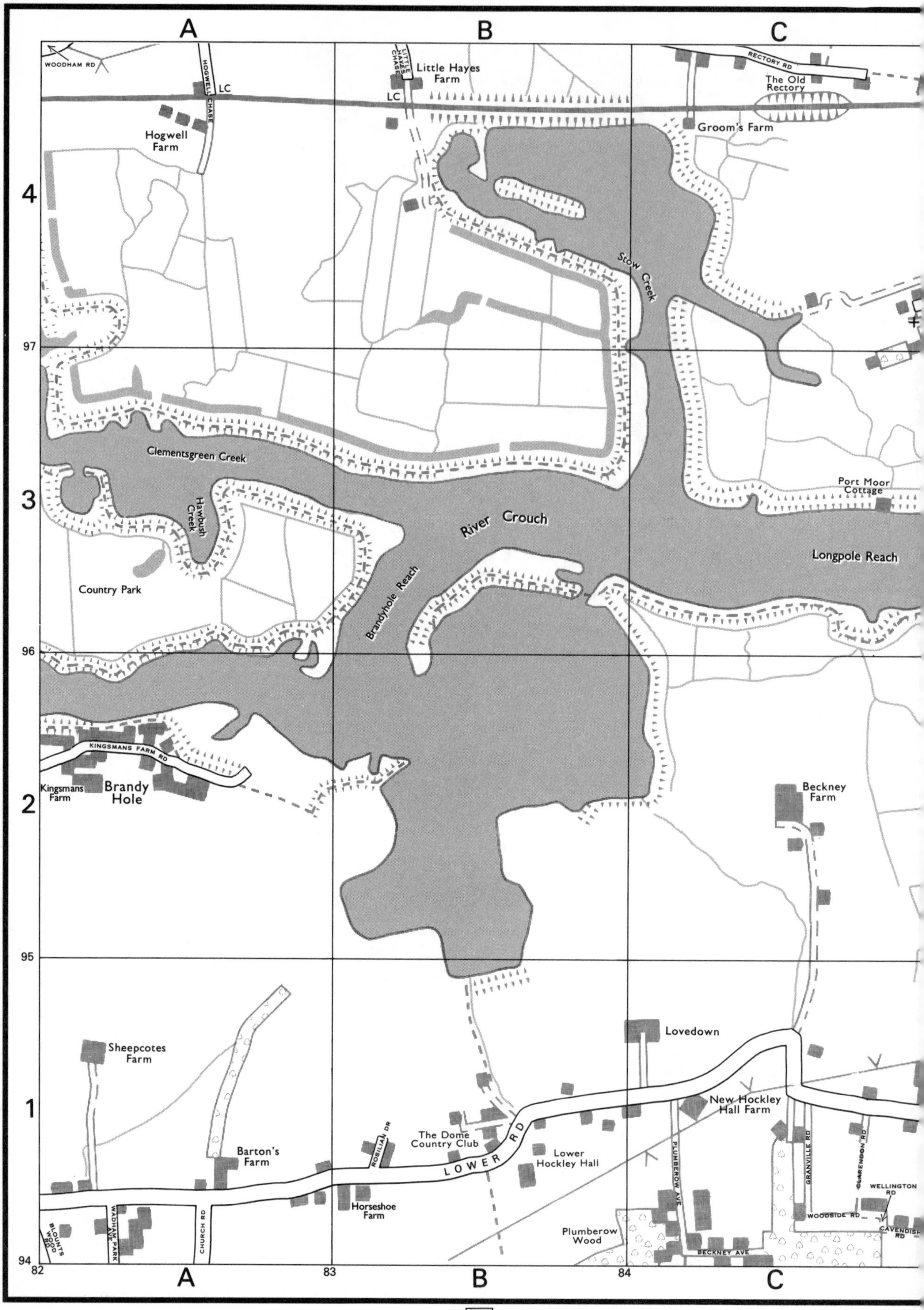
A
B
C
4
3
2
1
97
96
95
94
82
83
84
WOODHAM RD
HOGWELL CHASE
LC
Hogwell Farm
LITTLE HAYES CHASE
Little Hayes Farm
RECTORY RD
The Old Rectory
Groom's Farm
Stow Creek
Clementsgreen Creek
Hawbush Creek
River Crouch
Brandyhole Reach
Longpole Reach
Port Moor Cottage
Country Park
KINGSMANS FARM RD
Kingsmans Farm
Brandy Hole
Beckney Farm
Lovedown
Sheepcotes Farm
New Hockley Hall Farm
The Dome Country Club
Lower Hockley Hall
Barton's Farm
ROBILIAN DR
LOWER RD
Horseshoe Farm
PLUMBEROW AVE
GRANVILLE RD
CLARENDON RD
WELLINGTON RD
WOODSIDE RD
CAVENDISH RD
Plumberow Wood
BECKNEY AVE
BLOUNTS WOOD RD
WADHAM PARK AVE
CHURCH RD

177

156

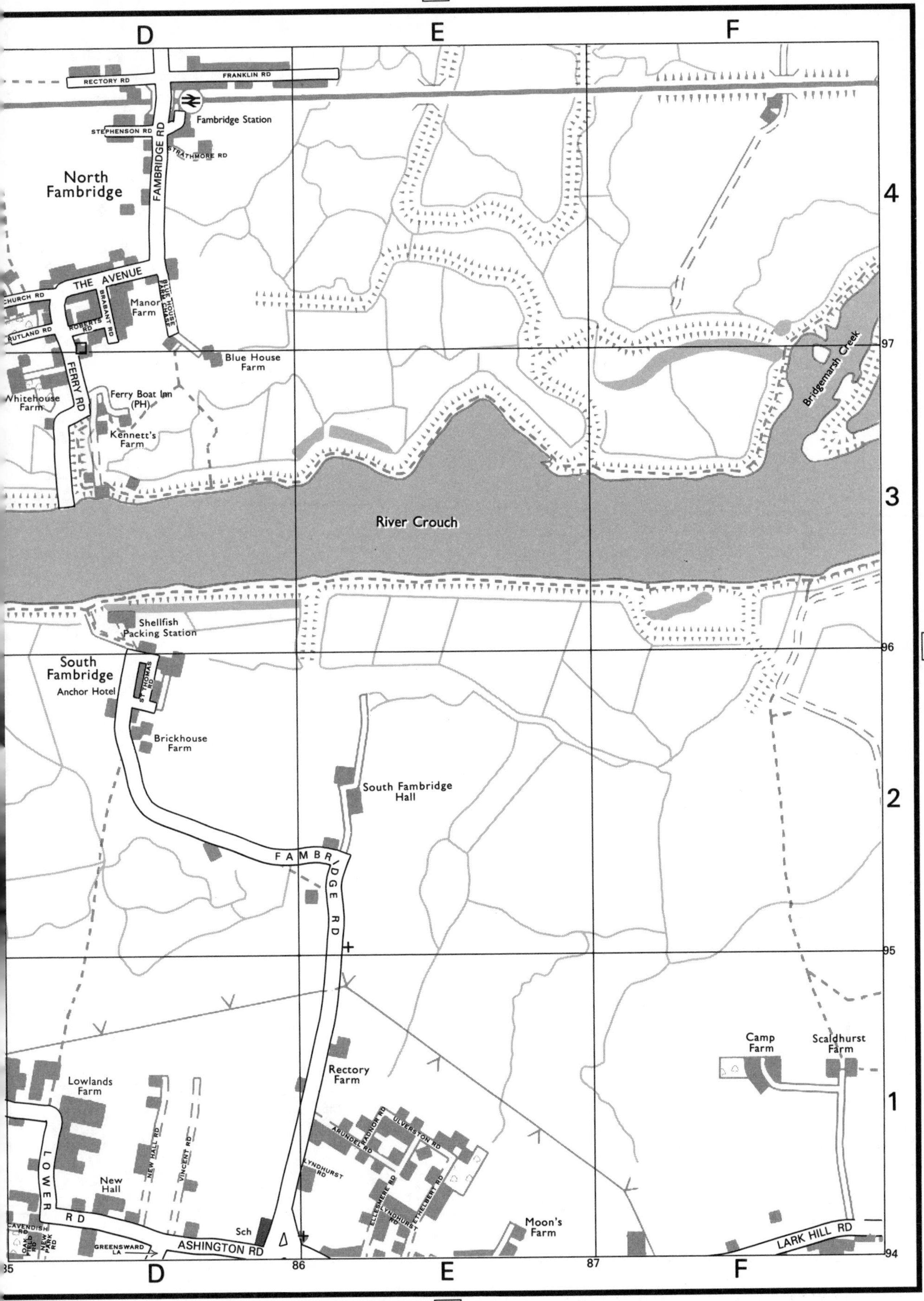
D
E
F
RECTORY RD
FRANKLIN RD
Fambridge Station
STEPHENSON RD
FAMBRIDGE RD
STRATHMORE RD
North Fambridge
4
THE AVENUE
CHURCH RD
BRABANT RD
BLUE HOUSE FARM CHASE
Manor Farm
RUTLAND RD
ROBERTS RD
97
Blue House Farm
FERRY RD
Whitehouse Farm
Ferry Boat Inn (PH)
Kennett's Farm
Bridgemarsh Creek
3
River Crouch
Shellfish Packing Station
96
South Fambridge
Anchor Hotel
ST THOMAS RD
Brickhouse Farm
South Fambridge Hall
2
FAMBRIDGE RD
95
Camp Farm
Scaldhurst Farm
Lowlands Farm
Rectory Farm
1
RADNOR RD
ULVERSTON RD
ARUNDEL RD
LYNDHURST RD
NEW HALL RD
VINCENT RD
ELLESMERE RD
ETHELBERT RD
LOWER RD
New Hall
Moon's Farm
LARK HILL RD
CAVENDISH RD
OAK FIELD RD
NEW PARK RD
GREENSWARD LA
Sch
ASHINGTON RD
94
85
86
87
D
E
F

168

178

157

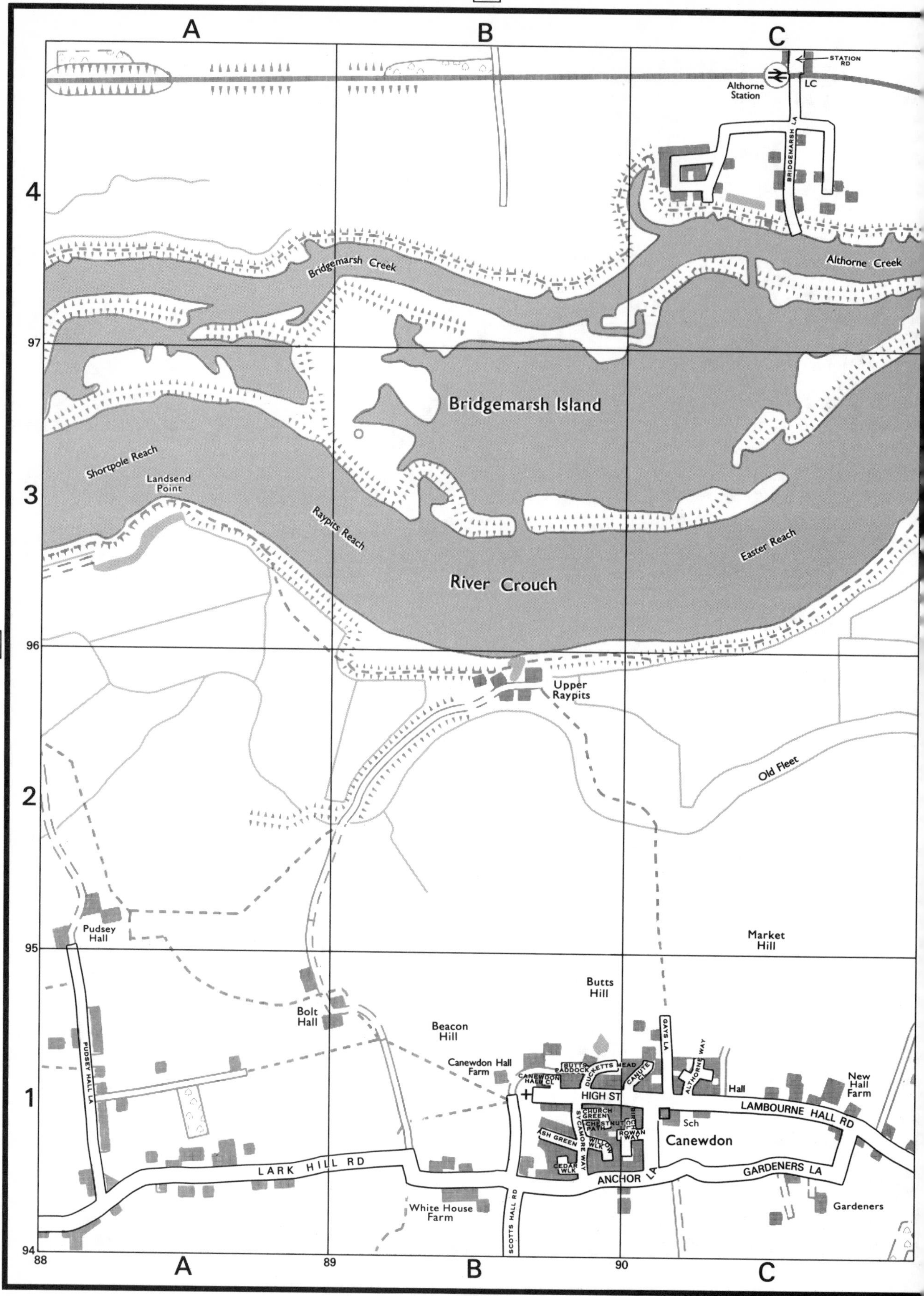
A
B
C
STATION RD
Althorne Station
LC
BRIDGEMARSH LA
4
Bridgemarsh Creek
Althorne Creek
97
Bridgemarsh Island
Shortpole Reach
Landsend Point
3
Raypits Reach
Easter Reach
River Crouch
96
Upper Raypits
2
Old Fleet
Pudsey Hall
95
Market Hill
Butts Hill
Bolt Hall
Beacon Hill
GAYS LA
Canewdon Hall Farm
BUTTS PADDOCK
DUCKETTS MEAD
CANUTE CL
ALTHORNE WAY
CANEWDON HALL CL
1
PUDSEY HALL LA
HIGH ST
Hall
New Hall Farm
LAMBOURNE HALL RD
CHURCH GREEN
CHESTNUT PATH
SYCAMORE WAY
ASH GREEN
WILLOW WLK
ROWAN WAY
Sch
Canewdon
LARK HILL RD
CEDAR WLK
GARDENERS LA
ANCHOR LA
White House Farm
SCOTTS HALL RD
Gardeners
94
88
89
90
A
B
C
167
179

158

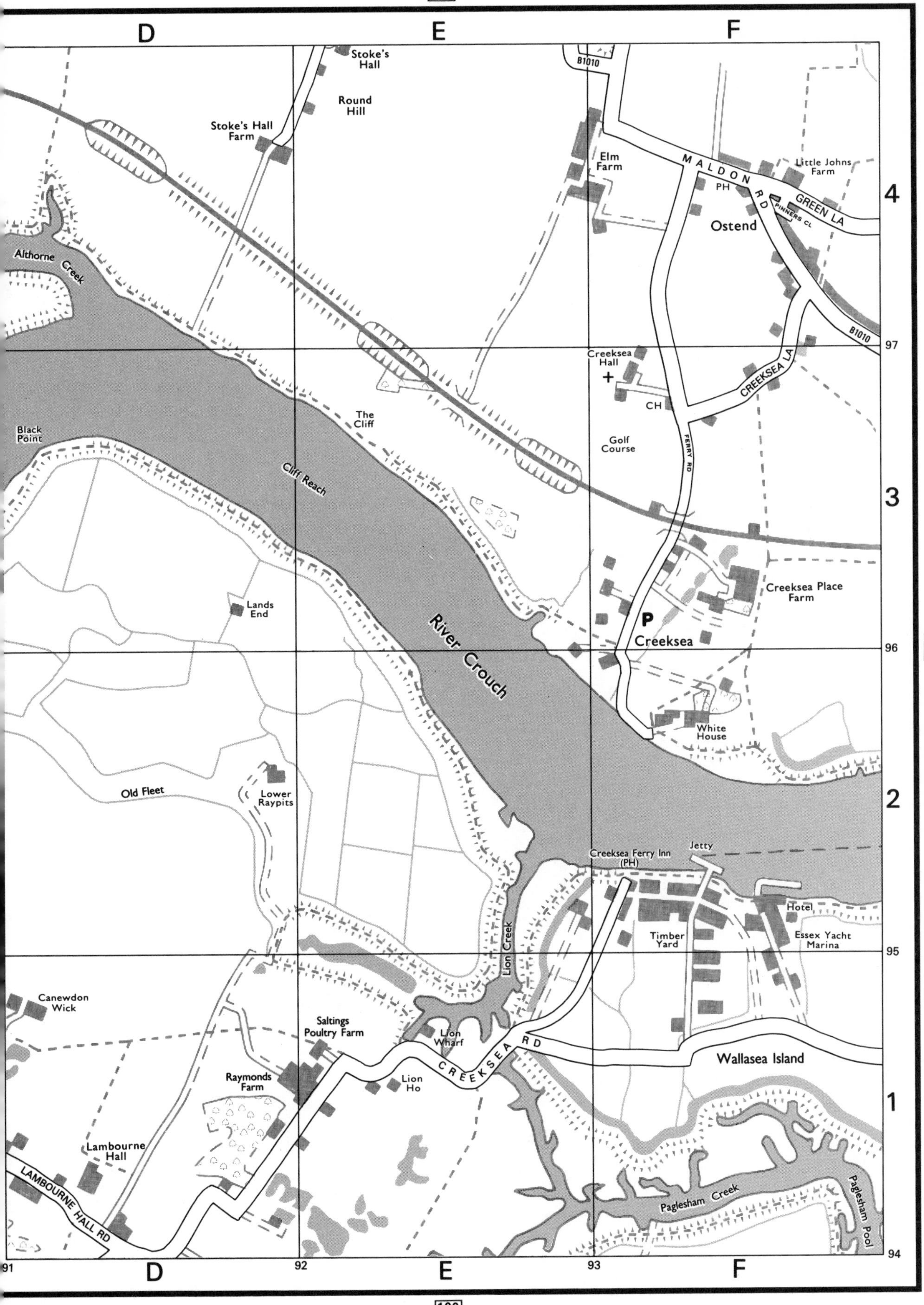
D
E
F
Stoke's Hall
Round Hill
Stoke's Hall Farm
B1010
Elm Farm
MALDON RD
PH
Little Johns Farm
GREEN LA
PINNERS CL
Ostend
Althorne Creek
B1010
Creeksea Hall
CREEKSEA LA
CH
The Cliff
Black Point
Golf Course
FERRY RD
Cliff Reach
Creeksea Place Farm
Lands End
P
Creeksea
River Crouch
White House
Old Fleet
Lower Raypits
Creeksea Ferry Inn (PH)
Jetty
Hotel
Timber Yard
Essex Yacht Marina
Lion Creek
Canewdon Wick
Saltings Poultry Farm
Lion Wharf
CREEKSEA RD
Wallasea Island
Raymonds Farm
Lion Ho
Lambourne Hall
LAMBOURNE HALL RD
Paglesham Creek
Paglesham Pool
4
3
2
1
97
96
95
94
91
92
93
170

180

159

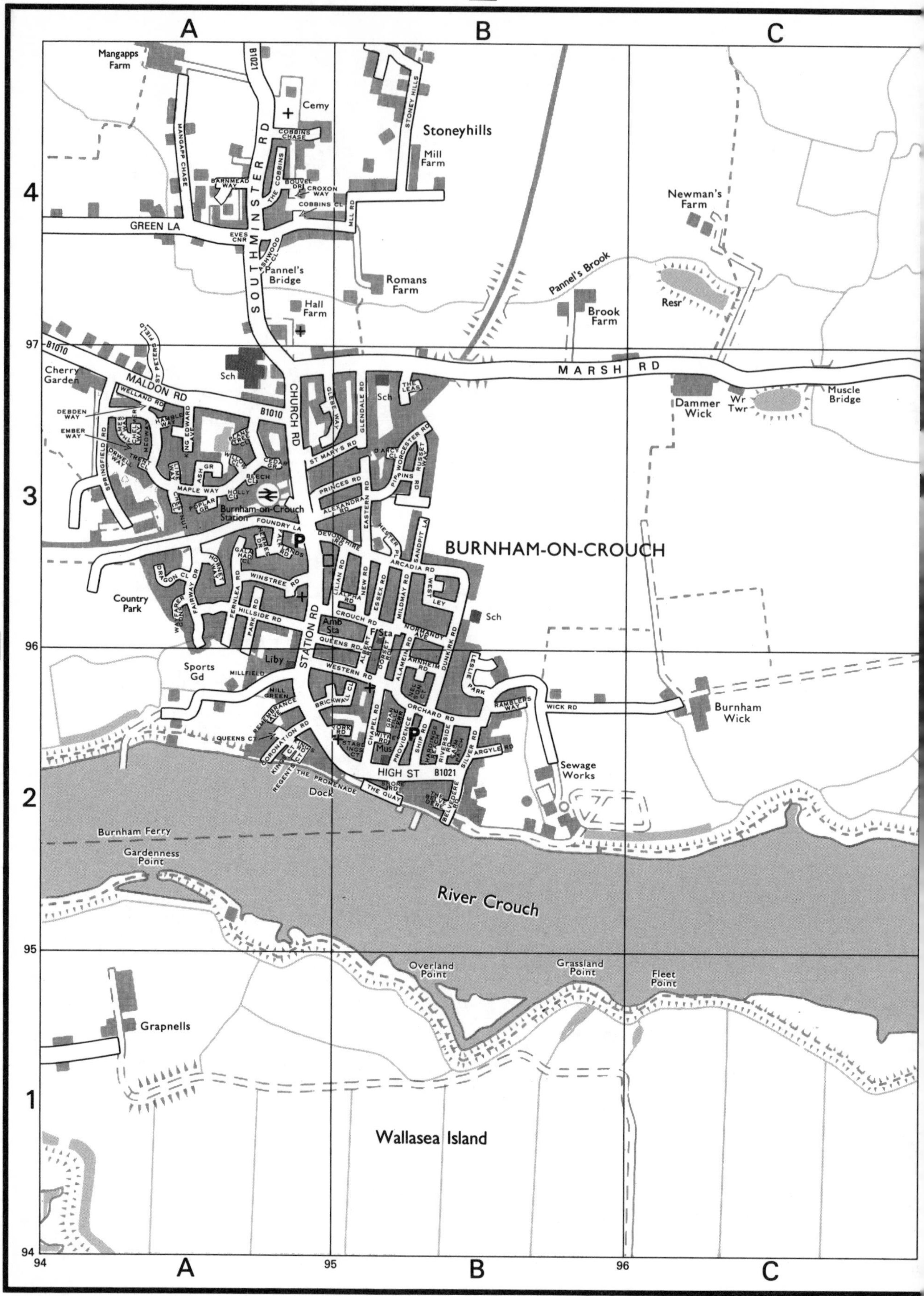

A
B
C
4
3
2
1
97
96
95
94
Mangapps Farm
B1021
Cemy
Stoneyhills
Mill Farm
STONEY HILLS
MANGAPP CHASE
COBBINS CHASE
SOUTHMINSTER RD
THE COBBINS
BARNMEAD WAY
BOUVEL DRI
CROXON WAY
COBBINS CL
MILL RD
GREEN LA
EVES CNR
ASHWOOD CL
Pannel's Bridge
Romans Farm
Hall Farm
Newman's Farm
Pannel's Brook
Brook Farm
Resr
B1010
ST PETERS FIELD
Cherry Garden
MALDON RD
Sch
CHURCH RD
MARSH RD
Dammer Wick
Wr Twr
Muscle Bridge
WELLAND RD
DEBDEN WAY
EMBER WAY
HAMBLE WAY
MEDWAY
SPRINGFIELD RD
ORWELL WAY
TRENT CL
KING EDWARD AVE
GLEBE WAY
GLENDALE RD
THE LEAS
ST MARY'S RD
DARCY CL
WORCESTER RD
RUSSET WAY
PIPPINS RD
CEDAR GR
BEECH CL
HOLLY CL
MAPLE WAY
POPLAR GR
ASH GR
WILLOW CL
PRINCES RD
ALEXANDRA RD
EASTERN RD
HESTER PL
SANDPIT LA
Burnham-on-Crouch Station
FOUNDRY LA
DEVONSHIRE RD
P
BURNHAM-ON-CROUCH
ARCADIA RD
HORNET WAY
DRAGON CL
FAIRWAY DR
WINSTREE RD
LILIAN RD
NEW RD
ESSEX RD
MILDMAY RD
WEST LEY
Country Park
WAYFARER GDNS
FERNLEA RD
HILLSIDE RD
PARK RD
CROUCH RD
Amb Sta
F Sta
NORMANDY AVE
Sch
QUEENS RD
ALBERT RD
DORSET RD
ALAMEIN RD
ARNHEIM RD
DUNKIRK RD
LESLIE PARK
STATION RD
Sports Gd
MILLFIELDS
Liby
WESTERN RD
MILL GREEN
BRICKWALL CL
REMEMBRANCE AVE
ORCHARD RD
RAMBLERS WAY
WICK RD
Burnham Wick
QUEENS CT
CORONATION RD
YORK RD
CHAPEL RD
PROVIDENCE
SHIP RD
HARBOUR
RIVERSIDE RD
SILVER RD
ARGYLE RD
KINGS CT
REGENTS CT
THE PROMENADE
Mus
HIGH ST
B1021
SHORE RD
THE QUAY
BELVEDERE RD
Sewage Works
Dock
Burnham Ferry
Gardenness Point
River Crouch
Overland Point
Grassland Point
Fleet Point
Grapnells
Wallasea Island
169

181

160

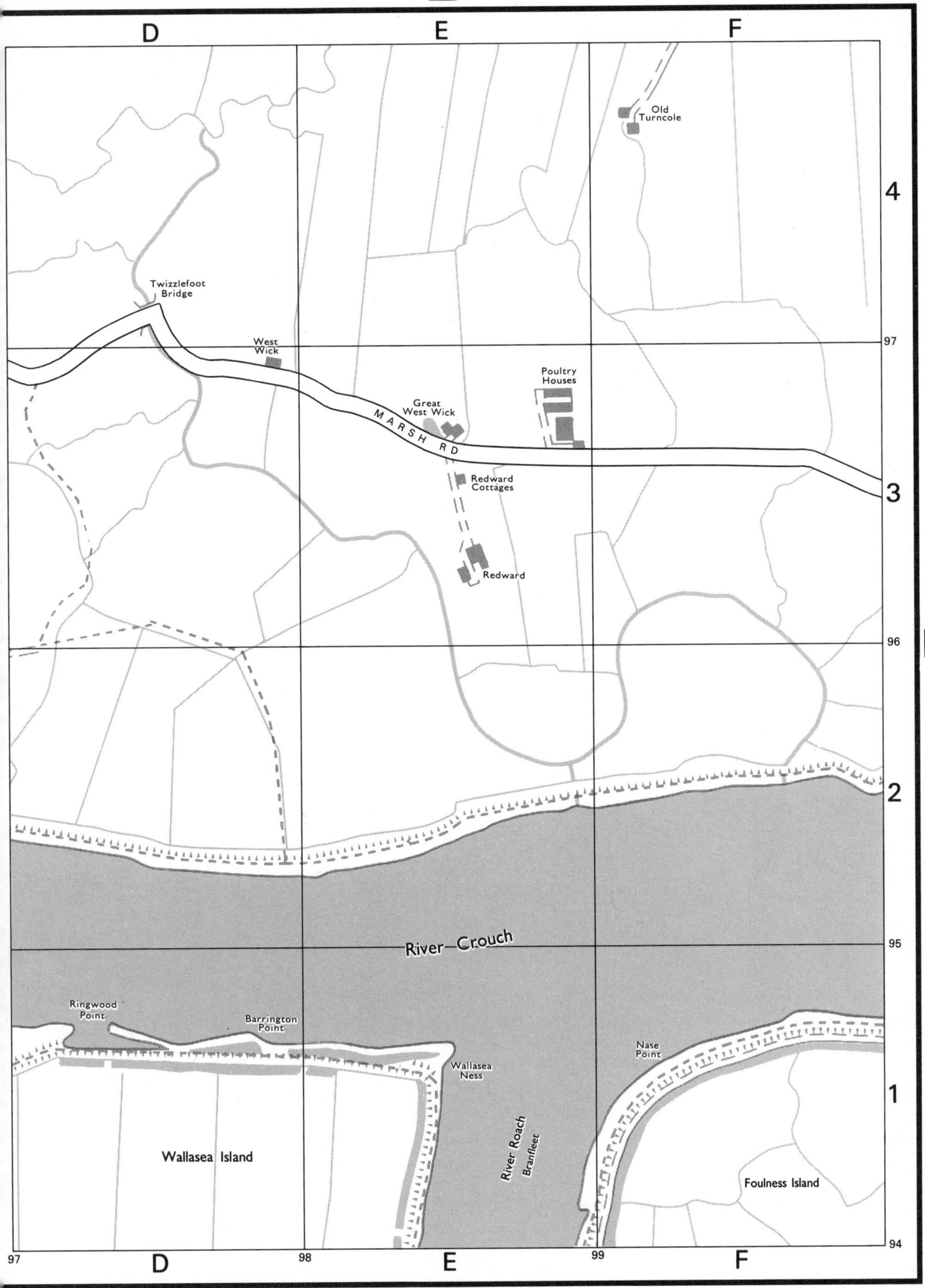
D
E
F
Old Turncole
4
Twizzlefoot Bridge
West Wick
97
Poultry Houses
Great West Wick
MARSH RD
Redward Cottages
3
Redward
96
2
River Crouch
95
Ringwood Point
Barrington Point
Nase Point
Wallasea Ness
1
Wallasea Island
River Roach
Branfleet
Foulness Island
94
97
98
99
D
E
F

172

182

161

171

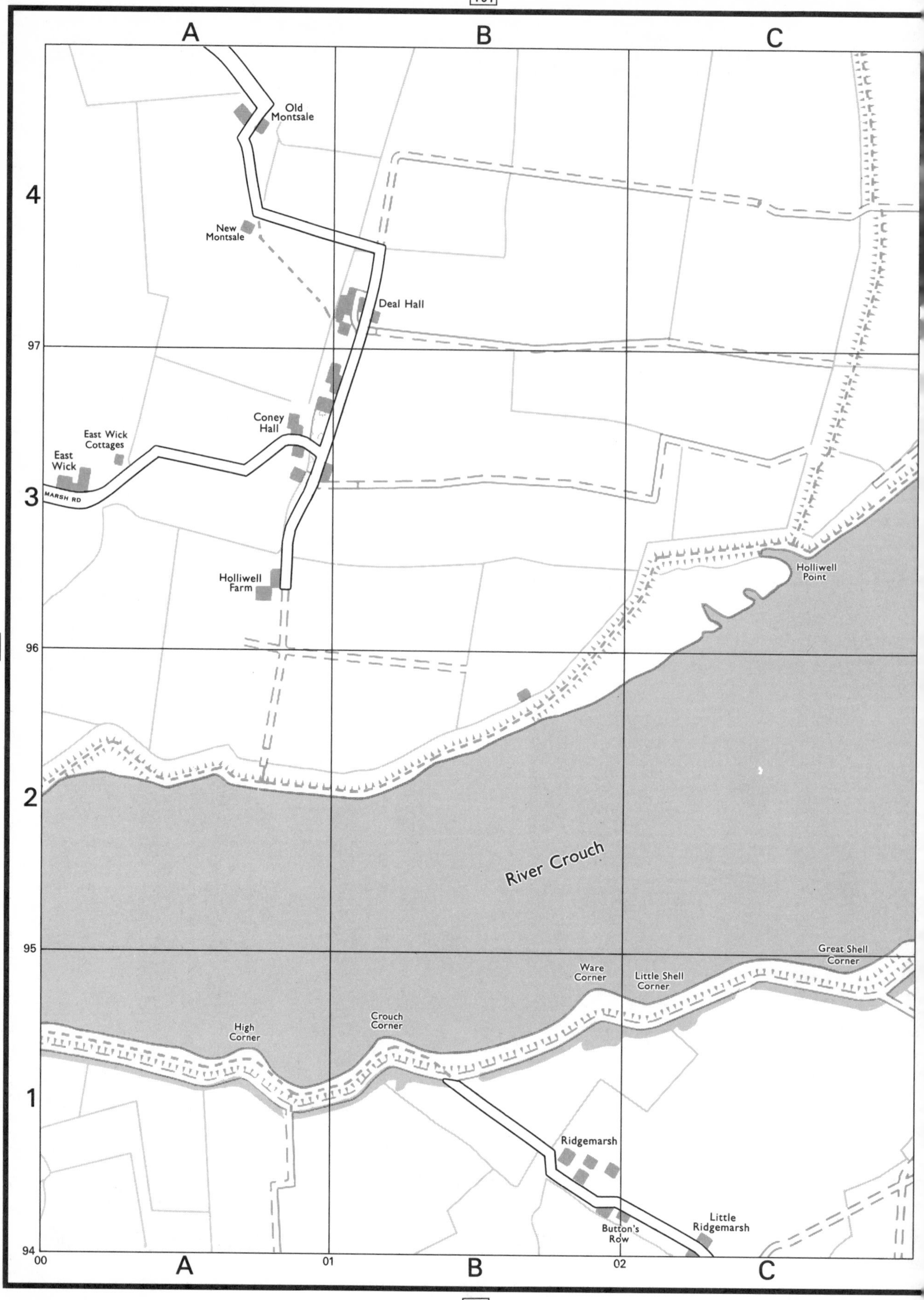
A
B
C
4
3
2
1
97
96
95
94
00
01
02
Old Montsale
New Montsale
Deal Hall
Coney Hall
East Wick Cottages
East Wick
MARSH RD
Holliwell Farm
Holliwell Point
River Crouch
Great Shell Corner
Ware Corner
Little Shell Corner
High Corner
Crouch Corner
Ridgemarsh
Little Ridgemarsh
Button's Row

183

162

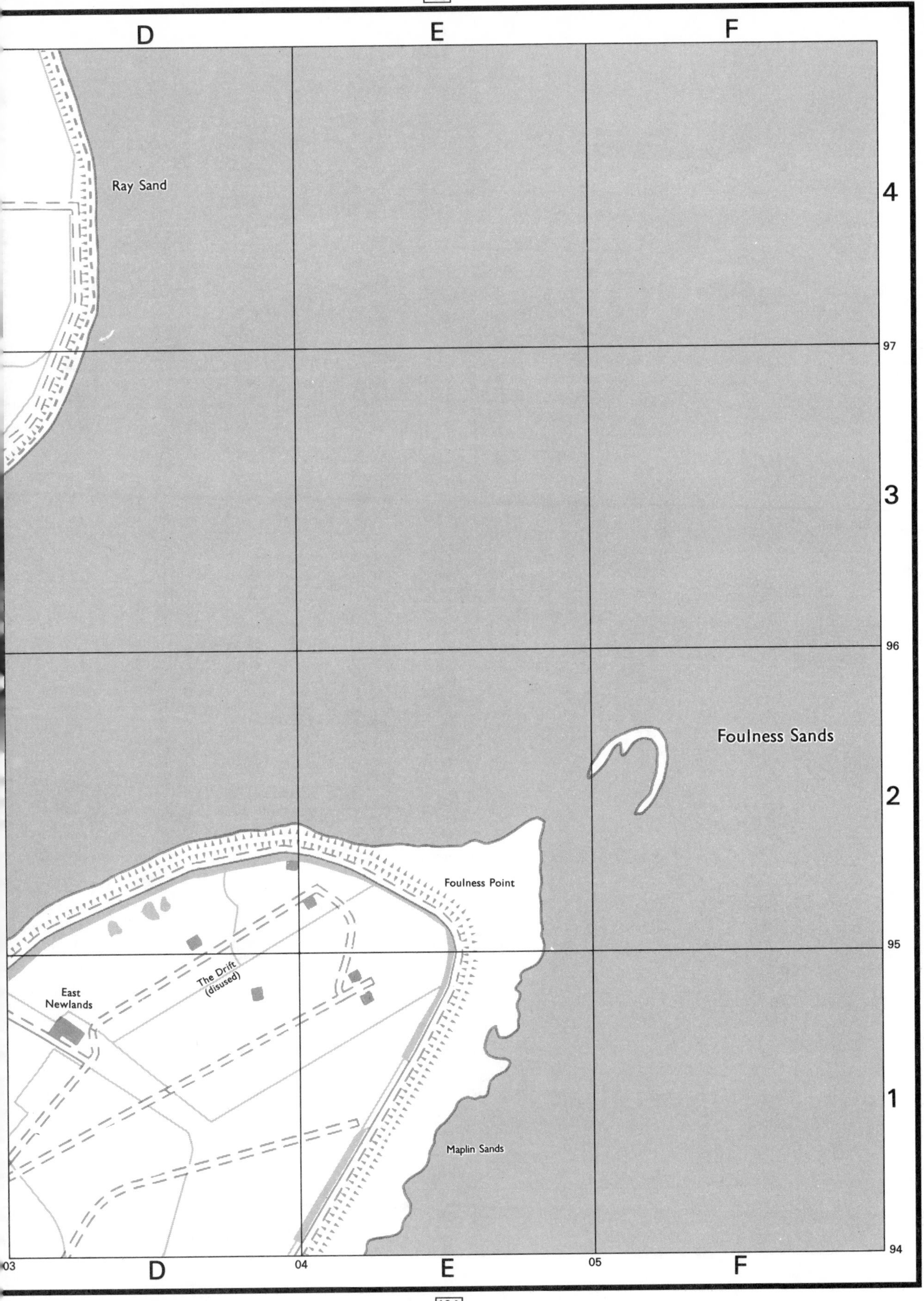
D
E
F
Ray Sand
4
97
3
96
Foulness Sands
2
Foulness Point
The Drift (disused)
East Newlands
95
1
Maplin Sands
94
03
04
05
D
E
F

184

163

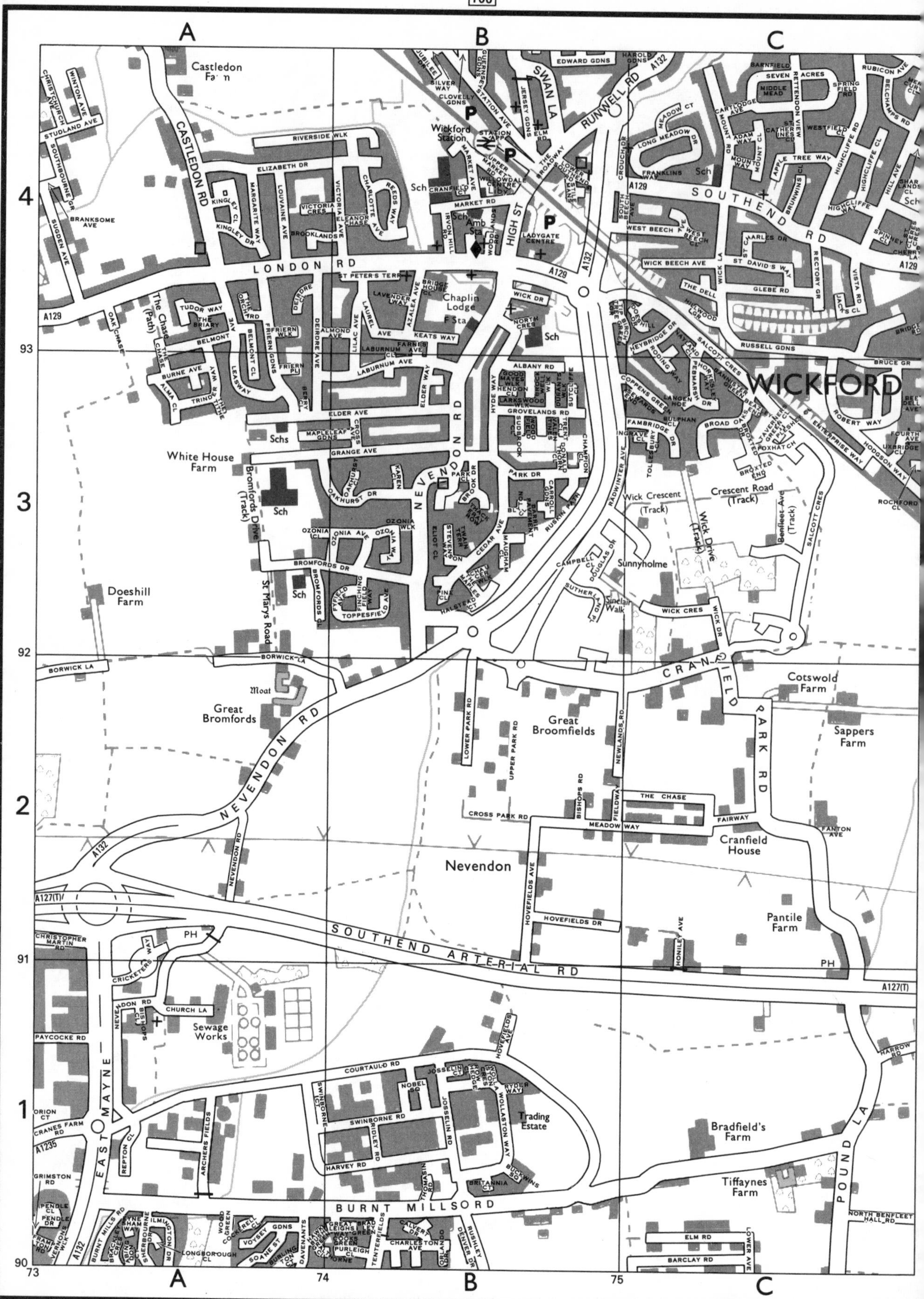
A
B
C
4
3
2
1
93
92
91
90
73
74
75
WICKFORD
Castledon Farm
CASTLEDON RD
RIVERSIDE WLK
ELIZABETH DR
KINGLEY CL
KINGLEY DR
MARGARITE WAY
LOUVAINE AVE
VICTORIA CRES
VICTORIA AVE
ELEANOR CHASE
CHARLOTTE AVE
REEDS WAY
BROOKLANDS
LONDON RD
A129
A132
A127(T)
A1235
Wickford Station
STATION APP
MARKET AVE
MARKET RD
CRANFIELD CT
IRVON HILL
Sch
Amb Sta
Liby
P
HIGH ST
SWAN LA
JERSEY GDNS
ELM RD
EDWARD GDNS
HAROLD GDNS
RUNWELL RD
THE BROADWAY
LADYGATE CENTRE
WILLOWDALE CENTRE
JUBILEE DR
SILVER WAY
CLOVELLY GDNS
GUERNSEY GDNS
STATION AVE
CROUCH DR
LONG MEADOW CT
LONG MEADOW DR
FRANKLINS WAY
SOUTHEND RD
WEST BEECH AVE
WEST BEECH CL
WICK BEECH AVE
WICK LA
ST DAVID'S WAY
CHARLES DR
GLEBE RD
THE DELL
HILLWOOD GR
RUSSELL GDNS
SALCOTT CRES
BARNFIELD
SEVEN ACRES
MIDDLE MEAD
CARTLODGE AVE
MOUNT RD
ADAM WAY
MOUNT WAY
MOUNT CL
APPLE TREE WAY
WESTFIELD
SPRINGFIELD RD
RETTENDON VIEW
BRUNWINS CL
HIGHCLIFFE RD
HIGHCLIFFE CL
HIGHCLIFFE WAY
RECTORY GR
VISTA RD
JACKS CL
SPINNEY CL
BELCHAMPS RD
RUBICON AVE
HILL AVE
BRUCE GR
ROBERT WAY
ENTERPRISE WAY
HODGSON WAY
ROCHFORD CL
WINTON AVE
CHRISTCHURCH AVE
STUDLAND AVE
SOUTHBOURNE GR
BRANKSOME AVE
SUDDEN AVE
The Chase (Path)
OAK CHASE
TUDOR WAY
THE BRIARY
THE ORCHARD
BELMONT
BELMONT CL
BURNE AVE
ALMA CL
TRINDER WAY
LEASWAY
FRIERN GDNS
FRIERN WLK
DEIRDRE AVE
ALMOND AVE
LILAC AVE
LAUREL AVE
AZALEA AVE
ST PETER'S TERR
BRIDGE HOUSE CL
LAVENDER WAY
Chaplin Lodge
F Sta
KEATS WAY
LABURNUM CL
LABURNUM AVE
FARNES AVE
ELDER WAY
ELDER AVE
MAPLELEAF GDNS
CROSS AVE
GRANGE AVE
Schs
White House Farm
Bromfords Drive (Track)
OAKHURST DR
KAREN CL
OZONIA CL
OZONIA AVE
OZONIA WLK
BROMFORDS DR
BROMFORDS CL
FYFIELD AVE
FINCHING FIELD WAY
TOPPESFIELD AVE
St Marys Road
NEVENDON RD
PARK DR
BROOK DR
ELIOT CL
STEVENSON WAY
CEDAR AVE
MAUGHAM
HALSTEAD CT
PINE CL
WICK DR
NORTH CRES
ALBANY RD
HYDE WAY
GOODMAYES WLK
HENDON CL
LARKSWOOD WLK
GROVELANDS RD
SUDBROOK CL
CHAMPION
RUSKIN PATH
CARROLL GDNS
Wick Crescent (Track)
Crescent Road (Track)
Wick Drive (Track)
Benfleet Ave (Track)
SALCOTT CRES
Sunnyholme
CAMPBELL CL
DOUGLAS DR
SUTHERLAND PL
Sinclair Walk
WICK CRES
RADWINTER AVE
TOLLESBURY CL
FAMBRIDGE CL
INGRAVE CL
COPPENS GREEN
HEYBRIDGE DR
ROWLAND
BULPHAN CL
BROAD OAKS
BANNISTER GREEN
BOXTED CL
FOXHATCH
Doeshill Farm
BORWICK LA
Moat
Great Bromfords
CRANFIELD PARK RD
Cotswold Farm
Sappers Farm
LOWER PARK RD
UPPER PARK RD
Great Broomfields
NEWLANDS RD
BISHOPS RD
FIELDWAY
THE CHASE
MEADOW WAY
FAIRWAY
CROSS PARK RD
Cranfield House
Nevendon
HOVEFIELDS AVE
HOVEFIELDS DR
Pantile Farm
HONILEY AVE
PH
FANTON AVE
SOUTHEND ARTERIAL RD
CHRISTOPHER MARTIN RD
CRICKETERS WAY
CHURCH LA
NEVENDON RD
BISHOPS CT
Sewage Works
PAYCOCKE RD
EAST MAYNE
ORION CT
CRANES FARM RD
GRIMSTON RD
PENDLE CL
PENDLE DR
REPTON CL
ARCHERS FIELDS
COURTAULD RD
JOSSELIN CT
JOSSELIN RD
NOBEL SQ
RYDER WAY
WOLLASTON WAY
SWINBORNE CT
SWINBORNE RD
RIDLEY RD
HARVEY RD
THOMASIN RD
BRITANNIA CT
BUCKWINS SQ
Trading Estate
HOVEFIELDS AVE
BURNT MILLS RD
LONGBOROUGH CL
ILMINGTON DR
SHERBOURNE DR
WOOD GREEN
COCKERELL CL
VOYSEY GDNS
SOANE ST
DAVENANTS
TENTERFIELDS
CHARLESTON AVE
CALVERT DR
RUSHLEY
DENVER DR
ELM RD
BARCLAY RD
LOWER AVE
Bradfield's Farm
Tiffaynes Farm
POUND LA
HARROW RD
NORTH BENFLEET HALL RD

186

not continued, see key diagram

164

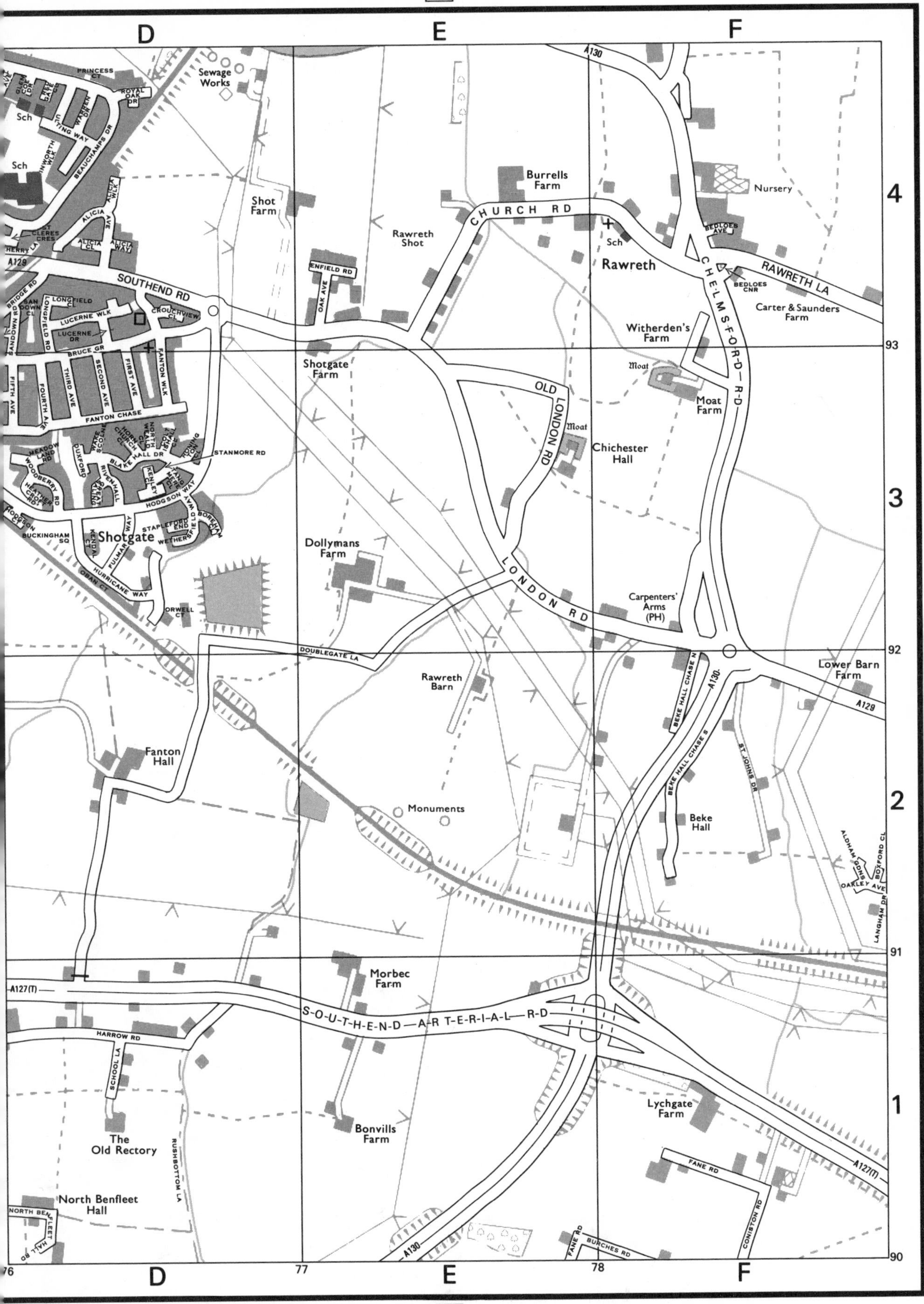
D
E
F
Sewage Works
Sch
Sch
PRINCESS CT
ROYAL OAK DR
UTTING WAY
WARREN DR
BEAUCHAMPS DR
ALICIA WLK
ALICIA AVE
ALICIA CL
ALICIA WAY
ST CLERES CRES
HENRY LA
A129
SOUTHEND RD
CROUCHVIEW CL
LONGFIELD CL
LUCERNE WLK
LUCERNE DR
BRUCE GR
SECOND AVE
FIRST AVE
FANTON WLK
THIRD AVE
FOURTH AVE
FIFTH AVE
FANTON CHASE
STANMORE RD
BLAKE HALL DR
HODGSON WAY
BUCKINGHAM SQ
Shotgate
HURRICANE WAY
OBAN CT
ORWELL CT
FULMAR WAY
STAPLEFORD END
WETHERSFIELD WAY
BOREHAM
Shot Farm
Rawreth Shot
ENFIELD RD
OAK AVE
Shotgate Farm
Dollymans Farm
DOUBLEGATE LA
A130
Burrells Farm
CHURCH RD
Sch
Rawreth
Nursery
BEDLOES AVE
BEDLOES CNR
RAWRETH LA
Carter & Saunders Farm
CHELMSFORD RD
Witherden's Farm
Moat
Moat Farm
OLD LONDON RD
Moat
Chichester Hall
LONDON RD
Carpenters' Arms (PH)
4
3
2
1
93
92
91
90
Lower Barn Farm
A129
Rawreth Barn
BEKE HALL CHASE N
BEKE HALL CHASE S
ST JOHNS DR
Beke Hall
Fanton Hall
Monuments
ALDHAM GDNS
BOXFORD CL
OAKLEY AVE
LANGHAM DR
A127(T)
Morbec Farm
SOUTHEND ARTERIAL RD
HARROW RD
SCHOOL LA
The Old Rectory
RUSHBOTTOM LA
Bonvills Farm
Lychgate Farm
FANE RD
A127(T)
CONISTON RD
BURCHES RD
North Benfleet Hall
NORTH BENFLEET HALL RD
76
77
78

176

187

165

175

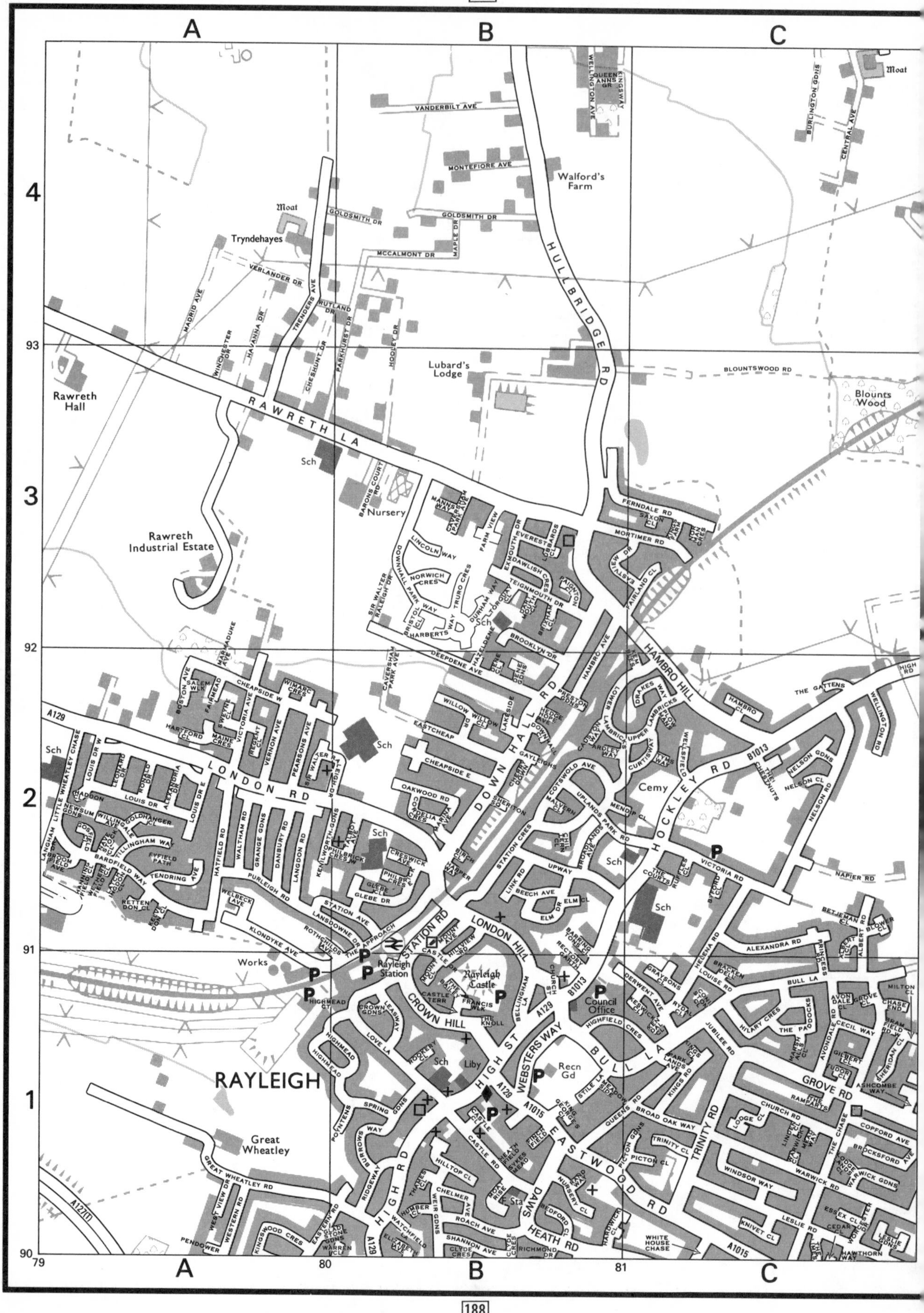
A
B
C
4
3
2
1
93
92
91
90
79
80
81
Moat
Walford's Farm
VANDERBILT AVE
MONTEFIORE AVE
GOLDSMITH DR
MCCALMONT DR
MAPLE DR
Tryndehayes
VERLANDER DR
TRENDERS AVE
RUTLAND DR
MADRID AVE
WINCHESTER DR
HAVANNA DR
CHESHUNT DR
PARKHURST DR
HOOLEY DR
HULLBRIDGE RD
Lubard's Lodge
BLOUNTSWOOD RD
Blounts Wood
Rawreth Hall
RAWRETH LA
Sch
Nursery
BARONS COURT RD
Rawreth Industrial Estate
LINCOLN WAY
NORWICH CRES
TRURO CRES
DURHAM WAY
BRISTOL CL
HARBERTS WAY
DOWNHALL PARK WAY
SIR WALTER RALEIGH DR
FARM VIEW
EVEREST
EXMOUTH DR
DAWLISH CRES
TEIGNMOUTH DR
FERNDALE RD
SAXON CL
MORTIMER RD
EASTVIEW DR
FAIRLAND CL
HAMBRO HILL
HAMBRO AVE
BROOKLYN DR
DEEPDENE AVE
HAZELDENE
CAVERSHAM PARK AVE
MARMADUKE AVE
BOSTON AVE
SALEM WLK
CHEAPSIDE W
WIMARC CRES
FAIRMEAD
VICTORIA AVE
REGENT CL
VERNON AVE
PEARSONS AVE
HARTFORD CL
MAINE CRES
A129
LONDON RD
LOUIS DR W
LOUIS DR
LOUIS DR E
ALEXANDRIA DR
LEONARD DR
HADDON
GOLDHANGER
TILLINGHAM WAY
BARDFIELD WAY
TENDRING AVE
HATFIELD RD
WALTHAM RD
GRANGE GDNS
DANBURY RD
LANGDON RD
KENILWORTH GDNS
TALBOT AVE
CRESWICK AVE
GLEBE DR
PURLEIGH RD
WELBECK AVE
STATION AVE
LANSDOWNE DR
KLONDYKE AVE
ROTHCHILDS AVE
THE APPROACH
LITTLE WHEATLEY CHASE
LANGHAM
WILLOW WALK
EASTCHEAP
CHEAPSIDE E
OAKWOOD RD
LAKESIDE
DOWNHALL RD
GAYLEIGHS
STATION RD
HEDGEHOPE AVE
PRESTON GDNS
COTSWOLD AVE
UPLANDS PARK RD
MALVERN
STATION CRES
UPWAY
LINK RD
BEECH AVE
ELM DR
ELM CL
BROADLANDS AVE
MENDIP CL
CURTISWAY
DRAKES WAY
UPPER LAMBRICKS
LOWER LAMBRICKS
WELLSFIELD
HOCKLEY RD
B1013
Cemy
THE CHESTNUTS
NELSON GDNS
NELSON CL
NELSON RD
WELLINGTON AVE
THE GATTENS
HAMBRO CL
HIGH RD
VICTORIA RD
NAPIER RD
BETJEMAN CL
ALEXANDRA RD
BULL LA
MILTON CL
PRINCESS
THE COURTS
RUFFLES CL
BYFORD CL
LONDON HILL
Works
Rayleigh Station
Rayleigh Castle
CROWN HILL
CROWN GDNS
HIGHMEAD
HIGHMEAD CT
LOVE LA
CASTLE TERR
THE BAILEY
FRANCIS WLK
THE KNOLL
BELLINGHAM LA
CHURCH ST
A129
B1013
Council Office
HIGHFIELD CRES
WEBSTERS WAY
Recn Gd
BULL LA
HIGH ST
Sch
Liby
RAYLEIGH
Great Wheatley
GREAT WHEATLEY RD
SPRING GDNS
POINTENS
BURROWS WAY
RIDGEWAY
A1015
EASTWOOD RD
QUEENS RD
BROAD OAK WAY
KINGS RD
JUBILEE RD
HILARY CRES
THE PADDOCKS
AVONDALE RD
CECIL WAY
GROVE RD
THE RAMPARTS
CHURCH RD
ASHCOMBE WAY
COPFORD AVE
BRACKSFORD AVE
WARWICK RD
WARWICK GDNS
WINDSOR WAY
LESLIE RD
KNIVET CL
ESSEX CL
CEDAR
HAWTHORN WAY
TRINITY RD
TRINITY CL
PICTON CL
PICTON GDNS
BEDFORD CL
NURSERY CL
HARDWICK CL
WHITE HOUSE CHASE
DAWS HEATH RD
RICHMOND DR
CLYDE CRES
SHANNON AVE
ROACH AVE
CHELMER AVE
WEIR GDNS
HILLTOP CL
CASTLE RD
F Sta
HIGH RD
WATCHFIELD
KINGSWOOD CRES
EASTERN RD
WESTERN RD
WEST VIEW DR
PENDOWER
A127(T)
DERWENT AVE
LOUISE RD
HELENA RD
GRAYSONS CL
RECTORY GARTH
Moat

188

166

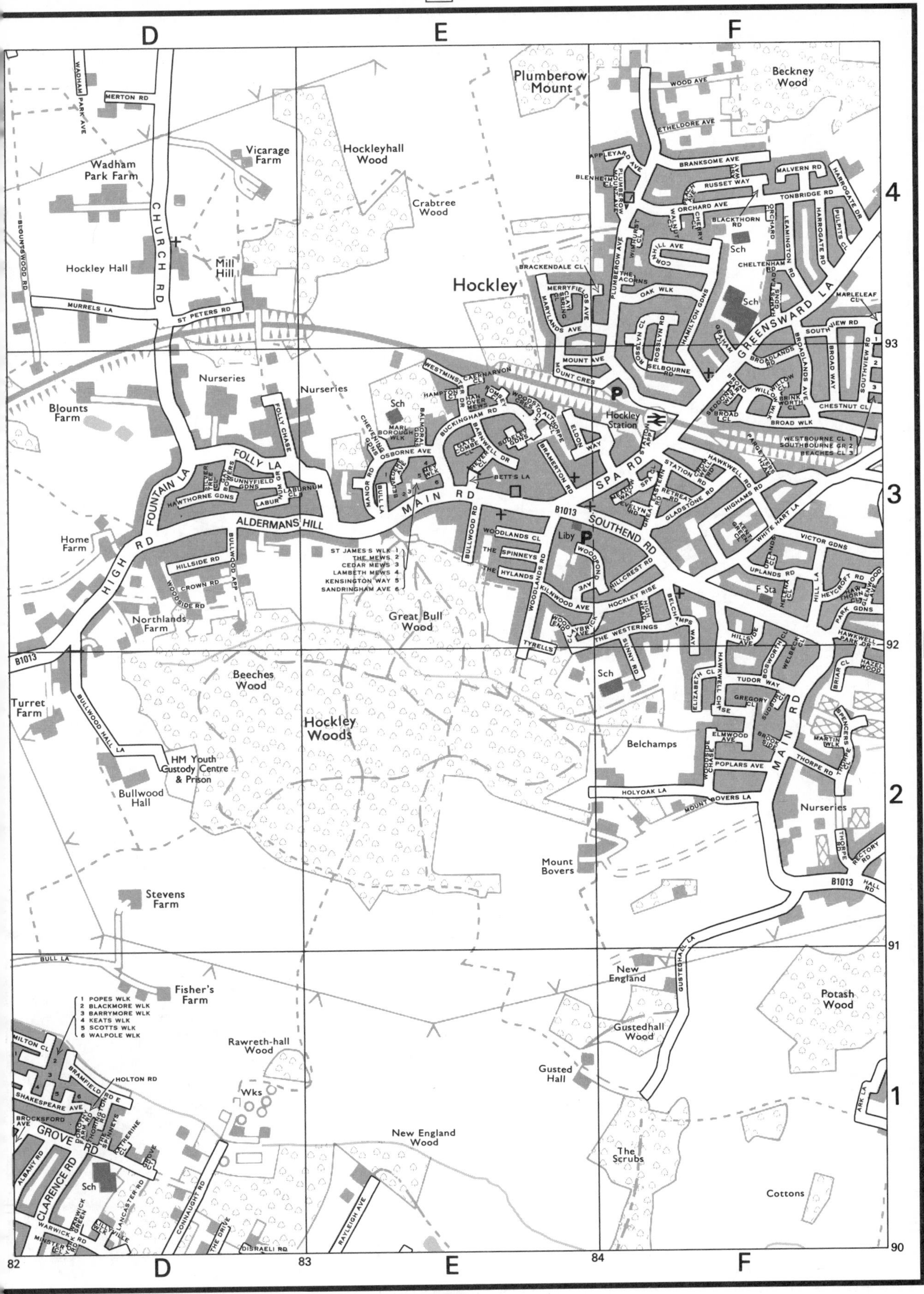
D
E
F
4
3
2
1
93
92
91
90
82
83
84
Plumberow Mount
Beckney Wood
WOOD AVE
ETHELDORE AVE
WADHAM PARK AVE
MERTON RD
Wadham Park Farm
Vicarage Farm
Hockleyhall Wood
Crabtree Wood
CHURCH RD
BLOUNTSWOOD RD
Hockley Hall
Mill Hill
MURRELS LA
ST PETERS RD
Hockley
APPLEYARD AVE
BLENHEIM CL
PLUMBEROW MOUNT AVE
BRANKSOME AVE
RUSSET WAY
MALVERN RD
HARROGATE DR
TONBRIDGE RD
ORCHARD AVE
WALNUT CT
CHERRY CL
BLACKTHORN RD
ORCHARD
LEAMINGTON RD
HARROGATE RD
PULPITS CL
Sch
WINDHURST CL
CORNHILL AVE
CHELTENHAM RD
BRACKENDALE CL
PLUMBEROW AVE
THE ACORNS
MERRYFIELDS AVE
CLAY SPRING
MARYLANDS AVE
OAK WLK
HAMILTON GDNS
HADSTEAD RD
GREENSWARD LA
MAPLELEAF CL
SOUTHVIEW RD
ROSSLYN CL
ROSSLYN RD
SELBOURNE RD
GRAHAM
BROADLANDS
BROADLANDS AVE
BROAD WAY
SOUTHVIEW CL
MOUNT AVE
MOUNT CRES
CHESTNUT CL
Nurseries
Blounts Farm
FOLLY CHASE
WESTMINSTER DR
CAERNARVON CL
HAMPTON CL
HANOVER MEWS
ROMSEY CL
WOODSTOCK CRES
ALTHORPE CL
Hockley Station
SEDGMOOR
BROAD CL
WILLOW WLK
WILLOW CL
BRINKWORTH CL
BROAD WLK
WESTBOURNE CL 1
SOUTHBOURNE GR 2
BEACHES CL 3
CHEVENING GDNS
MARLBOROUGH WLK
BALMORAL GDNS
BUCKINGHAM RD
GAYS COMBE
BARNWELL DR
SUDELEY GDNS
ELDON WAY
STATION APP
SPA RD
FOLLY LA
SILVER TREE CL
SUNNYFIELD GDNS
HAWTHORNE GDNS
LABURNUM GR
LABURNUM
OSBORNE AVE
MANOR RD
BULL LA
BELVEDERE
KEVER CL
BETT'S LA
BRAMERTON RD
MEADOW WAY
SPA CL
EVELYN RD
GREAT EASTERN RD
STATION RD
RETREAT RD
HAWKWELL RD
PARGETERS HYAM
GLADSTONE RD
HIGHAMS RD
WHITE HART LA
FOUNTAIN LA
MAIN RD
ALDERMANS HILL
B1013
SOUTHEND RD
Home Farm
HIGH RD
HILLSIDE RD
BULLWOOD APP
CROWN RD
WOODSIDE RD
ST JAMES'S WLK 1
THE MEWS 2
CEDAR MEWS 3
LAMBETH MEWS 4
KENSINGTON WAY 5
SANDRINGHAM AVE 6
BULLWOOD RD
WOODLANDS CL
THE SPINNEYS
THE HYLANDS
WOODLANDS RD
Liby
WOODPOND AVE
HILLCREST RD
KILNWOOD AVE
HOCKLEY RISE
HIGH MEAD
BELCHAMPS WAY
VICTOR GDNS
UPLANDS RD
HELENA CL
F Sta
HILL LA
HEYCROFT RD
HAWTHORN CL
GLENWOOD
PARK GDNS
Northlands Farm
Great Bull Wood
WOODEND
CLAYBRICK
THE WESTERINGS
HAWKWELL PARK DR
TYRELLS
SUNNY RD
HILLSIDE AVE
BOSWORTH CL
WELBECK CL
HAZELWOOD
BRIAR CL
B1013
Turret Farm
Beeches Wood
Sch
ELIZABETH CL
HAWKWELL CHASE
TUDOR WAY
GREGORY CL
Hockley Woods
BULLWOOD HALL LA
HM Youth Custody Centre & Prison
Belchamps
WOODSIDE CHASE
ELMWOOD AVE
BROOKSIDE
SPENCERS
MARTIN WLK
THORPE RD
THORPE CL
POPLARS AVE
Bullwood Hall
HOLYOAK LA
MOUNT BOVERS LA
Nurseries
THORPE
RECTORY
Mount Bovers
B1013
HALL RD
Stevens Farm
BULL LA
Fisher's Farm
New England
GUSTEDHALL LA
Potash Wood
1 POPES WLK
2 BLACKMORE WLK
3 BARRYMORE WLK
4 KEATS WLK
5 SCOTTS WLK
6 WALPOLE WLK
MILTON CL
Rawreth-hall Wood
Gustedhall Wood
Gusted Hall
BRAMFIELD RD E
HOLTON RD
SHAKESPEARE AVE
Wks
BROCKSFORD AVE
GROVE RD
SPINNEYS
CATHERINE CL
GROVE CL
ALBANY RD
CLARENCE RD
Sch
LANCASTER RD
CONNAUGHT RD
New England Wood
The Scrubs
Cottons
ARK LA
WARWICK GREEN
WARWICK RD
MINSTER
THE DRIVE
DISRAELI RD
RAYLEIGH AVE

178

189

167

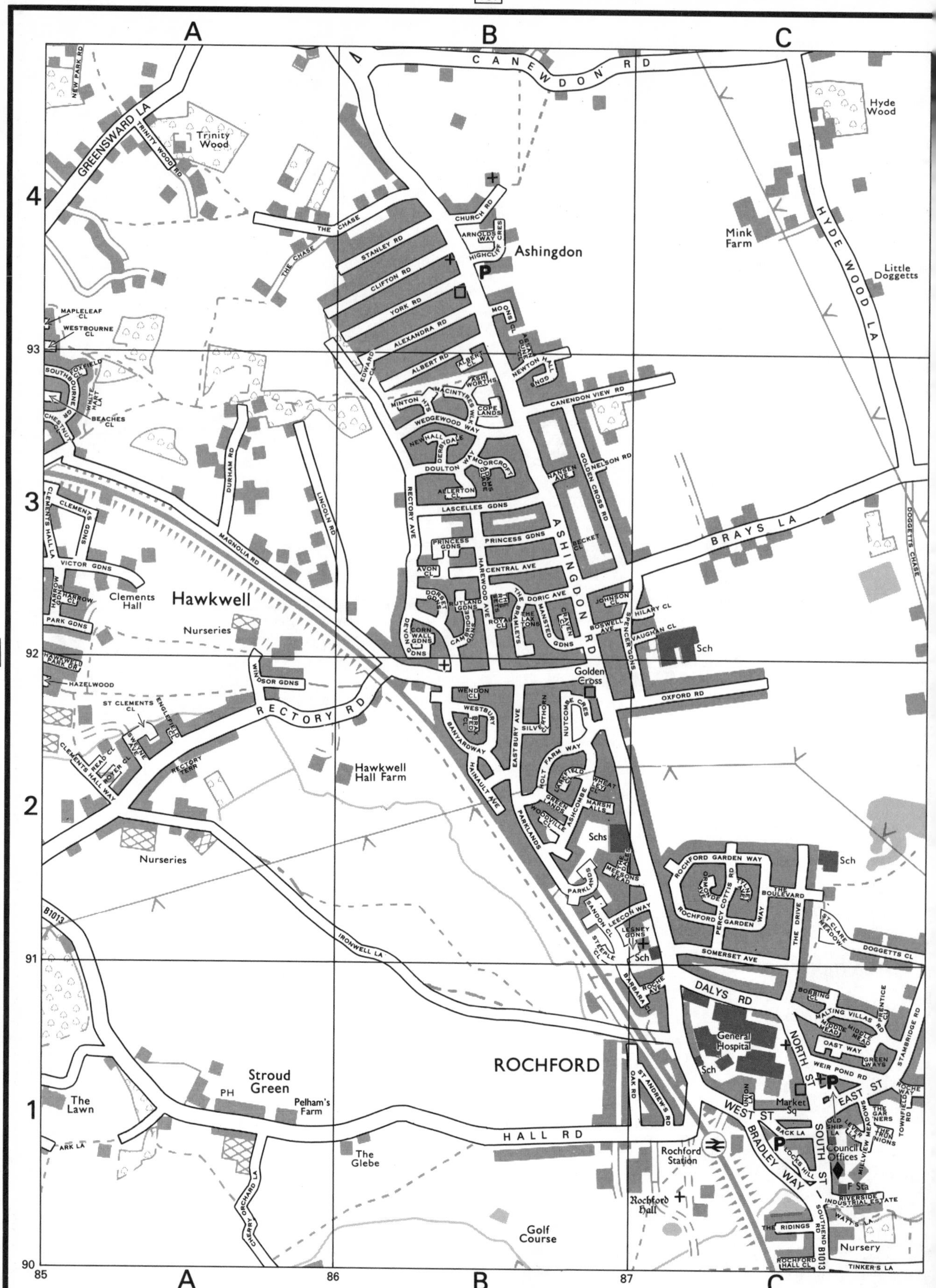

A
B
C
4
3
2
1
93
92
91
90
85
86
87
CANEWDON RD
NEW PARK RD
GREENSWARD LA
TRINITY WOOD RD
Trinity Wood
Hyde Wood
HYDE WOOD LA
Mink Farm
Little Doggetts
THE CHASE
CHURCH RD
ARNOLDS WAY
HIGHCLIFF CRES
Ashingdon
STANLEY RD
CLIFTON RD
YORK RD
ALEXANDRA RD
ALBERT RD
EDWARDS CL
ALBERT CL
MOONS CL
NEWTON HALL GDNS
CANENDON VIEW RD
MAPLELEAF CL
WESTBOURNE CL
OXFIELD
SOUTHBOURNE GR
WHITE HART LA
BEACHES CL
CHESTNUT GR
MINTON HTS
MACINTYRES WLK
ASHWORTHS
COPELANDS
WEDGEWOOD WAY
NEWHALL
DERBYDALE
DOULTON WAY
MOORCROFT
ADAMS GLADE
ALLERTON CL
NELSON RD
HANSEN AVE
GOLDEN CROSS RD
DURHAM RD
LINCOLN RD
MAGNOLIA RD
RECTORY AVE
LASCELLES GDNS
ASHINGDON RD
BRAYS LA
DOGGETTS CHASE
CLEMENTS GDNS
CLEMENTS HALL LA
VICTOR GDNS
HARROW CL
MOWBRAY
PARK GDNS
Clements Hall
Hawkwell
Nurseries
PRINCESS GDNS
BECKET CL
AVON CL
CENTRAL AVE
HAREWOOD AVE
DORSET GDNS
RUTLAND GDNS
THE BRAMLEYS
DORIC AVE
JOHNSON CL
HILARY CL
CORNWALL GDNS
DEVON GDNS
CAMBRIDGE GDNS
ROYAL CL
THE LAXTONS
MANSTED GDNS
CRAVEN CL
BOSWELL AVE
SPENCER GDNS
VAUGHAN CL
Sch
HAWKWELL PARK DR
HAZELWOOD
WINDSOR GDNS
Golden Cross
OXFORD RD
ST CLEMENTS CL
ENGLEFIELD CL
RECTORY RD
WENDON CL
WESTBURY
BANYARDWAY
EASTBURY AVE
SILVER
NUTCOMBE CRES
SWEYNE AVE
CLEMENTS HALL WAY
ROYER CL
RECTORY TERR
Hawkwell Hall Farm
HAINAULT AVE
HOLT FARM WAY
WHEATLEY CL
ASHCOMBE
GREENLANDS
MARSH WALLS
WOODVILLE CL
PARKLANDS
Schs
Nurseries
ROCHFORD GARDEN WAY
PERCY COTTIS RD
THE BOULEVARD
THE DRIVE
ST CLARE MEADOW
Sch
MEESONS MEAD
LEECON WAY
SANDON CL
STEPLE CL
LESNEY GDNS
SOMERSET AVE
DOGGETTS CL
B1013
IRONWELL LA
BARBARA CL
ROCHE AVE
DALYS RD
BOBBING CL
MALTING VILLAS RD
PRENTICE CL
MIDDLE MEAD
General Hospital
NORTH ST
STAMBRIDGE RD
EAST WAY
GREEN WAYS
WEIR POND RD
ROCHFORD
Stroud Green
PH
Pelham's Farm
The Lawn
OAK RD
ST ANDREW'S RD
WEST ST
Market Sq
EAST ST
ROCHE WAY
TOWNFIELD RD
HALL RD
ARK LA
The Glebe
Rochford Station
BRADLEY WAY
BACK LA
OLD SHIP LA
LOCKS HILL
SOUTH ST
Council Offices
MILLVIEW MEADOWS
THE GARNERS
THE TRUNNIONS
F Sta
RIVERSIDE INDUSTRIAL ESTATE
WATT'S LA
Rochford Hall
THE RIDINGS
SOUTHEND RD B1013
Golf Course
CHERRY ORCHARD LA
ROCHFORD HALL CL
Nursery
TINKER'S LA

177

190

168

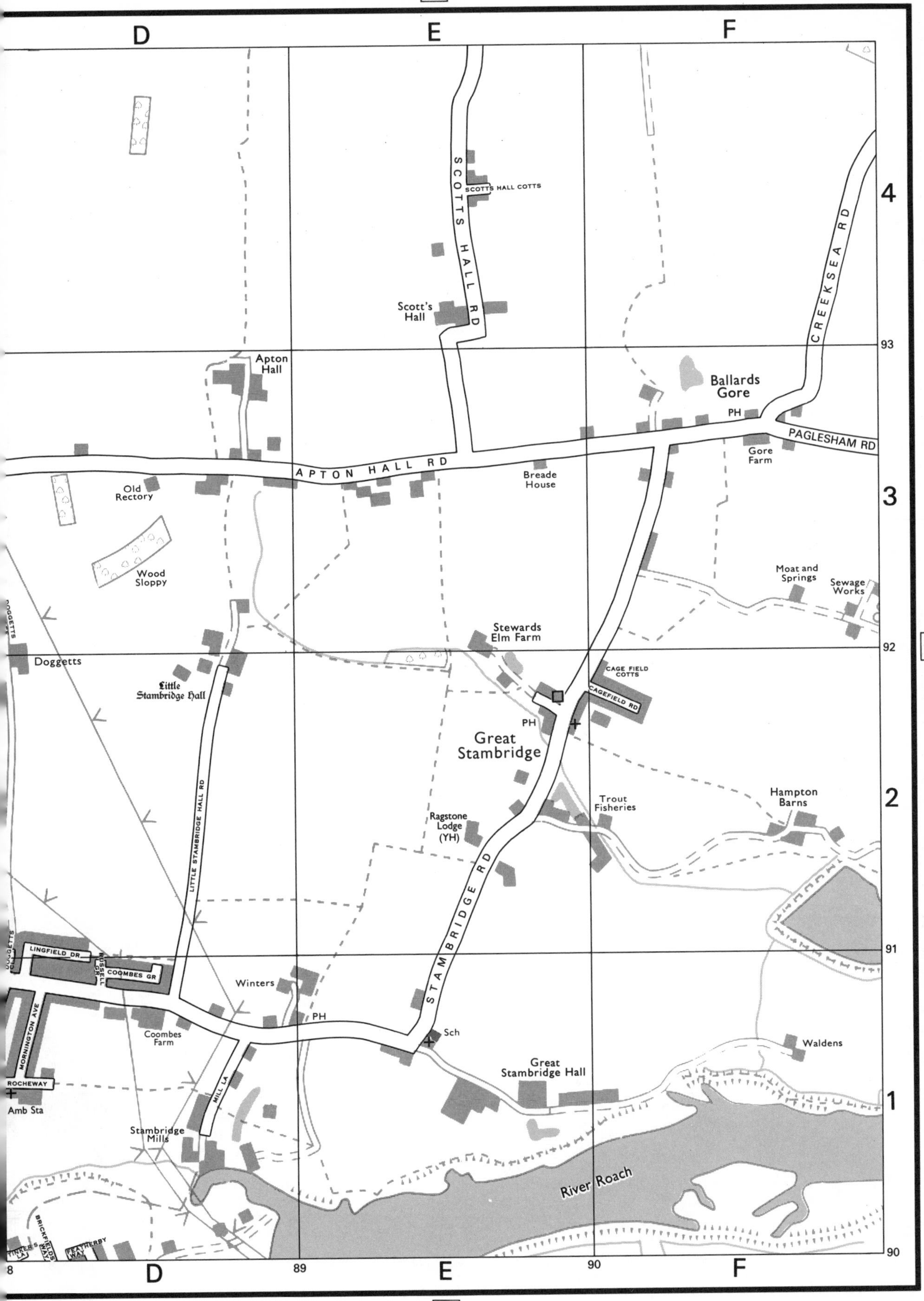
D
E
F
SCOTTS HALL RD
SCOTTS HALL COTTS
Scott's Hall
CREEKSEA RD
Apton Hall
Ballards Gore
PH
PAGLESHAM RD
Gore Farm
APTON HALL RD
Old Rectory
Breade House
Wood Sloppy
Moat and Springs
Sewage Works
DOGGETTS
Stewards Elm Farm
Doggetts
Little Stambridge Hall
CAGE FIELD COTTS
CAGEFIELD RD
PH
Great Stambridge
LITTLE STAMBRIDGE HALL RD
Trout Fisheries
Hampton Barns
Ragstone Lodge (YH)
STAMBRIDGE RD
LINGFIELD DR
RUSSELL GR
COOMBES GR
Winters
PH
Sch
MORNINGTON AVE
Coombes Farm
MILL LA
Waldens
ROCHEWAY
Amb Sta
Great Stambridge Hall
Stambridge Mills
River Roach
BRICKFIELDS WAY
FEATHERBY WAY
TINKERS LA
4
3
2
1
93
92
91
90
8
89
90
D
E
F

180

191

169

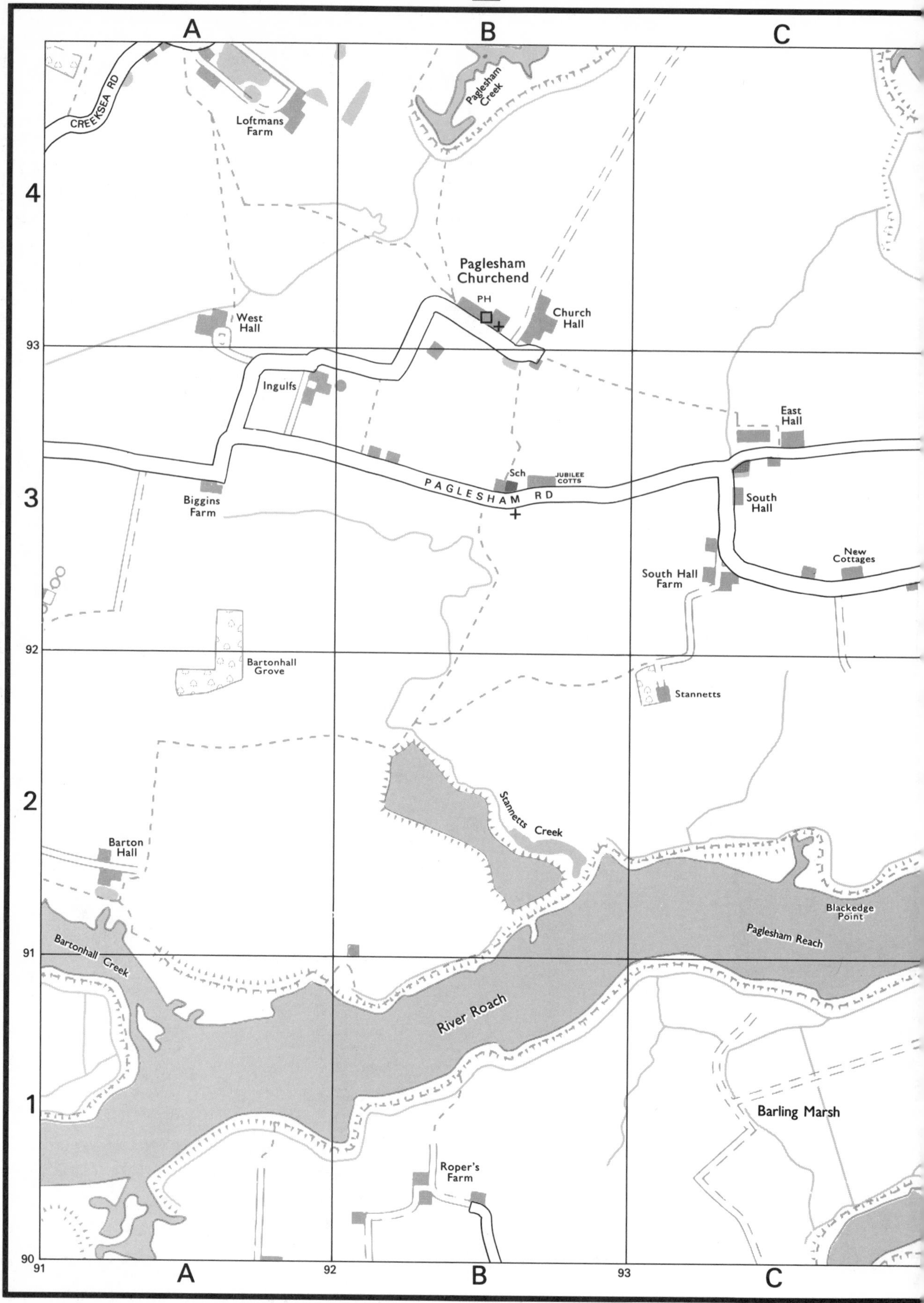
A
B
C
4
3
2
1
93
92
91
90
91
92
93
CREEKSEA RD
Loftmans Farm
Paglesham Creek
Paglesham Churchend
PH
Church Hall
West Hall
Ingulfs
East Hall
Sch
JUBILEE COTTS
PAGLESHAM RD
Biggins Farm
South Hall
New Cottages
South Hall Farm
Bartonhall Grove
Stannetts
Stannetts Creek
Barton Hall
Blackedge Point
Paglesham Reach
Bartonhall Creek
River Roach
Barling Marsh
Roper's Farm

179
192

170

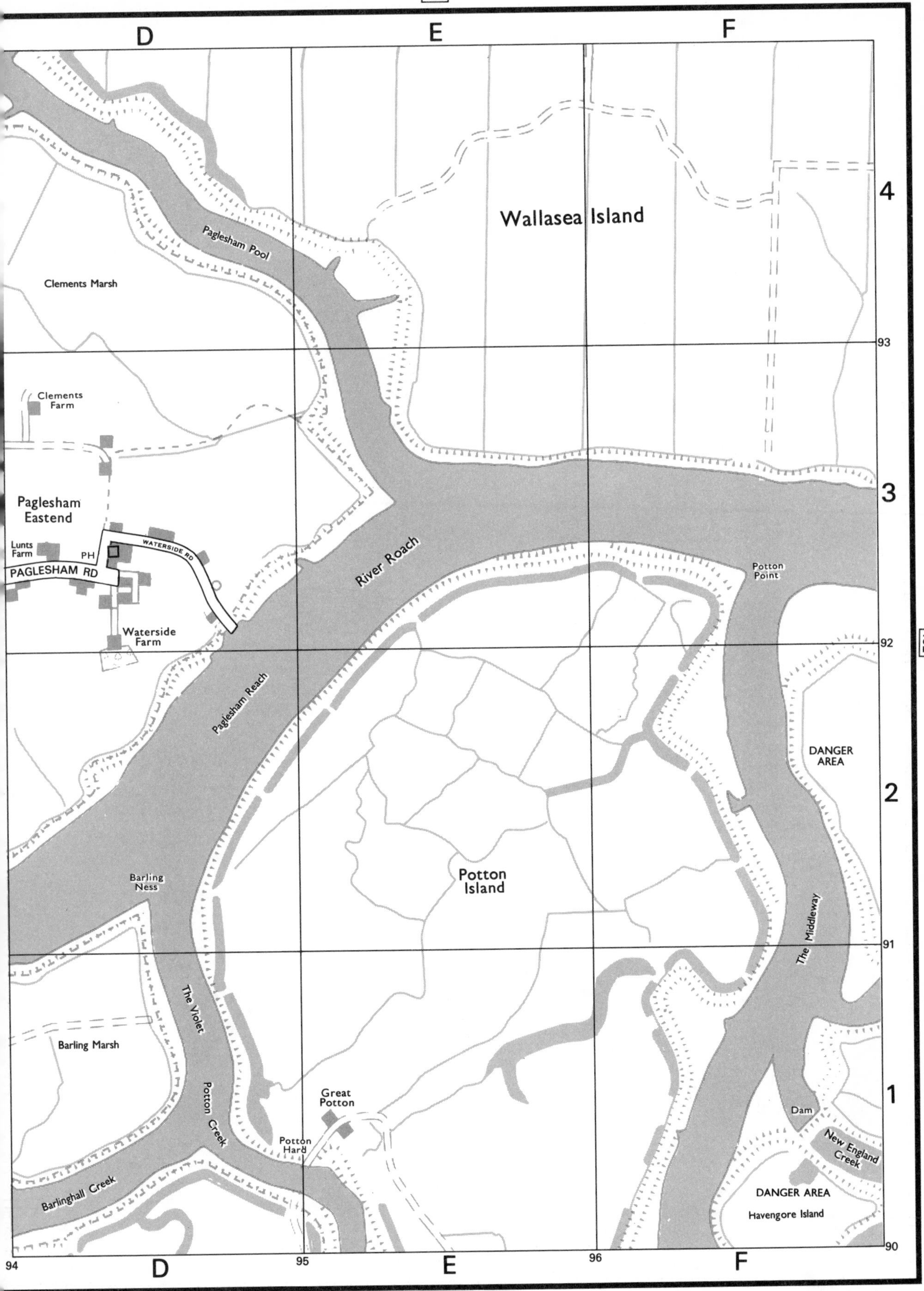
D
E
F
4
3
2
1
93
92
91
90
94
95
96
Wallasea Island
Paglesham Pool
Clements Marsh
Clements Farm
Paglesham Eastend
Lunts Farm
PH
PAGLESHAM RD
WATERSIDE RD
Waterside Farm
River Roach
Potton Point
Paglesham Reach
DANGER AREA
Barling Ness
Potton Island
The Middleway
The Violet
Barling Marsh
Potton Creek
Great Potton
Potton Hard
Dam
New England Creek
Barlinghall Creek
DANGER AREA
Havengore Island

182

193

171

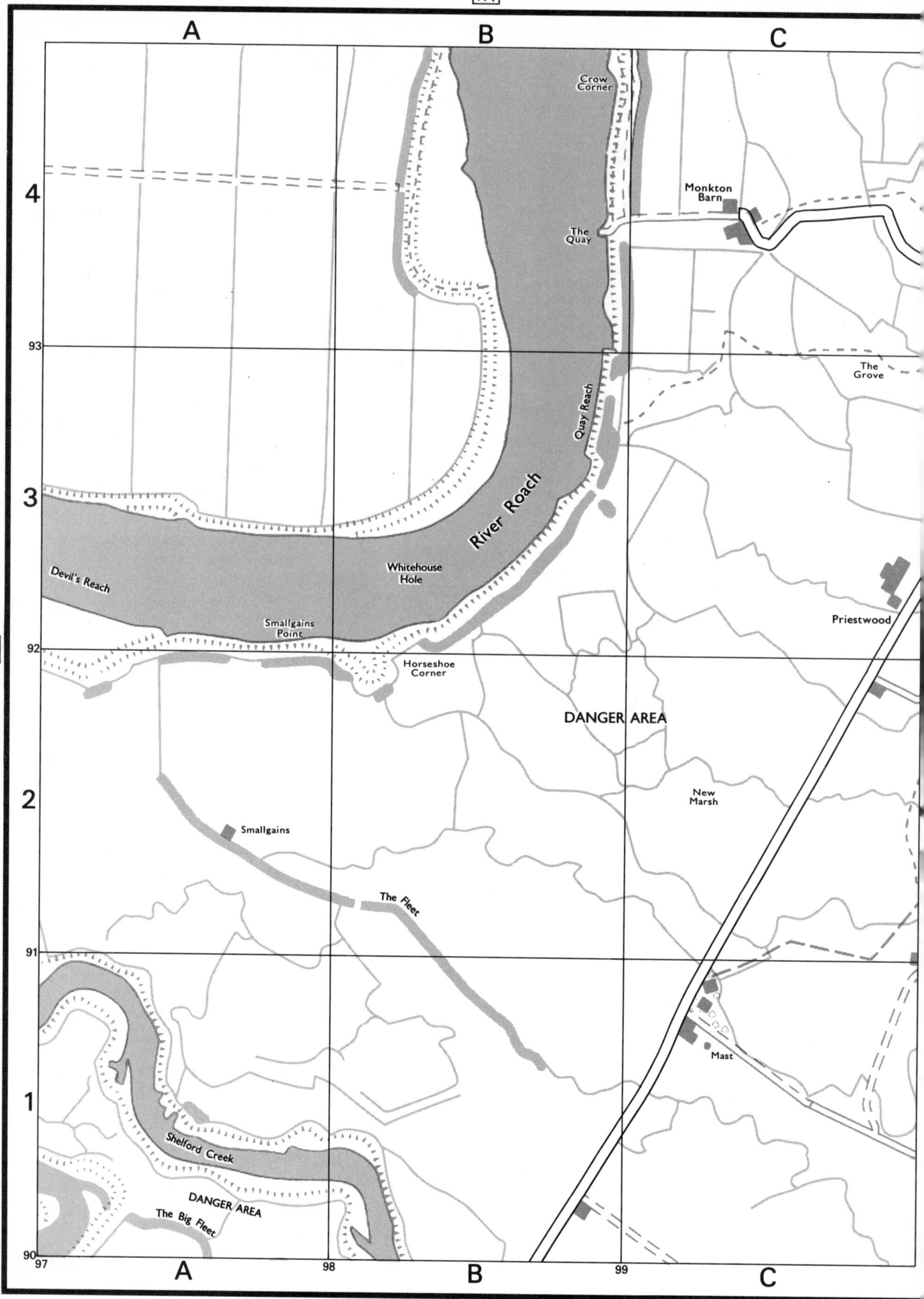
A
B
C
4
3
2
1
93
92
91
90
97
98
99
Crow Corner
Monkton Barn
The Quay
The Grove
Quay Reach
River Roach
Devil's Reach
Whitehouse Hole
Smallgains Point
Horseshoe Corner
Priestwood
DANGER AREA
New Marsh
Smallgains
The Fleet
Mast
Shelford Creek
DANGER AREA
The Big Fleet

181

194

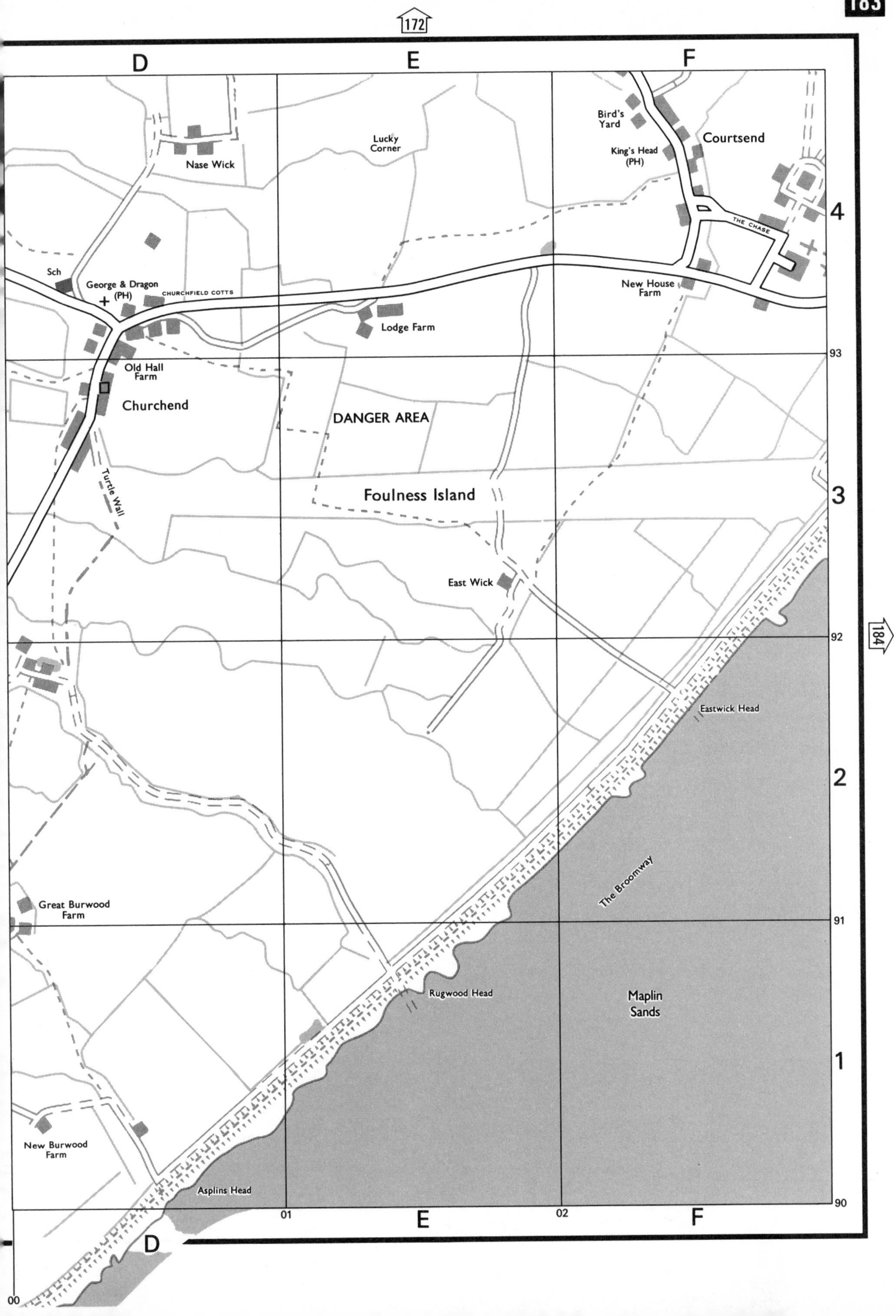
172
D
E
F
Bird's Yard
Courtsend
King's Head (PH)
Lucky Corner
Nase Wick
THE CHASE
4
Sch
George & Dragon (PH)
CHURCHFIELD COTTS
New House Farm
Lodge Farm
93
Old Hall Farm
Churchend
DANGER AREA
Turtle Wall
Foulness Island
3
East Wick
92
184
Eastwick Head
2
The Broomway
Great Burwood Farm
91
Rugwood Head
Maplin Sands
1
New Burwood Farm
Asplins Head
90
01
02
00

173

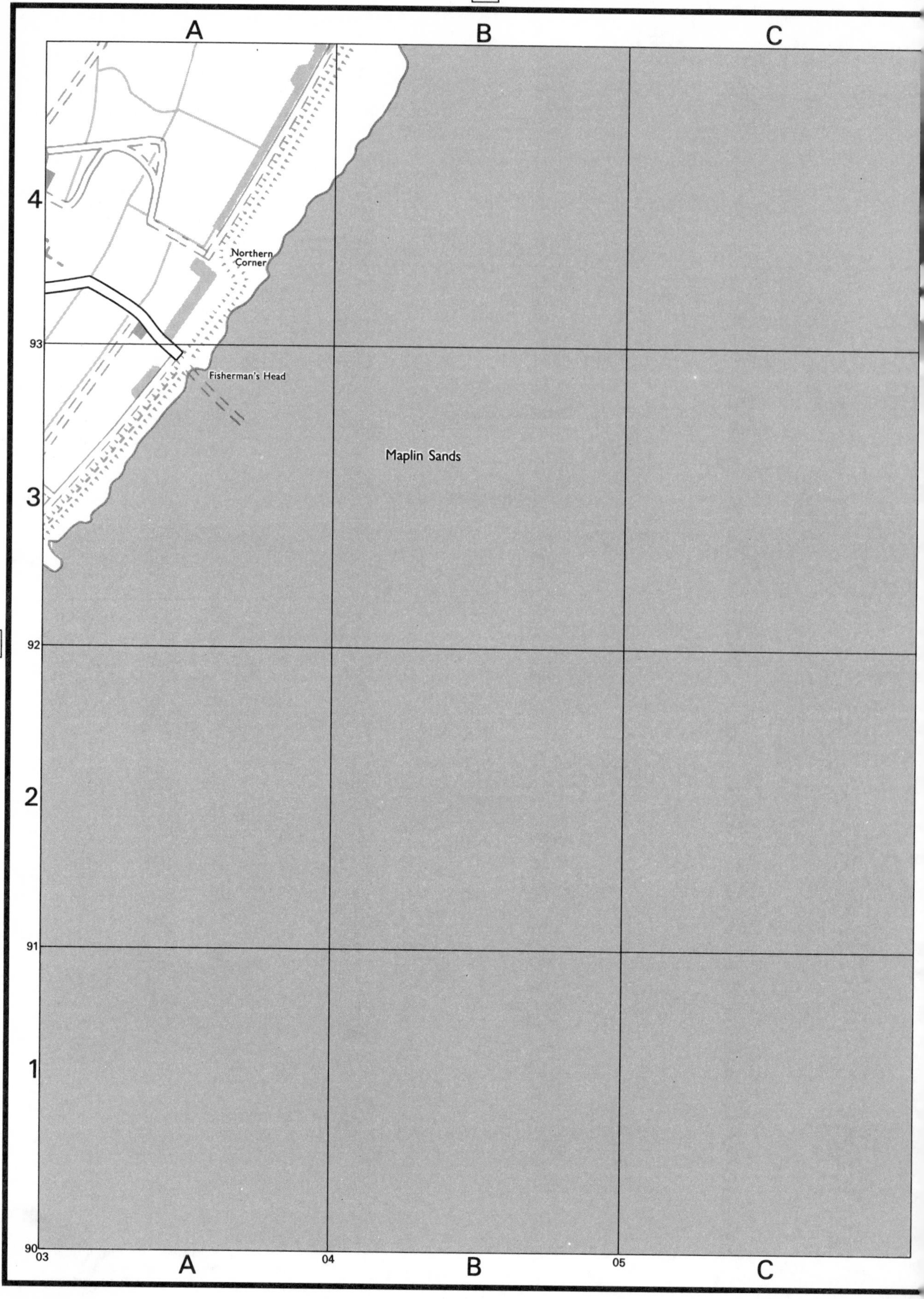
A
B
C
4
3
2
1
93
92
91
90
03
04
05
Northern Corner
Fisherman's Head
Maplin Sands

183

not continued, see key diagram

186

not continued, see key diagram

174
185

A
B
C
4
3
2
1
89
88
87
86
73
74
75
Nevendon Bushes
Felmore
Lanhams
Longmead (Path)
Northlands Park
East Mayne
Felmores
Ashlyns
Tyefields
Chalvedon
Eversley
Louisa Cottage
Recn Gd
Wickford Ave
Pitsea
Pitsea South Mayne
Rectory Rd
High Rd
Bull Farm
Bowers Gifford
Jackaman's Farm
London Rd
Little Chalvedon Hall
North Benfleet
Smiler's Farm
Pound La
Church Rd
Moat
Bowers Hall
Cemy
Church Hill
Hazelmere
Pitsea Station
Wks
Pitsea Marsh
Pitsea Creek
Sewage Works
Wat Tyler Way
Pitseahall Fleet
Picnic Area
Wat Tyler Country Park
Timberman's Creek
Tip (dis)
Manor Way
Great Mussels
Bowers Marshes
A132
A13
B1464
Sch
Schs
Liby
PH
LC
195

175

D
E
F
4
3
2
1
89
88
87
86
76
77
78
Nursery
FANE RD
A130
North Benfleet Hall Wood
Great Burches Farm
Caversham Farm
Braeside Farm
Wks
Cemy
CONISTON RD
BURCHES RD
HORNBEAMS
OAK WLK
THE LARCHES
THE BIRCHES
OAK WALK
WOODSIDE VIEW
WOODSIDE AVE
PARSONS
ULLSWATER RD
GRANGE RD
BIRCH CL
STANSFIELD RD
ROSEMEAD
WARWICK
MAY FLOWERS
WOODCOTE WAY
MARLBOROUGH
FULTON RD
BRUNEL RD
Manor Trading Estate
THIRLMERE RD
CROSSFELL
WINDERMERE RD
SHREWSBURY DR
CARTWRIGHT
New Thundersley
Schs
RUSHBOTTOM LA
EVERSLEY RD
MORELAND AVE
ROSEBERRY AVE
MANOR RD
ARMSTRONG RD
SEAMORE AVE
LAWNS COURT
MEADWAY
BLYTHE WAY
ARUNDEL RD
Wks
Sch
KESWICK RD
BASSENTHWAITE RD
Thundersley
SILVERDALE
GRANDVIEW RD
GLEBELANDS
CHURCH RD
LANGFORD CRES
RAYMONDS DR
SADLERS
OVERTON RD
OVERTON WAY
BARNCOMBE CL
PARK RD
STEEPLE HEIGHTS
Recn Gd
SEAMORE
CHURCH VIEW
GRASMERE RD
BORROWDALE RD
AVINGTON WLK
LOWER CHURCH RD
CHESTERFIELD AVE
IVY RD
ALBERT RD
BARTLEY RD
LOUISA AVE
ELGAR CL
LINDEN RD
MAY TREE WLK
WAVERLEY RD
SELBOURNE RD
HAZELMERE RD
KENTS HILL RD N
SPENCER RD
STANLEY RD
HART RD
Sch
FOXMEADOWS
KINGSTON WAY
PRINCES AVE
HYDEWAY
BROADLANDS
Sadlers Hall Farm
WYCOMBE AVE
BARTLEY CL
LYNDENE
Liby
LAMBETH RD
KENNINGTON AVE
DOWNER RD N
THUNDERSLEY CHURCH RD
KINGS PARK
B1464
LONDON RD
LONDON RD
A13
B1006
EASTERN AVE
COOMBEWOOD DR
KENNETH RD
THE CHASE
ROMSEY DR
ROMSEY RD
HOMEFIELDS AVE
MALWOOD DR
NORTHERN AVE
NEW PARK RD
STANWAY RD
GIFFORD RD
RHODA RD N
Coombe Wood
LAKE DR
THUNDERSLEY GR
HATLEY
SOUTHWOLD CRES
GLEN RIDDING
BREAD AND CHEESE HILL
DOROTHY GDNS
MALWOOD RD
LEA RD
DOWNER RD
GLEN RD
BRADLEY AVE
BRADLEY
BOULDREWOOD RD
CROFT RD
ST CLEMENTS RD
Council Offices
Sch
Tarpots
BOWERS RD
PEAR TREES
KILN RD A13
SAXON VILLE
ELMHURST AVE
THE SPINNAKERS
THE WILLOWS
ALBION RD
Sch
RHODA RD
JARVIS RD
MOUNT CRES
KENTS HILL RD
FELSTEAD RD
Sch
CATHERINE RD
Sch
HAWTHORNS
DENESMERE
VILLA RD
THE CHIMES
TIPPERSFIELD
MOUNT RD
CHESTNUT GR
HOLTYNGE
OAKLEIGHS
LIME RD
LIMETREE AVE
SYDNEY RD
MERTON RD
CLIFTON AVE
KALE RD
CLARENCE RD N
SOUTHWELL RD
Thundersley Glen
WAVERTREE RD
SOUTH CLIFF
CLIFTON WAY
EARLS WOOD
CLIFTON CL
CLARENCE CL
HILL RD
DURLEY CL
UPLANDS CL
KIMBERLEY RD
CLARENCE RD
AVONDALE RD
THUNDERSLEY PARK RD
FERNLEA RD
HIGH BEECHES
ELM VIEW RD
UPLANDS RD
OAKFIELD RD
SOUTH VIEW RD
GREEN OAKS CL
Jotmans Hall
SHORE FIELD
CUMBERLAND AVE
UNDERHILL RD
Cemy
WINCOAT DR
MELCOMBE RD
CONSTITUTION HILL
DOWNE STANS
South Benfleet
CANVEY WAY
JOTMANS LA
B1006
HIGH RD
MEGGISON WAY
PERRY RD
SANDERLINGS
Liby
GROVE RD
RICHMOND AVE
CRESCENT RD
Golf Course
WATLINGTON RD
PHILMEAD RD
TYRRELL RD
APPLETON RD
BENFLEET PARK RD
MERRIVALE
BOYCE VIEW DR
HILLTOP AVE
Hilltop Farm
LOTEN RD
SAXON WAY
Sch
DANESFIELD
Playing Field
GREENWAYS
Club House
BOYCE GREEN
QUEEN'S RD
RIVER VIEW RD
KINGS RD
VICARAGE HILL
B1014
SWALLOW DR
RAVEN DR
WOODHAM RD
KINGFISHER DR
CURLEW DR
Hope's Green
BROOK RD
HALL FARM RD
HOPE RD
FLEET RD
HILLSIDE RD
Benfleet Marsh
SIDWELL LA
SIDWELL PARK
NORWOOD DR
GREEN RD
GREENWOOD AVE
SIDWELL CHASE
SIDWELL AVE
Reeds Hill
Benfleet Creek
Sewage Works
ST MARY'S CL
HALL FARM CL
ST MARY'S DR
ADELAIDE GDNS
ESSEX WAY
A130
B1014
HIGH ST
THE CLOSE
EASTLEIGH RD
THE GLYDERS
188

196

176

187

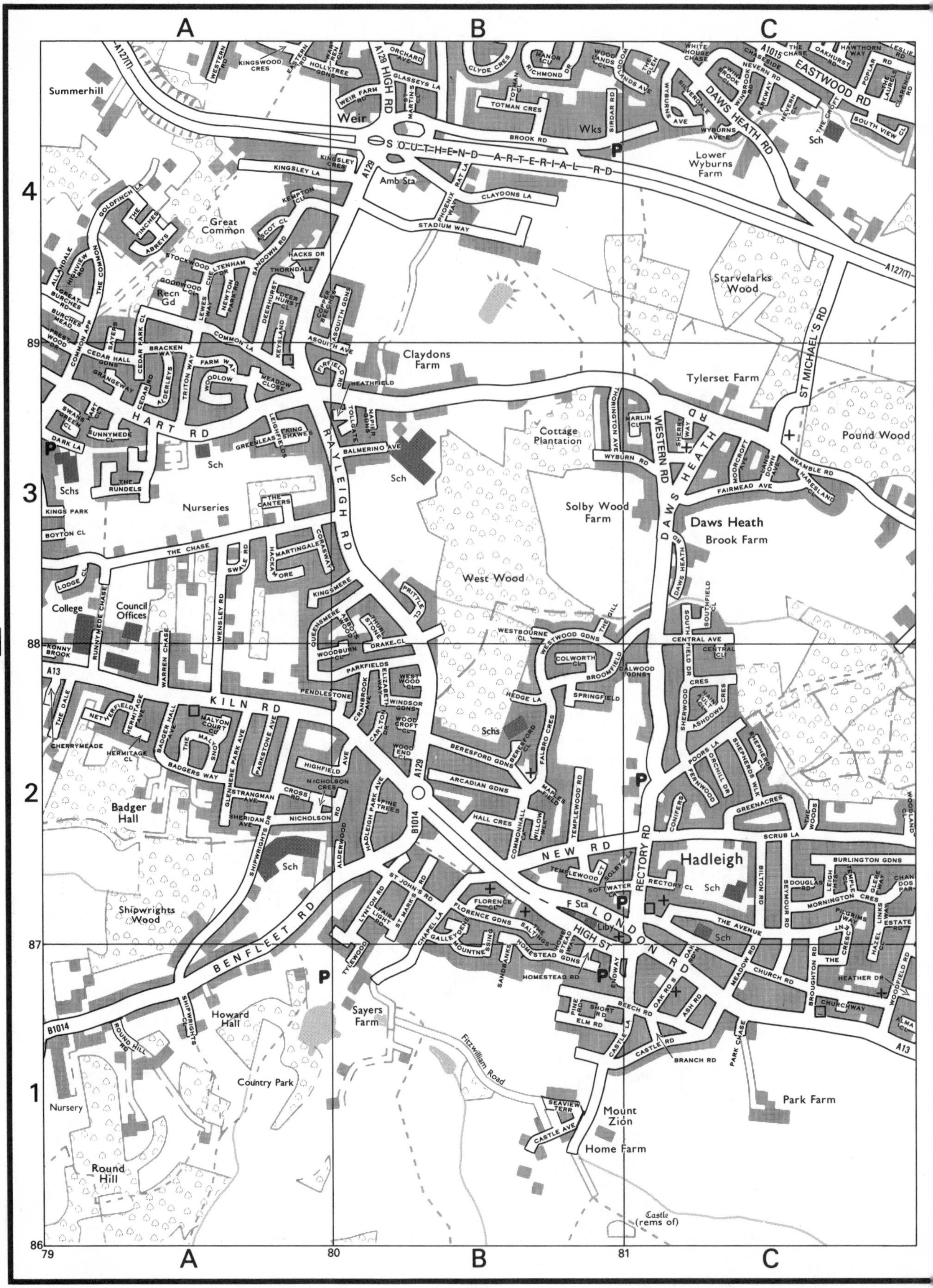
A
B
C
4
3
2
1
89
88
87
86
79
80
81
Summerhill
Weir
Wks
Lower Wyburns Farm
Sch
Amb Sta
SOUTHEND ARTERIAL RD
A127(T)
A1015
EASTWOOD RD
DAWS HEATH RD
A129 HIGH RD
KINGSLEY LA
CLAYDONS LA
STADIUM WAY
PHOENIX WAY
BROOK RD
TOTMAN CRES
RICHMOND DR
CLYDE CRES
GLASSEYS LA
WEIR FARM RD
KINGSWOOD CRES
HOLLYTREE GDNS
WESTERN RD
ORCHARD AVE
SIRDAR RD
WYBURNS AVE
WYBURNS AVE E
SILVERDALE
PARKWAY
NEVERN RD
SOUTH VIEW CL
POPLAR RD
HAWTHORN WAY
OAKHURST RD
THE CHASE
Great Common
Recn Gd
GOLDFINCH LA
THE FINCHES
ABREYS
STOCKWOOD
SCOT CL
SANDOWN RD
CHELTENHAM DR
GOODWOOD CL
LEWES WAY
NEWTON PARK RD
HACKS DR
THORNDALE
DEERHURST
DEER HURST CL
COPPER BEECHES
ASQUITH GDNS
ASQUITH AVE
KEYSLAND
COMMON LA
ALLANDALE
HIGHVIEW RD
THE COMMON
GREAT BURCHES RD
BURCHES MEAD
PRESTWOOD DR
COMMON APP
CEDAR HALL GDNS
SAYERS
CEDAR PARK CL
BRACKEN WAY
FARM WAY
GRANGEWAY
CEDAR RD
ALDERLEYS
TRITON WAY
WOODLOW
MEADOW CLOSE
FIRFIELD RD
HEATHFIELD
TOLLGATE
NAPIER GDNS
Claydons Farm
Tylerset Farm
Starvelarks Wood
ST MICHAEL'S RD
Pound Wood
Cottage Plantation
HART RD
SWANS GREEN CL
SUNNYMEDE CL
DARK LA
GREENLEAS
KING SHAWES
LEIGHFIELDS
BALMERINO AVE
RAYLEIGH RD
THE RUNDELS
Schs
Sch
Nurseries
KINGS PARK
BOYTON CL
THE CANTERS
THE CHASE
SWALE RD
MARTINGALE
CORASWAY
HACKAMORE
Solby Wood Farm
THORINGTON AVE
MARLIN CL
WYBURN RD
WESTERN RD
SHERBY WAY
MOORCROFT AVE
LANSDOWN AVE
FAIRMEAD AVE
BRAMBLE RD
HARESLAND CL
Daws Heath
Brook Farm
West Wood
KINGSMERE
PRITTLE CL
QUEENSMERE
THURSTONE
DRAKE CL
WOODBURN CL
LODGE CL
College
Council Offices
RUNNYMEDE CHASE
WARREN CHASE
WENSLEY RD
KONNY BROOK
WESTBOURNE CL
WESTWOOD GDNS
THE GILL
COLWORTH CL
BROOMFIELD
DALWOOD GDNS
SOUTHFIELD CL
SOUTHFIELD DR
CENTRAL AVE
CENTRAL CL
A13
THE DALE
NETHERFIELD
HERMITAGE AVE
HERMITAGE CL
BADGER HALL AVE
MALYON COURT CL
KILN RD
PARKSTONE AVE
PARKFIELDS
PENDLESTONE
CRANBROOK AVE
ELIZABETH WAY
WEST WOOD CL
WINDSOR GDNS
WOOD CROFT CL
CARLTON DR
WOOD END CL
HEDGE LA
SPRINGFIELD
FALBRO CRES
BERESFORD CL
BERESFORD GDNS
SHERWOOD CRES
ASHDOWN CRES
POORS LA
ORCHILL DR
SHEPHERDS WLK
SHEPHERDS CL
CHERRYMEADE
BADGERS WAY
GLENMERE PARK AVE
STRANGMAN AVE
HIGHFIELD AVE
NICHOLSON CRES
CROSS RD
NICHOLSON RD
SHERIDAN AVE
HADLEIGH PARK AVE
PINE TREES
A129
ARCADIAN GDNS
HALL CRES
COMMONHALL CL
WILLOW WLK
MAPLES FIELD
TEMPLEWOOD RD
FERNWOOD
CONIFERS
GREENACRES
THE WOODS
Badger Hall
SHIPWRIGHTS DR
ALDERWOOD
B1014
NEW RD
RECTORY RD
SOLBYS LA
TEMPLEWOOD CT
SOFTWATER LA
Hadleigh
RECTORY CL
BILTON RD
SEYMOUR RD
SCRUB LA
BURLINGTON GDNS
DOUGLAS RD
LEIGH CL
TEMPLE CL
GLEBE WAY
MORNINGTON CRES
PILGRIMS WAY
LINKS WAY
ESTATE RD
Sch
Shipwrights Wood
ST JOHN'S RD
LYNTON RD
FAIRLIGHT RD
ST MARK'S RD
FLORENCE CL
FLORENCE GDNS
CHAPEL LA
GALLEYDENE
MOUNTNESSING
THE SALTINGS
HOMESTEAD WAY
HOMESTEAD GDNS
HOMESTEAD RD
SANDBANKS
F Sta
Liby
HIGH ST
LONDON RD
THE AVENUE
MEADOW RD
CHURCH RD
BROUGHTON RD
THE CRESCENT
HAZEL CL
HEATHER DR
WOODFIELD RD
CHURCHWAY
ALMA CL
BENFLEET RD
TYLEWOOD
ENDWAY
OAK RD N
OAK RD S
ASH RD
PINE RD
SHORT RD
ELM RD
BEECH RD
CASTLE LA
CASTLE RD
BRANCH RD
PARK CHASE
A13
B1014
SHIPWRIGHTS CL
ROUND HILL RD
Howard Hall
Sayers Farm
Country Park
Fitzwilliam Road
SEAVIEW TERR
CASTLE AVE
Mount Zion
Home Farm
Park Farm
Nursery
Round Hill
Castle (rems of)

177

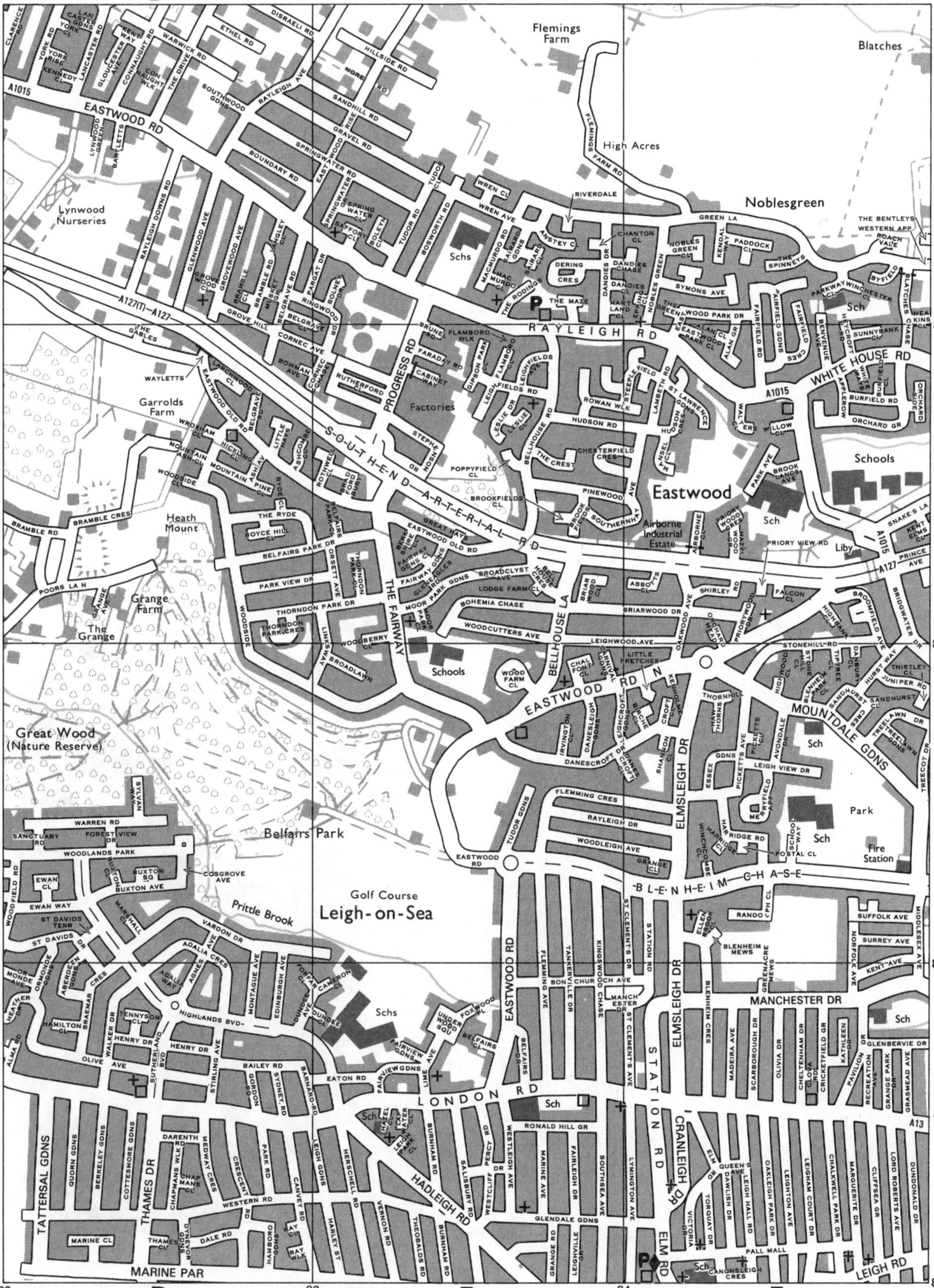

D
E
F
Flemings Farm
Blatches
High Acres
Noblesgreen
Lynwood Nurseries
Garrolds Farm
Heath Mount
Grange Farm
The Grange
Great Wood (Nature Reserve)
Belfairs Park
Golf Course
Leigh-on-Sea
Eastwood
Airborne Industrial Estate
Factories
Schools
Park
Fire Station
EASTWOOD RD
RAYLEIGH RD
SOUTHEND ARTERIAL RD
WHITE HOUSE RD
LONDON RD
BLENHEIM CHASE
MOUNTDALE GDNS
THE FAIRWAY
BELLHOUSE LA
ELMSLEIGH DR
STATION RD
HADLEIGH RD
MARINE PAR
LEIGH RD
MANCHESTER DR
HIGHLANDS BVD
THAMES DR
TATTERSAL GDNS
Prittle Brook
A127
A1015
A13
82
83
84
86
87
88
89
1
2
3
4

190

198

178

189

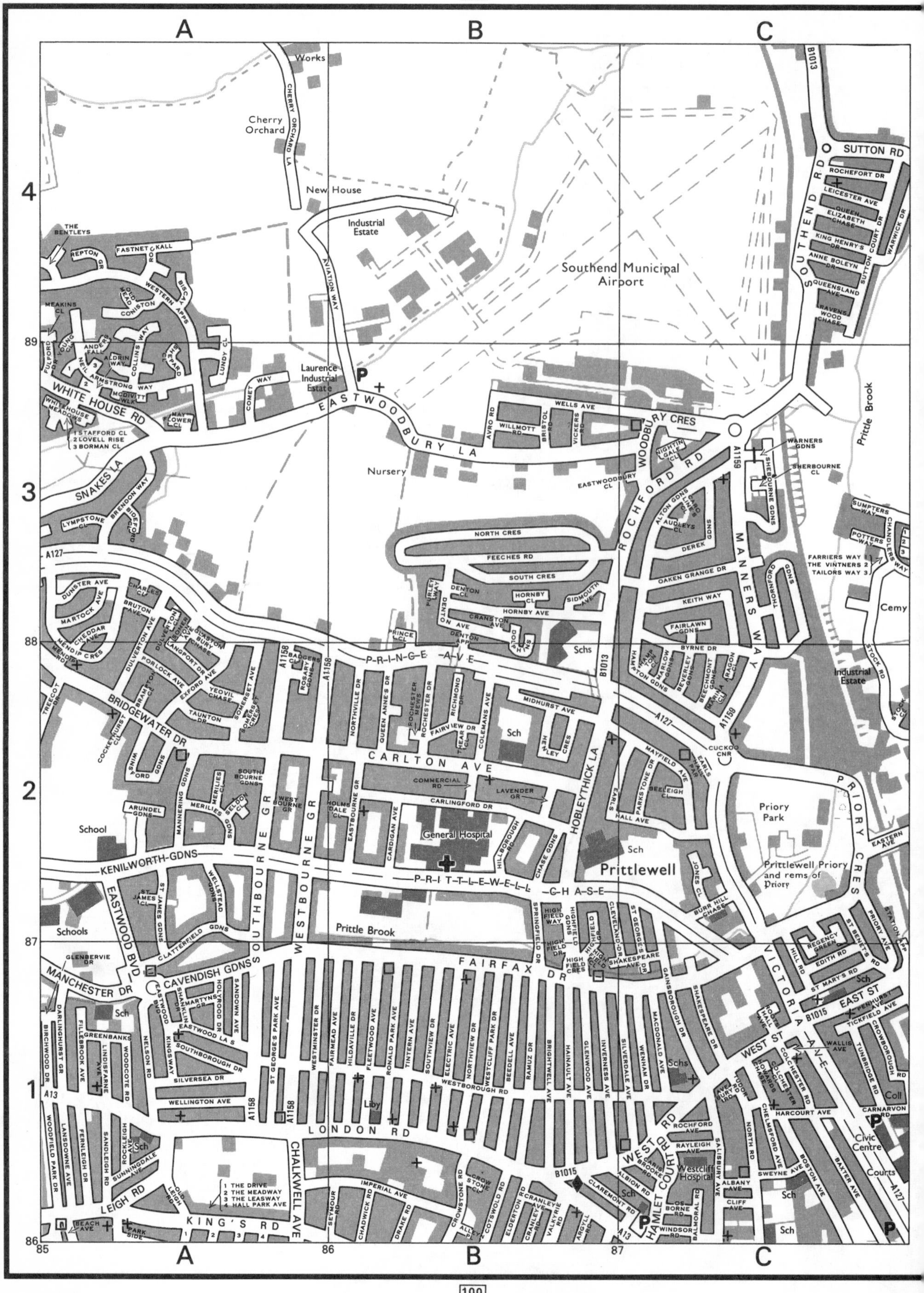
A
B
C
4
3
2
1
89
88
87
86
85
Works
Cherry Orchard
CHERRY ORCHARD LA
New House
Industrial Estate
AVIATION WAY
Southend Municipal Airport
SUTTON RD
ROCHEFORT DR
LEICESTER AVE
QUEEN ELIZABETH CHASE
KING HENRY'S DR
ANNE BOLEYN DR
QUEENSLAND AVE
RAVENSWOOD CHASE
SOUTHEND RD
SUTTON COURT DR
WARWICK DR
B1013
THE BENTLEYS
REPTON GR
FASTNET
KALLO
WESTERN APPS
CONISTON
MEAKINS CL
LUNDY CL
COLLINS WAY
ALDRIN WAY
ARMSTRONG WAY
MCDIVITT WLK
WHITE HOUSE RD
WHITEHOUSE MEADOWS
1 STAFFORD CL
2 LOVELL RISE
3 BORMAN CL
MAYFLOWER CL
COMET WAY
Laurence Industrial Estate
EASTWOODBURY LA
AVRO RD
WILLMOTT RD
BRISTOL RD
VICKERS RD
WELLS AVE
WOODBURY CRES
NIGHTINGALE CL
ROCHFORD RD
A1159
WARNERS GDNS
SHERBOURNE CL
SHERBOURNE GDNS
Prittle Brook
Nursery
EASTWOODBURY CL
SNAKES LA
BRENDON WAY
BIDEFORD CL
LYMPSTONE CL
A127
NORTH CRES
FEECHES RD
SOUTH CRES
DENTON CL
HORNBY CL
HORNBY AVE
SIDMOUTH AVE
CRANSTON AVE
DENTON AVE
DENTON APP
PURLEY WAY
ALTON GDNS
AUDLEYS CL
DEREK GDNS
MANNERS WAY
OAKEN GRANGE DR
KEITH WAY
FAIRLAWN GDNS
BYRNE DR
HAMPTON GDNS
MARLOW GDNS
BEVERLEY GDNS
BEECHMONT GDNS
ARAGON CL
THORNFORD GDNS
SUMPTERS WAY
CHANDLERS WAY
POTTERS WAY
FARRIERS WAY 1
THE VINTNERS 2
TAILORS WAY 3
Cemy
Industrial Estate
STOCK RD
DUNSTER AVE
CHARLES CL
MARTOCK AVE
BRUTON AVE
CHEDDAR AVE
MENDIP CRES
MENDIP RD
DULVERTON AVE
GLASTONBURY CHASE
LANGPORT DR
PORLOCK AVE
EXFORD AVE
YEOVIL CHASE
SOMERSET AVE
SOMERSET CRES
TAUNTON DR
BRANSTON
BRIDGEWATER DR
TRESCOT CL
COCKETHURST CL
WINSFORD GDNS
PRINCE AVE
PRINCE CL
A1158
BADGERS CL
ROSARY GDNS
NORTHVILLE DR
QUEEN ANNE'S DR
ROCHESTER MEWS
ROCHESTER DR
RICHMOND DR
FAIRVIEW DR
THEARLE DR
COLEMANS AVE
Sch
Schs
MIDHURST AVE
HENLEY CRES
B1013
HOBLEYTHICK LA
MAYFIELD AVE
EARLS HALL PAR
CUCKOO CNR
PRIORY CRES
Priory Park
Prittlewell Priory and rems of Priory
EASTERN AVE
CARLTON AVE
COMMERCIAL RD
LAVENDER GR
CARLINGFORD DR
General Hospital
HILLBOROUGH RD
CHASE GDNS
PARKSTONE DR
BEELEIGH CL
EARLS HALL AVE
Prittlewell
JONES CL
BURR HILL CHASE
SOUTHBOURNE GDNS
MERILIES CL
MERILIES GDNS
SELDON CL
MANNERING GDNS
ARUNDEL GDNS
School
WEST BOURNE GR
HOLME DALE CL
EASTBOURNE GR
CARDIGAN AVE
SOUTHBOURNE GR
WESTBOURNE GR
KENILWORTH GDNS
PRITTLEWELL CHASE
ST JAMES CL
ST JAMES GDNS
WELLSTEAD GDNS
EASTWOOD BVD
CLATTERFIELD GDNS
Schools
Prittle Brook
SPRINGFIELD DR
HIGHFIELD WAY
HIGHFIELD GDNS
HIGHFIELD CRES
HIGHFIELD GR
CLEVELAND DR
ST GEORGE'S DR
SHAKESPEARE AVE
GAINSBOROUGH DR
SHAKESPEARE DR
VICTORIA AVE
HILL RD
REGENCY GREEN
EDITH RD
ST BENETS RD
PRIORY AVE
ST MARY'S RD
EAST ST
STATION APP
GLENBERVIE DR
MANCHESTER DR
CAVENDISH GDNS
FAIRFAX DR
DARLINGHURST GR
BIRCHWOOD DR
FILLEBROOK AVE
GREENBANKS
LINDISFARNE AVE
WOODCOTE RD
NELSON RD
EASTWOOD BVD
SHANKLIN DR
MARTYNS GR
HOLYWOOD RD
SANDOWN AVE
KINGSWAY
EASTWOOD LA S
SOUTHBOROUGH DR
SILVERSEA DR
WELLINGTON AVE
ST GEORGE'S PARK AVE
WESTMINSTER DR
FAIRMEAD AVE
HILDAVILLE DR
FLEETWOOD AVE
RONALD PARK AVE
TINTERN AVE
SOUTHVIEW DR
ELECTRIC AVE
NORTHVIEW DR
WESTCLIFF PARK DR
BEEDELL AVE
RAMUZ DR
BRIGHTWELL AVE
HAINAULT AVE
GLENWOOD AVE
INVERNESS AVE
SILVERDALE AVE
WENHAM DR
MACDONALD AVE
Schs
WEST ST
B1015
FERNHURST AVE
TICKFIELD AVE
WALLIS AVE
CROWBOROUGH RD
TUNBRIDGE RD
COLCHESTER RD
HOWARDS CHASE
AVEBURY RD
TUDOR RD
WESTBOROUGH RD
Liby
A13
A1158
Coll
CARNARVON RD
HARCOURT AVE
CHELMSFORD AVE
NORTH RD
ROCHFORD AVE
RAYLEIGH AVE
LONDON RD
WEST RD
HAMLET COURT RD
Westcliff Hospital
SALISBURY AVE
Civic Centre
Courts
SWEYNE AVE
BOSTON AVE
BAXTER AVE
A127
WOODFIELD PARK DR
LANSDOWNE AVE
FERNLEIGH DR
SANDLEIGH RD
ROCKLEIGH AVE
SUNNINGDALE AVE
LEIGH RD
LOUIS DR
1 THE DRIVE
2 THE MEADWAY
3 THE LEASWAY
4 HALL PARK AVE
CHALKWELL AVE
IMPERIAL AVE
SEYMOUR RD
CHADWICK RD
DRAKE RD
CROWSTONE RD
CROWSTONE CL
COTSWOLD RD
ELDERTON RD
CRANLEY RD
CRANLEY AVE
VALKYRIE RD
ARGYLL RD
CLAREMONT RD
ALBION RD
CARISBROOKE RD
ALBANY AVE
CLIFF AVE
OSBORNE RD
BALMORAL RD
WINDSOR RD
KING'S RD
BEACH AVE
PARK SIDE
ALLEYN PL
B1015

199

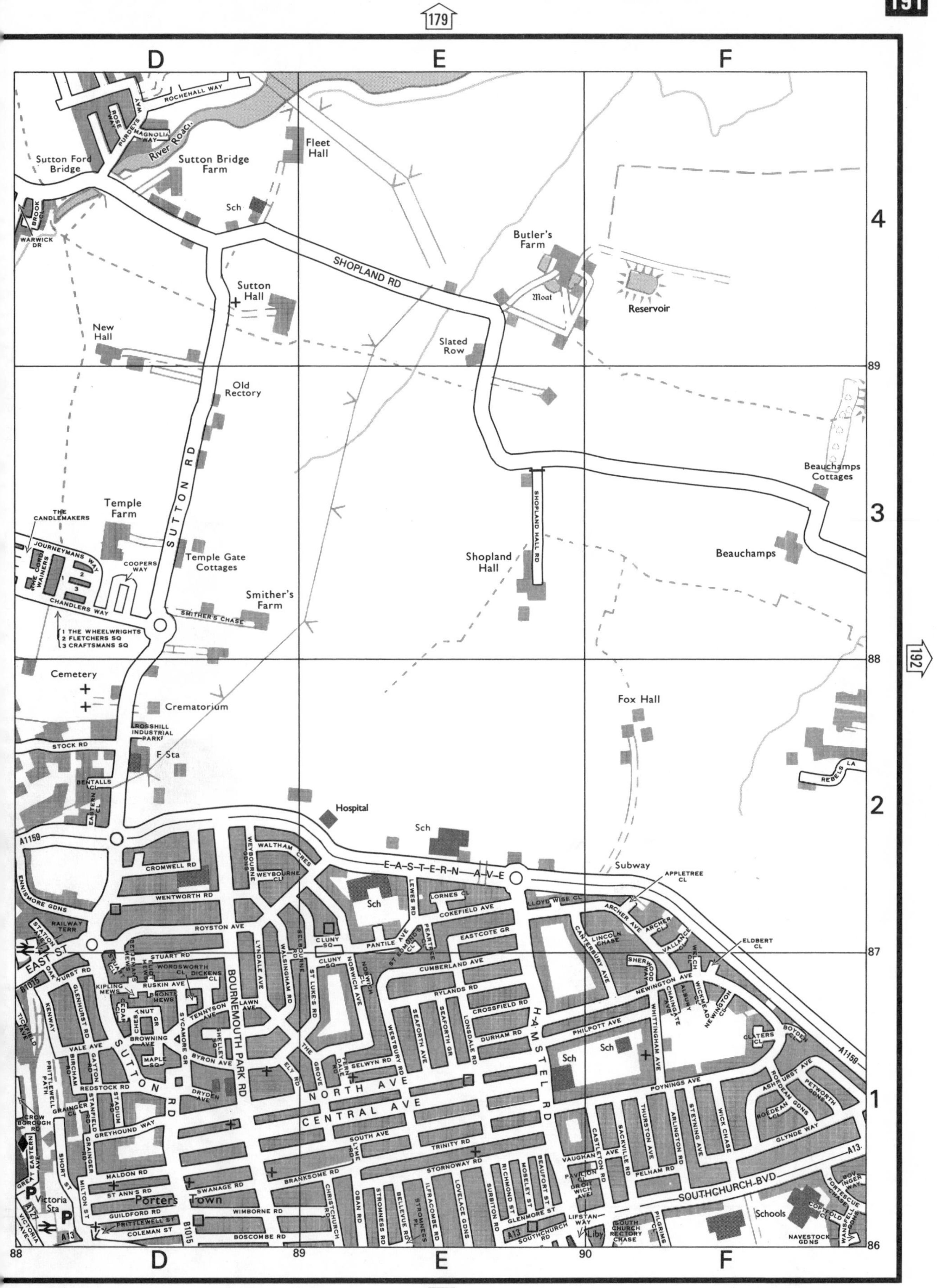
179
D
E
F
4
3
2
1
89
88
87
86
88
89
90
192
200
Sutton Ford Bridge
Sutton Bridge Farm
Fleet Hall
ROCHEHALL WAY
River Roach
Sch
SHOPLAND RD
Butler's Farm
Moat
Reservoir
Sutton Hall
New Hall
Slated Row
Old Rectory
SUTTON RD
Beauchamps Cottages
Beauchamps
Temple Farm
Temple Gate Cottages
Smither's Farm
Shopland Hall
SHOPLAND HALL RD
SMITHERS CHASE
CHANDLERS WAY
JOURNEYMANS WAY
COOPERS WAY
1 THE WHEELWRIGHTS
2 FLETCHERS SQ
3 CRAFTSMANS SQ
Cemetery
Crematorium
Fox Hall
STOCK RD
F Sta
REBELS LA
Hospital
Sch
EASTERN AVE
Subway
A1159
CROMWELL RD
WENTWORTH RD
ROYSTON AVE
EAST ST
NORTH AVE
CENTRAL AVE
SOUTH AVE
TRINITY RD
STORNOWAY RD
SOUTHCHURCH BVD
BOURNEMOUTH PARK RD
HAMSTEL RD
PHILPOTT AVE
POYNINGS AVE
GLYNDE WAY
Victoria Sta
Porters Town
Schools
A13
B1015
WIMBORNE RD
BOSCOMBE RD
GUILDFORD RD
COLEMAN ST
Liby

180

191

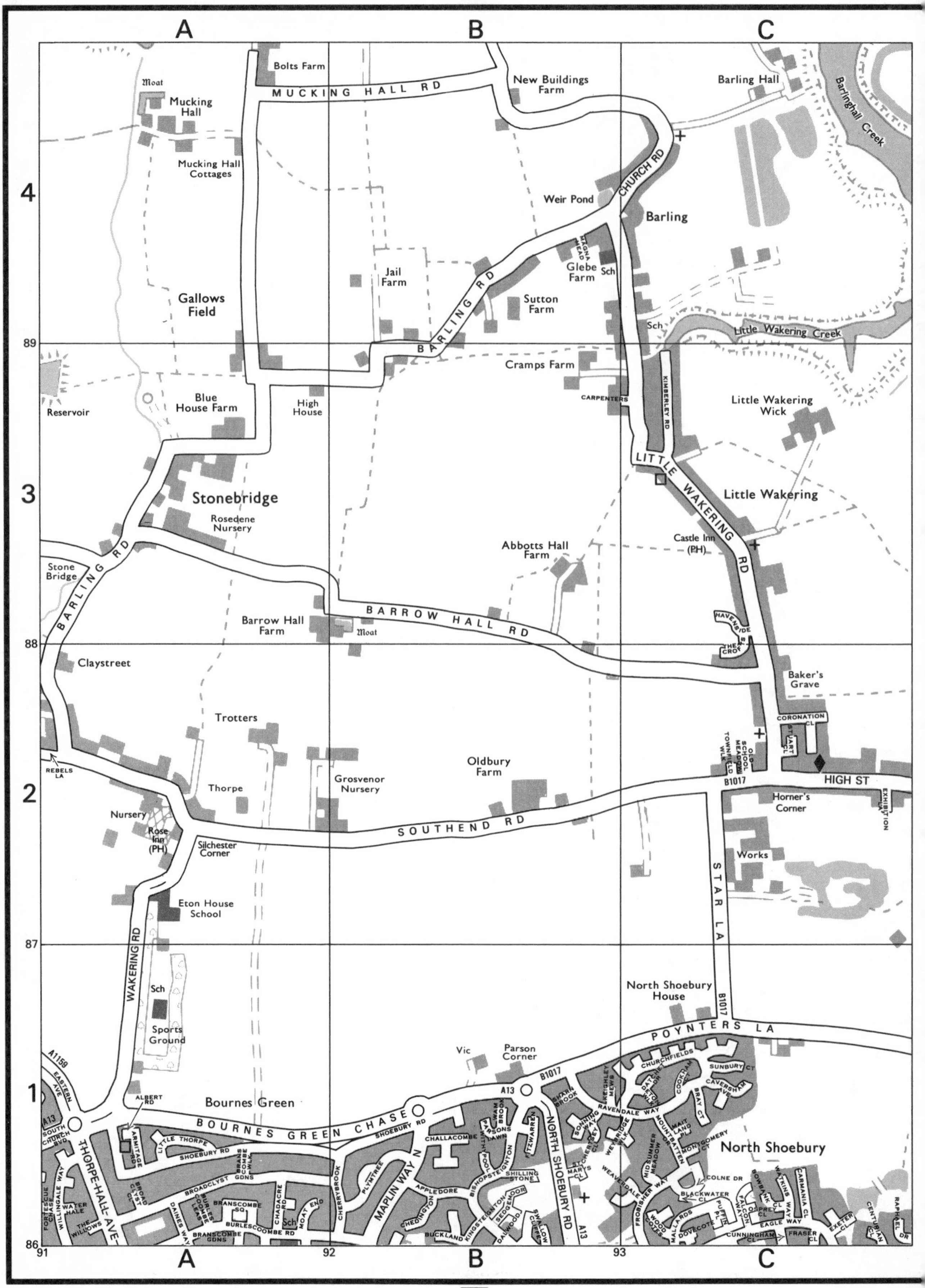
A
B
C
4
3
2
1
89
88
87
86
91
92
93
Bolts Farm
MUCKING HALL RD
New Buildings Farm
Barling Hall
Barlinghall Creek
Moat
Mucking Hall
Mucking Hall Cottages
CHURCH RD
Weir Pond
Barling
MAGNA MEAD
Glebe Farm
Sch
Jail Farm
Gallows Field
BARLING RD
Sutton Farm
Little Wakering Creek
Cramps Farm
Reservoir
Blue House Farm
High House
CARPENTERS
KIMBERLEY RD
Little Wakering Wick
LITTLE WAKERING RD
Little Wakering
Stonebridge
Rosedene Nursery
Castle Inn (PH)
Abbotts Hall Farm
Stone Bridge
BARROW HALL RD
Barrow Hall Farm
HAVENSIDE
THE CROFT
Claystreet
Baker's Grave
Trotters
CORONATION CL
STUART CL
TOWNFIELD WLK
SCHOOL MEADOW
OLD
REBELS LA
Oldbury Farm
Grosvenor Nursery
B1017
HIGH ST
Thorpe
Horner's Corner
EXHIBITION LA
Nursery
Rose Inn (PH)
SOUTHEND RD
Silchester Corner
Works
STAR LA
Eton House School
WAKERING RD
Sch
Sports Ground
North Shoebury House
POYNTERS LA
A1159
Vic
Parson Corner
CHURCHFIELDS
SUNBURY CT
EASTERN AVE
A13
ALBERT RD
Bournes Green
SOUTH CHURCH BVD
BOURNES GREEN CHASE
SHOEBURY RD
NORTH SHOEBURY RD
RAVENDALE WAY
North Shoebury
THORPE-HALL-AVE
ARMITAGE RD
LITTLE THORPE
SHOEBURY RD
CHALLACOMBE
PARSONS LAWN
FITZWARREN
MOUNTBATTEN
MONTGOMERY CT
MIDSUMMER MEADOW
MAPLIN WAY N
BROADCLYST GDNS
BROADCLYST CL
CHERRYBROOK
PLYMTREE
APPLEDORE
BISHOPSTEIGNTON
SHILLING STONE
WEAVERDALE
FROBISHER WAY
COLNE DR
BLACKWATER CL
WATKINS WAY
CARMANIA CL
FORTESCUE CHASE
WILLINGALE WAY
WATERHALE
THE WILLOWS
BRANSCOMBE SQ
CHADACRE RD
MOAT END
BRANSCOMBE GDNS
BURLESCOOMBE RD
DAINES WAY
CHEDINGTON
BUCKLAND
KINGSTEIGNTON
SEDGEMOOR
DALWOOD
SWALLOW CL
MALLARDS
DOVECOTE
CUNNINGHAM CL
EAGLE WAY
FRASER CL
EXETER CL
CENTURION
RAPHAEL DR
OSPREY CL
FALCON WAY

201

181

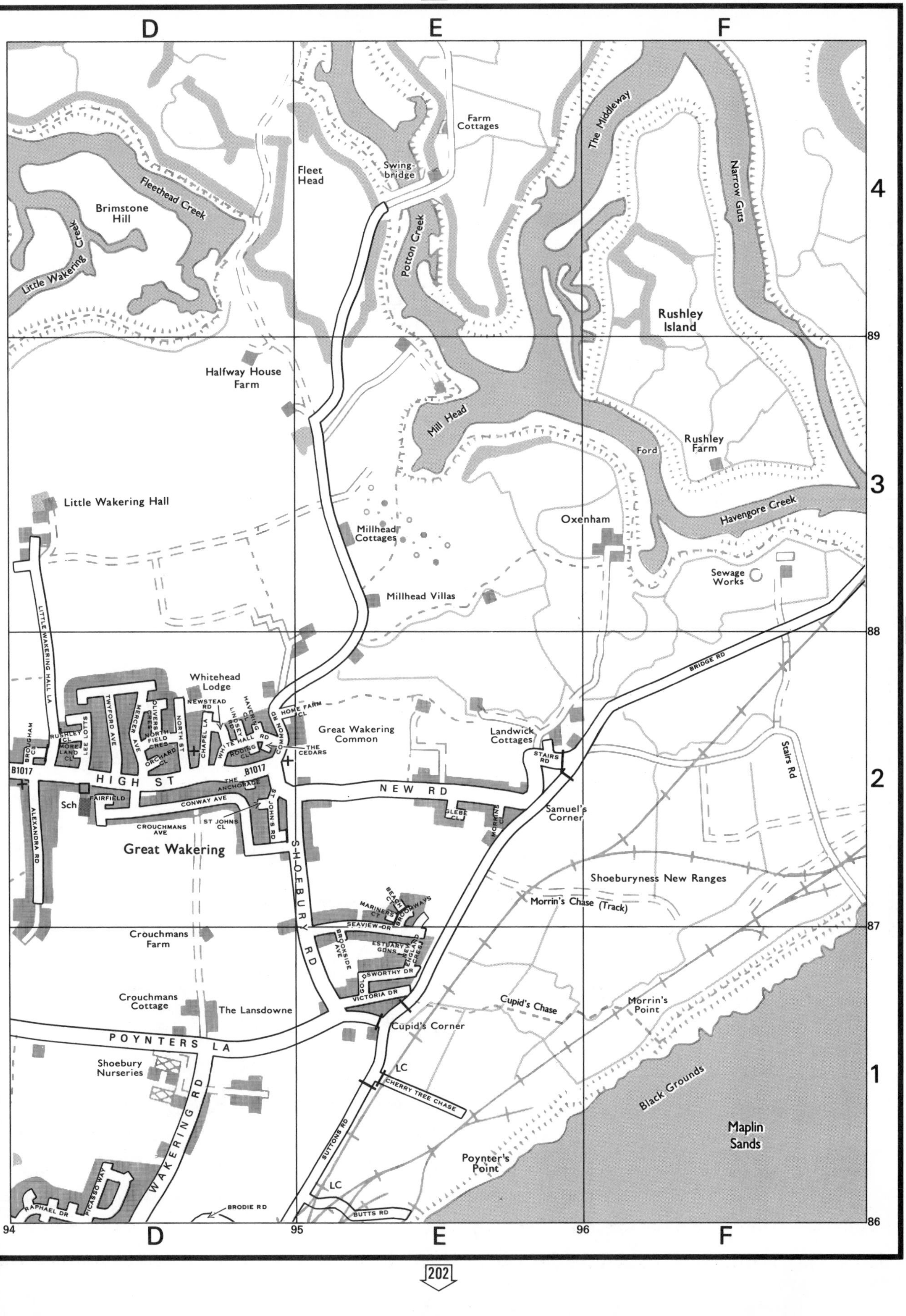

D
E
F
4
3
2
1
89
88
87
86
94
95
96
Farm Cottages
Fleet Head
Swing-bridge
The Middleway
Narrow Guts
Brimstone Hill
Fleethead Creek
Little Wakering Creek
Potton Creek
Rushley Island
Halfway House Farm
Mill Head
Rushley Farm
Ford
Little Wakering Hall
Havengore Creek
Oxenham
Millhead Cottages
Sewage Works
Millhead Villas
LITTLE WAKERING HALL LA
BRIDGE RD
Whitehead Lodge
NEWSTEAD RD
HOME FARM CL
Great Wakering Common
Landwick Cottages
Stairs Rd
STAIRS RD
BROUGHAM CL
RUSHLEY CL
MORELAND CL
LEE LOTTS
TWYFORD AVE
MERCER AVE
OLIVERS CRES
NORTHFIELD CRES
ORCHARD CL
NORTH ST
CHAPEL LA
LINDSEY CT
HAVERING CL
WHITE HALL RD
RODING CL
COMMON RD
THE CEDARS
B1017
HIGH ST
THE ANCHORAGE
NEW RD
Samuel's Corner
Sch
FAIRFIELD
CONWAY AVE
ST JOHNS RD
GLEBE CL
MORRINS CL
ALEXANDRA RD
CROUCHMANS AVE
ST JOHNS CL
Great Wakering
SHOEBURY RD
Shoeburyness New Ranges
BEACH CT
MARINERS CT
BROADWAYS
Morrin's Chase (Track)
SEAVIEW DR
Crouchmans Farm
BROOKSIDE AVE
ESTUARY GDNS
KINGSLAND CRES
GOLDSWORTHY DR
Crouchmans Cottage
VICTORIA DR
Cupid's Chase
Morrin's Point
The Lansdowne
Cupid's Corner
POYNTERS LA
LC
Shoebury Nurseries
CHERRY TREE CHASE
Black Grounds
WAKERING RD
SUTTONS RD
Maplin Sands
Poynter's Point
PICASSO WAY
RAPHAEL DR
BRODIE RD
BUTTS RD

194

202

182

193

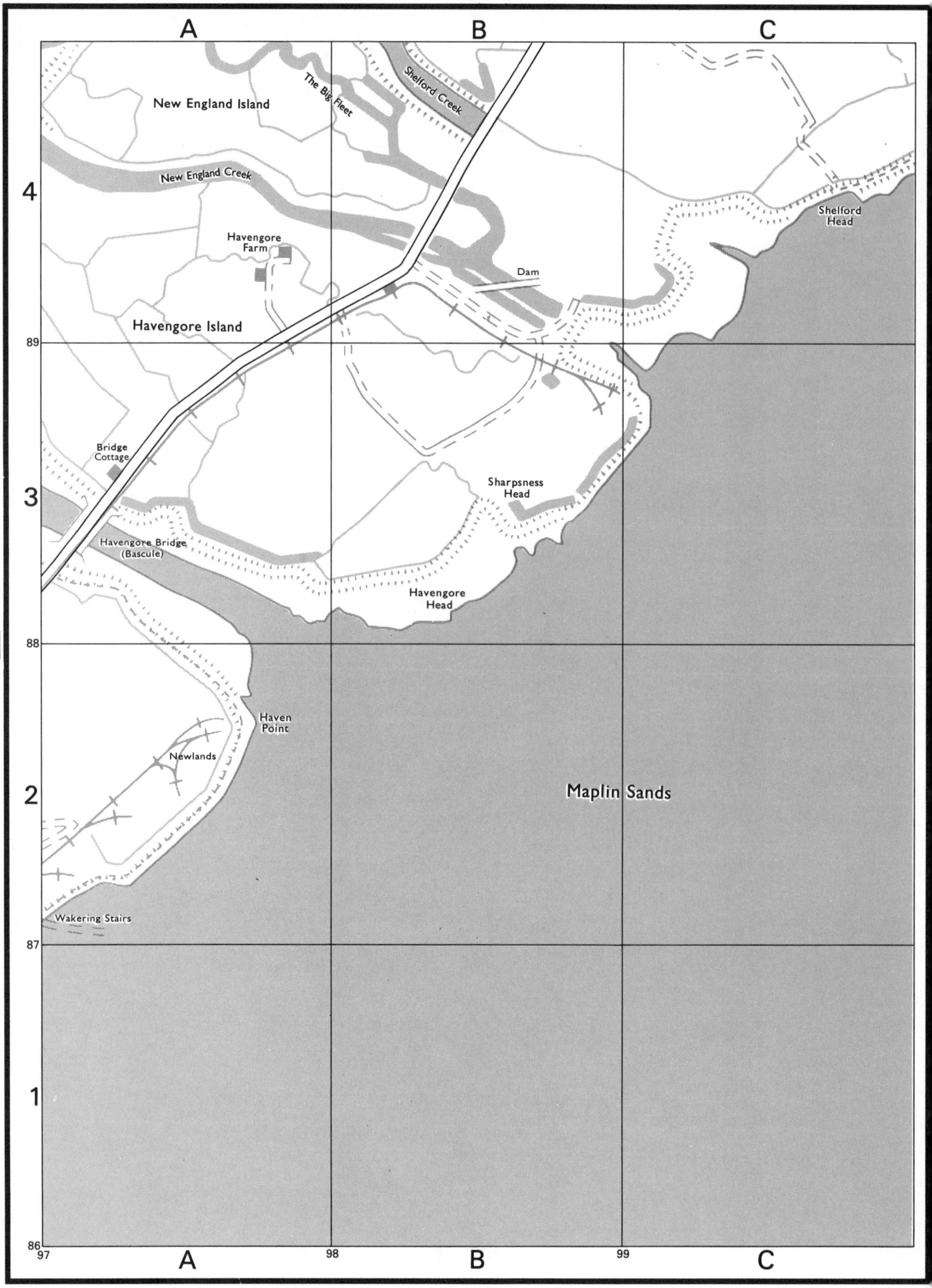
A
B
C
4
3
2
1
89
88
87
86
97
98
99
New England Island
The Big Fleet
Shelford Creek
New England Creek
Havengore Farm
Havengore Island
Dam
Shelford Head
Bridge Cottage
Sharpsness Head
Havengore Bridge (Bascule)
Havengore Head
Haven Point
Newlands
Maplin Sands
Wakering Stairs

186

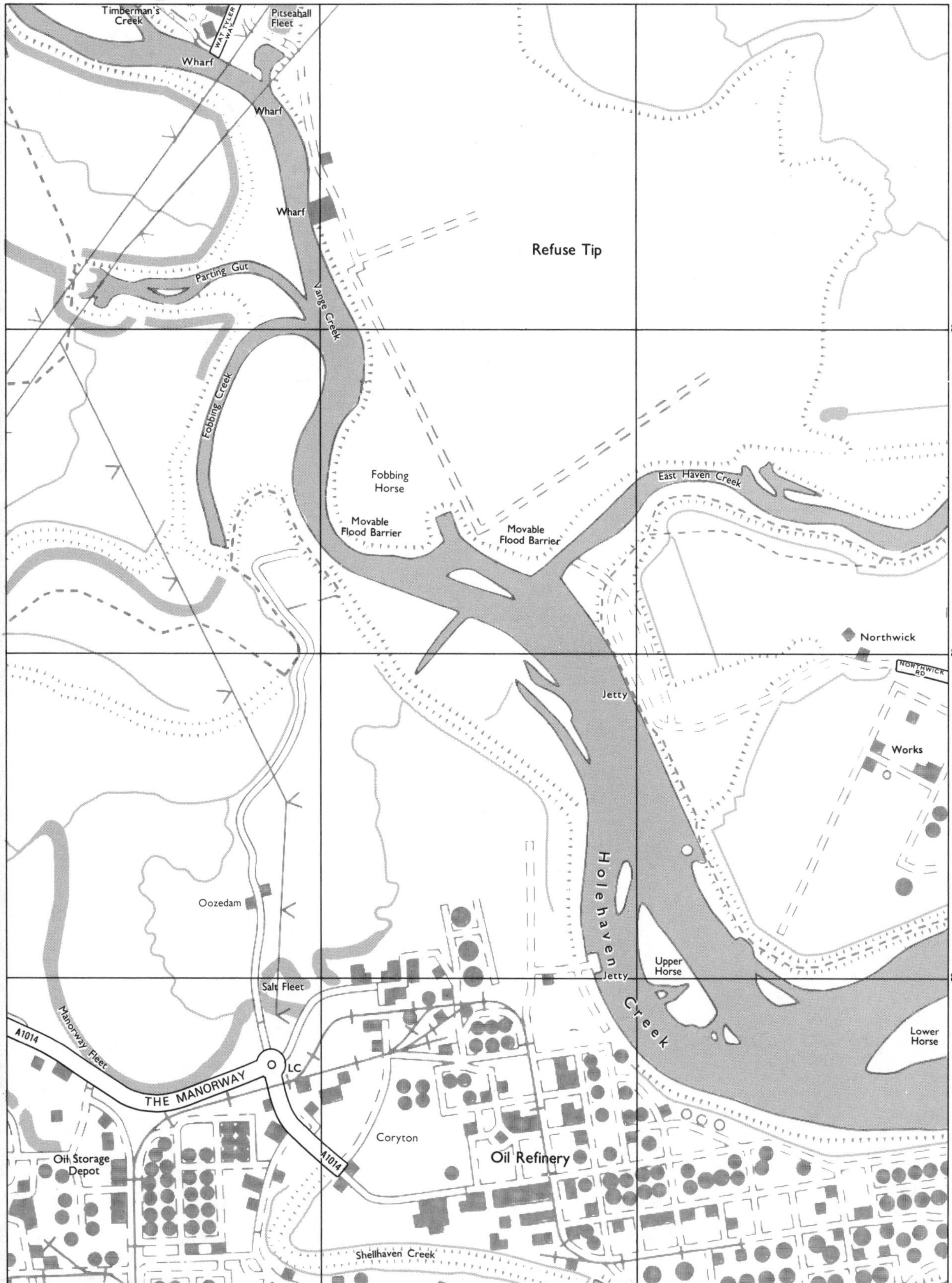
D
E
F
Timberman's Creek
Pitseahall Fleet
WAT TYLER WAY
Wharf
Wharf
Wharf
Refuse Tip
Parting Gut
Vange Creek
Fobbing Creek
Fobbing Horse
Movable Flood Barrier
Movable Flood Barrier
East Haven Creek
Northwick
NORTHWICK RD
Jetty
Works
Holehaven Creek
Oozedam
Upper Horse
Jetty
Salt Fleet
Lower Horse
Manorway Fleet
A1014
LC
THE MANORWAY
Coryton
Oil Refinery
Oil Storage Depot
A1014
Shellhaven Creek
4
85
3
84
2
83
1
82
73
74
75
D
E
F

196
203

187

195

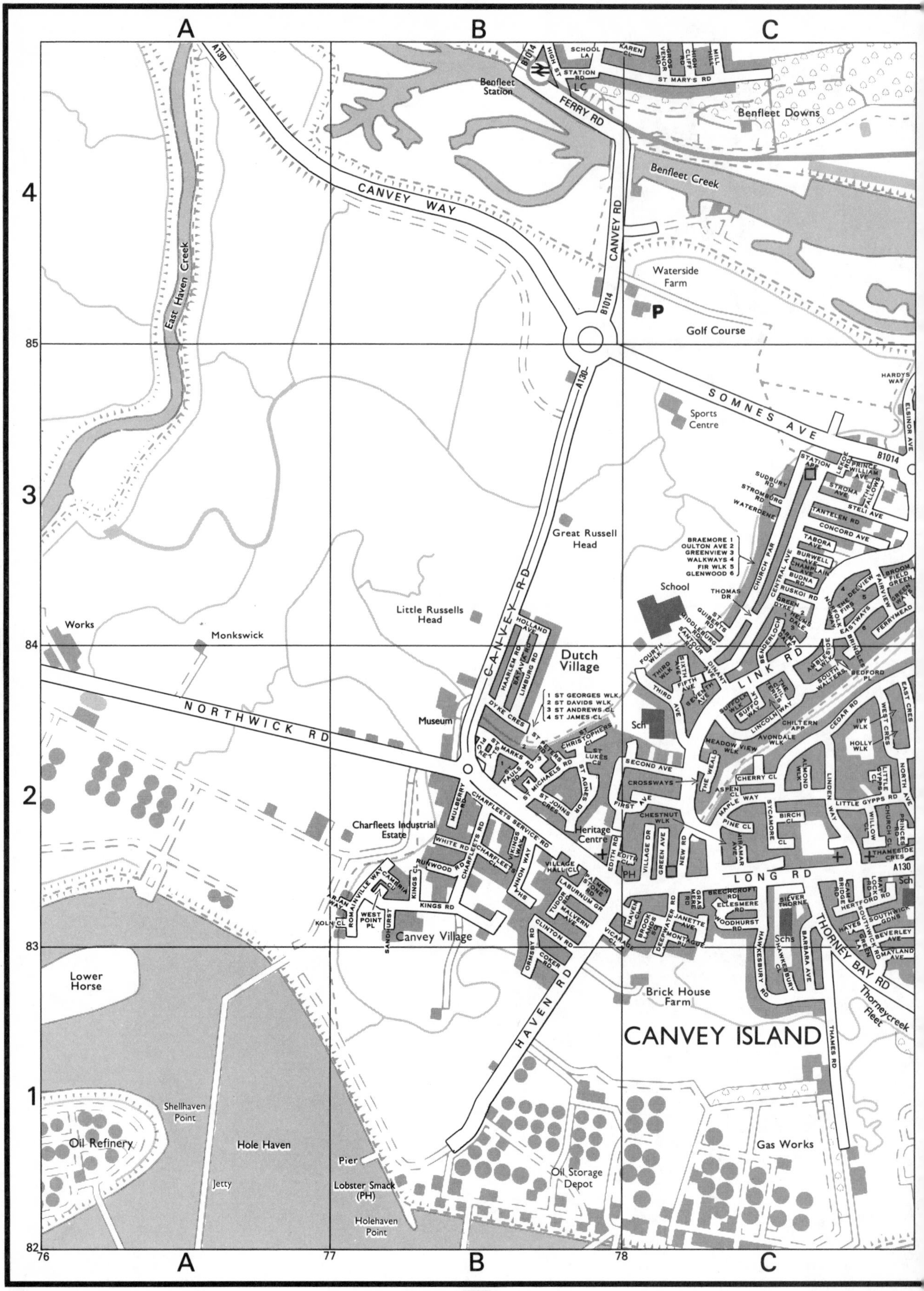
A
B
C
A
B
C
4
3
2
1
85
84
83
82
76
77
78
A130
B1014
CANVEY WAY
CANVEY RD
FERRY RD
Benfleet Station
HIGH ST
STATION RD
SCHOOL LA
KAREN CL
ST MARY'S RD
LC
Benfleet Downs
Benfleet Creek
East Haven Creek
Waterside Farm
P
Golf Course
SOMNES AVE
Sports Centre
HARDYS WAY
ELSINOR AVE
STATION APP
PRINCE WILLIAM AVE
STROMA AVE
THE FALLOWS
STELI AVE
TANTELEN RD
CONCORD AVE
TABORA AVE
BURWELL AVE
CHAMPLAIN AVE
BUDNA RD
RUSKOI RD
SUDBURY RD
STROMBURG RD
WATERDENE
CHURCH PAR
CENTRAL AVE
BRAEMORE 1
OULTON AVE 2
GREENVIEW 3
WALKWAYS 4
FIR WLK 5
GLENWOOD 6
THE DELVIEW
FAIRVIEW
BROOMFIELD GREEN
FERRYMEAD
EASTWAYS
Great Russell Head
School
THOMAS DR
ST GUIBERTS RD
MIDDLEBURG
SANTOUR RD
BENDERLOCH
LINK RD
BRINDLES
BEDFORD PL
SOUTH WALTERS
FOURTH WLK
THIRD WLK
SIXTH AVE
FIFTH AVE
SEVENTH AVE
DNANT AVE
THIRD AVE
SUFFOLK WLK
SUFFOLK WAY
LINCOLN WAY
CHILTERN APP
AVONDALE WLK
CEDAR RD
IVY WLK
WEST CRES
EAST CRES
HOLLY WLK
NORTH AVE
Little Russells Head
HOLLAND AVE
HAARLEM RD
BATAVIA RD
LIMBURG RD
Dutch Village
DYKE CRES
1 ST GEORGES WLK
2 ST DAVIDS WLK
3 ST ANDREWS CL
4 ST JAMES CL
Works
Monkswick
NORTHWICK RD
Museum
ST MARKS RD
ST PETERS
ST CHRISTOPHERS CL
ST LUKES CL
ST PAULS RD
ST MICHAELS RD
ST AGNES DR
ST JOHNS CRES
Sch
SECOND AVE
CROSSWAYS
FIRST AVE
MEADOW VIEW WLK
THE WEALD
ASPEN CL
MAPLE WAY
CHERRY CL
ALMOND WLK
LINDEN WAY
LITTLE GYPPS RD
PINE CL
SYCAMORE CL
BIRCH CL
CHESTNUT WLK
Charfleets Industrial Estate
MULBERRY
CHARFLEETS SERVICE RD
WHITE RD
RUNWOOD RD
CHARFLEETS RD
CHARFLEETS CL
VIKINGS WAY
SHANNON WAY
VILLAGE HALL CL
Heritage Centre
EDITH RD
EDITH CL
VILLAGE DR
GREEN AVE
NEW RD
PH
LONG RD
A130
THAMESIDE CRES
CAMBRIA CL
ROMAINVILLE WAY
KOLN CL
WEST POINT PL
KINGS CL
KINGS RD
SANDHURST
Canvey Village
LABURNUM GR
TUDOR
MALVERN RD
CLINTON RD
ORMSBY RD
COKER RD
HAVEN CL
BROOK LANDS
DEEPWATER RD
JANETTE AVE
MONTAGUE
BEECHCROFT RD
ELLESMERE RD
WOODHURST RD
SILVER THORNE
VICARAGE CL
Schs
HAWKESBURY RD
HAWKESBURY CL
BARBARA AVE
THORNEY BAY RD
HERTFORD RD
HAYES
SOUTHWICK GDNS
BEVERLEY AVE
MAYLAND AVE
Sch
Lower Horse
HAVEN RD
Brick House Farm
CANVEY ISLAND
THAMES RD
Thorneycreek Fleet
Shellhaven Point
Oil Refinery
Hole Haven
Jetty
Pier
Lobster Smack (PH)
Holehaven Point
Oil Storage Depot
Gas Works

204

188

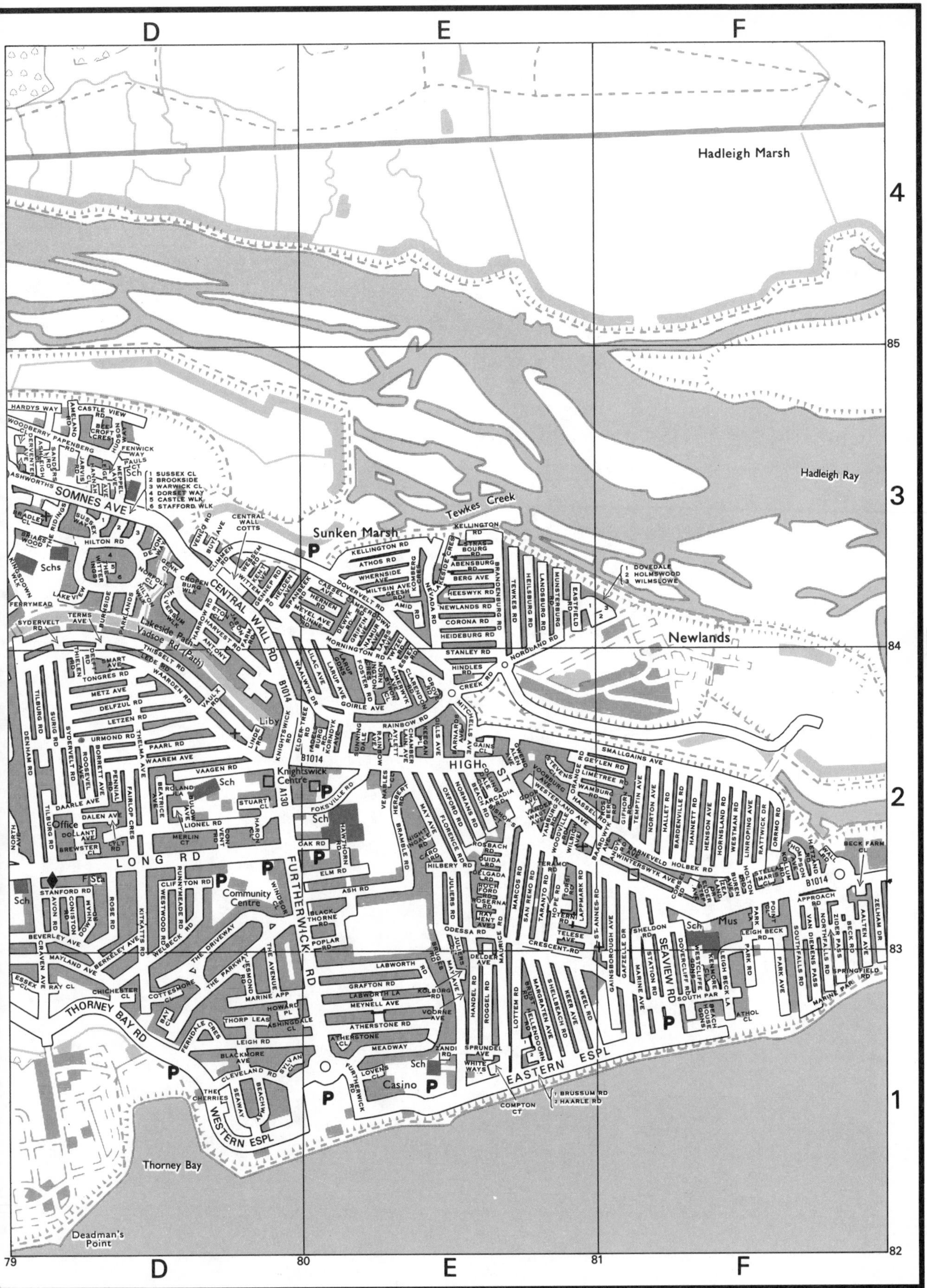
D
E
F
Hadleigh Marsh
4
85
Hadleigh Ray
3
Tewkes Creek
Sunken Marsh
Newlands
84
2
83
1
82
79
80
81
Thorney Bay
Deadman's Point
HARDYS WAY
CASTLE VIEW RD
WOODBERRY
PAPENBERG RD
FENWICK WAY
PAULS CT
Sch
1 SUSSEX CL
2 BROOKSIDE
3 WARWICK CL
4 DORSET WAY
5 CASTLE WLK
6 STAFFORD WLK
ASHWORTHS
SOMNES AVE
BRADLEY CL
SUSSEX WAY
THE RIDINGS
BRIARS WOOD
HILTON RD
Schs
KNIGHTSWICK CENTRE
LAKE VIEW
FERRYMEAD
CENTRAL WALL COTTS
CENTRAL WALL RD
KELLINGTON RD
ATHOS RD
WHERNSIDE AVE
MILTSIN AVE
DOVERVELT RD
NEVADA RD
ABENSBURG RD
BERG AVE
HEESWYK RD
NEWLANDS RD
CORONA RD
HEIDEBURG RD
STANLEY RD
HINDLES RD
CREEK RD
TEWKES RD
HEILSBURG RD
LANDSBURG RD
MUNSTERBURG RD
EASTFIELD RD
NORDLAND RD
1 DOVEDALE
2 HOLMSWOOD
3 WILMSLOWE
SYDERVELT RD
TERMS AVE
Lakeside Path
Yadsoe Rd (Path)
THISSELT RD
TEDE RD
WAARDEN RD
SMART AVE
TONGRES RD
METZ AVE
DELFZUL RD
LETZEN RD
URMOND RD
PAARL RD
WAAREM AVE
VAAGEN RD
TILBURG RD
SURIG RD
DENHAM RD
B1014
Liby
MORNINGTON RD
GOIRLE AVE
RAINBOW RD
MITCHELLS AVE
HIGH ST
SMALLGAINS AVE
GEYLEN RD
LIMETREE RD
WAMBURG RD
Sch
Knightswick Centre
A130
FOKSVILLE RD
STUART CL
LIONEL RD
MERLIN CT
DAARLE AVE
DALEN AVE
Office
DOLLANT AVE
BREWSTER CL
LONG RD
F Sta
STANFORD RD
AVON RD
CONISTON RD
ROSE RD
CLIFTON RD
Community Centre
FURTHERWICK RD
OAK RD
ELM RD
ASH RD
HAWTHORN RD
BLACKTHORNE RD
POPLAR RD
LABWORTH RD
GRAFTON RD
LABWORTH LA
MEYNELL AVE
ATHERSTONE RD
MEADWAY
Casino
HERBERT RD
BRAMBLE RD
MAY AVE
OXFORD RD
FLORENCE RD
NORMANS RD
BEACH RD
HILBERY RD
JULIERS RD
ODESSA RD
ROSSBACH RD
MARCOS RD
SAN REMO RD
TARANTO RD
HOPE RD
LAPPMARK RD
CRESCENT RD
ST ANNES RD
GAINSBOROUGH AVE
GAFZELLE DR
MARINE AVE
STATION RD
SEAVIEW RD
SHELDON RD
DOVERCLIFF RD
WINTERSWYK AVE
HOLBEK RD
LEIGH BECK RD
PARK RD
PARK AVE
Mus
NORTON AVE
HALLET RD
BARDENVILLE RD
HANNETT RD
HENSON AVE
HORNSLAND RD
WESTMAN RD
LINROPING AVE
RATTWICK DR
ORRMO RD
BECK FARM CL
APPROACH RD
SOUTHFALLS RD
VAN DIEMENS PASS
NORTHFALLS RD
ZIDER PASS
BECK RD
AALTEN AVE
ZELHAM DR
SPRINGFIELD RD
MARINE PAR
SOUTH PAR
ATHOL CL
LOTTEM RD
MARGRATEN AVE
SHELLBEACH RD
KEER AVE
WEEL RD
EASTERN ESPL
1 BRUSSUM RD
2 HAARLE RD
COMPTON CT
WHITE WAYS
SPRUNDEL AVE
HANDEL RD
ROGGEL RD
DELDER AVE
LOVENS CL
ZANDI RD
ATHERSTONE CL
ASHINGDALE CL
LEIGH RD
BLACKMORE AVE
CLEVELAND RD
SYLVAN CL
THE CHERRIES
SEAWAY
BEACHWAY
WESTERN ESPL
THORNEY BAY RD
CHICHESTER CL
COTTESMORE
THE PARKWAY
THE DRIVEWAY
THE AVENUE
MARINE APP
HOWARD PL
THORP LEAS
FERNDALE CRES
BAY CL
ESSEX CL
RAY CL
MAYLAND AVE
BERKELEY AVE
BEVERLEY AVE
CRAVEN AVE
WESTWOOD RD
WELBECK RD
KITKATTS RD
RUNNYMEADE RD
WINDSOR

198

189

197

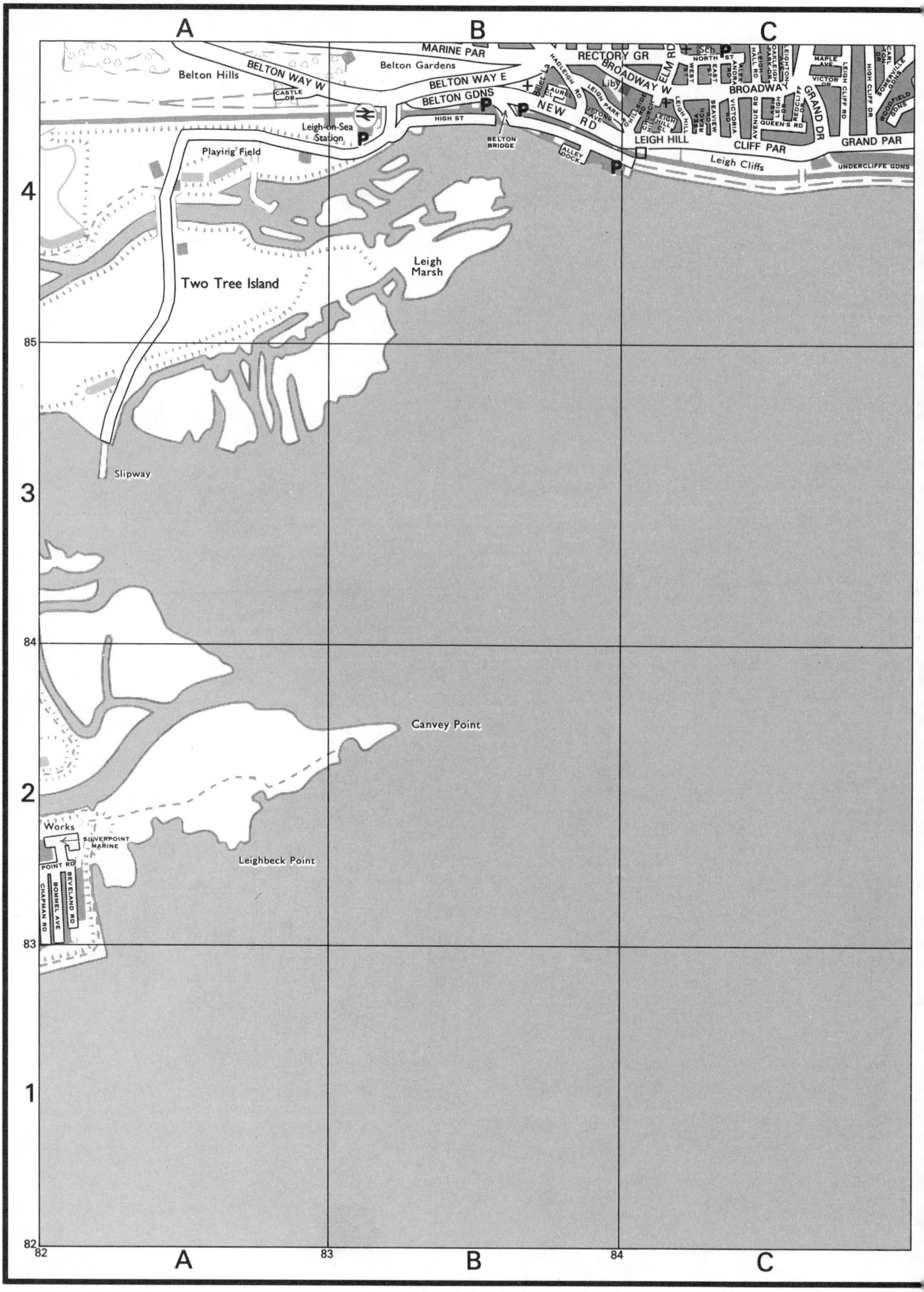
A
B
C
MARINE PAR
Belton Gardens
Belton Hills
BELTON WAY W
BELTON WAY E
BELTON GDNS
CASTLE DR
HIGH ST
Leigh-on-Sea Station
P
BELTON BRIDGE
RECTORY GR
BROADWAY W
ELM RD
Sch
NORTH ST
BROADWAY
MAPLE AVE
VICTOR DR
GRAND DR
LEIGH CLIFF RD
HIGH CLIFF DR
SOMERVILLE GDNS
WOODFIELD GDNS
HADLEIGH RD
LEIGH PARK RD
LAUREL CL
Billet La
Liby
NEW RD
ALLEY DOCK
LEIGH HILL
CLIFF PAR
GRAND PAR
QUEEN'S RD
VICTORIA RD
AVENUE RD
REDCLIFF DR
SEAVIEW
SEA REACH
WEST ST
EAST ST
LEIGH HALL RD
Leigh Cliffs
UNDERCLIFFE GDNS
Playing Field
Two Tree Island
Leigh Marsh
Slipway
Canvey Point
Works
SILVERPOINT MARINE
POINT RD
BEVELAND RD
BOMMEL AVE
CHAPMAN RD
Leighbeck Point
4
3
2
1
85
84
83
82
82
83
84

190

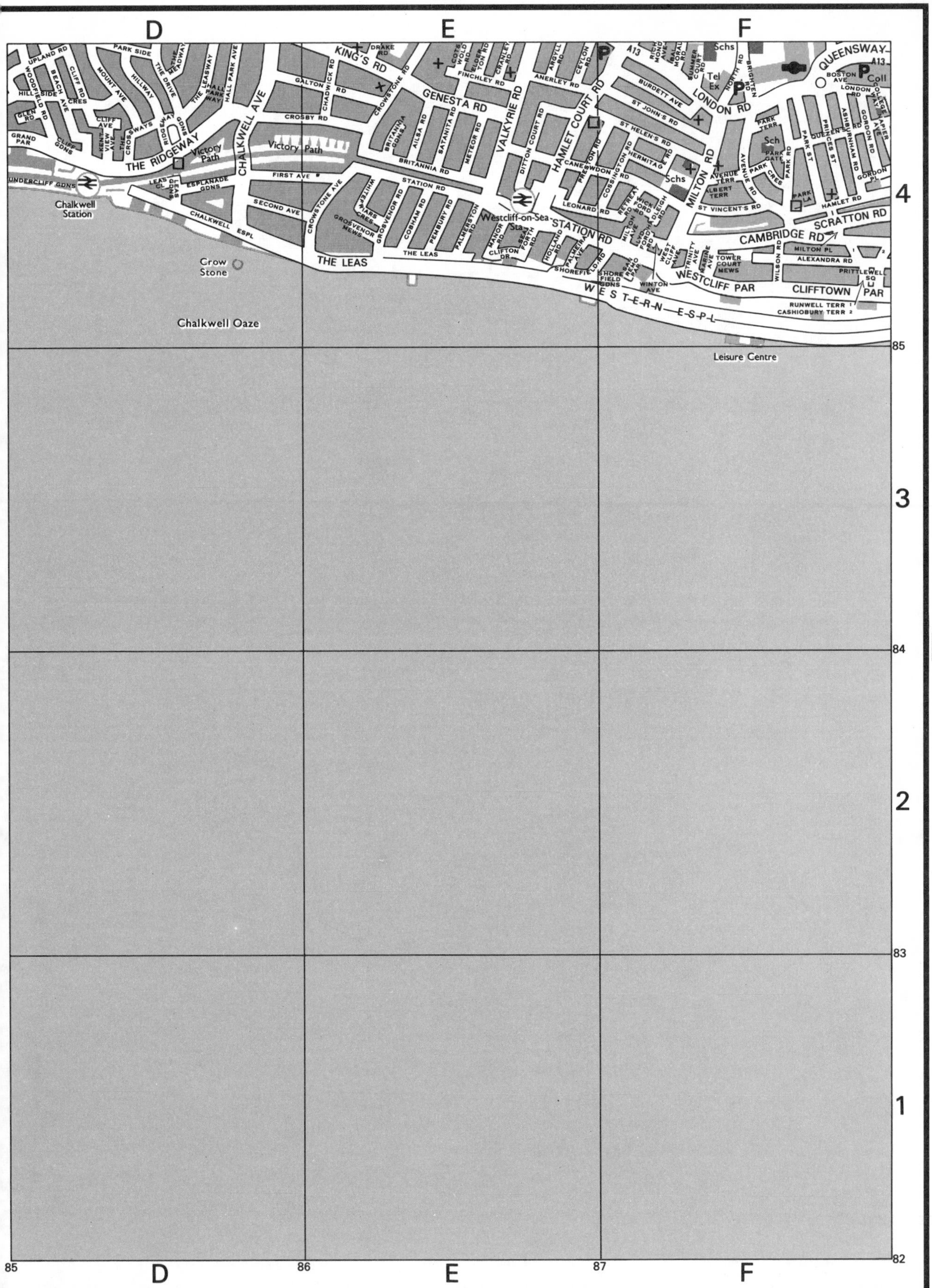

D
E
F
UPLAND RD
PARK SIDE
THE MEADWAY
THE LEASWAY
HALL PARK AVE
HALL PARK WAY
THE DRIVE
HILLWAY
MOUNT AVE
CLIFF RD
BEACH AVE
WOODFIELD RD
HILLSIDE CRES
GLEN RD
GRAND PAR
CLIFF GDNS
CLIFF AVE
KENT VIEW AVE
THE CROSSWAYS
RIDGEWAY GDNS
THE RIDGEWAY
Victory Path
CHALKWELL AVE
UNDERCLIFF GDNS
Chalkwell Station
LEAS CL
LEAS GDNS
ESPLANADE GDNS
FIRST AVE
SECOND AVE
CHALKWELL ESPL
Crow Stone
Chalkwell Oaze
GALTON RD
CROSBY RD
CHADWICK RD
KING'S RD
DRAKE RD
CROWSTONE RD
BRITANNIA GDNS
BRITANNIA RD
AILSA RD
SATANITA RD
METEOR RD
GENESTA RD
COTSWOLD RD
RIDGERTON RD
FINCHLEY RD
CRANLEY RD
VALKYRIE RD
ANERLEY RD
ARGYLL RD
CEYLON RD
DITTON COURT RD
HAMLET COURT RD
STATION RD
CROWSTONE AVE
WHITEFRIARS CRES
GROSVENOR RD
GROSVENOR MEWS
COBHAM RD
PEMBURY RD
PALMERSTON RD
THE LEAS
Westcliff-on-Sea Sta
MANOR RD
CLIFTON DR
SEAFORTH RD
HOLLAND RD
PALMEIRA AVE
SHOREFIELD RD
SHOREFIELD GDNS
CANEWDON RD
LEONARD RD
PRESTON RD
COSSINGTON RD
RETREAT RD
MILTON AVE
WICKFORD RD
LYNTON RD
ADLEIGH RD
HERMITAGE RD
ST HELEN'S RD
ST JOHN'S RD
BURDETT AVE
A13
RICHMOND AVE
IMPERIAL AVE
SUMMERCOURT RD
Schs
Tel Ex
NORTH RD
BRIGHTON RD
LONDON RD
MILTON RD
AVENUE TERR
ALBERT TERR
AVENUE RD
PARK TERR
Sch
PARK GATE
PARK CRES
PARK RD
PARK ST
PARK LA
ST VINCENT'S RD
WEST CLIFF AVE
WINTON AVE
TRINITY AVE
MARINE AVE
TOWER COURT MEWS
WESTCLIFF PAR
WESTERN ESPL
CAMBRIDGE RD
SCRATTON RD
HAMLET RD
QUEENSWAY
BOSTON AVE
Coll
LONDON RD
QUEEN'S RD
PRINCES ST
ASHBURNHAM RD
GORDON RD
NAPIER AVE
GORDON PL
MILTON PL
ALEXANDRA RD
WILSON RD
PRITTLEWELL SQ
CLIFFTOWN PAR
RUNWELL TERR
CASHIOBURY TERR
Leisure Centre
4
3
2
1
85
84
83
82
85
86
87
D
E
F

200

191

199

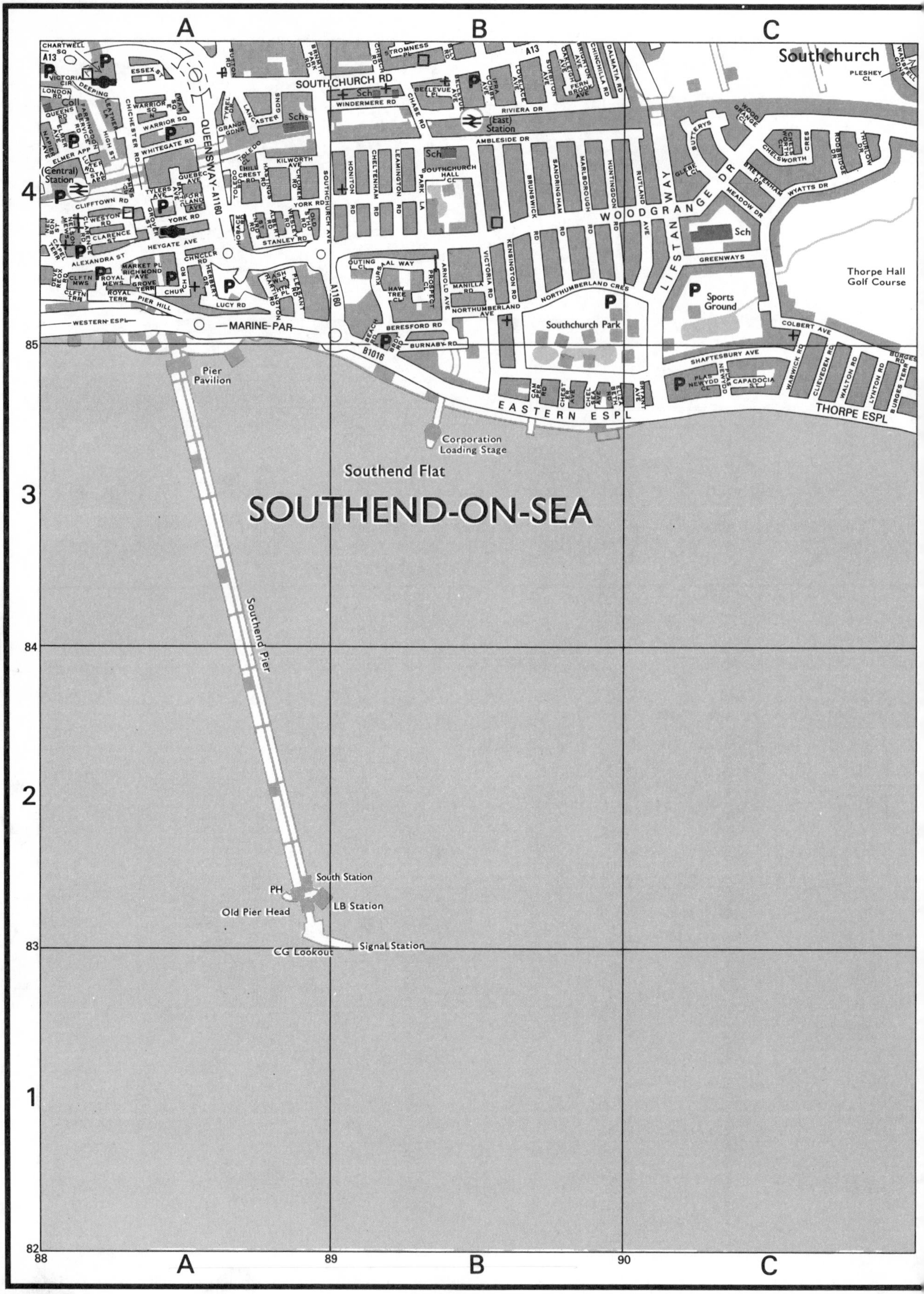
A
B
C
Southchurch
SOUTHCHURCH RD
WINDERMERE RD
RIVIERA DR
(East) Station
AMBLESIDE DR
QUEENSWAY-A1160
(Central) Station
CLIFFTOWN RD
YORK RD
HEYGATE AVE
ALEXANDRA ST
PIER HILL
WESTERN ESPL
MARINE PAR
LUCY RD
A13
A1160
B1016
WOODGRANGE DR
LIFSTAN WAY
GREENWAYS
NORTHUMBERLAND CRES
Southchurch Park
Sports Ground
Thorpe Hall Golf Course
COLBERT AVE
SHAFTESBURY AVE
EASTERN ESPL
THORPE ESPL
Pier Pavilion
Corporation Loading Stage
Southend Flat
SOUTHEND-ON-SEA
Southend Pier
South Station
PH
LB Station
Old Pier Head
Signal Station
CG Lookout
4
3
2
1
85
84
83
82
88
89
90

192

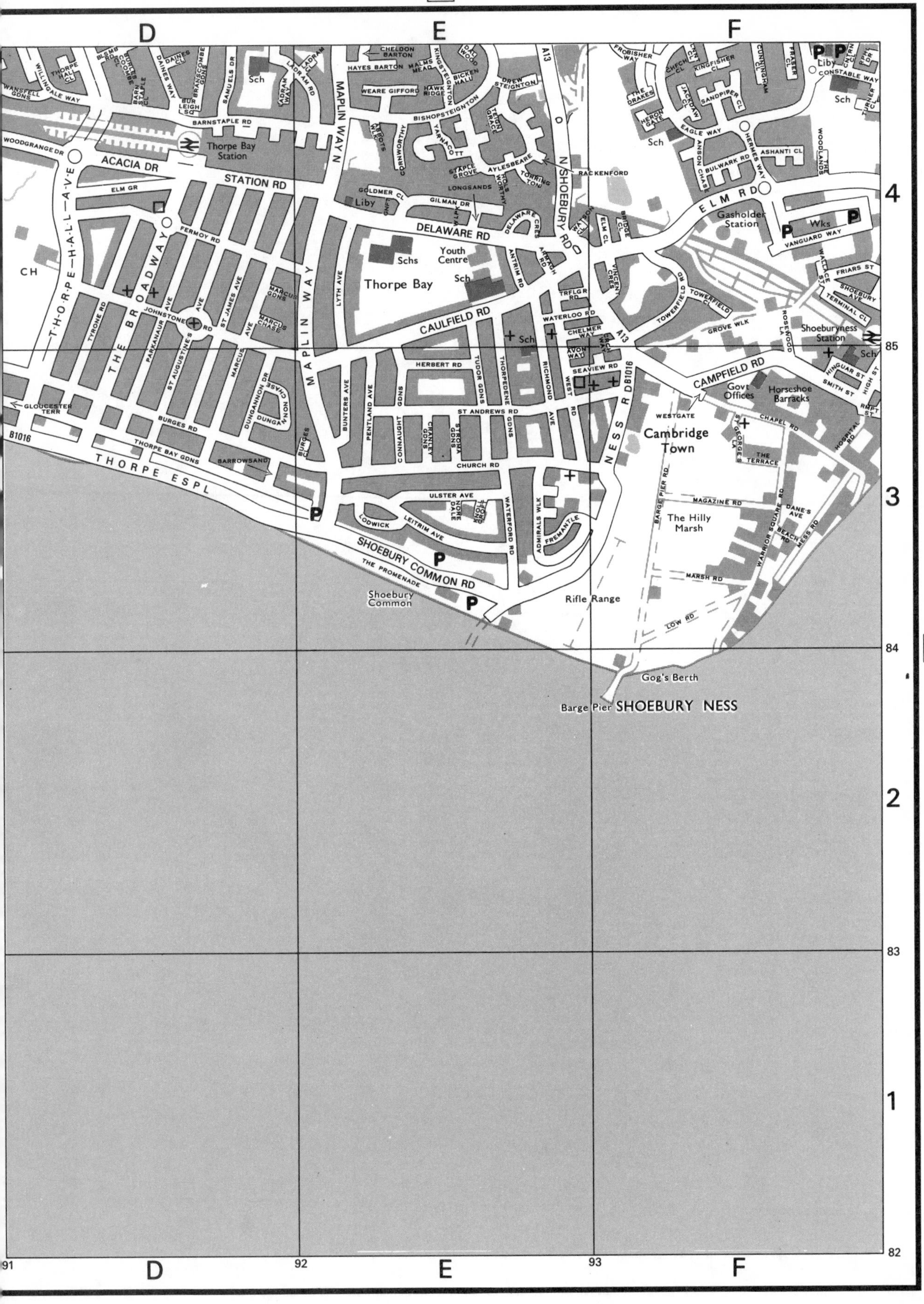
D
E
F
Thorpe Bay Station
ACACIA DR
STATION RD
ELM GR
FERMOY RD
BARNSTAPLE RD
WOODGRANGE DR
WILLINGALE WAY
THORPE HALL CL
WANSFELL GDNS
BARNSTAPLE
DAINES WAY
DAINES CL
BRANSCOMBE GDNS
BURLEIGH SQ
SAMUELS DR
Sch
LADRAM WAY
LADRAM RD
LADRAM
CHELDON BARTON
HAYES BARTON
MALMSMEAD
WEARE GIFFORD
HAWK RIDGE
BICKEN HALL
DREW STEIGNTON
BISHOPSTEIGNTON
KINGSTEIGNTON
YARNACOTT
CORNWORTHY
ABBOTS WLK
STAPLE GROVE
AYLESBEARE
TORRINGTON
RACKENFORD
LONGSANDS
GOLDMER CL
GILMAN DR
Liby
MAPLIN WAY
DELAWARE RD
DELAWARE CRES
ANTRIM RD
ARMAGH RD
Youth Centre
Schs
Sch
Thorpe Bay
CAULFIELD RD
LYTH AVE
CH
T·H·O·R·P·E-H·A·L·L-A·V·E
THE BROADWAY
TYRONE RD
PARKANAUR AVE
JOHNSTONE RD
ST AUGUSTINES AVE
ST JAMES AVE
MARCUS AVE
MARCUS GDNS
MARCUS CHASE
DUNGANNON DR
DUNGANNON CHASE
GLOUCESTER TERR
B1016
BURGES RD
THORPE BAY GDNS
BARROWSAND
THORPE ESPL
BURGES
BUNTERS AVE
PENTLAND AVE
CONNAUGHT GDNS
CRANLEY GDNS
STROMA GDNS
HERBERT RD
TUDOR GDNS
THORPEDENE GDNS
RICHMOND AVE
ST ANDREWS RD
CHURCH RD
ULSTER AVE
NORE DALE
LODWICK
LEITRIM AVE
WATERFORD RD
ADMIRALS WLK
FREMANTLE
SHOEBURY COMMON RD
THE PROMENADE
Shoebury Common
Rifle Range
A13
N SHOEBURY RD
WATSON CL
ELM CL
BRIDGE CL
TRFLGR RD
WATERLOO RD
CHELMER WAY
AVON WAY
SEAVIEW RD
WEST RD
NESS RD B1016
VINCENT CRES
FROBISHER WAY
THE DRAKES
HERON GATE
KINGFISHER CL
SANDPIPER CL
EAGLE WAY
CUNNINGHAM CL
FRASER CL
Liby
CONSTABLE WAY
TURNER CL
Sch
ANSON CHASE
BULWARK RD
HERMES WAY
ASHANTI CL
WOODLANDS
ELM RD
Gasholder Station
Wks
VANGUARD WAY
TOWERFIELD RD
TOWERFIELD CL
GROVE WLK
ROSEWOOD LA
FRIARS ST
SHOEBURY AVE
TERMINAL CL
Shoeburyness Station
WALLACE ST
HINGUAR ST
SMITH ST
HIGH ST
CAMPFIELD RD
Govt Offices
Horseshoe Barracks
WESTGATE
Cambridge Town
CHAPEL RD
ST GEORGES LA
THE TERRACE
RMPT ST
HOSPITAL RD
BARGE PIER RD
MAGAZINE RD
The Hilly Marsh
DANE'S AVE
WARRIOR SQUARE RD
BEACH RD
NESS RD
MARSH RD
LOW RD
Gog's Berth
Barge Pier
SHOEBURY NESS
4
85
3
84
2
83
1
82
91
92
93

202

193

201

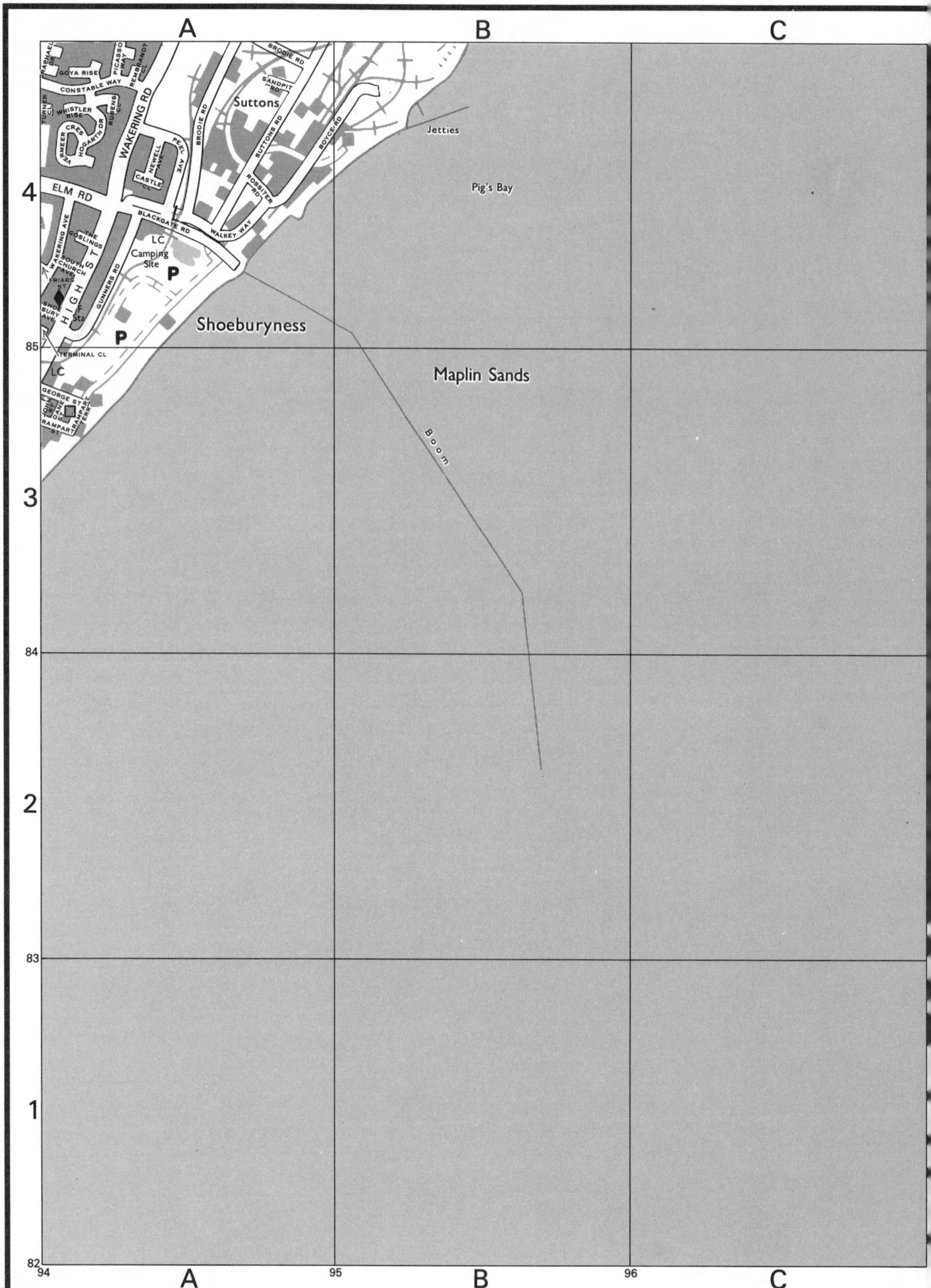
A
B
C
RAPHAEL DR
GOYA RISE
PICASSO WAY
REMBRANDT CL
CONSTABLE WAY
TURNER CL
WHISTLER RISE
RUBENS CL
CRES
VERMEER
HOGARTH DR
WAKERING RD
NEWELL AVE
PEEL AVE
CASTLE CL
BRODIE RD
BRODIE RD
SANDPIT RD
Suttons
SUTTONS RD
BOYCE RD
ROSSITER RD
Jetties
Pig's Bay
4
ELM RD
BLACKGATE RD
WALKEY WAY
WAKERING AVE
THE GOSLINGS
SOUTHCHURCH AVE
FRIARS ST
SHOEBURY AVE
HIGH ST
F Sta
GUNNERS RD
LC
Camping Site
P
P
Shoeburyness
85
TERMINAL CL
LC
GEORGE ST
JOHN ST
DANE ST
RAMPART TERR
RAMPART ST
Maplin Sands
Boom
3
84
2
83
1
82
94
95
96
A
B
C

195

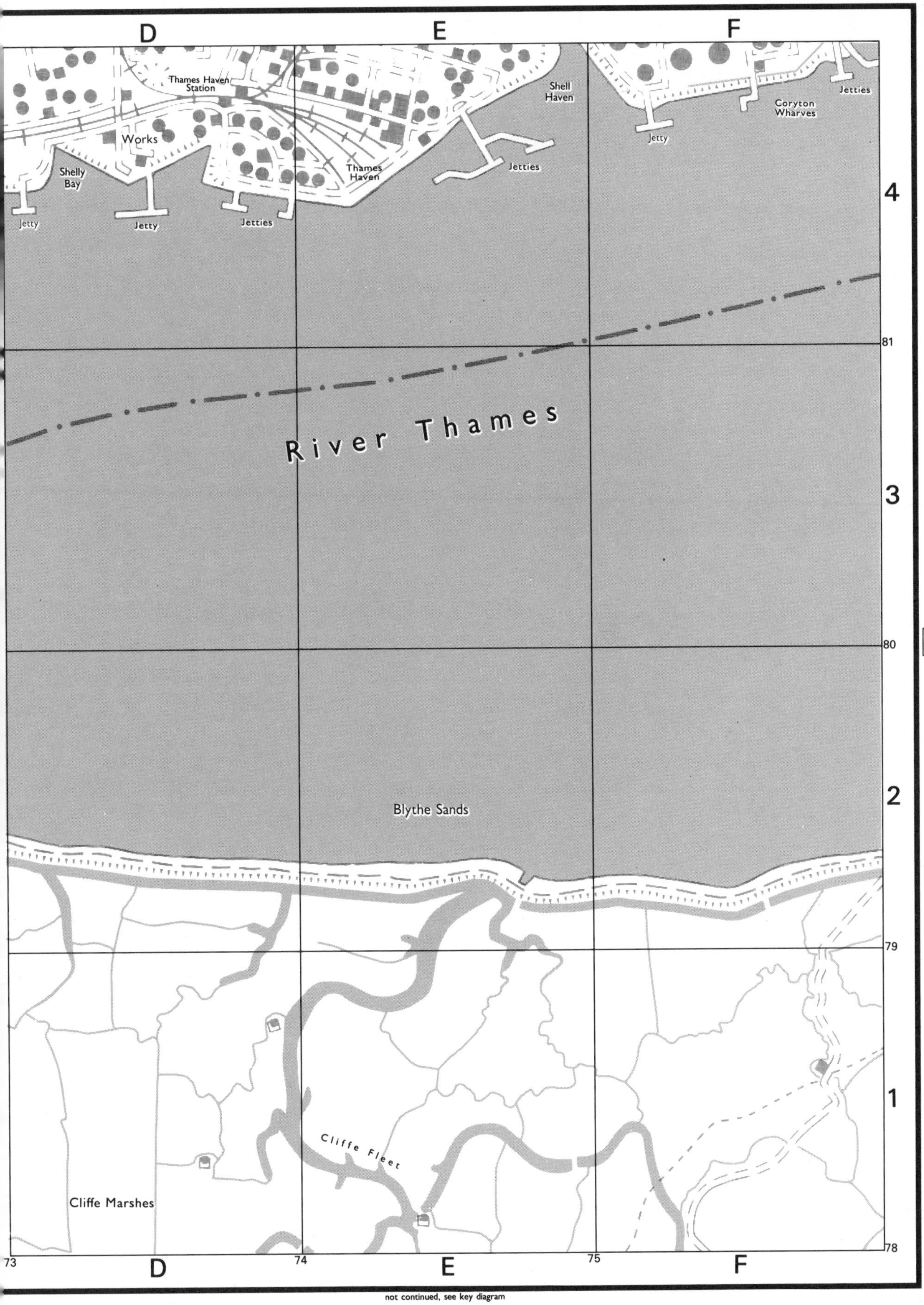
D
E
F
Thames Haven Station
Works
Shelly Bay
Jetty
Jetty
Jetties
Thames Haven
Jetties
Shell Haven
Jetty
Coryton Wharves
Jetties
4
81
River Thames
3
80
2
Blythe Sands
79
1
Cliffe Fleet
Cliffe Marshes
78
73
74
75
D
E
F

204

not continued, see key diagram

196

203

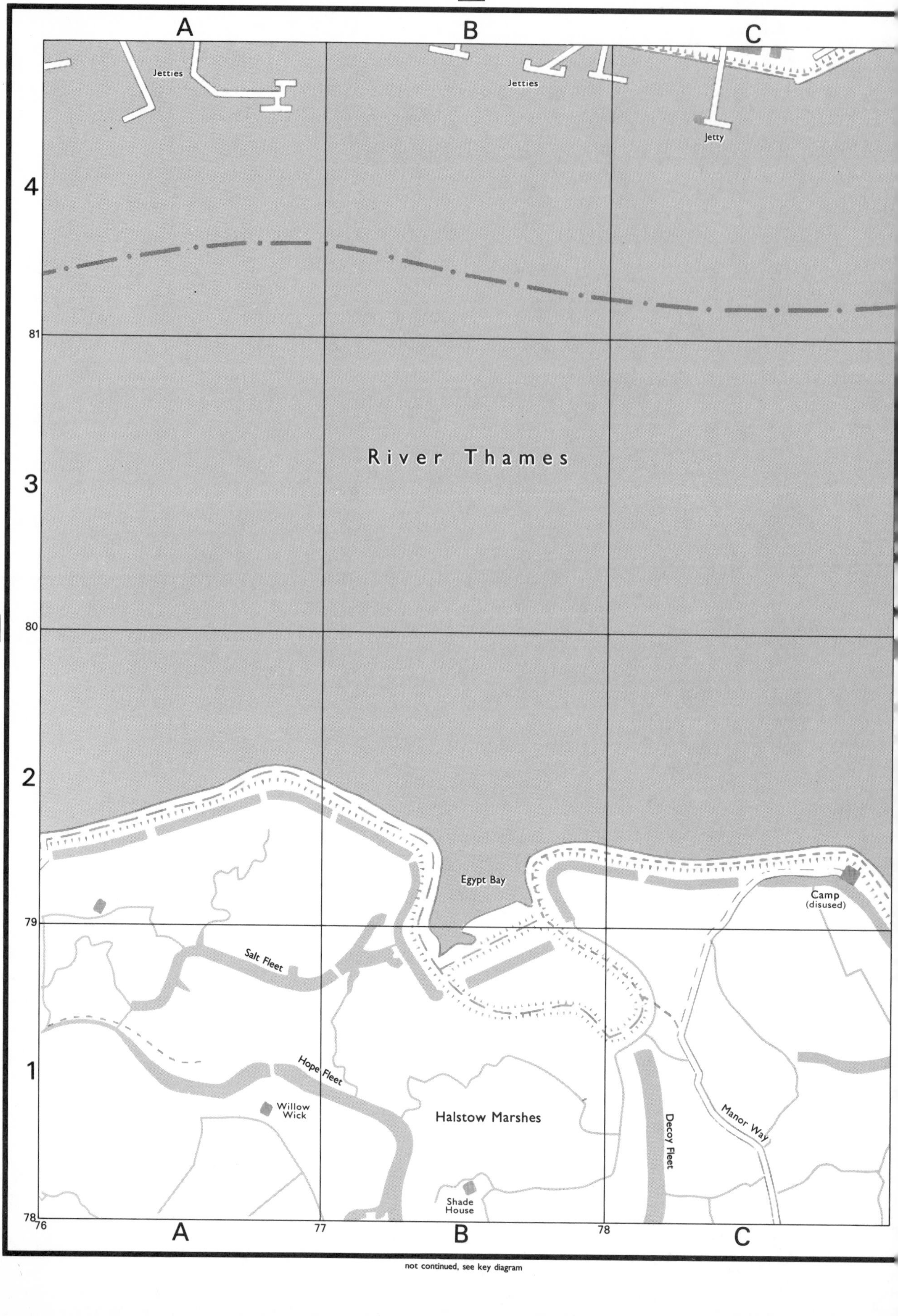
A
B
C
Jetties
Jetties
Jetty
4
3
2
1
81
80
79
78
River Thames
Egypt Bay
Camp
(disused)
Salt Fleet
Hope Fleet
Willow
Wick
Halstow Marshes
Decoy Fleet
Manor Way
Shade
House
76
77
78
A
B
C

not continued, see key diagram

JSER'S NOTES

EXPLANATION OF THE STREET INDEX REFERENCE SYSTEM

Street names are listed alphabetically and show the locality, the page number and a reference to the square in which the name falls on the map page.

Example:	Cedar Way. Gt Ben...89 F4
Cedar Way	This is the full street name, which may have been abbreviated on the map.
Gt Ben	This is the abbreviation for the town, village or locality in which the street falls.
89	This is the page number of the map on which the street name appears.
F4	The letter and figure indicate the square on the map in which the centre of the street falls. The square can be found at the junction of the vertical column carrying the appropriate letter and the horizontal row carrying the appropriate figure.

ABBREVIATIONS USED IN THE INDEX

Road Names

Approach....................................App
Avenue..Ave
Boulevard....................................Bvd
Broadway...................................Bwy
By-Pass...................................By-Ps
Causeway................................Cswy
Common................................Comm
Corner...Cnr
Cottages..................................Cotts
Court...Ct
Crescent...................................Cres
Drive...Dr
Drove..Dro
East..E
Gardens...................................Gdns
Grove...Gr
Heights..Hts
Lane..La
North..N
Orchard.....................................Orch
Parade...Par
Passage......................................Pas
Place..Pl
Pleasant....................................Plea
Precinct.....................................Prec
Promenade...............................Prom
Road...Rd
South..S
Square..Sq
Street,Saint...................................St
Terrace.......................................Terr
Walk..Wlk
West...W
Yard..Yd

Towns, Villages and Rural Localities

Boleyn Way. Bore 112 C1
Boleyn Way. Clact 124 C4
Boleyns Ave. Brain 59 F3
Bolls La. Lay H 84 C3
Bolney Dr. Rayl 189 E4
Bommel Ave. South 198 A2
Bonchurch Ave. South 189 E1
Bond St. Chelm 127 E1
Bonham Cl. Clact 110 A3
Bonington Chase. Sprin 127 F3
Bonnygate. Basil 185 E4
Boone Pl. With 98 A1
Booth Ave. Colch 68 B4
Borda Cl. Chelm 127 D3
Boreham Cl. Wick 175 D3
Boreham Rd. Gt Le 95 D2
Borley Rd. L Mel 7 D2
Borman Cl. South 190 A3
Borrett Ave. Canv 197 D2
Borrowdale Cl. Thund 187 F3
Borrowdale Rd. Thund 187 F3
Boscawen Gdns. Brain 60 B2
Boscombe Rd. South 191 D1
Boston Ave. Rayl 176 A2
Boston Ave. South 190 C1
Boswell Ave. Roch 178 B3
Boswells Dr. Chelm 127 E1
Bosworth Cl. Hawk 177 F2
Bosworth Rd. Rayl 189 E4
Botanical Way. St O 108 A3
Botany La. Weel 91 E3
Bouchers Mead. Sprin 127 F4
Bouldrewood Rd. S Ben 187 D3
Boulevard The. Roch 178 C2
Boulton Cotts. Mald 132 A3
Boundary Rd. Colch 68 C2
Boundary Rd. Rayl 189 D4
Bounderby Gr. Chelm 126 C3
Bounstead Hill. Lay H 85 E3
Bounstead Rd. Colch 85 E4
Bourchier Way. Hals 43 E4
Bourne Cl. Hals 43 E4
Bourne Rd. Colch 68 A2
Bourne Rd. W Berg 48 C1
Bournebridge Hill. Hals 43 D3
Bournemouth Park Rd. South 191 D1
Bournemouth Rd. Clact 110 C3
Bournes Green Chase. South 192 A1
Bouvel Dr. Burn 170 A4
Bouverie Rd. Chelm 140 A4
Bovingdon Rd. Brain 41 E1
Bovinger Way. South 191 F1
Bowbank Cl. South 192 C1
Bowdens La. Worm 29 F4
Bower Gdns. Mald 131 F2
Bower Hall La. W Mers 104 C1
Bower La. Basil 185 F4
Bowers Cl. Silv E 79 F2
Bowers Court Dr. Basil 186 C3
Bowers Rd. S Ben 187 E3
Bowes Rd. Elmst M 69 E1
Bowman Ave. Rayl 189 D3
Bowman's Park. Ca Hed 15 F2
Box Mill La. Hals 25 F2
Boxford Cl. Rayl 175 F2
Boxhouse La. Ded 33 E3
Boxted Church Rd. Gt Hor 31 E2
Boxted Rd. Colch 49 F3
Boxted Rd. Gt Hor 31 E2
Boyce Green. S Ben 187 E1
Boyce Hill Cl. Hadl 189 D3
Boyce Rd. South 202 A4
Boyce View Dr. S Ben 187 E1
Boyden Cl. South 191 F1
Boydin Cl. With 114 C4
Boyles Ct. Rowh 86 A4
Boyne Dr. Sprin 127 E3
Boyton Cl. Thund 187 F3
Brabant Rd. N Fam 167 D4
Brace Wlk. S Woo F 165 F3
Bracken Dell. Rayl 176 C1
Bracken The. Colch 50 A2
Bracken Way. Lang 86 A1
Bracken Way. Thund 188 A3
Brackendale Ave. Basil 186 B2
Brackendale Cl. Hock 177 F4
Brackenden Dr. Sprin 127 E4
Brackley Cres. Basil 174 A1
Bradbourne Way. Basil 186 B3
Bradbrook Cotts. W Berg 48 C2
Bradbury Dr. Brain 59 E2
Bradfield Rd. Wix 55 D4
Bradford St. Brain 60 A3
Bradford St. Chelm 127 D1
Bradfordbury. Hadl 189 E3
Brading Ave. Clact 110 A4
Bradley Ave. Thund 187 F3
Bradley Cl. Canv 197 D3
Bradley Cl. Thund 187 F3
Bradley Green. Basil 174 B1
Bradley Hill. Ovi 4 A3
Bradley Way. Roch 178 C1
Bradleyhall La. Th L S 73 E2
Bradwell Ct. Brain 78 B4
Bradwell Rd. Brad O S 149 D4
Bradwell Rd. St L 148 C3
Bradwell Rd. Steep 148 A2
Bradwell Rd. Till 149 F3
Braemar Ave. Chelm 140 A4
Braemar Cres. Hadl 189 D1
Braemore Cl. Colch 50 B2
Braemore. Canv 196 C3
Braggon's Hill. Glems 2 A4
Brain Rd. With 97 F2
Brain Valley Ave. Bl Not 78 A3
Braintree Rd. Gos 42 C3
Braintree Rd. T Gr 78 C4
Braintree Rd. Terl 96 A2
Braintree Rd. With 97 F2
Braiswick La. Colch 49 E2
Braiswick. Colch 49 D1
Bramble Cl. Rayl 189 D4
Bramble Cres. Hadl 189 D3
Bramble Rd. Canv 197 E2
Bramble Rd. Hadl 188 C3
Bramble Rd. Rayl 189 D4
Bramble Rd. With 97 F2
Brambles The. Colch 66 C2
Brambles. Walt 94 A4
Bramerton Rd. Hock 177 E3
Bramfield Rd E. Rayl 177 D1
Bramfield Rd W. Rayl 176 C1
Bramley Cl. Alres 88 A4
Bramley Cl. Brain 60 A1
Bramley Cl. Colch 67 D4
Bramley Way. May 146 C1
Bramleys The. Cogg 63 D2
Bramleys The. Hawk 178 B3
Brampton Cl. South 190 A2
Bramston Green. With 97 F2
Bramston Wlk. With 97 F2
Bramstone Cl. Gt Bad 140 C4
Bramwoods Rd. Gt Bad 140 C4
Branch Rd. Hadl 188 C1
Brandenburg Rd. Canv 197 E3
Brandon Rd. Brain 59 E1
Brands Cl. Sud 13 E3
Branksome Ave. Hock 177 F4
Branksome Rd. South 191 E1
Branscombe Cl. Frin 93 F3
Branscombe Gdns. South 201 D4
Branscombe Sq. South 192 A1
Branscombe Wlk. South 192 A1
Branston Rd. Clact 109 E2
Brantham Hill. Catt 35 E4
Braxted Cl. Hawk 178 B2
Braxted La. Gt Tot 116 B4
Braxted Rd. Gt Brx 99 E1
Braxted Rd. Lit Brx 116 A3
Bray Ct. South 192 C1
Braybrooke. Basil 185 D3
Brays La. Roch 178 C3
Braziers Cl. Chelm 140 B2
Breachfield Rd. Colch 67 E1
Bread and Cheese Hill. Thund 187 F3
Bream Ct. Colch 50 C1
Brecon Cl. Basil 186 B4
Bree Ave. Mks T 64 C2
Bree Hill. S Woo F 165 E3
Brempsons. Basil 185 D4
Brendon Pl. Chelm 126 C1
Brendon Way. South 190 A3
Brent Ave. S Woo F 154 B1
Brent Cl. Walt 93 F4
Brent Cl. With 97 F1
Brentwood Rd. Clact 110 B3
Bressingham Gdns. S Woo F 165 E4
Brettenham Dr. South 200 C4
Bretts Bldgs. Colch 68 A3
Brewster Cl. Canv 197 D2
Brian Bishop Cl. Walt 76 B2
Brian Cl. Chelm 140 A3
Briar Cl. Hawk 177 F2
Briar Rd. Gt Bro 52 A2
Briardale Ave. Harw 39 F2
Briarfields. Walt 93 E4
Briarswood. Canv 197 D3
Briarswood. Sprin 127 E4
Briarwood Ave. Clact 110 C3
Briarwood Cl. South 189 E3
Briarwood Dr. South 189 F3
Briarwood End. Colch 50 A2
Briary The. Wick 174 A4
Brices Way. Glems 2 A3
Brick House La. Bore 112 C1
Brick House Rd. Toll M 117 D4
Brick Kiln Cl. Cogg 63 D2
Brick Kiln La. Alres 88 C3
Brick Kiln La. Gt Hor 49 E4
Brick Kiln Rd. Colch 49 F1
Brick Kiln Rd. Sand 141 E4
Brick St. E A Gr 48 A1
Brickfield Rd. Basil 185 E1
Brickfields Rd. S Woo F 165 F4
Brickfields Way. Roch 179 D1
Brickhouse Cl. W Mers 121 D4
Brickhouse Rd. Col En 27 D2
Brickman's Hill. Brad 36 B2
Brickspring La. Gt Tot 116 B4
Brickwall Cl. Burn 170 A2
Bridewell St. Cla 4 A4
Bridge Cl. South 201 F4
Bridge Hall Rd. Bradw 61 E2
Bridge Hill. Ford 47 E4
Bridge House Cl. Wick 174 B4
Bridge Pl. Catt 35 E4
Bridge Rd. Wick 175 D4
Bridge St. Bures 19 F1
Bridge St. Cogg 62 C1
Bridge St. Gt Y 9 D1
Bridge St. Hals 25 F1
Bridge St. With 97 F1
Bridge St. Writ 126 B1
Bridgebrook Cl. Colch 50 B1
Bridgefield Cl. Colch 68 B4
Bridgemans Green. Latch 157 D3
Bridgemarsh La. Alth 168 C4
Bridgend Cl. S Woo F 165 F4
Bridgewater Dr. South 190 A2
Bridgewick Rd. Deng 161 D3
Bridon Cl. E Han 153 D3
Bridport Rd. Sprin 127 E3
Bridport Way. Brain 60 B2
Brierley Ave. W Mers 121 F4
Bright Cl. Clact 109 E3
Brighten Rd. South 199 F4
Brightlingsea Rd. Thor 88 C2
Brightlingsea Rd. Wiv 69 E2
Brighton Ave. South 200 B4
Brighton Rd. Clact 110 C3
Brightside. Walt 93 F4
Brightwell Ave. South 190 B1
Brindles. Canv 196 C3
Brindley Rd. Clact 110 A4
Bringey The. Gt Bad 141 D3
Brinkley Cres. Colch 50 B1
Brinkley La. Colch 50 B3
Brinkworth Cl. Hock 177 F3
Brisbane Way. Colch 68 A1
Briscoe Rd. Basil 186 A4
Brise Cl. Brain 60 A1
Bristol Cl. Rayl 176 B3
Bristol Ct. Silv E 79 F2
Bristol Hill. Sho G 40 A4
Bristol Rd. Colch 68 A4
Bristol Rd. South 190 B3
Bristowe Ave. Gt Bad 141 D3
Britannia Cr. Wiv 69 D1
Britannia Ct. Basil 174 B1
Britannia Gdns. South 199 E4
Britannia Rd. South 199 E4
Brittany Way. Colch 68 A2
Britten Cl. Colch 68 C3
Britten Cres. Gt Bad 140 C4
Brixham Cl. Rayl 176 B3
Broad Cl. Hock 177 F3
Broad Green. Basil 185 E4
Broad La. Gt Hor 31 D1
Broad Oak Way. Rayl 176 C1
Broad Oaks Park. Colch 50 C1
Broad Oaks. Wick 174 C3
Broad Par. Hock 177 F3
Broad Rd. Brain 60 A4
Broad Rd. Wic S P 17 D4
Broad Street Green Rd. Gt Tot 116 A1
Broad Street Green Rd. Mald 132 B4
Broad Way. Hock 177 F3
Broad Wlk. Hock 177 F3
Broadclyst Ave. South 189 E3
Broadclyst Cl. South 192 A1
Broadclyst Gdns. South 192 A1
Broadfields. Wiv 69 E2
Broadlands Ave. Hock 177 F3
Broadlands Ave. Rayl 176 B2
Broadlands Rd. Hock 177 F3
Broadlands Way. Colch 50 A1
Broadlands. Thund 187 F3
Broadlawn. Hadl 189 D2
Broadmayne. Basil 185 E3
Broadmead Rd. Colch 50 C4
Broadmere Cl. Clact 110 C4
Broadstrood. St O 108 A3
Broadwater Gdns. Sho G 40 A4
Broadway Ct. Silv E 79 E3
Broadway North. Basil 186 A3
Broadway The. Runw 174 B4
Broadway The. South 201 D4
Broadway W. South 198 B4
Broadway. Clact 125 D4
Broadway. Glems 2 A3
Broadway. Silv E 79 E2
Broadway. South 198 B4
Brock Cl. With 114 C4
Brock Hill Dr. Runw 163 E2
Brock Hill. Runw 163 E2
Brockenhurst Way. S Woo F . 142 C1
Brockham Cl. Clact 109 D3
Brockley Rd. Chelm 127 E1
Brocksford Ave. Rayl 176 C1
Brockwell La. Kelv 81 E1
Brockwell Wlk. Wick 174 B3
Brodie Rd. South 202 A4
Brograve Cl. Chelm 140 B2
Broman's La. E Mers 106 A1
Bromfords Cl. Wick 174 A3
Bromfords Dr. Wick 174 B3
Bromley Rd. Ard 51 E2
Bromley Rd. Colch 50 C1
Bromley Rd. Elmst M 70 A3
Bromley Rd. Frat 71 D2
Bromley Rd. Lawf 35 D1
Brompton Gdns. Mald 144 C4
Bronte Cl. Brain 78 A4
Bronte Mews. South 191 D1
Bronte Rd. With 97 F3
Brook Cl. Brain 59 E1
Brook Cl. Gt Tot 116 A2
Brook Cl. Roch 191 D4
Brook Cl. Tipt 100 C2
Brook Cl. Woo Wa 130 B1
Brook Dr. Basil 185 E1
Brook Dr. Wick 174 B3
Brook End Rd. Sprin 128 A2
Brook Farm Cl. Hals 26 A1
Brook Hall Rd. Fing 87 D3
Brook La. Chelm 140 C2
Brook La. Sprin 128 A1
Brook La. W Han 140 C2
Brook Meadow. Si Hed 15 E1
Brook Pl. Hals 25 F1
Brook Rd. Ald 65 D4
Brook Rd. Gt T 64 B4
Brook Rd. Rayl 188 B4
Brook Rd. S Ben 187 E1
Brook Rd. Till 149 E3
Brook Rd. Toll K 101 D1
Brook St. Col En 26 C1
Brook St. Colch 68 A4
Brook St. Ded 33 F4
Brook St. Glems 2 A3
Brook St. Gt Bro 52 C1
Brook St. Mann 35 E2
Brook St. Wiv 87 D4
Brook Terr. Si Hed 15 F1
Brook Vale. St O 108 A2
Brook View. Sand 141 E3
Brook Wlk. With 114 C4
Brooke Sq. Mald 132 A1
Brookfields Cl. South 189 E3
Brookfields. South 189 E3
Brookhouse Rd. Gt T 64 A4
Brookhurst Cl. Sprin 127 E2
Brookland. Tipt 100 B2
Brooklands Ave. South 189 F3
Brooklands Gdns. Clact 124 C3
Brooklands Rd. Catt 35 E4
Brooklands Rise. Catt 35 E4
Brooklands Sq. Canv 196 C2
Brooklands Wlk. Chelm 140 A4
Brooklands. Clact 124 C3
Brooklands. Wick 174 A4
Brooklyn Dr. Rayl 176 B3
Brooklyn Rd. Harw 40 B2
Brookside Ave. Gt Wak 193 E1
Brookside Cl. Colch 68 A2
Brookside. Canv 197 D3
Brookside. Hawk 177 F2
Broom Hill. Hals 25 F1
Broom Rd. Hull 165 F1
Broom St. Sud 13 D3
Broom Way. Lang 86 A1
Broome Gr. Wiv 69 D1
Broomfield Ave. Rayl 176 A2
Broomfield Ave. South 189 F3
Broomfield Cres. Wiv 69 D1
Broomfield Green. Canv 196 C3
Broomfield Rd. Chelm 127 D3
Broomfield. Hadl 188 B2
Broomfield. Silv E 79 E3
Broomfields. Basil 186 A3
Broomhills Rd. W Mers 121 E3
Broomways. Gt Wak 193 E2
Broton Dr. Hals 25 F1
Brougham Cl. Gt Wak 193 D2
Brougham Glades. Stanw 66 B3
Broughton Cl. Colch 67 E2
Broughton Rd. Hadl 188 C1
Broughton Rd. S Woo F 165 F3
Browning Ave. South 191 D1
Browning Cl. Colch 66 C3
Browning Rd. Brain 78 A4
Browning Rd. Mald 145 D4
Brownings Ave. Chelm 127 D3
Brownlow Bend. Basil 185 E3
Brownlow Cross. Basil 185 E3
Brownlow Green. Basil 185 E3
Browns Ave. Runw 163 F1
Brownsea Way. Colch 67 D2
Broxted Dr. Wick 174 C3
Broxted End. Wick 174 C3
Bruce Gr. Chelm 140 A4
Bruce Gr. Wick 175 D4
Bruce Rd. Writ 126 A1
Bruff Dr. Walt 94 A4
Bruges Rd. Canv 197 E1
Brundells Rd. Gt Bro 71 D3
Brundish. Basil 186 A3
Brundon La. Sud 12 B4
Brunel Rd. Brain 60 A1
Brunel Rd. Clact 110 A4
Brunel Rd. South 189 E3
Brunel Rd. Thund 187 E4
Brunel Way. Colch 50 B3
Brunel Way. S Woo F 165 E4
Brunswick House Cut. Mist 36 A2
Brunswick Rd. South 200 B4
Brunwins Cl. Wick 174 C4
Brussum Rd. Canv 197 E1
Brust Rd. Canv 197 E1
Bruton Ave. South 190 A3
Bryanstone Mews. Colch 66 C3
Bryant Ave. South 200 C3
Bryant's La. Woo Mor 143 E4
Bryce Way. Basil 186 B3
Buchan Cl. Brain 78 A4
Buchanan Way. Latch 157 D3
Buck Hill. Bl Not 77 F3
Buckeridge Way. Brad O S .... 137 D
Buckerills. Basil 186 A3
Buckfast Ave. Walt 93 E3
Buckhatch La. Rett 153 E2
Buckingham Dr. Colch 68 C4
Buckingham Rd. Hock 177 E3
Buckingham Sq. Wick 175 D3
Buckland Gate. S Woo F 165 E3
Buckland. South 192 B1
Bucklebury Heath. S Woo F 165 E3
Buckley's La. Gt T 63 E3
Buckleys Cl. Wic Bis 115 F3
Buckleys. Gt Bad 140 C4
Buckwins Sq. Basil 174 B1
Buckwoods Rd. Brain 60 A1
Buddleia Ct. Wiv 69 D1
Budna Rd. Canv 196 C3
Buffett Way. Colch 68 C3
Buglers Rise. Writ 139 D4
Buick Ave. Clact 124 B3
Bulbecks Wlk. S Woo F 165 E3
Bulford La. Bl Not 78 B3
Bulford Mill La. T Gr 78 B3
Bull Hill Rd. Clact 109 F3
Bull La. Hock 177 E3
Bull La. L Mel 7 E4
Bull La. Mald 132 A2
Bull La. Rayl 176 C1
Bull La. Tipt 100 B2
Bull's Hill. Ca Hed 15 F2
Bullace Cl. Colch 50 B2
Bullen Wlk. Chelm 140 B2
Buller Rd. N Fam 156 A1
Bullfinch Cl. Colch 68 C4
Bullock Wood Cl. Colch 50 B2
Bullocks La. Sud 12 C3
Bullwood App. Hock 177 D3
Bullwood Hall La. Rayl 177 D2
Bullwood Rd. Hock 177 E3
Bulmer Rd. Sud 12 B3
Bulmer St. Bul 11 E2
Bulow Ave. Canv 197 D2
Bulphan Cl. Wick 174 C3
Bulwark Rd. South 201 F4
Bumfords La. Hat Per 130 A4
Bumfords La. Ult 130 A4
Bundick's Hill. Chelm 126 C2
Bung Row. Gt Brx 99 E1
Bunters Ave. South 201 E3
Bunting Cl. Chelm 140 A3
Bunyan Rd. Brain 59 F2
Burches Mead. Thund 188 A4
Burches Rd. Thund 187 F4
Burdett Ave. South 199 F4
Burdett Rd. South 200 B4
Burdun Cl. With 114 B4
Bure Dr. With 97 E2
Buren Ave. Canv 197 F2
Bures Rd. Bures 30 A4
Bures Rd. Sud 13 D2
Burfield Cl. South 189 F3
Burfield Rd. South 189 F3
Burgate Cl. Clact 109 D2
Burges Cl. South 201 E3
Burges Rd. South 201 D3
Burges Terr. South 200 C3
Burgess Field. Sprin 127 F2
Burgundy Gdns. Basil 186 A4
Burkitts La. Sud 12 C4
Burleigh Sq. South 201 D4
Burlescoombe Cl. South 201 D4
Burlescoombe Leas. South 192 A1
Burlescoombe Rd. South 192 A1
Burlington Ct. Basil 174 A1
Burlington Gdns. Hadl 188 C2
Burlington Gdns. Hull 176 C4
Burlington Rd. Colch 67 F3
Burmanny Cl. Clact 109 E2
Burnaby Rd. South 200 B4
Burne Ave. Wick 174 A3
Burnham Ave. Col N 156 A3
Burnham Cl. Walt 94 A4
Burnham Rd. Alth 158 A1
Burnham Rd. Hull 165 F1
Burnham Rd. Latch 157 E3
Burnham Rd. Mund 156 B4
Burnham Rd. S Woo F 154 B1
Burnham Rd. Soum 159 E1
Burnham Rd. South 189 E1
Burnham Rd. Sprin 127 E3
Burnham Rd. Woo Mor 143 F3
Burns Ave. Basil 186 A3
Burns Ave. Colch 66 C3
Burns Cl. Mald 132 A1
Burns Cres. Chelm 140 B4
Burns Green. Gt Tot 116 A2
Burnside Cres. Chelm 127 D4
Burnside. Canv 197 D3
Burnt Dick Hill. Box 31 F4
Burnt Mills Rd. Basil 174 B1
Burnthouse Rd. Ea Col 45 F1
Burr Cl. Lit Oak 39 E1
Burr Hill Chase. South 190 C2
Burroughs Piece Rd. Sud 12 C4
Burrow's Rd. Ea Col 45 D4
Burrows Cl. Clact 109 E3
Burrows Cl. Lawf 35 D2
Burrows Way. Rayl 176 B1

Estella Mead. Chelm 126 C4
Estuary Cres. Sho G 40 A4
Estuary Gdns. Gt Wak 193 E1
Estuary Mews. Tolle 119 E1
Estuary Park Rd. W Mers 121 F3
Estuary Rd. Sho G 40 A4
Ethel Rd. Rayl 189 D4
Ethelbert Rd. Ashi 167 E1
Etheldore Ave. Hock 177 F4
Ethelred Gdns. Runw 163 E1
Eton Cl. Canv 197 D3
Eton Rd. Clact 109 F2
Eton Rd. Frin 94 A3
Eton Wlk. South 192 C1
Eudo Rd. Colch 67 E2
Europa Way. Rams 39 F2
Evelyn Rd. Hock 177 F3
Evelyn Wood Rd. T Gr 78 C3
Everard Rd. Basil 186 A4
Everest Way. Mald 132 A3
Everest. Rayl 176 B3
Evergreen Dr. Colch 50 B2
Everitt Way. Si Hed 15 F1
Eversley Rd. Basil 186 B3
Eversley Rd. Thund 187 E4
Eves Cnr. Burn 170 A4
Eves Cres. Chelm 127 D3
Eves Ct. Harw 39 E1
Ewan Cl. Hadl 189 D2
Ewan Cl. Stanw 66 B3
Ewan Way. Hadl 189 D2
Ewan Way. Stanw 66 B4
Ewell Hall Chase. Kelv 81 E1
Exchange Way. Chelm 127 D1
Exeter Cl. Basil 185 F4
Exeter Cl. Brain 60 A3
Exeter Cl. Gt Hor 49 D4
Exeter Cl. South 192 C1
Exeter Dr. Colch 68 A4
Exeter Rd. Sprin 127 F3
Exford Ave. South 190 A2
Exhibition La. Gt Wak 192 C2
Exmoor Cl. Chelm 126 B1
Exmouth Dr. Rayl 176 B3
Eynesham Way. Basil 174 A1

Faber Rd. With 114 C4
Fabians Cl. Cogg 63 D2
Factory Hill. Tipt 100 C2
Factory La E. Hals 25 F1
Factory La W. Hals 25 F1
Factory Terr. Hals 25 F1
Faggots Yd. Brain 59 F3
Fair Cl. Brigh 107 D3
Fair Green. Glems 2 A3
Fair Mead. Basil 185 E4
Fairfax Ave. Basil 186 B4
Fairfax Dr. South 190 B1
Fairfax Mead. Sprin 127 F1
Fairfax Rd. Colch 67 F3
Fairfield Cres. South 189 F3
Fairfield Gdns. South 189 F3
Fairfield Rd. Brain 59 F1
Fairfield Rd. Chelm 127 D2
Fairfield Rd. Clact 109 F2
Fairfield Rd. South 189 F4
Fairfield. Gt Wak 193 D2
Fairhaven Ave. W Mers 121 F3
Fairhead Rd. Colch 68 B4
Fairhouse Ct. Basil 185 E3
Fairland Cl. Rayl 176 C3
Fairlawn Gdns. South 190 C3
Fairleads. Dan 142 C4
Fairleigh Ave. Basil 186 B3
Fairleigh Dr. South 189 E1
Fairleigh Rd. Basil 186 B3
Fairlight Rd. S Ben 188 B2
Fairlop Cl. Clact 109 F4
Fairlop Cres. Canv 197 D2
Fairlop Gdns. Basil 185 E3
Fairmead Ave. Hadl 188 C3
Fairmead Ave. South 190 B1
Fairmead. Rayl 176 A2
Fairstead Hall Rd. Fair 96 A3
Fairstead Rd. Fair 96 B3
Fairstead Rd. Terl 96 B2
Fairstead. Basil 185 D3
Fairview Cl. Thund 187 E4
Fairview Cres. Thund 187 E4
Fairview Dr. South 190 B2
Fairview Gdns. Hadl 189 E1
Fairview Rd. Basil 185 F3
Fairview Wlk. Thund 187 E4
Fairview. Canv 196 C3
Fairway Dr. Burn 170 A3
Fairway Gdns Cl. South 189 E3
Fairway Gdns. South 189 E3
Fairway The. South 189 E3
Fairway The. Thund 187 E4
Fairway. Gt Bad 140 B4
Fairway. Wick 174 B2
Fairways The. Col N 155 F3
Fairy Hall La. Ray 59 D1
Fal Dr. With 97 F1
Falbro Cres. Hadl 188 B2
Falcon Cl. South 189 F3
Falcon Cres. Colch 68 A3
Falcon Fields. Mald 144 C4
Falcon Mews. Mald 144 C4
Falcon Rd. Soum 159 E2
Falcon Sq. Ca Hed 15 F2
Falcon Way. Basil 185 E2
Falcon Way. Chelm 140 A3
Falcon Way. Clact 109 F3
Falcon Way. South 192 C1
Falcon Yd. Wiv 87 D4
Falkenham End. Basil 185 E4
Falkenham Path. Basil 185 E4
Falkenham Rise. Basil 185 E4
Falkenham Row. Basil 185 E4
Falkland Cl. Bore 128 C4
Falklands Dr. Mann 35 E2
Falklands Rd. Burn 170 A3
Fallowfield Cl. Harw 39 F2
Fallowfield Rd. Colch 67 E1
Fallows The. Canv 196 C3
Falmouth Rd. Sprin 127 F3
Fambridge Chase. Wh Not 78 C1
Fambridge Cl. Mald 132 A1
Fambridge Dr. Wick 174 C3
Fambridge Rd. Alth 157 F1
Fambridge Rd. Ashi 167 E2
Fambridge Rd. Col N 156 A2
Fambridge Rd. Mald 156 A2
Fambridge Rd. N Fam 156 A2
Fambridge Rd. Purl 156 A2
Fane Rd. Thund 187 E4
Fanny's La. St O 90 B1
Fanton Ave. Wick 174 C2
Fanton Chase. Wick 175 D3
Fanton Wlk. Wick 175 D3
Faraday Cl. Brain 59 F1
Faraday Cl. Clact 110 A4
Faraday Rd. South 189 E3
Farford Field. Sud 13 E3
Farm Cres. Rett 164 C2
Farm Rd. Canv 197 D3
Farm Rd. Gt Oak 56 B2
Farm View. Rayl 176 B3
Farm Way. Thund 188 A3
Farm Wlk. Brigh 106 C4
Farmers Way. Clact 109 D2
Farmfield Rd. Gt T 46 A1
Farmleigh Ave. Clact 109 F4
Farnes Ave. Wick 174 B4
Farriers End. Stanw 66 B3
Farriers Way. South 190 C3
Farrington Way. Lawf 35 D2
Farrow Rd. Chelm 139 F4
Farthing Centre The. Chelm 127 D1
Fastnet. South 190 A4
Faulkbourne Rd. Faulk 97 E2
Faulkbourne Rd. With 97 E2
Fauners. Basil 185 D3
Fawkner Cl. Sprin 127 F1
Featherby Way. Roch 179 D1
Feeches Rd. South 190 B3
Feedhams Cl. Wiv 69 E2
Feering Dr. Basil 185 F3
Feering Green. Basil 185 F3
Feering Hill. Fee 81 E2
Feering Rd. Fee 63 D1
Feering Row. Basil 185 F3
Felixstowe Cl. Clact 109 D2
Fellcroft. Basil 186 B3
Felmores. Basil 186 A4
Felstead Cl. Colch 86 A4
Felstead Cl. S Ben 187 E2
Felstead Rd. S Ben 187 E3
Fen La. Ard 33 E1
Fen St. Nay 20 A1
Fenn Cl. S Woo F 165 E4
Fenn Rd. Hals 26 A1
Fennell Cl. Tipt 100 B3
Fennes Rd. Brain 41 F1
Fennfields Rd. S Woo F 165 D4
Fennings Chase. Colch 68 A4
Fenno Cl. Colch 66 C2
Fenwick Way. Canv 197 D3
Ferdinand Wlk. Colch 68 C4
Fermoy Rd. South 201 D4
Fern Hill. Glems 2 A4
Fern Way. Clact 124 C4
Fernbrook Ave. South 200 B4
Ferndale Cl. Clact 109 F4
Ferndale Cres. Canv 197 D1
Ferndale Rd. Harw 40 B3
Ferndale Rd. Rayl 176 C3
Ferndale Rd. South 191 E1
Ferndown Rd. Frin 93 F3
Ferndown Way. Hat Pev 114 A2
Fernie Rd. Brain 59 E1
Fernlea Rd. Burn 170 A3
Fernlea Rd. Harw 40 B3
Fernlea Rd. S Ben 187 F2
Fernlea. Colch 49 E1
Fernleigh Dr. South 190 A1
Fernwood Ave. Clact 110 C3
Fernwood. Hadl 188 C2
Ferrers Rd. S Woo F 165 E3
Ferris Ave. Col N 155 F3
Ferry Rd. Burn 169 F3
Ferry Rd. Canv 196 B4
Ferry Rd. Fing 87 D3
Ferry Rd. Hull 165 E1
Ferry Rd. N Fam 167 D3
Ferrymead. Canv 196 C3
Festival Gdns. Toll D 118 B2
Feverills Rd. Lit Cla 91 E2
Fiat Ave. Clact 124 B3
Fiddlers Folly. E A Gr 47 F1
Fiddlers Hill. E A Gr 47 F1
Field Way. Wiv 69 E1
Field Wlk. Walt 94 A4
Fields Cl. Weel 90 C3
Fields Farm Rd. Lay H 85 D2
Fieldway. Basil 186 B2
Fieldway. Wick 174 B2
Fifth Ave. Canv 196 C2
Fifth Ave. Chelm 127 D3
Fifth Ave. Frin 93 F3
Fifth Ave. Wick 175 D3
Filey Rd. Soum 159 D2
Fillebrook Ave. South 190 A1
Filliol Cl. E Han 153 D3
Finch Dr. Gt Ben 71 E1
Finch Hill. Bul 12 A4
Finch's. Lit Brx 115 F3
Finchdale. Clact 109 F3
Finches The. Thund 188 A4
Finchfield. Rayl 176 B1
Finchingfield Way. Colch 86 A4
Finchingfield Way. Wick 174 B3
Finchland View. S Woo F 165 E3
Finchley Ave. Chelm 140 A4
Finchley Rd. South 199 E4
Finer Cl. Clact 109 E3
Fingringhoe Rd. Colch 68 B1
Fingringhoe Rd. Lang 86 A2
Finham Cl. Colch 68 C4
Fir Tree Cl. Colch 50 A2
Fir Tree La. Lit Bad 129 F1
Fir Tree Rise. Chelm 140 A3
Fir Tree Wlk. Mald 132 B3
Fir Way. Clact 125 D3
Fir Wlk. Canv 196 C3
Firecrest Rd. Chelm 140 B3
Firecrest Rd. Gt Bad 140 B3
Firfield Rd. Thund 188 B3
Firlie Wlk. Colch 68 A1
Firmins Ct. W Berg 48 B2
Firs Chase. W Mers 121 D3
Firs Dr. Writ 126 A1
Firs Hamlet. W Mers 121 D3
Firs Rd. Tipt 100 B2
Firs Rd. W Mers 121 D4
Firs The. Canv 196 C3
Firs The. Lay H 85 D3
First Ave. Canv 196 C2
First Ave. Chelm 127 D3
First Ave. Clact 110 A2
First Ave. Frin 93 F2
First Ave. Glems 2 B3
First Ave. Hals 26 A1
First Ave. Harw 40 B2
First Ave. Hull 165 F1
First Ave. South 199 D4
First Ave. Walt 76 B2
First Ave. Weel 72 C1
First Ave. Wick 175 D3
Firstore Dr. Colch 66 C4
Firwood's Rd. Hals 43 F4
Fish St. Gold 133 F3
Fisher Way. Brain 60 B2
Fishponds Hill. Lit Hor 30 C2
Fisin Wlk. Colch 66 C2
Fitch's Cres. Mald 132 A1
Fitzgerald Cl. Lawf 35 D2
Fitzgilbert Rd. Colch 67 E2
Fitzwalter La. Dan 142 B3
Fitzwalter Pl. Chelm 126 C2
Fitzwalter Rd. Bore 128 C4
Fitzwalter Rd. Colch 67 D3
Fitzwarren. South 192 B1
Fitzwilliam Rd. Colch 67 D4
Five Acres. S Woo F 142 C2
Five Acres. Walt 94 A4
Fiveash La. Bradw 61 F1
Flag Hill. St O 89 F1
Flagstaff Rd. Colch 67 F3
Flail Cl. Elmst M 69 F3
Flambird's Chase. Purl 154 C4
Flamboro Cl. South 189 E3
Flamboro Wlk. South 189 E3
Flanders Cl. Brain 59 F3
Flanders Field. Colch 68 A2
Flatford Dr. Clact 109 D3
Flatford Rd. Str S M 34 B4
Flax La. Glems 2 B2
Fleet Rd. S Ben 187 E1
Fleetway. Basil 185 F2
Fleetwood Ave. Clact 110 C4
Fleetwood Ave. South 190 B1
Fleetwood Cl. Clact 110 C4
Fleming Cl. Brain 59 F1
Flemings Farm Rd. Rayl 189 E4
Flemming Ave. South 189 E1
Flemming Cres. South 189 E2
Fletchers Sq. South 191 D3
Flintwich Manor. Chelm 126 C4
Flixton Cl. Clact 109 D2
Flora Rd. With 97 E2
Florence Cl. Hadl 188 B2
Florence Gdns. Hadl 188 B2
Florence Neale House. Canv 197 D2
Florence Rd. Canv 197 E2
Florence Rd. Walt 76 C1
Florie's Rd. Gt T 63 F4
Flowers Way. Clact 125 D4
Fobbing Farm Cl. Basil 185 D2
Fodderwick. Basil 185 D3
Foksville Rd. Canv 197 E2
Fold The. Basil 185 D3
Folkards La. Brigh 106 C4
Folley The. Lay H 85 D3
Folley The. Stanw 66 B3
Folly Chase. Hock 177 D3
Folly La. Hock 177 D3
Folly The. Toll K 100 C1
Folly The. Wiv 87 D4
Ford La. Alres 88 A3
Ford La. Colch 49 E3
Ford Rd. Clact 109 E2
Ford St. Ald 47 E1
Fordham Rd. Ford 29 F1
Fordham Rd. M Bure 28 C1
Fordham Rd. Worm 29 F1
Fordson Rd. Bore 128 A3
Fordstreet Hill. Ald 47 E1
Fordwich Rd. Brigh 88 C1
Forefield Green. Sprin 127 F4
Foresight Rd. Colch 68 B1
Forest Dr. Chelm 126 C1
Forest Park Ave. Clact 109 F4
Forest Rd. Colch 68 B4
Forest Rd. With 98 A3
Forest View Dr. Hadl 189 D2
Forfar Cl. Hadl 189 E1
Forfields Way. T Gr 78 C3
Forge Cres. Bradw 61 E2
Forge St. Ded 34 A3
Forrest Cl. S Woo F 165 E4
Forsythia Cl. Sprin 127 F4
Fort William Rd. Basil 185 D1
Fortescue Chase. South 191 F1
Fortune Cl. Gt Le 95 D4
Fossetts La. Ford 47 F2
Fostal Cl. South 189 F2
Foster Rd. Canv 197 E2
Foster Rd. Gt Tot 116 A2
Foster Rd. Rams 39 F3
Foulgar Cl. S Woo F 165 F4
Foundry La. Burn 170 A3
Foundry La. Copf 65 E3
Foundry La. Ea Col 45 D3
Fountain La. Copf 83 F4
Fountain La. Hock 177 D3
Fourth Ave. Canv 196 C2
Fourth Ave. Chelm 127 D3
Fourth Ave. Clact 110 B2
Fourth Ave. Frin 93 F2
Fourth Ave. Glems 2 A3
Fourth Ave. Hals 26 A1
Fourth Ave. Wick 175 D3
Fox Burrows La. Writ 126 A1
Fox Cl. Thund 187 F3
Fox Cres. Chelm 126 C2
Fox's Rd. Ashe 3 F1
Foxden. With 98 B3
Foxes La. E A Gr 47 E1
Foxfield Cl. Hock 178 A3
Foxglove Cl. With 97 E2
Foxglove Way. Sprin 127 F3
Foxhall Rd. Steep 159 D4
Foxhatch. Wick 174 C3
Foxholes Rd. Gt Bad 140 C3
Foxmead. With 98 B3
Foxmeadows. Thund 187 F3
Foxwood Pl. Hadl 189 E1
Frampton Rd. Basil 174 A1
Frances Cl. Wiv 69 D1
Francis Cl. Tipt 100 B2
Francis Ct. Silv E 79 E3
Francis Mews. Mald 145 D4
Francis Rd. Brain 59 E1
Francis Rd. Sud 12 C4
Francis St. Brigh 106 C3
Francis Way. Colch 50 B1
Francis Way. Silv E 79 E2
Francis Wlk. Rayl 176 B1
Frank Clater Cl. Colch 68 A4
Franklin Rd. N Fam 167 D4
Franklins Way. Wick 174 C4
Fraser Cl. Chelm 140 B4
Fraser Cl. South 201 F4
Frating Hill. Frat 70 B2
Frating Rd. Ard 52 A2
Frating Rd. Frat 89 D4
Frating Rd. Gt Bro 70 C3
Fratting Abbey Farm Rd. Thor 89 E3
Freebournes Rd. With 98 A1
Freeland Rd. Clact 109 F1
Freelands. Brigh 107 D3
Fremantle Cl. S Woo F 154 B1
Fremantle Rd. Colch 68 A1
Fremantle. South 201 E3
Fremnells The. Basil 185 E4
French Rd. Stow M 155 F1
Frensham Cl. Stanw 66 B4
Frere Way. Fing 87 D3
Freshwater Dr. Basil 185 F2
Frettons. Basil 185 F3
Friars Cl. Clact 109 F3
Friars Cl. Colch 50 B1
Friars Cl. Elmst M 87 E4
Friars Ct. Colch 68 B2
Friars La. Brain 60 A2
Friars La. Mald 131 F1
Friars St. South 201 F4
Friars St. Sud 12 C4
Friars Wlk. Chelm 127 D1
Friday Wood Green. Colch 85 F4
Friends Field. Bures 19 F1
Friern Gdns. Wick 174 A4
Friern Pl. Wick 174 A3
Friern Wlk. Wick 174 A4
Frietuna Rd. Walt 93 F3
Frinton Rd. Clact 110 B3
Frinton Rd. Th L S 92 B4
Frinton Rd. Walt 93 E3
Frobisher Dr. Clact 108 C1
Frobisher Rd. Harw 39 F1
Frobisher Way. Brain 60 B2
Frobisher Way. South 192 C1
Frog Hall Cl. Fing 87 D3
Fronk's Ave. Harw 40 B1
Fronk's Rd. Harw 40 A1
Frowick La. St O 90 A1
Fryatt Ave. Harw 40 A2
Fryth The. Basil 185 F4
Fulford Dr. South 190 A3
Fullbridge. Mald 132 A2
Fuller's Cl. Kelv 81 D1
Fuller's Rd. Colch 68 B1
Fulmar Cl. Colch 69 D4
Fulmar Way. Wick 175 D3
Fulton Rd. Thund 187 E4
Furlongs. Basil 185 E2
Furrow Cl. Colch 66 C3
Furrowfelde. Basil 185 D2
Further Meadow. Writ 139 D4
Furtherwick Rd. Canv 197 E2
Furze Cres. Alres 88 A4
Furze La. Gt Bro 71 D3
Fyfield Ave. Wick 174 B3
Fyfield Path. Rayl 176 A2
Fyfields. Basil 186 B4

Gablefields. Sand 141 E3
Gables The. Basil 186 A4
Gables The. Hadl 189 D3
Gadwall Reach. Kelv 81 E1
Gafzelle Dr. Canv 197 F1
Gage's Rd. Bel S P 4 C1
Gager Dr. Tipt 100 C3
Gaiger Cl. Sprin 127 E4
Gains Cl. Canv 197 E2
Gainsborough Ave. Canv 197 F2
Gainsborough Cl. Clact 109 D3
Gainsborough Cl. W Mers 121 E3
Gainsborough Cres. Sprin 127 F2
Gainsborough Dr. Lawf 35 D2
Gainsborough Dr. South 190 C1
Gainsborough Rd. Colch 67 D3
Gainsborough Rd. Sud 12 C4
Gainsborough St. Sud 12 C4
Gainsford Ave. Clact 110 A2
Gainsford End Rd. Topp 14 A3
Galahad Cl. Burn 170 A3
Galleydene Ave. Chelm 140 B2
Galleydene. Hadl 188 B2
Galleywood Rd. Chelm 140 A3
Galleywood Rd. Gt Bad 140 C3
Galliford Rd. Mald 132 A2
Galloway Dr. Lit Cla 91 E2
Galsworthy Cl. Brain 78 A4
Galton Rd. South 199 E4
Gambleside. Basil 185 F2
Gandalf's Ride. S Woo F 165 E3
Ganges Rd. Sho G 40 A4
Gaol La. Sud 12 C4
Gap The. Clact 111 D3
Garden Cl. Alth 157 F2
Garden Farm. W Mers 121 E4
Garden Field. Hat Pev 113 F2
Garden Fields. Gt T 64 B4
Garden Fields. Steep 147 F2
Garden Pl. Sud 12 B4
Garden Rd. Clact 125 D4
Garden Rd. Walt 94 A4
Gardeners La. Cane 168 C1
Gardeners Rd. Hals 25 F1
Gardeners. Gt Bad 140 B3
Gardenia Pl. Clact 109 D2
Gardenia Wlk. Colch 68 C4
Garland Rd. Rams 39 F3
Garners The. Roch 178 C1
Garnons Chase. Worm 30 A3
Garrettlands. Sand 141 F3
Garrod Ct. Rowh 86 A4
Garthwood Cl. W Berg 48 C2
Gascoigne Rd. Colch 68 B4
Gate St. Mald 131 F1
Gatefield Cl. Walt 93 F4
Gateway. Basil 185 D3
Gatscombe Cl. Hock 177 E3
Gattens The. Rayl 176 C2
Gauden Rd. Brain 59 F4
Gay Bowers La. Dan 142 C3
Gay Bowers Rd. Dan 142 C2
Gay Bowers Way. With 115 D4
Gay Bowers. Basil 185 E4
Gay Bowers. Hock 177 D3
Gay Links. Basil 185 D4
Gayleighs. Rayl 176 B2

Hillview Cl. Rowh 86 C4
Hillview Rd. Rayl 176 B2
Hillway. South 199 D4
Hillwood Gr. Wick 174 C4
Hilton Cl. Mann 35 E2
Hilton Rd. Canv 197 D3
Hilton Way. Si Hed 24 C4
Hilton Wlk. Canv 197 D3
Hilton Wlk. Si Hed 24 C4
Hilversum Wlk. Canv 197 D3
Hindles Rd. Canv 197 E2
Hines Cl. Ald 65 D4
Hinguar St. South 201 F3
Hitcham Rd. Cogg 62 C2
Hitchcock Pl. Sud 7 F1
Hitchin Mews. Brain 78 A4
Hither Blakers. S Woo F 165 E4
Hitherwood Rd. Colch 67 E1
Hobart Cl. Chelm 126 C3
Hobbiton Hill. S Woo F 165 E3
Hobbs Dr. Box 32 A3
Hobbs La. Glems 2 B1
Hobleythick La. South 190 B2
Hockley Cl. Basil 185 E3
Hockley Cl. Brad O S 137 E1
Hockley Green. Basil 185 F3
Hockley Rd. Basil 185 E3
Hockley Rd. Brad O S 137 E1
Hockley Rd. Rayl 176 C2
Hockley Rise. Hock 177 F3
Hodges Holt. With 115 D4
Hodgson Ct. Wick 175 D3
Hodgson Way. Wick 175 D3
Hoe Dr. Colch 67 D3
Hoe La. Pent 5 F4
Hoe La. Rett 164 A3
Hoe Mill Rd. Woo Wa 130 C2
Hog's La. Str S M 34 C4
Hogarth Cl. W Mers 121 E3
Hogarth Dr. South 202 A4
Hogarth End. Walt 93 F4
Hogwell Chase. Stow M 166 A4
Holbech Rd. Basil 185 F4
Holbek Rd. Canv 197 F2
Holborough Cl. Colch 68 C4
Holbrook Cl. Clact 109 D2
Holbrook Cl. S Woo F 165 E4
Holdsworth Cl. Glems 2 A2
Holgate. Basil 186 B4
Holkham Ave. S Woo F 165 E3
Holland Ave. Canv 196 B3
Holland Park. Clact 110 A2
Holland Rd. Clact 110 A2
Holland Rd. Frin 93 F2
Holland Rd. Lit Cla 91 F1
Holland Rd. South 199 E4
Holland Rd. Walt 93 D3
Hollands Wlk. Basil 185 E1
Holledge Cres. Walt 93 F3
Hollies Rd. Bradw 61 D1
Holliland Croft. Gt T 64 B4
Hollis Lock. Sprin 128 A2
Hollow La. Broom 126 C4
Hollow La. Bures 19 F2
Hollow Rd. Ashe 3 F2
Hollow Rd. Kelv 80 C1
Holloway Rd. Mald 132 A3
Holly Bank. With 97 F1
Holly Cl. Burn 170 A3
Holly Cl. Colch 67 E1
Holly La. Gt Hor 31 E2
Holly Oaks. Worm 29 F2
Holly Rd. Stanw 66 B3
Holly View Cl. Tend 72 C3
Holly Way. Chelm 140 B4
Holly Way. Elmst M 70 A3
Holly Way. Tipt 100 B3
Holly Wlk. Canv 196 C2
Holly Wlk. With 98 A3
Hollybush Hill. Gt Ben 89 F1
Hollymead Cl. Colch 49 F2
Hollytree Gdns. Rayl 188 B4
Hollywood Cl. Gt Bad 140 C3
Holm Oak. Colch 68 A2
Holman Cres. Colch 67 D2
Holman Rd. Hals 43 F4
Holmbrook Way. Frin 93 F3
Holmes Rd. Hals 43 F4
Holmsdale Cl 190 B2
Holmswood. Canv 197 F3
Holmwood Cl. Clact 109 D3
Holsworthy. South 201 E4
Holt Dr. Rowh 86 A4
Holt Dr. Wic Bis 115 F3
Holt Farm Way. Hawk 178 B2
Holt's Rd. Lit Hor 30 A2
Holton Rd. Canv 197 F2
Holton Rd. Rayl 177 D1
Holtynge. S Ben 187 E2
Holybread La. Lit Bad 129 E2
Holyoak La. Hawk 177 F2
Holyrood Dr. South 190 A1
Holyrood. Harw 39 F1
Home Farm Cl. Gt Wak 193 D2
Home Farm La. Ard 52 A4
Home Mead. Chelm 140 B1
Home Mead. Writ 126 A1
Homefield Cl. Chelm 126 B3
Homefield Rd. Colch 67 E1
Homefield Rd. With 98 A2
Homefield Way. Ea Col 45 D4
Homefield Way. T Gr 78 B4
Homefield. Soum 159 F3
Homefields Ave. S Ben 187 D3
Homerton Cl. Clact 109 F4
Homestead Gdns. Hadl 188 B1
Homestead Rd. Basil 186 C4
Homestead Rd. Hadl 188 B1
Homestead Way. Hadl 188 B2
Homestead. Sprin 127 D4
Homing Rd. Lit Cla 91 E2
Honey Bridge Rd. Nay 20 B4
Honey Cl. Gt Bad 140 B3
Honey Pot La. Stow M 155 E2
Honeypot La. Basil 185 D4
Honeypot La. St O 91 D2
Honeypot La. Toll K 101 D1
Honeypot La. Wix 54 C2
Honeysuckle Way. Colch 68 C4
Honeysuckle Way. Thor 89 D3
Honeysuckle Way. With 97 E2
Honeywood Ave. Cogg 63 D2
Honeywood Rd. Hals 26 A2
Honiley Ave. Wick 174 B2
Honington Cl. Wick 175 D3
Honiton Rd. South 200 B4
Honywood Cl. Mks T 64 C2
Honywood Rd. Colch 67 E3
Honywood Way. Walt 93 F4
Hood Gdns. Brain 60 B2
Hooley Dr. Rayl 176 B4
Hop Gardens La. Woo Wa 130 C2
Hope Rd. Canv 197 E2
Hope Rd. S Ben 187 E1
Hopkin's La. Harw 40 B3
Hopkins Cl. Walt 93 F3
Hopkins Mead. Sprin 128 A1
Hopkirk Cl. Dan 142 C4
Hopper Wlk. Colch 68 B3
Hopping Jacks La. Dan 142 C4
Hoppit Mead. Brain 59 F1
Horace Rd. South 200 A4
Hordle Pl. Harw 40 B2
Hordle St. Harw 40 B2
Horkesley Hill. Gt Hor 31 D4
Horkesley Rd. Box 49 F4
Horkesley Way. Wick 174 C3
Horley Cl. Clact 109 E3
Horn La. Cogg 63 D1
Hornbeam Cl. Chelm 140 A3
Hornbeam Cl. Colch 67 E1
Hornbeam Wlk. With 98 A2
Hornbeams The. Lit Oak 57 D4
Hornbeams. Thund 187 D4
Hornby Ave. South 190 B3
Hornby Cl. South 190 B3
Hornchurch Cl. Wick 175 D3
Horne Row. Dan 142 B3
Horner Pl. With 98 A1
Hornet Way. Burn 170 A3
Hornsland Rd. Canv 197 F2
Horrocks Cl. Colch 68 A2
Horse and Groom La. Chelm 140 A2
Horsey Rd. Walt 93 E4
Horsley Cross. Basil 185 D4
Hospital La. Colch 67 E3
Hospital Rd. Colch 67 E3
Hospital Rd. South 201 F3
Houblon Dr. Chelm 140 B1
Houchin's La. Cogg 63 D2
Hovefields Ave. Wick 174 B2
Hovefields Dr. Wick 174 B2
Howard Ave. Harw 39 F1
Howard Chase. Basil 185 D4
Howard Cl. Brain 60 B2
Howard Cres. Basil 186 B3
Howard Dr. Sprin 128 A1
Howard Pl. Canv 197 D1
Howard Rd. Clact 110 B2
Howard Vyse Ct. Clact 109 F3
Howards Chase. South 190 C1
Howards Cl. Bore 128 C4
Howbridge Hall Rd. With 114 C4
Howbridge Rd. With 114 C4
Howe Chase. Hals 25 F2
Howe Cl. Colch 68 B4
Howe Green Rd. Purl 155 F4
Hoxton Cl. Clact 109 E2
Hoyners. Dan 143 D4
Hubbards Chase. Walt 94 A4
Hubert Rd. Colch 67 D4
Hucklesbury Ave. Clact 110 C4
Hudson Cl. Clact 109 E3
Hudson Cl. Harw 40 A1
Hudson Cres. South 189 F3
Hudson Rd. South 189 E3
Hudson Way. Canv 197 D3
Hudsons La. High 21 D3
Hugh Dickson Rd. Colch 49 F1
Hughes Stanton Way. Lawf 35 D2
Hull La. Terl 96 A1
Hull's La. Sand 141 F4
Hullbridge Rd. Rayl 176 B4
Hullbridge Rd. S Woo F 154 B1
Hullbridge Rd. S Woo F 165 E4
Hulton Cl. Bore 128 C4
Humber Ave. Clact 124 C3
Humber Cl. Rayl 176 B1
Humber Rd. Sprin 127 E3
Humber Rd. With 97 E1
Humphry Rd. Sud 12 C4
Hundred La. Box 32 B2
Hundred La. Langh 32 B2
Hungerdown La. Lawf 34 C1
Hunnable Rd. Brain 59 F1
Hunt Ave. Mald 132 A3
Hunt Cl. Fee 81 E2
Hunt Dr. Clact 109 E3
Hunt Rd. Ea Col 45 D3
Hunt Way. Walt 93 F3
Hunt's Cl. Writ 139 D4
Hunt's Dr. Writ 139 D4
Hunter Dr. Lawf 35 D2
Hunter Rd. Brain 60 B1
Hunter's Chase. Ard 33 F1
Hunters Ridge. Colch 50 A2
Hunters Way. Sprin 127 F4
Huntingdon Rd. South 200 B4
Huntingdon Way. Clact 109 F3
Hunts Farm Cl. Tolle 119 E1
Hunts Hill. Glems 2 A2
Hunwicke Rd. Colch 68 C4
Hurnard Dr. Colch 67 D4
Hurrell Down. Bore 112 C1
Hurrell Down. Colch 50 A2
Hurrells La. Lit Bad 128 C2
Hurricane Way. Wick 175 D3
Hurst Cl. Brigh 107 D3
Hurst Way. South 189 F2
Hurst Way. Sprin 127 F1
Hyacinth Cl. Clact 109 E2
Hyacinth Cl. Tolle 119 D1
Hyacinth Ct. Sprin 127 F4
Hyde Chase. Purl 143 E2
Hyde Farm Chase. Dan 143 D2
Hyde Green. Dan 143 D4
Hyde La. Dan 143 D3
Hyde Rd. Sud 12 C4
Hyde Way. Wick 174 B3
Hyde Wood La. Ashi 178 C4
Hydeway. Thund 187 F3
Hydewood Rd. Lit Y 9 D2
Hylands The. Hock 177 E3
Hythe Cl. Brain 59 F3
Hythe Cl. Clact 125 E4
Hythe Gr. Brigh 88 C1
Hythe Hill. Colch 68 B3
Hythe Quay. Colch 68 B3
Hythe Station Rd. Colch 68 B3
Hythe The. Mald 132 A1

Iceni Way. Colch 67 D2
Ifracombe Ave. South 200 B4
Ilex Cl. Colch 67 E1
Ilfracombe Ave. Basil 186 B3
Ilfracombe Rd. South 191 E1
Ilgars Rd. Runw 163 F1
Ilmington Dr. Basil 174 A1
Imogen Cl. Colch 68 C4
Imperial Ave. May 146 C1
Imperial Ave. South 190 B1
Imphal Cl. Colch 67 E1
Inchbonnie Rd. S Woo F 165 F3
Ingarfield Rd. Clact 110 C3
Ingelrica Ave. Hat Pev 114 A2
Ingestre St. Harw 40 B3
Inglenook. Clact 110 A4
Inglis Rd. Colch 67 E3
Ingram Mews. Brain 78 A4
Ingram's Piece. Ard 51 F4
Ingram's Well Rd. Sud 12 C4
Ingrave Cl. Wick 174 C3
Inkerpole Pl. Sprin 127 F2
Inverness Ave. South 190 B1
Inverness Cl. Colch 68 A4
Inworth La. Wa Col 28 B1
Inworth Rd. Fee 81 F2
Inworth Wlk. Colch 68 A1
Inworth Wlk. Wick 175 D4
Ipswich Rd. Clact 110 B3
Ipswich Rd. Colch 50 B2
Ipswich Rd. Langh 32 C1
Ipswich Rd. Str S M 22 C2
Ireton Rd. Colch 67 E3
Iris Cl. Sprin 127 F3
Iron Latch La. E A Gr 66 B4
Iron Latch La. Stanw 66 B4
Ironwell La. Hawk 178 B2
Ironwell La. Roch 178 B2
Irvine Rd. Colch 67 E3
Irvington Cl. South 189 E2
Irvon Hill Rd. Wick 174 B4
Isbourne Rd. Colch 68 C4
Ishams Chase. With 115 E4
Island La. Walt 75 F1
Island Rd. Walt 75 F2
Ivy La. E Mers 106 A2
Ivy Lodge Rd. Gt Hor 49 E4
Ivy Rd. Thund 187 D3
Ivy Wlk. Canv 196 C2

Jacaranda Cl. Sprin 127 F3
Jack Hatch Way. Wiv 69 D2
Jackdaw Cl. South 201 F4
Jacks Cl. Wick 174 C4
Jackson Pl. Gt Bad 140 B3
Jackson Rd. Clact 109 F1
Jaggards Rd. Cogg 63 D2
James Carter Rd. Colch 66 C2
James Cl. Wiv 69 E2
James Gdns. St O 108 A3
James Rd. Clact 109 E1
James St. Brigh 106 C3
James St. Colch 68 A3
Jameson Pl. Sud 12 C4
Jameson Rd. Clact 109 E2
Jameson Rd. Sud 12 C4
Janette Ave. Canv 196 C2
Janmead. With 98 A2
Jaques Cl. Glems 2 B3
Jardine Rd. Basil 186 B4
Jarmin Rd. Colch 67 F4
Jarvis Field. Lit Bad 129 E3
Jarvis Rd. Canv 197 D3
Jarvis Rd. S Ben 187 F2
Jasmine Cl. Colch 68 C4
Jasmine Cl. Sprin 127 F4
Jasmine Way. Clact 125 D4
Jason Cl. Canv 197 D3
Jays La. Mks T 64 C2
Jays The. Colch 50 A2
Jaywick La. Clact 109 D1
Jeffcut Rd. Sprin 127 F1
Jefferson Cl. Colch 66 C3
Jeffery Rd. Gt Bad 141 F4
Jeffrey Cl. Colch 66 C3
Jeffrey's Rd. T Gr 78 C3
Jellicoe Way. Brain 60 B2
Jenkin's Hill. Brad 36 B2
Jenner Cl. Brain 59 F1
Jenner Mead. Sprin 128 A2
Jersey Gdns. Runw 174 B4
Jersey Rd. Mald 132 A1
Jersey Way. Brain 59 E1
Jesmond Rd. Canv 197 D1
Jessica Cl. Colch 68 C4
Joes Rd. Sud 13 F4
John Ball Wlk. Colch 67 F4
John English Ave. Brain 59 F2
John Harper St. Colch 67 F4
John Henry Keene Meml Hms. Chelm 127 D2
John Kent Ave. Colch 67 D1
John Raven Ct. Fee 81 E2
John Ray Gdns. Bl Not 78 A3
John Ray St. Brain 60 A2
John St. Brigh 106 C3
John St. South 202 A3
Johnson Cl. Brain 78 A4
Johnson Cl. Roch 178 B3
Johnson Rd. Gt Bad 141 D3
Johnson Rd. St O 108 A2
Johnson's Dr. Elmst M 70 A3
Johnston Cl. Clact 110 C3
Johnston Cl. Hals 43 F4
Johnstone Rd. South 201 D4
Jones Cl. South 190 C2
Jonquil Way. Colch 49 E1
Joseph Gdns. Silv E 79 F2
Josselin Cl. Ea Col 45 D4
Josselin Ct. Basil 174 B1
Josselin Rd. Basil 174 B1
Jotmans La. S Ben 187 D2
Journeymans Way. South 191 D3
Joyce's Chase. Gold 134 A4
Jubilee Ave. Clact 109 F4
Jubilee Cl. Harw 39 F1
Jubilee Cotts. Pag Ch 180 B3
Jubilee Ct. Si Hed 24 C4
Jubilee Dr. Runw 174 B4
Jubilee End. Lawf 35 E3
Jubilee La. Ard 51 E2
Jubilee Rd. Rayl 176 C1
Jubilee Rd. Sud 12 C4
Jubilee Rise. Dan 143 D3
Jubilee Way. Walt 93 F3
Julien Court Rd. Brain 60 A2
Juliers Cl. Canv 197 E2
Juliers Rd. Canv 197 E2
Junction Rd. Basil 186 A2
Junction Rd. Col N 156 A3
Juniper Cl. Hals 43 E4
Juniper Cres. With 98 A2
Juniper Dr. Chelm 140 A3
Juniper Rd. Bore 128 C4
Juniper Rd. South 189 F2
Juniper Rd. Stanw 66 B3
Juniper Way. Colch 68 B4
Jupe's Hill. Wa Col 28 B1
Jupes Hill. Ded 34 B2
Juvina Cl. With 114 C4

Kale Croft. Stanw 66 B3
Kale Rd. S Ben 187 F2
Kamerwyk Ave. Canv 197 E2
Karen Cl. S Ben 196 C4
Karen Cl. Wick 174 B3
Katherine Cl. Rayl 177 D1
Katherine Rd. Basil 186 C4
Kathleen Dr. South 189 F1
Katonia Ave. May 146 C1
Kay Cl. Gt Le 95 D4
Keable Rd. Mks T 64 C2
Keating Cl. Lawf 35 D2
Keats Ave. Brain 77 F4
Keats Cl. Mald 145 D4
Keats Rd. Colch 66 C3
Keats Sq. S Woo F 165 F3
Keats Way. Wick 174 B4
Keats Wlk. Rayl 177 D1
Kebbles. Glems 2 A3
Keble Cl. Colch 67 E3
Keddington Hill. Sud 13 D1
Keeble Cl. Tipt 100 C3
Keeble Park. Mald 144 C4
Keegan Pl. Canv 197 E2
Keelars La. Elmst M 69 F1
Keelers Way. Gt Hor 49 D4
Keelings La. Deng 160 C4
Keelings Rd. Deng 160 C4
Keene Way. Chelm 140 A2
Keer Ave. Canv 197 E1
Keighley Mews. South 192 B1
Keith Ave. Runw 163 E1
Keith Cl. Clact 110 A4
Keith Way. South 190 C3
Kellington Rd. Canv 197 E3
Kelly Rd. Basil 186 C3
Kelredon Rd. Mess 82 B1
Kelso Cl. Gt Hor 49 E3
Kelvedon Cl. Chelm 127 D3
Kelvedon Cl. Rayl 176 A2
Kelvedon Hall La. Gt Brx 99 F2
Kelvedon Rd. Cogg 81 D4
Kelvedon Rd. Lit Brx 115 F3
Kelvedon Rd. Toll D 100 A4
Kelvedon Rd. Toll D 118 B3
Kembles. Rayl 176 C2
Kempson Dr. Sud 13 E3
Kempton Cl. Thund 188 A4
Kemsley Rd. Ea Col 45 D3
Ken Cooke Ct. Colch 67 F4
Kendal Cl. Hull 165 F1
Kendal Cl. Rayl 176 C1
Kendal Ct. Wick 175 D3
Kendal Rd. Colch 68 A3
Kendal Road Folley. Colch 68 A3
Kendal Way. South 189 F4
Kenholme. South 189 F2
Kenilworth Gdns. Rayl 176 B2
Kenilworth Gdns. South 190 A2
Kenilworth Gr. Th L S 74 A1
Kenilworth Rd. Clact 110 C3
Kenley Cl. Wick 175 D3
Kenmore Cl. Canv 197 F1
Kennedy Cl. Rayl 189 D4
Kennedy Cl. Thund 187 D4
Kennedy Way. Clact 110 A3
Kennet Way. Chelm 126 B3
Kenneth Rd. Basil 186 B4
Kenneth Rd. Thund 187 F3
Kennington Ave. Thund 187 E3
Kensington Rd. South 200 B4
Kensington Way. Hock 177 E3
Kent Ave. Canv 197 D3
Kent Ave. South 189 F1
Kent Cl. Brigh 106 C4
Kent Elms Cl. South 189 F3
Kent Gdns. Brain 60 A2
Kent Green Cl. Hock 177 F3
Kent View Ave. South 199 D4
Kent View Rd. Basil 185 F2
Kent Way. Rayl 189 D4
Kent's Ave. Clact 110 C3
Kentings The. Brain 59 F1
Kents Grass. Tolle 119 E1
Kents Hill Rd N. Thund 187 E3
Kents Hill Rd. S Ben 187 E2
Kenway. South 191 D1
Kenworthy Rd. Brain 59 F1
Kenyon Cl. Str S M 22 B1
Kerby Rise. Sprin 127 F1
Kerridge's Cut. Mist 36 A2
Kerry Ct. Colch 68 B4
Kersey Ave. Sud 13 D3
Kersey Dr. Clact 109 D3
Kestrel Way. Clact 109 F3
Kestrel Wlk. Chelm 140 A2
Keswick Ave. Clact 110 B3
Keswick Ave. Hull 165 F1
Keswick Cl. Rayl 176 C1
Keswick Cl. Walt 93 F4
Keswick Rd. Thund 187 F4
Ketleys View. Pan 59 D4
Ketleys. Chelm 140 B2
Kew La. Frin 93 D2
Key Rd. Clact 109 F2
Keyes Way. Brain 60 B2
Keymer Way. Colch 66 C2
Keynes Way. Harw 39 F1
Keysland. Thund 188 A3
Kilburn Gdns. Clact 109 E3
Kildermorie Cl. Colch 50 B2
Kilmaine Rd. Harw 39 F1
Kiln Barn Ave. Clact 109 F4
Kiln Dr. Sud 13 D3
Kiln Rd. Thund 188 A2
Kilns Hill. Cogg 62 C3
Kilnwood Ave. Hock 177 E3
Kilworth Ave. South 200 A4
Kimberley Rd. Barl 192 C3
Kimberley Rd. Colch 68 A3
Kimberley Rd. S Ben 187 E2
Kincaid Rd. St O 108 A2
King Charles Rd. W Mers 121 E3

Little Meadow. Writ 126 A1
Little Nell. Chelm 126 C4
Little Oaks. Basil 185 D3
Little Searles. Basil 186 A4
Little Spenders. Basil 185 E2
Little Sq. Brain 59 F2
Little St Mary's. L Mel 7 E4
Little Stambridge Hall Rd.
Gt Stam..............................179 E2
Little Stile. Writ 139 D4
Little Tey Rd. Fee 81 F3
Little Thorpe. South 192 A1
Little Totham Rd. Gold 117 E1
Little Totham Rd. Lit Tot 117 E1
Little Wakering Hall La. Gt Wak193D2
Little Wakering Rd. Barl 192 C3
Little Wheatley Chase. Rayl .. 176 A2
Little Wood. Walt 93 F3
Little Yeldham Rd. Lit Y 9 E2
Littlebury Ct. Basil 186 A4
Littlebury Gdns. Colch 68 B2
Littlebury Green. Basil 186 A4
Littlecotes. Colch 49 E2
Littlecroft. S Woo F 165 E3
Littlefield Rd. Colch 67 E1
Littlethorpe. Basil 185 F2
Llewellyn Cl. Sprin 127 E2
Lloyd Rd. Sho G 40 A4
Lloyd Wise Cl. South 191 E2
Loamy Hill Rd. Toll M 117 D4
Lobelia Cl. Bore 128 A3
Locarno Ave. Runw 163 F1
Lock Rd. Hals 43 F4
Lockhart Ave. Colch 67 E4
Lockram La. With 97 F1
Lockram La. With 98 A1
Locks Hill. Roch 178 C1
Lodge Ave. Gt Bad 140 C4
Lodge Cl. Clact 109 F2
Lodge Cl. Lit Oak 57 E4
Lodge Cl. Rayl 176 C1
Lodge Cl. Thund 188 A3
Lodge Cres. Bore 128 C4
Lodge Ct. W Berg 48 C2
Lodge Farm Cl. South 189 E3
Lodge Farm La. St O 108 B2
Lodge Farm Rd. Glems 2 B2
Lodge La. Ard 51 D3
Lodge La. Ard 51 E3
Lodge La. Brigh 106 C4
Lodge La. Lang 86 B1
Lodge La. Langh 50 B4
Lodge La. Peld 103 E4
Lodge La. Purl 144 B1
Lodge La. Tend 72 C3
Lodge Rd. Brain 59 F1
Lodge Rd. Haze 144 A3
Lodge Rd. Lit Cla 92 A2
Lodge Rd. Lit Oak 57 E4
Lodge Rd. Mald 131 F2
Lodge Rd. Mess 82 B2
Lodge Rd. S Woo F 153 F3
Lodge Rd. Writ 139 D4
Lodgelands Cl. Rayl 176 C1
Lodwick. South 201 E3
Loftin Way. Gt Bad 140 B4
Lombardy Cl. Basil 186 B3
Lombardy Pl. Chelm 127 D2
London Hill. Chelm 139 F1
London Hill. Rayl 176 B2
London Land Cotts. Worm 29 F2
London Rd. Basil 185 E2
London Rd. Basil 187 D3
London Rd. Bl Not 77 E3
London Rd. Brain 59 F1
London Rd. Chelm 139 F4
London Rd. Clact 109 F4
London Rd. Copf 65 E2
London Rd. Fee 81 F2
London Rd. Gt Hor 30 C2
London Rd. Gt Le 77 E3
London Rd. Hadl 189 E1
London Rd. Kelv 81 D1
London Rd. Mald 131 E2
London Rd. Mks T 64 C1
London Rd. Rayl 176 A2
London Rd. South 190 B1
London Rd. Stanw 66 C4
London Rd. Thund 187 D3
London Rd. Wick 174 A4
London Rd. Wick 174 A4
London Rd. Wick 175 E3
Long Acres. Fee 81 F3
Long Brandocks. Writ 126 A1
Long Gages. Basil 185 D4
Long Green. T Gr 78 C4
Long La. Frin 93 D2
Long La. Hull 165 F1
Long Meadow Dr. Wick 174 C4
Long Meadows. Harw 39 F1
Long Melford By-Ps. L Mel 7 F3
Long Pastures. Glems 2 B2
Long Rd W. Ded 33 F2
Long Rd. Canv 196 C2
Long Rd. Lawf 35 D2
Long Rd. Mist 35 D2
Long Riding. Basil 185 E3
Long Wyre St. Colch 67 F4
Longacre. Basil 185 E4
Longacre. Chelm 139 E4
Longacres Rd. T Gr 78 C3
Longacres. Brain 60 A1
Longbarn Hill. Brad 37 D1
Longborough Cl. Basil 174 A1
Longcroft Rd. Colch 68 B4
Longfellow Rd. Mald 132 A1
Longfield Cl. Wick 175 D4
Longfield Rd. Gt Bad 140 C4
Longfield Rd. S Woo F 165 E4
Longfield Rd. Wick 175 D4
Longfield. With 97 F3
Longfields. St O 108 A2
Longhams Dr. S Woo F 165 E4
Longleaf Dr. Brain 77 F4
Longleat Cl. Chelm 126 C4
Longmead Ave. Gt Bad 140 C4
Longmeads Cl. Writ 126 A1
Longmeads. Wic Bis 115 F3
Longmore Ave. Gt Bad 140 C4
Longridge. Colch 68 C4
Longsands. South 201 E4
Longship Way. Mald 144 C4
Longstomps Ave. Chelm 140 A4
Lonsdale Rd. South 191 E1
Lord Holland Rd. Colch 67 F2
Lord Roberts Ave. South 189 F1
Lordship Rd. Writ 126 A1
Lordswood Rd. Colch 67 E2
Lorien Gdns. S Woo F 165 E3
Lorkin's La. Twin 18 B2
Lornes Cl. South 191 E2
Loten Rd. S Ben 187 D1
Lott's La. Brad 54 B4
Lott's Rd. Clact 91 D2
Lottem Rd. Canv 197 E1
Lotts Yd. Colch 68 A3
Louis Dr E. Rayl 176 A2
Louis Dr W. Rayl 176 A2
Louisa Ave. Thund 187 D3
Louise Cl. Walt 76 C2
Louise Rd. Rayl 176 C1
Louvaine Ave. Wick 174 A4
Love La. Brigh 106 C4
Love La. Rayl 176 B1
Love Way. Clact 109 E3
Lovelace Ave. South 200 B4
Lovelace Gdns. South 191 E1
Lovell Rise. South 190 A3
Lovens Cl. Canv 197 E1
Lover's La. Gt Ben 90 A4
Loves Wlk. Gt Bad 140 C4
Loves Wlk. Writ 139 D4
Lovibond Pl. Sprin 127 F2
Low Rd. Harw 39 F1
Low Rd. South 201 F3
Low St. Glems 2 B3
Lowe Chase. Walt 94 A4
Lowefields. Ea Col 45 E3
Lower Anchor St. Chelm 127 D1
Lower Ave. Basil 186 C4
Lower Burnham Rd. Purl 156 B1
Lower Chase. Alth 157 F2
Lower Church Rd. Thund 187 D3
Lower Farm Rd. Box 21 D1
Lower Green. Chelm 140 B1
Lower Green. Wa Col 28 B1
Lower Harlings. Sho G 40 A4
Lower Holt St. Ea Col 45 E3
Lower Lambricks. Rayl 176 B2
Lower Langley. Gt T 46 B1
Lower Marine Par. Harw 40 B1
Lower Park Rd. Brigh 106 C4
Lower Park Rd. Wick 174 B2
Lower Rd. Ashi 166 B1
Lower Rd. Ashi 167 D1
Lower Rd. Birch 84 A3
Lower Rd. Fox 7 D2
Lower Rd. Hull 166 B1
Lower Rd. Lay Br 102 A4
Lower Rd. M Bure 29 D3
Lower Rd. Peld 103 E3
Lower Southend Rd. Wick 174 B4
Lower St. Cav 1 B1
Lower St. Glems 2 C3
Lower St. Str S M 33 E4
Loxford. Basil 186 A4
Luard Way. Birch 84 A2
Luard Way. With 97 F1
Lubbards Cl. Rayl 176 B3
Lucas Ave. Chelm 140 B3
Lucas Ave. Ford 47 E3
Lucas Rd. Colch 67 F3
Lucas Rd. Sud 12 C4
Lucas's La. Beau 73 E3
Lucerne Dr. Wick 175 D4
Lucerne Rd. Elmst M 70 A3
Lucerne Wlk. Wick 175 D4
Luces La. Ca Hed 15 F2
Lucksfield Way. Gt Bad 140 C3
Lucy Cl. Stanw 66 B3
Lucy La N. Stanw 66 A4
Lucy La S. Stanw 66 B4
Lucy Rd. South 200 A4
Ludgores La. Dan 142 B3
Ludgrove. Latch 157 D3
Ludham Hall La. Bl Not 77 E4
Luff Way. Walt 93 F4
Lufkin Rd. Colch 49 F2
Lugar Cl. Colch 68 C3
Luker Rd. South 200 A4
Lumber Leys. Walt 94 A4
Luncies Rd. Basil 185 F3
Lundy Cl. South 190 A3
Lunnish Hill. Rams 38 C1
Lupin Dr. Sprin 127 F3
Lupin Mews. Sprin 127 F3
Lupin Way. Clact 109 E2
Lushington Ave. Walt 93 F3
Lushington Rd. Lawf 35 E2
Lutus Cl. Cla 4 A3
Lydford Rd. South 199 F4
Lydgate Cl. Lawf 35 D2
Lydia Dr. St O 107 D1
Lylt Rd. Canv 197 D2
Lyme Rd. South 191 E1
Lymington Ave. Clact 110 A4
Lymington Ave. South 189 F1
Lympstone Cl. South 190 A3
Lyndale Ave. South 191 D1
Lyndene. Thund 187 D3
Lyndhurst Dr. S Woo F 142 C1
Lyndhurst Rd. Ashi 167 E1
Lyndhurst Rd. Clact 110 B2
Lynfords Ave. Runw 164 A2
Lynfords Dr. Runw 163 F1
Lynfords Dr. Runw 164 A2
Lynmouth Ave. Chelm 140 B4
Lynmouth Gdns. Chelm 127 E1
Lynn View Cl. S Ben 187 E3
Lynne Cl. Walt 93 E3
Lynstede. Basil 186 A3
Lynton Cl. Harw 40 A2
Lynton Dr. Sprin 127 F3
Lynton Rd. S Ben 188 B2
Lynwood Green. Rayl 189 D4
Lyon Cl. Chelm 140 A2
Lyon Cl. Clact 110 A2
Lyons Hall Rd. Brain 60 B4
Lyster Ave. Gt Bad 141 D4
Lyth Ave. South 201 E4
Macbeth Cl. Colch 68 C4
Macdonald Ave. South 190 C1
Macintyres Wlk. Hawk 178 B3
Mackay Ct. Colch 68 A1
Maclarens. Gt Tot 116 A3
Macmurdo Cl. South 189 E4
Macmurdo Rd. South 189 E4
Madeira Ave. South 189 F1
Madeira Rd. Clact 110 B2
Madeline Pl. Chelm 126 C3
Madgements Rd. Stis 61 D4
Madrid Ave. Rayl 176 A4
Magazine Farm Way. Colch 67 D3
Magazine Rd. South 201 F3
Magdalen Cl. Clact 109 F2
Magdalen Rd. Clact 109 F2
Magdalen St. Colch 68 A3
Magdalene Cres. Silv E 79 E2
Magna Mead. Barl 192 B4
Magnolia Cl. Chelm 140 A3
Magnolia Cl. With 98 A4
Magnolia Dr. Colch 68 C4
Magnolia Rd. Hawk 178 A3
Magnolia Way. Roch 191 D4
Magwitch Cl. Chelm 126 C4
Maidenburgh St. Colch 67 F4
Maidment Cres. With 114 C4
Main Rd. Alth 157 F2
Main Rd. Bore 128 B4
Main Rd. Dun 142 B4
Main Rd. E Han 153 E3
Main Rd. Frat 70 C2
Main Rd. Frin 93 D2
Main Rd. Harw 40 A2
Main Rd. Harw 40 C3
Main Rd. Hawk 177 F2
Main Rd. Hock 177 E3
Main Rd. Rams 39 D1
Main Rd. Rett 164 A3
Main Rd. S Woo F 154 A3
Main Rd. St L 148 B4
Main Rd. Worm 29 F2
Maine Cres. Rayl 176 A2
Maitland Pl. South 192 C1
Makins Rd. Rams 39 F3
Malard Cl. Tolle 119 E1
Maldon Ct. Sud 13 D4
Maldon Rd. Birch 83 F2
Maldon Rd. Brad O S 149 E4
Maldon Rd. Burn 169 F4
Maldon Rd. Colch 67 E3
Maldon Rd. Dan 143 D3
Maldon Rd. Dan 143 D4
Maldon Rd. Gold 133 E3
Maldon Rd. Gt Bad 141 E4
Maldon Rd. Gt Brx 99 F1
Maldon Rd. Gt Tot 116 A2
Maldon Rd. Gt Wig 102 C1
Maldon Rd. Hat Pev 114 B1
Maldon Rd. Kelv 81 E1
Maldon Rd. Langf 131 E3
Maldon Rd. Latch 156 C3
Maldon Rd. Marg 139 E1
Maldon Rd. Sand 141 E4
Maldon Rd. South 191 D1
Maldon Rd. Stanw 66 B1
Maldon Rd. Steep 147 E1
Maldon Rd. Tipt 100 B2
Maldon Rd. Toll D 118 B1
Maldon Rd. Toll M 118 B1
Maldon Rd. With 115 D4
Maldon Rd. Woo Mor 144 A4
Maldon Way. Clact 109 D2
Malgraves Pl. Basil 186 A4
Malgraves. Basil 186 A4
Mallard Cl. Kelv 81 E2
Mallard Cl. Lay H 85 D3
Mallard Rd. Chelm 140 A3
Mallard Way. Sud 13 E3
Mallards. May 158 A4
Mallards. South 192 C1
Mallow Field. Hals 25 F1
Malmsmead. South 201 E4
Maltese Rd. Chelm 127 D2
Malthouse Rd. Mann 35 E2
Malting Farm La. Ard 33 E1
Malting Green Rd. Lay H 85 D3
Malting La. Cla 4 A4
Malting La. Walt 75 E1
Malting Rd. Colch 67 E1
Malting Rd. Peld 103 F3
Malting Villas Rd. Roch 178 C1
Malting Yd. Wiv 87 D4
Maltings Cl. Bures 19 F1
Maltings Ct. With 114 C4
Maltings La. With 114 C4
Maltings Rd. Brigh 88 C1
Maltings Rd. Gt Bad 141 D3
Maltings Rd. Rett 164 C1
Maltings The. Ray 59 D1
Maltings The. Soum 159 F2
Malvern Ave. Canv 196 B2
Malvern Cl. Chelm 126 B3
Malvern Cl. Rayl 176 B2
Malvern Rd. Hock 177 F4
Malvern Way. Gt Hor 49 D4
Malwood Dr. S Ben 187 D3
Malwood Rd. S Ben 187 D3
Malyon Court Cl. S Ben 188 A2
Malyon Rd. With 114 C4
Malyons Cl. Basil 186 A4
Malyons Green. Basil 186 A4
Malyons La. Hull 165 E1
Malyons Mews. Basil 186 A4
Malyons Pl. Basil 186 A4
Malyons The. S Ben 188 A2
Malyons. Basil 186 A4
Manchester Dr. South 189 E1
Manchester Dr. South 189 F1
Manchester Rd. Clact 110 C3
Mandeville Rd. Mks T 64 C2
Mandeville Way. Thund 187 E4
Mandeville Way. Walt 93 F3
Manfield Gdns. St O 108 A3
Manfield. Hals 25 F1
Mangapp Chase. Burn 170 A4
Manilla Rd. South 200 B4
Mannering Gdns. South 190 A2
Manners Way. South 190 C3
Manningtree Rd. Ded 34 A3
Manningtree Rd. Lit Ben 71 F4
Manningtree Rd. Str S M 35 D4
Manns Way. Rayl 176 B3
Manor Ave. Basil 186 B3
Manor Cl. Cav 1 B1
Manor Cl. Gt Hor 49 E4
Manor Cl. Rayl 188 B4
Manor Dr. Gt Bad 140 C4
Manor House Way. Brigh 106 C4
Manor La. Harw 40 A1
Manor Rd. Chelm 127 E1
Manor Rd. Colch 67 F4
Manor Rd. Deng 149 E1
Manor Rd. Frin 93 D2
Manor Rd. Harw 40 A2
Manor Rd. Hat Pev 114 B1
Manor Rd. Hock 177 E3
Manor Rd. S Woo F 165 E4
Manor Rd. South 199 E4
Manor Rd. Sud 7 F1
Manor Rd. Thund 187 E3
Manor Rd. W Berg 48 C3
Manor Rd. Wiv 69 E1
Manor Rd. Woo Wa 131 D2
Manor St. Brain 60 A2
Manor Way. Clact 111 D3
Manors Way. Silv E 79 E2
Manse Chase. Mald 132 A1
Mansel Cl. South 189 F3
Mansted Gdns. Hawk 178 B3
Maple Ave. Brain 59 E1
Maple Ave. Mald 132 B3
Maple Ave. South 198 C4
Maple Cl. Clact 109 E2
Maple Cl. Hals 26 A1
Maple Cl. Harw 40 A2
Maple Dr. Chelm 140 A3
Maple Dr. Rayl 176 B4
Maple Dr. Walt 93 E3
Maple Dr. With 98 A3
Maple Leaf. Tipt 100 B4
Maple Rd. Sud 13 D3
Maple Sq. South 191 D1
Maple Way. Burn 170 A3
Maple Way. Canv 196 C2
Maple Way. Colch 68 A2
Mapledene Ave. Hull 165 F1
Mapleford Sweep. Basil 185 E2
Mapleleaf Cl. Hock 177 F4
Mapleleaf Gdns. Wick 174 A3
Maples The. Wick 174 B3
Maplesfield. Hadl 188 B2
Maplestead. Basil 185 E4
Maplin Cl. Thund 187 E4
Maplin Gdns. Basil 185 F3
Maplin Way N. South 192 B1
Maplin Way. South 201 E3
Marasca End. Rowh 86 A4
Maraschino Cres. Rowh 86 A4
Marconi Rd. Chelm 127 D2
Marcos Rd. Canv 197 E2
Marcus Ave. South 201 D4
Marcus Chase. South 201 D4
Marcus Gdns. South 201 D4
Marennes Cres. Brigh 106 C4
Mareth Rd. Colch 67 E1
Margaret Cl. Brigh 106 C3
Margaret Rd. Colch 67 F4
Margaretting Rd. Chelm 139 F1
Margaretting Rd. Writ 139 D3
Margarite Way. Wick 174 A4
Margraten Ave. Canv 197 E1
Marguerite Dr. South 189 F1
Maria St. Harw 40 B3
Marigold Ave. Clact 109 E3
Marigold Cl. Colch 68 C4
Marigold Cl. Sprin 127 F3
Marina Ave. Rayl 176 B2
Marina Cl. South 190 C2
Marina Gdns. Clact 110 B3
Marina Mews. Walt 94 B4
Marina Rd. Hat Pev 114 A2
Marine App. Canv 197 D1
Marine Ave. Canv 197 F1
Marine Ave. South 189 E1
Marine Ave. South 199 F4
Marine Cl. Hadl 189 D1
Marine Par E. Clact 110 A2
Marine Par W. Clact 109 F1
Marine Par. Canv 197 F1
Marine Par. Hadl 198 B4
Marine Par. Harw 40 B2
Marine Par. May 146 C1
Marine Par. South 200 A4
Mariners Ct. Gt Wak 193 E2
Mariners Way. Mald 145 D4
Marion Ave. Clact 109 F3
Mariskals. Basil 186 A3
Mark Rd. Till 149 F3
Market Ave. Runw 174 B4
Market End. Cogg 62 C1
Market Hill. Cla 4 A4
Market Hill. Cogg 63 D2
Market Hill. Hals 25 F1
Market Hill. Mald 132 A2
Market Hill. Sud 12 C4
Market Pavement. Basil 185 D3
Market Pl. Brain 59 F2
Market Pl. Mald 131 F1
Market Pl. South 200 A4
Market Rd. Chelm 127 D1
Market Rd. Wick 174 B4
Market Sq. Basil 185 D3
Market Sq. S Woo F 165 F4
Market St. Brain 59 F2
Market St. Harw 40 C3
Markland Cl. Chelm 140 B2
Marklay Dr. S Woo F 165 E4
Marks Gdns. Brain 60 B1
Marks Hall Rd. Cogg 62 C3
Marks La. Rett 163 F4
Marland Dr. Mald 131 F1
Marlborough Ave. Till 149 F2
Marlborough Cl. Clact 109 E2
Marlborough Cl. Thund 187 E4
Marlborough Dr. Sud 12 C4
Marlborough Rd. Brain 60 A2
Marlborough Rd. Chelm 127 D1
Marlborough Rd. South 200 B4
Marlborough Wlk. Hock 177 E3
Marlin Cl. Hadl 188 C3
Marlow Gdns. South 190 C2
Marlowe Cl. Brain 78 A4
Marlowe Cl. Mald 145 D4
Marlowe Rd. Clact 109 D1
Marlowe Way. Colch 66 C3
Marlpits Rd. Purl 143 F2
Marmaduke Ave. Rayl 176 A2
Marne Rd. Colch 67 F2
Marney Cl. Gt Bad 140 C4
Marney Dr. Basil 185 F3
Marney Way. Frin 94 A3
Marram Cl. Colch 66 A3
Marsh Cres. Rown 87 D4
Marsh Farm La. Thor 89 E1
Marsh Farm Rd. S Woo F 165 E3
Marsh Rd. Burn 171 E3
Marsh Rd. High 21 F3
Marsh Rd. South 201 F3
Marsh Rd. Till 150 A2
Marsh Way. Brigh 106 C3
Marshall Cl. Fee 81 E2
Marshall Cl. Hadl 189 D2
Marshalls Cl. Rayl 176 C1

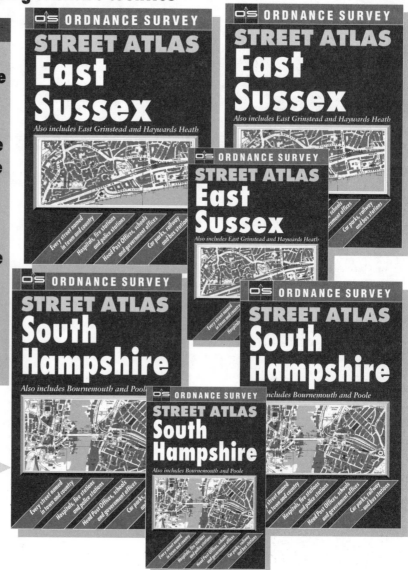

STREET ATLASES

CSA94

	Hardback	Softback	Pocket
	QUANTITY TOTAL		QUANTITY TOTAL
	£12.99	£8.99	£4.99
East Essex	ISBN 0-540-05848-3	ISBN 0-540-05866-1	ISBN 0-540-05850-5
West Essex	ISBN 0-540-05849-1	ISBN 0-540-05867-X	ISBN 0-540-05851-3
North Hampshire	ISBN 0-540-05852-1	ISBN 0-540-05853-X	ISBN 0-540-05854-8
South Hampshire	ISBN 0-540-05855-6	ISBN 0-540-05856-4	ISBN 0-540-05857-2
Nottinghamshire	ISBN 0-540-05858-0	ISBN 0-540-05859-9	ISBN 0-540-05860-2
East Sussex	ISBN 0-540-05875-0	ISBN 0-540-05874-2	ISBN 0-540-05873-4
West Sussex	ISBN 0-540-05876-9	ISBN 0-540-05877-7	ISBN 0-540-05878-5
	£10.99		£4.99
Berkshire	ISBN 0-540-05738-X		ISBN 0-540-05835-1
Buckinghamshire	ISBN 0-540-05660-X		ISBN 0-540-05711-8
Hertfordshire	ISBN 0-540-05720-7		ISBN 0-540-05840-8
East Kent	ISBN 0-540-05661-8		
West Kent	ISBN 0-540-05662-6		
Oxfordshire	ISBN 0-540-05665-0		
Warwickshire	ISBN 0-540-05642-1		
	£10.99		£3.99
Surrey	ISBN 0-540-05694-4		ISBN 0-540-05708-8

I enclose a cheque/postal order for £ . *made payable to* ***Reed Book Services*** *or please debit my* ◂ *Access* ◂ *American Express* ◂ *Visa* *account by* £ .

Name

Address

Postcode

Account number

Expiry date

Signature

Please tick this box if you do not wish your name to be used by other carefully selected organisations that may wish to send you information about other products and services

◆ ***Free postage and packing*** ◆ *All available titles will normally be dispatched within 5 working days of receipt of order, but please allow up to 28 days for delivery.*

Registered office: Michelin House, 81 Fulham Road, London SW3 6RB. Registered in England No 1974080